Fish for All

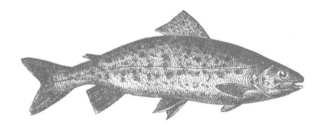

Fish for All

An Oral History of Multiple Claims and Divided Sentiment on Lake Michigan

Michael J. Chiarappa & Kristin M. Szylvian

Michigan State University Press • *East Lansing*

∞ The paper used in this publication meets the minimum requirements
of ANSI/NISO Z39.48–1992 (R 1997) (Permanence of Paper).

Michigan State University Press
East Lansing, Michigan 48823-5202

Printed and bound in the United States of America.

08 07 06 05 04 03   1 2 3 4 5 6 7 8 9 10

LIBRARY OF CONGRESS CATALOGING-IN-PUBLICATION DATA
Chiarappa, Michael J., 1985–
Fish for all : an oral history of multiple claims and divided sentiment
on Lake Michigan / by Michael J. Chiarappa and Kristin M. Szylvian
p. cm.
ISBN 0870136348 (cloth : alk. paper) —ISBN 0870136542 (pbk. : alk. paper)
1. Fishery management—Michigan, Lake—History. 2. Fishing—Political aspects—Michigan, Lake.
3. Fisheries—Economic aspects—Michigan, Lake. I. Title
SH219.7.M5 C45 2003
338.3/727/09774 21
2002154981

This book was published with financial support from the Great Lakes Fishery Trust.

Cover and book design and production by Sharp Des!gns, Lansing, MI

Visit Michigan State University Press on the World Wide Web at **www.msupress.msu.edu**

Contents

v

Acknowledgements

I N ASPIRING TO MAKE *Fish for All*—both the book and public history project—a multi-faceted endeavor, we have incurred numerous intellectual, professional, and social debts. This effort would never have been possible without
a generous grant from the Great Lakes Fishery Trust. From the start, Jack Bails, manager of the Trust, facilitated the development of this project with exemplary profes-
sionalism and vision. His support, along with the larger endorsement of the GLFT,
has help establish new benchmarks for how the study of fisheries history and culture can stand together with fisheries science in the advancement of new stewardship perspectives.

In addition to the GLFT, we enjoyed the support of the Michigan Maritime
Museum and its former curator, Kenneth R. Pott. Ken recognized the possibilities of
a project supported by the GLFT and we are grateful for having had the opportunity
to work with him. Now the executive director of the Ft. Miami Heritage Society, Ken
is among the most eloquent and devoted advocates for the study of Great Lakes history and culture. We owe Ken special thanks for his help, professional collegiality,
and friendship. We would also like to thank Fish for All's advisory board: Ellie Coon,
U.S. Fish and Wildlife Service–Ludington Biological Station; Cindi John, Grand
Traverse Band of Ottawa and Chippewa Indians; Forrest Williams, Michigan Fish
Producers' Association; Earl Wolfe, Michigan Department of Natural Resources; and
Bruce Wojcik, Michigan United Conservation Clubs.

While carrying out *Fish for All*'s scope of work, many individuals and institutions assisted us in conducting research and fieldwork, collection and interpretation of artifacts, and preparation of public programs. These individuals and institutions include: Erik Alexander, Public Museum of Grand Rapids; Charles Allers and Judy Borke, Wisconsin Conservation Law Enforcement Museum; William Cashman, Beaver Island Historical Society; William Casper, University of Chicago Library; Clarke Historical Library, Central Michigan University; William Cullerton and Jennifer Dale, Sault Ste. Marie Tribe of Chippewa Indians; Jerry Dennis, George "Skip" Duhamel, and Tom Gorenflo, Chippewa-Ottawa Treaty Fishery Management Authority; Great Lakes Fishery Commission, Illinois Department of Natural Resources; Indiana Department of Natural Resources, Lake Michigan Field Office; Eric Jeska, Gerald LaFreniere, and Paul LeClair, Leelanau Historical Museum; Little Traverse Bay Bands of Odawa Indians; Sherri Lucas, Win Awenen Nistotung Photographic Archives/Sault Ste. Marie Tribe of Chippewa Indians; Michigan Department of Natural Resources, Lansing Office; Christine Mitchell, Grand Traverse Band of Ottawa and Chippewa Indians Fisheries Office; Helen Allers Nicolen and Erik Olsen, Grand Traverse Band of Ottawa and Chippewa Indians Fisheries Office; Scott Peters, Michigan Historical Center; Babette Duhamel Patton and Molly Perry, Museum of Ojibway Culture; Joel Peterson, Barry Pischner and Christine Randall, Door County Maritime Museum; State Archives of Michigan; Brandon Schroeder, Michigan United Conservation Clubs; Tanya Schwartz, John VanOosten Library; Great Lakes Science Center, USGS; Norm Spring and Ann Thousand, Garden Peninsula Historical Society; Traverse City *Record-Eagle*; Al Vanderburg and Robert VerDuin, University of Wisconsin-Milwaukee; Wisconsin Arts Board, Folk Arts Program; Wisconsin Department of Natural Resources; State Historical Society of Wisconsin; Roger Martin, Wolf Lake State Fish Hatchery/ Michigan DNR; Michael Zimmer, Rogers Street Fishing Museum; and Yvonne Keshick Walker.

The genesis and completion of this project can be traced to the inspiration and guidance of our teachers and colleagues. Those who have left a mark on this work are many; but, in particular, we would like to acknowledge: Brian Black, Janet Gilmore, Henry Glassie, Edward Ives, Paula Johnson, LuAnne Kozma, the late Eugene Levy, Dane Morrison, Laura Quackenbush, Bill Rastetter, Robert St. George, Samuel Schrager, David Taylor, Joseph Taylor III, and Don Yoder. We are particularly thankful for the insights that Robert Doherty, Professor of History at the University of Pittsburgh, offered during the course of this project. Bob was one of the first historians to seriously address the fishing rights disputes of the Great Lakes Region. We appreciate his permission to use his interview with the late Arthur Duhamel.

At our own institution, Western Michigan University, a number of colleagues warrant particular mention. This project stems, in part, from the vision of our former chair, Ronald Davis. Ron's interdisciplinary vision for the Department of History and its Public History Program provided us with the framework to creatively pursue new connections between cultural history, environmental history, and public history. We are thankful for his support in bringing this project to fruition, as well as that of subsequent chairs Bruce Haight and Judith Stone. Other colleagues at Western Michigan University, who contributed in more ways than they might imagine, include: Jose Brandao, Sharon Carlson, Nora Faires, James Ferreira, Cheryl Lyon-Jeness, Catherine Julien, James Palmitessa, and Larry Syndergaard. Katherine Joslin, director of WMU's American Studies Program, reached out and gave *Fish for All* even greater programmatic reach within the university. We would also like to express our thanks for a grant from the Department of History's Mac Millan-Burnham Fund. This grant helped underwrite the expenses of student-oriented fieldwork exercises in the spring of 1999. At Western Michigan University's National Public Radio affiliate, WMUK, we had the opportunity of working with WMU Public History student Abraham Hohnke and Andy Robins and Gordon Evans on the *Fish for All* radio documentary. Our thanks to both of them for exposing our students to yet another realm of public history and environmental studies. Our work would have been far more difficult without the help of Christine McDowell, Project Fiscal Analyst in Western Michigan University's Grants and Contracts Office. Her noteworthy oversight of the *Fish for All* grant allowed us to work more efficiently on other aspects of the project. We would like to extend the same thanks to Jennifer Churchill for her efforts in transcribing *Fish for All's* oral histories. Her genuine interest and detailed attention to these oral histories was a great asset to the *Fish for All* project. The positive contributions of Christine and Jennifer regularly influenced the day-to-day conduct of *Fish for All* and left a mark on it in more ways than we can possibly acknowledge.

A particular benefit of this project was its capacity to introduce a new generation of students to the cultural/environmental history and folklife of the Great Lakes

Region. Paula Lange, our former graduate student and now an exhibit curator with the National Park Service, became *Fish for All*'s project coordinator and helped move it forward in its earliest, and sometimes, most difficult stages. James Clay Johnson joined the *Fish for All* team first as a research assistant and then as its web master. Clay's unique talents improved *Fish for All* in immeasurable ways. Other students who worked on *Fish for All* made equally vital contributions. Matthew Anderson, Clair Gornowicz, Abraham Hohnke, Cindy Olsen, and Jason Wintersteen assisted in the collection of oral history. Matt and Cindy, along with Michael Martin and David Bird, provided valuable assistance with documentary research. Dan VandenHeede conducted research on Beaver Island. The noteworthy fieldwork skills of all these students exemplified the wide-ranging impact that history, culture, and environmental research can have on the larger community. As this book neared completion, Joshua Cochran provided careful assistance in the preparation of the manuscript.

While the *Fish for All* project was underway, we had the opportunity to present our work at two conferences: The World Marine Millennial Conference at the Peabody Essex Museum in March/April 2000 and the Organization of American Historians Midwestern Regional Conference in August 2000. Participants at both conferences offered commentary that greatly assisted our thinking in this book.

We would like to thank each of the museums that hosted the exhibit *Fish for All*: the Dennos Museum Center in Traverse City, Michigan; the Michigan State University Museum in East Lansing, Michigan; the Door County Maritime Museum in Sturgeon Bay, Wisconsin; and the Michigan Maritime Museum in South Haven, Michigan. We would like to extend our additional thanks to the Michigan Maritime Museum for agreeing to house the original tape recorded interviews and transcripts at its Marialyce Canonie Great Lakes Research Library in South Haven, Michigan.

Fisheries History, Oral History, and Public History

Historical Voice and the Representation of
Lake Michigan's Contested Fisheries

I N 1997, THE GREAT LAKES CENTER for Maritime Studies—a partnership between Western Michigan University and the Michigan Maritime Museum— began considering a historical documentation project and museum exhibit on Great Lakes fisheries. When we approached the Great Lakes Fishery Trust for funding to conduct such a project, we were encouraged to focus our efforts on the history of fisheries management on Lake Michigan. From these deliberations emerged the research and public history project entitled *Fish for All: The Legacy of Lake Michigan Fisheries Policy and Management.* The compelling and wide-ranging nature of this topic lent its treatment to any number of approaches. Foremost among these considerations was the relevance of the topic to current debates concerning the use of Lake Michigan's resources; indeed, if there ever was an area of historical discourse or historical consciousness that made the phrase "living history" far more literal than its role in museum interpretation, this was it.

Among those groups that are considered Lake Michigan's principal fisheries stakeholders—commercial fishers, sport fishers, Native Americans, and government—the past is very much alive. But the perceptions and sentiment that each brings to this history diverges in significant ways. Not unlike other situations in the United States, the fish-using groups of Lake Michigan have endured fractured relations for the past half-century. One of the great travesties of past and present environmental policy is that its participants often seek to advance solely their own self-interest in the allocation of natural resources rather than look for broader consensus among all user groups. These dynamics have afflicted the relations among Lake Michigan's fisheries stakeholders for the past fifty years and have resulted in four different historical views that each group uses to substantiate its claims to Lake Michigan's fish.

Because of this legacy, *Fish for All*'s central objective was the examination of the different management and conservation viewpoints exercised by Lake Michigan's principal fishing constituencies since the late-nineteenth century, placing particular emphasis on the post–World War II era. A number of factors framed our focus on this time period. During these years, significant capital investment led to more industrial, volume-oriented harvesting of Great Lakes species and, in time, the development of the largest freshwater commercial fishery in the world. These same economic forces, and the ecological changes they fostered, helped lead to the demise of Lake Michigan's commercial fishery.

At the same time, while Euro-American commercial fishers reduced Lake Michigan's stocks, marginalized Native American groups in the region attempted to retain their economic and cultural connection to the resource. By the close of the twentieth century, they had reclaimed their treaty-rights fishing through recourse in federal court. But these groups were hardly alone in laying claim to Lake Michigan's fish. Sport fishers increasingly descended upon Lake Michigan's fisheries resources. Their aspirations assumed unprecedented proportions when a salmon fishery was successfully established in the 1960s. For Lake Michigan's sport fishers this represented a rebirth, a situation that took on greater meaning as their Upper Midwest lives were reshaped by the changed, often difficult, postindustrial economic realities of the late twentieth century. At the same time, and apart from these divergent agendas—divergences that often mask important common ground—state and federal government became more involved in Lake Michigan's fisheries. The dissipation of Lake Michigan's fisheries resources put new emphasis on the public trust doctrine and government's role in managing natural resources for the greatest public benefit. Thus, starting in the 1870s, state and federal government assumed the more visible "official" role of guardian of Lake Michigan's fisheries resources. By managing the

The centerpiece of the *Fish for All* exhibit was a fish emblazoned with images gathered from each of the groups that historically lay claim to Lake Michigan's fisheries resources. Photograph by Michael J. Chiarappa.

fish, government was mediating relations among each of the aforementioned groups. Not surprisingly, this role evolved in dramatic ways over the course of the twentieth century.

Since the historical debate over the use of Lake Michigan's fisheries resources concerns so many sectors of society, the *Fish for All* team's first charge was to present this research, and the stewardship issues it raised, to as wide an audience as possible. To this end, in a spirit of public history scholarship that seeks to extend historical discourse beyond the academy to similarly interested groups in society at large, we constructed the museum exhibit entitled *Fish for All: Perspectives on the History of Lake Michigan Fisheries Management and Policy*. This exhibit traveled to four different venues around Lake Michigan over the course of a year (March 2000 to March 2001). An interpretive booklet guided visitor interaction with the presentation. Educational programs (on- and off-site), a radio documentary (collaboratively prepared with Western Michigan University's National Public Radio affiliate, WMUK), and an internet site supplemented the exhibit and made the findings of the *Fish for All* project more accessible. The collection of oral histories that follows was prepared to provide an interpretive and substantive contribution that would endure beyond the previously mentioned components of *Fish for All* and assist in maintaining historical awareness of the social, cultural, and political nature of Lake Michigan's fisheries. Indeed, when historians write the story of late-twentieth-century fishing policy, as historian Margaret Beattie Bogue has recently done for the period prior to 1933, the material gathered as part of *Fish for All* will provide them with a rich source of perspectives from those who made and administered policy as well as from those whose everyday livelihood and lives were affected by it.[1]

The topic broached by *Fish for All* casts a wide net, but we focused on the fish-using interests that have been the most visible, vocal, and longstanding stakeholders on Lake Michigan—state and federal government, and commercial, sport, and tribal fishers. While this field unites the fields of cultural, economic, environmental, and policy history, our objective was to use these areas to clarify the historical division that resounds so frequently in the voices of Lake Michigan's fish-using groups. In short, we wanted our audience to understand the historical antecedents and cultural rationales that shaped these contested voices. This is hardly a historical scenario limited to the shores and waters of Lake Michigan. American history—indeed,

Erik Olsen (center), fisheries biologist for the Grand Traverse Band of Ottawa and Chippewa Indians, conducted one of the public programs offered in conjunction with the Fish for All exhibit on 29 April 2000. Photograph by Michael J. Chiarappa.

world history—is dotted with episodes where multiple claimants and decision-makers clashed over the use of natural resources that were presumably common property. The penchant of industrial and corporate capital to extricate natural resources and utilize them in focused market-driven schemes fosters the fragmentary process that sets one user group off against another. Allocation schemes vary in profile. Some are blatantly politicized, others are reactionary, while some are truly remedial in intent. But like the issues surrounding other natural resources, fishery priority schemes can be so subtle and, at times, so seemingly benign and justified, that when problems have arisen throughout history the voices are even more strident.

From the preparation of the museum exhibit to the collection of oral history, these factors suited the research and presentational aims of *Fish for All*. Our goal was to integrate new directions being charted in fisheries history with oral and public history's ability to "share authority" with those groups who will continue to bear the burden of fisheries management and policy in the future. We recognized that the strident positions of each group could not be fully or thoroughly understood by relying on the

Western Michigan University students Clair Gornowicz and Matthew Anderson interviewed perch fishing/charter boat captain Don Nichols on-board the *Captain Nichols* on 21 May 1999. Photograph by Michael J. Chiarappa.

documentary record. In this debate, and countless other fisheries deliberations, written documentation falls short of clarifying the histories of each group and does not explain the in-depth historical basis for each constituency's emphatic claim to both use the resource and participate in the governance of its allocation. We thus saw it as ethnographically remiss not to structure the presentation of *Fish for All* around formats or genres that would illuminate the highly vocal or oral dimensions of historical expression in each of these fishing communities; in short, the ability to talk about fishing history is precisely what makes it so socially and politically meaningful for each of the concerned groups. These stories are powerful place-based narratives that complexly reveal the myriad manifestations of everyday ecological consciousness. To have not placed oral testimony at the forefront of this project would have sorely impeded our ability to ethically exercise "shared authority" and make it a worthwhile framework for future fisheries history and policy-making.[2]

The themes that our informants emphasized not only offered us a means of understanding the development, implementation, and debate of fisheries policy and values from their unique perspective, but also began to shape the interpretive framework we imposed on the project. Rather than just examine the traditional policy-making process, the project recast the issue with a more holistic perspective in mind and asked: What historical factors shape the resource-use values that are the basis for each group's claim to the resource? This examination of a more expansive notion of fisheries management and policy required the use of written documents, photographs, fishing technology, and the cultural landscape as source material. But the traditions and decisions that guide the use or allocation of fisheries resources are also engulfed in daily deliberations, casual talk, and highly vocal debates—a social and cultural process that plays out on the streets, in homes, on the docks, in fishing boats, at community meetings, in government offices and legislatures, and in adjudicative bodies throughout the world. Within this oral culture circulate an extensive array of historical perspectives that either go undocumented or are not carefully interpreted in the process of fisheries policy debate. These circumstances made the collection and interpretation of oral history a focal point of this documentation project. As expected, these narratives convey the divided opinion of a fifty-year fisheries debate. Of greater significance, however, these narratives show the differences in how each group historically perceives and expresses what can variously be called their resource-use values, their policies, or their management methods.

The content of the oral histories gathered by the *Fish for All* team indicate how each group's resource-use priorities are shaped through a multifaceted occupational and environmental experience, but the "official," longtime debates over the use of Lake Michigan's fish were consistently waged through a reductionist dialogue of selected economic and allocation issues. Within this framework, each group's oral history was not adequately recognized or evaluated as expressing an environmental position—an ethnographic oversight in the policy-making process that failed to account for the diverse ways in which fish-using groups justify their claim to the resource. Furthermore, when these voices were enlisted in the debate, they were unevenly heard depending on the priorities or mediating role of state government. This evidence amplifies recent arguments, particularly those advanced by Joseph Taylor's work on the salmon fisheries of the Pacific Northwest, that natural resource debates can actually tell much more complicated ecological stories than those that are unidimensionally framed around "the tragedy of the commons" thesis. The status of Lake

Western Michigan University student Jason Wintersteen (left) conducted fieldwork on-board the trap-net boat *Robyn B.* on the waters of Lake Michigan off of Wisconsin's Door Peninsula. Photograph by Matthew Anderson.

Michigan's fish as common property is firmly entrenched, but to assume that this has meant equal access, widely shared protection, or the propensity to use the resource at all costs grossly oversimplifies the human and ecological relationships that have transpired on this lake. The stories that follow, particularly their juxtaposition as the collective memory of competing groups, is a first step toward interpreting this complex ecological legacy.[3]

As *Fish for All* got under way, it was ironic that a 1985 Federal Consent Agreement (settling Native American treaty fishing rights disputes in Michigan's Great Lakes waters) was being re-negotiated. Once again, the clamorous voices of Lake Michigan's fishing constituencies were all about and the cries were all too familiar. Echoing across the past 175 years were the continuing concerns of various fishers that their resource, or their ability to pursue it, would be diminished, obstructed, or threatened. For the *Fish for All* research group, this was one of those rare situations where past and present significantly converged. In the midst of this unfolding historical event, we were immersed in documentary evidence, photographs, and artifacts that bore similar marks, and told stories similar to, the fishing episode that was playing out right before us. From the start, we estimated that oral histories would be critical to the *Fish for All* story; indeed, these materials comprised the audio component of the exhibit. What became apparent with each and every oral history we collected was the compelling insight offered by the historical voices of those who actually participated in Lake Michigan's fisheries. Aside from the act of taking fish, much of fisheries history is consumed by the debate or contest over who will exercise such agency. Heightened by the fishing negotiations taking place at the dawn of a new millennium, these oral histories underscored the need to understand the nuance of fisheries debate. In 1999, as a new century beckoned, a heightened sense of retrospection surrounded these dilemmas. What factors shaped this historical consciousness and gave its oral expression a polemical tone?

Embedded in these oral histories—in the themes emphasized, in the points made, in the resonating reflections—is the critical nuance that endures as the measure of any fishing legacy. *Fish for All* went forward with an expansive notion of fisheries management and policy, a practice consisting of more than just lists of regulation, scientific reports, and uses of harvesting technology. Hardly ignoring these standard considerations, our intent was to suffuse them into a discussion of Lake Michigan fisheries management and policy with far more embrace: the idea, often obscured or even overlooked, that fisheries management and policy is the exercise and expression of values, needs, and relationships. Much of the material embodied these intentions, but oral history most thoroughly synthesized them. Oral history's synthetic dimension revealed fisheries policy, fisheries management, or fisheries custom as being socially operative—a driving, poignant sentiment. Taking this form, oral history shows that a fishery's historical consciousness is actually a pervasive sentiment whose daily effect in innumerable situations far transcends the immediate appearance of management or policy. Instead, these curatorial notions are a widely shaped historical temperament guiding the daily contemplation and dramatic rituals of the Lake Michigan fishing experience.

The oral histories presented in *Fish for All* are not just accounts; they simultaneously function as an ongoing historical debate—oral history illuminating the longstanding politics and culture of claiming Lake Michigan's fisheries. As in many debates, there have been points of striking division and surprising agreement since these groups began asserting claims or authority over the basin's fish. Competing claims to natural resources are scarcely unique in broad historical perspective, and historians are just starting to take note of how the threshold or liminal nature of the maritime environment shapes these dynamics. During the late-nineteenth century, the seeds of a complex array of claims or authority over Lake Michigan's fisheries began to take root. The major fishing constituencies on Lake Michigan began this self-referential (at times, polemical) claiming exercise by describing their administrative prerogative, natural heritage, economic livelihood, or cultural birthright. More commonly, they expressed these claims simply by acting. The essays that follow will examine themes and episodes since the late-nineteenth century that help clarify how an ethos or culture of fisheries claims developed on Lake Michigan in the modern age. The oral histories that follow—in their factual details and human depth—stand on their own in delineating this contested legacy. More important, however, these oral histories verbally corroborate the past and verbally continue the endurance and revision of claims in the present. By looking at the verbal expression of the history of fisheries values, this particular dimension of the *Fish for All* project reveals paradoxical considerations that will continue to inform the evaluation of fisheries history and the formulation of future fisheries policy and stakeholder relations. In sum, these oral histories not only reinforce the fact that fisheries management on Lake Michigan is a contested legacy among fish-using groups, but also strikingly show how each group is undeniably linked by the resource and the lake that produces it.

NOTES

1. Margaret Beattie Bogue, *Fishing The Great Lakes: An Environmental History, 1783–1933* (Madison: University of Wisconsin Press, 2000).

2. Michael Frisch, *A Shared Authority: Essays on the Craft and Meaning of Oral and Public History* (Albany: State University of New York Press, 1990). Other works that have informed the methodological and interpretive basis of this collection include Robert Perks and Alistair Thomson, eds., *The Oral History Reader* (London: Routledge, 1998); Samuel Schrager, "What is Social in Oral History," *International Journal of Oral History* 4, no. 2 (1983): 76–98; Charles L. Briggs, *Learning How to Ask: A Sociolinguistic Appraisal of the Role of the Interview in Social Science Research* (Cambridge: Cambridge University Press, 1986); Stephen Caunce, *Oral History and the Local Historian* (London: Longman, 1994); Henry Glassie, "The Practice and Purpose of History," *Journal of American History* 81, no. 3 (December 1994): 961–68; Michael Keith Honey, *Black Workers*

Remember: An Oral History of Segregation, Unionism, and the Freedom Struggle (Berkeley: University of California Press, 1999). Folklorists have presented compelling methodologies that advance the collection and interpretation of ecologically framed narratives. See Mary Hufford, *One Space, Many Places: Folklife and Land Use in New Jersey's Pinelands National Reserve-Report and Recommendations to the New Jersey Pinelands Commission for Cultural Conservation in the Pinelands National Reserve* (Washington, D.C.: American Folklife Center-Library of Congress, 1986). For more on the historical and folkloristic implications of oral tradition and its capacity to convey natural resource debates, see Edward D. Ives, *George Magoon and the Down East Game War: History, Folklore, and the Law* (Urbana: University of Illinois Press, 1988). See *Orion Afield* 5, no. 4, and its section entitled "Saving Stories," for efforts to enlist oral history and oral tradition in contemporary, locally oriented environmentalism.

3. Joseph E. Taylor III, *Making Salmon: An Environmental History of the Northwest Fisheries Crisis* (Seattle: University of Washington Press, 1999), 3–12; Garrett Hardin, "The Tragedy of the Commons," *Science* 162 (13 December 1968): 1243–48. For more on the complex use and interpretation of common property rights see Bonnie J. McKay and James M. Acheson, eds., *The Question of the Commons: The Culture and Ecology of Communal Resources* (Tucson: University of Arizona Press, 1987); Bonnie J. McKay, *Oyster Wars and the Public Trust: Property, Law, and Ecology in New Jersey History* (Tucson: University of Arizona Press, 1998); Arthur F. McEvoy, *The Fisherman's Problem: Ecology and Law in the California Fisheries, 1850–1980* (Cambridge: Cambridge University Press, 1986).

Tribal Fishing Claims

From Fishing First to Cultural Revitalization

T HE OTTAWA AND CHIPPEWA bands of Lake Michigan have always relied on oral tradition to transmit and preserve the historic management values they bring to the lake's fisheries. Euro-American efforts to document traditional Native fisheries management practices began in the 1820s with the collection of Chippewa legends by Henry Rowe Schoolcraft. Such ethnohistorical research sheds light not only on this specific issue, but the capacity of oral tradition to describe the historical ecology of Indian society in the Great Lakes region.[1] When combined with ethnographic description, material culture analysis, and archival sources, oral history provides a richly textured portrait of how bands of Ottawa and Chippewa fishers gathered on or near Lake Michigan's shores during the spring, summer, and fall months. In terms of recent history, this oral testimony illuminates the broad context in which contemporary fishing technologies, work organization, and target species fit into a centuries-old Indian tradition.

With the exception of work by historian Robert Doherty, oral history has seldom been utilized in attempts to understand how Ottawa and Chippewa fishers managed political and cultural change from the later nineteenth century to the turn of the twenty-first century.[2] The tribes' litigious efforts to reassert treaty rights fishing in the 1960s and 1970s added new chapters to this oral history. These events also fostered a new narrative tradition that historicizes the modern Indian's negotiating position in contemporary fisheries policy debate.

John Boucher and son, Sault Ste. Marie, c. 1917. Tribal fishers used large dip nets to harvest whitefish and other fish. Fishing traditions connected the Ottawa and Chippewa people to Lake Michigan and represent the essence of how these bands characterize themselves as "Anishnabeg" or "the people of this place." Courtesy of Clarke Historical Library, Picture File, Central Michigan University.

The use of oral tradition in fishing rights cases, court-ordered scrutiny of treaties, and ethnohistorical research affirms the personal and inherited memories of these Native American groups.[3] In spite of this, however, oral tradition was disparaged by opponents of tribal fishing claims who viewed these narratives as being solely empowered by the whims of contemporary political fashion rather than by a distinct and enduring cultural consciousness that was first shaped by the struggle to avoid being removed from lakeshore areas by federal authorities in the nineteenth century.[4] Michigan's Ottawa and Chippewa Indians were, for the most part, able to remain in place and preserve their fishing connections to Lake Michigan. Their traditional use patterns were, however, not immune from the social and economic transformations that engulfed the region. Both the location and operation of temporary seasonal fishing camps were altered by declining fish stocks and the use of lakeshore and tributary property for commercial and industrial use.

By the late-nineteenth century, Lake Michigan's Native American fishers were employed as wage earners by Euro-American gill-net and pound-net fishing operations.[5] Others operated as small clusters of independent commercial fishers on the periphery of "fishtowns," "fish stations," or "fishing centers" established by European immigrants to Lake Michigan's shores.[6] Most of Lake Michigan's tribal fishers drew a modest fishing subsistence by venturing out in the simplest of rigs from any available launching site. These circumstances strained the ethos of Native American fishing on Lake Michigan, but it nonetheless endured to find renewed purpose in the closing decades of the twentieth century.

The transformations that altered the exercise and appearance of Ottawa and Chippewa fishing tradition are seldom acknowledged by those who contest the modern claims of Lake Michigan's Native American communities. Choosing to fixate on the fishery's inconsistent appearance with "noble savage" stereotypes, they

Chippewa Indian village, Sault Ste. Marie, c. 1850. The roots of Ottawa and Chippewa fisheries regulation can be traced to the creation of fishing villages. The establishment of mutually respected fishing territories is one of the traditional ways in which bands of Great Lakes Indians managed and shared fisheries resources. Courtesy of Clarke Historical Library, Picture File, Central Michigan University.

5643. INDIANS FISHING IN THE RAPIDS SAULT STE. MARIE. MICH.

This scene, depicting tribal fishermen dip netting at the rapids of the St. Mary's River, was widely reproduced on postcards during the early-twentieth century. While Lake Michigan's Indians had largely lost access to many of their traditional fishing grounds, the popularity of this image reflected America's antiquarian interest in traditional tribal resource-use patterns and management systems. Courtesy of Michael Chiarappa.

either misunderstand or refuse to consider the cultural view that informed the negotiating positions of nineteenth-century Indians who reserved fishing rights in ceded territories when they signed the Ottawa-Chippewa Treaty of 1836.[7] Unfortunately, state and federal government agencies failed to establish policies that overtly acknowledged the fishing codicils of this treaty. Oral testimony shows how these usufructuary rights remained ensconced in the collective memory of Lake Michigan's Indian groups well into the twentieth century. Based on these perspectives, opponents of Lake Michigan's tribal fisheries continually lack an appreciation of the historical evolution of Native American fishing tradition or the manner in which it is expressed. Due to these factors, many older historical narratives were unable to get a balanced or open-minded hearing in the 1960s and 1970s when Lake Michigan tribes became more politically assertive in reclaiming their treaty fishing rights. This contested forum shaped the content of oral history that emerged in the 1980s and 1990s.

When expressing their stake in Lake Michigan's fisheries, Native American fishers' oral histories cite the political toll they have paid over the past thirty years. Geographically, these civil-rights-oriented fishers were not far removed from the racial unrest and economic decline that took place in Detroit during the late 1960s and early 1970s. Ironically, however, although three Michigan tribes, the Bay Mills Indian Community, the Sault Ste. Marie Tribe of Chippewa Indians, and the Grand Traverse Band of Ottawa and Chippewa Indians, were in the midst of events that captured national headlines and instigated social reform, their efforts to reassert treaty-rights fishing on Lake Michigan met a hard line of opposition from the Michigan Department of Natural Resources (DNR).[8]

Until the middle of the twentieth century, Indians found or pursued few instances upon which to invoke their fishing rights under the Ottawa-Chippewa Treaty of 1836 (formally known as the 1836 Treaty of Washington). In a manner similar to non-Indian residents of the Great Lakes region, they frequently fished Lake Michigan's waters and tributaries for home use or for additional income by selling their catch to tourists or local markets.[9] Notwithstanding their awareness of treaty fishing rights, Native Americans who independently entered Lake Michigan's commercial fishery during the first half of the twentieth century conformed to federal and state Americanization policies and purchased state-issued commercial licenses along with their Euro-American counterparts. For years, the tribal descendants of treaty signatories claimed the right to fish on Lake Michigan, but a state court in Michigan rejected this petition in 1930 and ruled that Indians were obliged to buy state-issued commercial licenses since they were granted U.S. citizenship in 1924.[10]

In the course of reasserting their fishing traditions on Lake Michigan, Indians found themselves simultaneously enmeshed in two of the most volatile issues of post–World War II America—the civil rights movement and growing federal and state government involvement in the management of natural resources. When the State of Michigan issued strict income, target species, and gear restrictions in the mid-1960s and early 1970s to encourage a more vibrant sport fishery on Lake Michigan, Indians were among the most severely affected.[11] Now, for the first time in more than 100 years, they stridently sought recourse in the treaties signed by their forebears.[12] In a number of federal court decisions in the Pacific Northwest that interpreted Indian treaty rights fishing, it was ruled that states could not deny

Indians an equitable allocation of fisheries resources. These court rulings also stip-ulated that Indians maintained the autonomy to self-regulate their fisheries resources and their respective fishers. The momentum generated by these court pro-ceedings encouraged Indians in Michigan to take similar steps. In *People v. Jondreau* (1971) and *People v. LeBlanc* (1976), the Michigan Supreme Court upheld the right of Michigan Indians to commercially fish in Lake Superior waters free of state control under treaties that were signed respectively in 1842 and 1836. In spite of these rul-ings, the State of Michigan refused to fully acknowledge treaty rights fishing until the federal courts forced its compliance in the 1979 case of *U.S. v. Michigan*.[13] In the course of pursuing this ruling, known as the Fox Decision, Indians became more familiar with county jails and courthouses, state and federal courthouses, and a wide range of other government venues. Although well-founded litigation and civil dis-obedience placed Indians in these environments, these high-minded goals hardly mitigated the discomfort they continue to feel in such surroundings. The oral histo-ries that follow shed light on how this reluctance painfully succumbed to their deter-mination to secure treaty rights fishing.

The testimony that follows includes that of modern Indian fishing rights advo-cates—the late Art Duhamel and Ron Paquin—who emerged in the course of these events to make Indian fishing's collective memory more stridently representational in the political arena.[14] Duhamel's life history struck a transcendent note within the Northern Michigan Indian community and politicized treaty rights fishing in a manner that went far beyond the extraction of fish from Lake Michigan. Born Buddy Chippewa in 1924 in the Leelanau County Indian community of Peshawbestown, Duhamel was removed from his family and placed in foster care. When Duhamel returned to Peshawbestown as a teen, he felt the same fragmented identity that afflicted other Indians who had been removed from their original cultural milieu. As a young man, he embarked on a career as a journeyman welder and traveled the world to various construction sites. These experiences, both in the United States and abroad, coupled with voracious reading habits, acutely awakened Duhamel's sense of cultural loss. After returning to Michigan in 1972, Duhamel became an advocate for federal recognition of the Grand Traverse Band of Ottawa and Chippewa Indians and the group's principal voice in its quest to reclaim treaty rights fishing. Duhamel was first arrested for violating Michigan fishing laws in 1974, three years after the arrest of Albert "Abe" LeBlanc of the Bay Mills Indian Community. Duhamel's resolve was strengthened when LeBlanc successfully challenged Michigan's right to deny members of his tribe fishing rights they claimed under the Treaty of Washington of 1836.[15]

The Arthur Duhamel testimony in this collection was gathered in 1980 by Dr. Robert Doherty, professor of history at the University of Pittsburgh, while doing research for his 1990 book, *Disputed Waters: Native Americans and the Great Lakes Fishery*. Its release in this volume is timely from a number of perspectives. When combined with the narrative of his son—George "Skip" Duhamel—it offers important insight on the evolving, intergenerational legacy of treaty rights fishing on the Great Lakes. Second, it sheds a valuable retrospective view on Art Duhamel's contribution to the legal, political, and cultural history of the fishing rights struggle. Finally, having seen the 1985 Consent Agreement as an example of an Indian community too willing to compromise to reach an agreement with federal and state government fisheries officials and sport-fishing interests, Art Duhamel yearned to participate in the recently concluded 2000 Consent Agreement deliberations.[16] His death in 1992 cut short this opportunity and his narrative in this collection is one of the few sources that provide some indication of how he would have proceeded.[17]

In describing a life that has many parallels with Duhamel's, Ron Paquin's testimony further augments existing oral histories chronicling his involvement in Indian treaty rights fishing in the Great Lakes region. Paquin, a member of the Sault Ste. Marie Tribe of Chippewa Indians, made an important contribution to Native American oral history and our understanding of the wider transformations of twentieth-century Indian life when he chronicled his experiences in *Not First in Nobody's Heart: The Life Story of a Contemporary Chippewa*, a work coauthored with Prof. Robert Doherty.[18] The testimony collected from Ron Paquin for this collection is one of the few existing narratives offering perspectives informed by thirty years of participation and observation of modern Indian treaty rights fishing.

Duhamel and Paquin describe how their involvement in the fight to reassert tribal fishing rights brought financial burdens, strained relationships, and great personal demands. The financial and personal cost of advocating treaty rights fishing was paid not only by the first generation of activists, but by later generations as well. Duhamel's son, George "Skip" Duhamel, sees himself as continuing the work of his

Ron Paquin (left) and his son Christopher (right) gill-net fishing for menominee whitefish in a small skiff on Lake Michigan near Brevort, Michigan, in the early 1980s. Photograph courtesy of Ron Paquin.

father and Joseph "Geeboo" Sands, an elder whose stories of earlier tribal fishing were inspirational to the elder Duhamel. Babette Patton (formerly Duhamel) recalled how local opposition to her late husband's work for treaty rights fishing affected her son at school and outside of the classroom. Paquin painfully recalls similar harassment of Indian children by non-native adults and children who were against Indian treaty rights fishing.

Second-generation advocates of modern treaty rights fishing such as "Skip" Duhamel and Cindi John, also a member of the Grand Traverse Band of Ottawa and Chippewa Indians, focus their oral history on the intractable position that the Michigan DNR has taken ever since proceedings surrounding the case of *U.S. v. Michigan* (Fox Decision). Even though the ruling favored Michigan's Indian fishers, actions on the part of the Michigan DNR and sport-fishing groups thwarted efficient implementation of the decision over the next twenty years and fostered widespread resentment within the Indian community. To overcome these tensions, Indians made significant compromises not to fish large areas of Lake Michigan in the Consent

Agreement of 1985. These gestures did not stem the sport-fishing community's long-time, highly vocal opposition to Indian gill netting or attempts by local municipalities to prohibit Indians from using public marinas and docking facilities.[19] Some sport-fishing interests and state fisheries officials alleged that the tribes would deplete Lake Michigan's fish stocks if they were allowed to regulate themselves.[20]

Members of Lake Michigan's Ottawa and Chippewa bands describe their adoption of modern regulatory schemes and scientific research methods as being a historic addition to a tradition of self-governance that never ceased.[21] Their narratives, however, ponder the misinterpretation of these evolutionary developments; in this role, oral history is seeking to give voice to the cultural nuance that guides the transformation of the resource-use values of indigenous peoples.[22] Focusing their narratives on developments of the past twenty years, they see the limited effect of the Fox Decision in ameliorating public misperception of the modern Indian fisher or in remedying problematic relations with state and federal government. The frustrated tone of their oral testimony ultimately turns on their lack of financial resources and their struggle to obtain fish tugs and trap net operations, which they regard as essential to better economic prospects and less occupational danger. Under the Consent Agreement of 1985, the State of Michigan agreed to provide financial assistance to Indians to facilitate their conversion to trap net fishing and to enable small-scale gill net fishers to better utilize tribal fishing zones. The State of Michigan's inaction and delay in implementing these measures from 1985 through 1999 is evident in the following oral histories. Ultimately, in spite of a judicially affirmed stake in Lake

"Save a Trout . . . Spear an Indian" bumper stickers appeared in Northern Michigan during the early 1980s in opposition to the 1979 U.S. District Court decision recognizing the treaty rights fishing of the Grand Traverse Band of Ottawa and Chippewa Indians and several other Northern Michigan tribes. Courtesy of Michael J. Chiarappa.

Brian Napont, a member of the Grand Traverse Band of Ottawa and Chippewa Indians, in the pilot house of his fish tug while moored at Beaver Island in 1999. Like his father and other family members before him, he fishes Lake Michigan's waters off of Beaver Island. Photograph by Michael J. Chiarappa.

Michigan's fisheries, the oral histories of Indian fishers delineate a continuing legacy of political and financial obstruction that impairs the modern cultural revitalization of their fisheries claims.[23]

Finally, these Indian oral histories portray a group that, despite obstacles, became politically adept. Over the course of a third of a century, it went from brokering fisheries resources to negotiating some of the most complex claims of indigenous peoples to their cultural patrimony. This provided the touchstone by which all of Lake Michigan's Indians could enter the debate. Oral testimony focuses on the collective efforts of the Indian community to press its fisheries claims. Most important, however, this oral tradition recognizes the voices of those elders who encouraged the activists of the 1960s and 1970s to return to fishing. Today, oral history forges the social inclinations of these activists into a seamless narrative of cultural identity and geographic affiliation. In daily discourse, the narratives of Lake Michigan's Native American fishers now attempt to translate a troubled past into a historically informed modern fishery that will be a more enduring legacy than the perceived benefits of gaming revenues and other token political concessions.[24]

Part I: Fishing, Economic Opportunity, and Cultural Identity: The Modern Face of Indian Tradition

Yvonne Keshick, a member of the Little Traverse Bay Band of Odawa Indians, began fishing with her father at a young age. She also fished with her husband John Keshick and worked onshore, cleaning and mending nets. Yvonne Keshick learned about fishing through family and community contacts.

I was born in Charlevoix in 1946. We lived there until about 1965, when I graduated from high school. My father used to fish. He did pole fishing when we were small. I remember being three and four years old in a rowboat learning how to pole fish. We did a lot of fishing with him and my mom. She would fish, too. When we got older, we got sent to Harbor Springs Holy Childhood to boarding school. But while we were home in the summertime, we would fish. And during that time my mom and dad separated. We stayed with my father and fished. He would go to work and we would go downtown. We would go to the little round lake around Charlevoix and go dock hopping. We would drop our lines on all the little docks unless they chased us out. We used to sit on Jack Cross's dock and fish down there. We would see the fish in the water swimming. The water was pretty clear. We would move all the way down towards the train bridge on that side of the lake, and then we would come back. Anything we caught we would take home, clean it, and give it to my dad for his lunch. By the time he got home at noontime, we would have the fish cleaned and cooked up. He would be really happy. Pole fishing was fun and it kept us busy.

We had friends whose families were fishing people. I knew this one boy named Freddy Wabanimkee. His father was a fisherman, his grandpa was a fisherman, and his uncle is a fisherman. We would go to Fred's place and sit outside their trailer. The family would be in there cooking, doing repairs, making plans and getting ready for work. A little ways away was a guy who we used to go over to see. His name was Simon Wabanimkee. He is gone now. He and Julius Wabanimkee used to mend nets and work on

Yvonne M. Walker Keshick (right) is a member of the Little Traverse Bay Bands of Odawa Indians. She is tribal archivist and a widely known quillwork artist and teacher of tribal traditions. Yvonne Keshick used to fish with her husband, John Keshick. Interview, 22 November 1999. Photograph by Michael J. Chiarappa.

the tugs. I have been around fishermen all my life. What we were doing was subsistence fishing. We were putting food on the table.

When I was small we would go down to John Crawford's fishery and ask for fish heads because we did not have any money but we knew we could always make fish head soup. So we would go down and get trout heads. We also used to spear fish in the spring. We would get suckers, trout, and whatever we could get out of the creek. My dad taught us how to spear fish. There were five of us and he was the only one working, so we would try to pitch in and do what we could, even though I was in my early teens. The first time he took me to the river I was about twelve. He made us gunnysacks and spears. He got us all rigged up and told us we were going to spear suckers. So he showed us how to spear the suckers and how not to get wet, but he was always the first one in. We would hear splash and much laughing and he would yell, "Come on in, the water's fine." So then we would go in waist deep. We got all wet and we would get out fish. We would spear the fish and put them in the gunnysack bag with a rope around it. The bag would float in the water except for the opening so the fish were still alive swimming around, trying to get out in the bag. We would take the bag home clean and gut the fish out. My father had a cousin, Clare Walker, who used to can them. He would take the fish over there and she would can them up. They would look just like pink salmon when she was done. Then he would get them back in the wintertime.

We used to go spearing at Inwood Creek. When we were kids we covered almost ten miles on foot all over the place. We were just a bunch of little wild girls in there fishing. We could be up in Belvedere in the morning and clear over Fisherman's Island in the afternoon. We did not hitchhike or anything. We were on the go all the time.

After I got out of college, I started dating John Keshick, who worked in commercial fishing. When the crew did not all show up, I would be a fill-in. So I just started in as a substitute. They would not have me go out in the lake right off the bat. They had me minding the equipment on shore. I cleaned the nets. We would spread them out to dry them. Then we would pick out crabs, sticks, or anything else that was caught in there. We would fix the big holes—John called them sporty holes because they were big enough to drive a truck through—put in there by carp. I washed the equipment while they were on the lake and made sure nobody came and messed around with our gear.

Ronald Paquin is a member of the Sault Ste. Marie Tribe of Chippewa Indians who chronicled portions of his life in a 1992 book, *Not First in Nobody's Heart: The Story of a Contemporary Chippewa*. During his 1999 interview, he recalled that his work in fishing began when he was a boy.

When I was young, I worked in a fishery down here called Colby's Fishery. When I was nine I cleaned smelt and herring. I had to stand up on a box so I could get high enough to the gut board. They would put the fish on the table for you. That is when I started buying my own clothes, too. If you read my book you know I had a little bad spell in there. I went to reform school. Later, I worked for Gessinger's and the fishery next door too. I worked for Fritz Halbert when I was twelve. He would call me "my boy." The first week when I got done work he said to me: "My boy, do you have a social security card?" I did not know what he was talking about, so they decided they would protect me and I would still work for them. Then I worked on several tugs. I

Ronald Paquin, a member of the Sault Ste. Marie Tribe of Chippewa Indians, began working in commercial fishing as a young man. A treaty fishing rights activist, Paquin co-authored *Not First in Nobody's Heart: The Story of a Contemporary Chippewa* with Robert Doherty in 1992. Interview, 28 May 1999. Photograph courtesy of the Great Lakes Center for Maritime Studies.

worked for Dick Hagen. I worked for Wes Sanders. I worked for Fritz Halbert and then Ray and Carl Halbert. I worked for them on a separate tug. I worked for Avella. I worked for Gustafson.

I worked on lots of tugs. I worked through the ice, too. I fished through the ice. We had the old-time machines like an old Arctic Cat with the steering wheel on it and big skis. It would go top end about nine miles an hour, but it was really powerful. We called Carl and Ray Helbert "the boys." What was so unique about them is that they were well crowding seventy when I worked for them. The younger brother would say to Carl, "You should retire." They were only a year apart. They worked on the lake until they were eighty. Fritz Halbert did a little bit of tugging when the bridge came in, but other than that, they were pretty much fishermen. All of them were old fishermen. Dick Hagen had a fishery down here. I worked for him down there, too. Plus I worked on the tug; I slept on it. I was at each fishery and on every boat.

I tried to go back to school when I was close to nineteen. I worked at King's Fishery just a few nights and dressed herring. Then I got married and the Indian fishing rights come up. I saw the chance to be independent and have my own business. I had my smoked fish business, too. I would smoke my fish up here. At the house I had two smokers and I sold wholesale all over.

Ed John recalled how he began fishing with a hook in line near his boyhood home in Elk Rapids, Michigan. Today, John fishes the waters of Grand Traverse Bay with his wife, Cindi John, in a trap-net boat.

I was born and went to school in Elk Rapids, Michigan. I used to do a lot of fishing, hook and lining, behind the dam in Elk Rapids. It is a good area for perch, bass, and trout. I dropped out of high school in ninth grade. I proceeded to move to this side of

Ed John and Cindi John are members of the Grand Traverse Bay Band of Ottawa and Chippewa Indians. They have worked in both the gill-net and trap-net fisheries and Cindi actively participates in proceedings concerning the formulation of Native American fisheries management policies for Lake Michigan. Interview, 26 May 1999. Photograph by Michael J. Chiarappa.

Grand Traverse Bay because this is where my wife Cindi lived. We got together, and I started commercially fishing with Art Duhamel, who broke into the fishing for the Grand Traverse Band. I worked gill nets with him for about five years. I started fishing for a living in 1975 or 1976. I worked for Art Duhamel for two summers. I do not like fishing in the winter. It is too cold to work in the winter. So we would work with him in the summertime. It was not a fair deal, actually. We were pulling nets by hand, and we would go out and maybe do twenty nets a day. The price did not seem right for doing all the work and not getting the hands on the money.

James Raphael lived near Grand Rapids until he was twenty-two, when he moved to Peshawbestown to live in the community where his father was raised. He found work fishing with his cousin and Indian rights activist Art Duhamel.

My father and my people are from here. I am Ottawa. The reservation is pretty much like one whole family. There are about five families everybody kind of originated from after a lot of people passed away at the turn of the century. I was not born up here. My father lived here. I have been here for sixteen years. I was born down state in Grant, Michigan. My father, Howard Raphael, did a lot of work with the farmers in the orchards and so forth. He was working in an area thirty to forty miles outside Grand Rapids, Michigan. I was pretty much raised down in the city.

When I was twenty-two, I got tired of the city and wanted to get away. I did not really know where to go, so I chose up here where my father was from. I came back to the reservation to see how life was, and to get away from the city life—the alcohol and drugs. I came up here around 1981, 1982, or 1983. It has probably been about sixteen years now. There was not a whole lot of work. I looked around for work and could not find a job. Somebody directed me to Art Duhamel—Skip's father. They said, "Go down and see him. He fishes and can probably put you to work." Art was my cousin. Skip is my cousin too.

I went down there and that was my first involvement with fishing. I introduced myself and he said, "Oh, you are my cousin." He had a crew of people working at the time. He was kind of old; he did not do a whole lot himself. When Art could, he would go out. Art said that everybody was out on the lake already that day. He hesitated a

James Raphael is a member of the Grand Traverse Bay Band of Ottawa and Chippewa Indians. He fishes with his sister, Rose Raphael, on the gillnet tug *Raven's Nest*. Interview, 27 May 1999. Photograph by Michael J. Chiarappa.

little bit and said, "Wait a minute, I do have another boat on the beach." And he had another gang of nets just across the bay, actually right down in Omena, just a couple miles from Peshawbestown, across the bay in Omena Bay. He said, "I have a gang of nets over here. I will put you in this boat and you can get them—we will see how you do and see where it goes from there." I had never been in a boat. I had not really pole fished down in the city. I just left the city life. I proceeded to get in the boat and look for the key to start the boat. Art was watching me and said, "What the hell are you doing?" I said: "I am looking for the key to start the boat." He said, "You pull on the rope on that motor."

So I shove off and pull on the motor and get it started. I am off. He pointed out the direction. Art said, "Go over there and you will find some buoys." He pointed across the bay. You could see things, but you could not see the buoys from there. So I went over there and took care of it all, came back in, and Art hired me. He caught a nice boatload of perch at the time. I later found out that the perch were making a comeback at that time. I worked with Art for a few years. Pretty much everybody worked for him. Art Duhamel was the man as well as a couple of other gentlemen from up north—tribal people—who fought for our fishing rights during the 1970s. They had to fish illegally and get it into court and draw up the procedures and steps. Boats got taken away and it finally got into local court, then in federal court and finally we won it in the 1970s. Everybody would work with Art in the beginning. I worked with him for two or three years off and on. I paid real close attention to what was going on, and learned about fishing.

There were a lot of new things to contend with but not enough to stop me. When I found fishing, I found out that it was in my blood. The history of my family and people goes back to a great grandfather from further north, from Cross Village, who lived in the early 1800s. His name was like Tall Fisherman with Spear in the Bay. He lived back when they fished with spears up in there. I found out in our history that my grandfather fished by pole and sold his fish. I liked to hear that. My sister traced our family to the 1700s. She found out that one of our grandfathers who lived in Cross Village fished up there and he was strictly involved as a fisherman. Part of his name was Naganashe— that is what he was called. He fished with a spear. He would go out spear fishing up there as well as gill netting. So it was good hearing about all the history, way back to them. We fished through our family.

My grandfather fished out of Peshawbestown. I barely remember him. He used to pole fish. We could not commercial fish at that time, probably in the 1920s and 1930s. He would go pole fishing at the back of the village where the marina is. He would bring in eight, ten fish and there would be people waiting to buy them on the shore. Now everybody in my immediate family is pretty much gone. I have one brother and seven sisters. My sister Rose works with me. We are partners. Rose will be on board and working all summer, wherever the fish bring us, maybe Beaver Island.

Skip Duhamel of the Grand Traverse Band of Ottawa and Chippewa Indians fishes with a twenty-six-foot tug named the *Dark Sea Emmet*. As a child, he moved with his father, Art Duhamel, and his mother, Babette Duhamel, to Peshawbestown, the community in which his father was raised. Skip Duhamel recalled that his father's activism was inspired in part by tribal elder Geeboo Sands, his fictive grandfather.

Rose Marie Raphael, a member of the Grand Traverse Band of Ottawa and Chippewa Indians, fishes on board the fish tug, *Raven's Nest,* with her brother, James Raphael. Photograph by Clair Gornowicz.

Duhamel regarded his father's treaty fishing rights activism as the beginning of the tribe's effort to gain federal recognition and renew the latent sense of community that focused on fishing.

My dad moved us back to the community, back to Shabbytown (Peshawbestown), so I would grow up and know the heritage. My grandfather was Geep Sands. Good old Geep was the one who got us going. He raised dad. At that time, we were not gill netting at all because you would promptly be arrested and jailed.

During the 1970s, the old man would come down and he would bug my dad. He had these boxes of nets. He would tell my dad we have got to put them in. He would tell him the time of year was right. We told my dad he had to do it. We knew it was going to mean jail. And finally my dad said, "Well that's it. Let's go put them in." He just could not stand the old man bugging him. It got to him. Geep told my dad that

George "Skip" Duhamel is a member of the Grand Traverse Bay Band of Ottawa and Chippewa Indians. He gill-net fishes in Lake Michigan's tribally managed waters. The son of the late Arthur Duhamel, Skip continues to be a vocal advocate of treaty rights fishing and its role in Ottawa and Chippewa cultural revitalization. Photograph by Michael J. Chiarappa.

he owed it to the people to do this and this is what he was supposed to do. And so my dad did it. We loaded her up. We sat and promptly got arrested. I cannot even count how many times they took our gear.

Geeboo is what we all called Joseph Sands. He is the first fisherman we met. He raised my father as sort of an uncle. He was the foster parent, he and Mary Sands. He was the one that had dad launch the first boat. He encouraged us and offered guidance as far as what fish to look for, and how they moved and traveled. Without that old man, my father would have probably never proceeded. But with him things were not really an option. They were a necessity and you had to move forward. You could not look in his eyes and not do it. And so no matter what the price, we decided—or my father decided—that this family was going to fish and we have been fishing ever since. My dad is dead now, but he raised me, him and Geeboo. Their influences were paramount to my growing up. I returned home to make sure that my father's work was done. We have been doing the best I can with the help with my crew and my brothers and cousins. And we are going to continue to do the best we can. There are many hard times ahead, but we look forward to the time when our children may not have to endure such hardships in order to make a livelihood on the Great Lakes.

There was no organized tribe as such when we first came here. Tribal government was kind of a fallout from my father fishing. Because we had to be licensed, you had to have a bureaucracy or government to license. Then you had to have a tribal council and you had to be federally recognized. All those things are things that he orchestrated. Geep was the instigator of the whole damn thing. It was kind of a neat thing because it showed you could do something if you wanted to. You could feel good about it after the battle was won. We never really had fishing until Dad fought for it and got it in the 1970s.

My dad's first ticket was in 1974, in December. The initial result was ninety days in jail for dad, but they were able to get an injunction through the federal court systems and he was released after a week. The end result of it was federal recognition for this tribe, decent housing, and jobs, not to mention further refinement of the treaty right itself. It spawned many things. The whole tribe here is based on fishing. When we first came here we found a community in despair. We found a community that was used to frequent visits from locals who tossed beer cans at its inhabitants. There were beatings in taverns that still had "No Indians" signs in the 1970s; there were outhouses and poor sanitation. Now we have our own water plant. Anybody in this community who needs a job can have a decent paying job, employed through their own community. Everybody has housing. We have seen a returning of our traditional ways. We have seen hope again. That is basically what was the end result out of that ticket.

My father knew the implications of his work absolutely. But, no, he never saw the payoffs. What it meant for him was a life of hardship, struggle, and disappointment. He knew the implications of listening to Geeboo's counsel. He knew what it all meant for us. During the early 1960s, my dad was making $50–$60,000 a year pipeline welding, top of the line. We wanted for nothing. And then he took the next ten to twenty years of his life and invested it in attorneys, not to mention jail time, incarceration, loss, and hardship you could not even fathom.

I am really proud to say that I am a lot like my father in the fact that the harder you pushed him, the harder he got. The day they took his first boat insured he would buy another two. The day they stole the first nets insured he would buy ten more. From time to time, he would have to go back to work on a pipeline to get more equipment so that we could continue to fish. Then they would confiscate that equipment. He had several boats sunk, chopped up with axes by local vigilantes. My father was a very stubborn man and was very determined. He would not be dissuaded. The more the opposition came and the harder the problems were to surmount, the more he struggled to meet them and deal with them. We had to have Bureau of Indian Affairs certification. We had to have federal recognition. All these things were a direct result of his efforts. We needed a tribal chairman. We needed somebody with business savvy. He recruited them. Name a program or a health service—everything was derived from us setting these gill nets. What it meant was a revision, a rebirth of the Ottawa-Chippewa, Grand Traverse Bands, as a rebirth of a nation. I am very, very happy that my father brought me home to do this and in his absence, I will do the best I can.

This is my life's work. I have no greater aspirations in my life than to be a fisherman. I am a member of the conservation committee. I advise our council on what our policy should be as a people and a tribe with respect to the resource. We decide what would be reasonable for us and what would not be reasonable for us. In my own community, my words do not fall on deaf ears. I have gained an amount of respect from my people for my own hardships and, of course, my family's hardships and my father's. My father was like the George Washington of the Grand Traverse Band. He was the one that founded this tribe and so I had the respect of my family name by following in my father's footsteps. Of course, the half a dozen arrests that the State of Michigan has imposed on me trying to inhibit these rights have confirmed everybody's belief in the community that I am my father's son. So that all helps. As far as recognition from our own community, I receive it gratefully. It is very appreciated and the tribal members support me. I am half-Irish, and not as dark-skinned as most community members and readily accepted. Prejudice in any form is wrong, whether it is against Mexican Americans, Indians, Hispanics, or Chinese; it is no good. My dad taught that to me. He instilled in me that you should judge a man by his works and not the color of his race. I found when we first moved here there were an awful lot of resentments from the Native Americans toward the dominant society. Over the last twenty-five years we have seen these lessen. We do not have to sulk and hide our heads. We can walk down the street and be proud of who we are. We have seen a rebirth of our culture, our language, our traditions, and our customs.

We have our sovereignty, employment, and housing. We have our own water quality expert. I see this tribe as a leader as far as preserving the Great Lakes ecosystem in the future, especially in our home area because we have jurisdiction over it. We are not afraid to exercise it. We have been able to block some major development areas in our spawning reef because we are the protectors of the Great Lakes. We are not the rapists of the resource. In fact, we are the protectors of this resource. And it is very encouraging to see things that we have been able to accomplish as far as our hatchery, the planting of fish, and the protection of some major spawning reefs that they intended to develop. We blocked the sale of the South Fox Island, a very, very special place out there. In the end, when it is all said and done, I will have made a difference just as my father did. It is just the second half of the job as she is not all wrapped up yet. I doubt that I will be able to accomplish all the goals and things that I want to achieve in my lifetime. I still have hopes that my daughter may help, although I would just as soon she became a professional person like an attorney. But we all have our own paths and whatever she does with her life will be good. If you can leave your mark in the world, it is to make it a better place for your people. What more thanks would anybody need, if you can just look around and see a difference in anybody's quality of life? That is what it is all about really—to still be an Indian is being able to have some sweet grass and make an offering before you get your catch, whether it is three boxes or thirty. There is always something to be grateful for. The lake is bountiful, the fish are many and we are few.

If I thought what I was doing had any harm to the Lake Michigan resource, I would quit as well we all should. That is true, too. I would quit. If there was something I was hurting out here, we would quit. But I have no problem sleeping at night catching the fish that I catch. As long as I feel in my mind and the biologists and the numbers work and there is no harm to the resource, there is no reason why we cannot continue to live like we have lived here on this land for hundreds of years. That about sums her up.

I see in print things like "Local Sports Groups Fear Duhamel May Deplete the Resource." I am one man. It is unfathomable that people would print things like that. We know that the lakes can produce millions of pounds of fish for all users. As aboriginal title holders to this state, our forefathers had the light and wisdom to know that if we could retain these rights to hunt and fish that we could still retain our identity. They were pretty wise because we have. So it is not just the fishing issue. This is not just a fishing issue or a resource issue or a social issue. It is an identity issue of our culture preservation. The main thing I want is to make sure that my father would be proud of the work that I have done by the time I am dead. He would be very pleased. So I have already got what I want. If I can get her all wrapped up where our kids can fish and still be part of these communities that are around us without facing the violence and things like that that accompany or have always accompanied us, it would be nice. It would be nice to see this end where things would be okay for everybody. It would be the ultimate goal.

The non-native community is becoming aware of violence and vandalism more and more. They have become outraged about this kind of thing. The people that do these things are not the majority. They are the minority. I find ever-growing support in the non-native communities. The worst thing I find is misinformation. I want people to understand what is really happening with the Great Lakes and what treaty fishing is involved in and that we do far more good than harm. We are no different than an osprey or an otter. We are just part of Mother Nature.

There are some fish that need to be kept in check, particularly salmon. If you have an overpopulation of salmon they will eat everything out here. The best I ever did was 80,000 pounds of salmon and your average fish was twenty-five to thirty pounds each. They counted every fish I caught, every one. The thing is they would of been dead three months from then anyway. Why in the hell not harvest them? They were going to be harvested by the State of Michigan at the weir at the end of their life cycle. As they pass by my home in my back yard, I am going to catch some of them for food to support three families. Right now it is just me and Vince Chippewa, but Donny Chippewa will come back to work here pretty quick, and the fishing supports his family too. He had to take a little time off. I put my dad's ashes right out in front here. That is where he wanted to be. When I am done, that is where I want to be, too, except a little further south, like Frankfort.

Yvonne Keshick (Little Traverse Bay Band of Odawa) fished in Grand Traverse Bay with her husband, John Keshick. She recalled the risks involved in fishing from a sixteen-foot boat. Keshick combined fishing with raising children and working as an artist.

One time, John and his son were almost swamped when the big waves were coming in. I was out there when the swells were huge. It looked like a big black wall coming, and they were not breaking, just swells. And I thought, what the hell am I

The fish aren't coming upstream like they used to

In this editorial cartoon, Grand Traverse Band of Ottawa and Chippewa Indians commercial fishing licensee Skip Duhamel was personally blamed for the demise of the salmon and lake trout sport fishery and the charter boat business in 1995. Cartoon by Gene Hibbard of the Traverse City, Michigan, *Record Eagle*. Courtesy of *Traverse City Record Eagle*.

doing out here? And I was rowing that boat faster and faster. John said, "Slow down, slow down." I looked behind me and there was another big one coming, big dark thing looming up in the dark. You could not see across the bay; you could not see the lights, the tower, or anything. I said, "The boat's filling up with water." Sure enough, we had a leak. Some of the rivets on the boat popped, and it was filling up with water. We were maybe a mile and a half from shore. We were just about done anyway, so John finished setting the nets and then he rowed in because he rowed a lot quicker than I could.

I am an artist. I am a quill worker. The fishing was done in between. I made quill boxes, little tiny one-inch to sixteen inches. I made quill boxes for twenty years and was self-supporting. But before I decided I was going do quill work full time, in the early years it was fishing. Physically, it was exhausting. We would go and set at eleven o'clock at night and we would stay out on the lake till about three. Then we would start loading up the fish. By six o'clock we were on the road going to market. The two guys would go to market with the fish and I would get dropped off with the equipment and stuff. I would start breakfast when they would go to market. I would feed them and they could go to sleep if they wanted or repair equipment. So while they were doing repair work and stuff, I would be cleaning the boat and we would unload the nets. John would pay his sons who helped him, but they would not clean the nets. We would work getting ready for the next day. Pretty soon it was three-and-a-half-hours. Sometimes we would have no sleep; the hours just start adding up. There were times when we wished it would storm so we could have a chance just to rest, but nobody would say so because we were always trying to ton up. I never met a rich Indian fisherman, never.

I planned on fishing when my children were old enough and they are getting close to it. I did not have a boat yet. But I had a heart attack so that kind of cuts out lifting nets. I had to find something else. I liked the work. I learned a lot from the fishermen. A lot of the fishermen are gruff and stuff like that, but they did not hesitate to put tobacco on the water. The fishermen I fished with, they usually used tobacco. And then they kind of did it on their own someplace quiet where everybody could not see. They were offering it for safety and a ton up. I do not know how you could do that in a six-teen-foot boat, but they would pray we would get a ton up.

I want to fish so that my kids can learn. I want to teach my kids. Their father is a fisherman and I feel they should learn that. One of my children is seventeen. She can get on the boat this summer if she wanted to start working. She has got older brothers who fish, so they are willing to put her to work. She could have a choice. My daughter is also a quill worker. I am trying to teach them everything I learned. All my children do quill work. The youngest one is twelve. I think it is important culturally and to be a part of the finest quill work in the world. It is really exclusive. There are a lot of quill workers up here, all at different stages of expertise. Each has their own style and ways of doing things because everybody is taught different, just like fishing. It depends on who taught you.

Who taught you determines where you are going to fish. John Case and John Keshick fished together. The knowledge combined between them helped them find good fishing spots. In Bay Harbor, we used to haul out fish out of there so big, we could only put two in a fish box. Sometimes they were so big, we would have to carry one at a time up the hill. We did not have a truck. It was really subsistence. We would throw them in the trunk of the car until the trunk fell through. It would happen; there were fish falling out on the roads.

There is some really good fishing out in the bay. The way we learned was just watching and decided for ourselves what we wanted to do. I was fishing when was I pregnant with my daughter who is now seventeen. I was three months pregnant and rowed the boat. After she was born, if we could not find somebody to watch her, she would go to the lake with us. I would go down to the lake for the lift. We would put her on a fish box, prop her up and wrap her up really good with just her face showing. Just her eyes and nose were sticking out of that bundle of clothing and blankets. She would watch us pick the fish out of the nets. When we were done, we would carry her with everything else. I wish I had had a camera then. The water was so clear and the big rocks down underneath were just huge, rocks the size of cars. You could look down in between the cracks and see fish. It was really nice.

We fished in the Little Traverse Bay, toward Charlevoix. We did not have any trouble getting whitefish. We would catch a lot of those great big gold fish, great big carp. They would get caught in the nets and just tear them up. Around the Big Rock nuclear plant, we caught suckers; they would get caught in our nets. They are the bottom feeders. They had growths on their bodies. They had lumps the size of marbles growing on the eyes, off the corners of their mouths, and where their fins attached to the back. There were growths on the more tender parts of their bodies. John would kill them and leave them on the beach. A sturgeon once got caught in the nets and just waited patiently while they were lifting. John untangled him and turned him loose. It did not thrash or anything. They were in a sixteen-foot boat and the sturgeon was about twelve foot. And he turned it loose. He untangled it real carefully and it just drifted away just as nice and smooth as could be, just drifted away. John always felt that this was one of his sons who had come to visit him.

We would see lamprey marks on trout when we got trout. And this was before they started telling us the target for each species of fish and who was going for trout, and who was going for whitefish. We had a mixture. It was not very often, but you would get a brown trout or a rainbow trout once in a while. John would give them to the old folks, people he knew who liked fish but do not get out. It made him feel good, like he was all right. That is how it was in the old days. If you got an extra amount of fish, then you gave away what you had because someday, you might need something to eat and somebody else might share their deer. It was support; the internet that helped pull people together was the food that they shared, so it was a real cultural thing. It was great when we got fish. When we got fish that was not for good sale or smoked fish, we would give it away. We would take boxes to pow wows and just give away chunks of fish.

We went to different markets, like Bell's Fishery in Mackinaw City, Kings up in Naubinway, and there was another one outside Mackinaw City. I forgot what it is called; it could be Big Stone Bay. Some customers were private people. John used to sell whitefish to a senior home. The seniors would have whitefish down there, and the fish was fresh.

<hr />

Cindi John, who fishes in Grand Traverse Bay in a trap-net boat, linked fishing to the larger issue of cultural endurance.

There is a perception that if you fish, you lack skills. Ed John has a lot of skills; he is an ironworker and a welder. He has worked on the road, but he never liked any of his jobs. Then Ed started fishing and he liked it. There was something about it. Then it evolved. It was something that he really liked doing. In 1989, he got off the big boat and we got back on the little boat. We would be out on a twenty-one-foot boat. You would be out there, and you could smell when the lake was turning. It would be real calm and then you would see the ripples and then you would see whitecaps. Ed would say, "No, we are finishing this gang, just keep picking."

In a twenty-one-foot boat, you are inside the lake. You are really fortunate lots of times to get back on the beach. For us, fishing was like a treatment plan. Ed quit drinking and I quit drinking with him. We got to go out and spend time together. It would be real stressful for us sometimes. We would fight and yell at each other, and then we would come back and we would have two or three boxes of fish. We were okay if we had enough fish to make the boat payment or the car payment. Then our lives really got swept along not only by the biological issues of the fishery, but the political issues as well. It was like a big storm in our life and we hung onto it. But for us, it has really freed us from having to be inside someplace from eight to five, and we are our own bosses. You really only accomplish what you go out to do. You know how to do. It is a good feeling to be able to go out and really know what the lake is and to smell it and to feel it. There is a lot more to it than just the financial part of it.

This year a deal was finally worked out where we could use a big boat because it was so unsafe working on our little boat. We decided that if we had to keep using a little boat, I was going to get off and work on the other boat, so that if one boat went down there would be one of us alive to raise our kids. These are the choices you make in that kind of situation. We thought about just getting out, but if we get out, what about the nearly fifty nephews and nieces we have between us. If we leave it, they will never have the opportunity to smell and feel the lake. You are really a doorway to your next generation. If we do not keep our operation, I know that these kids will never have an opportunity to feel that. We have had young people work for us who will never fish again, but they have felt and experienced the lake. They go on and they work other occupations, but they hang onto that experience and it is a satisfaction. So we continue fishing both for the satisfaction and for the ones that are coming up yet. You get a lot of things that people cannot get with money. Some people work really hard and go on vacation. They come up here for a vacation and they go home. We get to live here and experience it totally—fishing is totally part of your being. We get to watch the seasons change, feel the wind, and watch the weather.

Ron Paquin discussed the dangers and economic uncertainty faced by tribal fishermen. At the time of his interview Paquin was not fishing because, in his view, the 1985 Consent Agreement had left the tribe with too few grids open to fishing. The treaty rights activist also gave up fishing because he cannot afford impoundment gear.[25]

There was someone from the DNR who wanted me to take the civil service exam so they could hire me and put me in a fire tower out in Moran. I am afraid of heights, so I would not have even been able to climb it. But they were willing to hire me; I always wondered after all this if I should have taken it. Fishing is a rough life; it is a terrible life. Most of us fished in rowboats. I damn near drowned, I do not know how many times. In fact, my nephew did drown when he fell through the ice while fishing with me in 1984.[26]

You could not insure your rigs because people were shooting holes in them and stealing your nets. What insurance company in their right mind would give you insurance? I could not even get life insurance because I was fishing in a sixteen-foot rowboat.

I do not fish now, but I think I would be awful tempted if they ever opened them waters up. I will give you an example. One time we went down there and I thought we had $369 in the bank. I called my wife and she said, "No Ron, it is $69." I said: "Okay, I got my nets in." Within four days, we had $2,700 in the bank. But it is called "feast or famine," and that is exactly what it is. I am glad I am not fishing now. But if I had a trap-net rig, I would stay and fish. It is a lot easier. You lift your nets up and dip the fish out, sew the spot back up and drop her back down.

I fished all the way into Frankfort, Traverse City, Charlevoix, and all the way back this way to Atwood. I have fished all the places where you can get in, like Nine-Mile. I fished up there to Lake Huron. There are some pretty prime waters in this area. There are more prime waters where we are not fishing now. The trap netter has impoundment gear. They want everybody to go to trap nets, but it costs you a good $100,000 or more just to get started. They wanted me to go into the trap nets. Well, buy me a trap-net rig. I tried it and I did not have enough money to do it.

Now that the tribes have the casinos I do not imagine that fishing is going to be of too much importance to some of them. It is quite comical, but it is really not comical. My wife and I knew a lot of the fishermen up at Bay Mills. I saw three of them are now working at the casino. You work in the casino if you can get a good enough job and cannot afford a trap-net rig.

In the early 1970s everybody was fishing. In the spring there would be fifty to sixty four-wheel drives on Rex Beach. By the time the fall came, Johnny Alexander and I were the only ones there. Right now, I can think of three of them that are doing it here. One is a trap-net rig and there are a couple of gill-net tugs—that is it.

This was a prime fishing area for most people fishing. We fished primarily whitefish. When the trout was on, we fished trout. Then we fished herring. I fished some perch. I made $10,000—almost $11,000 on four nets in a month and a half, but I was a pretty damn young man. It is a lot of tough work. Then I made another $2-$3,000 on the whitefish run that fall. But we fished primarily whitefish.

They are trying to get a better outlet for menominees. They are very perishable fish, but they are really good. If they could do that, I would maybe even go back to fishing. But only if they could ever get a good outlet for the menominees—like the Japanese. They had a bunch of Jewish people. They had to say a prayer for every cut they made on the fish. We are working with perishable fish here. There was too much praying and not enough putting them on ice. But that would have been a nice outlet. The Jewish people eat the whitefish; this is very good for the fishermen because we get a better price. Now our tribe is starting a co-op for our fishermen and they are starting to get a better price for their fish.

There are lots of things they could do to improve this fishery. For instance, get some more waters. We are supposed to get the whole twenty-two percent so we can fish it. I would not encourage a young fellow to become a fisherman now. I would encourage it if they had their heart set on it. I told my son: "If you want to fish the fall run, I will go with you. We could make some money in the fall run." Why not? So maybe we can have gravy two times a year, in the spring run and the fall.

They can call me a "gravy fisherman" if they want. This is what has happened. A lot of fishermen who first started out did it during the "gravy time." Then all of a sudden, they had to think about how to put a net in the water and where to put it. You have to follow these fish—you have to learn their habitat and the depth of the water and the weather. The moon has a lot to do with it. There are all sorts of things you have to know. Then you have to know the bottom of your lake, what you are going to get, like green moss. Now the zebra mussels are coming in. So there is a lot to look at. An old fisherman, Carl Halbert said, "Ron, when you stop learning on this lake, you are dead." That is the case with everything. You never can stop learning. I am quite a talker, but I have learned that to get some wisdom you have to listen, too. I believe in being honest and I believe in compassion. So you get these instilled in you and what does it do? It builds up your self-esteem. And you know how important that is. I will tie it into the fishing rights. You are getting knocked down and trying to get back up and be nice at the same time. Then pretty soon you get radical and it all stems from the fact that you are trying to make a living for your family.

James Raphael sees the Grand Traverse Band's ability to retain and expand its fishing grounds as essential to the tribe's economic and cultural revitalization. The growth of tribal gaming facilities has made it even more important for the Indians to maintain their fishing cultural traditions.

We do not have many people fishing right now. We follow our conservation rules—they are right on us daily. We have heavy-duty fines and have been in court several times for not turning in a catch report. So the things that are talked about as far as unregulated fishing are totally untrue. We follow all the rules and regulations. If I did not, I would be in a brand new house. We would have more fish. We would be making more money than we do in the middle of all the struggles. We also have to abide by state rules and regulations; they have got us boxed up in. One of the reasons why I stayed fishing was I knew that there was money to be made. But it is to a point where it is just getting by. We lose gear and gear gets stolen. We have to deal with the state. They have us in a corner. After fifteen years, it is not all that I thought it would be. It is a lot of hard work. You have to know what you are doing to keep yourself and your crew safe. Then you have to deal with everything else.

It has been proven that we have been fishing for over 1,000 years. If a person has been fishing for 1,000 years it seems like the fish would be gone if they were going to be gone. But they are still here and we are still fishing, so it is just a bunch of talk of theirs. They have nothing real to talk about. It does not make sense that we should use the same equipment we used in the 1830s. Why would we? We have got machines today.

The state should be pleased with the way our tribe is and what we are doing. My own belief is we should be the richest people in the world. This is the most prime spot in the whole world. I believe that the state wants it. They would like to see us stop fishing. They did not want our land in the beginning when Michigan came into the Union. It was all swamp. But it was our paradise. We fished here. Animals were here and we hunted. They said leave that to the Indians. It is just all swamp. All Michigan was all Ottawa land. It was our people here. We allowed Chippewas to come in and Potowatomies to live down state. This whole territory was ours. There was more than enough fish. Chippewas came in and we said you can camp here and take fish. There is more than enough.

James Raphael at the net lifter of his fish tug, the *Raven's Nest,* 1999. Photograph by Clair Gornowicz.

Then the government came along and made these so-called treaties. I do not believe in one of them. They were all falsified. I do not go by any treaties. I only look to them because it is the only way I can fish right now and make a living and do what I like to do. It takes the head group of people to make an agreement and all of our heads had left and walked away. They decided this is a bunch of talk. We are not talking to you and we are not signing anything. So they would go back to their little offices and make the agreement or pull some Indians out of the woods—they were not the head people, they were not the chiefs, the ones who had left the negotiating table. Every treaty was done like that. They were always falsified. There has not been one true treaty. That is why people doubt them. Our people dealt with the creator, God, whatever. They had sacred, spiritual ways of doing things. They used a pipe, and whatever was done with that was between God and what was going on. It was not between a pencil and a paper and a thought from the mind alone. So our people were not stupid. But then the government would go back and figure out how to make the treaty happen. To make the treaty that we go on now, they got all of the Indians drunk and sick. They said they would cut them off. They were sick. They said, "Sign this and we will get you some more." They were not chiefs. They were just nobodys forced to sign the treaties. So I do not really believe in the treaties, but I have to follow them. I believe in things like my people would have back then. Good things come out of my heart like that.

Our people should be fighting. They accept what is going on. They give in to them. The more you give in, the more they want, and the more they take, which is what got us as fishermen into this position. You give them a little bit, and they take more and they got us down to hardly any fish. We are fish people or we would not be living by the lake. Our camp would not be on the lake. Fish was our main diet. It is why we came here so we could harvest fish. Our people were kind of forced to give into the gaming interests. If you keep giving into them without a fight, they are going to want to take whatever they can get. What has happened in past history is what is happening now. They have gaming compacts just like our fishing agreement and they have to abide with the state. All tribes, any people, would want the kind of money that it generates. So they have to deal closely with the state and government—so that is kind of in the middle of everything that they agree upon.

Cindi John observed that her involvement in fishing is a result of family and community influences. Fishing is, in her view, integral to the identity of the Chippewa-Ottawa people.

When I was little, my dad fished. He was a sports fisherman. We lived up north. My dad was a truck driver who owned a small airplane and took people up to the bush for camping and hunting expeditions. He had a powerboat, a cabin cruiser and an aluminum boat. I was my dad's fishing buddy and so I learned. I know and love that end of doing it recreationally.

Fishing issues were relevant for our tribe—our becoming a tribe depended on it. It was something we knew about, but it was kind of distant because it was not right in our face—in our house. When Ed started working for Art Duhamel, he stunk from the work. There are a lot of native people that do not have any more of a clue about fishing than non-native people. I worked in the planning department, and I had to give him a ride home. I complained about it all the time because we lived in Traverse City, and he worked out here. He was gill netting and he stunk from the work. I had the perspective of what it is like for a regular person to encounter the smell in people.

When I went back to school, Ed was fishing all along. I was taking a photography class as part of the commercial art course, and so they said you have to do a final project. So I did a comparison of gill-net fishing to trap-net fishing. All along, I had a younger sister—she has passed away now—that had been in the fishery right along with Ed since it started up with Art Duhamel. She was always saying, "Come out, come out, take pictures. You need to get out here on the lake." And so I went out on the lake in the gill-net boat with her and Art Duhamel, and then out on the trap-net operation with Ed and their crew. I took pictures of each operation. School abruptly ended because our car got wrecked and we lived in the country. But I could get a ride to Shabbytown (Peshawsbestown), and I started sewing nets for Art Duhamel. The following year, Ed and the guys on trap-net crew were drinking a lot, and he got in trouble for it and had to get off that boat. We got a skiff and started fishing out of a skiff. I went out and picked fish for him. We started out in a twenty-one-foot steel skiff that we use for our trap-net skiff right now. Ed pulled twenty-eight nets by hand that first season. Then he came back and spent a couple years training the other trap-net crew.

PART 2. COMING BACK TO THE WATER: THE POLITICAL AND ECONOMIC STRUGGLE OF INDIAN FISHING RIGHTS

Skip Duhamel (Grand Traverse Band of Ottawa and Chippewa Indians) uses both gill and trap nets. He has spent most of his time fishing on Lake Michigan in smaller boats, and has narrowly escaped serious injury.

My dad gave me his first tug, a 1935 thirty-foot wooden tugboat with a seventy-horse motor made in 1946. We threw a rod in the engine and locked her up tighter than hell about ten o'clock in the morning on the tip of Old Mission Peninsula. The wind started increasing and increased all day and our anchors broke. The wind took us just to the outer skirts of Grand Traverse Bay. The helicopters did not find us until the next morning around nine o'clock. My dad had been out looking for me all night long in his tugboat. He finally found us and he headed across the bay against the orders of the Coast Guard because the weather was so severe. He saved us and brought us back in. That was pretty harrowing. We drifted from the inner part of Grand Traverse Bay, damn near to Charlevoix. And it was wintertime.

Today we use #12 mono, heavy stuff, five-and-a-half-inch mesh gill net that is set shallow, real shallow for lake trout and salmon in the spring and fall. The fish move into the deep in the summer, so we have got some gill nets in the deep. We are really fortunate that there are fish stocks that are pretty goddamn good. It is the planting.

We got one of those trap-net things out there, too. It encompasses the whole boat.It is really hard to lay out a trap net. If we do not have a proper set on it you have got to put it back out and do it all over again. My new boat is a 1949 Chris Craft. I got a diesel engine for it, a Volvo Penta. I have invested about $8,000 bucks into it. I have had this boat six, seven, eight years now. My brother and I built the cabin. There was nothing.

The trap net is huge. It has not caught shit so far, but that is because we do not have it set properly. We have got to have a calm day to come out here and move it in this little boat. We are asking this boat to do something it does not really have the capacity to do. It does it because we make it do it. The trap net comes right over the edge of the boat, across the back. My bigger boat is for gill nets. It is closed and it will be nice and warm. And it is safer because it is a lot larger boat and will take the seas better, especially here.

I can only go to the 45th parallel with the gill net. That is part of the reason we bought the trap-net thing. It is also because they steal our nets every year. A vandal cannot get it to the surface without a capstan winch. It is too heavy. It relies on tension. It is tight. It would be like if you took a rubber band and stretched it tight and tried to pull it up. It would tip any smaller boat; it tipped this one. Your average Joe does not understand the mechanics of it.

Economically, there is no comparison between a gill net and a trap net. I paid $1,000 for a used trap net. I spent $300 repairing it, another $1,000 for the anchor, $400 for the rope, and it has not caught one fish yet. And I had to get another skiff to set it. It takes two boats to set it, but we will make it work. We would have been starved out if we had been counting on it.

When a gill net gets away, they will catch fish and fill up. The fish collapse the net. And it rolls up with dead fish and collects sticks and zebra mussels. Basically it looks bad when somebody finds it. As far as repeating a cycle or something like that, continuing to kill—whatever it catches it will catch. It will collapse if they are not regularly attended.

We got a lake trout once that was thirty pounds. We got a forty-pound sea salmon and a sturgeon that weighed about 110 pounds. It was amazing he even came to the surface. He just came floating up. I thought it was a log. There are no native fish there. They are all planted. All except the whitefish. The salmon have brought BKD, bacterial kidney disease. It is killing our whitefish now. They introduced that foreign fish and it brought a foreign disease. The whitefish pays twice as much as the lake trout fish. The bad part is that they planted fifteen million lake trout here. They are so abundant a majority of the time, we are dependent on lake trout. We usually come here in the spring because there are so many lake trout. It is their rules that bring us to this area. Whitefish are valuable. They denied us the areas where we need to go to fish whitefish, so we fish trout. We have a wholesaler who will pick them up for us. The fish he bought yesterday he filleted. And then he will bring them back and drop them to the restaurants in several cities all along the way to Charlevoix.

———

James Raphael recalled how access to capital, including his share of tribal gaming revenue, has enabled him to invest in better equipment. He is worried that if whitefish stocks continue to go down, he will be unable to make his payments.

I got tired of working for somebody else and thought I can do this. I can get my own boat. I found a sixteen-foot aluminum boat, gathered up some nets from some of the fishing people—some used equipment—and put it all together and started fishing on my own. Soon, everybody started following that procedure. Anyway, I ended up getting my first boat and started fishing. Other little boats came after that. They were all pretty much little boats until I got the boat that I have now—the *Raven's Nest*. I acquired it in October after talking with the banks for quite some time—maybe six months—and using some influence from the per capita payments we get from gaming revenues. It was hard. I did not have much credit. Finally, I convinced them that I was the person that this boat should go to—that I would make it work. The boat had been repossessed. I won the bid and finally got it.

We have been fishing the *Raven's Nest* for eight months, since October. I have been doing all right, staying alive and paying the note. I had one hell of a time. I got the boat to pursue fish and get out into expanded areas, which I could not do with a little boat, especially on the open water side into Lake Michigan, out of Leland. For fourteen or fifteen years, I had small boats. The boat I have now has a net lifter that pulls the net up. it is a regular fish tug operation. Pulling nets up out of the water by hand for fourteen years was pretty tough. Now I can make it toward the islands because some of the fishing is not good inside the Grand Traverse Bay where our village of Peshawbestown is. Our village was located there so we could cover the inside of the bay. The village was able to get fish when we established these grounds in 1800s.

This is my first major investment—the boat, truck, and equipment. It is used gear, but it is still a major investment; I have to pay the bank back for this equipment. I just keep hoping every day for enough fish to carry off what I am trying to do.

Ed John, who fishes from a trap-net boat in Grand Traverse Bay with his wife Cindi John, recalled his participation in a training program that introduced tribal fishers to trap-net fishing as an alternative to gill-net fishing.[27]

They started a trap-net program working out of Omena. They got a boat from the feds. The boat's name was the *Lady Hilma*. I worked on that boat on a training program for about four years or five years. About three different crews went through the training program but nobody actually took over the vessel. It kept on being like a training program. I think the feds and the state funded it. I am not sure what was to take place after the program was over. It got to a point where the tribe no longer wanted to continue the program and it ended. The end of the fishing season came and we got these pink slips saying that the program was over. We did not know what to do. We went to a tribal council meeting of the Grand Traverse Band of Ottawa and Chippewa Indians. We addressed the tribal council and asked them about fishing the boat. There were three of us that were working on the boat at the time. They would allow us to fish it for a year. We had to get a lease agreement for the boat, and pay about $10,000 a year. But the crew could not lease it; the lease had to be in an individual's name. Then the effort went down the drain.

I ended up going into business working off a twenty-one-foot steel skiff, pulling

The *Lady Hilma* served as a training vessel for tribal fishers learning how to use trap-net gear as an alternative to traditional gill nets. Cindi John and Ed John worked on board the *Lady Hilma* during the late 1980s. Courtesy of the *Traverse City Record Eagle*.

the nets by hand for about two years or three years. Then they started up another training program with the *Lady Hilma*. I got back on there because Brian Price, who was the trap-net training coordinator, wanted me to be on the boat. He needed help with the crew because he had a different job in Leland and did not want to do the training job on a full-time basis.

After about two years, Cindi and I had a personal conflict with the people that were working on the boat. So we got off the boat, and went back to fishing gill nets again. We did that for a couple more years. We ended up getting into the small trap-net boat program with the states and the feds and the tribes. We had the boat built for us and this is where we ended up. We are working on a deal with the state to get the *Hilliard*, a bigger boat, because the small trap-net boat was crowded. It did not have a lot of working space for the three people working on the boat, Cindi, William Fowler, and myself.

When we were setting the traps in the fall, there was a lot of moss and debris floating in the water. It was getting stuck in the mesh of the trap nets and they were pretty hard to pull up over the top of the small boat without actually getting to the point where you might flip the boat over. So if we ran into problems like that, we would end up leaving nets in until the next year. We are trying to work out the deal with this boat because it is a lot safer, and has more room to work. It does not create the problems that the small boat would.

Cindi John of the Grand Traverse Band fished on the *Lady Hilma* with her husband Ed, before they purchased a small trap-net boat. She used her photographic skills to show U.S. District Court Justice Richard Enslen how they had been pressured to buy a boat that was too small to pull traps nets safely.

We were always in this controversy over trap netting and gill netting, small boat trap netting, large boat trap netting, and gear being provided to the tribe from the state. The *Lady Hilma* was part of trying to work out those differences. There was another training program, so we went to work on the *Lady Hilma*. Ed John went back and trained crews on the trap-net boat he had worked on previously. Ed helped the state train the crew on that boat in the hope of being able to apply to lease that vessel, but it did not get leased. So we went back to fishing out of the twenty-one-foot boat until they closed the east side of Grand Traverse Bay down on us. When the small trap-net experiment came along, we were told to have the boat builder look at our twenty-one-foot boat and to see if it could be converted into a trap-net boat to work ten-foot trap nets. The boat builder said it could be done, but it would cost $35,000. So he recommended spending $45,000 for a boat that is built specially for that purpose.

We were faced with needing a safer vessel because of how they crammed us all up into this area. We built the boat, and were led to believe that if it did not work out that the project would take it over. We learned different about five years ago. Finally, we are coming to a solution by trading boats. We went through a lot since the trap-net operation transpired. In one of the all-time management highlights of the 1985 Consent Decree, they put together a group of biologists representing the state, tribe and federal governments, and told them that they were to manage the project. All the usable data that they had and used to go to court was derived from us desperately trying to stay in the business and financing our own vessel. But doing that was good, because it showed them the realities of things that occurred to us that they would not have encountered if they had just had the state or the tribe write a check. We showed them that if you got a small trap-net vessel, it had to be built for its intended purpose. It had to be insurable. A boat builder will only build down to a certain size boat because of liability and all of the realities and nuts and bolts of it. But when we got the boat built, they did not have us work ten-foot trap nets off it. They had us work sixteen-, twenty-, and thirty-foot trap nets which, in essence, are the same size nets that you would work off of a forty-five-foot vessel, except they made them skinny so that they would fit over the back of the little boat. So the gear did not change, but the boat size changed, and we worked in really unsafe conditions.

What we went through is documented. We could not remove gear from the water and we were held liable for it. At the same time, we showed them that you could go out and catch 100,000 pounds of fish with that vessel. But the true cost of the operation was the same as a large trap-net operation. We never could have gotten into trap netting if we were not allowed to use the state's nets. That was the business part of it for us. They provided nets for the experiment, and we were able to go and find out the problems. If it was just a matter of setting and tending nets, our boat could handle it. It was when nets got mossed and rolled up in storms that we could not. We could not pull them back on the boat and so we gave them a pictorial report of that problem.

I went in front of Judge Enslen on the small trap-net boat issue. We went down to the courthouse. I took pictures of it and made a photograph collection because few people realize that when we go to court, you have to go to Kalamazoo. You do not go to Leland. You go through the metal detector and down the marble floors. We were in front of the judge, and he looked at all the evidence. He stated right off noting that we are not subsidized. He realized that if we had to buy all this equipment, we would lose $26,000 a year. Even if the equipment was bought for us and we were allowed to use it, he realized that we would lose $26,000 a year. We used my report and photographs to get this point across to him. It was not written in legalese; it was just written and presented straight, and flat-out to explain what took place from our perspective. We wanted to show what happened to us and how it unfolded.

Trap nets require larger boats than many of Lake Michigan's Native American fishers can afford. Cindi John, a member of the Grand Traverse Band of Ottawa and Chippewa Indians and tribal fishing license holder, took this photograph to build the tribe's case in U.S. District Court for aid to obtain larger, safer boats for trap-net fishing. Photograph courtesy of Cindi John.

We answered their questions very completely about the true cost and using a crew that was experienced. Initially it was a question of whether the crew knew what they were doing. But it was pretty plain from the beginning. It was like using a van to do a semi's job. Sure, you can haul groceries with a van. It is just that you are going to have to go up and down the road twenty times more and your van is going to wear out faster.

James Raphael expressed concern about whitefish stocks. He feels that because the Ottawa have lost their land, greater state, federal, and tribal resources should be spent in restoring the whitefish fishery central to tribal culture.

This is supposed to be a good time to be fishing but it is not. We used to have whitefish in here. They planted so many lake trout, they chased them and their predators away. They should be trying their damnedest to restore the whitefish. I think they have in the past, but they are not putting a lot of effort into it. We should be try-ing. We should have a hatchery on the lake, with a pipe fish into the lake. I do not think anybody is going to do much of anything. Not with all this gaming operations in place. We are pretty much on our own. You rely on your boat and if you can get into a big-ger boat, you can get to more places as opposed to out in the big sea. My grandfather, Joseph Raphael, fished here. Back then the 1920s and 1930s, they could not commercial fish. He would go out with a pole and get them and there would be people standing on the beach waiting to buy his eight or ten fish, whatever he caught. My great-grand-father, Neganashe, fished in Cross Village with a spear.

My father did not fish. He mostly picked apples and drank. When they took away the fishing, it left people in a hopeless state. We never had anything because they have been trying to train us out of here since the 1800s. Anyway, they could not stop us from having a village here. In my own opinion, we should be the richest Indians in the whole United States because the Great Lakes is one of the most prime resources in the world. We are not rich because the government did not abide by anything. The state did not abide by anything. We should be getting paid royalties, but everything was stolen. We are knocked into a corner with nothing. We are struggling. They should be paying us beaucoup. All this whole area was ours—all of Michigan. We let all these other tribes, the Chippewas and Potowatomies, come in here. All Michigan was Ottawa land. I do not know where they get their maps and pictures and all that bullshit from. I know for a fact, from oral traditional history and stuff, that we allowed the Chippewa people to come in here to fish. They would not have been here if we did not allow them to come in here and fish. There was more than enough fish. I would sneak people in here just so they could get some fish and go feed their families. Other people did not like it.

Ronald Paquin is a member of the Sault Ste. Marie Tribe of Chippewa Indians. He maintained that sport fishing adversely affected fish stocks.[28] He indicated that many of the Ottawa people were reluctant to press for treaty fishing rights out of fear of retribution from sport-fishing interests and other opponents.

The DNR says they are for conservation. For instance, when they are taking an assess-ment on spawning years of fish, they should do it when the fish are spawning. But they will go in there a month earlier when there are no fish in there. These are the ploys they pull all the time. You have to go when they are spawning.

I told them after a meeting, if you take a small number—100,000 sportsmen—and they catch three fish a day—that is low, too—how many fish are you going to catch in a day? Now multiply that into a year. That is a lot of fish. But we have to realize that they are catching five, ten and eleven pounders. They cleaned this area out right over here.

The sportsmen came in and caused a lot of problems, especially further south. They had them here as well. Further south there was more trout. We called the area from Petoskey south, "the badlands." We would say: "We are going down to the badlands to fish tonight." First, we started fishing at night. We even put lights on our buoys so we could go early and get away from the crowds.

We were down at Rex Beach one day. I got done a little late and got set to go. Ed Moses, who has since passed away, and I were coming in. We heard this weird noise. We could not see the beach. I thought somebody swallowed it up. It was swallowed up by people. There were so many people on the beach they covered it. They were coming down to protest the fishing. Half of them did not know what a whitefish looked like. A guy is looking at the whitefish in the boat and he says: "Look at all them trout." So I pulled a dollar out of my wallet and I gave it to him and said: "Here, go buy a book on fish so you can learn how to identify them."

One guy held a little baby over our boat. It was about twelve o'clock and he said: "Now son, isn't this a shame?" The baby was so young, it could not talk yet. But that is how radical it got. It got quite bad. There were about 500 people that day. But I was not afraid of them. Crowd-pleasers do not bother me. You have to worry when there are three, four or ten of them and they are loaded with guns. Then they found out that we started carrying them, too. But the boats got shot up at that one place. Mine did not. But this is what was happening. The sad part was that they were picking on children if your dad fished.

That is why the Ottawas were quite reluctant to fight too hard. They were supposed to convert to trap nets, too, but nobody gave them any money so they had some battles over that.[29] There were so many stories on all that happened. I started out fishing with a little twelve-foot boat with a three-horse engine on it. You can imagine the close calls. I had no truck. I went down to the lake with my car and packed fish three or four trips. But anyway, people did not care so much at that point; there was not much talk. When we got enough money to buy a Mirrocraft and a four wheel drive truck, all of a sudden people started to say: "Oh, they are making a million dollars now." There is a lot of jealousy. If I cannot do it, I am going to be peeved if you can do it. There are 26,000 members in the Sault Ste. Marie Tribe of Chippewa Indians. There are not that many Indians in Michigan.

Ronald Paquin (Sault Ste. Marie Tribe of Chippewa Indians) discussed the sense of territoriality of both tribal and nontribal fishers. The Consent Agreement of 1985 imposed a new set of territorial boundaries for both tribal and state-licensed fishers. He maintained that treaty fishing rights are a matter of economic necessity.

Years ago, the fishing that was going on here by Gros Cap was done by those of Indian and French extraction. This is way back in the 1800s. An Ottawa Indian who was made a chief gave the white commercial fishermen a place called Point aux Chenes. There is a nice reef there. We fish it every fall when we fish whitefish. From Point Au Chenes to Millecoquins Lake is one of the oldest known reservation areas in history. Every time they dig around there they find things. Anyway, there was one hell of a battle when the Ottawa who was made a chief gave the white people permission to fish the Indian grounds out there which they had been fishing for years. That was the first battle over fishing they say. I do not know if it was fist fighting or ramming boats or whatever, but that was the first battle.

It has changed quite a bit from when you fished for the white man. I like to say non-Indian. I fished for them a lot and worked on every tug in every fishery that has ever been in this area in this town and there were a lot of them. I fished a good part of Lake Michigan and Lake Huron. I have done some fishing in Lake Superior, but not much. We did not bother with up there. We had a lot of pretty prime waters down here, and we went after the fish of course. Our fishing area went into Wisconsin, into Canada, down to Grand Haven. Michigan's got 36,000 square miles of Great Lakes. We had all of that according to the treaty rights of 1836.

During the negotiations for the Consent Order of 1985, they took seventy-eight percent and left us twenty-two percent of our grids even before we started dealing with the state to get our rights. We ended up with twenty-two percent and we are fishing ten percent of that now till the year 2000. I went to the negotiations down in Charlottesville, Virginia—to the federal court building. I was sitting next to the Assistant Attorney General of the United States. He said, "Ron, what do you think we can do?" I said, "Present company excepted, every time you deal with the white man—dealt with the white man back then—if they were dealing for a canoe the first thing they would do is cut the canoe in half and they would take half. Then they would deal for half of our half. They would end up with three quarters then."

I do not know why this happens. I explained it the best I could explain it. Perhaps it is because of academics. Everybody is getting rich off this. They get a mediator. He gets paid lots of money. Then you get your historians. Of course, the newspapers make a lot of money off of it, too. There are bylines all over TV. But the most important one is the lawyers. The lawyers get the money.

I had written a petition one time and had 126 Indian people sign it. And I sent it to the federal judge. I said, "You guys lost your perspective on all this. You forgot that you are fighting for the Indian fisherman. At least you, your Honor, have to make a choice. In fact, you might have to break a few rules now and then by listening to the poor people, not all these ethics of big words."

I said, "I want to let you know that I am an Indian person, a man trying to raise money for my family. I do not get what is going on here. The words you should pay attention to in the treaty are when the Indians said 'We will hunt and fish until the water stops flowing and the birds stop flying.'"

Now, how much plainer can you get? You cannot argue that. It is like trying to argue two and two is not four. It took fifteen years to decipher what the white people put in the treaty. It is only three to four pages long. There is nothing to it. I said, "There's all these people making money and we are going broke. I have lost my home. I do not know what to do." Anyway, they decided to invite me to the negotiations. We got more waters after certain negotiations by me being there.

When the court put a "stay" on us, I thought it meant stay fishing, so I kept fishing. They busted me, of course. Then I got busted on purpose to fight it. It was in the appellate court then. I did everything. I fought it hard. I started studying the history and the treaty. I did not want to go fat mouthing around. I did not know what I was doing. But I found out the treaty was fairly simple. They argued against commercial fishing by the

Indians. Well, common sense will tell you that if you are going to give the Indians salt barrels, leads, and a blacksmith shop, then it is commercial fishing.

They tried all sorts of sneaky things to classify us as subsistence fishermen. I stopped that in a meeting up here in Escanaba. A fellow and I went up there and stopped that. I had nets in at the time and we would do a lot of sneaking. We would find writings and the game wardens would stop us and had no idea what to do about it. They tackled me one time. They took my nets. I had seven game wardens around my neck and legs. They went out and pulled my nets. Well, I found out about it, so I went out and started pulling the other end. So we were pulling from each end. There were a lot of things that happened. I got my nets back and I left one for evidence. But they did not want me in court because they did not know what the hell was going on yet. But they were doing it as long as they could get away with it. I would go down and meet with the Ottawas. They would say, "Let's get Ron to talk to us." I said, "What you do not do is you do not run—you are doing nothing wrong. Do not run. If you run, you are acting guilty. So you are giving them an advantage in a lot of ways."

When they grabbed me, they tried to get me for obstruction of justice, which is a pretty serious charge. They were trying everything. But I was different than most people. I would fight it verbally and physically, but I would not go in there hot-tempered. I always had something.

So there is all this compassion and honesty, but the academics throw common sense out the window. You read the treaty. They will take that and try to twist it and turn it. You got to talk to an Indian in terms of how he was educated at that time. If you use these big words, he will not know what you are talking about. It is the same way today. We are going to make a deal. Then all of a sudden, we are going to make up a contract and add some fine print. It is trickery. That is what they did with the treaty. It sounded good on paper. So if you take the treaty and put all these other words around it, it is still a damn treaty. You cannot take that away. Then you have to start looking at a treaty for what? Look for fishing rights. So they took treaty, fishing, and rights and ruined them. They just mutilated it. There was so much proof of all this.

One time in court they had a piece of pottery with mesh on it. It was considered about 3,000 years old. It proved that mesh was around. But who cares how we fish them? They say, "Ron goes out and gill nets. What a horrible man." So it just went on and on like that. They used every bit of trickery. Then along comes a guy like me or

Abe LeBlanc and a few other guys that would voice it—and there were very few that would voice it. A lot of people do not like to talk in front of anybody. I do not like to do it too, but in this case we needed more Rons, we needed more Abes, and we needed a hell of a lot of honest lawyers. Dan Green was our lawyer. There was so much politics involved and everything else, he did not have time to do what he had to do.

I was interviewed by an economist named Richard Bishop and by Chuck Cleland. They got into it for the money. Anyway, they had it all written up and I read it.[30] I said this is not right. You did not expound enough on the Indian's living and a few other things. That was the first time anybody ever told Chuck Cleland he was wrong. And so he did not belong in there. He is a historian. He is not an economist. So what was he doing in there? You might as well not even showed up. You might as well he stayed home. That is why I mentioned education.

The fisheries are for people like me. I am never going to operate a computer or be a doctor or engineer. I am going to be a fisherman. I need this. This is for our people. I could not get it into their head that we were not just fighting for a right. We were fighting for a job. That is what it is all about. You have to feed your family. At many meetings I told them, "Why don't you guys study and then we can talk?" I told them this lake out here is like my bank. I can draw money out of it any time I want through my fishing rights.

Even if I did not have a big fishing rig—if we had all our waters—I could make a really decent living because I know my skill. I could fish practically every night and if the wind is blowing from the east, I will go over in the lee. I will do it all the time. I am going to make some money. And that is what they stopped us from doing. I am not vindictive. But I feel vindictive about it when I start talking about it. I do not let it run my life now, but when I start talking about it, I am very angry with these people and they know it. There were such terrible things in the first five years. The treaty fishing issue made people start talking about Indians again. Before, they just knew we were around. Then it got a little better when they figured they were going to get something out of it by being one. But it made them fight against each other. That is why the children were catching heckle all the time and that is sad.

When I fished for the non-Indian, I would go into a bar or a restaurant and people would say to me, "How's fishing Ron? What did you guys get?" And I would tell them. Then the Indian fishing rights start. We are using the same nets and same boats.

Gill nets have been used by tribal fishermen in Lake Michigan for centuries. Tribal fishermen prefer gill nets because they offer greater fishing flexibility and do not require as much capital investment as trap nets. Courtesy of the Great Lakes Fishery Research Station, Michigan Department of Natural Resources.

We are fishing in the same water. Now, we are no good Indian fishermen. So there is your prejudice.

Tribal fisher James Raphael, of the Grand Traverse Band, has been fishing for about sixteen years. He indicated that opponents of tribal fishing rights have continually stolen and vandalized his gear and tried to intimidate him not to fish. He noted that the lack of access to capital kept many tribal fishers working in boats that were too small or dangerous for the job. At least two communities in the Grand Traverse Bay area, Leland and Northport, tried to block tribal fishers from launching fishing boats from municipally owned dock facilities designed for recreational boaters.[31] The case ended when the U.S. Supreme Court refused to hear the case brought by the two municipalities.

One particular time in Leland, they stole everything. I put five gangs in and they were all gone the next day. When we first started going over there, I was out by myself lifting nets and a whole fleet of them, eight, ten of them came out on boats with intentions to sink me or do away with me because that is what they had said on shore.

We got to do away with him. I do not know what the problem was. Their objective is to stop us, which they did not. I gathered up some more nets and was right back in the next day. One way or the other they try to stop us, take our nets, make us fight and go to jail—another way of stopping us. We cannot let anything get to us. Everything and everybody is against us no matter who it is—our own, state, conservation, sport, government, and FBI. We report everything all the time and you might as well take a match to it or throw it in the trash can.

The majority of the local people are not against us. There is always a handful, a vocal, violent, vandalism-prone minority who ends up with the sport group organizations. They talk about it day and night. The Grand Traverse Sports Fishing Association, the Hammond Bay Anglers for the Alpena area, and the Michigan United Conservation Clubs (MUCC) are destructive in their own right as far as pressing legislation, as far as clout and money. Out of all of them, the MUCC is the least vocal but in turn, the MUCC has money and the backing of the local chamber of commerce. They are gathering any kind of support and moneys that they can use to take what little we have away from us.

My boat is a 1968; it is about thirty years old. It is not too bad. I have not had problems parking anywhere. They told me not to. I went to go do it. I never had a problem. I try to get along with them. Before, I could not get out of here until I got this boat. It is not quite a year yet that I was able to move a distance where I might be able to catch some fish. Other than that, I was in small boats, sixteen-foot boats and stuff. I talked and talked to banks.

Our reservation is here is because it is hidden from the wind. Now we got the state trying to say we cannot fish from here, which forces us to open water. I mean we were riding in ten- to fifteen- foot seas just to catch some fish last fall going into winter. We were looking straight down into the water. Some of those waves were coming over the boat. They forced us out of here over there into open water. Anybody with any good sense would go and put their village and camp where there is some shelter so they could do what they had to do. And then comes the state forcing us into the situation.

Ron Paquin (the Sault Ste. Marie Tribe of Chippewa Indians) fished on Lake Michigan for most of his life either as a crew member of a nontribal-owned boat or on his own after treaty rights were re-established.

We had one real irrational game warden. He did his job, I will say that. We would get into it verbally all the time. He was bound and determined Ron Paquin was going to get arrested. So I said, "I will take the ticket. Do you want me to tell you what you should write on it?" Well they wrote I was fishing in illegal waters with gill nets in closed waters. They said this because the waters had been closed to the white commercial fishermen. So finally I had my ticket and I said, "Well what should I do with it?" I never went to court. They pulled a lot of that. And for the same thing that they got me, other people were getting busted and getting convicted. That is why I told them not to run because they are not doing anything wrong. We fished right in Frankfort at night.

One time we were setting nets in Petoskey. We were cruising along and had the spreader on. The corks will clink on there. We looked and Ed said, "Ron, look over." I had my back turned because I was spinning the nets. We almost ran into this porch that was out on the lake with glass in it. This guy is setting there watching TV. He just about swallowed a sandwich. So we had to hurry up and get out of there because there were cops all over the place. They did not know where we went in. We would drive the truck down and brush the truck tracks out of there so they would not know we were down there. It was night. We had to do stupid things like that. But we would always find a place to fish. This is before it was settled in 1985.

When they put the stay on us this game warden came up. He came in and said, "Ron, I got some good news and I got some bad news." I said: "Well, give me the bad." He said, "We have to pull your nets today, Ron. You have been fishing a couple weeks now since that stay. The good news is I was supposed to take your truck, your nets—everything but you can just go." He said, "You treat me right down there." I said, "You did the same, too. Okay, I will pull them."

Then I went out and got intentionally arrested after that to bring it into court. We might as well have been in kindergarten. Nobody knew what was going on anyway. The judges around here were trying to bust us because they had a lot of pressure on them. They wanted me pretty bad. You know what they ended up getting me on? Dipping smelt. They got me on dipping smelt, a $20 fine. They finally got me on that.

Skip Duhamel recalled that during the years leading up to their State of Michigan and U.S. District Court cases in the middle to late 1970s, his father, Art Duhamel, would compare notes and stories with "Big Abe" LeBlanc of the Bay Mills Indian Community.

As Big Abe LeBlanc was getting arrested, we were getting arrested. My Dad and Abe used to joke with each other on the phone. They would ask, "How many nets did they take from you this week?" We would tell him so many. That was the beginning. My dad was never one to sneak and leave. He felt we had the right to do this and it was going to be a struggle. He knew there were going to be some hardships and he was going to do it no matter what. When he told the old man, Geeboo, "Let's go," he knew damn well he was going to jail amongst other things. He did, of course. They arrested him and brought him before Judge Benedict, the judge in Leland who is retired now. He ordered the old man not to fish in Lake Michigan under court order, so we went to Lake Superior. This was not the first time. It was just one of many. They found out what the old man was to up in Lake Superior, they hunted him down and dragged him back here in handcuffs. His own attorney fees were in the tens of thousands. There were many times when they took our poles and our nets and all that stuff. It cost us in thousands.[32]

Yvonne Keshick of the Little Traverse Bay Band of Odawa discussed how the issue of tribal fishing rights and the division of fishing areas had sparked controversy within the Native community and resulted in rising tensions with some non-natives.[33]

There is another rivalry between Grand Traverse and this tribe besides fishing, but it was more like a joking or teasing type of thing. We would draw cartoons about them and they would draw one about us. One of John Keshick's friends would draw cartoons and pass them on to him. John would change things on them, and the cartoons would go back and forth. Then, whoever gave up first, they would not accept the cartoon back. One of the cartoons we had was a Grand Traverse Indian watching the Ottawa fishermen on the lake. And he says, "I can't believe it. They do walk on water." The cartoon showed an Indian standing on the lake. His nets are coming up, but he's just flat on top of the water. Most of the cartoons are old, from about 1977.

Artist and former fishing boat crew member Yvonne Keshick drew cartoons, sometimes while on board, to express the views of tribal fishermen. In this 1982 drawing, Keshick, who is a member of the Little Traverse Bay Bands of Odawa Indians, features activist Ron Paquin of the Sault Ste. Marie Tribe of Chippewa Indians. In this depiction, Keshick comically counters accusations from sport fishers and government officials that Indians, such as Paquin, are depleting Lake Michigan's fish stocks with well-equipped vessels. In commenting on the cartoon, Keshick provided interesting insight on the politics of Lake Michigan fishing and new forms of Indian oral tradition: "Look at the hat on the head of the guy in that small boat. That is Ron Paquin. We had been hearing what he was going through. People were complaining about him, so that is why I drew the cartoon. He just had a little 16-foot boat and here the big charter boats are yelling at them for depleting the lakes. That is why I did it. Ron has never seen the cartoon. It was drawn before I met Ron. I just read the stories and heard the other fishermen talking." Courtesy of Yvonne Walker Keshick.

All the fishing people used to go to different places to fish. They would go to Lake Huron, Lake Superior, or Lake Michigan. Back then, you fished wherever you felt like fishing. Then the lines started being drawn because of the controversy and the tribes allowed the government to divide and conquer. When Brimley and Bay Mills were fighting to get their fishing rights, at the start, we supported them. Years later when it came our turn to apply and get the ability to enforce our fishing rights, they opposed us. We could not understand that because they were fishermen. By then they

This editorial cartoon by Gene Hibbard of the *Traverse City Record Eagle* depicts how differences in tribal economic and political power, along with the role of the federal government, influence Great Lakes fishing policy. Courtesy of the *Traverse City Record Eagle*.

had been established, and had run of the lakes. They would be down here fishing and it caused a problem with the tribes. And then later on, just recently even, we supported them when they went for their casino. Letters of support went in and then when it came our turn, they turned on us. So I do not know if it is a cultural thing or what it is, but we do not understand why they do that. We were surprised when they went against us in fishing. Our people assume just because we are Indian that we are all fishermen. My sister put a bumper sticker on her car that said "Indian Proud." Her tires got slashed because of that. They assume that they are slashing a fisherman's, but there are not that many fishermen.

I was walking down by the courthouse in Petoskey in 1987. This boy ran out of his house and saw me on the sidewalk. He yelled, "Go home gill netter."[34] I did not even look like a gill netter. I was in a skirt and blouse and carrying books. He ran around the house. The kids learn it from someplace.

Our neighbor was anti-fishing and anti-casino. She is so against us and it shows up in her kids. Her kids come over and say our mom said you guys are different. My boy said, "We are different. We are special." The kid said my ma says you guys get special treatment. And Jacob said, "We are special. You are special too." He just turned it around but the kid was looking for something else.

Even though I fished and was not the best fisherman, I did a lot of hard work. I have seen fishermen just drive themselves. I know this one girl who literally fell asleep standing up leaning against the wall waiting for her dad to fix the coffee. They had been on a fishing streak and they did not want to quit. We told them they had better go to sleep. They said, "We will be all right." They were on their way to market. They made it to market and back home and were laid up for about three days resting. When it is time to fish, you fish.

We must respect nature. You have to learn to respect all living things and let them be the way they are, without trying to shape and mold it the way you want it because it may not be good for it. I tell my kids respect everybody whether they deserve it or not. In your lifetime you are going to meet people who might not really deserve respect now, but I told them do it anyway because it is going to make a difference.

Ronald Paquin discussed how the struggle for treaty fishing rights both unified and divided the tribal community.

As far as the fishing went, it was very strange when it started to turn people, commercial fishermen, sportsmen, and natives too, friend against friend. Natives got scared. The elderly people thought they were going to lose everything they had. They are scared of the government because a lot of times, we did not get any backing. We lacked having the right people on our boards and committees and that goes back to the academics again. They think you have to be an academic to be on the board. You do not. It really got people riled. It brought out the prejudices. People were pretending they were your friends. I know the Catholic priest down here very well. He gave everybody that sermon on Sunday and gave them a lot of hell. "What are you people doing? You claim love. You claim all this." He was for the fishermen but he said: "What are you people doing? You should be ashamed of yourself."

The lack of cooperation between the educated and noneducated was a fault. It was a terrible fault. I am an elder in the tribe and I told them that. I said I know for a fact that no uneducated man ever gave our rights away. I know that. The judge told me later, he said: "I am not even supposed to be talking to you, off the bench." But he said: "I have to do this." That was down in Lansing. It was before we even got our rights in 1985. We were down in Lansing talking to the West Coast people who were fishing salmon. They got their treaty fishing rights, but it took eighteen years. It took us fifteen.

Why does it take you fifteen? I watched through the years. I would go to meetings and I straightened them out one time. I told them they use such big words in that meeting and they totally confused me and that was probably intentional. So when we got outside during intermission a bunch of us were talking. I said, "You used some pretty big words in there. Could you do me a favor? See that big tree out there? Could you write what that means and I will walk around the tree with you?" Well, he gets part way around the tree and he disappears. Well you know why? When they are using big words, they are being evasive. It is similar to Indians up west of here. They cut timber in the 1990s. They thought they owned the land and the old Indian just told them: "You might have the tree but you do not own the roots." It is the same with these waters. We gave away too much. I thought you had to go to court to see what you should get. You do not give it away, go and fight for what's left. Now is that my fault as a fisherman? You ask me what grids I want, where I prefer to fish. Time after time in court, everything was so ambiguous when you read the rules. They are called loopholes, I guess. But there should not be any loopholes.

They voted me fisherman-at-large. I represented the tribe's fishermen on a committee. My main job really was tabling things to keep them out of the voting process. I would have liked to have done more, but that was the main thing because I was the only fisherman on the board, so you had a lot to deal with. So my main job ended up being to table things to keep them from being voted on which would not have done the fishermen any good.

We were trying to get down here in "the badlands"—in Lake Michigan waters. Bay Mills was a little better at working for their fishermen, so they were down there already. We went up to the meeting and finally, I just tore up the notes. The meeting got all riled. I knew it would. They had to go into a closed session. We did get to go down there the next day. They had to let us get down there. Everyone was so afraid. I said, "Why should you be afraid? We are the ones who are going down there." Then they made a rule that we could not carry guns. I said, "Well, how come the game wardens carry guns?" They said, "What are you carrying it for?" I still brought a gun with me. I did not want to shoot anyone.

One time we were out and there was this big cabin cruiser. We were twelve miles out in the lake. What were we supposed to do? Call a cop? This big cruiser was coming towards us. I took the gun and I laid it on the bow and away they went. They turned away. So it is a psyche. I would like to try to take the game warden's gun away from them. What do they need one for if I do not have one? But we have to worry about other people. So there were lots of things that went on. When we went to the negotiations in Charlottesville, I knew what we had. I found out they mark it down differently. But they took our water—we went and fought and they took the grids away and rewrote things. So you had to constantly watch. I can see where academics would get scared. They worry more about other academics squeezing them than me yelling at them. So after a while you are going to get a little smart. You have to figure out how this can be done and then I wrote a petition. I wanted them to at least see what a fisherman looked like. It was for the specific tribe. We are members of the tribe, so you cannot go individually. It is for everyone. It covers everyone. But what we were worried about—we did not want to end up fishing in a washtub—which, I think, that is where we are now, pretty much in a washtub. Because I know there are fish down there.

———

James Raphael (Grand Traverse Band) opposed proposals to reduce tribal gill-net use raised during the renegotiation of the 1985 Consent Agreement.

I do not know how things are going to go. Hopefully, we will get some waters back where we can get to some good fishing. When they made this agreement in 1985, they blocked us off and made boundaries and lines. Wherever there was fish they made a line. They knew exactly what they were doing—the State of Michigan—trying to decide where to let us go and not to let us go. Even now, toward the end of this agreement, they have us boxed right up into nothing. I would not want to make another agreement with them. The bottom line with everything is ignorance and prejudice. We have been fishing for a thousand years or better with gill nets. It has been proven by historians. They have dug up nets—we used to make them out of bark and trees. I can imagine in those days it took a whole year to make a net to go fishing. Make the twine

57

and then sew it together. But with rocks and corks—this has been presented. There are 1,000-year-old gill nets which helped what we were fighting for.

———————

Ron Paquin maintained that the protracted nature of the negotiations over treaty fishing rights played a role in encouraging the Indians to agree to the provisions of the 1985 Consent Agreement.

I am not on the same level with the academics, but I guess it is called a little bit of wisdom. They brought in this intermediary. He was going to solve this. They paid him like $200,000. But by this time, we were ready to kiss our worse enemy, so he did not have much of a job. We wanted to get the damn thing over with. Here is what happened. In 1985 the agreement came down and went to the tribal board. I went to our board members and I said, " I am not going to show up." There were a lot of fishermen there. We have our political types in the fishery, too. Indians, too. They kind of perturbed me a lot of times where they had chances to be in there, and then blew it. But I found out they were pretty much educated, too. All of a sudden someone said, "What does Ron think?" I said, "It is not the best we are going to get but at least we can fish now. You can go out there and make a living. That is the best we can do. We were not going to get any better. Because if you prolong it and fight for more, you are going to be poorer than you are now. But at least we can go out and fish. Not everybody is happy with the areas."

There was just a hush in the whole building. Then they voted on it and passed it. I did not want to go up, because too many people were depending on me. Now they lost their area. They said let us get Ron to fight for it back. Well, I am not going to hold up the whole negotiations for one area. That is the way I looked at it. But in perspective, we got a pretty bad deal and you can understand by figuring areas. We got a pretty bad deal. But what I was getting at—we fought for twenty-two percent and we are fishing on ten percent of it and they are trying to take more.

———————

Tribal fisher Skip Duhamel of the Grand Traverse Band discussed several photographs taken when he was arrested for launching his fishing boat from a public recreational fishing dock in Northport.

George "Skip" Duhamel, 1999. The son of the late treaty rights activist Art Duhamel, Skip Duhamel waged a successful legal effort to establish the right to use public docking facilities for tribally licensed commercial fishing vessels. Photograph by Michael J. Chiarappa

There is a photograph of when we were waiting for them to come arrest me. We had been told that if I did not leave Northport marina immediately, it was their intent to arrest me. One of the tribal conservation officers, Jim Chambers, who is highly respected and honored among fishermen for his help, was there to make sure that local law enforcement did not physically abuse me in the arrest. There were some other people from the community who were bidding me farewell prior to my arrest. That is a nice picture. I like that picture. There is also a picture that shows the law enforcement people telling me that I have to immediately leave a marina that is open to the public because I am a tribal fisherman and they do not allow tribal fishermen in their facility. They wanted me to step aboard land and I shook my head no. I never did respond to them with a word. And they came aboard my vessel and tried to pull me out by my arms. I just went limp, kind of Ghandi type, noncooperation, nonresistance, and nonviolent. Those things hurt a person's feelings; it is not good for your soul to have people do that. So they decided that they could not get me out of the boat without coming aboard my vessel which is a direct violation of the federal law. They were interfering with my federally protected right. This is exactly what these people did. Jim Raphael was there trying to talk to me. Jim was telling me let us not make it hard, Skip. It was them making it hard, not me. They dragged me out of the boat. There was a woman who pulled on my arm. One pulled and one pushed and they grabbed me in handcuffs. They dragged me down the dock. This was on July 2nd. There were a lot of people. There were a lot of spectators—perhaps a hundred people were there. They loaded me in the car, shackled and handcuffed and away we went.

I was vindicated in the federal court system. They tried procedures in courts, the circuit court, district court, and the State of Michigan where they do not have any jurisdiction. They were all unsuccessful. The end result is we prevailed and can now park in the Northport and Leland marinas free of charge. In fact, it is a federal violation of a court order for them to inhibit or interfere with my access to the waters right where we live. These were civil rights violations. They knew it when they were doing it, and they just did not care. The effect it had was to ensure that I was to return the very next day. I mean, but they inhibited our fishing for a while but not for very long, but that was just because we did not allow them and we just came back no matter what. Just prior to being arrested the next time, we did think that it would be better for us to leave instead of going to jail, and we did leave that day. But it was also promised to me that we would have an injunction against some of the municipalities within the next two days. And we were successful in getting the injunctions against them so that they could not just prohibit us. Basically what it meant was no Indians.

Cindi John recalled that when the 1985 Consent Agreement was being negotiated she realized the importance of scientific data. Knowledge about the fisheries was, at least in part, key to gaining political influence.

When we went into the initial talks about allocation and resource management, we did not have a database. Now with the way that we are monitored, everybody files their catch reports. The tribal management holds up a pretty strong standard for fisheries management and their data is real credible. It has been through the legal test. This is not just a matter of being in the best interest of the tribal group, because the lake community is a bigger community than one user group and they understand that. When people look at the fishery, a lot of people think of the fishing people. But the fishery really is run at the management level. The people who do the best and really have the best income from the fishery are your biologists and your lawyers and your politicians across the board.

I was really frustrated with the reign of the biologists. It was really poorly run. We felt that they were shoving everything down our throats. We have a financial interest in the fishery. We are the ones that have a financial and personal interest in it; it is important to us. The grid up north, south of Charlevoix 616, should be opened up. It is a good gill-netting area. The bottom of it is not really suited for trap nets. It is a real flat ledge.[35] Judge Enslen went through it and he said: "I am still not going to open the grid." So it was all for naught, sort of, except it solved some issues, and we would not have to jump over certain hurdles during the next go-around (the renegotiation of the 1985 Consent Decree in 2000). I thought he was going to open our waters and I left crying. I just thought—I could not believe that he would look at it that way but he sees things from a different viewpoint. That was my experience with Enslen.

The people who manage the fishery think that trap netting is the answer. Trap netting takes up a big area. With two trap net boats in the bay, they are on top of each other because of the limited areas suitable for setting the traps. There is a lot of area that is suitable for gill nets. Gill nets are real selective if tended properly. The fish that we catch on a trap-net boat are generally twenty-one to twenty-two inch whitefish. Those fish will go through a gill net—seventeen inches is the size that you need to legally catch them. I hope that we get to continue to manage our area. We do not have a lot of new people entering the fishery because of all the other employment. I think we only have, at the most, seven fishing operations in our whole tribe from here to Charlevoix. So we do not put the pressure on the resource. It is a misconception when people feel that there's a whole bunch of us out here.

The tribes signed onto the 1985 Consent Decree without a database and thought, in good faith, that they would be provided with training in trap-net rigs. They did not know what type of areas would be required for these rigs to sustain themselves. They should have come up with a plan that would have allowed our fishermen to use smaller boats with feasible gear. But this plan was not followed, particularly the way tribal fishers thought it would unfold—and a whole area of Grand Traverse Bay got shut down.

And subsequently, it has been real difficult. If the east side of Grand Traverse Bay was never closed, the things that people were complaining about in Leland would not be talked about because Skip Duhamel would probably be fishing over on the east side.

Yvonne Keshick recalled efforts among the Little Traverse Bay Bands of Odawa Indians to organize to promote tribal fishing interests.

I was secretary for the Northern Michigan Association Fishing Committee. We have some original minutes from our meetings. The largest amount of money we had in our coffer was thirty dollars. We were a small-time group working to preserve the fishing for the people, for the fishermen. They were all fishermen. There were men and women in that group. Everybody tried to do what they could to protect and preserve the fishery.

James Raphael fishes in a gill-net tug, the *Raven's Nest,* with his sister and business partner, Rose Raphael. He supports changes to the 1985 Consent Agreement. Raphael wants more grids open to tribal fishing.

We are hoping that the lake will work out better than Grand Traverse Bay has. The fishing has gone right downhill. I do not even expect whitefish. That is the majority of what we can catch in the bay because of trout rehabilitation zones. We recently had to convince our tribal government to help us because there were no more whitefish. They plant so many lake trout they scare the whitefish away. They are predators and they plant so many, it drives the whitefish out. In addition there are no whitefish because of the zebra mussels and other predators that have gotten into the bay and all around the lake. We had a thirty percent rule—we could only bring in thirty percent trout to 100 percent of our total catch. Once there was no more whitefish, it was pretty much it. We had to stop fishing in here. In the beginning, when they made the Consent Agreement of 1985 with the State of Michigan, we had like thirty-five grids, which was quite a bit of water. Slowly, they worked us down to like three grids. Two of them are right in front of our village. There are no whitefish, so we cannot fish there.

This leaves us with Leland and we are neck to neck with charter boat fishermen and sport-fishing groups. It is a hassle in itself being over there. There is also the wind factor, dealing with the wind. Anyway, it has been a struggle the whole fifteen years that I have been fishing. It was a struggle with all the rowboats—pulling by hand. Now, it has gotten really bad.

Hopefully things can change once the Consent Agreement expires in the year 2000. The state would just love to come in and put another agreement on us. They would like to see us just stop. But we are trying to tell them that we are going to manage this. We do not want to make any agreements with you. We cannot afford to. It is a matter of survival for us. It is what we do. We cannot afford to so-call "negotiate" with them. Look at how they boxed us up. So we are trying to come with an approach which will end up in federal court. A federal judge always ends up hearing everything. We want to show them that we are going to manage the resources and protect the resources. We want to show them that we can do that without making an agreement and they are going to try to force us into one again. Hopefully, things will get a little bit better from what they are now. We want to get some of our waters opened up so we can move around and catch some fish. They have us boxed right into this area where we cannot catch fish.

Cindi John, a trap-net boat fisher, discussed the 1985 Consent Agreement and its policy implications for tribal fishers in the Grand Traverse Band of Ottawa and Chippewa. She also noted how the rise of local real estate values resulted in greater political scrutiny of tribal fisheries management.

What led to our Consent Decree was that people from up north, Michigan's Upper Peninsula tribes, came and fished down here when it was wide open. It was not wide open per se; they had a quota. They came down here and fished their quota and then they went home. But our tribal people could not fish, and we were left with the fallout from the perception that we were down here abusing the resource. A lot of people do not realize, but if it was shown that we were not managing fisheries resources responsibly, the state could take management back. It is the only reason that the state could enter in through the court and resume management. A lot of decisions that get made about the fishery are not about economics; they are political decisions. And the fishing issue is more politically volatile because of the location of our reservation. Our people are getting the brunt of the scrutiny. We live in probably one of the most volatile areas that exists within all the tribal fishing zones. To a big extent, dealing with the other user groups does not have to do so much with the fishers that are using the resource as it does with the impact on the community. All these issues need to be taken into account.

Well, the treaty specifically stated that they were allowed to progress. It was stated in the written agreement—it in no way bound them to the current methods. There has been a lack of information for the public that has caused a lot of the problems. All sides are guilty for not getting information out. The tribes are growing so fast; they are trying to keep up with all the changes in economics and social life. I have not seen the state being very helpful or even the feds being very helpful in getting out accurate information about why this took place, why it is happening, and what the laws are. Really, the question is: "Do the people of United States have to follow their own laws or is it all right only to follow them selectively?"

James Raphael indicated that opponents of tribal fishing rights have tried to keep him from fishing or try to provoke trouble for tribal fishers with law enforcement officials.

Fishing is pretty much a livelihood but in my heart I see things as more than just that. It is a means of living for me right now. With all the struggles—the state and sport people taking nets and destroying property—it makes it really hard. Over in Leland they stole all my nets. I had about five different gangs out. A gang is one separate amount of nets that are strung out. I had troubles with my truck and it broke down. I was running fish up in the UP and had to stop in the middle of the trip to get my truck fixed. I dashed back and put the nets in the water and went back up to grab my truck. By the time I got back, all my nets were gone. It was a real peaceful and calm night. I try to do everything legal—speaking for myself. I am a peaceful person. I go into a place in a good way with the sport groups, charter boat people, the municipal government or whatever. I come in a good way so they know me like that. It makes a point for people to know me like that. Anyway, they took my gear. I followed proper procedures and reports. I reported it to our conservation office as well as to the sheriff's. And then it went on to FBI—every report that has been done just gets filed. Nothing ever gets done because the people pretty much have to be caught right in the act. It is hard to prove anything unless somebody has been caught with some gear and nobody ever really is. You cannot be out there twenty-four hours. It has happened from time to time—not a whole lot with me—but it has at several different times. But that was one time that I could not believe they got away with it.

One way or another, they will try to stop you. They will try to provoke you and have you end up in jail. They will steal your gear just to try to stop you. I got more gear and had it in the water the next day or two because fish were there. I could not afford to just stop fishing. I got more gear and put it back in the water just to let them know that they did not stop me. I continued on because seasons or a run do not last too long. Three or four weeks and then it is over. So we struggled through that time. We struggle through work and then to deal with all of that. I am still at it. I have been at it for fifteen years.

———————

Skip Duhamel of the Grand Traverse Band recalled how opponents of tribal fishing would target boats and gear used by his father, Art Duhamel, for vandalism or theft. He maintained that he and other tribal fishers still have their gear vandalized and stolen today.

My father's boats were about twenty-foot, open boats. Most were made of door plywood. He had an old craft with an old Evinrude on it. It was really quite like a joke. Anyway, he had about eight different boats all with the same name. Of course, he did not want to put a lot of money into them because they were gonna come and take them. Then someone took an axe to my father's boats in Northport Harbor. They whacked them up and sunk them.

We were too afraid to launch down here in Leland because of the violence, so we launched down at an open sand beach at Sugarfoot. We set ten nets. Then we went down the beach and set ten more. By the time we came back, there were two men in the boat lifting the first nets that we had already set. I was about seventeen and pretty hot-tempered. I wanted to put the boots to them, but my father would never allow something like that. He felt that was not the way to go. You should try to seek prosecution. He really believed in that. My father told me we would report it. They promptly went to shore and got a gun and trained it on him as we tried to repair the damage they had done. They never did fire the weapon, but we were real close to shore. They trained it right on us the whole time we were there. We reported it. Of course, nothing was done. The prosecutor's people were the people that were doing it. So that was the man in charge of prosecuting choosing not to prosecute his own family. At that time the feds were not taking a very active role as far as the FBI reporting. He considered us more of a nuisance. Just go away. And so that did not happen either. Nothing, nothing happened except that we got our nets ruined and they pointed guns at us. Right here out of this area, they still ruin them every spring. It has been an organized effort. They take 10,000 feet at a lick. One morning we will come to work and all this gear will be gone. The real race of the thing is to get the net, have them make the money and get the profit out of them before they steal them.

I had a kid call me up. Actually, he is not a kid. He's as large as me, and a little bit younger. He called me up the middle of the night and told me if I came down here to the Bluebird, he was gonna beat my ass. I told him, "Why don't you just give me your name and number? It is the middle of the night right now. In the morning I will be more than happy to accommodate you any way you want to." He said, "I will be there in ten minutes." So I went down there. There were six, seven people there. I said, "Which one of you guys called me out of bed? You got me down here. Now let's get to her."

They waited for probably half an hour or forty-five minutes, to make sure I was alone. Then finally this guy who's a mate on one of the charter boats came up and accosted me. He said, "Want to step outside?" I said, "Well, that is what I came down here for. You want to get beat up, let's get with her because I am a very angry person." You could see in his eyes there that he probably was not going to win. Then he decided that he did not want to take that course of action. He was concerned about the net markings. So I told him that if he would talk with his people and if they would give me assurances that they would not steal my gear, that I would mark them so folks could see them, and you would not lose your fishing lures. And a year or so went by and he called me back and told me that he had talked with all of them. He gave me his personal word nobody would molest them. We promptly put on the buoys that we are using now and two days later, they stole them all.

We decided that we were going to keep marking the buoys the way we do because if one percent of the population does this, it does not matter what size buoy I got on there. They are going to find them and steal them. And meanwhile the average Joe Blow who is out trying to have a little weekend fun fishing has a right to be able to see them and not lose his lure. The buoys make us very vulnerable though. But it is a lot easier to find that thing in the dark.

A month or so ago we fished up here and I was catching 3—400 pounds of whitefish and maybe one box of trout. We are trying to catch the fish that are more valuable. The trout will ruin this fine net. I got to try to get away from them. This is real fine mesh that is fine for the whitefish. We replace them constantly. We can one time, tie up the big holes and stuff like that. We make them ourselves. I am in the process of making them at home and I should have a new one every other day until I get it built back up. Then I will go up north and buy some more, too. It depends how the nets make her through the weekend. If not, I will go buy some more and keep making them.

You cannot let those things be the determining factors on where you fish. If they are going to call you some names, threaten you, steal your stuff, break your windows and you leave, then it shows them that that is an effective way to prevent you from your livelihood and/or your area. When they stole this 3,000 feet from me up north, that secured it that I was going to stay here another month. And even if they steal every one of them this weekend, what I will do is I will—they will not steal the trap because they cannot and we will replace it and I will replace them and we will continue on. So it is just part of it. One time the DNR were right here with a lowboy loading up boats and nets. They busted us one day and threw a little rowboat and a couple boxes of nets in the back of an enforcement truck. Dad told them we were launching two more in the morning so bring a bigger truck. They came with a semi and a lowboy, and they loaded up both of the other boats. They took three boats and about ten boxes of nets in two days.

————————

Both Skip Duhamel and his late father, Art, ran into conflict not only with Michigan DNR enforcement officials but with tribal wildlife law enforcement officials as well.

One time we went up to Brimley to go to court. Damn, the old man beat the case. When we walked by, he said "Thank you. We will get our nets. Better luck next time. Give us a check for all our fish and our nets." That was their own conservation. We have got five different groups of officers, tribal officers.

Our tribal fisheries people will take every damn net you got and all your catch. You will never see nothing out of it. If you actually have done wrong here, you are going to be dealt with at least fairly. Obviously there are times when we're not complying with the regs. There are so many. We were dealt stiff fines. Jimmy Raphael can tell you about that. He has set nets right by the breakwall of the Art Duhamel marina. You have got to be half a mile away from creeks and designated rivers. The fines range anywhere from $100 to $1,000. There is no time when you were stepping in front of the tribal judge that he is not taking a couple hundred dollars away from you. I left a fish box with some beer cans on the dock and he gave me a ticket, $100 fine. I was charged $50 plus court costs for leaving a fish box on the dock. I asked the tribal judge, "Can't you find a better reason to write me a ticket than this?" I think they try to issue a ticket for every rule they had in the book. The judge is kind of like an Indian redneck because he grew up in Honor.

Skip Duhamel maintained that the entire Grand Traverse Band benefited as a result of his father's activism. Federal recognition of the tribe and the re-establishment of treaty fishing rights were major turning points. At the same time, new problems and a new or different sense of community emerged. As a tribal representative to the team negotiating the renewal of the 1985 Consent Agreement, Skip Duhamel expressed support for increasing the area open to tribal fishing.[36]

A lot of people weren't Indians before, were they? They were not Indian before. All they wanted to do is get along. After they found out everything was planted in here, now everybody wants to become an Indian. This never was. They were all whitefied. After they found out that the government recognized us as an Indian nation, bam, here they come, just like flies on shit.

They brought their assimilated ideas and their ethics. The first rule of being is you do not cause any problems. If you done wrong, you keep your mouth shut. If somebody

68

causes a problem, you let it go. You walked down the road. People would ask are you hungry? You go to their house and you eat. When you visited them, you never left without eating. And people's cupboards were pretty bare to begin with, that was the thing. They would always offer you something to eat. That is the way the nation was and the way it ought to go back, like the old people used to do. It would be beautiful. I am hoping we can walk down the road like everybody used to. You never see an Indian up and down this road walking. Just walking up and down this road. Now our generation now, you do not see nobody going up and down. We used to talk about that a long time ago. All these people that moved into this community now, you do not see anybody.

In some ways some my dad rubbed off on me when we opened this harbor up. There were a lot of threats of violence and a lot of name-calling. I was just thinking about it because men like me and Vince Chippewa, who works with me, have pride. I had absolutely forbidden anybody on the boat to respond back to anything as far as verbal. We do not respond. Now if somebody touches us, they are going to find that is different. They made it real clear that when I go below the 45th parallel in the year 2000 they are going to shoot me.

I am part of the government. I am the tribal representative. It is going to be up to me what we sign on to and we are willing to be reasonable in some forms, but we are not willing to give them everything. I do not want to hear any promises because they are empty.

There are a bunch of different kinds of people involved in the negotiations. They got a gag order on them or they might do a little saber rattling. All the money we are spending on litigation could be doing something about habitat preservation. The zebra mussels are destroying the bottom of the food chain. The tribe is going to spend a few million dollars to litigating this. If we could take the millions the tribe will spend and the millions the feds are going to spend, all that money that they are gonna waste on trying to stop this poor little boat from catching a fish, we could do something.

We are going to fish with our gill nets from Charlevoix to Arcadia. It is going to be the next area that this tribe has control over and the other tribes that agreed that we have control over the area. The Chippewa are going to establish a limited entry area. Mainly what we are trying to do is preserve the operations that already exist. A lot of things in the Consent Agreement were messed up. We want back the waters that we gave up in 1985.

We have grids 714 and 715. We got these two grids out of hundreds of grids in our particular area because they say this is an area of importance to them. They do not want any fishing at all. What they do not understand is this is our home. This is where we live and I am not inclined to move. The only reason we settled here is because it was good fishing and it still is. To some people it does not matter. They do not want to know the truth anyway. And they never will. If they did know the truth, they would not accept it. It is real easy for them to point the finger at something. Of course, I can and they cannot and on and on. I guess if I had my druthers, I would just as soon be off in Platte Bay right now.

Cindi John rejects claims by critics of tribal fishing rights who assert that tribal fisheries are unregulated. She expressed hope for greater coordination of fishery management resources.

We are really managed. Every month, we file a catch report. On a daily basis you tell where you fished, how much net you fished, species caught, the number of pounds of species caught, whether it was whole or gutted, and the price per pound. You tell where you launched. Then, to really make those figures credible, when you sell your fish, there is a wholesale report. There are three copies of the report. There is a copy that goes to the fishing person, a copy that goes to the tribes, and a copy that goes to the state. There are certain areas that you can use. Our code books define where you can fish, how you can fish, how deep you can fish, and when you can fish there and that was really dissected. Being a fishing person turns you into a mini lawyer. We are enforced by the state and by our tribal conservation officers. Other tribes can enforce each other, as well as the federal officials and Coast Guard. We have been boarded by all of them although not frequently. They boarded more frequently when we were gill netting than trap netting.

People need to understand more about the biological management of the lakes and the way that they manage and plant fish. A lot of users do not look at it that way. I think they look at each other as user groups. Who is getting this trout, who is getting this perch, or who is getting this whitefish is an issue that does not lie with us. It lies with the way the lake is being biologically managed. There are a lot of big issues taking place. It is difficult to get scientific information and it is hard to get reports about the Ludington Consumer's Power plant. I think it is hard to get reports because the Ludington plant drives funding projects—and that is a true issue. I think about the impact of planting salmon and planting lake trout on the native self-sustaining species. As fishing people, we have watched our fishing grounds change from the lake trout. It is alarming how loosely organized the scientific community is; there is not a data center. You have your Great Lakes meetings and all the scientists get together and they give their reports, but you do not have one distinct database that people can go to.

Skip Duhamel (Grand Traverse Band of Ottawa and Chippewa) rejected claims of lack of regulation made by opponents of tribal fishing rights, including many charter boat operators based in Leland and other ports on Grand Traverse Bay.

They think we are unregulated. We are the most highly regulated fishery. There is a fish council for every one of us. I mean, our own, and that is not county, the state, and higher ups. That is tribal fishing. We have our own Fish and Wildlife. They call me up to find out if I am working on a weekend to find out whether or not they have to go to work or not. It is quite funny really. We do not get away with anything. As soon as they know I am here, they will be here every day checking and trying to figure out any way they can stop me.

What the real main bitch is that the sports fishermen want all the fish. They want every one, and it does not matter whether it is a whitefish, a lake trout, or a salmon. We are catching lake trout and they have sixteen charter boats there that are catching lake trout and they want all of them. There are plenty, but that is not their mentality. Their mentality is every one I catch is one they do not catch.

The charter boat operators are running a business for profit and I am running a business for profit, too. We are competitors for the same resource. They feel their vandalism and theft is justified because what they do protects the resource even though sixteen boats can go out and limit out three times a day. They are making $5–600 a trip and doing two a day. If I walk away with $300 a day and my mate, Vincent Chippewa, gets $100 bucks, we are happy. Some days it is real good and some days, such as yesterday when a storm with forty-mile-hour winds came through here, are not. The wind twists the nets up, ruins them, and breaks them, especially in the shallows. I am in the business of killing fish, so I am trying to catch fish.

The DNR does not want to come over here because they cannot enforce the lake trout rule because this is a deferred lake trout rehabilitation zone. When the law enforcement is present, it discourages vandalism so hence, we do not have any. They are leaving us out here hanging, waiting for them. To me that is an open call for violence and vandalism. These are people that have been charged by the State of Michigan as law enforcement people with badges and guns. The bottom line is we let them create the State of Michigan, but we reserve the right to live here and produce our livelihood. There are not very many of us to do it. It does not lend itself for new entries. I know one guy who started fishing a few years ago. He made it about two weeks and quit. He lost his gear; it got all wrecked up. We ended up recovering all that junk out of the lake.

PART 3. AN INTERVIEW WITH ARTHUR DUHAMEL AND BABETTE DUHAMEL PATTON

By Robert Doherty, Collected 1980

The late Art Duhamel discussed the importance of fishing to the cultural revitalization of the Grand Traverse Band of Ottawa and Chippewa Indians. He observed that helping to re-establish their treaty rights had come at a cost to both him and his family.

When we came back to Peshawbestown in 1972, we cut our ties with our old life. I used to wear neckties and white shirts and suits. I had a Cadillac in the yard. We had snowmobiles and all those appurtenances which people value, but are not worth much. I wear jeans now and flannel shirts. I always felt my roots were here. This was my home even when I was living other places. I was uneasy in your world. Skip was going into high school, so Babs and I felt that we should settle down for a while. We decided to return to the village.

Choosing to come here was a complex thing. I wanted to finish out my years in the place I was born and I was tired of the sort of life that goes on in construction camps.

Arthur Duhamel (1924–92). Treaty rights fishing activist Art Duhamel was born in Peshawbestown, Michigan. Art Duhamel supported his family by working as a welder both in the U.S. and abroad. During the 1970s, shortly after his return to northern Michigan, he began a legal challenge which culminated in the U.S. District Court's recognition of tribal treaty fishing rights and self-regulation on the Great Lakes. Art Duhamel was interviewed by Prof. Robert Doherty of the University of Pittsburgh in 1980. Photograph courtesy of the *Traverse City Record Eagle*.

I wanted to be with my people and my family—with Babs and Skip and all the rest of my family too, my brother and my cousins.

Looking back on it now, maybe it was not good for Skip to come back here. We made the decision to return to Peshawbestown with his best interest in mind. As parents, we wanted to do the best we could for our son. It was not long after we settled in when people started making trouble for Skip. It never really stopped until he quit school.

Schools are like the courts. And if Michigan State Court of Appeals Judge Richard Benedict was trying to impose his WASP standards on me, the teachers in Sutton's Bay High School were doing the same thing to Skip. I rebelled and so did he. We were sort of on parallel tracks. It got so bad we had to threaten to sue the school for denying Skip's rights.

Another time, people shot at Skip with a shotgun. Nothing came of it. After I protested, the cops caught them and they went to trial in a closed hearing in front of

Art "Buddy" Duhamel, Susan Miller, Babette Duhamel, and George "Skip" Duhamel. The family photograph was taken in the early 1970s when Art Duhamel began working as an activist for treaty rights fishing for the Grand Traverse Band of Ottawa and Chippewa Indians. Courtesy of Babette Patton.

Judge Benedict. At the time, I was in jail. They were juveniles, and Benedict let them off with probation. It may sound like we have thin skin, go around looking for trouble, and turn every little affront into something big. A few years ago, if I read what I am saying now, I might not have understood. But being here in the midst of hostility has given me a stronger sense of myself and what I believe in. It has made me more an Indian than I ever was before.

When Babs and I came back here after years of working in the outside world, the people here had little self-respect. They had very little drive or ambition. That is the way they felt about themselves. Let us pick our cherries. Let us chop our wood. Let us trap a few muskrats. Indians just did the shitwork and survived. They were afraid to hope for anything better.

People's spirits are up now. They are proud of themselves and what we have done. It was hard to convince people that the way to dignity was through the fishing rights struggle. With federal help maybe we can get a fish hatchery and some technical assistance. This body of water, Lake Michigan, is all this village needs. It should be treated as a garden, with proper management and the plantation of lake trout, fish that evidently do not reproduce naturally any longer. If we could participate in the replanting of this bay on a regular basis, it would take care of the lake trout problem. And this would have a fallout for the white sport fisherman. The Northwest Indians have hatcheries and aquaculture programs to farm the coastal waters. We could do that here. We need a hatchery.

If I were to envision a future for this village, it would be for the village to have a viable, continuous fishery. We have to plant, harvest, and conserve so we have fish in the future. We need a tribally operated fish processing plant, and wholesale outlet. In time, I hope those things will come. That is my dream. There is room for everybody if they were not so pigheaded.

Treaty fishing rights activist Art Duhamel used this chart to navigate the waters of Grand Traverse Bay he sought to place under tribal control. Duhamel made notations directly on the chart. Courtesy of Babette Patton.

It is hard to plan when you are fighting day-to-day to fish and to stay out of jail. It is difficult to accomplish much when you can hardly get a boat in the water without it being seized. Usually, you get your stuff back after a lot of effort. But meanwhile, they have kept you off the water.

All this is a bunch of dreams until the courts decide once and for all. We are beat—tired. Fishing is not that good and it is hard work. I am not catching that much fish. Last month we got only about 4,000 pounds—for three people. We are only getting about fifty cents a pound. We are not making much money, but you know somebody sure is. In the supermarket, whitefish is five times what we get.

My boat is small. It will only handle so much fish. I can only handle so much net. There are no big-time operators around here. We are subsistence fishermen. In the future, maybe we can get some assistance from the feds and get geared up properly. That is probably our best hope really, if we are ever going to have an economic base as a fishing village. Fishing could save this village and bring the people out of the economic doldrums. It could bring some dignity to the people. That is really the important thing: self-respect. I am not sorry about what I have done. Once in a while, I have certain regrets about the effects it has had on my family. If you asked me why I did it, I guess I would say to find dignity for myself and for my people. I hope that years from now my people will look back on all this and they will say, "Buddy Duhamel was Big Medicine."

It probably sounds like I am just full of myself. I do not mean it to be like that. We would never have achieved anything without help—Michigan Indian Legal Services, Eleesha Pastor, Bill Rastetter, Barry Levine, and Jim Olson all pitched in. I would probably be in jail now if it were not for them. They deserve a lot of credit.

Babette Patton, former wife of the late Art Duhamel, discussed the effects of prejudice.

One of my reasons for agreeing to come to Peshawbestown was that Skip had always been raised in white communities. The only connection he had with being an Ottawa was visiting the village a few times each year. I wanted him to marry an Indian woman and have a chance to become part of the Indian community here.

White mothers would not let their daughters date Skip. He did go out with one white girl from Suttons Bay. On senior prom night after they had been to the dance, they went to a friend's house. On the way back, some white kids in a car tried to push them off the road. Finally, they stopped in front of the girl's parents' house. Skip got out and grabbed a club. The girl's parents called the law. The cops talked with Skip and her parents. I called the sheriff and they said: "Well you know it is senior prom night."

The late Ottawa activist Art Duhamel recalled the beginning of his effort to re-establish treaty fishing rights following the 1971 Michigan Supreme Court case *State of Michigan vs. Jondreau.*

Jondreau's case was decided in 1971. There was a lot of fishing activity. I came up and visited people and talked with them. Pretty soon the attorney general said: "Well, O.K., Jondreau can fish but nobody else." So then Abe LeBlanc went to court and it came out in the state supreme court that perhaps Abe LeBlanc could fish, fine, but nobody else. Where did that leave us? Out in the cold that is where. So we had to have an advocate here to press the case for the Ottawa people.

I started fishing out here in August of 1974. Everybody knew we were fishing. We were out in broad daylight, right out in the open where people could see us. Our net buoys were visible from shore. Everyday we would set our nets and go lift them. Everyone in Leelanau County had to have known we were fishing. But they bided their time. Then on December 20th, I got picked up in Traverse City for illegally transporting fish. Skip and I had made a lift of 200 or 300 pounds of fish. We loaded them on the trailer and we were going to deliver them to Mackinaw City, to Bell's, a wholesale fish house up there. We stopped in Traverse City. I had to get a check cashed at the bank in order to get some gas. Apparently someone looked in the trailer and saw the fish. We had had them covered with a canvas to keep the wind off of them, but we had not made any effort to hide the fish. We had them iced down under the canvas.

Up drove Ellis Barber. I guess he was one of the DNR supervisory officers. "Say," he says, "have you got a license to transport fish?" I was a member of the Northern Michigan Ottawa Association (NMOA). We had already formed a fisherman's committee and written a fishing code. Mrs. Waunetta Dominic, the chairwoman, had issued cards

77

to NMOA fishermen.[37] So when he asked me did I have a license to transport fish I said, "Yes I do. I am a member of an Indian tribe and here's my card." I presented him with my NMOA card. He was quite contemptuous of it and just as much said I could wipe my ass with it. He gave me a ticket and took the fish. That is where the whole thing began for us. I told him, "Well you have not exactly caught me fishing yet. But, if you would like to, come to the village tomorrow, you will have a good opportunity because we are going to continue to fish."

The next day they came with I cannot remember how many officers. They just swarmed over here. Ultimately there came trucks and other vehicles to take all our gear away. Taking our gear was an outrageous, vicious tactic. They grabbed all our gear as evidence and held it for trial. Meanwhile, we could not fish without spending another two or three thousand dollars for equipment which would just get confiscated next time they came around.

That day did not seem different. It was like any other day until they arrived here in force. We knew they would be here. Skip and I were out in the boat. I told him there are eyes on us from shore right now. But I said, "We will lift our nets and take the fish in." Sure enough, when we got close to shore, they came running out like something on TV—a riot or something, not a couple of Indian fellows catching a few hundred pounds of fish. It was strange, really strange, to see all those police in my back yard.

I talked to the officer. I told him: "We have a right to fish. You are the one violating the law, not us. You are violating our treaty. One day—it may take a little while but one day you are going to have to back up." "Well," he said, "I am going to give you this ticket. You will have to appear in court on the 10th of January."

I said, "O.K., it does not make any difference to me. We intend to fish anyway." We did fish the next day, and they did the same thing. By then, they had cleaned us out of boats and nets. They wiped us out. They took everything and I mean everything. They took nets away that were not even being used. Some of them did not even belong to me. Unbelievably, on December 23rd, they returned a truckload of stuff.[38] Someone must have told them they had illegally seized my equipment. They returned it all and put it back in my fish shanty. I would not have known the difference because I did not know anything about the law. They took everything that was in there related to fishing.

We did not have an attorney at that time. We knew that we would need legal help, but we just did not want to go down to Suttons Bay and hire an attorney. We wanted somebody who had some commitment, a person who would prove to be an advocate, not just someone interested in the fee. Finally, Jim Olson of Olson and Dettmer was recommended to us. We had said to the press that we needed someone to take our case. Someone named Bowers from the American Civil Liberties Union in New York contacted Olson and Dettmer. Michigan State District Court Judge Richard L. Benedict agreed at a pretrial conference that we will take this one case and we will go through with it and all the rest, we will forget. But it did not turn out that way. In due time, the judge broke his word, and insisted that we be prosecuted on every one of these cases.

In 1980 Art Duhamel looked back upon the events of May 1975 when he again challenged the Michigan DNR's right to enforce laws which infringed on treaty fishing rights.

My cousin Albert and I had set nets off Gull Island near Northport, in May 1975. Indian people from Bay Mills were fishing and the Michigan State Appeals Court had upheld treaty right fishing.[39] So we were within the law, within our rights, to be fishing out there. We would drive from here and camp on the island so we could lift our nets early in the morning before the wind came up. We wanted to be off the water early to avoid trouble. Somebody called the Coast Guard and said there are people on the island. A helicopter came out. Albert and I were setting nets and Albert said: "What should we do? Should we take the nets up and go in?" I said: "No." So we went ahead and set them.

Coming in to my place in the fog, we saw there were two DNR boats. They caught us out on the water. Albert was hard of hearing and his motor was loud too. He kept chugging along. The guy yelled, "Stop, shut that boat down or I will blow you out of the water." This was that DNR from Benzie County, a hard-nosed lawman, who thought he was John Wayne.

After they had threatened to blow Albert away, I came on in. I heard that, so I came on in. I was not evading them in any case. We came in and you know how conversations go—"Got you again, didn't we! See you are fishing some more." I said: "Yeah sure, that's right. We were fishing." They took two fourteen-foot rowboats and the gear down to Suttons Bay. We were sitting around the beach watching them. We were kind of morose. We were really devastated because there went two more boats and all our nets and everything. My uncle was sitting on the beach and I told him "Well, you are going to get a fish out of this by God, you are going to have something to eat out of this." I went down there and took a nice whitefish. They insisted that they wanted that one too. But I said, "No, this is my uncle's." I gave it to him. They did not do anything. Hell, what were they going to do, tackle an old man, put him down, and take a fish away from him? They took the fish, menominees and whitefish, except that one.

I sat around there and, God, it just pissed me off that they had done that. So I went down to Suttons Bay to the dock. I told them, "Look, you guys are in the wrong here. You are the ones who are violating the law, not me." I said: "I want this boat. It belongs to me and you have no right to take it. It is mine." So I jumped in my boat and started it up. They just stood there with their mouths open. I pushed off and headed north toward Peshawbestown.

The DNR had already trailered their boat so they had to put it back in the water. By that time, I was maybe a half-mile on my way toward Peshawbestown. I could see them coming. Man, they had it wide open. It was not long before they caught up with me. I was just putting along in my rowboat. They said, "Well are you going to go in?"

"No," I said. "No, I am taking this boat home." Later, they said I threatened to ram them, which would have been a pretty silly thing for me to do in that wooden rowboat. I would have sunk if I had hit them. That boat was not very strong and it had only about twelve inches of freeboard. Hell, they got so close to me that I thought they would swamp me. For that reason alone, I tried to avoid them. I was not going to ram them. I just wanted them to leave me alone. The DNR guy pulled out his gun. He said, "Are you going to come in?" I saw that gun and I did not know if he might use it. I turned around and headed back to Suttons Bay. "OK" I said, "Let's go in."

I went back to Suttons Bay and sat on the dock there waiting to see what they would do. I did not even speak to the DNR people. There were several witnesses there— one ex-state police officer who told me he would testify for me. I gathered up some witnesses. "Did I resist these people?" I asked them. By this time, I realized I had done something foolish, and I figured they would say I was resisting arrest or something like that. They charged me with obstructing justice. But I was seeking justice. How can you obstruct what you cannot find?

I was just sitting on the dock waiting. They never arrested me until they got all done. I think they were hoping maybe I would flee. They ignored me all that time. I figured I would just sit there and watch and see what they would do with my stuff. Finally, after they were all done, they said: "Get in the car."

They took me to the county jail in Leland. I was booked there. It was not until late that afternoon when they set bond of $2,000 cash. We did not have that much money right there. We had been doing this for a while, and had several thousand dollars tied up in confiscated gear and bail money. My wife, Babette, had to scramble around to get the money. She had to hock some jewelry. The sentence was sixty days in jail. They had me all locked up in a cell in Leland. If it had not been for Babs, I would have been stuck there. But she got me out by evening. In a lot of cases here, they merely issue the ticket and hope you will appear in court. In my cases, except at first, they gave me the ticket, then took me right to jail. I went directly to jail.

I do not remember what was on my mind that day. I was depressed and angry, angry as hell. The Department of Natural Resources (DNR) had seized my gear again, boats, motors, nets, everything. And I could not fish without that stuff. They broke the law, stole my equipment, and took away my livelihood, but I ended up in jail. How is that for justice?

Dean Robb volunteered his legal services. We did not use those witnesses or argue at all. When it came time for the hearing in front of Judge Forster, we thought it would be best to plead no contest and take our chances. They charged me with obstruction of justice, a felony offense. It was scary. You can get two years for a felony.

I got sixty days for taking my boat in Suttons Bay. They said I was obstructing justice. I pled no contest. That case was assigned to Judge Forster in January 1976. I was going to return to Alaska to my job welding on the pipeline. I took a leave from my job to come here to court. I was scheduled to go back, but it did not turn out that way because he sentenced me to jail. They took me right from the courthouse in Traverse City to jail. I cannot describe what I felt at that moment—nausea, strangulation. I like to be outdoors in the open, on the water. I cannot express how awful I felt with the idea of being locked up for sixty days. But the guilty sentence held. And I spent five days in jail before they got Forster's sentence postponed. I think it was five days. I am not sure. I do not like to remember that time.

There was a possibility I could have gotten two years out of it, which scared me pissless. I probably should have fought that obstruction charge rather than plead no contest. It was hard for us to decide which way to go. I was locked up in a cell in the Leelanau County Jail. Then I got sick. I could barely walk. I had to go to the hospital for an operation. I had served about half of my sixty days because I got sick. God, was I glad to get home. I do not like being locked up. You know, for years I really got into work being the white man. I worked my ass off. I worked just as hard and often as I could on a daily basis—ten, twelve hours a day for ninety days in a row. God damn, how I wasted my time, working like that! I guess I was lucky to find out when I did that there was more to life than work.

Art Duhamel reflected upon his view of Indians' treaty fishing rights as a legal issue and not the political issue it would become.

If I were to go through the whole record, the whole sorry record of the injustice and prejudice toward me, my family, the village, the Indian people—if I recounted all of those things, we would end up writing a whole bunch of books. God, I am not going into that. It is too depressing.

We have to rely on the courts. The higher up the court system we go the better. After all, we have got a low level of jurist in the lower courts. It is only when you get into the higher tribunals that you begin to see some thought and reflection.

Judge Richard L. Benedict of the State's 26th District Court prosecuted me at every turn. He did his best to bury us, but he did not succeed because of the law. Even though he is a representative of the law, and a very poor one in my estimation, there were other representatives of the law who devoted more thought and less passion to my case. I respect the law. That is why I broke it, you know. A man without faith in the law does not engage in civil disobedience.

Everyone came to see Judge Benedict and my trial. The courtroom was packed. Lots of Indians came. They flocked in. Benedict tried to hurry it up a bit. He stated from the bench that he wanted to go fishing the next day. I did not realize it then, but that statement said a lot about Benedict's commitments. In a way, Indians and sports fishermen are struggling to control the fishing resource. Benedict certainly revealed his sympathies when he tried to hurry the trial along so he could go fishing. His sport fishing was more important than my trial.

Helen Tanner's testimony was really effective in *United States vs. Michigan*, but was not as effective as it might have been in my case because Benedict tried to hurry her along so that he could go fishing.[40] But it probably would not have made any difference. Benedict was not going to pay much attention to her testimony anyway.

At first, I thought we had a chance to win. Benedict had not shown his prejudice yet. And he had seemed like a fair jurist before. I had some contact with him when I worked as a volunteer probation officer. He had commended me. But I did not know him very well did I? Actually, I had high hopes. But since then, I have lost hope of obtaining justice for Indian people in this county or in the state for that matter. The state courts will not treat Indian people fairly. It is only in the federal courts that we are going to find justice.

I do not recall what I told them at my sentencing after the Suttons Bay incident. I just do not remember what I said. I was worked up and upset. I did mention that there were other courts and other justices. There was justice along the way—somewhere—even if not in Benedict's court. And I told him I was going to continue to fish.

When my first trial was over, it was pretty clear that Benedict would do me in. We complained to the press about his unfairness. But Benedict never did anything for the longest time; he did nothing. He could have issued an opinion the next day but he just let it drag on. I do not know why he did that. There were political reasons I suppose. He wanted to take advantage of all the good press he was getting. Everybody was jumping on his bandwagon saying, "Oh, what a good judge we have in Leelanau County." Well, Benedict was aware that this was not an ordinary case. He wanted to make a landmark decision—a decision of landmark quality. Benedict said so in a speech he gave to the Grand Traverse Area Sportfishing Association at the Holiday Inn in Traverse City. This was in the spring of 1978. The newspaper said, "Benedict expressed hope that his decisions would ultimately come to be regarded as landmark quality."

Benedict was chasing votes and hobnobbing with his friends just the way he was when he let those sport fishermen submit a brief in my case as friends of the court. They were friends of the court all right. They had just organized three days before. Friends of the judge is what they were. When in 1974 the decision in LeBlanc came down and the Michigan Supreme Court had affirmed the Indian's right to fish, I called up Benedict and asked for my gear—I asked him to return my gear. He told me right over the phone, "Art, I have got you by the short hairs and I am going to keep you there." He was really wrought up. I could imagine that he was just livid that I had the guts to ask for the return of my gear.

Benedict just twisted things around so the jury had to find me guilty. Benedict is one of these straight-laced White Protestants or WASPS. He had represented his class of people very ably and he still does. But us? Never! He will hold us down just as long as he can. Local police, sheriff's departments, DNR, have been just vile to us, just awful. They are a lot like Benedict. Those cops represent the values of the dominant members of the community but do not worry much about right and wrong. I do not think they have ever heard the word justice.

I was naive when I started all this. I thought we would violate a state law. We would set a gill net and catch a few fish. We would go to court. In the court it would probably be a one-day trial. We would present our treaty and we would walk out of the courtroom that evening with the right to fish. Well, it has not been like that. I have been at this six years now and we still have not won.

Boy, we were dumb back then. No kidding, I thought we would walk out of that court with the right to fish. I had such a firm belief I told Babs the judge is just bound to rule in our favor. How could he decide against us? Babs was always the skeptic. She was right. She said, "Benedict will hang you." Sure enough, he did. But Benedict had not shown his true character yet. I thought it would be a simple matter of violating the statute, going to court with the treaty, and then walking out of the court a free man and a hero to the people. After the first trial, Judge Benedict ran around the courthouse saying, "Arthur Duhamel is nothing but a common crook."

Art Duhamel discussed his belief that the judge in one of his treaty fishing rights cases was prejudiced against him. He was in possession of a letter he maintained was written by Judge Richard Benedict.

Sportsmen," the letter said, "vote for Glenn Aylsworth." Longtime Leelanau County Prosecutor Glen Aylsworth thought he would move up to the bench so in 1976, he ran for district judge against James R. McCormick. A letter was circulated in support of Aylsworth. It read:

Dear Outdoor Sportsman:

You and I, as hunters and fishermen, have been taking lumps from everyone lately. We have been smeared in the media, blamed for the murder rate, and the resources we have fought to preserve and recreate have been and are being taken from us and being turned over to minorities and anyone and everyone to our exclusion.

Sometimes it seems we are powerless to slow or reverse the tide. But occasionally we get the chance to protect ourselves and our sport. Such an opportunity is presented in the race of the 2nd District Judge for Leelanau and Grand Traverse Counties. One candidate is not known as a hunter and fisherman, but as a champion of minority rights, real or imagined, and a member of the American Civil Liberties Union Legal Panel. The other is Glen Aylsworth, who, when presented with the first Indian netting case in 1971, [got the offender to remove his nets from Grand Traverse Bay] . . . and who as Leelanau County Prosecutor was vigorous in the protection of our natural resources.

You can see where our best interests lie. It will not be enough to vote for Glenn, talk to your relatives, friends and hunting and fishing partners. Don't let us in for further abuse, when we can nip it in the bud.

The letter was signed by nine men. Pressed about the widely circulated letter, Aylsworth accepted responsibility for it. Tight-lipped and crew cut, Aylsworth said yes, the letter was sent through his campaign office which had paid the postage. Aylsworth talked with reporters and said he had read the letter and believed that what is in there is true. He claimed neither he nor the nine men who signed the letter had written it. The author? Judge Richard L. Benedict wrote the letter.

Babette Duhamel Patton was convinced prejudice influenced the way her late husband was treated in the criminal justice system.

Historian Helen Tanner was our expert witness. Her testimony was really important to our case. We needed her to establish the legitimacy of the treaty and Ottawa rights guaranteed by the treaty. She was put on last. Everybody was very tired. She was tired. She is a nervous person. It was late at night, but Benedict insisted that she testify. He insisted she testify because fishing season opened the next morning and he was not going to miss opening day.

All during the trial when witnesses were up on the stand, Benedict would slump back in his chair with his eyes shut, just contemptuous of the whole proceeding. The first day of the trial when we broke for lunch, we went to the Bluebird Restaurant. Benedict said something to Art. I cannot remember just what he said. At first Art ignored him and Benedict said, "You asked for it!" Everything is so political. I never realized just how political judges are.

Benedict rendered his decision after that incident at Suttons Bay when Art took his boat back. During the trial, Benedict insulted Mrs. Waunetta Dominic, chairwoman of the Northern Michigan Ottawa Association.[41] He ridiculed her position and the organization. He demeaned the identification cards, and the association's conservation code. I cannot remember all that he said, but I remember his attitude. I was getting angry. I had to sit there and do nothing, but I was angry. I told the lawyers one day: "I have sat quietly in Benedict's court for the last time. I am not going to listen to that man insult my husband any more. I am not going to do it. I am going to tell him off." They laughed and told me I would end up in jail if I did that.

Benedict got ready to sentence Art and he said, "First of all, I want you to know that you sneak around. You sneak around and fish. You stole these fish from the people of the State of Michigan. You sneak around to do this." I stood up and I told him, "My husband does not sneak around. He was fishing in broad daylight. He has been fishing since last August in broad daylight. The whole community knew he was fishing."

When he sentenced Art he said: "I want you to know you stole. You stole these fish from the people of the State of Michigan." I got up and said, "My husband stole nothing." I went on something of a tirade. I cannot remember all of what I said. I stomped out of court. I thought they would throw me in jail for sure. They had guards at every door. I burst out of that place and tried to smack those guards with the doors. I waited in the lobby for them to come and take me away.

Judge Benedict would only let the jury decide on the state law; nothing was said about the treaty. Now that is the whole issue, the treaty. When he charged the jury, he told them they should just decide did it happen or not, and pay no attention to any treaty. We got hit with a summons to come into Traverse City to deal with the illegal transporting of fish. Benedict said it was up to his discretion. That is when we tried to have him disqualified.

Judge Benedict showed Art's record to people who had no business seeing it. June Soper phoned me and told me about it. "Nothing but a common crook." Those were Benedict's actual words. Art got in some trouble when he was fifteen years old but Benedict brought all this out thirty-six years later. "Look at this," he said. "Look, at the type of person who is fighting for you Indians—a crook." That was the first time we said he was prejudiced and should not sit on Art's case. That was in July 1975. All these years Art's never been in trouble. He raised his family and helped me raise mine. A common criminal—where do you get that?

We had no warning. Our lawyers had said Art would get maybe probation or a fine, but no jail. He will not go to jail over this. We were just stunned. Dean Robb (Art's attorney) was so upset he began to cry. But they got busy that night and drove to Lansing with an appeal. During his sentence, Art was in the hospital two weeks. He was weak from surgery and had not fully recovered yet. They came and took him back to jail from the hospital.

They took him back to jail. The doctor called them up and said: "I will not be responsible. You are going to kill that man." Hell, when the deputy came, he told Art to pick up his case and put it in the car. I was there and I said: "Wait a minute. He is not supposed to pick up over five pounds. If you want that case carried, you carry it." It was so callous. "Well," he said, "he does not look so bad to me." They released Art that night. I went over and got him out of jail.

Benedict had said that Art was not to fish in Lake Michigan as a condition of his bond. So Art went to fish in Lake Superior. They confiscated Art's boat and nets, and all his fish. Everybody else was fishing, but they got Art's stuff. Benedict had him transported in handcuffs. They left his truck up there and brought Art back to jail. I had to go in that night and post $200 bond. But when it came down to it Benedict said, "If you will forget about it, I will forget about it." There's still $200 up there somewhere. You know this case is still on appeal in Forster's court. He has had it all these years and has never done a thing. In the meantime, while Art was here, people up there wrecked his truck.

Art Duhamel discussed the relationship between fishing and efforts to help win federal recognition of the Grand Traverse Band of Ottawa and Chippewa.

Right after my wife Babs, my son, Skip and I moved back to the village I realized that recognition had to come about. Partly it was my problems as a fisherman that convinced me. I could not establish myself as a treaty rights fisherman unless the federal government acknowledged the legitimacy of the Grand Traverse Band. But there were all sorts of other advantages that would derive from recognition—most of all, we would have a chance to be sovereign people again.

After I thought about tribal recognition and talked with people, I decided that recognition was the thing to do. I went to Leelanau Indians, Inc. They were our representatives then—a business corporation that been formed to look after our interests. I made my pitch for recognition and they appointed me to head up a campaign for federal acknowledgement.

This all happened several years ago and it has been a long slow process. That is the way Indian politics usually go. We do not do things in a hurry. I got a committee together and we began to lobby for recognition. We held meetings all over the area where we explained the advantages of recognition and answered questions. We would have a meeting here and a meeting there. Sometimes, only a couple people would show up. But we kept at it. There were times when it seemed like we were not getting anywhere. I remember once we had a meeting in Traverse City. We were all psyched up because we thought there would be a lot of people there—a big crowd. After all our efforts, just one person showed up.

We got better results lobbying informally, talking up recognition every chance we had. The young people helped. When they ran into problems or people asked them questions they could not answer, they would come to me to see if we could work it out. But mostly they were on their own. We would never have prevailed without the young people. They are flexible and open to change and they have more education so they could see that recognition was the right thing to do.

Apathy was our biggest problem. Most of the older people, people my age and older, were indifferent. They did not care. They did not oppose us but they did not help us either. We had to try to overcome their lack of interest and that was hard to do. Some of the board members of Leelanau Indians were not very supportive of recognition either so I tried to get the people to elect board members who were sympathetic to recognition. In time, the board came around to our side. I guess we won them over.

Some people really fought to prevent recognition. People who owned property in the village worried that they might lose it. Others thought that we were selling out to the feds and that recognition would have the BIA (Bureau of Indian Affairs) running our lives. Some people still feel that way and a few families are still working against recognition.

I can see why some people think that we have to conform to white institutions in order to be recognized. They are right. We do have to abide by BIA guidelines. We do have to create a government patterned after non-Indian institutions. But I believe that those are compromises worth making. Without recognition, we would just exist as we always have without control over our lives—powerless. With recognition, we can exert ourselves and take initiative. We can be sovereign people as we were long ago.

People from Northern Michigan Ottawa Association (NMOA) opposed our efforts too. The group had formed around claims and money due from an Indian Claims Commission judgment. They had come to feel that they spoke for the Indian people of that area. To be honest, NMOA had performed well in the past, but they had become ineffective. They could not protect our rights. They did not have the sort of clout we could get from recognition. I guess they saw us as usurpers.

We would never have made it without Michigan Indian Legal Services. They helped us every step of the way. They did the technical and legal work. They prepared the petition for recognition. Without Michigan Indian Legal Services, there would not be any Grand Traverse Band. It is that simple. And without Michigan Indian Legal Services, we would be hard pressed to go on even now.

Twelve years before his death, Art Duhamel recalled how neither arrest nor the theft or vandalism of his boat and gear kept him from fishing.

I was fishing in Grand Marais—about 200 miles north of Traverse City on Lake Superior. Michigan State Court of Appeals Judge Richard Benedict said if I was fishing in Lake Michigan, it would be a violation of his probation orders. The DNR officers came up there and arrested me. They brought me back down here in handcuffs and charged me with what, I do not know exactly, because nothing ever came of it.

While I was gone, everything went to hell. They smashed my truck and chopped holes in my skiff. Vandals sunk a twenty-six-foot sport boat that we had converted. Nobody knew a thing about what happened. Oh, they knew who did it, but nobody was talking. I complained to the local constable. He acted very disinterested and indicated to me that I had it coming. Somebody from the Munising Sheriff's Office came out, but he got nowhere. Now we know who did it. Most everyone around there brags about who did it. But the guy from the sheriff's office never could find out what happened. I guess you have to look at it from their point of view. People need tourist business and they thought we would drive the fishermen away. So there was no way they were going to help us.

People, vigilantes, have harassed us, smashed our boats, torn up our nets. The sheriff will come out and investigate, but he never finds anything out. Not one of those cases has been solved as far as I know. Attitudes like that are common – not just among enforcement people, but ordinary citizens, business interests, and the resort owners who rely on the tourist dollars. I never knew before that they had become so twisted, so warped in their attitude toward Indians, but I know now. Years ago, I do not think they held these attitudes.

When we began to assert our rights, their attitudes began to change. Prior to that they had a more or less bemused attitude toward us. We were Indian people, so what? Whites knew they had robbed us and dispossessed us. Fine! Whites are superior people who are entitled to all of this, who have a God-given mandate to improve this country and put it to higher use. I get worked up at times; maybe I get over-emotional about it.

Babette Duhamel discussed how her husband's civil disobedience created a financial strain on their family.

I had some gold jewelry Art had bought for me when he was working in Algeria. I used that for Art's bond, for the collateral to get him out. They kept my jewelry for about a year until that case was settled. The case was settled by Art going to jail for sixty days.

Art sold fresh and smoked fish out of the fish shack in his back yard. He claimed he did not need a license. The state said otherwise. They came at nine o'clock and took

Art to jail. They fingerprinted him and everything. He had to have $100 cash bond or they were going to lock him up all night. Generally they would know that most people do not have $100 cash at 9:30 at night. But Art's lawyer was here; we are good friends and we went right over to the courthouse.

NOTES

1. Philip P. Mason, ed., *Schoolcraft's Ojibwa Lodge Stories: Life on the Lake Superior Frontier* (East Lansing: Michigan State University Press, 1997); Frances Densmore, *Chippewa Customs* (Washington, D.C.: Smithsonian Institution, 1929; reprint, St. Paul: Minnesota Historical Society Press, 1979), 22–28, 42–43, 124–25, 150, 154, 165; Charles E. Cleland, *Rites of Conquest: The History and Culture of Michigan's Native Americans* (Ann Arbor: University of Michigan Press, 1992), 45–47, 99, 148, 240–41, 243, 256–57; "The Inland Shore Fishery of the Northern Great Lakes: Its Development and Importance in Prehistory," *American Antiquity* 47 (October 1982): 761–84; Helen H. Tanner, ed., *Atlas of Great Lakes Indian History* (Norman: University of Oklahoma Press, 1987), 5, 19, 22, 132; Harold Hickerson, "The Southwestern Chippewa: An Ethnohistorical Study," *American Anthropologist*, Memoir 92, vol. 64, no. 3 (June 1962); Shari Dann, *The Life of the Lakes: A Guide to the Great Lakes Fishery* (East Lansing: Michigan Sea Grant Extension/Michigan State University, 1994), 21–23; Richard White, "Ethnohistorical Report on the Grand Traverse Ottawas," History Department, Michigan State University, [n.d.]; Charles E. Cleland, "The Prehistoric Animal Ecology and Ethnozoology of the Upper Great Lakes Region," (Ph.D. diss., University of Michigan, 1966); Andrew J. Blackbird, *History of the Ottawa and Chippewa Indians of Michigan* (Ypsilanti, Mich.: Ypsilantian Job Printing House, 1887).

   On tribal fishing traditions, see Margaret Beattie Bogue, *Fishing the Great Lakes: An Environmental History* (Madison: University of Wisconsin Press, 2000), 5–15, 76–81; James Clifton, George L. Cornell, and James McClurken, *People of the Three Fires: The Ottawa, Potawatomi, and Ojibway of Michigan* (Grand Rapids: Grand Rapids Inter-Tribal Council, 1986); William J. Gribb, "The Grand Traverse Land Base: A Cultural Historical Study of Land Transfer in Michigan" (Ph.D. diss., Michigan State University, 1981); Donald J. Hanaway, *History of the Chippewa Treaty Rights Controversy* (Madison: Wisconsin State Department of Justice, 1989); Donald J. Hanaway, *History of the Chippewa Treaty Rights Controversy* (Madison: Wisconsin State Department of Justice, 1990); Lawrence Bobo and Estela B. Garcia, *The Chippewa Indian Treaty Rights Survey: A Preliminary Report* (Madison: Robert M. Lafollette Institute of Public Affairs, 1992); Patty Loew, *Voices From the Boatlandings in the Chippewa Treaty Rights Dispute: Source Selection and Bias in the Coverage of Two Very Different Newspapers*, (n.l.: 1995); *Chippewa Treaty Rights: A Guide to Understanding Chippewa Treaty Rights* (Odanah, Wisc.: Great Lakes Indian Fish and Wildlife Commission, 1990); *Chippewa Treaty Rights: A Guide to Understanding Chippewa Treaty Rights* (Odanah, Wisc.: Great Lakes Indian Fish and Wildlife Commission, 1994); *A Guide to Understanding Chippewa Treaty Rights: Rights, Regulation and Resource Management* (Odanah, Wisc.: Great Lakes Indian Fish and Wildlife Commission, 1995); *Report of the Governor's Special Task Force on Indian Fishing Rights* (Lansing, Mich.: Governor's Special Task Force on Indian Fishing Rights, 1971); Beman Greenway Neubeck, *The Public's Right of Hunting and Fishing on Michigan Waters* (Detroit: Principle Publication, 1934).

   On women and tribal fishing, see Bogue, *Fishing the Great Lakes*, 7. On origins of tribal treaty rights, see U.S. Indian Commission, *Commission Findings on the Chippewa Indians* (New York: Garland Publishing., 1974), 504–24; Robert Doherty, *Disputed Waters: Native Americans and the Great Lakes Fishery* (Lexington:

University of Kentucky Press, 1990), 7–37, 67–85; William W. Warren, *History of the Ojibway People* (St. Paul: Minnesota Historical Society Press, 1984), 97; James M. McClurken, *Gah-Baeh-Jhgwah-Buk: The Way it Happened* (East Lansing: Michigan State University Museum, 1991); *Ojibway Heritage* (Lincoln: University of Nebraska Press, 1976); R.W. Dunning, *Social and Economic Change Among the Northern Ojibway* (Toronto: University of Toronto Press, 1959), 31; Mike Norton, "Traverse City History Full of Indian Traditions," *Traverse City Record Eagle*, 14 November 1999; Owen S. Cecil, *History of Small Working Sailboats Among Native American of Manitoulin Island, Ontario* [unpublished manuscript], February 1994, Michigan Maritime Museum Collection, South Haven, Michigan.

2. Doherty, *Disputed Waters*.

3. George Weeks, *Mem-ka-weh: Dawning of the Grand Traverse Band of Ottawa and Chippewa Indians* (Traverse City, Mich.: Grand Traverse Band of Ottawa and Chippewa Indians), 41–45; Chippewa-Ottawa Treaty Fishery Management Authority, *Michigan's 1836 Treaty Fishery Guide* (Sault Ste. Marie, Mich.: Chippewa-Ottawa Treaty Fishery Management Authority), 4–14; Dann, *The Life of the Lakes*, 34–35; Linda S. Parker, *Native American Estate* (Honolulu: University of Hawaii Press, 1989), 172–87; Helen Hornbeck Tanner, "History vs. The Law: Processing Indians in the American Legal System," *University of Detroit Mercy Law Review* 76 (spring 1999): 693–708; Doherty, *Disputed Waters*, 67–104.

4. Cleland, *Rites of Conquest*, 234–63; McClurken, *Gah-Baeh-Jhgwah-Buk: The Way it Happened*, 73–86.

5. James M. McClurken, "Wage Labor In Two Michigan Ottawa Communities," in *Native Americans and Wage Labor: Ethnohistorical Perspectives*, ed. Alice Littlefield and Martha C. Knack (Norman: University of Oklahoma Press, 1996), 66–99; Doherty, *Disputed Waters*, 1–37.

6. Hugh M. Smith and Merwin-Marie Snell, "Review of the Fisheries of the Great Lakes in 1885," U.S. Commission of Fish and Fisheries, *Report of the Commissioner for 1887* (Washington, D.C.: U.S. Government Printing Office, 1891), 1–333

7. Kevin Joseph Hill, "An Analysis of Michigan Chippewa Treaty Fishing Rights in the 1836 Ceded Waters of Lake Superior, Lake Huron, and Lake Michigan" (Master's Thesis, Eastern Michigan University, 1988); Cleland, *Rites of Conquest*, 283–84.

8. Cleland, *Rites of Conquest*, 280–85; Doherty, *Disputed Waters*, 67–85.

9. McClurken, *Gah-Baeh-Jhgwah-Buk: The Way it Happened*, 50–59.

10. Ibid., 83; Dann, *The Life of the Lakes*, 29–30; Cleland, *Rites of Conquest*, 267–68.

11. Tom Kuchenberg, *Reflections in a Tarnished Mirror: The Use and Abuse of the Great Lakes* (Sturgeon Bay, Wisc.: Golden Glow Publishing, 1978), 88–92; John A. Scott, "A Historical Review of the Productivity and Regulation of Michigan's Fisheries," in *Michigan Fisheries Centennial Report, 1873–1973*, Fisheries Management Report No. 6, April 1974 (Lansing, Mich.: Fisheries Division, Michigan Department of Natural Resources), 81–82; Arthur W. DeClaire, "Chronology of Important Events in Michigan Fisheries History," in *Michigan Fisheries Centennial Report, 1873–1973*, Fisheries Management Report No. 6, April 1974 (Lansing Mich.: Fisheries Division, Michigan Department of Natural Resources), 183–85; Dean A. Brege and Niles R. Kevern, *Michigan Commercial Fishing Regulations: A Summary of Public Acts and Conservation Commission Orders, 1865–1975* (Michigan Sea Grant Program Reference Report 78–605, November 1978), 55–62; Doherty, *Disputed Waters*, 51–66.

12. For more on the symbolic and legal context of resource use rights in Indian treaties, see: Fredrick E. Hoxie, "Why Treaties?" in *Buried Roots and Indestructible Seeds: The Survival of American Indian Life in Story, History, and Spirit*, ed. Mark A. Lindquist and Martin Zanger (Madison: University of Wisconsin Press, 1993), 85–105

13. For more on *People v. Jondreau* (1971), *People v. LeBlanc* (1976), and *U.S. v. Michigan, 1979*, see Cleland, *Rites of Conquest*, 279–87; Parker, *Native American Estate*, 179–82; Doherty, *Disputed Waters*, 67–104; McClurken, *Gah-Baeh-Jhgwah-Buk: The Way it Happened*, 84–86; Weeks, *Mem-ka-weh: Dawning of the Grand Traverse Band of Ottawa and Chippewa Indians*, 41–45; Diane Conners, "Federal Judge Will Rule on Tribal Fishing," *Traverse City Record Eagle*, [n.d]; Marcellas S. Kreiter, "2 Ways of Life Clash in Fishing Court Battle," *Grand Rapids*

Press, [n.d.] 1978, Michigan Department of Natural Resources Charlevoix Research Station Scrapbooks [hereafter CRSS]; Marcellas S. Kreiter, "Indian Fishing Trial Will Resume Tuesday in U.S. Court," *Petoskey News Review*, 14 August 1978; Marcellas S. Kreiter, "Says Indians Didn't Know, Understand Treaty Terms," *Petoskey News Review*, 14 August 1978; "Judge Fox Raps Attorney In Indian Gill Net Trial" *Petoskey News Review* 21 August 1978; "Fox Appalled at Broken Treaties, Indian Case Ends," *Petoskey News Review*, 4 October 1978; "Rule 2 Tribes Have 'Unlimited' Fishing," *Petoskey News Review*, 8 May 1979, CRSS; "LeBlanc, Mrs. Dominic, Comment on Decision," *Petoskey News Review*, 8 May 1979; "Indian Fishing Rights Upheld," *Traverse City Record Eagle*, 8 May 1979; Rick Haglund, "Indians Ecstatic; Prosecutors Dour," *Traverse City Record Eagle*, 8 May 1979; Eric Sharp, "Indians Win Court Fight on Fishing Rights," *Detroit Free Press*, 9 May 1979; Jim Doherty, "Judge Fox's Decision is Law of the Land," *Petoskey News Review*, 9 May 1979; Marcellas S. Kreiter, "Fox Warns Against Fishing Violence," *Petoskey News Review*, 9 May 1979; "MUCC Terms Fox Decision 'Outrageous,' 'Prejudiced,'" *Traverse City Record Eagle*, 9 May 1979; "Rule Treaties Don't Cover Planted Fish," *Petoskey News Review*, 10 May 1979; "Milliken: Appeal Fish Ruling" *Traverse City Record Eagle*, 10 May 1979; "Indians: Law, Environment, and People are Tangled in the Fish Nets," *Detroit Free Press*, 10 May 1979; Marsha Robinson, "Tribal Leader Says Ruling Defines Rights and Privilege," *Petoskey News Review*, 14 May 1979; Marsha Robinson, "Bay Mills Shows Little Sign of Windfall Fishing Profits," *Petoskey News Review*, 15 May 1979; Pete Sandman, "Indian Rights Decision Will Affect Multi-Million Dollar Business," *Great Lakes Steelheader*, July 1979; "Treaties Must be Abrogated," *Detroit Free Press*, 29 July 1979; "Anglers to Appeal Fox Ruling," *Petoskey News Review*, 18 September 1979; "State Appeals Judge's Gill Net Ruling," *Detroit Free Press*, 23 September 1979; "Fox Lets Grand Traverse Indians into Treaty Case," *Petoskey News Review*, 15 November 1979; Rick Haglund, "Officials Still Confused on Indian Fish Ruling," *Traverse City Record Eagle*, 7 December 1979; Rick Haglund, "Fish Conservation Loses with Defeat of Art LeBlanc," *Traverse City Record Eagle*, 10 December 1979; [Nancy Kida], "Treaties: Yesterday Lives On," 17 March 1984, Typewritten Report, Mackley Public Library, Muskegon, Michigan; "Our View: Courts Moving to Clarify Hunting and Fishing Rights," *Traverse City Record Eagle*, 2 April 1999; "Court Limits Indian Fish Rights," *Detroit Free Press*, 31 August 1971; "Only U.P. Indians Covered by Treaty," *Petoskey News Review*, 1 September 1971; George Anthony Interview Transcript, 4 August 1992, clip reel #28, Public Museum of Grand Rapids, Grand Rapids, Michigan.

On tribal fishing rights in the Northwest United States, see Elizabeth Ann O'Brien, "Tribal Hunting and Fishing Rights Fail to Survive Cession of Treaty Land: Oregon Department of Fish and Wildlife v. Klamath Indian Tribe," *Ecology Law Quarterly* 13 (1986): 593–608; Donald L. Parman, "Inconstant Advocacy: The Erosion of Indian Fishing Rights in the Pacific Northwest, 1933–1956," *Pacific Historical Review* 53, no. 2 (May 1984): 163–89.

14. On tribal fishing, treaty rights, and cultural and political revitalization, see Joane Nagle, *American Indian Ethnic Renewal: Red Power and the Resurgence of Identity and Culture* (New York: Oxford University Press, 1996), 29, 129–30, 161–64, 170; Donald L. Fixico, *The Invasion of Indian Country: American Capitalism and Tribal Natural Resources* (Niwot, Col.: University Press of Colorado, 1998), 103–22; Melissa A. Pflug, *Ritual and Myth in Odawa Revitalization: Reclaiming a Sovereign Place* (Norman: University of Oklahoma Press, 1998), 189–221.

On the issue of Indian fishing tradition, ecological concerns, and geographic affiliation, see Donald A. Grinde and Bruce E. Johansen, *Ecocide of Native America: Environmental Destruction of Indian Lands and Peoples* (Santa Fe, N.M.: Clear Light Publishers, 1995), 145–69; Pflug, *Ritual and Myth in Odawa Revitalization*, 15–65.

15. Weeks, *Mem-ka-weh*, 42–49, 61–64.

16. Ibid., 49.

17. On Arthur Duhamel, see David Averill, "Activist Art Duhamel Helped Tribe Gain Federal Recognition," *Traverse City Record Eagle*, 13 November 1992; Doherty, *Disputed Waters*, 68; Grand Traverse Area

Sportsfishing Association, "The Treaty of 1836 and the Fishing Case" [n.l.] 17 February 1976, CRSS; Letter from Joseph Lumdsen, Arthur Duhamel, and Wade Teeple to Michigan Governor William Milliken, 22 September 1982 [original in the possession of Chippewa Ottawa Tribal Fishing Management Authority, Sault Ste. Marie, Mich.]; [Nancy Kida], "Indians, Fishing and the Economy," 17 March 1984, Typewritten Report, Mackley Public Library, Muskegon, Michigan.

18. Ron Paquin and Robert Doherty, *Not First in Nobody's Heart: The Story of a Contemporary Chippewa* (Ames: Iowa State University Press, 1992), 166–207.

19. Doherty, *Disputed Waters*, 105–51; Weeks, *Mem-ka-weh*, 43–52. On conflict over treaty fishing rights, see Grand Traverse Area Sportsfishing Association, "The Treaty of 1836 and the Fishing Case" [n.l.] 17 February 1976, CRSS; Richard C. Widman, "Indian Fishing Could Spawn Bloodshed by White Vigilantes," *The Plain Dealer*, 9 October 1977; Mark E. Dixon, "Indian Netters Reap Large Trout Catch at Charlevoix," *Petoskey News Review*, 10 August 1977; "Why Violence on Beaches," *North Woods Call*, 24 August 1977; "No Room Here for Racist Tactics," *Traverse City Record Eagle*, 21 April 1979; Rick Haglund, "New Threats Anger U.P. Indians," *Traverse City Record Eagle*, 21 April 1979; Doreen Fitzgerald, "SGN—Both Good and Bad," *Antrim County News*, 26 April 1979; Doreen Fitzgerald, "Anti Gill Net Group Formed," *Antrim County News*, 26 April 1979; "District Judge Comments on Editorial Opposing Violence," *Petoskey News Review*, 27 April 1979; Doreen Fitzgerald, "SGN—Prosecutors Meet with DNR," *Antrim County News*, 3 May 1979; Jeff Blake, "Dismayed Gill Net Foes Warn Will See Depletion of Fish," *Petoskey News Review*, 8 May 1979; "Our Gill Net Position," *Traverse City Record Eagle*, 9 May 1979; "MUCC Terms Fox Decision 'Outrageous,' 'Prejudiced,'" *Traverse City Record Eagle*, 9 May 1979; Marcellas S. Kreiter, "Fox Warns Against Fishing Violence," *Petoskey News Review*, 9 May 1979; Jim Doherty, "Judge Fox's Decision is Law of the Land," *Petoskey News Review*, 9 May 1979; Eric Sharp, "Indians Win Court Fight on Fishing Rights," *Detroit Free Press*, 9 May 1979; "Student Gives Views on Gill Net Fishing," *Petoskey News Review*, 11 May 1979; "Statement of Thomas L. Washington on Behalf of the MUCC," [Presented before the House subcommittee on Fisheries and Wildlife Conservation, 6 June 1980, Traverse City, Michigan] Michigan Department of Natural Resources File, Michigan State Archives, Box 8, Lansing, Mich.; John Broder, "Vigilantes Greet Gill Net Fishers," *Detroit News*, 24 June 1982; Dennis Knickerbocker, "Gillnetters Bitter Over Vandalism," *Lansing State Journal*, 24 October 1989; "Judge OKs Indian Commercial Fishing in Grand Traverse Bay," *Weekly News: Fishery News of the Great Lakes Basin*, 8 September 1997; "Are Contaminated Fish Being Sold," *The Sport Fisherman's Friend*, November 1997.

   On opposition from sport-fishing organizations, see Kuchenberg, *Reflections in a Tarnished Mirror*, 123–25; Cleland, *Rites of Conquest*, 279–87; Tom Opre, "Gill Neting: Will the Indians Catch Cost Lake Michigan Too Much?" *Detroit Free Press*, 5 August 1979; Tom Opre, "Abusing Indians Over a Fish Makes No Sense," *Detroit Free Press*, 23 March 1980; "Rally Against Gill Net Fishing is Slated," *Muskegon Chronicle*, 25 April 1982; Barry L. Levine, "Indian Fishing Rights," *The Muskegon Chronicle*, 15 September 1982; "Threat to Fishing," *Michigan Out of Doors*, April 1984, p. 1; [Nancy Kida], "The Gill Net and State Policy," 17 March 1984, Typewritten Report, Mackley Public Library, Muskegon, Michigan; "State Asks U.S. Court to Halt Indian Fishing," *Lansing State Journal*, 29 April 1988; "Gill-Netting Limit Sought in Grand Traverse," *Detroit News*, 29 April 1988; "Press Release from the Grand Traverse Area Sport Fishing Association on Native American Fishing Regulations," 24 April 1995; Diane Conners, "New Fishing Dispute Flares Over Fishing Rights," *Traverse City Record Eagle*, 8 August 1996; Ric Zehner, "Instead of Fishing Rights, It's Discrimination by Feds," *Traverse City Record Eagle*, 7 September 1997; John Block, "Truce on Indian Gill Fishing in Jeopardy," *Kalamazoo Gazette*, 4 October 1997; "Salmon are Not a Native of the Great Lakes," *The Sport Fishermen's Friend*, November 1997; Diane Conners, "State Wants Ruling on Salmon Fishing," *Traverse City Record Eagle*, 2 February 1998; Steve Kellman and Diane Conners, "Grand Traverse Band Loses Bid to Expand Fishing," *Traverse Bay Record Eagle*, 5 February 1998; Diane Conners, "Attorney: Tribe May Boycott Fish Talks," *Traverse City Record Eagle*, 6 February 1998; Larry Sawicki, "As I

See It . . . ," *The Sport Fisherman's Friend*, November 1997; "Discontent is Being Shared Among Traverse Bay Sports Fishermen," *The Sport Fishermen's Friend*, November 1997; "A Boating Hazard is Being Created in Grand Traverse Bay and Lake Michigan," *The Sport Fisherman's Friend*, November 1997; Lawrence J. Thornhill, "An Invasion of Gill Nets Could be Awaiting the Great Lakes," *The Sport Fisherman's Friend*, November 1997; Larry Sawicki, "Some Blame Should Fall on Our Governor's Office," *The Sport Fisherman's Friend*, November 1997; Richard M. Zehner, "Congress Must Act on Gill Netting Issues," *The Sport Fisherman's Friend*, November 1997.

On disputes over tribal gill nets and fishing gear, see Michigan Indian Legal Services, "Facts About Treaty Fishing" (Traverse City, Mich.: Michigan Indian Legal Services, [n.d.]; Chippewa-Ottawa Treaty Fishery Management Authority (COTFMA), *Chippewa-Ottawa Treaty Fishery* (Sault Ste. Marie, Mich.: COTFMA, [n.d.]); Dave Borgeson, "Negotiator Says Tribal Net Deal Does Not Include Floating Nets," [n.l.][n.d.], CRSS; Fred Vanden Brand, "Indian Fishermen Net Another Big Catch Here," *Grand Haven Tribune*, 7 July 1971; "Hearing Scheduled on Indian Fish Rules," *Traverse City Record Eagle*, 29 December 1979; N.B. Sawyer, "Watt Outlines Indian Gill Net Zoning Proposal," *Grand Rapids Press*, 8 May 1982; John Broder, "Vigilantes Greet Gill Net Fishers," *Detroit News*, 24 June 1982; John Block, "More Gill-Net Fishing Controversy Surfaces," *Kalamazoo Gazette*, 8 February 1997; Diane Conners, "Court Won't Heat Gill-Net Dispute Until December," *Traverse City Record Eagle*, 28 August 1997; John Block, "Truce on Indian Gill Fishing in Jeopardy," *Kalamazoo Gazette*, 4 October 1997; Diane Conners, "Fishing for Some Answers," *Traverse City Record Eagle*, 1 February 1998; Gordon Charles, "Indian Fisherman Setting Gill Nets in West Grand Traverse Bay," *Detroit Free Press*, 28 June 1971; Tom Dammann, "Indians Gill Net Little Traverse Bay Lake Trout," *Grand Rapids Press*, 5 June 1977; "Next Round in Fishing Battle Before Judge Fox," *Petoskey News Review*, 14 July 1977; "Arrest 3 Indians for Netting in Antrim," *Petoskey News Review*, 5 April 1979; Gordon Charles, "Indians Fish 800 Miles of Nets," *Traverse City Record Eagle*, 7 April 1979; Doreen Fitzgerald, "Indian Gill Netting Resumes," *Traverse City Record Eagle*, 12 April 1979; Kendall P. Stanley, "UP Indians to Net North of Good Hart—Until Mid May," *Petoskey News Review*, 19 April 1979; Rick Haglund, "New Threats Anger U.P. Indians," *Traverse City Record Eagle*, 21 April 1979; Kendall P. Stanley, "Prosecutors Warn Gill Netters, Vigilantes," *Petoskey News Review*, 30 April 1979; Rick Haglund, "2 Indians Guilty in Landmark Case," *Traverse City Record Eagle*, 3 May 1979; "Carte Blanche for Indians?" *Traverse City Record Eagle*, 9 May 1979; "To Set Nets in Area May 15," *Petoskey News Review*, 11 May 1979; Rick Haglund, "Indians Make Big White Fish Catches," *Traverse City Record Eagle*, 19 July 1979; "Indian Gill Netting Action on Grand Traverse Bay," *North Woods Call*, 25 July 1979; "Depletion of Traverse Bay Fishery Predicted by Fall," *North Woods Call*, 25 July 1979; Mike Ready, "Gill Netting to Double in Grand Traverse Bay," *Traverse City Record Eagle*, 26 July 1979; Tom Opre, "Gill Net Fishing Worries State," *Detroit Free Press*, 29 July 1979; Tom Opre, "Gill Neting: Will the Indians Catch Cost Lake Michigan Too Much?" *Detroit Free Press*, 5 August 1979; "Responds to Arguments on Indian Gill Netting," *North Woods Call*, 20 August 1979; Rick Haglund, "Indians Urged to Change Nets," *Traverse City Record Eagle*, ?? September 1979; Tom Opre, "No Hope for Stocks if Netting Continues," *Detroit Free Press*, 2 September 1979; Tom Opre, "Kelley Asks New Ban After Gill Net Tangle Deepens," *Detroit Free Press*, 30 September 1979; "Grand Traverse Indians Ask Fox Ban DNR Gill Net Curbs," *Petoskey News Review*, 14 November 1979; Rick Haglund, "Court Decides Gill Net Ban is Limited to 1 Indian Band," *Traverse City Record Eagle*, 5 December 1979; Nancy Zeno, "Milliken Speaks Out With Gill Netting Opponents," *Antrim County News*, 16 March 1980.

20. "Statement of Howard Tanner to U.S. Department of Interior Concerning Amended Rules for Off-Reservation Treaty Fishing on the Great Lakes," 13 May 1980, Lansing, Michigan, Michigan Department of Natural Resources File, Michigan State Archives, Box 8, Lansing, Mich.; [Nancy Kida], "Indians, Fishing and the Economy," 17 March 1984, Typewritten Report, Mackley Public Library, Muskegon, Michigan; Mike Petoskey Interview Transcript, 17 June 1992, clip reel #30, Public Museum of Grand Rapids, Grand Rapids, Michigan; George Anthony Interview Transcript, 4 August 1992, clip reel #28,

Public Museum of Grand Rapids, Grand Rapids, Michigan; Jennifer Dale [Letter to the Editor], "Tribes Working to Conserve Great Lakes Fishery," *Benzie County Record Patriot*, 24 December 1997; Michigan Legislative Service Bureau, *Michigan Indian Rights Controversy*, by Paul G. Connors, Legislative Research Division Report vol. 19, no. 3 (Lansing: Michigan Legislative Service Bureau, July 1999).

21. Dann, *The Life of the Lakes*, 34–35; COTFMA, *Michigan's 1836 Treaty Fishery Guide*, 17–25.

22. On contemporary Native American land and natural resource issues, see Winona LaDuke, *All Our Relations: Native Struggles for Land and Life* (Cambridge, Mass.: South End Press, 1999); Thomas Vennum, Jr., "Survival This Way: Indian Policy and Living Tradition," in *Buried Roots and Indestructible Seeds: The Survival of American Indian Life in Story, History, and Spirit*, ed. Mark A. Lindquist and Martin Zanger (Madison: University of Wisconsin Press, 1993), 109–25.

On fishing grounds and traditional ecological knowledge (TEK), see George Anthony Interview Transcript, 4 August 1992, clip reel #28, Public Museum of Grand Rapids, Grand Rapids, Michigan. On tribal management of fisheries resources, see Doherty, *Disputed Waters*, 141–51; James W. Oberly, "Tribal Sovereignty and Natural Resources: The Lac Courte Oreilles Experience," in *Buried Roots and Indestructible Seeds*, 127–53; U.S. Department of Interior, State of Michigan, COTFMA, *Status of the Fishery Resource: A Report by the Tripartits Technical Working Group on the Assessment of Major Fish Stocks in Treaty Ceded Waters of the Upper Great Lakes*, 1982–2000 (n.l.: U.S. Department of Interior, State of Michigan, COTFMA, 1982–2000); Chippewa-Ottawa Treaty Fishery Management Authority, Inter-Tribal Fisheries and Assessment Program *Bi-Annual Report: July through December 1998* (Sault Ste. Marie, Mich.: COTFMA, 1998); Chippewa-Ottawa Treaty Fishery Management Authority, "Chippewa-Ottawa Treaty Fishery" (Sault Ste. Marie, Mich.: COTFMA, n.d.); Diane Conners, "Federal Judge Will Rule on Tribal Fishing," *Traverse City Record Eagle*, [n.d]; Bill McCulloch, "Chippewas to Renew Spring Fishing Ban," *Traverse City Record Eagle*, 18 April 1979; Rick Haglund, "Chippewas Support Fishing Ban Extension," *Traverse City Record Eagle*, 9 May 1979; Rick Haglund, "Limit Catches, Biologist for Indians Urges," *Traverse City Record Eagle*, 30 July 1979; [Nancy Kida], "Fishing Controversy Myths," 23 March 1988, Typewritten Report, Mackley Public Library Vertical File, Muskegon, Michigan; Mike Petoskey Interview Transcript, 17 June 1992, clip reel #13A, Public Museum of Grand Rapids, Grand Rapids, Michigan; Russell W. Brown, Mark Ebner, and Tom Gorenflo, *Great Lakes Commercial Fisheries: Historical Overview and Prognosis for the Future* (Woods Hole, Mass.: National Oceanic and Atmospheric Administration, 1995); Diane Conners, "Court Won't Hear Gill-Net Dispute Until December," *Traverse City Record Eagle*, 28 August 1997; "Nets Pulled for Weekend," *Traverse City Record Eagle*, 31 August 1997; Gordon Charles, "Astroturf Helps to Develop Lake Trout," *Traverse City Record Eagle*, 23 November 1997; Jennifer Dale [Letter to the Editor], "Tribes Working to Conserve Great Lakes Fishery," *Benzie County Record Patriot*, 24 December 1997; "Regulations Enforced," *Traverse City Record Eagle*, 8 January 1998; Diane Conners, "Fishing for Some Answers," *Traverse City Record Eagle*, 1 February 1998; Diane Conners, "State Wants Ruling on Salmon Fishing," *Traverse City Record Eagle*, 2 February 1998; Steve Kellman and Diane Conners, "Grand Traverse Band Loses Bid to Expand Fishing," *Traverse Bay Record Eagle*, 5 February 1998; Kevin Clark, "Close Monitoring by the DNR Is Called For," *Traverse City Record Eagle*, 7 March 1998; Bill O'Brien, "Marina Dedication Recalls Tribal Fisherman's Battles," *Traverse City Record Eagle*, 29 June 1998; Bill O'Brien, "Walleye Stocking Dispute Ignites," *Traverse City Record Eagle*, 3 July 1998; Connie Stafford, "Gill Nets in the Water for Assessment," *Alpena News*, 24 October 1998; Don Ingle, "Banquet Centered on Tribal Fishing," *Traverse City Record Eagle*, 18 April 1999; Chippewa-Ottawa Treaty Fishery Management Authority, "Chippewa-Ottawa Treaty Fishery Management Authority" (Sault Ste. Marie, Mich.: COTFMA, n.d.); Chippewa-Ottawa Treaty Fishery Management Authority, *Michigan's 1836 Treaty Fishery Guide* (Sault Ste. Marie, Mich.: COTFMA, n.d.); Chippewa-Ottawa Treaty Fishery Management Authority, "Rules and Regulations Governing Tribal Commercial and Subsistence Fishing Activities in the 1836 Treaty Ceded Waters of Lake Superior, Huron, and Michigan" (Sault Ste. Marie, Mich.: COTFMA, 1 September 1995);

William H. Eager, *Lake Trout Rehabilitation Management Plan for the Michigan Waters of Lake Superior, Huron, and Michigan: 1985–2000* (April 1984), Michigan Department of Natural Resources File, Michigan State Archives, Box 8, Lansing, Mich.; Diane Conners, "New Fishing Dispute Flares Over Fishing Rights," *Traverse City Record Eagle*, 8 August 1996; John Block, "More Gill-Net Fishing Controversy Surfaces," *Kalamazoo Gazette*, 8 February 1997; "Tribal Fisherman's View of the Conclusion of the 1985 Consent Decree," *Win Awen Nisitong* [newspaper of the Sault Ste. Marie Tribe of Chippewa Indians], 21 April 1997; Eric Sharp, "DNR, Indians Should Compromise to Avoid Fishing Battle," *Traverse City Record Eagle*, 4 September 1997; Steve Kellman, "Tribe Ends Talks for New Fishing Agreement," *Traverse City Record Eagle*, 10 September 1997; John Block, "Truce on Indian Gill Fishing in Jeopardy," *Kalamazoo Gazette*, 4 October 1997; Jennifer Dale, [Letter to the Editor] "Tribes Working to Conserve Great Lakes Fishery," *Benzie County Record Patriot*, 24 December 1997; "Regulations Enforced," *Traverse City Record Eagle*, 8 January 1998; Diane Conners, "Fishing for Some Answers," *Traverse City Record Eagle*, 1 February 1998; Steve Kellman and Diane Conners, "Grand Traverse Band Loses Bid to Expand Fishing," *Traverse Bay Record Eagle*, 5 February 1998; Diane Conners, "Attorney: Tribe May Boycott Fish Talks," *Traverse City Record Eagle*, 6 February 1998; "Tribe Makes a Mistake by Refusing to Negotiate," *Traverse City Record Eagle*, 8 February 1998; Bob Gwizdz, "A Negotiated Settlement on Indian Fishing?" *Kalamazoo Gazette*, 21 February 1998; Diane Conners, "Cool Outlines Indian Fishing Issues," *Traverse City Record Eagle*, 28 April 1998; Bill O'Brien, "Plan for Fishing Treaty Unveiled," *Traverse City Record Eagle*, 27 June 1998; Bill O'Brien, "State, Tribes Ordered Back to the Bargaining Table," *Traverse City Record Eagle*, 9 September 1998; Connie Stafford, "Gill Nets in the Water for Assessment," *Alpena News*, 24 October 1998; Bill O'Brien, "Mutual Respect Urged in Fishing Talks," *Traverse City Record Eagle*, 24 March 1999; "Inland Hunting, Fishing likely Part of Pact—U.S. Attorney," *Lelanau Enterprise*, 15 April 1999; Cari Noga, "Rumblings in Air Over Tribal Fishing Rights," *Traverse City Record Eagle*, 22 June 1999; John Flesher, "Tribal Fishing Rights on Great Lakes Muddled," *Kalamazoo Gazette*, 3 September 1999; John Block, "Indian Fishing Dispute Heads Back to Court," *Kalamazoo Gazette*, 2 October 1999; Lynette A. Kalsnes, "Federal Judge in Kalamazoo Delays Action on Indian Fishing Rights Case," *Kalamazoo Gazette*, 16 October 1999; Bob Gwizdz, "Negotiations with Tribes at Critical Juncture," *Kalamazoo Gazette*, 26 February 2000; John Block, "Indian Fishing Dispute Near End," *Kalamazoo Gazette*, 29 April 2000; John Block, "Indian Fishing Case Settled—Almost," *Kalamazoo Gazette*, 3 August 2000; "View from Elsewhere (*The Muskegon Chronicle*): Fishing Settlement is Probably Best for All," *Kalamazoo Gazette*, 5 September 2000.

23. Diane Conners, "New Fishing Dispute Flares Over Fishing Rights," *Traverse City Record Eagle*, 8 August 1996; John Block, "More Gill-Net Fishing Controversy Surfaces," *Kalamazoo Gazette*, 8 February 1997; "Leelanau: Judge Makes Ruling," *Traverse City Record Eagle*, 7 September 1997; Steve Kellman, "Tribe Ends Talks for New Fishing Agreement," *Traverse City Record Eagle*, 10 September 1997; John Block, "Truce on Indian Gill Fishing in Jeopardy," *Kalamazoo Gazette*, 4 October 1997; Steve Kellman and Diane Conners, "Grand Traverse Band Loses Bid to Expand Fishing," *Traverse Bay Record Eagle*, 5 February 1998; Diane Conners, "Attorney: Tribe May Boycott Fish Talks," *Traverse City Record Eagle*, 6 February 1998; "Tribe Makes a Mistake by Refusing to Negotiate," *Traverse City Record Eagle*, 8 February 1998; Bob Gwizdz, "A Negotiated Settlement on Indian Fishing?" *Kalamazoo Gazette*, 21 February 1998; Bill O'Brien, "Plan for Fishing Treaty Unveiled," *Traverse City Record Eagle*, 27 June 1998; Bill O'Brien, "State, Tribes Ordered Back to the Bargaining Table," *Traverse City Record Eagle*, 9 September 1998; Bill O'Brien, "Mutual Respect Urged in Fishing Talks," *Traverse City Record Eagle*, 24 March 1999; Cari Noga, "Rumblings in Air Over Tribal Fishing Rights," *Traverse City Record Eagle*, 22 June 1999; Lynette A. Kalsnes, "Federal Judge in Kalamazoo Delays Action on Indian Fishing Rights Case," *Kalamazoo Gazette*, 16 October 1999; John Block, "Indian Fishing Case Settled—Almost," *Kalamazoo Gazette*, 3 August 2000.

24. On economic and cultural revitalization of fishing, see Bill O'Brien, "Marina Dedication Recalls Tribal

Fisherman's Battles," *Traverse City Record Eagle*, 29 June 1998; Dick Hatch, "Anishinabek: The People of This Place" [Public Museum of Grand Rapids], *Museum* (spring 1995): 10–14; Charles E. Cleland and Richard C. Bishop, *An Assessment of the Economic Conditions of the Bay Mills Indian Community, Sault St. Marie Indian Community, and Grand Traverse Band of Ottawa and Chippewa Indians, and a Cost-Return Analysis of Treaty Commercial Fishermen—1981* (Michigan State University, April 1984).

25. "April 4th Meeting of the Executive Council of the 1836 Treaty," *Win Awen Nisitong*, 21 April 1997.

26. Paquin and Doherty, *Not First in Nobody's Heart*, 202–6.

27. Doherty, *Disputed Waters*, 71, 149–50; Anne Stanton, "*Lady Hilma*," *Traverse City Record Eagle*, 17 July 1990.

28. Mike Ready, "Gill Netting to Double in Grand Traverse Bay," *Traverse City Record Eagle*, 26 July 1979.

29. Dennis Knickerbocker, "Tangled Issues: Tribes Improve Relations by Switching to Trap Nets," *Lansing State Journal*, 24 October 1989.

30. Cleland and Bishop, *An Assessment of the Economic Conditions of the Bay Mills Indian Community*.

31. Bill O'Brien, "Court Rules in Favor of Mooring Right," *Traverse City Record Eagle*, [n.d] 1995.

32. [Nancy Kida], "The Gill Net and State Policy," 17 March 1984, Typewritten Report, Mackley Public Library, Muskegon, Michigan.

33. Doherty, *Disputed Waters*, 71.

34. Richard C. Widman, "Indians Seek Economic Progress," *The Plain Dealer*, 11 October 1977; Diane Conners and Rich Wertz, "Petoskey Tribe Revives Gill Net Issue," *Traverse City Record Eagle*, 25 April 1995.

35. On tribal efforts to open other sections of the lake for fishing see, Jim Vander Maas, "Tribes File Motion to Gill Net South to Arcadia," *Great Lakes Steelheader*, February 1994.

36. Diane Conners, "New Fishing Dispute Flares Over Fishing Rights," *Traverse City Record Eagle*, 8 August 1996.

37. Dave Pitt and Dave Guzniczak, "Police Arrest 3 Gill Netters Who Lack Indian ID Fish Cards," *Petoskey News Review*, 12 October 1978; "Indian Netter Pleads Innocent," *Petoskey News Review*, 17 October 1978. On George "Skip" Duhamel, see "DNR Plan Would Close Boardman Fish Weir," *The Sport Fisherman's Friend*, November 1997; Bill O'Brien, "Marina Dedication Recalls Tribal Fisherman's Battles," *Traverse City Record Eagle*, 29 June 1998; "Cost, Benefit Don't Balance in Tribal Mooring Right Case," *Traverse City Record Eagle*, 18 July 1998; Bill O'Brien, "Fishing Case at End of Line," *Traverse City Record Eagle*, 8 December 1998; "Mooring Rights Lawsuit Wasted Time and Money," *Traverse City Record Eagle*, 14 December 1998.

38. "Fishing Nets Returned After Confiscation," *Traverse City Record* Eagle, 26 December 1974.

39. On Bay Mills Indian fishing rights, see Kuchenberg, 122–33; Cleland and Bishop, *An Assessment of the Economic Conditions of the Bay Mills Indian Community*; Marsha Robinson, "Indians, DNR Draw Battle Lines on Gill Nets," *Petoskey News Review*, 10 November 1975; Grand Traverse Area Sports Fishing Association, "The Treaty of 1836 and the Fishing Case" [n.l.] 17 February 1976; "Gill Netters May Draw Line at Good Heart," *Petoskey News Review*, 15 September 1978; Kendall P. Stanley, "Gill Netters Active in Area," *Petoskey News Review*, 30 October 1978; "Bay Mills Amends Fines, Revocation," *Petoskey News Review*, 1 December 1978; Kendall P. Stanley, "4 More Facing Fishing Charges," *Petoskey News Review*, 4 December 1978; Mike Ready, "Police Surprise 10 Indian Netters," *Traverse City Record Eagle*, 6 December 1978; Gordon Charles, "Indians Fish 800 Miles of Nets," *Traverse City Record Eagle*, 7 April 1979; Rick Haglund, "Indians May Fish When May 15 Ban Expires," *Traverse City Record Eagle*, 19 April 1979; Rick Haglund, "New Threats Anger U.P. Indians," *Traverse City Record Eagle*, 21 April 1979; "New Study May Ease Indian Fishing Dispute," *Traverse City Record Eagle*, 28 April 1979; Rick Haglund, "Indians Make Big White Fish Catches," *Traverse City Record Eagle*, 19 July 1979; "Indians Sentenced for Trespass," *North Woods Call*, 2 August 1979; Rick Haglund, "Court Decides Gill Net Ban Is Limited to 1 Indian Band," *Traverse City Record Eagle*, 5 December 1979; Jon Halberg, "Bay Mills Indians Refuse October Gill Netting Season," *Alpena News*, 1 October 1990; Jon Halberg, "Bay Mills Indians: 'In the Year 2000 We Get Our Waters Back,'" *Alpena News*, 12 October 1990.

On Albert LeBlanc, see Kuchenberg, 122–33; Cleland, *Rites of Conquest*, 279–87; Doherty, *Disputed*

Waters, 69, 86–104; Clifford Ross Gearhart, *Pity the Poor Fish, Then Man* (Au Train, Mich.: Avery Color Studios, 1987), 149, 199–200; "Indian Commercial Fisherman Issued Compassion Licenses in Michigan," *The Fisherman* 24, no. 2 (February 1972): 10; "Norwood Report an 'Indian Fish Story,'" *Petoskey News Review*, 24 August 1978; Mike Ready, "Pact May End Fishing Dispute," *Traverse City Record Eagle*, 13 September 1978; Mike Ready, "Indians, Too, Clash on????" *Traverse City Record Eagle*, 14 September 1978; "LeBlanc, Mrs. Dominic Comment on Decision," *Petoskey News Review*, 8 May 1979; Rick Haglund, "Some Chippewas to Resume Fishing," *Traverse City Record Eagle*, 10 May 1979; Marsha Robinson, "Tribal Leader Says Ruling Defines Rights and Privilege," *Petoskey News Review*, 14 May 1979; Marsha Robinson, "Bay Mills Shows Little Sign of Windfall Fishing Profits," *Petoskey News Review*, 15 May 1979; Rick Haglund, "Milliken Asks Halt to Fishing, New Rules for Indian Netters," *Traverse City Record Eagle*, 15 September 1979; Tom Opre, "Plan Suggests Millions to Buy Indian Fishing Rights," *Detroit Free Press*, 23 September 1979; Rick Haglund, "Fish Conservation Loses with Defeat of Art LeBlanc," *Traverse City Record Eagle*, 10 December 1979.

40. "Indian Expert Testifies," 1 March 1978, Garden Peninsula Historical Society Scrapbook [hereafter GPHS scrapbook]; "Indian Fishing Rights: More Testimony," 28 February 1978, GPHS scrapbook.

41. Robert E. Hardenburgh, "Will Be Remembered," *Traverse City Record Eagle*, 12 December 1998.

2

Commercial Fishing Claims

Modern Dilemmas of Harvesting the Inland Seas

THIS SECTION'S ORAL HISTORY features the testimony of men and women whose identity and economic livelihood is, or was, directly derived from Lake Michigan's commercial fisheries.[1] Taken together, these oral histories show the role that family, ethnicity, and community played in shaping the commercial fishery's claim to Lake Michigan's fisheries resources.[2] Members of Lake Michigan fishing families and communities historically developed, and gradually adapted, informal, traditional systems of fisheries management within an ever-changing set of working contexts, government regulation schemes, markets, and environmental conditions.[3] As part of an effort to manage the resource on their own, commercial fishermen moved to new or different fishing grounds, altered their target species, and changed gear.[4] The set of management practices or codes commercial fishermen imposed upon themselves was intended to maximize their earnings and, at the same time, preserve fishery stocks for future use. In historical terms, commercial fishermen connect their claim to fisheries resources to their ability to establish their own occupational standards and expectations; it is a worldview they see validated in their families' enduring tenure in the occupation of fishing. The price paid for "being your own boss" was high and included economic uncertainty, occupational danger, and a host of long-term, occupationally related health risks.

The Lake Michigan fishermen whose testimony follows were, in most instances, introduced to a set of attitudes and beliefs regulating fishing practices and fishing grounds at an early age. The locally based criteria that defined a "good" fisherman—one who earned the respect of the community—was typically learned at the dinner table, the docks, the fish sheds, and other public and private gathering places, long before one set forth on the lake to fish. Once a family or community member began fishing, he developed a reputation of his own; a label based on how hard and honorably he fished. Status and reputations were not, however, only personally earned but socially deliberated and forged in the collective memory of the lake's wider commercial fishing community. In short, one's standing among other fishermen and state and federal fisheries authorities was a function of extended family and community affiliations. Certain fishing families and communities in both Michigan and Wisconsin had reputations—both favorable and unfavorable—that were readily recognized by the broad-based fisheries network that encircled Lake Michigan.

Traditional ecological knowledge (TEK)—occupationally derived insight that is necessary for understanding fish behavior, the contours and composition of the lake bottom, weather, currents, and wind direction—was shared with youth and others in order to help gain their support for the informal fisheries management systems that existed among fishermen. This knowledge, historically derived from work experience, not only equipped and empowered commercial fishers to harvest Lake Michigan's waters, but also, in any number of fishing communities, defined the parameters of what constituted a "good" fisherman and responsible resource use.[5] With such hard-wrought knowledge as the basis of the Lake Michigan commercial fishers' management prerogative, it is hardly surprising that the tools of that experience figured prominently in the oral testimony.[6]

The testimony that follows indicates that commercial fishers understood that economic survival depended on carefully crafted adjustments to TEK—closely scrutinized modifications in fishing behavior that could help them address decreased fish stocks and increased fishing costs. While not abandoning longstanding fishing codes or ethics, they looked to new technologies that would reasonably conform to traditional use strategies and assist them in countering difficult economic circumstances; in sum, a set of factors that provided a tempered, traditionally measured crucible within which TEK could be reconfigured to meet evolving demands. Recognizing the need for both tradition and innovation within their occupation, family and community members instructed the uninitiated in fishing techniques

The reel yard at an unidentified Charlevoix, Michigan, fishery shows how employment in the fisheries existed on shore as well as out on the lake. Fishery workers dried gill nets on large wooden reels and returned them to net boxes that were brought on board the fish tugs. Courtesy of Michigan United Conservation Clubs.

and offered the use of new or different boats and fishing gear through gifts, inheritance, and favorable purchasing agreements. Some elder fishers, reluctant to totally sever their ties to the occupation, assisted their sons or sons-in-law by leasing them fish tugs and harvesting gear upon retirement. At a minimum, each generation of Lake Michigan's commercial fishers was expected to reciprocate the favors of their elders by acquiring the knowledge and mastery of those technical skills necessary to safely and efficiently operate fishing boats—particularly their navigation and fishing gear—in all types of weather.[7] In addition, many also acquired the skills necessary to design, build, repair, and overhaul boats. Some also mastered the rebuilding and repair of engines, powered net lifters, and other types of mechanical gear.

TEK and technical knowledge and skills combined to make it possible for fishermen to respond to changes in policy, market conditions, fishing stocks, or other factors that could endanger their fishing livelihood. Lake Michigan commercial fishers gave numerous details that portray the everyday work experience—tending nets, discovering rich fishing grounds, observing fluctuations in fish stocks, and allocating human and financial resources. These oral histories show that the learning process began early. Numerous testimonies recalled boyhood days on the docks

Beaver Island, Michigan, fishery workers drying gill nets on wood reels. The net drying reels, frame sheds and outbuildings, and docks constituted the typical Great Lakes fisheries landscape prior to the introduction of salmon in the mid-1960s. Courtesy of the Michigan Maritime Museum.

where one might be assigned the job of cleaning nets, filling mending needles, or working on a fish tug or trap-net boat on a fill-in basis. Even when they were not working, the informants remarked on the indelible experience of simply being in the midst of dockside flurry or being captivated by the overpowering presence of Lake Michigan's waters.

While Lake Michigan's commercial fishers instructed subsequent generations in the everyday tasks required for occupational survival, they underscored these lessons through references to informal, traditional systems of fisheries management. In their oral testimonies, these consistent references serve to historically contextualize the fisher and the fishing community; it is a narrative technique that culturally and politically upholds the intergenerational value of local ecological knowledge.[8] This oral history project's informants grew up hearing stories of how their parents, grandparents, and great-grandparents balanced Old World fishing experience with New World aspirations in order to maintain a living that was often shrouded in economic and biological uncertainty.[9] Their photographic collections show not only family members who fished, but also contain copious images of the boats, gear, and fishing buildings they used. Artifacts and mementos relating to past fishing operations and endeavors dot the walls and shelves of homes, fish sheds, taverns, and restaurants and link their owners to the lake or those who spent their days fishing upon its waters. They evoke memories of male and female family members and countless others in the community, who shared in the numerous tasks that had to be completed before a fishing crew ever left the harbor.

The stories contained in this volume—along with each informants' personal or family collection of photographs and memorabilia, their accumulations of obsolete or outlawed boats and gear, and the abandoned or adapted fisheries landscape—all play a didactic role in their lives and provide continuity with the past. Vividly alive in their memories, these stories help Lake Michigan's commercial fishers understand that many of their contemporary fishery problems are neither isolated nor new. During the late-nineteenth and early-twentieth centuries, as the Lake Michigan shoreline became more industrialized and a larger percentage of its fish was marketed by large commercial brokerages, Lake Michigan's commercial fishers faced the

This model of the fish tug *Susie Q* is representative of a variety of expressions that have been created by Lake Michigan's commercial fishing community to celebrate its occupational tradition and show its technological and ecological adaptation. This model shows a hauling/lifting ramp projecting from the boat's stern. This feature was installed on fish tugs to make them safer and more efficient when trawling for alewife, smelt, and chubs. Daniel "Pete" LeClair was instrumental in devising this feature and its inclusion on this model is an important commentary on the occupation's adaptive legacy. Courtesy of Daniel "Pete" LeClair and Paul LeClair.

Retail fish markets and wholesale fishing buying or processing operations helped commercial fishermen recoup their costs. Kenneth Vanderberg is shown with his son Kenneth and daughter Judy behind the counter of the family's fish market on Pine Street in Muskegon, Michigan, circa 1942. Courtesy of Allan Vanderberg.

specter of debt, unpredictable fish harvest, environmental degradation, and dangerous working conditions. A pervasive form of work organization—the framework of family, ethnicity, and community—mitigated these challenges somewhat and, with the passage of time, allowed these fishers to gain measures of financial success and the desire to stake more elaborate claims to the resource.[10] This collective activity historically led to corresponding family, ethnic, and community participation in the development and implementation of a code of fisheries governance wrought in shared experience. This combination of human, economic, and environmental conditions created the regionally distinct social and cultural features chronicled in this volume's oral history.

In contrast to the commercial fishermen's informal, traditional systems of fisheries management, state and federal government gradually began to introduce more institutionally formal fisheries regulation to Lake Michigan in the late-nineteenth century. The importance of family and community to the successful implementation of fisheries policy was suggested by the U.S. Fish Commission, which examined these factors in its earliest economic surveys of Lake Michigan's fisheries. By the late twentieth century, state government in both Michigan and Wisconsin closely regulated gear use and enacted fishing quotas and distinct management zones throughout Lake Michigan's waters. Once again, the traditional strategy of family and community cooperation helped fishermen respond to these changing economic, political, and environmental conditions.

Several informants expressed concern over whether there would be any Lake Michigan fishermen in the future. The eldest fishers—those who fished in the 1930s, 1940s, and 1950s—noted that during the 1960s and 1970s young men from fishing families frequently decided to pursue other types of work. Since Michigan and Wisconsin began severely limiting entry to the commercial fishery in the late 1960s/early 1970s, there have been virtually no newcomers to the commercial fishing business. These oral histories show that the anxiety of these recent events caused commercial fishers to examine the challenges posed by fish stock depletion, pollution, and new technology—such as electronic fish finders and automated navigational instruments—to their informal, traditional management system. By self-consciously examining their past through oral narrative, commercial fishermen see themselves as being better able to successfully revise and adapt their informal system of resource management to meet changing political, economic, social, and environmental conditions. In this sense, oral history's evaluative function within this occupational community abets its quest to remain fishing.[11]

Oral history shows that the family and ethnic ties upon which Lake Michigan commercial fishermen base their resource-use claims is a vernacular fisheries management strategy that fuses enduring communal sentiment with uncompromising economic necessity. As the testimony that follows shows, Lake Michigan commercial fishing is regarded as a way of life and a measure of financial success is required to maintain that tradition. In both the past and the present, fishermen characterize their work as a vocation or calling, not simply an economic investment that offers the abstract loss and gain of real estate speculation or the stock market. Specifically these fishers distinguish the time in their lives spent fishing from other times when they worked in other occupations or fields with fixed hours of work, performance standards, and levels of responsibility and compensation, even if it offered more lucrative monetary gain.

The fishermen whose testimony is presented below chose not to focus on the larger and more fundamental economic restructuring that took place in the Great Lakes region after World War II. They were not oblivious to the decline of manufacturing, the lack of public and private investment in the aging urban and rural infrastructure, and the pollution that contributed to the region's reputation as America's "Rustbelt." Viewed perhaps as factors largely beyond the control of individuals and their local communities, they chose to focus on market conditions and fishery stocks; in short, Lake Michigan was their paramount point of economic and political reference. Such issues were more familiar to them and, from their perspective, could be addressed through individual or small-scale collective action.

The informants understandably and logically focused on the problems of declining fish stocks, low market prices, and the high cost of purchasing and maintaining boats and gear and hiring crew when discussing how economic conditions affected them. A small handful drew analogies between their situation and the farming economy. They noted how financial and personal investment in crew, boats, gear, docks, storage sheds, fish processing, marketing, transportation, licensing fees, and insurance helped legitimize—from their economic and political perspective—their fisheries claim.[12]

Commercial fisheries management is a far more entrenched claim whose historical effect is only minimally gauged by the printed word of the policy-making process. Not surprisingly, when asked to provide oral history on their view of the relationship between fisheries management and their economic livelihood, most commercial fishers chose to do so through the objects and technologies of their occupation. Lake Michigan's waters and landscapes were, and continue to be, dotted with vestiges of the commercial fishing industry—buildings and objects that expressed and facilitated the fundamental economic use patterns. Oral history takes measure of these historic resources and shows how fisheries management played out on a daily basis in the lives of those who were, arguably, the most intimately connected to the resource.[13] These historical narratives show that Lake Michigan's commercial fishers consider harvesting technology to be the most tangible determinant of their financial success; for them, it is the mechanism that mediates a variety of place-based variables that historically affect occupational endurance and the cultivation of fish stocks.

With these criteria in mind, commercial fishing technology becomes a point of affirmation and, at times, a point of contention, regarding economic decisions over the use of Lake Michigan's fish. The oral histories show that for fishermen, technology is not just an extractive tool but also a broader representation in the justification of economic claims to the resource. Commercial fishermen debated their technological options among themselves, evidence that fishing technology was far more complexly expressive of resource-use values than the sole appearance of mechanical function. Because the skillful manipulation of commercial fishing technology was often a critical factor in occupational survival, it thematically arises in oral history to identify economic options and benchmarks.[14] Celebratory, nostalgic photographic displays, folk art, and the sheer desire to be surrounded by their old fishing boats complement these expressions and equipment no longer used. Many of the informants for this oral history project, most notably ninety-one-year-old Howard Weborg of Gills Rock, Wisconsin, insisted on providing economic commentary by showing interviewers the technology while they spoke. By focusing much of their oral histories on fishing technology, commercial fishers illuminate the economic context of the fish harvest and clarify the fishery's broader ecological and cultural relationship along the shoreline, and on the water, of Lake Michigan.[15]

It was the availability of capital, the desire to pursue certain target species, or the allowances imposed by governmental policy that determined whether Lake Michigan's nineteenth- and twentieth-century commercial fishers entered the pound-net, gill-net, trap-net or trawl fisheries.[16] The high overhead costs of maintaining a pound-net fishery limited participation during the nineteenth century. Pound nets required a significant outlay of capital and fishing families were understandably wary of acquiring such gear on credit from large fish brokerage firms such as the Booth Company of Chicago.[17] However, as more modestly capitalized fishers gained financial resources, however, they established small- to medium-sized pound-net fisheries through the mid-twentieth century.[18] These initiatives became longstanding family operations at particular pound-net sites; in other situations, partnerships were formed between families to operate pound nets. Today, Dennis

Hickey operates the only surviving pound-net fishery on Lake Michigan in waters immediately adjacent to Wisconsin's Door Peninsula.

In the 1880s, the gill-net fishery was characterized as not requiring "the possession of any considerable amount of capital," a factor resulting in a workforce with "all classes of fishermen employed."[19] Open to a wide array of independent fishermen, the gill-net fishery's participants relied on the mobility of their equipment to realize a profit. In contrast to the more stationary pound-net fishery, gillnetters roved the Great Lakes in Mackinaw boats, Huron boats, Norwegian boats, steam tugs and, eventually, diesel-powered tugs. Able to readily move to more productive fishing grounds or shift to different target species, gill-net fishermen developed a reputation as "perhaps the most venturesome men, and at the same time the most skillful seamen, of the lakes."[20] Originally, the Mackinaw boat was the mainstay of gillnetters who could not afford the initial overhead costs of the pound-net fishery and needed more versatile fishing technology. The vessel fostered the initial environmental engagement that became the inheritance (traditional ecological knowledge) of subsequent generations of Lake Michigan commercial fishers. Although its use is now three to four generations removed from the collective experience of Lake Michigan's contemporary commercial fishermen, the Mackinaw boat is more alive in this group's collective memory than one might expect.[21]

Once steam-powered towing tugs were introduced into the Great Lakes during the mid-nineteenth century, it was only a short time before they became the desired vessel of the region's gill-net fishery. Gradually, the fish tug's deck space became more enclosed as it was tailored to the region's gill-net fishery and earned the name it bears today. Quite simply, the unique design and appearance of this boat type was a function of the Great Lakes gill-net fishery's longtime and emerging demands: (1) protection from the difficult weather conditions of the Great Lakes; (2) the ability to set and tend large numbers of gill nets; and (3) greater versatility in the selection and range of fishing grounds. Initially powered by steam engines and later by internal combustion engines, these boats allowed fishers to cruise from their respective "fishtowns" or ports and work ten- to fifty-mile ranges in what were considered their customary or "home waters." The fish tug's propulsion system, its mechanical net lifters, and its enclosed space allowed it to cruise this range, and at the same time, enabled the crew to utilize permanent processing and maintenance structures on

The *Herbert*, a steam-powered, steel-hulled tug, was prominently featured on the letterhead of the Mollhagen & Company Fish Catchers of St. Joseph, Michigan. Great Lakes fish tugs, which represented a significant capital outlay for most fishermen, would later be modified in design and feature a totally closed deck. Courtesy of Kathryn Chappel.

The *H. J. Dornbos* was used by the Dornbos family to fish the waters of Lake Michigan off Grand Haven, Michigan. Compared to the earlier Herbert, owned by the Mollhagens of St. Joseph, Michigan, the *H. J. Dornbos* is almost completely enclosed. Courtesy of Robert and Fern Ver Duin.

The *Susie Q* (bottom) was owned by Joseph and later Pete LeClair of Two Rivers, Wisconsin. It represents later functional and stylistic changes in fish-tug design with openings for the pilot-house and for the setting and retrieval of gill nets. These design features, most fully embodied in the modern steel fish tug, were intended to mitigate the difficult economic, harvesting, and weather variables faced by Great Lakes commercial fishers. The *Susie Q* was seized by the Wisconsin Department of Conservation in December 1947 after an incident involving warden Don Euers. The tug was later returned to the LeClairs. The LeClair's second *Susie Q* (top) was outfitted for trawling, including a stern ramp that facilitates the lifting of the net. Over the past fifty years, the LeClairs have been among the most adaptive commercial fishers on Lake Michigan. Photograph (bottom) courtesy of Robert and Fern Ver Duin and (top) Daniel "Pete" LeClair.

shore. Furthermore, the fish tug's dependable, slow-turning steam- and diesel-powered engines allowed commercial fishers to more readily relocate to other Great Lakes locations when seasonal conditions or stock fluctuations warranted.[22]

During the late 1940s and 1950s, Lake Michigan commercial fishermen compensated for the problems created by overfishing and non-native species by holding to the pre-World-War-II pattern of building larger, steel-hulled fishing tugs. These vessels allowed them to more aggressively pursue chubs, perch, and Lake Michigan's other increasingly limited commercial fishing stocks.[23] As the ranks of Lake Michigan's commercial fishers thinned even more in the 1960s, new economic options were pursued. The trap net (a submerged version of the pound net), which was condemned in the 1930s and 1940s for its excessive harvesting capacity, was now used by commercial fishers to pursue rejuvenated whitefish stocks. Since it caught fish alive, fisheries authorities saw it as a more selective entrapment device that allowed the return of endangered lake trout and tremendously popular sport species such as the introduced salmon.[24]

With state encouragement, Wisconsin commercial fishers adapted their gill-net tugs to stern trawling in order to massively harvest overabundant stocks of alewife, smelt, and chubs from Lake Michigan for the pet food market. The depletion of fish stocks caused Lake Michigan states to revise their commercial fishing policies. Surmising that sport fishing would provide greater economic gain from limited fisheries resources, states drastically reduced or eliminated the use of gill nets in various sections of the lake.[25] Wisconsin adopted quota systems that made it unfeasible for smaller-scale commercial fishers to endure. When the federal courts upheld Native American treaty fishing rights in Lake Michigan in 1979, the State of Michigan began a process of further restricting the options of state-licensed fishers in favor of the sport-fishing industry. Today, most of the remaining members of Lake Michigan's commercial fishing community make their living by marketing, processing, and smoking fish. A small handful of former Lake Michigan commercial fishermen such as Bob "Coho" Maynard of Pentwater, Michigan, and Lyle Teskie of Ellison Bay, Wisconsin, became charter boat captains or worked in other services that supported the sport-fishing industry.

Realizing that many people are interested in the nostalgia that surrounds their work, a number of commercial fishers integrate elements of their occupation into heritage and cultural tourism. William Carlson—a commercial fisherman who is acutely aware of the romantic hold his occupation exerts on the public at large—owns the majority of surviving fish sheds that constitute Leland, Michigan's "Fishtown." Tourists flock to this site and, while Carlson's fishing boats still ply Lake Michigan, he is selling the history of the lake's commercial fishing industry as much as he is selling fish. Although it sits demurely on the outskirts of Ludington, Michigan, the historically charged atmosphere of Bortell's Fisheries and its take-away meals make it a sought-after tourist location. In Wisconsin's Door County, fisherman Neil Teskie attracts the attention of both local residents and tourists to his food market by playing on the fish tug's status as one of the region's most recognizable cultural icons; in a most post-industrial gesture, he built his market around the family's retired fish tug, *Gem*. In short, tourists who visit Lake Michigan's port communities in Michigan and Wisconsin want to see what remains of the commercial fishing landscape and some commercial fishermen are more than happy to parlay their cultural patrimony into a vicarious occupational foray or consumer experience for the willing purchaser.[26]

Based on both their personal and collective life histories, commercial fishers acknowledge that their ability to adapt to changes in fisheries stocks, market conditions, and other factors depends, in part, on their ability to influence state and federal law and policy makers. Aware that their livelihood depends on the health and vitality of Lake Michigan's fisheries resources, commercial fishers became politically active during the late-nineteenth and early-twentieth centuries. They sought to shape policy by channeling their long-standing interest in fisheries management and conservation into the century's progressive environmental debates. Although their observations were frequently ignored, they developed their own environmental ethic based on TEK derived from personal observances and family and community networks.

When it was ecologically appropriate or legally necessary, fishermen changed target species, sought new or different fishing grounds, and devised other ways of preserving fishing stocks. Far from being a consensus-based occupation, these oral histories show the amount of capital one possessed or the type of gear one employed often pitted fishers against each other. Such internal disagreement naturally extended to their viewpoints over the principles and practices of fisheries regulation

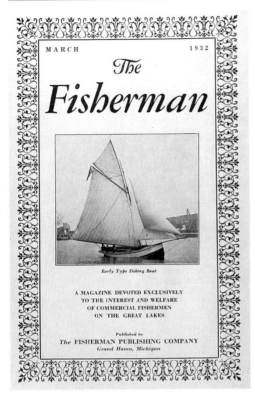

MARCH 1932

The

Fisherman

Early Type Fishing Boat

A MAGAZINE DEVOTED EXCLUSIVELY
TO THE INTEREST AND WELFARE
OF COMMERCIAL FISHERMEN
ON THE GREAT LAKES

Published by
The FISHERMAN PUBLISHING COMPANY
Grand Haven, Michigan

The Fisherman circulated throughout the Great Lakes and beyond as the voice of the region's commercial fishing industry. The first issue was published in 1931 by Grand Haven's Claude Ver Duin, a member of a commercial fishing family. Courtesy of Robert and Fern Ver Duin.

by state government. For example, in 1915 Lake Michigan fisherman David LeClair of Two Rivers, Wisconsin, sought stronger enforcement of existing laws on closed seasons and a prohibition on permits for commercial fishing during spawning season—a viewpoint that many current-day observers might not necessarily associate with a member of the commercial fishing community.[27] Twelve years later, the eleven commercial fishermen serving on the advisory committee to the Wisconsin Department of Conservation remained divided on the issue of taking spawn.[28]

During the final years of the nineteenth century and throughout the first half of the twentieth century, Lake Michigan's commercial fishermen attempted to influence fisheries policy by directly appealing to their respective state legislatures. These political efforts were significant since Great Lakes states controlled vast territorial waters—much more than the states on the east and west coasts. To this end, commercial fishermen sought to elect officials to represent their interests and created

A meeting of the West Lake Michigan Commercial Fishermen's Association in Two Rivers, Wisconsin, c. 1930. Lake Michigan fishermen formed numerous organizations and met regularly to promote their political and economic interests in state legislatures and beyond. Courtesy of the Rogers Street Fishing Museum.

lobbying organizations to work with state legislatures and state conservation officials. A few Lake Michigan commercial fishermen suspended or curtailed their fishing activity and sought election to public office.[29] Frank LeClair of Two Rivers was a member of the Wisconsin State Assembly from 1946–56.[30] Prior to that time, he was active in the Wisconsin Commercial Fishermen's Association and the Lake Michigan Protective Association. Everett "Butch" LaFond served as secretary-treasurer of the Wisconsin Commercial Fishermen's Association in the late 1930s before he was elected to the Wisconsin State Senate where he served from 1948–56. Both LeClair and LaFond helped organize the Wisconsin Commercial Fishermen's Association and helped secure the appointment of commercial fishermen to advisory committees created by the Wisconsin Department of Conservation.[31] The Lake Michigan Commercial Fishermen's Association, which represented the political and economic interests of fishermen on both sides of the lake in the early part of the

Wisconsin commercial fisherman Frank LeClair (right) served as a Wisconsin State Assembly-man and Everett "Butch" LaFond (left) served in the Wisconsin State Senate during the 1950s. LeClair and LaFond attest to the political activism of the commercial fishing industry and were closely allied with the numerous organizations created by Lake Michigan commercial fisher-men. Courtesy of Rogers Street Fishing Museum.

century, was responsive to the needs of fishing families and their communities. William Ver Duin, a Grand Haven fisherman of Dutch ancestry, served as secretary and treasurer in 1908. A generation later, his son Claude would play a leadership role in the Michigan Fish Producers Association, founded in July 1939.[32]

After producing record harvests of lake trout during World War II, Lake Michigan's commercial fishers were panic-stricken by the virtual elimination of these stocks due to sea lamprey predation. As Lake Michigan's principal fish-using group, commercial fishers also watched as their other notable target species, the whitefish, was dangerously reduced in number by this parasite, along with walleye, burbot, and steelhead stocks. Lake Michigan commercial fishers were arguably in the midst of the worst recorded crisis to afflict the human use of their particular fisheries resources. With rates of occupational attrition running high, Lake Michigan commercial fishers turned to the federal government for aid, and tempered their longstanding opposition

The *Butch LaFond* docked at the Jensen Fishery on the Black River in South Haven, Michigan. Named in honor of Wisconsin commercial fisherman and State Senator Everett "Butch" LaFond, the fish tug was operated by South Haven fisherman Glenn Richter during the late 1930s and early 1940s. Photograph by Roy S. McCrimmon, Roy S. McCrimmon Collection, Michigan Maritime Museum.

to international co-management schemes with Canada by supporting the 1955 establishment of the Great Lakes Fishery Commission under Pres. Dwight D. Eisenhower.[33] More specifically, commercial fishers who found their traditional management systems both marginalized and incapacitated by the sea lamprey problem could do little but watch as state and federal fisheries managers assumed an increasingly aggressive stance in guiding the future of Lake Michigan's fisheries. Finding themselves forced to coexist and, at times, totally capitulate to fisheries managers in a manner that was unprecedented on the Great Lakes, commercial fishers saw the beginning of a fractured relationship with government regulators that culminated with the planting of Pacific salmon.

The stocking of salmon in Lake Michigan by both Michigan and Wisconsin during the mid-1960s set into motion a chain of events that dramatically weakened the political influence of Lake Michigan's commercial fishers and put their advocacy

Claude Ver Duin (top right), the foremost promoter of Great Lakes commercial fishing, confers with Cong. Gerald Ford and Sen. Richard M. Nixon in Grand Haven, Michigan, during the 1952 presidential campaign. In 1956, Pres. Dwight D. Eisenhower appointed Ver Duin to the Great Lakes Fishery Commission. A member of a Grand Haven, Michigan, fishing family of Dutch ancestry, Ver Duin was active with the Michigan Fish Producers Association and published *The Fisherman* from 1931 until his death. Howard Tanner, formerly of the Michigan DNR and Michigan State University, recalled Claude Ver Duin: "Claude Ver Duin was a gentleman. He had his position, which was totally opposite that of mine, but I always respected Claude. He was born and reared to what he was, and that was his perspective. And he fought hard." Retired U.S. Fish and Wildlife Service fisheries biologist Stan Smith recalled that Ver Duin knew all of the federal policy makers and scientists on the Great Lakes: "John VanOosten worked with Claude Ver Duin. Everybody worked very closely with Claude Ver Duin. Before Claude Ver Duin was one of the first Great Lakes Fishery commissioners, he was the spokesman for the fishermen of the state of Michigan. He was the secretary of the Michigan Fish Producers Association. There was a very good relationship between Claude Ver Duin and all of the people who had worked on the Great Lakes Fishery Investigations." Courtesy of Robert and Fern Ver Duin.

organizations in a secondary position to those of sport-fishing interests. Even the appointment of Great Lakes commercial fishing advocate Claude Ver Duin of Grand Haven, Michigan, to the Great Lakes Fishery Commission in 1955—a position he held for thirty-two years—could not stem these developments.[34] Having sought to preserve Great Lakes commercial fishing traditions during a period of rapid decline,

Ver Duin hoped that progressive management schemes would ultimately reconcile the differences between commercial and sport-fishing interests.[35] Not surprisingly, as commercial stocks and the number of people employed in the industry dwindled, the economic and political influence of Lake Michigan commercial fishing organizations similarly diminished.[36] Crippled by sea lamprey predation, pollution, and overuse of available target species, commercial fishers were hardly in a position to seriously challenge the plan announced by the State of Michigan in the mid-1960s to begin stocking Pacific salmon—a nonindigenous species—in order to create a sport fishery.[37] Having been occupationally weakened on an unprecedented ecological scale, commercial fishers struggled to find a voice in the emergent environmental politics of the 1960s.

Michigan's decision to begin stocking salmon marked the beginning of significant differences between its commercial fishing policies and those of Wisconsin. With remarkably little fanfare and minimal public input, the Michigan Department of Conservation reached the conclusion that the viability of the fledgling sport fishery depended on the virtual elimination of the commercial fishery. Commercial fishermen whose families and communities had depended on Lake Michigan fisheries for several generations found the Michigan Department of Conservation, later the Department of Natural Resources (DNR), to be both unresponsive and, at times, hostile to their concerns. When, in the late 1960s, the state refused to renew licenses for commercial fishers who did not meet minimum income requirements, this policy effectively eliminated small-scale, modestly capitalized fishing operations. This included Indian fishers who, at the time, had to be licensed by the state to fish on Lake Michigan.

In 1969 Michigan's DNR, politically empowered by its successful salmon program, further restricted commercial fishing opportunity on Lake Michigan by dividing its waters into management zones. The overwhelming majority of the state's territorial waters were designated as rehabilitation zones or sport-fishing development zones where commercial fishers were permitted to use only trap nets (live entrapment gear) for whitefish, and in the former zone, gill nets solely for chubs. Since fish remained alive once they were in a trap net, the Michigan DNR viewed it as a more selective harvesting method that allowed the return of the incidental catch of lake trout and salmon.

Commercial fishermen had little enthusiasm for the Michigan DNR's 1969 ruling. They had long-standing concerns—dating to the 1920s and 1930s—over the sheer volume of the fish caught in trap nets. Trap nets were also prohibitively expensive for many commercial fishers and vast areas of the zones open to commercial fishing were ill-suited for this type of gear. While permitted to use a wider variety of gear in specifically designed commercial fishing zones, this benefit was offset by the small geographical scale of these areas and the difficulty of avoiding incidental catch of prohibited sport species in gill nets. With such tightly delineated boundaries, commercial fishers saw these zones as susceptible to overfishing; rather than being a fishing opportunity, it was a situation that might compromise their already fragile bargaining position with state regulators.

Stricken by the curtailment of their most affordable and versatile harvesting method—the gill net—commercial fishers had even fewer options when the Michigan DNR took yellow perch and walleye off the commercial list and reclassified them as game species. When the closure of the lake herring fishery accompanied the reallocation of these former market species, commercial fishers grew apprehensive with the prospect that sport fishing's popularity might totally supplant their occupation. These fears were scarcely allayed when Michigan withdrew support for the industrial use of alewife and emphasized its value in sustaining the sport fishery. Consequently, by rejecting alewife's industrial use, the Michigan DNR put itself in a stronger position to deny requests to allow commercial harvesting of salmon. Responding to a host of recreational fishing interests, the DNR's stance was succinct: salmon were needed to control the proliferation of alewife and contribute to the development of a world-class sport fishery.

Commercial fishers saw efforts by Lake Michigan states in the late1960s and 1970s to drastically curtail or eliminate gill nets as further evidence of a conspiracy to eliminate their occupation or blame the demise of the lake's fisheries solely on them.[38] When the DNRs of both Michigan and Wisconsin decided to curtail or stop the practice of selling commercial fishing licenses to non-residents, it was viewed by many commercial fishermen as a factor that limited their ability to adapt to changes in fishery stocks and fishing policy. These territorial measures alarmed commercial fishers who realized that their living was contingent on their ability to use Lake Michigan's waters as flexibly as possible. In Michigan, much of the commercial

WHAT the LORD GIVETH the D.N.R. TAKETH AWAY

Bumper Sticker: "What the Lord Giveth, the D.N.R. Taketh Away." Since the late 1960s, this phrase has frequently been the rallying cry of Lake Michigan's commercial fishing community. Courtesy of Michael Toneys.

"Yes, you commercial fishermen may still use nets. However . . ."

The key to Lake Michigan is taken from the "low-budget fish fry," commercial fishermen and presented to the sport-fishing community by the DNR. Wisconsin commercial fisherman Don Stiller clipped the cartoon by Lyle Lahey from the Green Bay *News Chronicle* in March 1989. Courtesy of Green Bay *News Chronicle* and Don Stiller.

This billboard was erected near Algoma, Wisconsin, by Wisconsin's commercial fishing community to contest newly implemented fishing regulations in the early 1970s. In it, Wisconsin DNR fisheries officials Ron Poff and John Brasch were shown applying pressure to a Wisconsin commercial fisher. The billboard created public sympathy for the fishermen and helped raise consciousness of commercial fishing's importance as a longtime tradition in Northeast Wisconsin. Former Wisconsin DNR fisheries scientist Jim Moore vividly remembered the sign: "There was a big billboard in Algoma painted by a local sign maker. It showed a picture of Ron Poff and a commercial fisherman with a big screw going through his belly. The commercial fishermen were saying they were getting screwed by Ron Poff, an official in Madison who early on was involved with the fisheries management of both Lake Michigan and Lake Superior. He was our Madison person. If we had had to go to our Natural Resources Board to present the work that the biologists did out in the field, he was the spokesperson, the number one person working with both the sport and commercial fishermen on those types of issues." Courtesy of

fishery's resentment stemmed from the Department of Conservation's accumulation of power throughout the 1960s and, upon its re-organization into the Department of Natural Resources, its even broader and more autonomous authority to dictate fisheries regulation. Thus, when Michigan and, to a lesser extent, Wisconsin, favored sport-fishing interests on Lake Michigan, commercial fishers saw this as the unfair and arbitrary use of the public trust doctrine's regulatory power.[39]

Commercial fishers resisted the loss of their livelihood and substantial investment in gill-net boats, gear, and crews. They appealed for assistance from state and federal officials such as Cong. Philip E. Ruppe.[40] Verbal and occasionally physical confrontation between commercial fishermen and DNR officials occurred. Resistance to DNR policy was especially strong in the more isolated regions of Lake Michigan such as the area around the Garden Peninsula where, according to a feature story in the *Detroit News*, the refrain from local fishermen was "just leave us alone."[41]

Due to its prominent position in the Great Lakes basin, Michigan's fisheries management scheme quickly influenced events beyond its borders. This was particularly true among neighboring states that shared the shoreline of Lake Michigan. The transformation of Wisconsin's conservation politics bore many of the same features exhibited by Michigan, so casual observers were presumably not surprised when it announced preferential status for sport fisheries in its future Lake Michigan management plans. Swept by the popular sentiment that accompanied Michigan's bold experiment, Wisconsin planted coho salmon in its Lake Michigan tributaries in 1968. Notwithstanding this context, those who were familiar with Wisconsin's fisheries policies recognized the tone and intent of this stance to be an abrupt departure.

Wisconsin did not duplicate Michigan's efforts to largely dismantle the Lake Michigan commercial fishing industry. Instead, it sought to maintain its record of helping its commercial fishers respond to emerging problems. In 1957, Wisconsin fisheries officials began investigating the use of trawls to remove rough fish and less highly prized food fish from its areas of Lake Michigan's watershed. By 1964, Wisconsin's commercial fishers were trawling for chubs on Lake Michigan and sheepshead on nearby Lake Winnebago.

Wisconsin commercial fishermen responded with anger to any suggestion that the state might retreat from this tradition. Wisconsin's Lake Michigan commercial fishers had been a force in state and regional politics for the better part of the twentieth century and, in addition to their professional organizations, two aforementioned Lake Michigan commercial fishermen served in the Wisconsin State Assembly and Senate in the 1940s and 1950s. Fearing the loss of their occupation, they used their experience in state politics to stem the type of sweeping reductions taking place in Michigan. Geographic proximity aided Wisconsin's commercial fishers in their efforts to contest fisheries policy and build a case for simultaneous management of sport and commercial fishing.[42] Most operated along Lake

Michigan's shores and their concentrated presence helped encourage the establishment of the Lake Michigan Fisheries Task Force—an effort to impose more flexible management schemes than those imposed by Michigan. From these deliberations in the mid-1970s, Wisconsin commercial fishers gained a less restrictive quota fishery and direct participation in the state's fisheries management and policy-making processes. This approach mitigated some of the friction between the Wisconsin DNR and the state-licensed commercial fishermen at least until the introduction of limited-entry fishing. Some commercial fishers alleged that quotas and the time allotted to fish for quotas were insufficient and amounted to putting them out of business. At the same time, however, Wisconsin fishermen were able to buy or sell their quota, a policy many have utilized to their advantage. While fighting to retain greater fishing prerogatives than their Michigan cohort, these stakeholders galvanized an issue that increasingly shaped an environmental and natural resource use debate in the last quarter of the twentieth century: what conditions should be placed on the state's power to regulate Lake Michigan's contested fishery resources?

Commercial fishers seek to shape Lake Michigan fisheries legislation and policy by attending meetings in Lansing, Madison, and other locations and by accepting appointments to advisory committees that serve state, federal, and tribal agencies. While their participation is motivated by self-interest, it is also driven by the belief that those who fish the inland seas are best equipped to offer advice. When Lake Michigan commercial fishers narrate their occupational histories, they convey a variety of social and cultural issues that govern the use of fisheries resources. Thus, in seemingly endless ways, these patterns historically account for the Lake Michigan commercial fishermen's managerial bearing. By actually, "living the fishing," commercial fishers created resource management histories by carrying out their daily round of work.[43] In the oral histories that follow, Lake Michigan commercial fishermen give numerous details that portray the acquired knowledge, rules, and working conditions that were, and continue to be, their most fundamental management framework. Most policy analysts and historians are unaccustomed to documenting and evaluating management schemes that are forged through work and, perhaps more important, are recorded principally in memory.

Michigan's commercial fishers shaped vernacular management policies through the process of tending nets, discovering rich fishing grounds, observing fluctuating fish stocks, and allocating human and financial resources. With the passage of time, these social and cultural dynamics created a management temperament that hung like a valence over every dimension of the fisher's life. As testimonies of a social and cultural claim to the resources, oral history becomes a configuration of fisheries management. Their oral testimony identifies the convergence of occupational tradition and Great Lakes fisheries ecology as a managerial inheritance dating to the nineteenth century.

1. IN THE BLOOD: OCCUPATIONAL ENDURANCE AND TRADITIONAL ECOLOGICAL KNOWLEDGE

Rick Johnson's father and grandfather both worked as fishermen before moving on to other economic pursuits. Raised in the fishing community of Gills Rock, Wisconsin, Johnson played at being a fisherman as a child. He began fishing one year after high school.

My grandfather was mainly a gillnetter and his fish tug was the *King*. It was an old wooden tug. An artist drew a picture of it from a black and white photograph. It is quite a unique looking boat. I guess it used to go just as fast in reverse as it did forward. Any more than an inch of ice and my father said, you were stuck. I think they had a twenty-five-horse engine. My father worked for the Weborgs gill netting and pound netting. Back then, there were not any trap nets around. It was just pound nets and gill nets.

I was born on November 19, 1956, in Sturgeon Bay. I have lived across the road from the fish docks here in Gills Rock my whole life. I used to hang around the docks as a kid, and ride on Marvin Weborg's pound-net boat. My brother and I used to ride along. They used to let us pull on the line and think that we were actually working. When we were growing up, we were down at Weborg's dock all the time in the summer. As soon as the school was out, we were down here bugging these guys. It becomes a way of life. You used to go along and it seemed like a fun way to make a living. Then they hired us to pick moss out of pound nets. I graduated from high school in 1974 and had a job as a carpenter. I got laid off after one year. I had just bought a brand new car,

Rick Johnson has been a commercial fisherman from Gills Rock, Wisconsin, since 1976. He is actively involved in the fisheries policy-making process in the state. Interview, 2 June 1999. Photograph by Michael Chiarappa.

so I needed a job. I came down here and I have been fishing ever since. I started working for Jeff Weborg around 1976. When I started working for Jeff Weborg, and I ran the boat, he owned it; but I ran it and so I got the feel of it. After a couple years, I figured, if I am doing all the work, why not make the extra money of owning it. So I bought out his half. He was in partnership with Tim Weborg. I bought out Jeff's partnership and then about nine years ago, I bought out Tim's. So now, I am sole owner of it.

The year I got married, we almost went bankrupt. There was just no fish to be had. It was just a tough go. You are all happy because you are getting married, and then you come back, and there are no fish. You could not catch enough to eat. Then a couple months later, all of a sudden, the fish seemed to come from nowhere and we started catching them again. That was around 1982.

Paul Goodman of Washington Island, Wisconsin, believes his father destined him for a life on the water. He discussed how fishing helped to unite the community.

My name is Paul Mariner Goodman. My dad gave me the name Mariner because he figured I would be on the water, so it is actually my real middle name. My grandfather was a commercial fisherman on Washington Island. His name was Tom

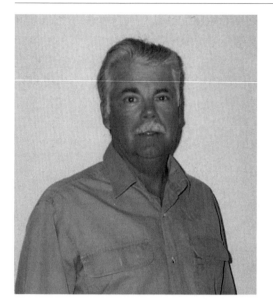

Paul Mariner Goodman, from Washington Island, Wisconsin's Icelandic community, was the third generation of his family to work in Lake Michigan's commercial fishery. He now works in the sport fishery as a charter boat captain. Interview, 2 June 1999. Courtesy of Paul M. Goodman

Goodman. His name was really Tom Goodmander, but he changed it to Goodman. It is Icelandic, so the "er" was always on it. He changed it to Goodman and his brother kept it as Goodmander, so there was always kind of a split there in the family. It works that way sometimes.

My grandfather, Tom Goodman, fished commercially on Washington Island. Then my father fished there. When I was young, there were a lot of boats on Washington Island. When my dad fished, I would be on the boats with them in the summer. At that time they had shore work going. I was not much for shore work because I was a kid. I would run around the docks and all the other commercial fishermen and their sheds, and joke with them and look at their Heidi calendars on the walls. There was still an icehouse when I was young. They took up ice and had sawdust in the buildings.

Joel Peterson discussed his family history and fishing history. He described how the family adapted to technological, economic, and environmental change.

It started in the 1800s with Elmer Peterson. Elmer came over from Sweden. Then he sent over and got a couple of his sons by his first marriage. Elmer's father worked

Joel Peterson (right) is a commercial fisherman of Swedish descent and has been fishing out of Fairport, Michigan, located on Michigan's Garden Peninsula, since 1972. Interview, 4 June 1999. Photograph by Michael J. Chiarappa.

for Jackson Iron Mine. Elmer fished and later they tell me, his brother Ben and his son fished—that's the Manistique group.[44] So then there was Elmer, my grandpa, Thomas Peterson, my father, Hector Peterson, me, Joel Peterson, and my son, Steven Peterson. There is my brother, Ben Peterson and his son, Lucas Peterson. We all fish together.

Originally, my great-grandfather and my grandfather fished gill nets and pound nets. After my dad was in the Second World War, he, his dad, and a lot of other people went down below to Michigan's Lower Peninsula for a while. They worked six or seven years in Detroit after the Second World War. When they came back, my Uncle Kenny, my father, and my grandfather all fished on a gill-net tug. It was probably in the 1950s or 1960s when they went down to Lake Winnebago and fished rough fish, sheepshead, for the State of Wisconsin. My father stayed in Fairport and ran the gill-net boat.

I was introduced to fishing when I was small. I was always down at the docks. I was a little snot-nosed kid running around, asking questions, and getting my butt kicked. I always liked fishing and I grew up fishing. When I graduated from high school, I stayed home and fished for a year. Then I decided I should go to the big city and see what was happening there. So I worked a few jobs down there. I worked for Buick for a while. Then I got drafted and served my two years in the service. When I got out of the service, I got married to a woman from up the road. Then my wife and I had our son Steven. I was working as a carpenter in Flint and carpentry was slow. So one day I came home and I told the wife, "I think we should move back up." She was not real receptive to the idea right away, but we moved back and have never been sorry.

I had a job working with my dad on the boat. Any time I wanted to come back, we could just jump in and start fishing again. My brother, Ben, who is a little younger than me, was just getting done with high school when I got back, and so it was my dad, Ben, and I. In the meantime, my uncle and his son went into the pound-net business. They stayed on in the pound-net business when my father was a gillnetter. Ben and I stayed in the gill-net business with my father until they started eliminating gill nets in the Great Lakes. Then we gradually slipped over into the trap net end of it.

After we got into the trap nets, my father only fished with us for maybe three or four years on the trap-net rigging. Then he retired. He came down one day and said: "Well, I have worked twenty-eight or thirty years with one hand and I am going to retire and this is what you owe me for the rig." That is how Ben and I got going on our own. We had a small trap-net boat and a gill-net boat, and then decided to build an aluminum boat. We had the second or third aluminum trap-net boat on the lakes. We had it built sometime around 1983 or 1985. It is over at Manistique right now. From there we have kept building up. Our sons got out of school. Now we have got my son, Ben's son, and my sister's son working for us. We have one other guy that fishes with us also.

My grandfather built the dock. My father and Uncle Kenny owned it. Then they passed it on. Kenny's got two boys, so the four of us own it now. If the boys stay fishing, they will probably end up with it. It is nothing fancy. I have seen people come in here and say, "Boy, it is messy." Well, you do not see many fish ports that have yachts in them. I come through here every day with a $150,000 boat, and it does not even have a bathroom in it. But in this day and age, that is what one of these new trap-net boats will cost you.

Fishing is a way of life that is passed down. My dad never said this is what you are going to do. In 1965 when I decided to go to the city and make my fortune, the one thing my dad told me was, "I will be here when you get back." I came back in 1972, and he was still here fishing. But you have got to try different things. I worked for Buick. I worked construction. I built houses. I enjoyed everything I have done and did the best that I could. But when you have been around fish, and you can be your own boss—if you can make a living at what you like to do, you are fortunate. Fishing gets in your blood. Probably the most valuable thing about fishing is that you are independent. What you make depends on how hard you work at it. You get out of it exactly what you put into it. If you do not put anything into it, you are not going to get way ahead. It is a lot of hard work. A lot of the time the fishing is not really great, but the rig always comes first. If you do not have a good fishing rig, you are not going to be able to harvest a good quantity of fish when they are there.

My wife has always been really supportive. Her father was a commercial fisherman; he fished up out of Garden. Fishing is also important because we live here. This is what people did in Fairport—they commercial fished. I used to think my dad did not know that much. I think more about what my dad has taught me over the years, and how much more that I know now than what I did twenty years ago. We have got some nets set out in the lake where my grandfather had told us that is a damn good spot to set a net. Well, we are setting nets there now and you know what? It is a damn good spot to set nets. It is just a different way of life.

As far as my son goes—it is going to be his choice. My dad never told me that this is what I had to do. If you like doing it and can make a living doing it, then do it. As far as the stability or the security of it, it is probably not good. You are playing the odds—you are the same as a farmer. It is the same culture as farming. How many family farms are falling by the wayside?

———

Gills Rock, Wisconsin, resident Leon Voight discussed his family ties to fishing. He reached the conclusion that fishing did not offer the quality of life he wanted for his son and has advised him against becoming involved in fishing.

My grandfather started commercial fishing back in the early 1900s. My father fished from the 1920s until he retired about eighteen years ago and we took over, us three boys. Our oldest brother quit about ten years ago and it is just the two of us left now. We will probably be the last fishermen in our family. I have a son, but I told

Leon Voight (front) has spent his life working in Lake Michigan's commercial fisheries. As a young man, he fished the waters of northern Michigan and Wisconsin with his father, Donald Voight, and his brothers. He now resides in Gills Rock, Wisconsin. and operates the fish tug *Faith II* with his brother Lyle Voight (back). Interview, 2 June 1999. Photograph by Jason Wintersteen.

him not to get into the business because it is too hard. We have been doing it for years. It is family tradition. We have fished here out of Gills Rock. We have fished out of Frankfort, Michigan. I have been doing it since I was probably six or seven years old.

Fishing is a backbreaking job. There is no doubt about that. You are bending over and lifting all this gear. You are out there rolling around in the big waves trying to do your job. It gets to be an awful hard job. We take people along on the lake when it is calm so they can stand and watch. Sometimes somebody will actually try and pick a fish out of the net. We try to explain to them, "Could you imagine doing this in ten- or fifteen-foot seas?" They just cannot comprehend that. It is a hard life. People do not understand it. That is why we like to show people once in a while what it is actually all about. I think it opens peoples' eyes up to actually see what a fisherman goes through to catch fish. They just think the fish are there and that it does not cost anything to go and get them. They do not realize the cost that is involved in all this. So we take people along so they can learn a little bit about it.

It's in your blood, especially when you are brought up with it. When you are just a child and you are doing it, it gets to be part of your life. You will never see a commercial fisherman move away from the water. He has been on the water his whole life. He can get up and see the water every day. You will never see him move away from it, no matter what he does. When he goes on a vacation, he goes where there is water and most likely fishing hook and line. You really have to love it. It gets in your blood. If you get a couple weeks off, sure it is fine. Your back kind of heals up. But then you are ready to get out fishing again. I would never move away from the water. It is in your blood and you cannot get rid of it once it is there.

I know how hard it is to be in the fishing business—to keep it going. I can see down the road into the future that it is going to be even harder. There will be fewer fishermen. I do not want my son to put up with those kinds of problems. It is too much hard work. He is really not built for it. He is a smaller guy and you have to be pretty husky to be throwing around fish boxes and nets constantly. It is backbreaking and I do not want him to go through that.

Steve Peterson is a commercial fisherman who works out of Fairport, Michigan. He began fishing as a boy to help his uncle. He later went into business with him.

I was born in Flint in 1971. We lived there for a few years and my family moved up here and started fishing because grandpa always did. They came up here and moved back home. I have been doing this for at least twelve or so years. Since I was young I would always go fishing with my uncle, Ben Peterson. It is not too bad. He never really wanted me to because you never know what is going to happen from year to year. We have uncles and cousins fishing. Ben Peterson's son Lucas is almost the same age as I am. He will be the sixth generation. We originated from Andrew Peterson from Sweden. He was a big logger around here in Fayette, the ghost town, who did fishing besides. He lived on the big Summer Island. The way they fish over on the island is the old way. Here, we got some of the newer stuff. My mother's dad was a fisherman on the Garden until he passed away. He fished pretty much until the end.

My uncle always wanted me to do something else, but as you go on, you enjoy it. A lot of times we get winters off where we cannot fish in the wintertime, which is nice,

Steve Peterson, son of Joel Peterson, is the sixth generation of Petersons to pursue commercial fishing as an occupation. Interview, 4 June 1999, with uncle, Ben Peterson, at his family's fishery in Fairport, Michigan. Photograph courtesy of the Great Lakes Center for Maritime Studies.

so it works both ways. You get used to doing certain things like going out on the water. I would never be able to sit in an office job. I would have to be outside all the time. I left here this morning. I lifted at big Summer Island, and I run all the way down to Manistique. So I got my miles in. Then I drove back home. When it is blowing, it makes it rough some days, but it is not too bad. You get used to that, too. You are real excited every day. You get to see the water. I like being on the water. When I am done working, I go back on the water with the powerboat. During the last few years the winters have been mild. There are a lot of deer running around. It works out nice. The fishing season ends in November and the deer season opens on the 15th.

Pete LeClair's decision to become a fisherman was influenced, in part, by his family and the local community.[45] LeClair indicated that his work for the family fishery began when he was a boy in the 1930s. At the time, the family was fishing with pound nets that were dried in nearby fields.

Daniel "Pete" LeClair (second from left) and his sons operate the Susie-Q Fish Market in Two Rivers, Wisconsin. LeClair has been involved in commercial fishing his entire life and has participated in the pound-net, gill-net, trap-net, and trawl fisheries. He, along with his sons, represents a long line of LeClairs who have fished from the Two Rivers area since the mid-nineteenth century. Interview, 11 December 1997. Photograph by Michael J. Chiarappa.

I was born on June 28, 1929, in Two Rivers, Wisconsin. My great-granddad, Charles LeClair, came from Canada and started commercial fishing out of Two Creeks, Wisconsin, about ten miles north of Two Rivers on the lakeshore. My great-grandfather, Charles LeClair, was one of the men who started the commercial fishing industry in this area. They started with long oars and skiffs. Then they went to sailboats and then they went to gas engines. My father was Joseph LeClair. He was a commercial fisherman. My father and my older brother Paul led me to become involved.

My dad originally started commercial fishing down near Two Creeks, Wisconsin, in a lakeshore town called Kidville. It got this name because there were five families there and they had forty kids. Everybody there more or less founded the fishing industry. I started when I was ten or eleven years old. I used to drive the truck for my dad while he worked with the nets in the fields. I have been in it since I was old enough to walk or really be useful for something. We fished pound nets out of Two Creeks for years

Brian Price is a graduate of the University of Michigan, where he studied geology. Today, he is manager of the Leelanau Conservancy. He worked as a commercial fisherman with the late Ross Lang and crewed with commercial fisherman Alan Priest. He has also worked with Lake Michigan's Native American fishers, serving as an instructor in the use of trap nets. Interview, 28 May 1999. Photograph by Michael J. Chiarappa.

and then it became obsolete. The lake trout kind of left and we had to go into a different fishery. We went into the trout fishery with gill nets.

I was ten or eleven when I was driving the truck while they were picking the nets up out of the field. So my dad got all he could out of me when I was young. I would back the truck up as they pulled the nets out. They were pound nets. It was an old 1929 Chevrolet truck with a big, long flat bed. All you had to do was let the clutch in and out and not touch the gas pedal. You just backed up when they told you to back up. So I was restricted in what I could really do—I really did not drive it around the field, I just operated the clutch. But that was the beginning of it.

Brian Price recalled how his attraction to the lakes compelled him to work as a commercial fisherman for fifteen years.

I was fascinated with the Great Lakes. That is what attracted me to go out on the water in the first place. I was trained as a geologist, but I also loved boats. And I worked on research ships when I was in college for the University of Michigan. When I got out of college, I did not want to go on to grad school. I was hanging around and it occurred to me that nobody knows the lakes like the fishermen know them. I thought I would fish for like a year or so, to get that perspective, and then I would decide what else to do. And then fifteen years later, I started casting around for something else to do. It is astounding to me because I found out I loved it too much.

———————

Jack Cross is the third generation in his family to engage in commercial fishing. He is now in the wholesale and retail business.

I was born and raised in Charlevoix. My grandfather came up here from the south end of the lake, around South Haven, back before the turn of the century. He sailed schooners up and down the lakes. They settled on Beaver Island when my dad was only about two years old at the time. My grandfather and father went into the fishing business. I grew up at it. So I have been at this for over forty years. In my time, whitefish, lake trout, perch and chubs have been our main fish.

Jack Cross, Jr. (right), worked as a commercial fisherman on Lake Michigan for more than forty years. He was the third generation of his family to work Lake Michigan's waters, but today he concentrates on buying and marketing Lake Michigan fish. Interview, 27 May 1999. Photograph by Michael J. Chiarappa.

My dad and I grew up using gill nets; we were primarily gill-net fishermen. At one time my father had two or three boats going. We had what was considered a large crew of twenty to twenty-five people. In the 1970s the state put us out of the gill-net business and we went into trap-net fishing. We did that until they put us out of business again in the mid-1980s, around 1983 or 1984. We have been out of business as far as the fishing end of it since then. We moved into the retail and processing operation in 1945. My dad always bought fish from other fishermen. We ran our wholesale and retail store here in addition to fishing with our own fish tugs. We just expanded it over the years. My son is kind of growing up in this as well.

Alan Priest, a commercial fisherman who works out of Leland, recalled that his interest in fishing stemmed from his boyhood experiences on the water off the Leelanau Peninsula. He began to learn the commercial fishing business in 1972, when he was hired by Ross Lang, a family friend, who died in a fishing accident in April 1998.

I was born on January 11, 1952, in Lansing, Michigan. My parents are originally from Leelanau County. My dad is from Suttons Bay and my mom is from Leland. She is now living in the house where she grew up. When my parents first got married, they went to Lansing because my dad could not find any work around here. We spent summers up here in Leland. My dad stayed in Lansing and worked, and mom and my other brothers and sisters spent the summers up here. When my grandpa and grandma died and my mom got the house, we decided to move back up to Leland. Thank goodness they did. We moved to Leland in 1966 when I was fourteen. It was good for me.

I have always loved the outdoors and hunting and fishing. I had a small fourteen-foot wood boat with an old ten-horse Johnson motor and was out in Lake Leelanau basically night and day. I would come down to Fishtown before the lodge and the cove were here. There used to be an old mail boat at the end of the dock. I would catch eighteen- to nineteen-inch small mouth bass all the time. I would get enough, go home, and clean them up for dinner. In the summer, I would snorkel and fin up and down the river, getting sinkers, swivels and odds and ends that the trout fishermen had lost during the spring. That would be my supply of sinkers and swivels for the summer. When they built the harbor, I snorkeled all out through there and spear-gunned

Alan Priest began working as a commercial fisherman in 1970 when he was hired by the late Ross Lang. Today, Priest concentrates his commercial fishing effort on Lake Michigan chub. He works out of Leland, Michigan, where he leases his fish tug from Carlson's Fisheries. Interview, 29 May 1999. Photograph by Michael J. Chiarappa.

carp, and put them under my ma's rosebushes. I never hung out with anybody. Mother Nature got a hold of me, and that was it, which I am thankful for. I have always loved the outdoors.

In the summers, when I was real young, I was down at Fishtown all the time. The Fishtown docks were only two planks wide. You could come down, look under the dock and see great big pike—three footers—laying under the dock. Across the river on the north side, used to be the Stallman Fisheries. There was a fishery that used to smoke fish back behind where we smoke jerky now for Carlsons. There was another tug across the river on the north side called the *Mary Anne*. The *Janice Sue* was back there and the *Frances Clark* was on the south side. There were four tugs that fished out of here. The *Mary Anne* just fished the summer. There were three others. The Bucklers had the *Sea Bird*, the Langs had the *Frances Clark*, and the Carlsons had the *Janice Sue*. We all fished chubs in the summer. In June, July, and August we got a permit from the DNR to fish menominees all around the islands. When the lake trout were planted, they ended that. They were afraid that we were going to catch too many lake trout, but that would never have happened.

When I was about to graduate from high school, I was going to be drafted into the service because my number was low. I did not go to college because I did not know exactly what I wanted to do. Ross Lang and his wife Joy were good friends with my mom and dad. Ross said, "You want to go fishing?" I said, "Oh yeah. I love to fish." Well, I did not have a clue. So my first job as a commercial fisherman was with Lang's Fisheries, with Ross and his dad, Fred. I started commercial fishing in 1970 and fished until 1972. Then I had to go into the service. I went into the Navy for three years. When I got out in 1976, I started up fishing right away.

The Langs came over from Alpena and needed a crew because the chubs out here were just thick. They were catching lots of fish. Ross and his dad could not handle it. I got on the boat on my first day. Oh God, I was so seasick. I crawled under by the stove and just laid there. Oh God, I was sick. I was puking and Ross's dad was laughing. But for some reason, I did not give it up. I stayed right with it. It would either cure or kill— I think that was what I had in my mind. I carried a dinner pail for a week. Anyway, that is where I started—on the *Frances Clark* with Ross and Fred. I buried them both. Ross's dad died of cancer and then Ross got killed in an accident out on the *Joy* a year ago April. It is still hard for me to understand why. All I can figure out is it was his time. I gill netted with him and his dad.

Ross and Fred Lang taught me how to work. If you want to be successful, you have to work at it. You cannot just show up for work, jump on the boat and go out, and catch chubs. It does not work that way. Here in the shed is ninety percent of your fishing—working on nets. If you do not keep up your nets, and fix the holes that are in them, you are not going to produce anything. I am not saying go out and rape the lake or take every fish that you can catch, no. But you have to keep your rig up, and you have to work at it. Even if I do not fish until I retire, they taught me how to work and be responsible.

Chuck Jensen of South Haven worked primarily in the marketing end of the family fishery. He discussed how fishing united various branches of the family. Jensen recalls many of the men who worked for his father more than half a century ago.

My dad started his fishing operation in Muskegon right after he got out of World War I. He had a brother in Muskegon and several friends who were from the

Prior to his retirement, Chuck Jensen (left) and his family harvested Lake Michigan's waters and operated a wholesale and retail fish market in South Haven, Michigan. Founded by Chuck Jensen's father, Chris Jensen (below, c. 1930s), a Danish immigrant, the Jensen fishery now houses a restaurant and marina. Interview, 20 May 1999. Photograph of Chuck Jensen by Michael J. Chiarappa, Photograph of Chris Jensen courtesy of the Michigan Maritime Museum.

same territory in Denmark. They all fished together and worked together for a while. My dad was sixteen or eighteen when he came over from Denmark. He was born in 1890. His father fished in Denmark from a little village on the North Sea. For some reason, my dad liked South Haven better, so we moved to South Haven in 1932. He continued fishing up until he retired. My grandfather did not fish too long in Muskegon. He had different jobs. He worked on the streetcars in Muskegon. I believe he fished on the side a little bit. But my uncle, Paul Jensen, was a steady fisherman. I think he worked with him for a while, and then after the streetcars went out, they decided to go fishing steady. Paul had two sons who were in business with him for many, many years. Jensen Brothers was quite a famous fishing name up in Muskegon.

I was pretty small when I started working for my folks. I was working in the fish market all the time then. Once in a while I would go out in a tug, but I was kind of raised in a fish market selling, cleaning and packing fish. Basically, I was always on shore operations. Every so often, I would either have to take a man's place on a boat if someone was sick or something. I would take over his job and go on. But basically, I was a shoreman.

In South Haven, the fishermen were pretty steady. They settled down and raised their families. My dad did not have too much trouble keeping regular, steady help. Jim, Walt, and Lloyd McCash and Mr. Julius Allers worked for him for many years. Allers skippered the tug. Ray Wakild also worked for my dad.

Mark Weborg of Gills Rock, Wisconsin, indicated that family, ethnicity, community, and a love of the water compelled him to make fishing his life's work.[46]

I have been in the fishery all my life. When I was eight or ten years old I spent a good share of my time down on the dock or on the boats helping my dad. I went full time on my own with my brother back in 1971. I am a fourth-generation commercial fisherman. My great-great-great-grandfather came over from Norway, and my great-grandmother made some of the first linen gill nets in this area. From there, it has progressed to quite a bit of different equipment.

I became interested in fishing at a very young age. We grew up fishing. That was all we did. We did a little farming, but mostly fishing. When you are around the docks and been on the water—it is a known fact—it gets in your blood. Once fishing is in your blood, it is hard to get it out. For many, many years fishing went in cycles. There were times when you could not make a living. At that time, you could move around the Great Lakes and still make a living. But now we are limited to this one area and if fishing got bad, we would be looking for a different job. We have been having good fishing now for about thirty years, and we do not know what is going to be in store down the road.

Mark Weborg is a commercial fisherman from Gill's Rock, Wisconsin. The great-grandson of Norwegian immigrants, Weborg's family has been involved in commercial fishing on the Great Lakes for four generations. Interview, 1 June 1999. Photograph courtesy of the Great Lakes Center for Maritime Studies.

I did try working at Sears for six months of my life after I got married, and that was all I lasted. I had to get back in the open air and out on the water.

Bill Carlson of Leland indicated that his family fished and farmed in Scandinavia before they came to Michigan. He is the fourth generation in the Carlson family to fish on Lake Michigan.[47]

I am the fourth generation of Carlsons to fish out of this port. My son works with me also, so he is the fifth generation. We have been here quite a while. We have moved around in different buildings in the port, but Leland has been pretty much our home port all this century.

My family members were emigrants from Norway and Sweden. In the 1870s they homesteaded on North Manitou Island, which is just twelve miles off the shore of Leland. They came over as fishermen and farmers and they continued that practice on North Manitou Island. They had a farm and fished off the island until about 1906. The

Lester William "Bill" Carlson (right) is the owner and operator of Carlson's Fishery, located in the Fishtown section of Leland, Michigan. Carlson and his son Clay represent the fourth and fifth generation of Carlsons to fish Lake Michigan's waters. Bill Carlson was interviewed on 26 and 27 May 1999. Photograph by Michael J. Chiarappa.

islands were settled in northern Michigan before the mainland because the mode of transportation was by water until the early 1900s. The railway had not reached northern Michigan, especially remote areas like Leelanau County. When the railroad came in and roads were brought up into northern Michigan, the islands were no longer quite as important. My family moved to the mainland in 1906. They had a farm north of Leland and they also fished out of the port of Leland. Commercial fishing started here in the late 1800s. My great-grandfather, Nells Carlson, was here pretty much at the beginning. He brought a large family with him from Sweden. Nells had quite a few children. Some of them were born on North Manitou Island. There was quite the Swedish immigration to the islands in the Great Lakes. There were Andersons, Firestones, and all the good Swedish-Norwegian names. These families intermarried. At that time, North Manitou Island had a population of about 300 people in Crescent City on the west side. So there was a good colony of immigrants over there.

The nucleus of our family started with just Nells and Sophie Carlson—she was a Firestone—and it went from there. So a lot of my family fished, but not all here. Some of them fished out of Northport and further south. The family started fishing in Leland and then branched out. My grandfather, Will Carlson, fished with my great-grandfather. Will and my father fished together until 1941, when there was a boating accident. Our boat caught on fire. My grandfather died of exposure in the water. My father swam for twenty-one hours and was rescued.

The *Diamond* burned to the water line and sunk. They waited to see if anything would float so they could hold onto it. They had a life jacket—a cork life jacket—the other one was partly burned. When my grandfather died of exposure, my father put it on his body. He took two of the floats out of the burned life jacket and tied them in his shirt and he swam with the floats in his shirt. A couple of fishermen found him about four o'clock in the morning. They had pretty much given up hope of finding them alive. It was a moonlit night and they followed the moonbeam and they just about ran him over. He could not talk anymore. He had lost his voice so he tried to splash the water. They thought they heard something, stopped the boat, and looked out. He was right there and they pulled him ashore.

When the *Diamond* burned and my grandfather Will died, people in the community took up a collection and raised enough money to pay for pretty much having the whole boat built so my father could get back into the fishing business. They did not want him to have a choice whether to continue to fish or not. They wanted to force him to continue to fish and so they built him a boat. That was a pretty neat deal.

My father, Lester "Pete" Carlson and I fished together until he retired in the late 1960s and early 1970s. I continued to fish. I was on my own until my son joined me in the business. His name is Christopher Clayton Carlson, but we call him Clay. He is working with me now.

When you have a family that has been in the fishing business like our family, you grow up with it. It is a way of life. It is not just a tradition. It is how you live; you are in the fishing business before you know it. I remember when I was eleven years old I worked, waited on customers in the fish market and went on the lake when they needed me. My first job was filling mending needles. I got a nickel apiece for doing that. I must of been about four, five, or six years old. I remember doing it in the attic of one of the buildings here where they mended nets. They would sit me in the corner and I would fill mending needles until my fingers were too sore to do it anymore. But I would make myself fifty or sixty cents in a good afternoon. Now we have machines that do it.

Don Stiller worked as a commercial fisherman in Wisconsin's Green Bay waters and tributaries. Interview, 31 May 1999. Photograph courtesy of the Great Lakes Center for Maritime Studies.

Don Stiller of Green Bay, Wisconsin, recalled that he had wanted to fish since he was a boy. He began fishing with his father in 1942 upon his graduation from high school. At that time, Don's father had been fishing for about twenty years.

My schooling was at the grade school right across the railroad tracks from my house here. I graduated from Green Bay West High School in 1942. Then I spent about two years in the Navy during World War II, and another year and a half during the Korean War. When I graduated from high school in 1942, I started fishing with my father full time. I just liked fishing right from the start. I just liked to fish; when I was in high school I do not know how I learned anything. My heart was out in the duck marsh or out on the water someplace. When I was in the navy the first time, I had an ensign who was bound and determined that I was going to go to college under the GI Bill. I resisted the whole time. I went right back into the fishing business again. That was my classroom out there.

Kenneth Peterson, from Michigan's Garden Peninsula, spent his life working as a commercial fisherman on Lake Michigan and Lake Winnebago. Interview, 4 June 1999. Photograph by Michael J. Chiarappa

Kenneth Peterson is a member of the fourth generation of Petersons to fish on the Great Lakes.

I was born in Fairport in 1920. I weighed right around thirteen pounds when I was born. My two brothers were not very small either. The middle one, he was better than twelve and my oldest brother he was better than ten. Hector and Stanley both were fishermen. My dad, Thomas H. Peterson, fished all his life. He fished out of Fairport just about all his life, ever since he was a little boy. My grandfather, Elmer Peterson fished too. I think my great-granddad, Andrew, fished, too. They got over 150 years in, I guess, in our whole family. I never did know my great-grandfather. He was gone before I was born. I never even saw my granddad. He went sailing on Great Lake boats and the ship went down and he got drowned.

I do not know what year it was when I started fishing. It had to be in the 1930s. I was just a young fellow, about fifteen or sixteen years old. I worked for different fishermen but I mostly fished with my dad. My dad taught me everything I knew. It was not much maybe, but he taught me everything he knew. He did everything. My dad had all different kinds of fishing equipment. He fished gill nets, pound nets, and trap nets. He had all of them. He did not have all that many trap nets and pound nets; he mostly fished gill nets. We had a regular gill-net boat. It was about a forty-five to fifty-foot fish tug, the *Clara S*. The *Eli* was the first one my dad had when I was a young fellow. But then he upgraded a little bit and got the old *Clara S* which was a used boat, too. I do not know where either one of them were built. I think it was in Milwaukee or down that way in Wisconsin somewhere. My dad used to make a lot of trips across the lake with her. He used to fish all around the Manitou Islands and Fox Island over there.

My gill-net boat, the *Alice*, was a used boat. I bought it from another Peterson in Marinette. I never did too much gill-net fishing. I did with my dad. My dad and I and my brother, Hector, fished gill nets together out of Fairport. My brother, Hector, and I fished gill nets later after my dad quit. I quit gill nets when I went to Lake Winnebago. First, we were fishing pound nets. We had three-pound nets in down there, and then we went to trap nets.

We fished sheepshead out of Lake Winnebago under the supervision of the state for about nine years, probably during the 1950s and the 1960s. Then I came back to Fairport and I went to fishing pound nets right up here in the bay. I would use, on an average, maybe ten pound nets at the most. I fished trap nets, too. My boy is fishing trap nets now. That is about all he can fish. They took the gill nets away from us.

We used to fish all around Lake Michigan. When my dad was living, he and my brother and I fished together. We made a few trips over to Manitou Islands. We would stay there two, three days. We would sleep right on the boat. We fished for whitefish.

We brought them back to Fairport. A lot of time you had to come home because you ran out of grub. No matter if it was blowing or not, you just took off for home. You can go back and reminisce about a lot of interesting trips that you made. My dad told me lots of stories, his fishing history. It was terrible. Some of the old leaky boats they had! They took a chance going out in the lake with them old leaky buggers. They had to bail with a five-gallon pail. It was terrible in a storm.

Over the years, I have had a lot of guys working for me. Oh yes, lots of them. But they were all younger guys than I was, too. Some were good fishermen, some were not. You had to break them in and teach them. As long as he was fast, quick on his feet, and quick at learning, you did not have time to tell him how to do things. They just had to learn by themselves. They just grab hold of it and go.

For nearly fifty years, Elaine Johnson has been involved in the commercial fishing business in the Wisconsin waters of Lake Michigan and Green Bay. Until April 2000, she provided fish products to numerous restaurants in Door County, Wisconsin. Interview, 2 June 1999. Photograph by Michael J. Chiarappa

Wisconsin fish processor Elaine Johnson, is among the more visible women involved in Lake Michigan fisheries. Ethnic, family, and community ties combined to create an interest in the fisheries.

Our family first came here from Norway. They landed on Eagle Island about 1852. In 150 years we have only gotten a quarter of a mile away from our seed—not too far. A lot of people think that we are unique—it is a unique profession, I guess. We are probably the biggest processing operation north of Green Bay and have been for all the years, ever since we started. But it has been really a good life. We have strong roots in the fishery. This is our forty-sixth year in the fishing business.

Community and family ties directed Neil Teskie of Gills Rock, Wisconsin, to commercial fishing. His family combined fishing with cottage rentals.

Neil Teskie graduated from Carroll College in 1971 and returned to his native Door County to work in the family fishing operation. During his youth, Teskie fished with his father and his brother, Lyle Teskie. Today, Teskie and his family operate orchards and Very Berry, a retail fish, produce, and gourmet foods shop in addition to their commercial fishing business. Interview, 1 June 1999. Photograph courtesy of the Great Lakes Center for Maritime Studies.

I was born on June 7, 1949. My family did not jump right into fishing. My father started fishing when he was around twelve years old, but did it off and on. He was in the shipyard business. He spent four years in the navy and was in the Kwajalein Islands near Australia. He came back here and married my mother and then Lyle and I came along. I remember my early days when we lived in Gills Rock in Cottage Three. I would walk over to Johnson's Smokehouse and get a fresh smoked fish or go down and see Howard Weborg and Emery, his brother. I would always go down by those guys and watch them clean their fish. I always was interested. There was not anything else to do but hang around the docks.

When I was four years old, my father and grandfather took me on the boat when they went fishing. I do not remember going, but they remembered it. I was around ten or eleven when I started going out with my father. When I was twelve, we did more and more fishing. We used this boat that we are sitting in here right now, the *Gem*, to run to Chambers Island to catch 100–200 pounds of whitefish. Three hundred pounds was a big lift of whitefish back then. After we caught the fish my father would go to the supper club in Ellison Bay and work there at night cooking the fish for the people. It was whitefish, caught and cooked by Frank Teskie. He did that off and on over the years and I just kept fishing.

My dad went to different parts of Michigan and Wisconsin. He spent some time in St. Ignace, Michigan, and Sault Ste. Marie because there was not any whitefish here. He went over there and fished chubs and whitefish. They did not get kicked out of there, but there was a botulism scare. Seven people died from botulism back at that time. They had eaten vacuum-packaged smoked fish sent on an unrefrigerated truck. My dad came home because they dumped his fish. Nobody would buy a fish. When he came back he fished some whitefish here for a while—off and on. Lyle and I helped him and fished with him.

When I was in high school, in my early years of high school, we went over to Frankfort, Michigan. He fished chubs out of Frankfort for about four or five years—maybe a little longer. I went to Carroll College in 1967 and my dad continued fishing in Frankfort until about 1970. In 1970, he came back because they had a scare with DDT. The DDT scare caused another fish dumpage. He had been buying salmon from the Michigan DNR and smoking them. They dumped all his salmon, his chubs, and whatever he had frozen. So he had to come home. When he was fishing out of Frankfort they called it DDT, but it may have been PCBs. On the spectrograms, they were seeing more than DDT but they were not really aware of PCBs. So he came back home. When I graduated in 1971 he said, "If you want to work I got a job for you." So I said, "I am going back there." All my friends said, "Why would you want to go back there?" I went back because I was born there. I spent four years in the city and I did not really care for it all that much. So I decided I would go back to go fishing for a while. My dad said I could leave at any time I wanted, but I never did leave. I just stayed there. I could see there was a future for me if I really wanted to do the work and stay committed. I realized even at that time—even though I was younger—that there had to be commitment to it. Otherwise, you were not going to be successful in it. So in 1971 I started fishing with my father.

Joy Lang owns the Leland-based trap-net boat *Joy*, which is leased to the Manitou Fish Company of Leland, Michigan. Her husband, Ross Lang—a respected, longtime Lake Michigan commercial fisherman— died in a fishing accident on Lake Michigan in April 1998. Interview, 29 May 1999. Photograph by Laura Quackenbush.

Joy Lang of Leland, Michigan, recalled her late husband's family fishing history. She discussed how the need to follow the fish and adopt new target species affected her marriage and family life.[48]

Ross's father and grandfather were fishermen. Ross was a third-generation fisherman. His grandfather came from Denmark when he was fourteen, and fished on the East Coast. His grandfather, John Lang, was the original immigrant. He came over here with his brother Fred and fished on the East Coast. From there, Ross's grandfather went to Pentwater, Michigan, and ended up in Fayette. Ross's father, Fred Lang, fished for a while, went to farming and then back to fishing. Both farming and fishing were pretty much the same in terms of the time that is involved. It is always steady, but you do not make a great amount of money. He ended up going back to fishing and Ross joined his father on the lake when he was fourteen. He would fish in the summer with his father and then go back to school. He knew then that fishing was what he wanted to do and all he would ever do. He tried construction for a while when he got out of school because the money was good. Ross tried factory work downstate, but none of it appealed to him. He said the best part of the day was getting up in the morning, getting out on the lake, and seeing the sunrise. He and his father fished together from the time Ross was fourteen, so we always moved together. We came here all at the same time. It was all a whole family thing.

When I first met Ross in 1957, he was fishing out of Manistique, Michigan. When I met him that was my first involvement with fishing. I never really knew anything about it before that time, other than I used to nail together a few wooden fish boxes for an uncle who worked in a sawmill. We married in 1960 and by that time, Ross had moved to Alpena, Michigan, where he was fishing out of Thunder Bay. That was my first experience with fishing. I cannot say it was a real good experience because Ross got up at four in the morning and got back at eight at night. He was in bed at nine, so we really did not have much of a life over there. It was a hard time. Fishing was not good at that time in Lake Huron. The very early experiences I found to be very difficult. Times were so bad in Alpena I can remember eating chubs, which are basically used for smoked fish. But times were pretty lean so Ross would bring chubs home and we would boil them with onions. You just put the water and the onions in the pot with some salt, put the fish in, and bring it to a boil. That is all it required. Then we would take some butter and scorch it and put it over the top. It was marvelous. It was good eating. He always said that I worked so he could fish. It was true for a number of years. In the fishing business, it is maybe seven good years, seven bad years, but it all equals out in time.

Ross left Alpena in 1968 because the stocks were depleted in Lake Huron and he was fishing strictly chubs at that time. So he came over to Lake Michigan to see if he could find a place to fish. I remember asking him why he chose Leland. He said that he started down by Frankfort to look for a spot to dock the boat. At that time there were not many docking facilities because that is when the coho was coming into the lakes. It was a big issue with the sports fishermen. The only place he found available was here in Leland. Ross was from Fayette, Michigan, up on the Garden Peninsula. If you stand on the dock in Leland on a clear day and look northwest, you can actually see where he grew up. It is only sixty miles across the water. So when he came here, he was actually familiar with these waters because he fished out of Fayette, but on the other side of the North and South Manitou Islands. He had fished on one side and then on the other.

Ken Koyen is a commercial fisherman from Washington Island, Wisconsin. As a young man, he fished with his father, Alexander Koyen, and brother, Tom Koyen, on the fish tug *Welcome*. The Koyen family has also owned the *Sea Diver* since 1984. Interview, 3 June 1999. Photograph by Michael J. Chiarappa.

Ken Koyen of Washington Island, Wisconsin, discussed how fishing and farming became woven together as part of a family strategy to adjust to economic and social change. He described some of the other activities fishermen engaged in to supplement their income.

Commercial fishing was not part of my life plan. I went to vocational school at Green Bay for one year. I came home and was working for the ferry line. One fall day my dad said to me, "Do you want to go fishing?" I said, "Let's go," and headed for the fishing poles. I thought he meant sport fishing. He said, " No, commercial fishing." And I asked: "Can I do it?" He said, "Hold out your hand." I held out my hand. He said, "They are big enough." That was twenty-seven years ago. That was how I got my start fishing with him. I fished thirteen years with my father on board the fish tug Welcome, which was built right here in Jackson Harbor—right over here in the shed in 1926. We fished together for thirteen years. When dad died, my brother and I took up fishing. My brother is now a part-time carpenter and pours cement and I fish alone. By next spring, I will probably be the last fisherman here on the island, the way it is going.

Jake Ellefson fished with the *Miss Judy*, but that rig has been sold now. In September it will be going to Baileys Harbor. Randy Sorenson took a job with the Power Company for insurance and all the good benefits of life that fishermen do not get. I figure when the *Welcome*'s 100 years old—I think I will be seventy-three—the two of us should go fishing if I live that long. We are doing a major rebuild on it, and when we get done, it will make it.

My father got me into fishing and I will not get out until they make me get out. It was something we did together. I also farmed with him. We had always been together in the dairy farm and I liked that. I liked dairy farming, too. I custom bail hay in the summer time down about Denmark, Wisconsin. I make big square bales and last year, I was gone all but two days the month of July baling hay.

Back then, if they did not fish, they sailed. In every family from Foss to Hagen to Bjarnarson, to Jacobsen to Jensen somebody in the family fished. Back then one rig—the boat, the nets—would support four or five families. They did not have synthetic nets. The nets had to be dried every day. Now you can put them in a box, keep them out of the sun, and they will last forever. You do not even have to dry them. It is all plastic corks instead of old cedar corks and nylon maitres and monofilament, same as fish line twine, all synthetic.

The B & H Fish Company was owned by Oliver Bjarnarson and Hannes Hanneson. Lindal and Young are well-known fishing family names. The Ellefsons have been at it forever. The *Osprey* and *Rainbow* are all old boats. A lot of them are sunk now or burned. The fish tugs went from wood to putting sheet metal on them in the fall. Now they are just steel. The *Welcome* and the *Jane* are wood with steel over it. There was a time when forty-two boats fished out of Washington Island. Now we are down to four, and we own two of them.

I would not tell my sons to go fish, but yet if one of them took a real liking to fishing and decided he was going do it, I would not tell him not to because it is pretty unique. I do not solely fish for a living anymore. I would not be here. You just cannot do it. In 1971 whitefish were thirty-five cents a pound. Twenty-seven years later they might hit thirty-five cents a pound. And your costs have increased; look at the value of the dollar. The volume of fish has gone down just in the last two years. There were times when you could set for however many pounds of fish you wanted. I have picked 1,500 pounds alone in three hours.

The Gunnlaugssons made the boxes for all the fishermen on Washington Island. They would nail the bottom on and then flip it over and nail the sides. One side was a little longer for handles. After these were nailed on, you would flip the box up and make sure you got the handle on the right side because that was all there was. The handles just stuck out a little further. There was a shorter board again on the bottom. And they were so short on timber, quite often the same day the tree was knocked down, it was made into a box. So instead of the boxes weighing twenty pounds, a lot of them were forty-five or fifty pounds. Then you put 100 pounds of fish in them and about thirty pounds of ice. So they were pretty heavy.

Rick Johnson (Gills Rock, Wisconsin) reflected on the fisherman as both capitalist and worker. Johnson's father instilled in him the belief that it is better to own your own gear than to work for someone else. Rick Johnson's father worked for the Weborg family's fishery because his father had sold his fish tug, the *King*, before he started fishing.

M y father said the biggest mistake he made was when somebody offered to buy him a boat, he turned the guy down. Of course, back in those days money was tight and you did not want to stick your neck out. He said that was probably his biggest regret; he had an opportunity to become an owner of something instead of just working for somebody. He definitely likes fishing. That is all he talks about, even when he is pounding nails.

I only have one son and he is talking about being a diesel mechanic. He likes going on the boat. I have a couple daughters who probably like it more than he does. I am certainly not going to push him into it. It is something that you have to want to do because it is a tough life. Sometimes you make a lot of money and sometimes you do not make much at all. I kind of hoped that he would give it a try. He is going to work with me this summer. He worked with me last summer. And who knows?

Hopefully there are enough young guys that are crewing on fishing boats that are interested in buying in. Whether they can make enough money or get enough backing from somebody to buy other guys out would be a good question. I know there is a guy on Washington Island who just sold his fish rig to a young guy who is interested in fishing. He graduated from the University of Wisconsin at Steven's Point with a degree in fisheries biology. He worked in Alaska and somewhere out west in a hatchery. He has wanted to get into the fishing industry. I have a young guy that works for me. When we get done fishing, he goes and throws a boat in and goes out with a hook and line for the next eight hours. He just loves to be on the water. He would be another guy who might continue if he can get the backing to buy in. That is what it is going to take. I am sure there are a few sons or son-in-laws who maybe will step in.

Neil Teskie (Gills Rock, Wisconsin) indicated that fishermen had to learn skills such as the ability to envision the lake bottom and the migratory patterns of their target fish. The desire to fish and to hone one's skills as a fisherman was both learned and inherited.

You learn to think like a fish after a while because you have a picture of the bottom in your mind. You know where the banks are. You know where the hard bottom is. Now, it is a little easier with the color sounders. Before, we used to have to take a bar with a rope on it and bang it and listen to it ring or stick a little bit of grease on it to see what the bottom was like. Now, with color sounders, I can run around and see mud bottom or clay or sand or rock. So it is a little easier, but you kind of get a mental picture and it is funny how whitefish have runways. Just like deer develop patterns, there are certain runways or areas and if you set the net a certain way, it seems like it fishes better. You could be just a little off and that net will not catch as much fish. It is amazing how it seems like the fish have a certain bottom pattern or whatever. But fishermen like Mark Weborg and myself develop somewhat of a mental picture of what the bottom is like. You have to in order to set your net right, to get it in the right place.

It is a knowledge of survival. It is not as if everybody can go out and catch fish. They always say that anybody can go out and catch fish. Well, yes and no. The guys who catch the most fish develop an approach to it. They picture it. You have to have a picture of what fishing is—Mark Weborg does, I do, and my dad does. You picture what is going to happen next. You do not go out, put out a net and hope it is going to fish. You develop a pattern to the way you fish. Everybody has a little different way of doing it. But you develop a system that is a matter of economic survival. It is hard for me to really explain it because I have been doing it full time for almost thirty years now. I thought I knew a lot about fishing thirty years ago. I knew nothing compared to what I know now and I still have more to learn. It is not something that you can grasp in four years. It is not a college course that you can take in four years. It is a long-term process. If you have been at it long enough, you will develop the patterns that you want to develop for catching fish.

You are not going to learn fishing overnight. You are not going to step on the boat and say I can run out here and catch fish. There is a whole pattern to fishing. First, you have to understand you are not sitting in the boat on dry land. You are sitting on the water and everything moves. You have current and drift. You approach a buoy from a certain way because of the wind and the current. You do this a certain way, you turn the wheel a certain way. Everything is done in a rhythm. It is like a basketball player that dribbles the ball down the court naturally. It is something that a fisherman does over the years. You do it without even thinking anymore. You see the boat, you look at the net, you turn the wheel and go back about your business.

My father enjoyed his work and he was creative. He is still very creative and has good ideas. Now we have begun to disagree a little because I may know a little more about fishing than he does now or because I have learned different ways of doing things, but not a whole lot. They used to say about my dad, "Frank Teskie can catch whitefish in a mud puddle." Then a few years ago, I was ice fishing and I was doing pretty well compared to everybody else. I was catching a lot of fish through the ice. Then I heard somebody say, "Neil Teskie can catch whitefish in a toilet bowl." I said, "I followed right in my dad's footsteps. He was the mud puddle; I was the toilet bowl."

My dad intrigued me because I saw how you could do things. I saw how you could fix something with nothing. You could repair something with a piece of rope or twine or vice grips. He taught me that you have to help yourself because sometimes when you are in the fishing business and on the water, you cannot call the tow truck. You cannot call somebody else to help you. You have to be independent. You have to be able to go out and get it done yourself. There is a thinking pattern. You have to develop a thinking pattern so that you are not doing things twice or three times. You only have X number of hours in the day. So my dad taught me how to organize when fishing.

When I come home at night, I do not just park the truck. I go out and make sure boxes are ready and all my phone calls are taken care of. I make sure the ice machine is running. I make sure that the lights are on and there is fuel for the boat. There is a whole checklist. The next morning when I get up, I can go right to the boat. If not, before you know it, a half an hour or an hour is gone. I could have been catching fish all that time. So you have to be ready in the morning. You just hope that everything goes well. My family knows that this has to be done tomorrow and that has to be done now. But it is a whole way of life. That is what it is. That is what my dad taught me—fishing is a way of life.

Bill Carlson (Leland, Michigan) indicated that every fisherman combines traditional ecological knowledge with new information.

A lot of the knowledge that we have on fishing grounds and things like that was passed down. Species that are indigenous to this area, to the Great Lakes, do things for a reason—reasons we may not know—but they do not change very often. We have had to learn about the exotic species, the species that have been introduced such as the salmon, for instance. We have had to learn their habits and why they react to things. The information that has been passed down to us, on traditional spawning grounds, traditional feeding areas, the ways fish move, is information that somebody learned the hard way. We have learned the easy way. We have used other techniques in catching fish that helped us learn quite a bit.

Pound-net stakes are still in the lake from seventy-five years ago and that was a problem because they were in traditional fishing grounds. If we went to those areas to set the purse seine, we would get tangled up in the pound-net stakes. So we had to send a diver down to cut the pound-net stakes off or to untangle the purse seine. But with each new technique there is a learning curve. But historically, we still have the advantage that my father and my grandfather and my great-grandfather passed onto us that gives us a lot of shortcuts. We know where the fish should be at certain times of the year. They were not sophisticated in that they relied on water temperature. I do not think they knew why fish came up shoal. I do not think they knew why fish went deep or why they came off the bottom. We have a better feel for that. I do not even remember my father saying much about water temperature being a factor. He said he knew when the fish came up—if the pollen is on the water the whitefish will be shoal.

Now whether he associated the pollen with the whitefish coming shoal, I have no idea, but that was how he gauged when to move his nets into shoal water. If there was a lot of east wind, he would tell me: "Well, we are going to have better fishing in shallow water." But the reason was that the wind blows the surface water away from this shore and brings colder water up from the bottom and the fish are temperature oriented. Whitefish like water that is in the forties and low fifties. Lake trout like it a little bit warmer. Salmon like fifty-five degrees. We learned that because of advances made in technology.

Most of the knowledge comes from observation and trial and error—putting things together. When I started fishing, we did not have sonar. We did not have sounders to tell us what the depth was. We had a line with window weight on it and we would drop that over the side and it was marked every six feet, or every fathom, and then every ten fathoms. So when we were fishing, we would drop that line overboard to find out how deep it was, reel it back up, and that is how we knew where we were. That was how that changed. It was a lot of work back then. When they had cotton nets, they had to bring the nets in about every ten days or two weeks to dry them, scald them, treat them so they would not rot. And now we can fish nylon nets and we never have to bring them in except to repair them. They just do not deteriorate. They wear out after a while.

Mark Weborg, a fourth-generation fisherman, has fished out of Gills Rock his entire life. He noted that fishermen share certain expectations of responsibility to the craft, the fishery, and the lake.

We used to have eighteen fishermen right out of this port. Now there are three. There used to be probably sixty commercial fishermen in Door County. Now we have about eight full-time fishermen in Door County. It is down so far that we understand each other and know what we want to do. We have our own spots and keep to our areas. We are in a cooperative with four other fishermen to market the fish. We get along very well. There is no problem.

We did have some problem fishermen back a ways. That is why we have many of the rules we have today. They just did not fish right and did stupid things and as a result, we get more rules to live by. One guy fished right in the prime sports fishing area in Whitefish Bay and hardly ever lifted. He never even pulled them out. He just left them in there. The nets started floating around here, there and everywhere and they were hooking into them all over. So he is out of the business now. In fact, he is banned from even being near a fishing operation.

Joel Peterson (Fairport, Michigan) expressed admiration for his father, Hector Peterson, who refused to allow the loss of his left hand during World War II to interfere with the development of his skill as a fisherman.

My father fished with us for a number of years. My father fished all the way from 1945 until he retired in the 1980s—something for someone with one hand. He had a hook on his left hand. There was not anything that any fisherman could do that he could not do. My father had his hand blown off in the Second World War. He lost his hand in Italy during the war. There were a lot of people who were amazed with my dad. I used to bet people when I hired them. I would say, "My dad could beat you with one hand." The guy would say, "I will bet you ten bucks he cannot." I would say, "Well, wait until we get in." So we got in and we were fishing chubs and I said to my dad, "Jump in the boat here and show this guy how to dress chubs." He would take a board and nail it to the boat's wooden deck. He would grab the fish with his hand, stick it through the eyes, hold it with the hook, take the guts out, and flip him off with the knife. My dad was good at it.

When stringing nets, they always figured that if you could string a box of nets a day you were really something. Well, my dad only did half a box, but he did it on both sides. So, if he worked by himself and he strung 600 foot of net on each side that was the same as doing the whole box of nets a day with one hand. He used to catch the twine, get it through, stand on the line, hold it up with his hook and throw a double half inch on. His hand was big—it was a good size hand. He would run the boat sometimes. He went out lifting when they would say you lifted one handed, well he did. He had already lifted by himself with one hand on a gill-net boat, which is a feat. When you can lift and set that back by yourself on a gill-net boat, you have really done something. But that was his life. He had four sisters and two brothers. Besides his family, fishing was it. He never hunted. He never fished hook and line. He had his little

Bob Maynard, known around Lake Michigan as "Coho Bob," is a native of Pentwater, Michigan, and owns a local fishing tackle shop. Maynard worked as a commercial fisherman on Lake Michigan and has been a careful observer of the changes that have consumed the industry over the past seventy years. Interview, 9 June 1999. Photograph courtesy of the Great Lakes Center for Maritime Studies.

things. He would garden a little bit, but as far as hobbies, as far as us quitting at noon and grabbing the golf clubs never; my dad worked from six till four, and then he went home. Those were the days of wooden boats and iron men.

Pentwater's "Coho" Bob Maynard, a charter boat operator, recalled his earlier years as a commercial fisherman. He does not anticipate much interest in fishing by future generations.

Fishing was a serious business, a risky business, but more of a neighborly business. We who lived along Pentwater-Ludington-Manistee were quite a ways from the markets where you could sell the fish. We had to get an overnight truck. They did that up on Lake Superior, too. The lake trout they are so famous for was trucked to Chicago fish markets overnight. It was serious business and they could make a livelihood of it. It was not a get-rich you would want to hand down to your children.

The older generation has long since passed away. The boats, the docks, and the equipment they used is worn out or discontinued. So we who have lived here these many years have many kind words to say and think of the commercial fishing people.

The line of thought, the line of thinking has changed so much. We lived more hand-to-mouth and day-to-day and paycheck-to-paycheck, so to speak. It is a long way from hand-to-mouth to the computer age. It is difficult for me to understand now. Now people think of computers, resorts and golf. The new generation coming up will have to learn totally different trades; they have to think of computers instead of thinking how to mend the nets. The way the world is running, I cannot see any increase in commercial fishing per se as a family. Kids grow up learning about computers rather than how to mend or repair a net, or fix the boat if it was not working just right. The line of thought is entirely different.

Kenneth Peterson (Fairport, Michigan) discussed how fishing has changed during his lifetime. Fishermen from his native Garden Peninsula traveled around the lakes searching for good fishing grounds.

There are probably more fishermen here than any port on Michigan. I would not say there are more boats, but there are more fishermen who own their own rigs. Once you are a fisherman, you would not want to be anything else really. You are your own boss for one thing. If you did not want to go out, you did not have to go. When my dad was a young fellow, he used to like to drink once in a while. If he did not feel good, he did not go out the next day. He stayed home in bed because he did not feel good. But he did not miss too many days. Nowadays, the younger generation is used to getting this fifteen to twenty dollars an hour. It is pretty hard to get them to work for you. You cannot pay them as much as they got to have in order to live, not on a fishing rig you cannot. You have too much expense. By the time you pay your expenses and your hired help, you have got nothing left for yourself unless you are awful lucky. You got to have a few good years where you are a little lucky and then you can make it. You can coast a little bit through the years if you watch yourself a little.

I like to fish the area right here off Fairport. When I was a kid, I used to like to move around with my dad. We fished out of Munising, Detour, and Sault Ste. Marie. We went to Manistique, the Manitous, and Fox Island. That was as far as he went. Of course, that was my dad trying to keep the screw going. Those men worked for three dollars a day, and you got good fishermen in those days, too. They could string nets, slug nets, fish, and set nets. In fact, there was not hardly a man on a boat that did not know the ranges and the time on your buoys. They all knew that. They all made it their business to know. In case they had to take the boat out, well they knew where the net was. That was the real sunshine of the fisherman game, the fishing game then, in the older days. Everybody was just as good as the captain. Of course, it was hard times then too; three dollars a day was lots of money at that time.

Fishing is interesting. There is something different every day. My dad had his eighty-third birthday just before he died. He said, "I learned something all the time, fishing." Somebody does something different and you learn that way. But he says you never know everything, because there is always something new comes up. It is true that you learn something new every time. I learn a lot of new stuff, new things about fishing pound nets or trap nets that make it a little easier on yourself.

A guy by the name of Reuben Nelson used to fish pound nets out of Fairport. He was always thinking up some way to make it easier on himself. And he had his pound-net boat rigged up he could go out there and set a net all by himself if he wanted. Reuben Nelson and I used to sit and talk for hours at a time. He showed me how to string twine. He had pound nets, too. He found different ways of hanging the twine that made a little difference in the fishing and he showed me all that stuff. I helped him a little bit, too. He fished out of Sand Bay up here. Sand Bay is just really a couple little points up from Fairport, with a little sandy bay. That was where his fish rig, house, shed, and field were. Then he moved down to Bayfield, Wisconsin. He had a boathouse for each boat. He had one big enough that he could pull a couple yachts in there for the winter. He would pull out his trap-net boats or pound-net boats and set them up in a little shed. He had a beautiful field there that he would lay his twine out in and he treated it. It was nice. Of course, he had all synthetic twine, too, and he did not really have to treat that much. He was always thinking, that guy. He was always looking for an easier way out.

Alan Priest, who began fishing in the early 1970s, discussed the knowledge and skills necessary to survive as a commercial fisherman.

Y ou have to learn the banks. Certain spots produce better in the summer than they do in the fall. Over the years, you just learn which spots produce better at certain times of the year and at what depth of the water. You keep a logbook. Ever since I started running the boat, I have had a big binder I call a logbook. I write down every day when we leave the dock. Sometimes I write the weather conditions, although I have gotten away from that a little bit. While we are lifting nets, I always have the sounder on so I can see where we are catching most of our fish. So, when you set back, you put most of your nets in that depth. But you do not concentrate on that depth. Say the fish are in fifty-seven to sixty fathoms. Well, you might start out in sixty-three, go down to forty-nine, and then go down to fifty-seven, fifty-eight, fifty-nine, or sixty, and set seven or eight boxes in that depth. You always have two or three that are up above or deeper because the chubs move up and down the bank.

Right now, fishing is terrible because I think they are off the bottom. There are no chubs being caught on Lake Michigan right now to speak of. We are averaging between 300 and 500 pounds a lift and those nets are a week out. Last year, if I had left my nets out a week, we would have had 1,500–1,600 pounds. I was fishing fewer nets. I was fishing two five-box gangs and this year, I am fishing two tens. With those nets I was catching between 700 and 1,000 pounds a lift. I was going out every three nights. I was catching 600 pounds a lift at Empire. I had my gangs close together. They were only about a mile apart. If I lifted one gang and had enough time, I would go over and lift a couple boxes off the other gang. This way, I would not have such a long day the next day. The fish were thick last year. At this point, they are not.

You just keep plugging away and keep trying. It does not pay to move around too much. In the wintertime, we try to fish close to home. There is a place called the Northeast Channel bank, which is off the northeast corner of North Manitou Island. It is about an hour and ten minutes out because of the weather. It blows just about every day starting the end of October, until the ice is out or spring comes. It is very rare, but we fished the last three winters, all winter. It is very seldom that we get to do that. The harbor freezes up with ice every once in a while. Then we take the boat up, turn it around at the falls, get her pointed down the river, and just give her the berries. We can go through lots of ice. When you hit the ice with the bow, you feel it. Then you give her the throttle and the tug goes up and breaks the ice. Always make sure you have a clear spot behind the boat so you do not get stuck. You can turn around, but it will take time. But right here in the harbor, we can get through anything that will build up. The problem is with the snowdrifts. I call them snowballs. You start with a snowflake and then it will freeze and roll. You can get some snowballs as big as a fish shed. You get a southwest wind and the snow just packs in here. You have to be careful if you are out on the lake and you get ice drifting around—you have to get home. Usually, we were pulled out by then and taking a break. Then if the wind shifts or you get a good forecast, then we will go out and set again. But about that time, you are ready for a break because we screen chub eggs for caviar in the fall—starting the first part of December through February or middle of March depending on how your season is.

On the way out in the morning, I will get the logbook from two years ago or a year ago and see what we were catching and where we were. Usually, you can remember because you do it enough times. But you think you are setting on a bank and you got it and you have known it for years and all of a sudden: where did the bank go? It has disappeared. Well, there is a turn in it I never saw. Or you were going down at a different angle or you were coming up at a different angle and it comes up too soon. You never stop learning about it. That is probably the one reason why I like to stay with it. And I am my own boss. If I do not produce I do not make any money.

Well, there have been many times I probably should have gotten out of it. Money is not the whole issue. You have to survive, but we are doing okay. We do not want a new car every couple years. My truck is eleven years old. I have over 200,000 miles on her. It is still ticking. It is simple. One of the reasons why I stay with fishing is because it is just like farming. You are going to have good years and bad years. Right now, this is turning into kind of a mediocre year but the fish could hit tonight in the nets. So I could go out Tuesday and have 1,000 pounds. You just never know. That is another thing I like. You just never know.

————————

Joel Peterson (Fairport, Michigan) observed how fishermen are often united by a collective mindset or management perspective and mutual respect.

I can see the Weborgs when we are out. I know where the Weborgs went today and lifted their nets is near where we were lifting. We were right off of Washington Island. We know the Weborgs and the boys across the lake. We know the boys here. We know them up on Lake Superior. There are so few of us left that you know everybody. It is sad because there are a few less every year. Take Ross Lang for example. He never had any sons to take over his end. He was only going to fish for another year or so and was going to retire. You have to like what you are doing. Hopefully, you can make a living out of it. My son, Steve, is a pretty good welder. He is not married yet and likes to play around here. He likes the freedom. They go over to Washington Island with the boat to party almost every weekend.

I think fishermen have a common bond. I guess fishermen overall probably bond together or stick together. You are in the same profession. You are battling the elements. You are battling politics, because when you get down into it, you start pitting the sportsmen against the commercial fishermen. Then they try to pit the Native American fishermen against the fishermen. When it gets down to it, a Native American fisherman is nothing but a state fisherman who was put out of business, and had to fall back upon something else to stay in business. You respect other fishermen. I think that is probably the one thing that is not important in a lot of other jobs. I respect each one of these guys. They have their own right to fish. One might be a half-assed fisherman, another guy is a fairly good fisherman, and this guy is an excellent fisherman. Competition is the name of the game. If you are out there and it is blowing twenty miles an hour, I will probably be alongside of you. You do not see that in many professions any more. At the end of the day you can walk in, sit down, and have a beer together and talk about what kind of a day it was. That is probably another reason why you will never get anybody to say anything bad about your fellow fishermen all over the lake. There is some mutual respect amongst us all.

Paul Goodman (Washington Island, Wisconsin) has worked both in commercial fishing and as a charter boat operator.

You are not going to see a lot of young people getting into the fishery. When they went into the quota system, they eliminated any young upstarts. It is too much for anybody to buy into it. The quota system really eliminated anybody from getting into it. There might be somebody who comes by, thinks it is a good life, and buys somebody's rig out. But the guys who buy those rigs better watch real close to make sure they sell before it goes past a certain point, because it can change real quick on them. Fishing can change in two years' time.

When I was commercial fishing, I loved it. I was out there and did not have to deal with people. I thought it was the greatest thing in the world. Now, I am dealing with people and am finding out people are pretty good. There are some pretty nice people out there, so it is not that bad. But they can get on your nerves if you are not catching a fish and they ask you 300 times where are the fish? But as a general rule, I think commercial fishing is great. You get up and are able to do different kind of things. You do not really have other people around and you are with your crew. I had a good time. I have pictures of being on the boat. I look at the pictures of the sunsets and there is no doubt, I had some pretty good times out there. It is hard on your family life because it is like an addiction. Fishing is a little bit like an addiction. Sport fishing is too, but commercial fishing is just as much. It is like going gambling, but not really gambling. The more nets you set the more you catch. How much do you want to do? You can get so you are working day and night. You have to control it and control yourself so that you are working sanely. I have only known a couple people that can go fishing for a certain amount of hours a day, go home and have a home life. But the rest of them do not seem to. All your friends end up being just commercial fishermen. If we ever get together with our wives, all we talk about is commercial fishing. The women hate that. But if you lost it, you would definitely lose a way of life—you would lose some of the culture. There is no doubt about it. I think that a time will come when it will happen.

When I became a charter fishing boat captain, I was surprised that nobody even mentioned it to me. I have been in both industries. When I am on a commercial boat— I help out once in a while—and a sport fish shows up in the nets dead the crew will joke about it saying, "There is one of yours." They know that I see the bigger picture. One fish here and there, or even a few fish does not make a difference. Some sportsmen will see you catch two or three fish in a net and they will say, "Oh man, you are ruining the fishery. It is the end of the world." That is how they are. But I know what kind of volume is out there. I do not think the incidental catch affects me as a charter boat operator.

According to Joy Lang, her husband, the late Ross Lang of Leland, Michigan, undertook special precautions when fishing in winter.

People often speak of the danger of being a commercial fishermen. I never felt that
danger because Ross always assured me that these boats would not fall apart. They
roll out there and have been in some terrible weather. I have been down at the dock
when they came in and all you could see was the antenna from the radio sticking out—
right at the dock in Leland Harbor. I have been down there when everybody in town
was down there with our lights on to guide them in at night, but I never, ever felt that
he was in danger because he was in control. He knew when it was time to cut the lines
and come home.

Daniel "Pete" LeClair (Two Rivers, Wisconsin) recalled the dangers of pound-net
fishing. He described the toll fishing took on the health of those who worked out on
the lake day after day, particularly before power lifters and other mechanical devices
became commonplace on board Great Lakes fishing vessels.

I puked for two summer vacations. My ma said, "You better not let that kid go. There
will not be anything left of him. He does not eat, then he eats and pukes it out." But
how are you going to get tough? You have to get over it. Two years after I graduated,
I puked everything before I got used to it.

It was cold working on the pound-net boat. At the most, the pound nets were set
two miles off shore. The deepest nets set by my father were in ninety feet of water. At
the time, I think my father was the only one pound-net fishing here. The posts were
long and hard to handle. If you got a storm they would tip over, but that was where
the fish were. So they innovated with their own equipment so they could fish in that
depth of water where the fish were. But it was very expensive and very dangerous handling these big poles on the lake when the boat is rolling around or in any sea. It got
to be a pretty dangerous operation. Three or four people worked in the pound-net boat.

My dad's hands all tightened up from pulling on the pound-net ropes. On pound
nets, all you do is pull. And if you could not pull, they would say you have got to pull.
They would pull and they broke all their tendons in their hands. Their hands were all

broken up and bruised. My dad could not even open his fingers to get a cup of water in it. He had to get his cut because his hands just closed right up. He had to cut his tendons so he could straighten his fingers back out. Fishing from an early age, their hands were all the same. They all had busted their tendons. All your tendons would give out on you. As you get older, they just close up. Mine are not that bad; they have been staying about the same. But the old-time fishermen that fished pound nets in the earlier years—it was always by hand. Later on, they got hydraulic neck drums to pull the rope. But in the earlier years, the fishermen really, really worked hard. It was a rough way to make a living. As fishing went on, they innovated and got better equipment. They used to pull gill nets by hand. When my great-grandfather started, they would go to the front of the boat and go to the back of the boat and then they would go back to the front of the boat and pull again until they got to the back of the boat. They left the nets on the deck. So it was all pulling by hand. Now they have the net lifter. That is how the fishery grew and got better.

"Coho" Bob Maynard, a retired charter boat captain who also worked in commercial fishing, noted that conditions on the lakes could be so hazardous that commercial fishermen would have to pull or even cut their nets and head ashore, resulting in a lost or diminished catch.

Way back we did not have the weather reports or radio contact. You had to depend on your weather-eye. This involved looking at the sky, watching the temperature, and watching the barometer drop. If the barometer started to drop suddenly, you better head for shore. You better head for safe shelter. But if you were out there working on a fish tug lifting nets and you had a little bit more to go, you might try it get it done and then head for home. The problem was, sometimes you did not pull the nets quick enough and you got caught out in the storm. There were many folks who met their fate on the lake. Historically, there are many stories. In 1940, the November eleventh storm, was when the Cross brothers boat went out and rescued eighteen people on the Canadian boat the *Novaduct*, which had gone aground. The fishermen themselves were the ones who did the hard work and got the credit for the rescue.

Joel Peterson of Michigan's Garden Peninsula has been involved in commercial fishing his entire life. He discussed how the weather and conditions on Lake Michigan affected fishermen.

There are still a few really hard-core fishermen such as Charlie Nylund in Menominee. He is a card. We always called him "Charlie Rough Water." He is a genuine, true, 100 percent fisherman. Weather is not a factor with this boy. But he is getting up there. He is about sixty-five now, but I would say he fishes eighty-five percent as hard now as he did when he was thirty or forty. I fished with him for one summer. He is a terror. There is no weather on Lake Michigan that will intimidate him, none.

Alan Priest, who began fishing in the 1970s with the late Ross Lang, noted that running time and danger in severe weather are costs commercial fishers must absorb.

We can go west to the Wisconsin border. We can go north from the middle of Lake Michigan, a little bit past Point Betsie, up to the sanctuary, and that was it. But it does not pay to fish any farther because of what we are running right now. It takes us two hours and forty-five minutes to get to Empire when we are fishing in that area. To get to one bank—I call it the outside of the outside bank at Empire—is three hours. So you have six hours running time and if you catch any fish, you are looking at getting done at nine-thirty or ten o'clock at night. I have not had a crew that is worth anything for years because fishing does not pay a lot of money. There are no benefits with it. You have to do it because you love it. And that is how I am. I make a living, but I cannot go out and be luxurious. But I love the water. I always have, ever since I was small. We used to joke about it. Ross Lang made up the saying, "Fishing is a boat ride and a picnic every day." Then we would laugh. People think we just go out and bring the fish in. They do not have a clue what is involved. Mother Nature plays a big part. If we could spread the spring days around into the fall and winter, it would make life a lot more pleasant.

To me, fishing offers a sense of freedom. You leave when the sun is coming up and it is beautiful. You get out on the water a ways and the sun is coming up. Then, all of a sudden, I am still out here and the sun is going down. It puts you in a kind of awe. It is also a bit of a challenge because we will be out there lifting and the water can be flat as the floor. Two hours later, you are lifting and you can have a four-foot sea wall. By the time you are done, they can be eight- and ten-footers. Then it is a challenge to set your nets back and keep lifting.

The worst sea I was ever in was with Ross Lang and Fred Lang in the *Frances Clark*. We left that morning and it was blowing hard, probably twenty knots. We had Ross's brother, Kent, with us. Our nets were on the northwest corner of North Manitou Island. We went out between the islands and then went north to the buoy on the backside of the island. The wind was blowing southwest and continued to pick up. I was throwing up. I was seasick looking out the window. We would go up on a great big wave and you could see North Manitou Island and everything else. Then, you would go down and all you could see was the next wave coming. It was about ten or eleven o'clock. The Carlsons and the Bucklers were out that day too. The Carlsons called and said they were heading in. A little while later, the Bucklers called. They were heading in. We were the only ones out there. The Langs were tough fishermen. They really stuck it out. They worked hard at it. Their boat was always the first boat out in the morning.

One wave hit us on the lee side of the boat, and halfway filled the lifter door with water. All you could see was green. A little while later, another wave hit us on the lee side of boat. Water filled the whole door up. All you could see was green. We took on about 50 to 60 gallons of water boom, just like that. Ross looked at Fred and Fred looked at Ross. The Langs did not have to say a word. They both knew it was time to go home. We used to have a knife stuck in the ceiling. Fred pulled it down, handed Ross the knife and Ross cut his nets off. We had about a box and a half to lift yet. Fred, who never wheels a boat—he always let Ross do it—wheeled all the way home and into the harbor.

We tried to go home on our course to the backside of the island. The waves hit us. The wind was coming from the southwest. It hit us and turned us right around. So we had to go on the north end of the island, cut back in the lee of the island, and then head fair wind home. In the lee of the island, it was blowing so hard that it was blowing the tops off the waves. There was a ten-foot sea in the lee of the island. We got out in the channel and it looked like it was snowing because it was just blowing the tops right off the waves. When we got in the harbor, the *Enterprise*, the local paper, was down there. They took a picture of us. All you could see of the boat was the top of the cubicle and a great big sea in front of us and a great big sea behind us. That was the only time that I had seen Fred's wife meet the boat at the dock. A lot of people were down here. We came in and Fred and Ross did not make any big deal of it—it was another day on the lake.

———————————

Brian Price, a former commercial fisherman, spoke about the relationship between the commercial fishing industry and fisheries resources.

Fishing is a unique kind of profession. There was a time when lots of epithets were thrown at commercial fishermen as being the people that rape the lake, take and take and take, and never put anything back. The fishermen are competitive not only with each other, but with themselves personally. They want to catch more fish than they did last year. They want to be more efficient about their operation. They want to use better equipment. They want to have a nicer boat. They want to have a well-oiled crew. They want people to respect what they do. That means that they continue to improve their efficiency and improve their catch from year to year to year. And unlike a farmer, who can delineate the 360-acre field that was his and plan for the long term, fishermen cannot do that. If I do not go out and take those fish that are available in April or this month, the next guy is going to.

There was a long period of time when fishermen were basically cowboys. They could move anywhere they wanted, take anything they wanted. There were very few restrictions on gear. For a hundred years, in response to one crisis after another, the state has placed restrictions on gear, closed seasons to protect certain spawning fish stocks, and created lake trout refuges not subjected to commercial fishing. Some state action has come at the request of the fishermen. I cannot tell Bill Carlson where to fish but the state can. I am his competitor, if he does not go out and get fish I am going to. Reasonable restrictions have been put in place, often with the encouragement of the fishing industry.

———————————

Ben Peterson (left), of Fairport, Michigan, on the Garden Peninsula, is a member of the fifth generation of Petersons who have made their living from commercial fishing. Interview, 4 June 1999. Photograph courtesy of the Great Lakes Center for Maritime Studies.

Ben Peterson now lives in Manistique, Michigan. He has fished the waters off Michigan's Garden Peninsula most of his life. His discussed how his reasons for fishing and the way he fishes have changed over the course of his life.

My nephew Steve and I both like the powerboat. When we get done, we take off in our powerboats. In the wintertime when I am not working, I take off for Mexico and I fish hook-and-line down there. I spend ninety percent of my time on the water. I like the water. When I was younger, I wanted to hurry up and get done. All the time, it was hurry up and get done. There are good, bad days. It is getting better as we go. You learn it. You get systems and get things worked out. You learn how to do it and it gets easier. There is still some work, unloading and loading the fish. The hardest part is handling the fish, moving them around back and forth. There is a lot of lifting. We try to come up with easier ways to do it, but sometimes, it just takes more time.

We know the commercial fishermen all around this area and pretty much the whole state. We know most of the guys in Wisconsin, too. Commercial fishermen are pretty much close-knit people. We lie when we are not catching fish and we lie when we are catching fish. You do not want anybody to know what you are getting because they will be right there.

A fisherman will do anything to fish. He will go anywhere. My grandpa went out to the coast when he was about fifteen or sixteen years old. That says a lot. The only fishermen I know of that stayed here through it all was the Devet brothers. There were two Devet brothers up here and my father. They fished down here for I do not know how many years with just a couple boats. Gordon Berbeau fished here also. But most of the other guys come and went and left. My dad had the whole family here. There were six kids. My dad lost his left arm in World War II, so he wore a hook on this hand. He was pensioned from the service. He got enough of a pension for us to survive. And he fished his butt off. It was like my dad had a point to prove all his life; he was going to make this thing work. So he stayed here.

When fishing was real bad there for a while, my grandfather and my uncle were fishing sheepshead in Lake Winnebago. They were down there for maybe ten years or so. When the fish started picking up, they came back here and they did real good. My dad did real good in the pound-net business. My grandpa started the fish buying business here. That was in the latter part of the 1960s. I can remember when I was a kid and we did caviar with him. We made caviar out of the chub roe. I think he retired out of the business when he was about eighty-two. My brother and I just kind of took it over. He wanted us to have it. So then we built this place. We had a fish house exactly like this one and a fire started in it. We had other buildings, too, and the fire burned everything down about 1975. So then we rebuilt and started all over.

I live on the family homestead in what was my grandfather's house. I only fish Manistique for the spring and then I will be back in Fairport. This year is a little different. I am back and forth like a yo-yo. I am all over the place. There is a lot of fish out there. There is a certain amount of luck involved. You never get rich, just make a living. I do not care what you do, if you go out here in the spring of the year and you have a really good spring, it seems like you have a terrible fall. Last year we had a terrible spring and a terrible summer and we were all starting to sweat it out a little bit and all of a sudden, fall came and September came and we just had a great September and it all worked out. We have been probably more fortunate or more lucky than most. When we make a dollar we put it back into the business, too. We buy new nets. We buy boats. We buy fillet machines, whatever it takes.

Don Bell, Jr. of Cheboygan, Michigan, is the third generation of his family to work in commercial fishing. Today, Bell focuses on the wholesale and retail sale of Lake Michigan fish. Interview, 28 May 1999. Photograph courtesy of the Great Lakes Center for Maritime Studies.

Don Bell, Jr. fishes out of Mackinaw City, Michigan. He emphasized how fishing continues to be affected by a multitude of factors outside of the control of the fisherman.[49]

I am the third generation in the business. My grandfather started out on the Cheboygan River in Cheboygan, Michigan. Back in 1949 my dad bought the place in Mackinaw City. I was only four years old when we moved to Mackinaw, so I spent all my school years here. Two other people had fish businesses in Mackinaw City before we bought it. August 1999 will make fifty years for us. We have seen a lot of ups and downs over the years. Back in the late 1940s and early 1950s you had the problem with the lamprey eels. We had to get fish sent in all the way from Lake Winnipeg to survive. Then they controlled the lampreys pretty well and the whitefish started coming back real strong. Then the DNR started planting lake trout back in the lakes. The lake trout have not reproduced on their own, so all the lake trout are planted. Then there was the botulism scare back in 1963. The lakes have their ups and downs. The lake level is way down. Last summer's production was the worst I have seen in a long time because the water temperature was warm all summer. The lakes were so warm, even Lake Superior. Normally, people swim in Lake Superior about three or four times in the summer. Last year, the people up there were swimming every day. Around the Fourth of July weekend, we were not getting much fish around here because the fish were going way out, too deep, where they could not find them.

Rick Johnson reflected on the thinning ranks of commercial fisherman working on Wisconsin's Lake Michigan waters. He maintained that for many, fishing was a business. He recognized that for others, working on the waters was an expression of self, family, and community.

The more fishermen you have, the more nets are out there. Trying to find a spot to set used to be a real chore. It used to look like a cedar forest out there with buoy staffs. Now, from a fishing standpoint, you can run anywhere and you never have anybody set over the top of your nets. It makes it a lot easier to fish now. You wish it was not getting as sparse as it is now. It is down to a real core group, which is good because you have mainly businessmen and guys doing it for a living. But by the same token, you think about the future of it. Is anybody else looking to get back into it? And if they do, will they get trampled too? If the numbers get down too low, the opportunities for somebody like that are limited. So there is some concern for the future.

There have been a few times where I thought something else sounded pretty good. For the guys that are in it right now, fishing is a business. It is still a tradition, but it is not as much as it used to be. There is a guy who fishes with me who is going to be ninety years old in June. He lives to fish. He goes to Florida in the wintertime. When he comes back, he is not in his house ten minutes before he is calling to find out what time the boat is going out the next day. He does not need any more money; he has made enough money in his lifetime. But to him fishing is a way of life. Hopefully, when I am ninety years old, if I get that old, I will be somewhere where it is nice and warm. I do not know. I guess it is a different perspective. I know I do not have the tradition that he does as far as wanting to be on that boat day after day. That is his life, right there, the water. He has slipped quite a bit in the last two years or so. But before that, up until about three years ago, I would have taken him over just about anybody around here as far as being on the lake. He would have been eighty-seven then. I have to give him credit for sticking it out. He was out there today, rolling around at eighty-nine years old. I kind of take him for granted. When you look at him you do not think eighty-nine. When you sit and think about it, to be rolling around on a gill-net tug on a day like today, is quite an accomplishment.

Rick Johnson discussed the relationship between commercial and sport fishers in northern and southern Wisconsin.

Our relations with sports fishermen are great. I cannot think of a time when we have had a real serious problem. Most of them are our neighbors. Quite a few of them such as Paul Goodman, Roy Elkquist, and Lyle Teskie were commercial fishermen. Gary Gross never owned a license, but he did commercial fishing. There are a couple more in Baileys Harbor. We try to stay out of their way. We know that they have a business to run just like we do. Most of the problems between sport and commercial fishermen occur from Two Rivers and south for some unknown reason. I cannot understand it. Obviously, a lot of the radical sports fishermen are from down in that area and the guys up here are a little more laid-back.

We have tried to do our part for the sport fishery. We have planted lake trout. Probably five or six years ago the commercial fishermen built Astroturf mats at our own expense for the planting of lake trout. I built them all for the first two years. We built the crates, bought the matting, and took the boats down to Algoma and harvested the lake trout. We had DNR people along. They stripped the eggs and fertilized them. Then we brought them in and put them in these mats. We figured we planted over seven million lake trout off the Jacksonport reefs. So obviously, the commercial fishermen are not just there taking. We try to put back and do things in the community too. Up at this end of the Door Peninsula, the relationship is real good as far as I know.

Lyle Teskie discussed the transition of Door County, Wisconsin, from agriculture and fishing to tourism. In his view, escalating property values and increased taxes helped to drive fishing families from the lakeshore.

Now there is a whole different ballgame in Door County. I live in a beautiful place. The taxes I pay are because of the view; they are not based on the value of what the land is worth because of the fishing. I live in my grandmother's house; it means a lot to me. But if somebody were to buy it—the price that they would pay for that piece of land is astronomical—they would bulldoze it and put up a new house. But see, the reason why it is so valuable is because of the scene, the view. But that is only for people who sell the land. I want to keep it for my family. We ought to pay taxes, but once they start to take the land away from you—your heritage from your children—it gets to the point where it is a little ridiculous. I am a law-abiding citizen, but if I am taxed out of here and my family has to sell it because they cannot afford it, no longer will there be any Teskies here to tell anybody about how dad used to fish. That is the way I look at it.

Neil Teskie, who has been fishing out of Gills Rock, Wisconsin, since 1971, maintained that the state should weigh the historical and cultural significance of commercial fishing and the knowledge of those who made their livelihood on the lake, and not evaluate it strictly from an economic perspective.

I do not know if they are real proud of it, but the DNR uses us to help take scale samples and monitor other species. We are one of their tools. If they want to go find out how many whitefish are out there, what the stocks are, they come along and they ride with us. If they want to monitor lake trout populations, they set pound nets and tag them down in Sturgeon Bay. They do not have all the resources that they need to operate and collect the data; they collect a lot of data through us. I have met with them and we have talked with them and we have tried to work through our problems together. It has gotten better over the years because we realize we need each other in some ways. It is not a cut-and-dried thing. Commercial fishing is more than just an industry to me. It is a history. It is something that should be passed on. I do not know if there are any men out there who are going to pick it up. When you are talking to me and the Weborgs, you might be talking to some of the last generation of fishermen. Maybe some younger guys will step in. I would like to see it preserved. I never want to see it die. It is a piece of history.

They always say fishing is in the blood. There is something to that. You cannot do it to make money. You can do it to make a living. Sometimes the living is good; sometimes it is poor. It is the law of averages. You do not get poor at it but you work more than forty hours a week. You work a lot longer and have to wear many, many hats.

You have to think about the days that you have when you can provide that joy for yourself or for somebody else. It is kind of a joyful experience to take somebody out there and say, "Here is what I do." There is more than just that buoy on the water and the fish in the store. This is how it is done. People need to be aware there is a real technique to being a commercial fisherman. I am not saying that to elevate anybody or myself, but you have to really know what you are doing. The guys who are in it for a living really know what they are doing. I like to take people out on the journey or take them up in the field and show them a net or whatever I can do so they understand that there is more to it than just buying the fish in the store. There is a man behind this. There is a family behind it. There is a history behind it. There is generation after generation behind the fish in the store. Many of the men and women of this area who are natives have somebody in their family who fished. There was fishing, farming, and logging here. The guy across the road here bought his farm through fishing. There is a whole past and I would like to see a whole future in it.

---

2. Making a Living: The Necessity
of Economic Adaptation

Bill Carlson is a member of a family that has been fishing out of Leland, Michigan, for four generations. The decline of fishing on Lake Michigan in the 1940s and 1950s prompted the family to increasingly supplement its fishing income with other economic activities such as real estate investment.

The fishing collapsed in this area in the 1940s. The lamprey eel took a devastating hold on the whitefish and lake trout. We were getting eighty percent scarring on the fish, which means the mortality rate was just enormous. Whitefish and trout were the bread and butter of the fishery. Our family struggled in the late 1940s and early 1950s. We switched our fishing techniques to fishing chubs. There was not a lot of money in fishing chubs, but it was a life. I remember my father getting other work as a hunting guide. He worked as a carpenter. He took care of people's yards and had a catering business. He tended bar. My mother opened a bakery. My father's sister had a restaurant in town and my mother went to work there. We did whatever we had to do, but we continued fishing. We were fortunate in that we had summer residents up here who came down and bought fish regularly. There was a bit of a tourist business at that time, too. So in the summertime, we were able to sustain ourselves by selling the fish directly to the consumer rather than shipping it in large volumes out of state or to processors. But a lot of the year, we were not fishing because there was either no market, no money, or no fish.

We switched from large mesh nets catching whitefish and trout, to smaller mesh nets in deeper water to catch chubs. We have continued to do so with the exception of when we were put out of business several times for different reasons. But we always were able to maintain ourselves and keep our boat, equipment, and property. It was a struggle through the 1950s and the early 1960s. Later in the 1960s fishing and the tourist business started to bounce back here a little bit. We started to do a little more direct consumer sales. I got involved on a full-time basis in the very late 1960s, about the time that the Department of Natural Resources decided that they were going to manage the resource for the sportsman because they offered the state the highest economic return. The DNR decided to set up certain criteria for being able to fish commercially. They set the criteria retroactively, so a lot of people did not qualify to continue to fish. At one time, we had eight fishing operations out of here. But the late 1960s, it was down to three. By 1970, it was down to two.[50]

We are pretty unique in that this has been our fishing area for over 100 years—for 125 years or more. We have not moved out of here except for some short periods of time when fishing got so bad back in the 1950s, and we moved to southern Lake Michigan to fish down there. But we continued to fish here part of the year. We took our boat and went to Saugatuck for a few years, and fished whitefish out of there. Leland has always been our homeport and our traditional base. A lot of the fishermen had to move around to different parts of the lake if they wanted to continue their business, but we have not had to do that. When fishing was really tough in the late 1960s, it took a while to try to figure out what to do. In the 1970s, I was pretty much operating the business with my father, though he was taking less and less part in it. In order to get the greatest economic return, I felt that we had to move our business into selling directly to the consumer. The highest economic return would be to catch the fish, process them yourself, and move them right to the consumer. So our business went that direction. We put in a store in Traverse City, which was the closest metropolitan area. We developed our tourism business here in Leland a lot more. We bought what property in Fishtown was available, and there was some available because of the fishermen being put out of business. We felt our future was in retail and local wholesale. And that is how we were able to stay in business and actually thrive in the business. The plan has worked well and still does, though our local wholesale business to restaurants is not very large anymore.

We have developed new products and new processing techniques. We have developed new markets, but all on a local basis. What we have found is that we have to stay as small as possible to run this as a family operation and hire seasonal help. If the overhead is too large, you get to a point of diminishing returns. We used to have twelve full-time employees processing and distributing. The workers' compensation rate for people in the fishing industry is twenty-three or twenty-five percent of the wage. You cannot operate on that. We are just a small family operation, basically operating seasonally. My brother has a store in Traverse City, which operates year around. My son works on a year-round basis here. But our Leland market is open from May through October. Our commercial operation, our chub fishing operation, goes year round but that is it. We have tried to find where we get our best bottom line and it has been direct to the consumer. Quality is number one, but you have to keep the overhead down. You have to be your own mechanic; carpenter, electrician, and plumber. You have to be able to do all those things yourself because you cannot live with the overhead costs.

As things come up, you face them and try to figure them out. I do not try to guess the future and worry anymore. I spent a third of my life worrying about whether I would be in business tomorrow or not. It is nothing you can worry about. It just makes you old fast. What I have found is that if it is out of your control, you do what you can with your resources. Then you just have to let it happen and adjust to it. We stopped putting all our eggs in one basket a long time ago. Fishing is not the only thing we have in our life anymore.

Elaine Johnson established herself in the fishing business at a time when commercial fishing stocks such as lake trout and whitefish were severely depleted. Johnson remained in the commercial fishing business because she helped to create a market for those types of fish that were still plentiful.

We had a little fishing business going in 1953. There was a fisherman by the name of Robby Keduncle who was really kind of a character to our town. We fished with him. He taught us how to set gill nets, spin them, slug them, and lift them. There were very, very few whitefish so we fished perch. He showed us how to pick perch. I never really was crazy about a tug. You are all enclosed. More or less, I was sick every day but I would not give up. A lot of times if my butt had not been so big, I would have crawled out through the porthole and swam to shore. We fished with Robby, and bought the perch from him. We processed everything he caught because there were not any whitefish.

Then we thought we could fish. We borrowed a little seventeen-foot skiff from a fellow that lived on the beach. We had some perch nets and our uncle had a five-horse outboard engine. We would go out to Sister Island, about three miles off shore down from Sister Bay. We would set our perch nets around the island there. We would take fish orders. There was a place down the road called the Hillside. It is different than what it is now. When we first started to sell perch up there, there were no perch fries. We went in the Hillside to sell these perch and I said, "How about doing some perch fries?" The owner really was not too excited about the idea, but I talked her into it. She finally conceded by agreeing she would take five pounds. Her husband was standing behind her and he held up ten fingers. We brought her ten pounds on Thursday. When she saw the ten pounds of perch she just hit the ceiling. I said, "What you do not use I will take back." The perch plate was seventy-five cents and you got a glass of beer with it. Of course, they just went like hotcakes. By the time we quit bringing perch to her, she was up to seventy-five to eighty pounds a week, every week. So, the perch fries really started at the C and C, Swedes, and Johnny's Cottage, which is Sister Bay Cafe now.

We had a place up in the country called Bastian's Nursing Home for old-timers, old fishermen. On Thursday, they would wait for our little truck to come in with the fish. They had a bunch of chairs or seats sitting in a row on each side of the sidewalk, and they would all be waiting there for us when we came with the fish. Then they would want to talk about the old days, the old fishing. They talked about how ice fishing went, how they used to set hooks, and that kind of fishing. Each one of them had an interesting story, but you heard the same story week after week. I could not understand it then, but I do now.

Don Stiller, a commercial fisherman from Wisconsin, recalled how the family fishery responded to the alewife problem in Lake Michigan and Green Bay.

The alewife made a great difference in the fishery. The first alewife I saw was in 1955, and they kept getting thicker and thicker. They seemed to knock down the perch population. We could not compete with them after a while. We could not set the gill nets for perch because the alewife were so thick, the nets would come up looking like a blanket or a sheet. So that is how we got into the alewife fishing with the pound nets. We fished two-pound nets and trucked the fish over to Oconto, to E. C. Swaer and Co., who used the fish for cat food. They also had a plant at Pensaukee that made fish meal and oil.

A lot of our fish went to Chicago for the Jewish market. Some fish, primarily suckers and carp, went to the eastern market. The Jewish holidays in the spring were always a good time for getting rid of that type of a fish. When the quota system came in during the early 1980s, the perch population was down and we were fishing alewife. So we were not fishing too much perch. Your percentage of quota was based on what fish you reported from 1978 until the early 1980s and as a result, my father and I had less than one-quarter of one percent of the perch quota. We had 420 pounds of perch to catch the first year. But when the quota first came in, it did not make any difference whether you caught the fish or not. You could still get your quota back the next year, so consequently we did not even fish those 420 pounds. We were fishing carp and doing fairly well on those at the time. But in 1984 the PCBs scares kept getting worse and worse. So they closed down the carp fishing on Lake Michigan and Green Bay on the 18th of June 1984.

———————

Ben Peterson emphasized the need for fishermen to pursue economic diversification. He processes his own fish and caviar. Peterson, who held both a tribal and a Michigan commercial fishing license until 2000. He now fishes out of Manistique and Fairport, under license from the Sault Ste. Marie Tribe of Chippewa Indians.

I decided that if we were going to stay in this business you have got to put some money in it. So far it has worked out. We do not even have to process as much as we thought we might have to. Because we have the machine, the other buyers know that we can process our own if we have to. We make whitefish caviar in September. We usually start around the 15th of September. The whitefish have to be just that right exact size. I cannot tell you the exact centimeter, but I can tell by looking at it because I have been around it enough. Elaine Johnson from Door County, Wisconsin, is our buyer. We went down there three years ago and helped her out and got her place kosher. I think they are the only kosher fish place in Wisconsin.

———————

Donald Voight of Gills Rock, Wisconsin, is now retired from commercial fishing. He indicated that the family was able to remain in fishing because they undertook various adaptive strategies such as relocation and alteration of target species.

My dad, Stanley Voight, was a commercial fisherman. He was in a partnership with my uncle, William Johnson. They had two boats. My uncle ran the fish tug *Hope*. My dad ran the other tug, the *Roamer*, which was built in 1936. The *Hope* was built in 1930. They employed about eight to ten men in those years. They moved to Lake Superior in 1940. My brother and I bought out my uncle in 1948, and we moved back to Gills Rock with the *Hope*. They had moved to Lake Superior because the state changed the size of the mesh and their whole rig was illegal. On Lake Superior it was legal. They went to Port Wing, Wisconsin, which is between Superior and Bayfield, and fished lake trout.

Donald Voight of Gills Rock, Wisconsin, began working as a commercial fisherman on Lake Michigan's waters in the 1940s. His sons, Leon and Lyle Voight, followed in his footsteps. Interview, 2 June 1999. Photograph by Jason Wintersteen.

Back in Gills Rock, we fished chubs. My brother passed away in 1958, so it was just me and my dad. We fished herring in the fall of the year, when there were a lot of twenty-hour days and a lot of hard work. When chub fishing got light, we moved over to Frankfort, Michigan. We were in Frankfort for eighteen years and in 1976, we came back here. In Frankfort, the chub fishing had gotten down low. The chub fishing went down after they planted all the cohos; I think the cohos ate up the chubs. The State of Michigan put us out of chub fishing, so we moved back to Gills Rock. Then we fished whitefish. When my health went, I got out of it in 1985. My boys took over and they are still fishing. When the DNR came out with this quota business, the three of them really could not make a living on it, so one of them got out.

Door County, Wisconsin's Howard Weborg has been fishing on Lake Michigan for more than seventy years. He discussed changes in target species over time.

Howard Weborg is from Wisconsin's Door Peninsula. He has been fishing on Lake Michigan for eight decades. Interview, 1 June 1999. Photograph by Michael J. Chiarappa.

I have to catch 13,000 pounds of whitefish. Otherwise, they will take the license away from me. My quota is 30,000 pounds of whitefish a year. That is all I can catch. When using gill nets, you measure from knot to knot. One sized gill net catches the smaller whitefish. Another mesh size catches the big whitefish. So when there is big whitefish, then we will set them. Today, it is all monofilament. Chub nets are a smaller mesh, two and one-half inches. That's the law. You have to have two and one-half inches.

We used to go all the way across to the Michigan side for herring. One day we had 13,000 pounds of herring. We sold them for mink feed for four and one-half cents a pound. We were catching so much—8,500 pounds every day. The herring are gone; there are none left. They were still in the nets and the women would help pick all the herring off when we came in. We would just pile the nets up in the boat with the herring in the webbing. I had a Michigan license and a Wisconsin license. As a Wisconsin resident, you cannot get a Michigan license any more. We would go way across to the Manitou Islands. We would leave here at two o'clock in the morning and by six-thirty, we would be over there, picking up our buoy and lifting. We pursued chub—big chub.

Oh man, that was many years ago. When the fishing got poor here, we went up to Mackinac Island and Cheboygan, Michigan, to fish for smelt. Then the smelt fishing got to be bad. So we had to quit and come back. Now we are lucky if we get five or six smelts a day. The alewife destroyed the type of chubs that were out in ninety fathoms of water. They were called mooneye chub. They had a bigger eye than regular chub.

South Haven's Chuck Jensen is a member of a third-generation fishing family. He discussed how fishermen adjusted to stock depletion and economic change.[51]

The amount of fish that were brought in depended on the time of the year and the species. For any one day, perch would be the biggest amount supplied from a certain length of net. You would probably get more perch than you would anything else. The chub nets—you would fish more chub nets and you might get a little more poundage but there would be more effort to it. So it was quite a change. At one time, you might go out and get fifty pounds of perch. The next day you might come in with 500, so it just varied from day to day.

Chub fishing was a little more consistent. If there were enough chubs out in the lake, you would have a pretty good chance of getting an average amount about every day. But as the population went down, then of course your average would go down. Chub fishing had its bad years too. They would have maybe a couple really slump years, bad years. Then all of a sudden it would pop back again and it would kind of change the other way. So it depended on year to year, you might say, and weather and so forth. Like a farmer, fishermen have their one or two good years and maybe have a bad one in between.

Chub were always pursued, but not in great quantity. Grand Haven was quite a chub fishing port, but when the trout were around, they fished for trout mostly. Our last chub permit I believe was in 1978. After that, one of the tugs in town received a research permit to catch chub. I think there were three tugs in town and they drew names out of a hat for it and the McCash brothers got it. It was mostly to study the population of the fish and they fished mostly out of South Haven. Then they had to move down to St. Joe. It was a research permit for fish population and pesticides. They could sell the fish they caught. It was a more restricted license than a research permit.

The market prices fluctuated all the time. If one market was flooded, you would try something else for a while. At certain times of the year, whitefish were really in demand, so we put all the pressure on whitefish we could. We would stay away from perch or whatever for a while. Ninety percent of our fish was shipped out—except during the three summer months when the tourist trade was on. Then we used a lot in the store, but otherwise a lot of it was shipped out. Years ago, most of it was shipped to Chicago, and then later on with the chub fishing, we started shipping to Brooklyn, New York, and Philadelphia.

We smoked fish here all the time. In the wintertime there were periods when you did not do much at all. At certain times, we did import some fish from other ports. Years ago, in the summertime, we would buy a lot of chubs from this dealer in Grand Haven. We would buy fresh chubs from him and smoke them ourselves because there was not any chub production. They were not fishing and harvesting chubs out here at that time. So we would buy chubs from one place and send them trout or something like that.

When smoking fish, we used just plain wood fire. Nowadays, they have a combination of gas and wood. Ours was all wood, mostly apple. You could use cherry, oak, and maple, but we usually used apple wood. It was plentiful and very good for smoking. First you would brine the fish in saltwater overnight. And then the next morning you would hang them on the racks and put them in the house and start the fire. By twelve or one o'clock, you would have hot smoked fish. The fish went in right away. But we had to leave the doors open for a certain length of time to let the moisture drain out of them. Then you would shut the doors and start the smoking process. But the fire was always there. It was just that you wanted to get some of the moisture out of the fish.

Daniel "Pete" LeClair (Two Rivers, Wisconsin) indicated that fishermen invest money not only to take economic advantage of changes in the fishery, but out of a spirit of competition as well.

Art Swaer started trawling smelt up in Green Bay. Then, when I developed the *Avis J*, he went and bought some Lake Erie boats. Things went so well for him, he built twin boats up in Pensaukee, Wisconsin. He was going to show me he was bigger.

He built the *Art Swaer VI* and the *Art Swaer VII*. He built them side-by-side. They are fifty-five feet long and twenty feet wide. He said: "I will show you how to fish, I will put in a bigger engine. I will show you." So he did. It is a nice trawler, but that is all it is really good for because it is so big and ox-like. You need a smaller boat for gill nets. So, they went out of business. Beautiful boats like that, now they are good for nothing. He lost the whole ship. He was out of Pensaukee, over by Oconto. Art Swaer was mainly a Green Bay fisherman. He built a meal plant. He built a million-dollar freezer plant. He really kept us going on the fishing end because he bought all of our forage fish. He froze them or made fishmeal out of them. He put a lot of money in it. But now the meal plant is gone and the freezer plant is gone.[52]

During the early 1990s, commercial fisherman Paul Goodman of Washington Island, Wisconsin, sold his fishing quota and became a charter boat operator and fish buyer.

I started charter fishing. I found that charters went pretty well. I opened a fish market too. I started dealing smoked fish and some fresh fish and that gave a draw to other tourist-oriented things you could sell. I have kind of justified the whole thing. Some of my neighbors who were fishermen were looking at ways to get rid of other fishermen so that maybe their livelihood could be better. But I kind of justified it by saying it gave me more time on land. It gave me more time to see what was really going on around here and realize this whole county is more tourism than anything else.

The problem is, when you are working real hard in the fishery and you are on the water, you are not paying attention to what is happening on land. If you do not pay attention, you can work so hard, you end up not making any money. You might not make a living because you are working so hard at a dying industry. So from that end, the charter industry has worked out pretty well for me. I do some commercial fishing now. During the spring and fall, I will jump on guys' boats if they want to hire me to help them out.

The fishery today is a lot easier fishing because of the equipment. The nets used to be linen and cotton and now they are monofilament. We used to have crews on shore, big crews boiling nets and doing all kinds of things. And now they tar the trap nets, but they have already figured how to tar them. Our gill nets are all monofilament. You can put them in a box and put them away. Nothing rots. You used to have to change nets all the time and boil them and reel them up and dry them. When I was young, we had three or four on the boat and we had a shore crew reeling nets and packing nets and having them ready. So commercial fishing employed a lot more people then because it took that many more people in the industry to keep up the equipment. But you could see the sentiment—even when I was fishing sometimes—I think we fished extra hard because we thought it was not going to last very long. You wanted to get a few dollars ahead before it collapsed.

I think the fishery will collapse if we have any contaminant problems, especially on the whitefish. That would be the end of the fishery. The other possibility of the fishery ending is because of the quota system. When fishermen just fished, it was always controlled. If you did not catch fish you did not fish. But you could always come back into it, or you would slow down. And then you had other fish. Now, there's not much other fish. There are some chubs, but the market for chubs is not real good because people do not know how to eat them anymore. You see chubs in the grocery store, but not like you used to. If they lose shelf space, they put something else from Iceland or from Greenland. So once you are off the shelf for a little while, you are in trouble nowadays. The marketing has changed. And years ago, you could have alternative fisheries like perch and chubs. But now, all that has changed with the quota on the whitefish. The state is allowed to raise the quota when there's a lot of whitefish around, so these guys always get increment. If you got 100,000 pounds, you might get—you would get 10,000 more. But if the fish disappeared or anything or fishing went the other way, they can diminish the quota.

Based in Gills Rock, Wisconsin, fisherman Leon Voight discussed the problems faced by fishermen who, in order to survive economically, become involved in retail or wholesale marketing.

Even if we are not fishing, we are still waiting on money. Some of it takes sixty days to get, some of it takes thirty days, depending on where we are shipping fish. There are times in the wintertime—you might have a whole month because of ice conditions where you will be working in the shed all the time—but you still have money coming from other places that has been out there. You are always waiting on money. You do not get any interest on it and you are always waiting on it.

Elaine Johnson and her cousin and business partner Gretna Johns were in the fish processing and brokerage business for forty-seven years. Today they operate Northern Lights Fish and Caviar International. Many of their caviar buyers are from Sweden. She recalled how the popularity of Door County whitefish boils among tourists assisted them in their attempts to economically diversify.

The restaurants were some of our first customers. Lawrence Wickman at the Viking Restaurant started fish boils. He chunked his own fish. Whitefish was hard to get. We went clear up to Naubinway and Epoufette, Michigan, to get whitefish at that time. The first customers we chunked for were the Pelletiers in Fish Creek. We chunked for our next customers, the White Gull Inn. I am speaking about whitefish chunk for boils now. Then we started to chunk for the Wagon Trail, and Village View in Egg Harbor. But the first three are the three major boilers in Door County. Among those three, they used around 90,000 pounds of chunks a year.

We were the first ones that used a band saw to chunk. Most fishermen would chunk by hand. We started right off with the meat saw, with a band saw. You would take the fish and grab it by the belly flap. Then grab the tail and make a little bend so you zip off the back. You turn it over and cut off the anus fin along with the rectum. Then you give it another flip and snap it into the saw. The record I have cut is 4,200 pounds a day. I have cut 100 pounds of fish in three minutes forty-seven seconds. I was hustling and everything went just right. I do not do that any more. It takes me four and a half minutes to chunk now.

We bought the grocery store in 1965. We had a really good grocery store business. As our business grew, Gretna was determined we should drop the fish business, but I would not do it. A trucking line out of Michigan picked up trout for us out of Slave Lake, and they would fly it into Chicago. They would drop it off at our store about midnight. He used to drop off 500 or 600 pounds. If I was chunking when they came through, I would take them up to our grandma's house, which is where we chunked for a while.

We had a building back here. Actually, our processing shed is where our garage is now. We had the egg room on one side and we did the perch on the other side.

Now, we just do whitefish. We do it down at Weborg's Fishery in Gills Rock. We did not have a filleter. We did it all by hand, filleting all by hand. Then we bought a scaler. We bought half a scaler—half the scaler down in Gills Rock is ours, half is the boys'. We have an older scaler down here that's ours for that perch. One scaler is for perch and one is for whitefish.

Rick Johnson (Gills Rock, Wisconsin) discussed how the Door County fish boil became commercialized and created a demand for local whitefish.

My grandfather fished and my father fished. Unfortunately, my grandfather sold out because my father was too young to get into the business. My father was in it for a while. He worked for the Weborgs. Actually, my grandfather sold his fish rig to the Weborgs, and then my father started working for them. That was probably in the 1950s when it was real tough fishing, so he became a carpenter. He has been a carpenter and building contractor for probably thirty years. So I am third generation, but unfortunately there was not anything passed on other than a little history. No boats or nets or anything like that. My grandfather was Richard Johnson and my father was Roger Johnson. They were both from Gills Rock. They were of Swedish background and my mother is Norwegian, so I am fifty-fifty. My mother's parents, my grandparents, started the fish boil at the Viking. The Wickman family owned the Viking in Ellison Bay and started the first commercial fish boil in Door County. Jeff and Mark Weborg's dad pitched the idea to my grandfather. They used to do fish boils down in the park in Gills Rock.

My grandfather died in the 1970s. My grandmother kept it for a year or two and then sold it. It has had two owners since then. I spent a lot of time picking up trays and cleaning up after fish boils. That was our job when we were eight, nine years old. The used to have fish boils Tuesday and Friday nights. It was nothing to have 600 or 700 people on one night from four to eight P.M. There were not as many tourists around at that time, so it was a big thing.

It is kind of neat seeing people from the city eat fish cooked outside in a big kettle with all the salt dumped in there. They used whitefish for the fish boil. They dump in ten pounds of salt and you do not even taste the salt—so it is quite unique. When my grandfather had it, they had homemade cherry pie with ice cream. Everything was top notch. It was a big doing. It still is. There are a lot of fish boils in Door County. Everybody has got one now, but back then, they were the only one.

First, they throw in the potatoes and you cook them for about eight, nine minutes. Then you throw the onions in, cook them for about another three or four. Then you throw the fish in and cook them for about ten minutes. It takes about forty minutes because you do not start timing the fish and potatoes until they start rolling boil. Then you dump in a considerable amount of salt. When it boils over—that's mainly for show. They throw the kerosene under the fire—on the fire—and it makes a big cloud of smoke and that—some people use it to get the oil off. There is a little oil that lays up in there and it is for that, but ninety-nine percent of it is for show.

The fishermen do not do as many commercial fish boils as the restaurants. But the Memorial Day fish boil at Gills Rock is a good time. Everybody gets together because you are working a lot of hours fishing and it is hard work. We invite legislators up and throw a fish boil for them. All the fishermen come. It is a way we can show off our industry and fill their stomachs too.

Donald Voight discussed the importance of the Door County fish boil to the local fishing and tourist-based economy.

This is kind of a fishing community through here. My neighbors over here, Mr. and Mrs. Lawrence Wickman, are the ones who really started putting out this fish boil. They used to serve 500–600 a night when they first started. Then they sold out. Of course, that was what really started the whole business here for the public, you know. You go to the fish boil and get your fish, potatoes, onions and cake or some dessert. If you want more fish, they charge you so much and you go up and get one or two pieces more. At the Viking Grill they have a fish boil pretty near every night. And the fish boil spread through the whole county. It is a big drawing card for our tourists.

Mark Weborg and his family have hosted fish boils for their employees and friends in the past and they still do today. He discussed the Weborg family's historic ties to the Door County fish boil. Popular with locals and tourists alike, fish boils provide a major market for the whitefish caught by Weborg and his crew.

Years ago, you used to have a big crew for fishing. This operation here used to fish pound nets. The fish boil in this area originated with my grandfather—it has its origins in Norway but we did not start doing it here until my grandfather and father started feeding the crew. Back then, when we had pound nets, you had a crew of eight, ten people. Then he had the families come down and some neighbors and they had a fish boil. They got the fish, potatoes, and onions together. People brought bread and a few goodies and we had a good old time. From there, we finally convinced the Viking Grill in Ellison Bay to do it commercially. The owner did not have any hope that it would ever succeed. After the first year, he was serving over 400 people a night. From there, it has progressed to the point that there are at least a dozen establishments in Door County that are doing it in the summer months. The ones we service use about 30,000 pounds a year.

We started our holiday fish boils about twenty-five or thirty years ago because everyone liked them so much, and it was a good way to invite our friends and have a good old time. So we started having a fish boil for our friends and family here every Labor Day and Memorial Day. It works out well. It is on Monday. No one has to go back to work until later that day. We started out with 100–200 people. Now we are running around 250 to 350 people every time we have it. We have a great old time.

Daniel "Pete" LeClair described the alterations that have been made to the family property in Two Rivers, Wisconsin, in response to changing economic and social conditions and fishing regulations and stocks. The fishery became an informal hangout for the family, its employees, and friends. With the construction of an adjacent tavern, the LeClair fishery became a gathering place for the local community.

My father's operation was located next door to our present location; it was where the tavern is now located. That is where it originally started. He bought an old house and then we built the fish shed below. We actually moved it from Two Creeks to Two Rivers in sections. We had to cut it in sections and then bring it down here and bolt it together.

The fish shed was for storing equipment for our gill-net operation. You had to have a cooler and ice bin for weighing your chubs and so forth. Our net reels were outside it. Inside we could patch our nets and dry them. We would string the nets on the maitres. The building got old and dilapidated and the water was halfway up in the building, so a couple of years ago, we knocked it down and bought the house next door. We needed it for our trawl nets. We just kept on going and expanding. But now we have to do something with it. We put all steel sheeting out on the front of our dock. When things were going good we developed the area and made it look like something. You blacktop the yard and you want to be proud of the operation. Then they put you out of business. This is what was so frustrating. It was stupid. If there was a good reason, but it was just totally ridiculous.

We built the tavern next door. It used to be my trawl shop. The back of the shop was supposed to be for repairing nets and so forth. We made it long, so we could stretch the whole net out in it. The basement was used for testing smelt. It was supposed to be a workshop, but we soon had to have a little social hall for all the workers. They put a little bar room in there and pretty soon everyone wanted to come in. They all wanted to have a tavern—so they took one part—they made a tavern and a social hall out of it. Then my son Dan took over and started expanding the tavern business. You cannot have a tavern and a net shop so we put up our new building and moved over here.

It all started just with our employees and pretty soon all the fishermen were coming to talk smart—to tell how many fish they caught and who was a better fisherman. It was really a fun place. It grew and grew and got so big that people were pounding on the door to get in. Before it was a tavern, we had a half-barrel of brew there. We still have the half-barrel of beer here for after work. You all sit down and have a beer and talk smart. That got so big up there that you could not afford to give away beer any more. So we had to start a private club and you had to be a member. It just got carried away. Soon, the cops came in and said, "You cannot do this here. You have not got a license."

Donald Voight (Gills Rock, Wisconsin) indicated that consumer fish demands and tastes have changed over time, making it necessary for fishermen to do more fish processing.

The chub market used to be the backbone of the fishery, but it does not seem to be as good as it used to be. I think the younger people are afraid to peel the skin off the fish. Years ago, you bought the whole fish. Now, you have to scale it and fillet it and everything for them. Next thing, you will have to help them chew it.

In order to remain in commercial fishing, Washington Island-based fisherman Ken Koyen has pursued various strategies, including adopting burbot, a freshwater cod known locally as a lawyer, as a target species.

I fish the waters around Washington Island but we are only allowed one mile north of Rock Island, and a mile and a quarter north of Boyer's Bluff to the Wisconsin-Michigan line. Our waters run west out to a point about eight miles northwest of Boyer's Bluff and then the line swings down to Whaleback Shoal which is basically northwest of Ellison Bay Bluff, and it takes another bend there. Sometimes we get thirteen miles out in the lake for chubs. That is a long run. It is tough when you fish chubs because you can get into pretty nasty weather out there. I have only been in one little tornado in all my years. The *Welcome* was hit by lightning. I had the roller out. The lightning hit the roller and came in and the whole thing glowed like a light bulb and I was standing right alongside it. So I set my knife down and I went to the back of the boat.

I have started specializing in lawyers. The sign on the window at my restaurant says "fresh lawyers." I will not say why they call them lawyers but if you look at the carcass of a lawyer I caught this morning you will see that its heart is actually next to its ass. That is a fact. The proper name for lawyers is burbot. The Indians call them meeseye. In Minnesota, they are eel pout. In some places they are called freshwater cod. They are roughly only one-third meat, but the meat is the best eating fish in the Great Lakes as far as quality. It is low in fat and high in protein. Right now some of the whitefish are really poor and skinny. Even some of the suckers, which are a rough fish, are poor. And I think lawyers are going to win out because they live on other fish. They are not bottom feeders. They do not have to live off of little worms, bugs, or other fishes' spawn like whitefish. I have cleaned lawyers with German brown trout in them that the DNR has planted, as well as perch, short whitefish, and chubs. The other day, I caught a lawyer with zebra mussels in it. But it also had a bunch of gelled eggs in it; I think maybe the zebra mussels were attached to those eggs and it just was sucking away and happened to get the zebra mussels. I cleaned a whitefish once with zebra mussels in it.

I have pretty much pursued the lawyer for my restaurant. I have started something there and it is going pretty good. We have people call nightly to see if we have fresh lawyers. You cannot market them because you cannot freeze them. They get tough and rubbery. It has got to have something to do with the methane or something in them, but they get just like rubber and lose their flavor if you freeze them. They are excellent fresh. I do my own fish boils. Quite often at a Saturday night fish boil, I will catch the fish Saturday morning. I will not boil frozen fish. I would sooner cancel.

Marketing and trying to catch the fish when they are worth something are problems. We are on a quota system, and I do not know if we will ever catch our quota again, the way the fishery is going. Years ago, we had to slow down fishing because there were so many fish. Three years ago, we set six boxes of nets at a particular location and we caught 7,500 pounds of whitefish, just the biggest lift we ever had or almost anybody had heard of around here. I went back a year later almost to the date and had 3,750 pounds, and I went back a year after that—almost to the date—and had two fish. So there is something going on and it is not good. My theory is it is the zebra mussel. They started in the south end of Green Bay. Then we saw an influx of perch and walleye around Washington Island we had never seen. This was five years ago when we started to see perch in chub nets in the bay in 160 feet of water. We had never heard of it. Then within a year or so after that, the south end of the bay dried up for perch fishing. They were hollering that the sport fishery caught too many and then they hollered that commercial fishermen caught too many. Well, it is neither. It is between the cormorants and the zebra mussels.

Based in Gills Rock, Wisconsin, Mark Weborg noted the difficulties presented in trying to diversify the target species.

We can keep lawyer, also known as eel pout, freshwater cod, or burbot, but you only save the meat on the tail. You get about a fifth return on the fish because it is a fish that is very hard to freeze. You must have a fresh market. If you could get a market started and then all of a sudden, you do not catch any—there goes the market. And if you do not have continuation, people are not going to be there to buy it. It just is not a very marketable fish. We can market it, but we would have to get lobster prices for it. Basically, its taste and texture is just like lobster. It is very good eating. Many people take the liver out of it. A regular size lawyer—a four- to five- pound lawyer—has got about a pound of liver in it. It is cod liver oil, of course, and it is very good for you. But I do not like it.

Dennis Hickey of Baileys Harbor, Wisconsin, discussed the importance of family in helping fishermen adapt to changes in economic and environmental conditions in the fishery.

Our family has been fishing since 1852. Our grandfather was a commercial fisherman who came from Norway. He was one of the original settlers in town and he farmed, logged, and fished, which was pretty typical of the first immigrants. My father and his brother fished and had a fish rig. Their fishery was over across the harbor, over across from the town hall. They fished until about 1929. During the Great Depression my dad and his brother had to make some decisions. Times were tough. They decided to sell the fish rig they had at that time, work for some other guys, and keep all the farms. And to this day, I am really happy they did, because we have got a lot of land because they kept the farms. My father and his brother later got another fish rig. They were involved in the fishery all the way up until the 1950s when the sea lamprey era came and the lake trout and whitefish stocks were pretty well down. They sold the fish rig. My dad worked in the shipyard and still had the farms. He also worked for Wenniger, one of the guys who owned the building where the fishery was located, the dock, and other surrounding property, which is where condos are today.

For a period of eight or ten years before my dad and his brother stopped fishing, there was not much happening at all. This was right about the time that my brother and I finished high school. We were both in the navy, went to trade school, and moved

Dennis Hickey is a third-generation fisherman of Norwegian descent. He has been fishing out of Baileys Harbor, Wisconsin, for more than thirty years and operates the last pound-net fishery on Lake Michigan. Interview, 2 June 1999. Photograph courtesy of the Great Lakes Center for Maritime Studies.

to California. We both had good jobs. One day we came home. It was hot. There were four lanes of traffic and accidents all over on the freeways. There were people everywhere. We lived in Sherman Oaks. It was beautiful with the climate and all, but we said, "We do not need this." So we quit and came home. A guy by the name of Cliff Wenniger had some pound nets on the other side of the harbor and come spring, he was going to fish for alewife because there was not any whitefish or trout to speak of at that time. And so we said, "We will work with you."

We did not know what we wanted to do once we got home. But we had the idea that we could fish, even though the whitefish stocks and all the good species were pretty well down. We said, "We will fish for alewives." So we started out fishing pound nets for alewife for about a cent and a quarter a pound over on the other side of the harbor. We sold them for cat food. They pressed them for fishmeal and took the oil out for paint. That summer we got interested in it and when fall came, Cliff was kind of excited. He had a young crew again. We decided to try one or two pound nets for whitefish. We helped him set them and we caught a few. Not a lot, but it was encouraging. The reason we got the idea is during that time we were fishing alewife, we were seeing a lot of small, six- to eight-inch whitefish mixed in with the alewife. I showed them to my dad and he said, "That's a good sign; the whitefish could come back."

As it turned out, the whitefish did come back and so then we got interested. The next spring, we bought our first gill-net boat, got our first license, and started ourselves. We gill netted for a year and had some lifts of maybe 400 or 500 pounds. We thought that was really a lot of fish. My dad was always interested in pound nets—big living trapping nets. He helped us string our first pound nets. We strung three, I think, the first couple of years and were pretty successful. We started to get some pretty good lifts of whitefish. There was a guy in his seventies who asked us if we would like to buy his rig. We bought his rig and combined it with ours. After that we probably totaled about fifteen other fishermen. We have gradually built the rig up from that. And now we are to the point where we have six boats and we fish every type of gear that is legal for Wisconsin fishermen. We have quotas for all the species that are available for commercial fishing.

Third-generation fisherman Paul Goodman (Washington Island, Wisconsin) recalled how his family struggled economically as fishing deteriorated and the botulism outbreak diminished the market for chubs.

After my father got back from the service, he came back to the island and fished. And he fished for quite a few years. In the 1960s, the fishing got pretty tough. I was born in 1952, so I was about twelve, thirteen, or fourteen years old. We were just fishing chubs. My family was not fishing whitefish at that time. It was just chubs off the island. About that time, there was a botulism scare in the chub industry. You could hardly sell a chub. Things really went bad fast. I am not sure who died, but I think the botulism claimed several lives. I think the fish came out of the State of Michigan. It was a smoked product that was transported improperly to Florida. It was enough to put a scare into the industry.

When the botulism scare happened, my father could not make a living for us anymore. I had two brothers, a sister, and my father and my mother. My father left the island and was actually out of the fishery at that time. There was no compensation program. There was nothing going on. So he got out of the fishery and moved just north of Milwaukee. He found a job working in a plant. He did that for a few years and finally, the rest of our family moved there for a while. We kept our house on the island. I kept coming back during summers and worked on the docks around here. My job was to be on the dock, smoking fish for other people in their smokehouses. Around 1975 or so, I bought back into the fishery myself. I worked my way back into the area through ship-building and got back into the fishery about 1975.

Don Bell, Jr. (Mackinaw City, Michigan), who both fishes and buys fish to sell on a wholesale and retail basis, discussed the changing nature of the fishing business.

I know this Canadian who fishes with his brother's boat, a big sixty-five-foot fish tug. They were fishing last summer and he called me up and said: "Donald, I have about 1,600 pounds of whitefish. Are you interested?" I said: "Yes. Nobody else around here is getting any." He brought them down and they were so soft, we could hardly hand-filet them or hand-scale them. They were good for smoking but that's about it. Normally, Lake Superior is so cold, the fish have a little bit longer shelf life.

Last summer—because of the bad winter—we had more tourists up here than we had ever seen before. There was so many times in July and August where we could not service our restaurants. We did not have fish to sell over the front counter. We had smoked fish because we had fish in the freezer we could bring out, but you cannot cut them to filets for restaurants. We service ski lodges in the area and, of course, we got a lot of restaurants that are open year around.

We sell perch and walleyes when we can get them. We sell salmon at certain times of the year when we can get it. We get most of our fish out of Lake Huron. At certain times of the year, we will get quite a few out of Lake Michigan. We have fishermen up in Lake Superior, around Whitefish Point, Bay Mills, and we also have Canadians that come down. A lot of times in the fall, Canadians who work different jobs will take time off from work and fish. They are allowed to fish through November where our people, even the tribal members, shut down for the month of November because it is spawning season. Poor little guppies, they only get to do their thing once a year, so they leave them alone. We need to have stock for next year and years to come.

In the summertime, we service the Grand Hotel on Mackinac Island and other restaurants over there. We go to Harbor Springs, Cross Village, Petoskey, and as far as Boyne City. We have about four or five places over in Gaylord and Indian River in the Cheboygan area. As far as restaurants go, we cover a pretty wide range here. We do not go across the Mackinac Bridge because there are fish outfits up there like ours, and they do not come down here. We do not bother each other. We kind of work together and respect each other's territory. They also realize that we have been here for fifty years. Right now, I think we are the oldest business in town. We work real closely with other fisheries in the area. Jack Cross called me yesterday. If we have extra fish and somebody is short, we help each other out. We got a pretty good reputation. We ship to New York, Chicago, Detroit, and Boston. I have shipped product to California. We are known all over.

In this industry, you almost have to have working relationships with a lot of different people. It is such a changing industry. Back twenty to twenty-five years ago, you had the real strong Catholic market. You do not have that strong Catholic market anymore. Every Friday night, every corner bar had a fish fry. People would say, "Let's go up to Susie's corner bar." Everybody has fish and a couple beers and they spent the evening together. When you did not have to eat fish on Friday, it closed up a lot of bars and their fish fries. You do not have your strong Orthodox Jewish market like you used to have either. We really noticed the difference in how they buy their fish. It is not the same as they used to do it. They do not buy in the large quantities like they used to. And another thing we have really noticed in our industry is that there are more women in the workforce. They have got good jobs. They are doctors, lawyers, and schoolteachers. You see them out running heavy equipment and driving semis. The women are not doing the cooking at home like they used to. It is a whole different ballgame. So the industry is really changing. There are so many different factors in it compared to twenty or twenty-five years ago. You can slowly, but surely, see the difference.

Daniel "Pete" LeClair, a commercial fisherman (Two Rivers, Wisconsin), discussed the adaptive strategies pursued in order to keep the family fishery and fish market going.

Since commercial fishing on Lake Michigan looks like it is going to go down the tubes, we are trying to develop our fish market. We have my son, Daniel, on the road trying to sell smoked chubs and smoked salmon. We buy perch from Lake Erie and try to sell to restaurants. My son likes being a salesman. But I still feel bad that we are going to lose this fishing on Lake Michigan. We know we can produce good eating fish for the fish consumer, but if it is not profitable, you have to give it up. It is something that we have worked hard and long to develop. I guess this is it. When they are gone, they are gone.

Jack Cross is a member of the third generation in his family to engage in commercial fishing. He is now in the wholesale and retail business. He discussed how changes in state policy required his family to concentrate their efforts on building their retail and wholesale business.[53]

When the state stopped us from gill netting and then, later, trap netting, they took us down. We had eighteen to twenty men in our crew when we quit working that time. Now we are down to probably five or six permanent people working. It was kind of hard because we were used to catching our own fish. We had our own boats and then we went into trap nets. The DNR said that it would be for a lifetime. Well, that did not last. It lasted not quite ten years and they put us out of the trap net business, and turned the northern end of the lakes over to Native Americans. After that, some of the fishermen went to work at small plants and some were getting old enough to retire. Then, after that trap-net business, some worked for the state on their boats because they had experience as fishermen and net makers. Some of them went to other places like mine—wholesale/retail outfits. So now we buy the fish from the Native Americans because they are the only ones here who can fish commercially.

I could not see myself doing anything else. I grew up with this. When I was just a young kid, twelve years old, my dad had the boats. He would be on the boat himself in the summertime. We had two or three boats. If one of the crew did not show up, they would come up and get me. I would go regardless of what boat needed a crew member. My dad would not even know what boat I would be on. It has been a way of life with us and so I do not know what else I would do. But I miss being on the water.

At one time there were close to a dozen boats in here. Everything has changed so much in the town. When I was a young kid, back in the 1940s, commercial fishing was one of the chief industries of the town of Charlevoix. Since then, the small factories, cement plants, and Consumers Energy have come in. When I was a kid, there were not any condos here. The water is one of the drawing cards of Charlevoix. Charlevoix is a big resort in July and August.

A lot of my customers have condos here. They come up for the summer and the holidays. I know a lot of them. I do get a few strangers in every once in a while, but a lot of my clientele I know. We furnish a lot of fish for the restaurants around here. That's a big part of our business. People come up here and they want fresh fish. It is a big part of our business. In another turn, people want fish for the health reasons. People are eating more fish today than they ever did and our problem is not selling the fish. Our problem is getting the fish to sell.

There are fisheries like mine up and down the lakeshore. There is one outside of Petoskey and one in Mackinaw City and Carlson's in Traverse City and Leland. They are scattered out along the lakeshore. I talk to them all the time. Most of them are like me, they were brought up in the business and they were fishermen before they started their wholesale/retail business.

Alan Priest noted that many fishermen, such as his first employer, the late Ross Lang, temporarily relocated in order to stay in business. Priest stayed in fishing by learning various skills and being willing to perform a variety of different tasks. He used his woodworking skills in the assembly of boxes for the shipment of fish and worked processing fish for other fishermen.

I came over and started to work for Ross Lang after he got back from Lake Superior. He was tired of Lake Superior fishing, and wound up here in Leland. He had been fishing in Munising. He came back, got his boat back, and he bought a license out from up north. Then he got a trap-net license and got into the trap- net business. I went to work with him and we would fish summers with the trap net. We would fish chubs in the fall, winter, and spring. I have fished on the *Frances Clark, Janice Sue,* and the *Joy* as a trap-net boat.

The building where Langs worked out of was not set up the way it is now. It was not insulated. There was a tarp across there and I worked on the backside of the shed in the wintertime. There's no heat back there. I would make eighty to ninety boxes a day just for the chubs. We used to have a semi come in here and all three fishermen had their trucks loaded to the max. You have a half-ton truck, you put 2,000 pounds on it, or 3,000, or just load her up till you cannot put another box on it. We were going out of here with a load of fish. Ross was driving and Fred and I were on the back tailgate, jumping, just bouncing her, just to try to get her to go.

I used to work at Carlson's but I got so busy with chub fishing that I could not do anything else. I used to clean charter fish for him too, but it just got so busy with just keeping the chub boat going. I worked at Carlson's when they filleted a lot of whitefish. They get most all their whitefish filleted now. We used to set up on a table at eight o'clock in the morning and fillet until four or five o'clock at night. Sometimes, when Bill Carlson was gone, we would have beers on the table at eight o'clock in the morning and just go to it and make a party out of it. My wife would not like that sometimes but that is part of the life of a fisherman. You could go through a lot of fish, too. My main job was ribbing—taking the ribs out. Sometimes you get going so fast, using a big knife, you stick your hand. You wipe it off, keep going, and think, God, I am getting behind.

Elaine Johnson, a fish processor based in Door County, Wisconsin, recalled that Michigan's hostility toward its commercially licensed fishermen created great concern among their Wisconsin counterparts. Johnson challenged the assumption held by both Michigan and Wisconsin—that sport fishing generated greater economic returns.

When Michigan shut down their fishery that time, I was the person that wrote the request for an emergency order to put a moratorium on issuing licenses in Wisconsin. At the time I wrote up the request, five fishermen had already come down here and taken up residency. They did not live here, but they paid rent and said this was their residence, so they qualified for a license. I am not saying our boys are clean and white, but more things happened to this fishery than you could ever believe after those Michigan boys came down. They fished perch, lots of perch out of the lake. They took them back to Michigan and handled them out of Michigan. The bunch of regulations now going into effect are the result of these boys were caught over-harvesting their quota of perch about two years ago. The regulations are being reworked on account of them.

I was so intense it seemed like all the fishermen's problems became my problems. They all called me. They said that they would have a meeting. The DNR would have a meeting to have public response, but they would fix it so that the notices they had to give out by statute would never get to the fishermen until the day after the meeting. That is how they lost the majority of their gill-net fishermen in the first round. They lost hundreds of commercial fishermen the first round. Michigan has only got about thirty left in the non-Indian, white fishery.

Fishing was a big industry up there at one time. I do not know how much revenue that would bring into the state, but with tax now on your meals—the tax that the state gets back just from fish dinners would have to be quite a bit. Many were employed in the commercial fisheries, if you count the shed work, the net work, the stringing, slugging, as well as the processing they did and the boxes they bought. I do not know what the dockside value of that fish would be if all this was accounted for.

Richard Bishop was an economist who worked for the State of Wisconsin. About twenty-five years ago he deemed that whitefish was worth twenty-five cents a pound on the dock. Now, what would it be worth twenty-five years later? Quite a bit, I would say. You watch the process the fish goes through from the time the fishermen catch it and get it on the board. You accrue what that pays, what your fuel takes, what the upkeep of that boat is—so a clutch goes out on you or a gear, I hope not an engine, but all these things can happen. The daily costs—the fuel costs and the upkeep and the nets—you take that cost and you take that fish after a person like me buys it, then I take that fish and I have employees that help me process that fish. I have a processing place that I have to pay for. My license is $100 to the state and $200 to the Department of Agriculture, so I meet all their specifications. That is $300 from every processor. Then you pay my delivery person, buy a truck, fuel, the oil, and your upkeep on the truck. Then you finally get it to where it is going and the customer pays you for that fish. But now he has a cook. He has got his waitress. He has got the insurance on his place. Now, you finally get that fish down there and the customer is about to eat it. So, if you count all those moneys from the very time that wild fish, and I mean wild, was taken out of that lake and brought ashore, it amounts to a lot of money. And it has been proven time and time and time again.

Sport fishermen buy a boat and a pole. But that does not compare to going out to a fish boil. Some of the places like Viking and Wicko, use about 30,000 pounds of chunks a season. They serve 120 people out of 100 pounds of fish. They get two pieces per serving. Now they are serving 30,000 pounds of fish. What kind of revenue does this bring to the waitress, to the place, to the state, to the fishermen? This money really circulates up here.

Daniel "Pete" LeClair (Two Rivers, Wisconsin) associated the fishery with employment uncertainty. Fishermen want to continue to work on the water not only for economic reasons, but for other reasons as well, including fear they lack the skills sufficient to get other employment.

Today, our captains are Kenny Kulpa and Greg Erickson. Kenny is on the *Susie Q* and Greg is on the *Avis J*. Greg has been with us since he graduated from high school. Kenny Kulpa has only been with us the last four years or so. He ran trawlers a while before he started working with us and is very knowledgeable. He knows how to adjust the nets and how to patch nets. He is really one of the few that are left. When these guys are gone, that is the end of it. That is a dirty shame.

Greg Erickson was a crew member with my son, Mike. He and Mike were my crew members. Then when Jerry Glaser retired off the boat and started smoking fish, Greg took over his boat because they worked together for a long time. Greg was interested in it and he learned from Jerry. So Jerry—he went into the smoked fish business—and then he retired all together. So, my youngest son, Paul, took over for Jerry. If I did not have my sons involved, I do not know where we would be. We probably would not have developed.

Greg Erickson is pretty frustrated and real disturbed with the fishery. He wants to finish his career here but he does not know if he can. And when you get to be forty-five, who is going to hire you? You know, you do not have any other trade. Most people, at forty-five, if you are a machinist or something, you know, you are guaranteed a job for life and a retirement plan. We have a profit-sharing plan for these guys and they would sure like to continue and retire in this profession. They know they are the last of the fisherman breed and we all would like them to continue. But I do not know;

it has really been bad the last two years. They have just been terrible. That's why we are trying to develop our fish market—to kind compensate for the lake fishery. We hoped, in the meantime, something would change. The fishery on the lake could come back and help support the other part of it and work as a unit—this is what we would really like to do but it is a rough road right now.

———————————

Neil Teskie (Gills Rock, Wisconsin) indicated that migration was a strategy employed by fishermen to survive when stocks were down in a particular geographical area.

When my father moved from one fishing location to another it was a matter of economics. You know, he needed money to feed us and to take care of everything and there was not the tourist industry here at that time. They would go to the Manitou Islands. They would leave here and get to the nets in the morning, lift the first gang of chub nets, dress the fish, park on the Manitou Islands, anchor out, sleep, cook, go to bed, lift the other gang of nets, put them back in the lake, then come back. They would spend a couple of days there lifting two gangs of chub nets because there were not any chubs or whitefish here to make it profitable. See, back then, you could have a Michigan license and hold them—my dad held one. So he went to the different ports to fish because there was not the production here to make enough money to just take care of us.

———————————

Rick Johnson saw the early 1980s, just before limited-entry and quota-based fishing was introduced in Wisconsin, as the end of the well-established practice among Great Lakes fisherman to follow the fish.

In the early 1980s, mainly in the summer months, there were probably thirty-five boats fishing out of northern Door County at that time. There were probably seven or eight boats from Racine, and five or six from Milwaukee. Everybody was here. There was a major influx and that was the start of the DNR's concern about the overfishing of whitefish. Prior to that time, there were mainly chub fishermen here. They would come in May. Some of them stayed right through October and fished the full season with the best fishing right before the closed season. They were fishing whitefish from May through October. There were no quotas. It was take as much as you want to take. At the time, they had nothing else to fish. It was mostly gill netting and pound netting. Trap netters soon got into it.

You would hear stories of fishermen in the past. They fished in Gills Rock for five years, then they went to Ludington, Michigan, to fish for five years, and up to Lake Superior for five more. They were just vagabonds. They just went wherever there were fish. But nowadays, you cannot do that. You are restricted to Wisconsin waters and even in Wisconsin you are restricted to certain areas. In terms of our fishing grounds, you like to stay in the bay as much as possible because the bottom is much softer. You go out in Lake Michigan, and you are dealing with lake trout, a lot more lake trout than you would in the bay. There are a lot of rocks on the bottom. Your nets get ripped up and torn; they are just a mess. So anytime we can fish in the bay, I would much rather be there. About a month ago we made a lift over there. We had seven fish out of eleven boxes of nets so obviously it did not pay to stay there. We have certain grounds that we just kind of traditionally fish. You kind of feel out the area. There are about three gill-net boats that regularly fish in our area. You kind of spread out and once you find the fish, you kind of let everybody else know and they come. My boat does not have a fish finder on it yet. Hopefully, I am going to get one. Some of the gill-net tugs and the trap netters have them. They are helpful in finding schools of fish. At times, they find schools that are not whitefish, but a pile of suckers or "lawyers." But to me, the bay is the best place to fish if you can. The less you fish in the lake, the better off your pocketbook—what you catch Mother Nature takes back sooner or later.

It was not uncommon, if you were setting gill nets north and south, for somebody else to set east and west right across you. It was probably in the early 1980s when all these boats were up here, my partner and I went out. We had to pass thirteen gangs of nets—other people's nets. We were setting in one direction and the rest of these guys were set in the other direction. The only way you can do it, is to bring their nets up and pull them in the boat and then pass your box underneath and clear yourself so you can keep lifting. It sounds easy, but it was not. We had to clear thirteen of those in one day—that is how many nets were out there in just that one little area where we were fishing. It is much simpler now. Basically, you can run out there. You can kind of just glance out your window and if you do not see a buoy, you can just go. Where before, they were real close together and they were just wall-to-wall. Obviously, it has helped the fishing industry from the standpoint of incidental catch, which is a big thing in the DNR's eyes. It has gone down dramatically from the heyday. I do not have the numbers. I know the DNR does. When all those guys were up here, there were millions of feet of gill nets being fished each year and now there is not. So that is one of the benefits. It has helped the fishing industry from that standpoint that the DNR can back off a little bit as far as incidental catch issue is concerned.

––––––––––

Daniel "Pete" LeClair (Two Rivers, Wisconsin) indicated that the depletion of the alewife stocks and DNR regulations curtailing inshore commercial fishing during the 1980s prompted him to expand into the business of smoking fish.

This building was a house. My son bought it for a residence. We needed the back-yard for processing, storage, and repairs. Then in the 1980s the fishing of alewife kind of disappeared—it started going all haywire. We thought we better get into something else, because it does not look like there is going be a big future here. So, we tore the house apart and put in two small smokehouses, just two small ones. We were just experimenting with them to see if we could get something going. We did not know anything about smoking or fixing them. We had to learn that profession. The demand for smoked fish started growing out of control so we had to put up the other big building and we put in four big smokehouses.

We were diversifying in the 1980s. The alewife had died, and everything was going haywire. Then they chased us off the beach. They made us stay outside of sixty feet of water. When our big operation was near the beach for eight weeks of the year, we would give her hell and we would make enough money to last a while. Then they took shore fishing away from us because they had to save the alewife for the salmon and trout.

We could not survive just fishing deep water. We had to do something else. We got the chubs. Why catch them and sell to somebody else to smoke and sell them? We will catch them, smoke them, and get another hand in the pie. So that is what we did and it kept growing and growing. It got so big that the house was too small. So we had to build some new buildings around it.

We had to develop the fish-smoking business. I went and looked at other people's smokehouses and I did not like the way they did it. So, I developed a way you could put the wood in from the back end instead of through the front end. Other guys would fire up in front, but why mess around with fire in the front where the carts go? You should put the fire in the back. Open a big door to get in there and regulate your fire with a damper all through the back end of it. I improvised a smokehouse where it is nice and easy when you have your wood and the fire is in the back. We developed a modern way of doing it. We thought that we would have to switch from using wood to gas for heat to cook the fish. Some of the modern guys are going with gas. They regulate their temperature and use wood chips on top of a steel plate. They use the gas for heat and the wood chips for smoke for the flavor. But my kids do not believe in gas. They think we have a good market—we have the best on the market. You get the full flavor of the smoke in the fish and they are leery to change. It would be up to the boys if they want to change or not. This is the old-fashioned way. Sometimes when you get modern, you lose some of your quality. Since we developed this market, we have stressed quality. If we cannot have quality, we are not going to handle this product. I think that is why our business is growing now, because we have quality. When we catch our chubs, instead of just freezing them, we wash them in cold water and lay them in boxes so they are all straight are not all crooked. We freeze them in twenty-five pound cartons. In twenty-four hours they are frozen solid. Some people freeze them in fifty-pound blocks and by the time the outside is frozen, the inside is rotten.

Joy Lang (Leland, Michigan), who was married to Ross Lang for more than thirty years when he died in a 1998 fishing accident, indicated that the Michigan Fish Producers Association unified fisherman both economically and socially.

We knew fishing people from all over the Great Lakes—particularly Lake Michigan. You networked a little more with those you knew. There were a few in Lake Superior. We socialized with those people a lot and visited back and forth. We went to the state conventions of the Michigan Fish Producers Association every year. Ross was on the board of directors for the Lake Michigan side. We got real involved with other fishermen. I admired some of those wives who were right in there working on the boat. Some of them were great net workers; they knew how to build nets.

I remember when they were putting the fisheries out of business the Michigan Fish Producers took it upon themselves to put notices in restaurants what the state was doing—taking fish away from the individual who was not able to go out there to do the sport fishing or buy it in the market. They were taking away a product that was such a good healthy product for the customers. I think that did have some effect.[54]

Rick Johnson (Gills Rock, Wisconsin) supplements his income working as a carpenter during the winter months. He noted that the unpredictability of fishing made it particularly difficult to gauge when and if he would make his quota. He and other local fisherman have created a marketing cooperative in order to get the best price possible for their fish.

I make my living fishing ten months of the year. During the winter months, when there is not much fishing, I go to work for my father in the construction business. Most of my living is made off of fishing, but it can be tough. About a month ago, we had a real bad blow. Our nets got all messed up and ripped pretty badly. Over the last month, the fishing has picked up again but it was looking like it was going to be a long spring and short summer. Most of the people in northern Door County are pretty much dedicated strictly to fishing. You get down in the southern bay with the perch fishermen—a lot of guys have second jobs. But I have enough quota where I can stay fishing. You almost have to stay fishing, especially if you have restaurants that you are selling to. They do not take too kindly to you saying, "Well, I will be back fishing in two weeks." They want a steady supply, so we try to provide it, even if fishing is not real great. Last summer was really poor but we stayed at it and filled our orders. You have to work at it a little bit harder. With a forty percent increase in our quota this year, I am not sure that we will make it. It could be close. Yesterday, I would have said yes and today I would have said no. Yesterday we had 1,400 pounds and today we had 100. You never know from one day to the next, especially with gill nets. It will be tough unless the fishing on the bay goes back to the way it was three years ago. We were catching 1,000 pounds on three boxes of nets. I have never seen fish like that before in my life, 400 or 500 pounds to the box. We were basically grading for size. We would throw the live ones back. They were all live. We just picked the size we wanted and everything else went over the side. You would fill up 800 to 900 pounds a day. It was just unbelievable fishing.

Jeff Weborg, Jake Ellefson from Washington Island, Dennis Hickey from Baileys Harbor, and Neil Teskie from Ellison Bay and I have a cooperative; it's our marketing tool. We hired a manager to market our fish in New York, Chicago, and wherever. Before we had a co-op, another individual owned the business and you sold the fish directly to him, and he marketed the fish by himself. Otherwise, each fisherman did it by himself. You would get in off the lake and had to call the fish buyer to see what he was going to give you today. The co-op is a better way of doing it. The co-op has worked out real well. It has cost us a few trips to New York, but we have a frozen market where we can freeze fish at a guaranteed price. At this time of the year, when the price is down a little bit and you have that guaranteed price, it makes a big difference as far as what the bottom line is concerned.

Some other fishermen are starting to sell fish through us. The Voights do it. Paul Saunders does it. A fisherman on Washington Island uses us once in a while. At different times, we buy chubs from fishermen in Kewaunee—so obviously we are trying to expand. The more we can sell, the more the co-op makes. Obviously we think we can do a better job of marketing their fish than they can. We can make more money for them by selling for them. The New York market is definitely more lucrative than the Chicago market, which is where the Voights pretty much exclusively sell. When they are selling on their own, they sell exclusively to Chicago. The problem is that over the last ten or fifteen years the fish houses in Chicago have declined. There are not nearly as many of them. Even if they are still there, you have to know if they are financially sound. A lot of money has been lost over the last ten years with fish markets that go bankrupt, and two days later they open up down the street under a different name. It is not fun sometimes.

Tom Kelly, a marine biologist and educator, reflected on the changes commercial fishing had undergone since the 1970s. He spent a decade after college working as a commercial fisherman.

If I were a commercial fisherman, I would be looking for something else to do. I think they are probably getting the same price per pound for fish now that they were twenty years ago. I do not think anybody is getting too rich doing that. Maybe a few people are doing okay. It is obvious that the trap nets work. You can catch fish with them, and they have the ability to be selective. And given our situation here with an intense sport fishery, that is the way the fishery is going to go. There is still a legal chub fishery out of Leland that uses gill nets, and will probably continue to because they are fishing deep for the chubs with small mesh nets. And I understand that bi-catch of sport fish is not that great. That is probably a gill-net fishery that could continue.

Ross Lang is gone. I have seen Terry Buckler up here quite a lot, but I do not know what his situation is right now. He was fishing perch out of Chicago for a while.[55] Somehow, some of those folks like Ross Lang and Bill Carlson managed to hold on. Of course, they had to diversify. Ross had fished chubs with gill nets primarily and then at some point, he bought a trap-net boat. Then he built his own trap-net boat, the *Joy*, so he was fishing two boats. Carlson does a lot of wholesale and retail business in addition to operating the fishing boat. They have more; they do not rely on just the boat. When the fishery closed down, it probably affected some of the fishermen in other ports more than those in Leland. Of course, there was a lot more commercial fishing in the years before I got here, you know, and was all gone when I got here.

———

Neil Teskie (Gills Rock, Wisconsin) and several other local fishermen organized the Door County Commercial Fisheries Cooperative as one of several ways of obtaining a better economic return on the fish they catch on their individually owed or leased fishing rigs.

Mark and Jeff Weborg, Mark Weaver of Weaver Fisheries, Rick Johnson, Dennis Hickey, Jake Ellefson on Washington Island and I market our fish through the Door County Commercial Fisheries Co-op. The co-op's building and cooler are down in Ellison Bay. Harvey Olson ran it before us. He was a commercial fisherman and fish buyer for a long time. We bought the cooler from him and put up a new building. We have a fellow that manages it. He markets our fish to the best of his ability. We have markets that we have developed. A lot of our fish are going to New York and some stay here. Some are for the fish boils this time of year. But the bulk of our fish go to New York. We have got about two or three good buyers up there who like our fish. We have good healthy fish—good size; they are not skinny. We dress and sort the fish. The smaller ones go one place and the bloodline is taken out of the bigger ones and they are frozen. We have a market for frozen whitefish—it has to be a certain size, the bloodline has to be out of it, and they go on to a smoker in New York. The co-op helps us maintain a more stable market. Sometimes you have to freelance. But it has stabilized our marketing. I would not want to go back to the old way where I was selling all my fish on my own and one buyer would call me up and say that this guy will sell it to me for five cents less. It is good because we deal with the people who pay. You deal with certain individuals who know who you are and know your product. They know our product is going to be good.

Changes in policy, fishery stock, and market conditions require commercial fishermen to constantly adjust to new conditions. Over the years, they have come to regard technology as an aid to assist them in meeting new demands. Many fishermen supplement their knowledge of present-day gear and techniques with information they have learned from their fathers, grandfathers, or other community members. Howard Weborg has fished the Great Lakes for more than eight decades. Ninety-one at the time of his 1999 interview, he still fishes the waters off Wisconsin's Door County. Weborg recalled when he and his family fished long lines. Rolls of set lines with hooks attached have now been in his storage shed for more than sixty years.

I was born on June 24th, 1909. I have three brothers—Glen, Wallace, and Emory. They all fished except one brother who worked down in Gary, Indiana, in the steel mills. When the Great Depression came, they all had to come back here. Then they trusted in fishing. We did good fishing. We did not suffer during the depression. Some fished on their own. Emory and I worked for our dad and uncle until our dad died. Then we worked for Ma for five years, and then our uncle did not want to keep the rig up. He wanted to quit fishing. Well then, we told him that does not leave anything for us to do. He either had to sell it to us or split the rig up. So he sold it to us. Emory and I later bought a rig from our uncle after he died. We bought the boat—the *Golden Girl*. It was built in 1918. It was wood and seasoned with a little sheet iron on the outside so they could run in ice and water. Otherwise, the ice would chew the boat to pieces.

I started fishing hooks. Four hundred hooks on each line—all cotton, too. When they wanted to lay them away, they put them on slats along the walls of the shed. We used hooks for lake trout. There is a hook every twenty feet on the heavy twine or maitre cord. Every twenty feet there is a four-foot line with a hook tied to it. They call the four-foot line a snooge, which might be a Scandinavian name. We had 10,000 baits and so we set 10,000 hooks. We started outside the bluff out there and went all the way across to Michigan—we had a Michigan license. Then they went up to Door County with the lines and came in by Chambers Island and Fish Creek and then back down. You only can lift 3,000 hooks a day so that took a little over three days to lift all of the lines. The lines would sit out for one or two nights. Then you would go out and pull them and take the trout off. They had pound nets that would catch little herring for bait. Then they would take the hook through the back and then come out through the cheek. We stopped using those hooks in the 1920s. There are about 400 hooks on each one of the lines. You tie them together. At that time we set 10,000 hooks, all in one line. We would have to run them hooks over, you know. The trout tangled the lines up, so then before they could set them again, we had to run them over and put them in hook boxes. Us kids, nine to ten years old, would take all the tangles out and run them. The boat could run almost full speed as they were setting them. We would space them out after they lifted them. They have been hanging here in the shed forever. Oh man, we set miles of them.

With pound nets, we had a forty-foot square pot. We had boats that were thirty feet long, and could put them right into the pot. You pull up the tunnel and then you work the fish over to one side where we had the smaller mesh. From there, we would scoop them. It was an open boat. We pursued whitefish and herring with those nets. We also set a box of nets that we called floating nets. Milk jugs were used for every ten floats and the nets hung in the water six feet below the surface. The last year we used pound nets was 1975.

The *Golden Girl* cost us $12,000 in 1945. Now it would be $60,000 or $70,000. It had a Kahlenberg engine. It only had 350 revolutions a minute—a three-cylinder Kahlenberg. You never broke down with them. Emory and I were partners in that boat. We also had a fish tug called the *Skipper*. It was built in Sturgeon Bay in 1945.

Daniel "Pete" LeClair (Two Rivers, Wisconsin) described how his family tended the now nearly obsolete pound net. LeClair worked with his father in the pound-net fishery until the 1940s, when they began gill netting.

When you tended the pound net, you started at the back end. You started in the back and took the net off the posts and pulled the net in the boat until you got to the back two corners. The fish would be all bunched up in here. And then you would scoop them into your boat. The tunnel of the net would just collapse. They had ropes on the top and bottom of the tunnel that would pull it and open it up. When you started, you let these lines all go and they would force the fish all to one side. Then you would scoop the fish out and then push this whole net down under water. Then you get your boat inside the net and your boat goes and follows with it. From your boat, you pushed the net down and the boat would go over the top and get inside the net. Then you scoop them out with a dip net.

As they set the net back, they would pull the boat back and all the net would go back into the water. Then they would go back outside the net and lay the boat outside of these posts and then they would pull all this tight and get the net back up to position again. Then you would go to the next one.

Neil Teskie (Gills Rock, Wisconsin) recalled how during the early 1970s he and his father worked together to tend pound nets with another Gills Rock fishing family, the Weborgs. Teskie remembered the labor involved in fishing before nylon was used in gill nets and trap-net operations.

We fished pound nets and gill nets. Actually, the first few years we fished with Marvin, Mark, and Jeff Weborg in the pound nets together. We went together. We did not have enough crew to individually do it, so we all went together. We fished anywhere from seven to eight pound nets in the spring. We did not fish the fifty-foot nets they fish now in North Bay. We fished up to eighty-foot nets. We had seven of them in the water at that time. We did fairly well in the pound-net fishery at that time from the early to middle seventies. When the pound nets were done in the spring, then we fished gill nets the rest of the year. We did not have a trap-net fishery at that time. This was in the early 1970s—1975 or 1976.

In about 1976 we bought the *Frances* and we started fishing trap nets. Before that time, the trap net had been a banned piece of gear and they legalized it again. They caught a lot more fish than the gill net did and you were able to go out in deeper water than with a pound net. I am not sure exactly why they were a restricted piece of gear. I believe gill-net fishermen got the trap net curtailed, but I cannot say that with any animosity because I fish gill nets as much as I do trap nets. We used to fish two pound nets at Chambers Island, two on the Horseshoe Reef, one at the Sister Island, one in the Porcupine Bay area, one in Ellison Bay, two in Gills Rock, probably one at Elstroms, just around from the Gills Rock area, and one or two in the Door. It was sometimes a trick to keep them upright there at Death's Door by Northport dock. We used to have two pound nets off of Northport pier next to the ferry landing. But it was hard to keep them standing there. The currents would take them down quite often, but we did not have the equipment we had then. Now I can take 200—300 foot lines and put them in a box and carry them by myself. But back then, we used to have one, two guys carry one 300-foot line because it was cotton, manila, and tarred. It was heavy. We used to have to put them on rope spinners and then spin them. We hardly had any nylon at all. Everything was cotton and manila rope. So things broke a lot easier and did not have the strength that nylon and the polypropylenes do nowadays. The equipment we were working with was a lot more backbreaking and a lot more time consuming than it is now. We fished pound nets in the lake at one time but it was not for a whole lot of years.

Dennis Hickey, a third-generation fisherman of Norwegian descent, fishes out of Baileys Harbor in Wisconsin's Door Peninsula. He discussed the challenges of remaining involved in the pound-net fishery. Hickey anticipates that pound nets will soon disappear from the Great Lakes altogether.

The cormorants have basically ruined our spring and summer pound-net fishery. We have the last pound-net rig on the Great Lakes. It is a tremendous piece of gear.

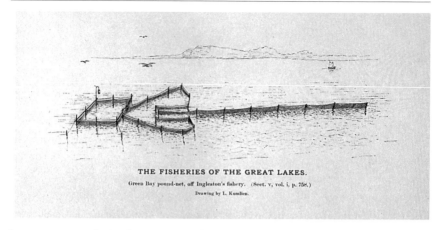

THE FISHERIES OF THE GREAT LAKES.
Green Bay pound-net, off Ingleston's fishery. (Sect. v, vol. i, p. 758.)
Drawing by L. Kumlien.

Large entrapment devices known as pound nets were anchored to long poles driven into the lake bottom. Pound nets were a common sight on Lake Michigan a century ago. Today, Dennis Hickey of Baileys Harbor, Wisconsin, maintains the last pound-net operation on Lake Michigan and Don Stiller was among the last commercial fishermen to use pound nets on Green Bay. This drawing originally appeared in a report of the U.S. Commission of Fish and Fisheries in 1887.

In the spring the cormorants get in the nets and spear all the whitefish. They slash and ruin them and chase the fish. We still fish the pound nets in the fall, but it is a lot of work. Basically, we maintain a trap-net rig for the springtime of the year so that the nets are down under the water where the cormorants cannot get them. If you set in shallow water they still get in there. Then we pull those out and set the pound nets back for fall fishing because they are just a heck of a nice piece of gear. If you get trout or salmon in there, it is real easy to release them. It is more of a volume-type fishery than trap nets—it is a lot easier to handle a bigger volume of fish faster. So we take seventy-five percent of our quota in the fall with pound nets. So if you are going to see pound nets, you have to come here because we are the last guys left.

When we quit, there will not be anymore. It will be the end of it. At one time, I think throughout all the Great Lakes and in all the little towns it was one of the best pieces of gear the fishermen used—the pound net. A lot of times two or three families would join together and one would have the boat, one would have a net, and the other one would cut the stakes or whatever and they would all work together and they would fish one or two pound nets. The whole Door Peninsula was just lined with them all the way around in the 1800s and early 1900s. And I think that was true on a lot of the lakes.

Kenneth Peterson, who fished out of Fairport, Michigan, for more than forty years, recalled when fishermen such as his father used a wide variety of gear and traveled around the lakes in search of fish. He discussed how fishing was more labor-intensive in the past before synthetics were used.

There are quite a few who fished out of here. I was fishing on the boats when A. D. Shaw was here. A. D. Shaw was from Cheboygan, Michigan, on the other side of the straits. He brought his whole crew and everything else here. He owned practically all of Fairport. The town was not that big, but he owned just about every building for housing for his crew. A. D. Shaw had a big fishing rig. I have no idea how many boats he had at the time, but he had at least ten or twelve boats of his own. They fished mostly pound nets. Then they got into trap nets, too. Years ago there was no limit on how deep the pot could be. The whole net was thirty to forty feet or whatever. Now they got a limit on the pots for fishermen that fish trap nets now. You cannot have anything deeper than a twenty-foot pot, but you can taper the hearts up to forty-five. You can have your hearts and your lead up to forty-five feet.

I liked to fish pound nets once we were all set up. We had anchors we attached to our stakes. Then we would sink the lines. In the fall when you pull your stakes out, we would leave the lines right there. Then you go back on your ranges. Old Joe LeClair used to call it a ranger—we used to take our rangers on our nets and, of course, you always got them back in the same spot. You would grapple up the lines and stand your stakes up and tie them up. Then we set the twine on them. But you had to wait till late in the spring, because you had to have all of the ice out of the bay when you went up there and set up your stakes and that.

The fall of the year would really raise hell with your cotton nets. You could hardly lift them sometimes. When you would get your fingers in them and you would tear up the twine a little bit. But then they got this synthetic twine. That was a little stronger. You could tug a boat with just one twine and almost tow it with it before it breaks.

I mostly fished in our own family, with my dad and my brothers. I worked for different fishermen like Ron Gauthier. I fished for him or worked on his boat with him. They called him Runny. I fished with a guy by the name of Lester Groll when I was a young fellow. That is when we worked for three dollars a day. We got fifteen dollars for five days a week in the 1930s.

When I was a real young kid, my dad and I went trolling for lake trout out of Munising. We had riggers on her and outriggers—big long poles. We trolled one day there, but I never did that too often. All the fishermen wanted to go and try it, so my dad said, "Well, we will go and try it." He went out and tried her. We got a few trout trolling like that. It was a nice day and it was fun doing it.

My dad fished for lake trout. He used set hooks; you put the bait on them. They used bloats for bait. Bloat are like chubs. They bloat up when you catch them, when you take them from deep water up to the shoal water. They were fresh. You just keep the bloat so it would float. They had barber hooks. They put barbers on them every so often that would keep them up so far off of the bottom. The set hooks had little stones on them once in a while, too, and then they would sink them down pretty close to the bottom. We fished hooks like that. I can see my old dad at the lifter there with his gaffe hook. He would snap the old bloats off, lifting hooks, anything that did not have a fish on it. You had to knock the bloat off. He always had a pet seagull there, one of his buddies would come and land on the roller and he would sit there. My dad would talk to him and feed him chubs or bloats. We used to go right out here in the lake from Fairport, down to the northern end a little bit. My father did more hook fishing than I did. I never fished too many hooks. My fishing was mostly gill nets until I started fishing this twine pound nets and trap nets. If you get a pretty good load on your boat, most trap-net and pound-net boats are decked off on top so the water will shed off them. You have to keep the scuppers clean so the water can run off of the deck. There are boats that swamped up in the bay pulling trap nets or pond nets. They get too loaded, too heavy. You can get into trouble pulling stakes too.

Bill Carlson, a fourth-generation fisherman and fish buyer who operates out of Leland, Michigan, reflected on changes and continuities in fishing and fishing gear. He indicated that despite numerous technological advances, fishermen still rely heavily on knowledge shared by or passed down from family and community members.

The native species that commercial fishermen pursued in the Great Lakes were lake trout, whitefish, sturgeon, chubs, perch, and menomoniees. The lake trout and whitefish were the most valuable so that was what they concentrated on. The techniques they used in the past are very similar to what we use now. They used a gill net. Gill netting was the primary fishing technique. They also used pound nets. Pound nets were nets that worked like a maze that were staked in place. The gill nets sat on the bottom like a fence and actually physically entrapped the fish by their gills. We use very similar techniques today. The main difference is the material that the nets are made of and the type of equipment we use to tend them. Originally, my grandfather used a sailboat. He fished out of a twenty-foot sailboat called a Mackinaw boat. Then they started using one-cylinder engines on smaller boats that still had the Mackinaw hulls, but had cabins put on them. Now we fish with larger steel boats and diesel engines. My father used to always say in the old days we had wooden boats and iron men. Now you have iron boats. I think he was telling me something. I am not sure.

The technique has not changed much. The netting material started out as cotton, then went to linen, and now is nylon or monofilament depending on the choice. But those changes have been here for the last fifty years. The entrapment gear like the pound net, has now been replaced by trap nets. Now you do not actually drive stakes in the ground, but use anchors to hold the net in place. We are using trap nets here now. But the technique, the idea, the concept, is still the same. We have improved on it some but mostly in the equipment that we use and the materials that we use. So that has not been a tremendous change. The species have changed. There's a lot of new exotic species in the lake and ones that were once abundant like sturgeon and other fish, no longer exist.

We are still entrapping fish the way they have for decades. The electronic equipment on the boat has become more sophisticated with GPS (Global Positioning System) and underwater sonar. We are looking at underwater television as a technique to find out things that we could not determine before as far as what the net looks like under water and why it is not fishing for a particular reason. It could be that part of it is collapsed, which we could not tell before. The cost of underwater television is coming down, so we can use it to see these problems with the nets. Basically, we are doing things pretty much the same as we always have. And a lot of what we do today is based on information that has been passed down from generation to generation.

When we use traditional gear like trap nets and pound nets, we are doing it on a historical level; there's not a lot of learning in a situation like that. We are learning a little bit, especially with trap nets, because we are fishing areas that were never fished with pound nets. Pound nets were out in the exposed part of the lake. You had to drive stakes in the ground. They stayed there. You strung your nets along those stakes. Trap nets use anchors instead of stakes to hold them in position, so they are much more flexible than pound nets. We are finding those things out through trial and error. We are also going over those areas with sonar. The other day we made a trip twenty-five miles from here to check to see if the slope of the bottom was conducive to setting our type of trap nets in those areas. We are still doing a lot of research and learning things, but when it comes right down to it, we are still going back to those traditional fishing grounds that have been passed on from generation to generation.

Chuck Jensen discussed how fishing practices and gear have changed over time. His family fisheries made adjustments according to larger environmental, economic, or resource policy realities.

Years ago they fished with hooks and gill nets for lake trout—especially gill nets, most of the year. Years ago, when they used hook lines, they could have them on the bottom or just off the bottom or they could float them up higher. They could regulate the depth of hook lines, but your nets were always on the bottom. There were tugs in the harbor in the 1930s and a couple of them fished hook lines for trout. They set a string of hooks in a line and they would come back and pick them up. They fished mostly hooks during the fall and winter. I do not think they did much in the summertime.

We would set a gang of chub nets and it might be eight boxes or ten boxes, sometimes twelve. With your perch nets, you usually just fish a three-box gang. Because of the currents, you would not want to have the nets too long or they would be at two different depths of water. So, instead of having one long gang for perch nets, you would set maybe three or four shorter ones so you would have the same depth of water. Perch or whitefish will usually stay in the same depth of water at different times of the year, depending on the temperature of the water, so you did not want the gangs of nets too long. You are better off to have two or three side by side instead of having one big long one.

It seems like we had more severe winters years ago than we have now. We had more ice in the lake, so we were shut down pretty well from the first of the year until about March. January and February and most of March was just about completely shut down. But if we had a break in the weather or if there was not much ice in the lake, they would fish when they could. Sometimes they would get stuck. The nets would be out longer than they should be. It did not hurt anything, just that you could not get the fish out there.

The only hassle in the winter would be your long runs out to the chub grounds. You might be running anywhere from an hour to a two-hour run out and one hour to two hours back and that made a lot of difference if the weather was bad. With perch fishing—you could have a short day. We did not have a very long run. Perch are hard on your hands when picking them out, but you did not have to dress them. You did not have to clean them at all. But all the chubs, whitefish, and trout were dressed out before shipping. The only other processing besides gutting was when we opened the retail counter, when we sold retail to individual customers. Then we would filet and cut and whatever.

The DNR used to have a closed season in the fall of the year for trout during their spawning season, which is usually in late October or November. If they had a closed season on trout, they would fish for whitefish, perch, or whatever they could catch, depending on the weather. In the spring there was a closed season on the perch during their spawning season, so they would fish for whitefish or trout. They had two or three choices during the year. When the trout disappeared, they switched over to chub fishing, so then it was chubs, whitefish, and perch. We never had much trap-net fishing down this end of the lake. They did not have the gear they have nowadays, the nylon and so forth. We had all the bad storms down here and it was not very profitable at that time.

The fishermen were in a transition changing from fishing trout to chubs in the late 1940s and early 1950s. It was probably about 1948 when the depletion really hurt—within a one- or two- year period. You could still fish for perch and whitefish but there was a transition from the type of nets you fished for trout to a smaller size for chubs. So we just had to get more gear and make more gear, but I do not think the transition was that bad.

There was always a restriction on the size of the mesh you could use to fish perch. I believe the perch mesh was anywhere from two-and-a-half- to two-and-three-quarters-inch mesh. You could not bring in anything under a seven-and-a-half-inch perch. Eventually, they took that restriction off for some reason. That was another thing that we could not understand. The DNR would allow us ten percent under size, but anything over that was considered illegal. They eventually took that restriction off and we never could figure out why. During that same period, the DNR let the other boats in and fish large amounts of perch. So I do not know if they had a special reason or not. I do not know. Between the size of mesh, the closed season, and size of the fish, we were restricted pretty good. The fishermen themselves had no complaints about that.

Now retired, commercial fisherman Howard Weborg recalled how change was reflected in both the gear used by fisherman and the use of space within the fishery complex.

One building was used when we fished pound nets. We would hang heavy twine in there and prepare tar for tarring the pound nets. The boiler made steam. There are small pipes in the bottom of that building there. There is a tank in there with tar in it and that heats the tar. And they had a rack in there. They pulled all the twine on there and then when the tar got hot, they would let her down because everything was cotton.

We had to boil the cotton gill nets every month to preserve them and kill the bacteria. We boiled the water in the tank. That is why we have the tank out there on the other side of the building. The tank has one of these wrought pipes. We fired it with oil, and heated the water. When it was boiling, we scooped the water on the nets. Otherwise, the nets will start to get black spots on them and then you could break them easily. When we fished cotton gill nets, we fished twelve boxes a day. We would reel up six and then we would have to pack off six boxes to take along until we got them all boiled and then we could go for a month again. My dad, Alfred Weborg, built this shed in 1913. Up here in the shed is where we made our gill nets. We spent $66,000 on the steel sheeting for the bulkheads on the dock. She was all cedar at one time—cedar logs—and a big blow washed them away.

Donald Voight (Gills Rock, Wisconsin) maintained that the equipment once used by commercial fishermen required considerable individual skill and judgment.

W hen I fished, all we had was a clock and a compass to navigate by. We did not have all the instruments they have now. You had to be a pretty good navigator. And you had to know your way around your engines. We had Kahlenberg engines and in 1986 we took the Kahlenberg out of the *Faith II* and put in a Cummins and that Kahlenberg sits out in my backyard and we run it once in a while.[56] I got it running last year after it sat for ten years.

At first we had cotton nets. Then it went to nylon and then to monofilament, which they are using now. The cotton nets had to be taken in and boiled. We boiled them once a month. We dried them all the time, or they would have rotted, you do not have to do this with the synthetic materials. I preferred the monofilament. It makes less work for you and you get less junk in them, like alewives. Alewives were hard on cotton and nylon nets.

Daniel "Pete" LeClair (Two Rivers, Wisconsin) noted how his family was forced to adopt new fishing gear and methods as a result of changes in fisheries stock and fisheries policy. He owns two of the five trawlers licensed to fish smelt in Wisconsin waters by the DNR.

S ome of our pound nets were in eighty feet of water, but most of them were for herring and whitefish in forty feet of water. We fished pound nets in the 1930s and 1940s. When I was young we used pound nets for lake trout and herring. Herring was a big fish in those years. Right now, the herring are obsolete; there are none. We used pound-net boats and scooped the net out. Then we fished with gill nets and later, with trap nets, which is a big industry for whitefish. The modern way—the way we are fishing now—we pull the trawl behind the boat. There are five trawlers on Lake Michigan that are operating under this method. Under the present controls with the DNR this industry is finally going to be eliminated, I believe. These are smelt trawlers. We have two of them.

When my father fished pound nets, he used an old wooden boat with a little gas engine in it. It was an open boat with an engine instead of sails. It had a hoist and a square stern and he pulled the net up and they bunched the fish and scooped them into the boat. The boat was about thirty-five feet long and ten feet wide. It was called a pound-net boat. This is how it was in the 1930s.

Don Stiller, who began fishing on Lake Michigan and Green Bay with his father in the 1940s, stayed in business by pursuing different target species and fishing in a nearby river. Each shift in target species and location brought new demands for skills and equipment.

On top of my cupboard is a replica of one of the boats we had. We bought a conventional gill-net boat in 1947 in Algoma. It was twenty-five feet long and we called her the *Dawn*. It did not have a power lifter in it. We did the lifting by hand. We bought her from Fred Michael and we re-powered it. We put a twenty-five-horse power Universal utility-four engine in it. It would not run an hour on a gallon of gas, but our range was mostly within three miles. We usually did not go out further than the net. When the water went down, we got a big flat-bottom boat we used for alewife fishing. It was a twenty-two footer and almost eight-feet wide. We had only about six inches of free board on it. We had up to 7,800 pounds of suckers in it.

For ten years or twelve years we fished suckers in the river with a pound net. We actually blocked it off two-thirds of the way and we caught fish going upstream and downstream and we caught 780,000 pounds of suckers over that period of time. We would catch them when they were going up and then we would turn the net around and get them when they were coming back after they spawned. Those fish went over to the Schilling Fish Company and were shipped south for crawfish bait. All these fish, like the alewife, were packed in fifty-pound paper boxes. The fish was put in a rack, which would hold 1,600 pounds. The racks were transferred into a quick freeze, and then into a big holding freezer, which could store 12 million pounds. Then they were shipped— 40,000 pounds a trip—down to Carnation in Jefferson, Wisconsin, and to Kalcan in Columbus, Ohio. That is where those fish went.

Brain Price discussed how commercial fishermen responded to changing economic, political, and environmental conditions by migrating to different fishing grounds and adopting new fishing technologies.

When the Michigan DNR closed the chub fishery in 1975, I went to work for the Sea Grant program in an office in Traverse City. I remember I was walking down the street and Ross Lang pulled over and asked me if I wanted to go fish up in Lake Superior. I was not doing anything that was making any money, so for a period of about a year and a half we fished on Lake Superior out of Munising. The fishing culture up there was somewhat different. We are pretty tame and civilized down here on Lake Michigan compared with those guys. It was a lot of fun.

Ross Lang had been a fisherman all his life as were his people before him. They had lots of experience with different kinds of fishing. All I knew was how to pick chubs, set nets, and do stuff on a gill-net boat. We still lived down here. We would go up to Manistique on Sundays and come back on Thursdays if the weather was good. We got all our work done by putting in twelve- or fourteen-hour days most of the time when we were up there. Heck, we did not have anything else to do but work. Ross did not drink. We just worked. We caught a lot of fish.

We showed those folks up there how to fish chubs because that is what we specialized in down here. They did not fish chubs up there, because there is no market for chubs on Lake Superior when there is any production out of Lake Michigan. The guys out East that buy the fish know the difference between Lake Michigan chubs and Lake Superior chubs and they prefer Lake Michigan chubs because they take the smoke better. They taste better. They are a different stock, even though they are the same species. If there is plenty of Lake Michigan chubs, you cannot even sell Lake Superior chubs really. It is a bizarre thing.

On Lake Superior at that time, there was still a large mesh gill-net fishery for whitefish. I learned a little bit about setting the large mesh gill nets. The only time I have ever fished with large mesh gill nets was up there. At the same time, we realized that in order to ever come back down to the Leland area, we were going to have to learn to fish something else and do it in a different way. The state had been pushing fishermen for a long time to convert to trap nets. Ross was always willing to try whatever to keep himself in the fishing business, so he bought a goofy little trap-net boat called

Seagull. It looked like the *Merrimac* or the *Monitor* with a telephone booth stuck on the bow. In that cabin we taught ourselves how to fish trap nets which are far more complicated, more costly, more difficult, and more interesting than gill nets. Ultimately, Ross probably came to prefer fishing trap nets. I know I came to prefer fishing trap nets; they are fun.

Fishing trap nets is a big shell game. The average operation has about ten nets out at any given time. The nets stay out in one location and are held down by these giant anchors. You go and empty the net every once in a while, which is fun. You never know what is in there and it is kind of enjoyable. You cannot fish trap nets in really terrible weather. I like that, too. I have seen enough terrible weather up on Lake Superior to last for a while. I like the idea that when the weather's bad, we will stay home today. You are out on the open deck instead of enclosed in the gill-net boat, so you are outside in the sun. You are always thinking, trying to figure out where the fish are going next, trying to outsmart them, even more so than with gill-net fishery. Gill nets are so easy to move. There is more strategy involved trying to figure out where the fish are going to move with the trap nets. When you hit it right, the trap nets can be wildly successful. I mean, it is like winning the lottery to find a new spot for a trap net where there is a huge number of fish that you did not know about before. That happened this spring. The guys who are fishing on the boat that I worked on with Ross and then I helped with last spring when Ross died, just found a spot. We never fished there. Ross and I never put a net there, and it is only like a half mile from where we did. But they found a new spot and they are just hammering them.

In 1999, Ben Peterson, who held a tribal fishing license and a commercial fishing license from the State of Michigan, discussed how the gear used by the Peterson family changed over time with policy and the availability of fishing stocks.

My brother, Joel, was in the service when the whitefish first started picking up a little bit, during the latter part of the 1960s. I graduated from high school in 1971, and that is when we kind of started as a partnership, my father, Joel, and I. My father was in the business and we both did it as kids, but from then on, it seemed like it was pretty good. Around 1974, 1975, and 1976 we first started into trap nets. We kept getting a little more efficient. We have had a couple down years but all in all they average out pretty near the same.

Joel knew this guy who knew another guy who had this boat in a yard down near East Tawas. We bought the boat for about $400. It cost us more to have it hauled home than it did for the boat. So we got it home here. We had a brother-in-law that was a really good welder and we fixed her all up and went into the trap-net business.

The trap net is by far, more efficient. The only problem is you catch so many at one time that you control the market so much—it knocks the price down. The gill net is more effective. The gill net is more selective. You are not handling everything with the gill net. You only catch the larger fish. You do not catch all the small fish like the trap net. It is a four-and-a-half-inch mesh but the fish do not swim through it. It was designed so he just sits there. The gill net's four-and-a-half-inch stretch of mesh only catches large fish. Small fish go through it. There are a lot of dumb people who are not educated in the fishing business and do not understand how the gill net works. If you go out here and set a gill net and let that thing go ten days or five days or whatever, you are going to have a lot of dead fish.

There is controversy with the gill net catching lake trout. Lake trout have teeth and they are gonna get caught in the gill net, so it closes their mouth and a lot of them die when they get caught in there because they twist. But we have caught a lot of lake trout that you can catch and release. There was a biologist named Jerry Peterson who retired out of Escanaba. And we took him out there and showed him I do not know how many times that we could release lake trout. How can we pound it into their heads? Besides that, I do not see the big thing. We should be able to keep some. We should have been able to keep some of the fish anyway because after all, it is tax dollars that paid for these fish and the fish-eating public definitely ought to be able to eat some of that fish, not only the licensed sport fishery. Where would you be without commercial fishermen? You would not have any fish fries on a Friday night.

Fairport, Michigan, native Kenneth Peterson fished with his father, and later his son, on Lake Michigan for more than forty years. He acknowledged the benefits of new technology, but cautioned against depending on it.

J ust like any other fisherman, you had to move around a little bit. Now they do not let you move. You got a fifty-mile radius and that's right from this port fifty miles one way. You cannot go any farther north. We can only go partly up the bay here. You cannot fish north on the lake there at all. It is all Indian territory now. It is legal for the Indians to fish there but not for a white man. Or they call them Indians, I do not know. Anything you can do to fish, I guess. That is the only way they can fish—is fish Indian rights. I guess I would be doing it too, if I could, or my family anyway. You cannot blame them for that.

I was on the boat until I was at least sixty-two. I was on the boat a little while after sixty-two—maybe a year or two. I broke my son in. He was like my dad. He can go anyplace with a boat, as long as he had water under him. It does not bother him at all. Foggy, blowing, or whatnot, he takes off and goes. Of course, he has got all that modern equipment. It is pretty hard to get lost if you get to know how to run it, but you have got to keep the thing to keep going and running proper. The radar goes to heck once in a while. You cannot get a correct reading on that, but he gets it fixed. That old radar is a lifesaver. It is good when you are in the steamboat channel. If you happen to be crossing the steamboat channel, you better be on the lookout, especially in the fog. A boat can get pretty close to you before they realize you are there. Of course, they got all that equipment on the big boats, too, you know. Accidents still happen—even happen when there is no fog and it is a clear day.

There was an ocean boat that ran over some fishermen in Lake Michigan, right off of Manistique, a ways out there. They saw that boat. They saw it right up to the time that they hit it. They knew it was there. I do not know why the captain did not just shut her right down. If he had to throw the anchor, it would of been a hell of a lot better than running over them. It was terrible. They had an American pilot on there, too. It is funny that he did not make them shut her down sooner than run over them and drown the whole bunch. I heard a crew member tried to swim, but by the time they got to him, he was gone, too, the way it sounded. The crew was partly at fault, too, I guess. They must have had her on automatic pilot. They were all down in the engine room and there was a blind side on that boat. They just got through setting their nets and they set the course for home. Some fishermen depend on those automatic pilots. They are magnetic. You know how a compass will go when a magnet will draw it. Maybe that steel boat drew the fishermen right towards them and it ran across their path. I do not trust a lot of automatic stuff. I was used to sailing with a compass and a watch. You had the window open with your head out there watching where you were going.

I went sailing with my oldest son across the lake. He had about a forty-foot yacht. He puts her on all this automatic stuff and he told me, "When them two numbers come together, let me know. I am going to go and take a shower." I said, "You are not going to do nothing like that until you show me how to kick this automatic pilot out in case I see something in the fog." It was a little foggy, you know. I wanted to be able to steer this thing around it, whatever it is. I do not want that automatic pilot holding me back. He showed me how to throw her out.

Bill Carlson of Leland recalled his involvement in the purse-seining experiment funded in the 1970s by Michigan Sea Grant.[57]

In the 1970s, we developed a technique that was used on the West Coast to catch salmon and adapted it to the Great Lakes to catch whitefish. It was called purse sein-ing. We developed it in a cooperative effort with Michigan Sea Grant. We built a boat, outfitted it, and got equipment made for the particular areas where we intended to fish and the areas that we were limited to. We had gear made to fit those conditions. We used the purse seine on the Great Lakes. It worked very, very well. We learned a lot about fishing doing it. We outfitted the boat with very sophisticated sonar that would scan around the perimeter of the boat up to 1,500 feet. We could see what was happening under the boat, which has become important in the gill netting operation and in sport fishing. With the sonar we could see what was happening all around the area we were in, not just under the boat, but to the sides. We learned a lot about whitefish and how they move and congregate or school and the strata of water they would be located in. Because it was a new technique on the Great Lakes—we were pioneering it—we had to do a tremendous amount of research. There was a lot of trial and error, but we were helped by sophisticated gear. The purse seine was very successful. It is no longer used here because we cannot fish in the waters where we used it. They are Indian waters and they have exclusive rights to those areas. The purse seine had its limitations in that it had to be fished in good weather. We looked for bays and areas where we could get protected waters to fish it in, and those areas we can no longer fish in. We

A purse-seining experiment was funded by Michigan Sea Grant during the late 1970s as an alternative to gill-net fishing. Commercial fishermen Ross Lang and William Carlson were among those who used the purse seine to fish the waters of Lake Michigan near Leland, Michigan. Courtesy of Thomas Kelly.

were lucky with the purse seine in that we just happened to hit it a couple of times. We continued to learn all the time we were fishing it.

Marine biologist Tom Kelly recalled his involvement with three commercial fishermen from Leland in the purse-seining project using Michigan Sea Grant funds.

Around 1975 when I was working with the Sea Grant program, the fishermen in Leland, Bill Carlson, Terry Buckler, and Ross Lang, were interested in trying a new fishing method called purse seining. It was new to the Great Lakes although it is commonly practiced in other parts of the world. The purse seine is a large net that you drag through the water. It is what is called actively fished—you have to be there to do it. It is not like a gill net or a trap net, you put it in the water, and go away and you come back to see if you caught any fish. Through the Sea Grant program, we put a research project together. The four of us flew out to Seattle and went out on some purse seiners out there, and talked to a lot of people out in Seattle and saw how the thing worked for salmon, which are pelagic species. Usually purse seining is done with pelagic schooling fish. And the whitefish here, people really were not sure whether they schooled or not; they are pretty much on the bottom and not up in the water column that much. So it was a question whether this method would work, but we were willing to try it. They purchased a boat, and had a seine made for us out in Seattle. Most of the gear, the hydraulic system and everything, was made in Leland by Nick Lederle.

The boat was modified to do the purse seining. The purse-seine net was put on the back of the vessel in sort of layers and so it would unfold properly. One end of the net is tied to the mother vessel which in this case was a forty-five-foot steel boat called *Argo*. We had a small boat, about twenty feet, that we used as the little tow boat. We would attach one end of the net to the tow boat and then the two boats would steam away from each other in opposite directions, and as they went away from each other, the net would pull off the back of the boat. The net was about 360 feet long and about 110 feet deep. We would go in a big circle, and when the two boats met, we would transfer the end of the net from the tow boat back to the mother vessel. And then we would have this sort of big curtain of netting hanging down in the water in a circle, and hopefully in the middle of the circle were the fish. And then at the bottom of the net, there were weights down there to keep it down and the nylon line called the purse line. The ends of those lines came back onto the ship and we would put them in a hydraulic winch and pull until we had basically the bottom of the net closed up like a purse. That is where the name comes from, purse seine. Hopefully, the fish are inside the net when you start pulling the net in from one end until you have all the fish concentrated in a small area of the net close to the boat. And then we had dip nets with long poles, so we would dip in the water and dip the fish out.

When we first went out, we had one of the captains from Seattle come out when the boat was ready and help us the first few days to learn how to set the seine and get it back in the boat and whatnot. I remember the first time we set the net, we caught two whitefish and I thought that was great because at least we knew we could catch something. And we came over into the bay, like when we started actually doing the experimental work. We came over into the Grand Traverse Bay in the northern part. And we had a special permit from the DNR, a research permit, to fish north of the 45th parallel. And at that time, nobody had commercially fished in Grand Traverse Bay since the mid-1960s. It was closed to commercial fishing so the whitefish population in this bay had had a chance to recover and build up. There was a sport fishery in the lower east arm that was pretty intense, but there really was not much fishing going on up here for whitefishing. And we were catching—we started catching these huge whitefish that were—some of them were twenty pounds and more. We commonly caught fish that were over the state record for sport-caught whitefish. They were over twenty pounds. And they just caught a slew of fish. Then we went down the coast. We fished out of Ludington, Grand Haven, and different ports, to see how it would work in different areas. We were pretty successful, so we did that for a couple of years. The project went on for a couple of years and I wrote two papers on it.[58]

I designed a fish-sorting table that folded up. It was a big table, maybe four feet by four feet or a little bigger. It was made out of wood and had sides that folded up. And along the sides we had the legal length of the fish. The whitefish we could keep had to be nineteen inches, so we marked off on there. So the fish would be dumped in that box, and you would just hold the fish up against the mark if it was close to being too small to see if it was legal or not. And then if it was a legal size fish, it would go down one shoot into the ice box, into the boxes that had ice in them. If not, they went down another shoot, which went over the side of the boat. And so if we got trout or suckers or other fish that we did not want to keep, they would go over the side. And then the whitefish would go down into the fish boxes. It was a pretty slick system. A couple times we got some sturgeon, which was kind of cool. We put them back, of course, but it was neat just to see them. That is basically the system that we used. They caught a lot of fish for a number of years.

They continued to fish that gear, some in the bay and some out in Lake Michigan, for a number of years after that, after the project was over. And then they sold the gear to Bayport Fishery in Saginaw Bay when the Indian commercial fishery started to pick up here in the late 1970s and early 1980s, when a lot of the boats were coming down from Lake Superior and other places. The majority of the fishing, I think, was not being done by the Grand Traverse Bay Indians.

The purse seine was most effective fishing along banks where there was an incline, submerged incline. The fish tended to congregate along the bank, the same places where the Indian fishermen want to put their gill nets. Their nets were laid there, so they really could not seine anymore. So they apparently felt that it was no longer a viable method to use in this area. The other problem with the purse seining was that it was fairly intensive in that it took four people on the larger vessel and one person in the little tow boat. You had a crew of five to maintain, whereas most of the gill netters worked two people in a boat and the trap netters work with maybe three, so you had more mouths to feed in that method. If you are working at a relatively simple piece of gear like a gill net, which is relatively inexpensive and you have already got all of your equipment, you are not going to change what you are doing unless you are forced to do it. That is the situation with the Indian fishery we have today. So it is a more labor-intensive fishery with specialized equipment, some of which is costly. The purse seine was not something that people were jumping at. I understand the folks at Bayport Fishery down in Saginaw Bay used it for walleyes and they did pretty well down there for quite a number of years. I do not know if they are still using it or not. But it was never duplicated by anybody else in the lakes. But we did at least show that it worked, it could be done.

I had a heck of a good time doing that project because I got to know a lot of those people and work with them. I guess that was probably the most satisfying work I have ever done as far as using my talents and working with that group of people. And I got to know Ross Lang really well, before he was killed in a 1998 fishing accident. I remember being impressed with him in that I had never really met anybody who was as dedicated to his given profession. Whatever the problem was, Ross and the other fishermen could improvise some solution out of stuff they had in their garage or on the dock and put in as many hours as it took to get the job done. I do not think anybody ever worried about what they were making per hour. They just worked and worked and worked until the job was done. And there were times when we would be out fishing and not doing very well and suddenly we would get into the fish at maybe two o'clock in the afternoon. We would call the fishery and have them send the truck over. We would go in maybe at six, unload all the fish, get more ice, go back out, and come back in at six o'clock the next morning. We would work twenty-four hours straight, whatever it took. So that was a fun job.

John McKinney has been a Michigan Sea Grant agent since 1979. The purse-seining project was already under way when he arrived in the Grand Traverse Bay area.

The purse-seining project was done in Leland. Bill Carlson and some others working with the Sea Grant got funding. A purse seiner was built and brought here. It was being looked at as an alternative type of fishing, to get away from the gill-net issue. Purse seining was an attempt to find an alternative way to fish for certain species because it can be very species-specific. You can target certain things like whitefish, and fish for them once you know how to do it without interfering with some of the other species. It proved itself. They could target whitefish and they were very successful. They had quotas and all. In the scheme of things, it just did not work out because of larger issues, the politics of it. Locally I think it could have worked, but I do not know that it was given the chance. Purse seining was tried and it was successful, but it never was implemented. The purse seiner is now gone, but I was out on that boat and worked with them a bit. It was actually going on before I got here.

Joy Lang recalled how her late husband sought to adapt to new technologies in order to remain fishing. She discussed Ross Lang's response to DNR policies and the political context of the purse-seine experiment he was involved in during the 1970s.

Then the Department of Natural Resources came along and said—probably five times—you cannot use gill nets any longer because they kill everything they catch. Therefore, they put us out of business. That did not deter Ross at all. He loved fishing so much that he always knew there would be another way. He could find a way. He was very innovative in that respect. He went out to the West Coast and researched how they fished with the purse seines. When he came back, the Department of Natural Resources said that if he could find another way of fishing and could meet their criteria, they would go along with him. He was only in Washington a day and a half, and he came back with all these plans to build a purse-seine boat. The Department of Natural Resources said it would never work in the Great Lakes because the lake bottom was not right—it was not the same. It did not deter him at all. He went ahead with it. As long as they said yes, he went ahead with it.

The purse seining was a very successful operation. I recall one time, I believe it was in 1977, in September of 1977, it was the only time I ever went out on the purse seiner with him. We went over by Northport Bay and they lifted 10,000 pounds of whitefish that day. The reason that all came to an end was the Indian issue. The areas that Ross purse seined in for whitefish were all north of Leland up towards Northport and in the bay, Grand Traverse Bay. But when the Treaty of 1836 became involved, the Indians were given all that territory. Again, Ross was without a way of fishing.

For most Lake Michigan fishermen, during the past century, the fish tug has been the most important tool used to manage fishery stocks both within their own informal systems and the formal system established by the states that license them. Fish tugs are more than just boats to most fishermen; they are practically a part of the family. Many commercial fishers can recall the intimate details of their boats the way they know their family genealogy. They know who built each boat, when it was built, where it was used, who owned it, and what alterations have been made to the boat over time.[59] Jack Cross of Charlevoix provided particularly poignant testimony revealing the extent to which fishermen see their individual, family, and community identity as tied to their boats.[60] A witness to the destruction of one of his family's boats after a state-financed buyout, Cross bought the remaining boat back again even though he did not plan to fish with it. Since the 1999 interview, he has sold the boat once again. In all likelihood, he will continue to keep tabs on her.

Fairport, Michigan fisherman Joel Peterson discussed the ties between the family's history and the fish tugs and trap boats they have owned over the years.

My grandfather had the fish tug *Clara S*, and then the *Dawn*. My father, Ben, and I bought the *Richard E*, which was originally from across the lake, out of Kenosha, Wisconsin. We had the *Arlene A*, which was a little trap-net boat that was out of Saginaw Bay. Then we built a boat called the *Martha Jean*, which is named after my brother's daughter who died when she was thirteen or fourteen. Then we purchased the *Proud Maid*, which was built for fishermen in Manistique, the Sellman brothers. They were put out of the business in the 1970s when they converted over from the gill nets and then came the tribal settlement in 1985. So we acquired that boat. Those are the boats that we have had so far. I do not plan on building any more. What the rest of the boys do is up to them, but we have got a fairly decent fleet. The aluminum boat is forty-five foot by twelve foot, the *Proud Maid* is forty-six foot by fourteen foot, and the *Richard* is fifty foot by fourteen foot.

South Haven resident Chuck Jensen, who is now retired, worked in his family's fish marketing business. He recalled how the purchase or sale of a fish tug was regarded as an important family decision. Jensen observed that when fishermen bought new fish tugs in the 1940s, they were made of steel instead of wood.

When we moved to South Haven around 1932, my father brought the *Tuscarora* with him. It was an old tug that was originally a sightseeing launch in Saugatuck. It is the tug he lost between here and St. Joseph in the storm on the day before or after Christmas 1933. My dad's tug and another tug were out that day. My dad beached his tug south of South Haven, between here and St. Joseph. The other one floundered out there in front of the Catholic Church, and three men drowned on that one. After that, he got the Ike and he had that for several years until 1940. In 1940 he got the *Buddy O*. In 1945 he got the *Elsie J*. He got it at the end of 1945, just after the war. These were gill-net tugs. Most were switching from wood to steel right at that time. There were a lot of good old wooden tugs, but towards the end, they preferred the steel ones because of the ice conditions and the upkeep.

Daniel "Pete" LeClair (Two Rivers, Wisconsin) discussed how fish tugs reflected changes in the fishery and larger economic, technological, and policy issues.

There were wooden fish tugs. They started with steam tugs and then they went to the Kahlenberg engine. Fish tugs have the little doghouse in the back, the area where you steer the boat. With the pilothouse at the stern, you could steer the boat and set the nets. If the powerhouse is further up, you have to have a man up here steering the boat and then somebody back here for the nets. With the aft pilothouse, you could steer the boat and set the nets back at the same time and eliminate one man. That is what I mean by improving the boats as time went on. It was better to have the pilot-house way in the back.

Around 1946–47, the lamprey got so thick they killed all the lake trout. That was the end of our pound-net operation. Then we had to go to gill-net fishing, for chubs and so forth. My dad bought an old wooden boat up in Door County, I believe in Sturgeon Bay, and fixed it up. It was a gill-net tug called the *Margaret*. It was all wood, with a wooden hoist and a small pilothouse and a little gas engine. It was about thirty-five to thirty-eight feet long and about eight feet wide.

The *Margaret* was built in a farmer's backyard up in Door County. It was a pretty crude machine. It had all oak frames, and they had to soak them in water to form them. Mainly, they built the boats themselves. It was something a farmer would build. In those days, you had to be a carpenter, welder, and a jack-of-all-trades to survive in the fishing industry. You had to develop everything yourself. There were not that many people who knew about these boats. You had to design it to fit the demands of the fishery. As they went along, they improved the method and style of different boats. When he brought it home, as he got it to the river, it was leaking so badly that we had to pull it out. My dad had to put all new boards in and rebuild the whole hull because she was so old and rotten. I know she had big oak frames. I remember my father soaking them and trying to bend them to fit the hull.

When he came home with the boat the wind was blowing. He got so seasick, he puked all the way home. He did not know what he had gotten into—buying a boat like this and trying to fish without getting seasick. But he stuck it out. It took a long time to get over it, but he got over it. He fished gill nets until 1953–54, and then I bought his boat and he went mink farming.

Joy Lang recalled the boats owned by her and her late husband. She indicated how each boat was a part of Ross's fishing strategy and an extension of himself. As a result, she has retained the last boat her husband built, which was named for her. The *Joy* is leased to Leland-based fishermen Bill Carlson and Jeff Houdek.

Ross brought the chub boat *Frances Clark* over here. Then the DNR decided that we could not fish chubs any longer because of the gill nets. In 1977 he went to the

Argo, the purse-seining boat, for about a year and a half.[61] Then Ross purchased a whitefish boat from up in the Detour Village area, and brought it back to Leland. He fished with that boat until he built the present boat, the *Joy*. He built the boat himself. Ross had the four boats while in Leland—two of which he built himself.

Ross designed some of his boats. He went up to Iron Mountain to see about buying a boat. It was $85,000 and he did not have the money at the time. So he decided he could make his own. I remember him sitting there with heavy cardboard designing the hull of the boat, getting just the right pitch. That is all he had. All the rest was in his head. He never had anything else on paper, only the hull and what the pitch was going to be. He did the same when he built the *Argo*. He was out in Seattle for a day and a half. He took a lot of pictures of boats and engines, came back, put this boat together. It always amazed me—he looked at boats for a day and a half and just had pictures. But it was there. It was in him. He cut the steel. They bent their own ribs.

George Stevens worked with Ross on the *Joy*. They built it in George's barn—actually a pole building. I cannot recall who they got the pole barn from. Some guy said you can have the pole building, so Ross, George, and Bill Carlson took it apart and put it over in East Leland. They used it for a workshop. That is where the boat was built. It took him about three months to make it when you put the days and the hours into it. He started in October and they finished in March. They had times when they had to wait for the engine and different parts. But in actual days and hours, it took him about three months to build the *Joy*. The *Joy* will stay here in Leland.

Fishing in Wisconsin waters where gill nets are still permitted, Ken Koyen of Washington Island uses two tugs. Koyen compared his 1926 fish tug to a more recently acquired vessel.

The *Sea Diver* came from Erie, Pennsylvania. It was converted into a fish tug about ten years ago. The first fish tug I worked on was the *Welcome*. She is the fish tug *Welcome*, the little *Welcome*. There are two of them in the history books. The ferry line owned both of the boats at one time. One *Welcome* was a car ferry, and the little *Welcome* was used for freight and mail in the wintertime. The fish tug *Welcome* is thirty-nine foot, nine inches long and nine-foot, nine inches wide. It is pretty long and narrow. It does a lot of rolling. Everybody always said it rolled two days before a storm and two days after. The *Sea Diver* is forty-eight foot by thirteen and a half, and is very stable. It is like going from a Volkswagen to a Cadillac; there's just no comparison.

The old fish tugs were designed with a real round stern. Some were made in Marinette, Wisconsin. They were called "Menominee rollers" because they were still pretty round. The back of the *Sea Diver* is square and flat making it a lot more stable. It does not repeatedly roll once it starts. It tends to stop after the first wave goes by. The *Sea Diver* has a Crossley net lifter. It is worn out like most of them. The jaws are worn out pretty bad. It needs to be rebuilt.

Alan Priest (Leland, Michigan) observed that when fish tugs rammed through the ice, mechanical and other equipment problems were not uncommon.

Before they had hydraulic steering on the boat, the boat had chain steering. Jeff Houdek and I were breaking out of the harbor for spring. It was tough going because the ice was really packed in there from winter and we backed up and just hit it and backed up. Anyway, a piece of ice—a big chunk of ice—got caught in the rudder and spun the wheel and broke the coal shut. On the boat's steering mechanism, there is a chain going one way and one going the other way. The coal shut connects them. You put it in there and bang it is shut. It was worn when the ice got in the rudder. We were going forward full blast it cranked the rudder around and snapped it. The ice broke the coal shut and we had no spare on the boat. Jeff said, "What are we going to do?" I said, "Well, I guess we are just going to have to jump on a piece of ice and go and get one." Jeff called the shed over here and Pete Carlson, Bill's dad, said, "I will get you one." So I jumped off the back of the boat on to a piece of ice and ran all the way down the breakwall to the shed to get a coal shut and come back. So we learned to carry a spare.

Now, everything is hydraulic, but you can always have problems. If there is a vibration of the boat and if you get two lines touching, you will vibrate a hole in the line—the copper tubing. After a time you have maintenance and you just have to look at things.

Daniel "Pete" LeClair (Two Rivers, Wisconsin), who owns two of the last trawlers operating in Wisconsin waters of Lake Michigan, recalled how his father improved upon the design of the fish tug used by one of the most prominent building firms, Burger Boats (see page 12).

My father must have had the *Margaret* in the late 1930s or early 1940s. The original *Susie Q*, a steel boat, was built around 1946 or 1947 by Schwarz Marine in Manitowoc. Some of the boats at that time were built with a round bottom. The old Burger boats were built like a bathtub. Every time you would go out there you would be rolling around getting seasick. My dad said, "Well, you look at a duck in the water and the duck just goes up and down, he does not flap around and roll." So, why not build a boat with a square bottom? It will be stiffer in the water because it is going to be flat like a pancake. So that is why he had built it flatter—with a slanted bow so you could break the ice. This boat would climb up on the ice and break it.

The previous boats had a straight bow—they would hit the ice and stop and break nothing. So he designed this boat that would climb up on the ice and the weight of the boat would break the ice and keep on going. We had a lot more luck fishing during the winter months because we could break the ice down. If you have this slant on the bow, it would hit the ice and it would slide up on the ice.

The original *Susie Q* was flat right behind the bow all the way to the back. It was built just like a square cracker box. She did not roll; she just went up and down. Burger boats were like a bathtub; they have to roll. There was nothing to hold them stiff. Our boat was amazing. She would just go up and down. She would hardly roll because of the flat bottom. He changed the boat-building method and developed one all his own. That is why I say my dad was a good inventor.

The original *Susie Q* was built around 1946–47. I know my father stuck me way up in the bow when I was little because I would fit in there to sandblast the steel. I damn near died up in there too. My dad used me for anything possible he could get out of me. He stuck me somewhere and taught me how to work. My dad fished with the *Susie Q* from 1946 until 1952. Then he wanted to retire and get out of it. So I bought the boat and he went into the mink farm business. I fished gill nets for ten years and in 1962 we developed this trawling mechanism.

We had the *Susie Q* and then we bought the *Avis J* as a second boat. Then we had the original *Susie Q* and the *Avis J* as trawlers. When we got the *Avis J*, Jerry Glaser ran it. He has been with me for thirty-five years. He was originally with me on the *Susie Q* and we got this boat so I kept on the *Susie Q* and I transferred him over to the other trawler. The *Avis J* was catching double what I was catching on my little *Susie Q*. That is not good—you cannot be the chief if that is the case. I needed to get a bigger boat to compete. So we sold the original *Susie Q* and we got the new *Susie Q*.

We had two or three people on the boats when we were trawling. When we were fishing for chubs, we had crews of three or four because of all the sorting and the twelve- to fourteen-hour days. When we trawled in the summer in shallow water, we would use a crew of three. When you have 100,000 to 200,000 pounds, you need someone for shoveling the load around.

———

Ben Peterson, a tribal and past Michigan-licensed fisherman, noted the difference in design in fish tugs.

The *Richard E* is our gill-net boat. I cannot even remember when she was built, maybe back in the 1940s. She is a Burger boat, with a Durning hull, a different design. The Burger is more round on the side than the Durning. At the water level, a Burger is rounded. The Durning comes up and has got a little teeny square part to it, which is a pain in the butt because it rusts out right there. We just had to repair all that. I did not realize that there was such a thing as a Durning hull, but a couple of old-timers told me about it. I think the original plan was to give it stability. Whether it worked or not, I do not know. When a gill-net boat stops rocking and rolling, it is time to get off. You are tied up to the dock. When there are about 1,500 chubs up in the front, the bow head will be tipping down in the front.

———

Neil Teskie (Gills Rock, Wisconsin) recounted how his boat preferences were affected by policy changes and fluctuations in fisheries stocks.

I like the deeper fish tugs; the heavier the better. If it rolls less, I can go out in rougher weather. The *Betty*'s pretty good in the weather. She is a good vessel—a worthy vessel. So it is not always a matter of how good the crew is. Of course, it pays to have some determination, but it also pays if you got it trimmed right and got it set up right. I have got that boat set up very, very nice for operating. It has good pilots and good lifters. I prefer a deep draft vessel. I put in a six-inch deeper keel on the *Betty* with a split I-beam because it did not have enough drag. It rolled too much. I put more drag on the bottom to keep her from flopping. It made a big difference. We redesigned her a little bit. The *Frances* is designed with a flatter bottom. It is not designed for fishing chubs or using gill nets. The gill-net boats are mainly designed for fishing chubs and whitefish, but mainly designed for chub fishing because you run out so much deeper and so much farther. When you fish chubs, you are ten to fifteen miles off shore and usually in December and January. So you have to have something that is a little more enclosed with a big coal stove in there to stay warm.

Leon Voight (Gills Rock, Wisconsin) discussed the fish tugs owned by the family and the strategies employed to use changing technology.

We have had two fish tugs. We had the wooden one, my grandfather's boat. I have seen where we have put logs through the side of it down in the waves, but it always popped back up. I think they are the safest boats on the lake because you can roll them on their sides and they will pop right back up.

Our grandfather had two boats. He traded one of them for the land up here on the point, up where I live, on the bluff. I think that the boat he traded it for was burned up. He had the *Hope* built. It has been restored and it is in the museum here in Gills Rock. Now we have the *Faith II*, which we bought down in St. Joseph, Michigan. It is the first steel boat we have owned. Everybody has always said there is not much upkeep on a steel boat, but it is just the same as the wood boat. You are constantly painting and scraping.

We sold the *Hope* quite a few years back because it was getting too hard to keep two boats running with all the paint and scraping and hauling them out of the water. It just gets too much, especially on a wooden boat because you got the metal that you have to pound on the wood bottom so that the wood does not get all ripped up in ice. They call it sheet metal. Some of the old fishermen call it ice tin. You have to pound it on. Then you have to countersink all these nails so that the twine does not catch on them, which is nice on the steel boats because it is smooth. But there are places it still catches—back on your shoe and on your rudder. Twine will get back in there and wrap up. There is an awful lot of upkeep on those boats.

———————————

Alan Priest discussed his attachment to the tug he leases and his reluctance to invest further in fishing until the renewal of the Consent Agreement of 1985.

I am married to my fish tug just like my wife. This year the fishing is kind of slow and she said, "I am going to blow that tug up." And I said, "Now honey." I have to butter her up a little bit.

My tug is the *Janice Sue*. I do not own it; Bill Carlson owns it. I lease it from him. He has got the license, which makes it even harder for me to make it because I have to pay him so much for leasing. He charges me for packing my fish over there. That makes it harder too. He wants too much for the boat; he wants way over what it is worth. And the Indian treaty rights issue—nobody knows what the treaty rights negotiations are going to come to in the year 2000. So I cannot afford to do it. At this point in my life, I do not know if I want to go way in debt. So I just keep plugging away.

I started right after they got into nylon. Right now, nylon is outdated. It is ancient. They are using all monofilament now. I am going to have to switch over to monofilament pretty soon because I can hardly find any nylon anymore. I am kind of old fashioned and want to stick with nylon. It is easier for me to work with. Monofilament is puffy. It gets all over and it does not lay down.

———————————

Kenneth Peterson recalled detailed information about his and other family members' boats. The boats were modified as changes occurred in the fishery.

We had mostly Cummins engines. My dad had Kahlenberg when he was younger. He had a Kahlenberg in the old *Clara S*. He had a two-cylinder; they called them 50/60. I had a seventy-five-horsepower Kahlenberg in the *Alice*. It was a three-cylinder. They were 325s. It was a good old engine. That old buzzard would go blub-blub all day long. My dad had a way with them. Something on the engine would make a little noise or something and he would know what it was. He could tell you how many revolutions it was turning up. The old timers were amazing. They could really tell you something.

We bought the *Dawn* around 1949. My brother, my dad, and I went in together on it. Dad and I went down and got the *Dawn* when we bought it. We ran her home from Milwaukee. He told me when I was steering to take a range on a star. "The star does not move," he said. "If you want to keep going in that direction, you just take a range on a star. Then you do not have to watch the compass all the time." And by golly, he was right. I would get her going in a certain direction, he would give me a course to steer on, and I would steer her right that way. I could look up at the sky and find a good bright star and go on. As long as I could look out there and see that star, I knew I was going in the right direction on the course. When we bought it out of Milwaukee, it had a Chrysler gas engine. We changed it over to a Kahlenberg. Then we got a four-cylinder Cummins in there. That boat is still going yet as far as I know. It is down in Wisconsin down at Little Suamico. It was tied up there for a while. I do not know where it is now.

Paul Goodman (Washington Island, Wisconsin) recalled the boats used by the family in commercial fishing and, more recently, as part of his charter boat operation.

My dad's first boat was the *Hance*. He bought her on Washington Island. I was on that boat when I was young. The next boat that my dad and his brother had was the *Charlene*. I was on that one on the island. That is the boat my dad had when he got out of the business. The *Hance* was probably about thirty-six foot or so and the Charlene was probably a forty-some-foot boat. It is the regular size that most of the commercial fish tugs are around here. The *Charlene* was a fairly new boat. It was not that old. The *Hance* was real old. She was an old wooden boat. I do not know the age of her. She had a Kahlenberg engine. It was probably a three-cylinder Kahlenberg. That is the boat I was on with my dad when I was young.

In 1975 I bought a boat with my cousin, Charlie Voight. I went into partnership with him, so I bought a share of a boat called the *Susie*. She was built in Saginaw,

Michigan, in the 1940s. It was a steel boat. When we got it, it had a gas engine in it. We converted it to a Volvo diesel, a TMV70B Volvo diesel engine. The *Susie* was a thirty-seven- or a thirty-eight-foot boat. It was a regular style fish tug. It was not a real heavy-duty boat as far as ice-breaking capabilities, but it was a real good boat. Economy wise, it was real easy on fuel, which I think helped us out a lot because I know a lot of guys were paying an awful big fuel bill. We were getting by pretty easy on fuel. We remained partners for quite a few years. Then I sold my share of that boat and bought another boat called the *Falcon* with Lyle Teskie. We owned the *Falcon* together for a few years. Then I ran the shoreline boat for the shoreline resort, one of their boats. There was a guy that owned two charter boats and I ran his one boat. It was an old navy boat—it was built for Vietnam. It was a river patrol boat. So I ran that for a few years. They still have it. They made it into a diving boat now and refurbished it. It is a pretty nice boat. That was about a thirty-three- or thirty-four-foot boat. Fifteen years ago I bought a Slickcraft, a twenty-eight-foot, twin-engine Slickcraft. It works out ideally for sport fishing. That's what I am still using. It has been re-powered but I am still using it.

Joel Peterson discussed changes in work routines that have come about as a result of the State of Michigan's determination to convert nearly all commercial fishing in its waters to trap-net fishing.

Trap nets are totally different than the gill nets. In the gill-net boat, I do not think there's any weather that you could not tough it out. A lot of fishermen that have toughed it out in sixty- to seventy-mile-an-hour winds, even eighty-mile-an-hour winds. You just button the gill-net boat up. With the gill nets, you actually get to a point where common sense prevails. But the trap-net boat has an open deck. I always lift until—I do not ever say until you get scared, but until you start thinking should I be doing it any more or quit and go home. That is an indication that maybe you should stop lifting and come in. Last Tuesday, it blew pretty good. We lifted five nets. We were one of the only boats that lifted. If you have got a good crew, and you have got a good boat, and everybody knows what to do, you could probably lift in difficult weather. But the whole fishing industry, the way you get paid is by what you produce, so that is another factor. I have a cellular phone, radar, GPS, loran, and an FM radio. I have survival suits. Some common sense is needed I guess. How safe do you really feel? You do not want to jeopardize somebody's life. Whether you stop lifting depends on the way the wind is blowing and the position of where your nets are set because the trap nets are fixed on the bottom. If you are lifting with the bow into the wind, you feel a hundred percent better than lifting with her big butt into it because the water just kind of shreds away in the bow and jumps over.

Jack Cross of Charlevoix recalled how his family responded to changes in fisheries policy by converting gill-nets boats into trap-net rig and buying new trap-net boats.

My dad probably had eight or ten different boats, maybe even twelve boats in his lifetime. The *Jackie C* and the *Jackie II* were the main boats that we built.[62] We had them built ourselves. When I was a young fellow, my dad had three boats fishing here. When I came out of the service back in 1958, my dad was starting the "big Jackie," the *Jackie II*. It was fifty-two foot. I fished that boat for him for nearly twenty years. Then I ran it myself and he was ashore. Then we kept just our two boats, the "Jackies." We had them in the late 1950s and 1960s. We fished with those two boats until they put us out of business. The state bought one from us on a buyout. We sold the *Jackie II* to fishermen up on Lake Superior. It went to Lake Superior. The state scrapped the *Jackie C*. It was kind of sad because we had it all those years. We had built it. It was a gill-net boat we had converted into a trap-net boat. We had done everything we could to preserve and keep it and then they destroyed it. The *Jackie II* went up to Lake Superior, but the state put them out of the gill-net business and I bought it back. So I own the boat but I am not using it.

Among the strategies employed by commercial fishers in Wisconsin to insure their economic survival was trawling. A handful of commercial fishers responded to the call of the Wisconsin DNR in the late 1960s for assistance in reducing stocks of alewife and other fish used not for human consumption, but for pet food and other uses, and outfitted their boats with trawling gear. Michigan never encouraged trawling because

DNR officials hoped that the enormous stocks of alewife would serve as the forage base for the newly stocked salmon. Today, alewife stocks continue to vary, but generally they are not considered as bothersome as they were in the late 1960s. In addition, greater awareness of bacterial kidney disease (BKD), which weakens or kills salmon when forage stocks are insufficient, has prompted the Wisconsin DNR to reduce the quotas assigned to trawlers. The small number of fishermen from Wisconsin who continue to trawl for smelt, alewife, and other forage fish, such as Daniel "Pete" LeClair of Two Rivers, complain that they will soon be unable to cover their costs. For now, however, for a brief few weeks, trawling still takes place in certain Wisconsin waters of Lake Michigan.

When LeClair began trawling the Wisconsin waters of Lake Michigan in the 1960s for forage fish including alewife, chub, and smelt, alewife comprised a significant percentage of the fish biomass of Lake Michigan. LeClair, who has invested considerable capital in trawling gear, opposed the trawling harvest cap placed on state-licensed trawlers in 1989. Two years later, the DNR ended trawling for flesh or forage fish except for smelt, which could be caught during certain designated seasons. LeClair and other state-licensed fishermen were assigned a quota, which was part of a total allowable catch of smelt determined by the Wisconsin DNR.

We used to fish for forage fish—alewives, smelt, and chubs. It was used for cat food. We also had big fishmeal plants that would make fishmeal and feed it to pigs, chickens, mink, and so forth. Forage fish were used for pet food and fishmeal. They dried the fish and used the oils for paints and so forth. That was a big operation for many, many years. The trawlers harvested around forty-five million pounds a year. Then the DNR took all of our forage fish fishing away from us. Now they only let us fish smelt. But you cannot go out there and just fish smelt because you are going to get some chubs and some alewife. So, instead of letting us fish twelve months of the year like we used to fish, we are down to five and a half months a year. We just cannot survive on five and a half months fishing time. We are trying to work with the state and the governor to give us more time to fish. The governor just vetoed it, so it looks like we are only going to have five and a half months a year and we just cannot survive. This industry is just about done.

Our most prosperous years for trawling were from 1962 to 1991. Then they planted salmon in Lake Michigan to control the alewife because they were so thick. They were dying on the beaches and the harbors. Then they planted chinook salmon. They planted so many chinook that they consumed the whole biomass of alewife. There was no more alewife.

Then the salmon got sick from a disease due to the lack of food and they all died. So it keeps going in cycles. When the salmon died, the alewife came back. Now the alewife are thick again and they are continuing to plant salmon and so it is up and down—a merry-go-round. It is hard to tell how many hundreds of fish to plant to control the alewife biomass because alewife explode within two years just like flies. They produce so fast, it is unbelievable.

Now the DNR will not let us have any of the forage fish. They are concerned that when we fish smelt, we catch too many of the forage species. They are trying to save these forage fish for the salmon and trout sport fishery. Whenever alewife are in your area, the season's closed. Now, in the winter months, the alewife go to deep water and they are not in our area where we fish smelt, but we do catch quite a few chubs. The DNR is not really that concerned about the chubs because we do not catch that many. If you do, you have to sort the smelt out from the chubs and there is so much labor involved, you cannot afford it, so you just have to quit fishing. So we are restricted in our operation.

We try to get a couple of weeks in during the summertime when the smelt is separated from the alewife and the chubs. But then, the sportsmen are out there and they scream and holler they do not want us in their way. We might catch a trout. They are so powerful they convinced the DNR to stop all summer fishing on Lake Michigan completely whether it was profitable for smelt fishing or not. They are so strong with their lobbyist and sport organizations that we do not have a chance to change the rules. So this is why we are only allowed five and a half months out of the year. We just cannot survive on it.

Perch is a delicacy. Smelt is too. It is just like eating popcorn. There is nowhere in the world that they have them like we have them here. Here, we have quality control so we catch them today and they are dressed tomorrow morning. The resource is going to be wasted if this is the only area on all of Lake Michigan that catches smelt. But that resource is going to be gone too. What a waste. Now, somebody should be accountable for this, but right now it does not look like anyone is or ever will be.

It is difficult to develop the whitefish market. If you get a warm winter the whitefish will come in earlier and if you get a cold winter you will have to wait for the water to warm up. You cannot control the temperature and neither can the DNR, but the season is set so you have to work around set times. So some years you can make it and the next year you cannot. You cannot be versatile according to the way the whitefish stocks are in the lake because the law says you have to get your nets out whether the whitefish are there or not. This is totally wrong. If you have a quota, you should be able to fish it when you want to fish. When the quota is caught, you quit. Why do I have a time period? That is not fish management; it is like a dictatorship. They are going to tell you when you can fish and when you cannot fish, right or wrong. And this is totally wrong.

Kenneth Peterson of Michigan's Garden Peninsula was among a small number of fishermen who responded to changes in the fishery by becoming involved in trawling operations during the 1950s and 1960s.

I was a trawler on Lake Winnebago.[63] We trawled for sheepshead on Lake Winnebago. Each individual had his own outfit, trap nets and whatnot. We fished for mink ranch feed. There were some winters when we used to fish under the ice with trap nets on Lake Winnebago too. The fish went for human consumption to Chicago.

I also trawled on Lake Michigan with Art Swaer out of Sheboygan, Wisconsin. I was one of the deck hands on one of his big trawlers. Art Swaer had a big trawling outfit; he had at least five or six trawling boats at one time. He built two brand new ones, right here in Little Suamico. They were pretty good size boats. Swaer trawled for alewife, chubs, bloats, and any kind of junk fish. It was used as feed for mink farms.

I went trawling on Lake Winnebago because things were getting a little rough here. It was getting pretty tough to make a living. I had a friend who was down there fishing on Lake Winnebago. He had a permit to fish there, so I went down and he gave me a job. In fact, he and I fished together for a while, because I had the pound nets. I took a couple pound nets down there, and we set them up. He had a few trap nets. We started with a little old white boat. They called it the *White Owl* or something like that. The old *Alice* might have been licensed in Wisconsin. They just transferred the license over to me because I fished out of Milwaukee there for a while with the old *Alice*.

I brought it home here, and then I took it down to Lake Winnebago. I made a trawler out of it down there. We trawled at night sometimes because it seemed like you got more fish, sheepshead anyway, at night.

I had a boom with a roller on it and it rolled up right on the deck. We dumped the fish right on the deck. When I fished with Art Swaer, there were puckering strings on his trawl bag. They could quarter it or put it into about three different sections and they would put the boom on it and pull in the bottom part of the bag. When you would put it back over, you would tie it up, put it back over and then they had to boom the fish back into the bag again and then lift that up and pull her in. The bag was in about three sections. It was interesting if you had never done it before. Of course, I fished quite a few years before I went out with him, but I never did trawl. He gave me a job and I went to work for him. I did not stay there too long before I went to work for Tecumseh, a little small-engine factory in New Holstein. I only worked there for two or three winters.

Daniel "Pete" LeClair observed how the Wisconsin DNR supported trawling as a means of helping to eliminate the alewife problem. LeClair worked with local machinists to develop a trawling apparatus. Through trial and error, they were able to develop a trawler that could be operated safely without swamping the fish tug. Ultimately, however, the practice prompted LeClair to buy bigger boats. LeClair recalled how during the 1960s, he helped to organize the fishermen who began trawling for alewife, chub, and smelt.

I was one of the first or second trawlers. There was a small boat up in Green Bay they were using for smelt. Then the lake got overpopulated with chubs and the smelt were stunted in growth. You could set gill nets, but you would not get fish big enough to use for smoking for human food. They would not grow. So the state said we have to clean out the chubs because there is not going to be enough food for all of them. We have to make them grow.

The DNR encouraged us to start this trawling business. The original trawlers pulled the type of trawl where you have got all the fish in the back end of the net. They turned around and got a rope and pulled the net over the side. Once they got the net over the side of the boat, they would untie the bag and the fish would fall on the deck. But while they were doing this, the boat was half tipping over and as the boat tipped, the bag would get further way from the boat.It became a pretty dangerous operation. When I saw that operation in Green Bay, I said there has got to be a better way. This is never going to work. They could only lift 3,000 or 4,000 pounds at a time. So we developed a trawler with a stern ramp.

You have a big net drum inside the boat that winds up the net. You have a ramp where the net and fish are pulled right up into the boat. Then we got a big pipe that we put up in the boat. We untie the back end and pull the net over the pipe and all the fish run onto the deck. Then we tie the bag again and you set it back again. You do not have a dangerous operation.

The net drum was developed in a small machine shop by me and two of my friends, brothers named Krueger from Hilbert, Wisconsin. I called them and they said, "We will come to Two Rivers. You show us what you want and we will build it." They were inventors. They developed the whole operation. Now they copy it worldwide. I had an idea, but I did not know how to put it all together. But I knew what I wanted—now how do you do it? We need to know how much power was needed on this drum to pull this net into the boat. They wanted to know how many fish we were going to pull in—25,000? 30,000? Well, I did not exactly know. I wanted them to build it heavy enough so that I could get it into the boat. So we built it heavy enough, but the net was so big and it got so full, we damn near sunk the boat trying to pull the net in the boat.

There is only so much free board on the boat. They put the ramp on but then the boat goes down. Then you get 20,000 pounds of fish on the back end, and pretty soon you are going to take on water. We almost sank a couple of times because the boat takes in the water. The water keeps coming in and cannot get out. The more water you get in, the lower the boat goes. So we had some very, very, scary experiences. The first boat was not good for our purpose so we had to get bigger boats. We went to the boats we have presently. They are fifty-five-feet long and sixteen-feet wide. It is a lot longer, and we can pull up to 25,000 to 30,000 pounds at one time right into the boat. We limit our trawl time. Instead of pulling for two hours, sometimes we only pull for half an hour. This way, it is easier to get the net into the boat and dump the fish out and set her back.

The new *Susie Q* was a Lake Erie boat. They had lots of larger fish tugs on Lake Erie. They were fishing walleyes and perch with gill nets and they had a real big deal going there. Then the walleye and perch disappeared. So they had lots of boats there for sale in Erie, Pennsylvania. We bought the *Avis J* in Erie, Pennsylvania, also. We paid $10,000 for it, but the engine was shot. We had to stick a lot of money into it to make it a trawler because it was a gill-net boat. We developed that boat with a net drum and winches inside it and a ramp on the stern for lifting the net. It is fifty-five long and sixteen foot wide. We can pull twenty-five to thirty thousand pounds and dump the load in the boat and set the net back with no problems. It is a real nice boat.

We wanted a boat that would run the winch and be able to pull up a trawl door from the bottom of the lake. We had to put a thousand feet of cable on each drum and you had to run that at the right gear ratio so that you would have enough power from the tractor engine. So it took lots of experiments and lots of different chains and sprockets to get the right ratio so that the tractor had enough power to actually pull the doors up off the bottom of the lake. You have to pull your net up while you still have full power on the engine. So we designed it all. It was very, very difficult and cost a lot of money and lots of labor to develop all these different theories and power mechanisms. As we got bigger, we found out that if you get a bigger trawl door, you catch more fish. Then the Cub tractor engine was too small, so we had to go to the next size engine. The whole operation was a growing experience. Now, instead of using a gas engine we have a big hydraulic pump in the front of the main engine and we run everything on hydraulic. So it is a real nice, neat operation. We developed it all ourselves. We did not get any grants. It was just trial and error and lots of hard work and lots of disappointments. We are proud of what we developed. But it is too bad this industry has to go down the drain to benefit a few sportsmen on Lake Michigan. It is a wasted shame, all the time and effort. We could produce good eating fish for the fish-consuming public but under the present condition it is like hitting your head against the wall and there is no future in it. I am afraid this is the end of it.

We started Wisconsin Trawlers Inc. when we had eighteen boats going. We thought that with this many trawlers, we should be organizing. We should have a game plan. So we worked with the DNR. The DNR asked us if we would get more boats to cut the chub population. Bob Ruleau built a big freezer up in Cedar River, Michigan, where he could freeze 200 thousand pounds a day. It was a growing business. We worked with the DNR to come up with a game plan that everbody could live with. It was working fine until the sportsmen came in and blew us right out of the water.We had a board of directors and we worked together with the DNR. We had DNR people riding the boats. We used to put out a big report every year on the fish monitoring on our trawlers. After a short time, the DNR said they did not have any more money and they let it all go.

Wisconsin Trawlers Inc. worked with the DNR monitoring programs. We had a real good thing going until all the sportsmen started taking over the lake and then our data did not mean anything. We tried to really do a good job with the DNR. When they first started planting lake trout we were the only ones that could catch these plantings to see if they survived. We would dump 5,000 to 6,000 pounds on the deck. We literally got on our hands and knees with the DNR people and tried to find any lake trout. We wanted to see how they survived and how fast they grew. They guaranteed us they would work with us through the whole fight for our fishery if we would help them to see how the lake trout were. How else would they ever have known if we were the only operation that could catch them? So, we got all that going, and eventually, they came to kill our industry. That is the thanks we got.

Daniel "Pete" LeClair describes how effective his crews became at trawling. During the trawling heyday of the 1970s and early 1980s, their biggest concern was keeping the huge loads of fish from swamping the boat or causing it to roll.

We hold the state record for 250,000 pounds in one day with the two boats. In the 1970s and 1980s was when we were really fishing. We fished for alewife, chubs, and smelt. It was all going for pet food or fishmeal. I got an elevator in the boat to dump the fish. We dumped the fish into the elevator, and from the elevator they went onto semi trucks. We would haul them to the pet food freezer plants or to the fishmeal plant.

We got an auger from the back of the boat that would run the fish up to the front. So we had the front full and the back full. This was what the farmers used for moving their feed—a big steel trough with an auger inside. We would push the fish into the auger in the back of the boat and auger them up to the front. Then we had to have a guy in the front to level them all off so the boat could stay level and not tip over. But a lot of times the planks came out and the fish started sliding around and we almost rolled over a couple of times. They are so slimy and juicy that they are all over the boat and they are hard to hold in any kind of a sea so we had to improvise to keep from rolling over or sinking. If we hauled 50,000 pounds for our boatload, it would be one semi load. But when they were really thick out there on a lot of days, we had 200,000 pounds with no problems. We caught the most alewife when we fished right along the beach in shallow water. Sometimes they were so thick we set the net going out of the river. By the time you got to the end of the harbor, you had 25,000 pounds in the bag. They were so thick we fished in about twenty feet of water right along the shoreline between Two Rivers and Manitowoc and north of Two Rivers Harbor. It is a good sand bottom and that is what you need for trawling. At a lot of ports, it is rock along the beach and shoreline and you cannot trawl there. You need good, clean, sand bottom for this type of operation.

The DNR stopped us from fishing for alewife to save the alewife for the salmon and trout. They still claim they saved them for the salmon and trout but they destroyed the perch fishery in the meantime because the alewife ate all the perch larvae. The alewife also ate the zooplankton, which is needed for the young perch to survive. Also, as perch spawn, the alewife come in from deeper water after the winter like a stampede of cattle. They go through this perch spawning area like a vacuum cleaner. They clean the perch spawn right out. Some people claim it is a small part of it, but all the biologists that I know and research data that I have indicates that you cannot have perch when you have a high abundance of alewife.

May and June is when the alewife are the thickest. We caught most of the fish in May and June along the beach. There was only a six- or eight-week period where you would catch this many fish, but they come to spawn in shallow water and they spawn and then they go back out again. Then they scatter all over the lake. In the fall when we would go out, we would get maybe one semi load all day in deeper water. You would only get 10,000 to 15,000 pounds in a one-hour drag. You would catch some, but they were not as concentrated like when they are near the beach and in shallow water. We tried in the other months, but it was very unprofitable.

In our nets we have a diverter—little grates that are about one inch and seven-eighths opening on the bars. The small fish can go through the slots in the diverter but the bigger fish hit this and are forced downward and forced out of the bottom of the net where they escape. So we do not catch any game fish at all. All the big salmon—all escape before they get to the net so all we really get at the back of the net is just chubs and smelt and ninety percent of the alewife is in deep water by November thirtieth. But if we get a lot of alewife we have to separate them from the smelt—all by hand. So you really cannot deal in volume like we did in the 1970s and 1980s. That is when we had elevators and you could handle some production. Right now, it is all done by hand and you cannot deal in volume by hand. Our trawlers have to shove all the fish on a table and sort them all by hand. So labor is really the big issue right now. When the smelt are out there and you just get pure smelt, then they have the season closed. This is very disheartening and it is hard to maintain a crew year round when you are only allowed to fish five and a half months out of your own port.

Daniel "Pete" LeClair discussed the process the family underwent working with a Biloxi, Mississippi, firm to adapt the ocean trawling apparatus for use in the Great Lakes. He expressed concern that the skills and knowledge utilized to develop and operate a cost-effective trawling operation on the Wisconsin waters of the Great Lakes will be lost as the generation of fishermen born in the 1920s and 1930s passes on.

We tried fishing up in Lake Superior a couple of times, but if you are not familiar with the grounds it is difficult. We took our trawlers up there and tried to catch smelt on Lake Superior. But we were not familiar with the bottoms. We tore our nets and lost some nets. There are clay balls up there and we got them in our nets and they destroyed the whole operation. It just did not work. You have to grow up in an area of the lakes and know your lake bottom. We started trawling here in the Two Rivers area in 1962. We started with the old small *Susie Q*. We did not have much money to buy a trawl net. At the time, trawl nets were $1,500, I believe. We went out the first day and lost her—our trawl net. We snagged a shipwreck and lost the whole works. We went out the next day, and lost another one. I said this is not going to work, so we had to go to our next plan. We got a hold of an old car ferry captain. He had been on the lake a long time, and he had a map of all the lakes showing shipwrecks, explaining the lake bottoms, where the rocks were, where the reefs were, and where the clay balls were. We worked with him for several weeks and mapped out an area that had a good sand bottom where we had half of a chance of fishing. This is what we did and we had to go borrow some more money to buy some more nets. So we tried her again. Finally, we developed areas where we could fish and not lose your net.

Right now, trawls are up to $5,000 to $6,000 and you cannot afford to lose them. Fortunately, now with loran and shipwrecks charted, you know where you can go and where you cannot go. So, all this was part of the development of the fishery. We went from charts to sounders to color TV sounders to fish finders. The only way you do all this is through experience. You cannot take a guy off the street, throw him in the boat, and say you are going fishing. Once in awhile we still get our nets torn up with logs and other debris on the bottom, but it has been a long time since we lost our trawl. We took a long time to develop the area that we can safely fish in. We went through lots of hills and a hollows to get where we are but I guess now it is all in vain.

We got our trawling gear from Biloxi, Mississippi. The Maronovich Trawling Company worked with us. At first, they had us try the fish trawls they used in the ocean. When we got them here, we could not get them to work because the salt water is different than freshwater. They pulled hard and the fish were gilling in the nets. We found the reason for this through trial and error. The front of the net is like a big funnel and then it tapers back to the cod end. The taper for ocean use cut down too fast. Instead of being led by the trawl and going into the bag, the fish were fighting the twine and going through the mesh. The mesh was bigger in the front of the trawl and they were not even gilling, they were just going through. So, then we cut the mesh size down and they put the cod end of the bag right behind the taper with the bigger mesh. When you would slow down to lift the net the fish would come out of the cod end because the water pressure did not hold them back. The fish would squiggle up ahead and go to the body of the trawl.

I knew we had to develop something better. So we developed an intermediate area on the net with a small mesh—a portion of the net about ten- to twelve-feet long between the body of the net and the cod end. This meant that the fish would have to go about twelve more feet before they would get out of the net. This kept them back in the bag and then our production practically doubled. So, we really developed our own trawl for our own special deal here on the lake. You have your cod end—which is the very far end—your intermediate area and then the body of the trawl and the wings with incrementally smaller mesh size for each part of the net. We created a slower taper rather than a quicker taper like the ocean type We worked with the net makers in Biloxi. We told them what we wanted and thought we needed and they would make it. They would send it up here and then we would put it on. If it did not work we would call back. They really worked with us 100 percent and as a result, he sold a lot of trawls. We had eighteen trawlers from Wisconsin at one time. They were from Two Rivers, Sheboygan, Kenosha, Sturgeon Bay, and Milwaukee. We did not have much money. The company in Mississippi sent us samples of net. In 1962, all we knew about trawling was what we had read about in the ocean.

All this work in developing the trawler has been done from our own trial and error—lots of experience and time. There has been lots of wasted time. Once all this knowledge is gone, if somebody does not continue this, it is never going to come back. Nobody is ever going to do what we did. The young are not innovative. They did not grow up from the bottom of the family through the whole operation to learn how it changes. You cannot take them off the street and throw them in your boat. They have not learned how all this started. My kids started during high school summer vacations. These other fishermen are from families that fished on the lakeshore. They all learned from their dad. Most kids are not growing up in the fishing business—they are not growing up with the family tradition. This is why this is the last.

Daniel "Pete" LeClair expressed dissatisfaction with the management of the fishery. In order to protect the lake trout, the U.S. Fish and Wildlife Service (USFWS) joins with the Wisconsin DNR to monitor LeClair's trawling operations.

The fishery is so up and down. It is almost impossible to manage it by sitting at your desk in Madison. The DNR says we have to put quotas on the fishermen when they do not even know what is out in that lake or what the biomass really is. The U.S. Fish and Wildlife Service people go around once a year with their small net and their boat. It is just a waste of time because if you go one week earlier or one week later, or if you go in a different depth of water, the whole project would be turned right around. You can get a ton of smelt, go out the next day, and you cannot find one even if you are in the same depth of water and same area. The current and the water temperature change. You cannot set quotas by going around the lake two weeks out of the year and say this is what is out in the lake. That is false. It is very, very, very disturbing when you try to manage a lake off this kind of data. You cannot do it. We would like to be part of a research program where we could go and make test drags with our nets. We know what the nets can catch because we proved it. The nets that U.S. Fish and Wildlife Service pulls are too small, and the people who do it do not understand how a trawl is supposed to work. We observed them on their boats and the net was not even on the bottom of the lake. On the trawl doors you have a towing point and the towing point on your trawl door has to be within a half inch so your door goes down to the bottom of the lake and pulls upward to spread your trawl. When we observed the trawl doors on the Fish and Wildlife boat when it was in Two Rivers, we noticed that the doors were painted. That is a no-no right away because your doors will not get water soaked and they will not go to the bottom unless they are water soaked. Also, you have to get your towing point right or your doors are going to lay down on the bottom or tip in and it is not going to spread your trawl. If you do not have experience with this, you are just wasting your time.

---

3. HOLDING THE LINE: THE POLITICS OF LAKE MICHIGAN COMMERCIAL FISHING

Brian Price, who once worked as a commercial fisherman on Lake Michigan, discussed the public trust doctrine as applied to fisheries. He discussed what he considers the near-destruction of the commercial fishing industry for the sake of developing a sport fishery on Lake Michigan as contrary to the public good.[64] Price observed how cultural and economic values need to be considered in the development and implementation of fisheries policy.

The state's role is to regulate for the benefit of the resource. The state is the only one that can speak for the resource and the fish. It is a tragedy. The recurring theme is when everybody owns the resource, nobody owns the resource. And when everybody owns the resource, the only one that can be the protector of the resource is the state. When the Michigan Fish Commission began in the 1800s there was not a real full understanding of the role of the state as protector of the resource. The Michigan Fish Commission ran hatcheries and introduced new species of fish thought to be of benefit to the former commercial or sport-fishing industry. They never took regulatory responsibilities very seriously.

Michigan is unique in that during the mid-1960s certain managers in the DNR decided that the Great Lakes were going to become a sport-fishing paradise. There was money in sport fishing in terms of tourism dollars. The DNR managers were also working in response to another ecological crisis, the alewife explosion. So the DNR had a reason for planting exotic species of fish. They were overwhelmed with the size of the salmon, the mania that surrounded it, and the write-ups that they got about it. The DNR went totally overboard and decided that the Great Lakes should be managed primarily, if not exclusively, as a sport fishery, neglecting the fact that the sport-fishing industry and the commercial fishing industry can survive very nicely side-by-side. They also neglected years and years of experience to show there is never going to be a sport fishery for whitefish that would be even close to utilizing the resource. And there is never going to be a sport fishery for chubs because the little suckers are 400 feet down and they do not bite on anything anyway.

With the development of the sport fishery on the Great Lakes, Michigan's fisheries managers went way, way overboard and they tried to reduce a thousand commercial licenses to a target originally somewhere around seventy or seventy-five. They managed to do it in a couple of years. And there was a huge amount of frustration and bitterness. Those were the years when it was actually dangerous to be a DNR officer in certain parts of the Great Lakes waters. Not only was harassment a problem, but also vandalism. Shots were fired occasionally.

The development of the Great Lakes sport fishery was a continuation of a long and needed trend of the state gaining more and more control over the resource and being more active in managing it. It was an extremely difficult thing for the state to do, which should not be minimized. The state's effort to control the resource was met by the culture of the fishing industry. All these guys bristle at authority or did. Many of them want to be responsible, but nobody likes to be told that they can only set their chub nets in forty fathoms or deeper when they know damn well that the fish are in thirty, and that happens. Or that the closed season on whitefish on a certain reef starts the first of November when the fish are not in there spawning, or have already spawned before the season is over. The fishery is closed for the whole month of November. The fishermen think they should be able to fish the last week of November. Because the regulations are never perfect and lots of other factors, there are always problems and grievances. But I think it was unprecedented for any unit of government, any body of government, to basically dismantle a commercial fishery on the scale that the state went after Michigan's commercial fishery.

The DNR launched a two-pronged attack against the commercial fishing industry. The first thing was to try to ban gill nets, the large mesh gill nets are set primarily for whitefish and also take lake trout as an incidental catch. They were concerned that they would also take salmon. That was one of the rationales for banning large mesh gill nets in the late 1960s and early 1970s. Second, they wanted to reduce the total number of licenses from over a thousand to something less than a hundred. I believe the target was around seventy. Now they have it down to less than forty.

The DNR wanted to make a transition from this troublesome, meddlesome, pain-in-the-butt commercial fishery that was hard to regulate and difficult to quantify the economic value, to a modern era when the Great Lakes was primarily a sport fishery. It was absurd. Managing the Great Lakes to be a sport fishery is like managing the Great Plains for grouse. It marginalizes the economic potential of a vast area. There are certain species of fish that will never be sport-fishing targets.

If you look at the last fifteen years of the commercial fishing industry, there are two things going on. One is that the white commercial licensed industry continues to shrink. And the Indian commercial fishery is growing, maybe not growing in terms of numbers of fishermen, but in terms of economic ability, better gear, and better equipment. It is the same progression that has always occurred. You start with the rowboat. You get some more nets and make a little money. You get a bigger boat that is safer, better, and you can do more from. Then your crew gets a little bigger. The tribal fishery has taken up that slack.

Second, it is important to look at the catch statistics. We have had a prolonged sustained great period for whitefish. In the last fifteen years in Lake Michigan the whitefish fishery has been strong, and it is reflected in the price that the fishermen get. When we were fishing for whitefish in the late 1970s, day in and day out, we got at least as good a price as they are getting right now. The price has not changed. By mid-summer, it will be down to forty or fifty cents a pound. And in the fall and in the spring, when there are not a lot of fish on the market, it will be over a dollar a pound. That is the way it was twenty years ago, and the reason is people are eating just as much or more fish, but the catch is greater. And there is no indication that the fish stocks are being particularly hammered. Whatever is going on in the ecology of the lake, we are not in a situation where the commercial fishery is on its last legs. There will be a commercial fishery. It just will not look like the one that we had.

Fisheries managers need more adaptability and flexibility. The state and tribal regulations need to control fisherman and make sure that they do not damage the resource, while at the same time, give them the flexibility to exploit this changing ecology and to put fish on the market. Flexibility has not always been the case in the past. When the fisheries managers think they have got a lock on what is happening out there, they create regulations that are too rigid and force the fishermen into violating them if they want to make a living at all. So they have got to somehow make sure that the people who stay in it will be smarter and better capitalized. They will be more efficient through better electronics. It will be a different fishery.

The really, really bad period was from the late 1960s through the early to mid-1970s. There was a huge amount of bitterness. You could say maybe the motivations were not right at that time and maybe they made a miscalculation about just turning the Great Lakes into a sport fishery. In some ways, it was perhaps the inevitable final gaining of control over the resource and the people that have the resource. With a thousand licensed commercial fishermen out there, many of whom were just part-timers working out of a rowboat, there is no way to know. In a way, a gill-net operation is not an expensive thing to run. It is hard work for the guys doing it. You fish almost year around as long as the ice does not get so thick that you cannot get back into port.

Dennis Hickey (Baileys Harbor, Wisconsin) discussed the role of commercial fishermen and their organization in the development and implementation of fisheries policies and programs.

I do not have any qualms about sport fishing. It is an important industry to have. It really gives a boost to Baileys Harbor and the whole county throughout the year. In the summertime, we process a lot of the sport-caught fish. I would say we probably process seventy-five percent of all of the fish caught out of Baileys Harbor. We filet, smoke it, and vacuum pack it. We help with the brown trout derby in the spring. The attitude of some sport fishermen is that a commercial fisherman will just fish until you cannot fish any longer. This is not necessarily so. The guys who are left have a tremendous investment in the fishery and are not going to ruin it. Then your whole investment is shot. Actually, a lot of times when there is an issue about protecting fish stocks, we are a lot more concerned than the sport fishermen are. For many of them, fishing is only recreation. If the stocks go down or something, they all go off turkey hunting or do something else.

Our fishery does a lot of the research for DNR and Fish and Wildlife. They ride with us. We have been involved with planting of Astroturf mats in a cooperative effort between the commercial fishermen, the DNR, and Fish and Wildlife.[65] We planted 7.1 million lake trout eggs on the reef out here in Astroturf mats. We donated hundreds of hours of boat time and our building down by the dock. For the last two weeks, the state research boat has been lying at our dock. They are monitoring whitefish and chubs, and are checking trout, salmon, and other fish at the same time. We donate a lot toward the benefit of the sport fishery as well as commercial fishing. Lake trout is the only species where there is an issue because they are generally in the same waters and the same temperature of water as the whitefish. The regulations are always designed to keep us out of that water. For example, for about eight or ten years now, Whitefish Bay has been closed down to commercial fishing for whitefish because they had salmon fishery down there. In the summertime, the sport fishermen would troll down and they did not want to be bothered by having nets there. If we cannot fish whitefish in Whitefish Bay, where should we fish? Just this last week, we were talking with the DNR to try to get that area back because of the decline in the amount of sport fishing and fewer commercial fishermen who would set nets there.

I am the treasurer for the whitefish association; we are on the board for the state commercial fishery. I am an advisor for all of Wisconsin for commercial fishermen on Great Lakes fisheries. During this last year we were able to get the chub fishery opened in the wintertime out here. For the last two years we have been doing research on the chub fishery with the DNR. They did not want the season open in the winter. They are concerned about opening it because of how many lake trout we will kill if we are fishing out there. They did not care what we did to the chub stocks. They were concerned we might kill some lake trout. As it turned out, it was not a problem as we told them in the first place, but it took about ten years to get it open.

Lake trout are always the biggest concern. And yet guys say to me, "Why in the world would you even cooperate with them to plant 7.1 million more lake trout in there?" I want to see the lake trout try and get back to natural reproduction. It would mean the lake was healthy again. The lake trout are a barometer of the status of Lake Michigan. Overall, things are pretty good. If we do not like a law, we go to Madison and we work on changing it. Actually, there are only about ten or fifteen commercial fishermen in the state who do a lot of the work regarding regulations. And the other fishermen are not involved, but that is pretty true with a lot of organizations. From that standpoint, when we go to tell our story in Madison or to the legislators, they are really interested because they do not talk to a lawyer or a lobbyist.

———————————

Bill Carlson, a fourth-generation fisherman and fish buyer, observed how the fishing operations that existed in Leland when he was a boy were gradually reduced to two by 1970. He maintained that fishermen informally managed the resource before the state became so heavily involved.

In Leland, the Buckler fishery was one fishing operation, Stephens and Stallman was another, and ours was the third. When the DNR passed the criteria around 1970, Stephens and Stallman did not qualify to be commercial fishermen anymore and they had to quit. So it was then just the Bucklers and us. Lang Fishery moved in during the very late 1960s, and Buckler went out.[66] Then it was the Langs and the Carlsons who were the fishermen here. The Langs and the Carlsons were the only fishermen here until last year, when Ross Lang was tragically killed in a fishing accident while lifting trap nets. So we lost Ross Lang, and so that put us back to one operation. We are basically still one operation though we fish two different fishing operations. The Lang Company is being taken over by the Manitou Fish Company of which I am a partner. The Carlsons still have our own fishing operation.

From 1968 through 1990, I was put out of business I think a total of eleven times for one reason or another. Some of it was the market, but that was a small part of it. Pesticides were found in the fish; DDT was the primary one. Later on, they found out that what they were calling DDT was a whole category of chemicals including DDT, PCB, and other chemicals. The fish were thought to be contaminated to the point where they should not be consumed. So they stopped the fishing or killed the market. There were times that they stopped the fishing. There were the times that publicity killed the market. They outlawed large mesh gill nets and put us out of business for a while. Then they thought the chub stocks were depleted to the point where they could not be fished anymore so we were out of business again. There were a multitude of things that stopped us from fishing for periods of time. Then the Indian fishery was acknowledged. A lot of people who were able to trace their ancestry back to the Indians were able to continue to fish, but the non-Indians north of the forty-fifth parallel were all put out of business. That took care of a majority of the non-Indian fishery.[67]

We are still in business here. We have been fishing here for 120 years or more. We are in business here not because we caught all the fish. The fishery has policed itself, but it cannot do that anymore. It cannot do it because we do not have the same things that we used to have. To give you an example, I am a big advocate of the commercial fishery, but at the same time, I can be critical of it because I believe that the resource is important—not the people and not the industry. In the old days, you could police yourself because you had a multitude of species to fish which were not all caught at the same time. If you fished whitefish and fishing got bad for whitefish, you would try another species. And then you would go to another one. You could fish them all. It gave the other species time to recover. Economics also came into play. If you caught too many of a particular species and fishing was too good, the price would go down. A lot of fishermen said, "If the price goes down, I guess I have to catch a whole bunch more fish," instead of saying, "I guess I will cut back and make the price come up." And that helped keep the stocks in balance. They would catch more to make the same amount of money. If they had let them go, maybe they would have overpopulated because there was not enough stress put on them. There are a whole bunch of factors involved.

Today, we cannot go for any fish because we are limited to two species. The state-licensed commercial fishery can catch whitefish and chubs here. The Indian fishery can catch anything they want, but we can fish whitefish and chubs. If we deplete the population of whitefish, we cannot fish anything else. One license says we can only fish whitefish. The other license says we can only fish chubs. We cannot switch to trout, perch, menominee, or some of the other fish that traditionally we were able to switch to. When our whitefish population was decimated here in the late 1940s and early 1950s, we started fishing menominee whitefish and we developed a market for them to replace the whitefish. We cannot do that anymore; that is how it works.

———————

Joel Peterson discussed how political interests favored sport over commercial fishing for economic reasons. He questioned the premise of the State of Michigan that sport fishing brought a greater economic return than commercial fishing.

They figured there was more money in the sports fishery than there was in commercial fishing. You as a taxpayer paid to put the sport fishing there but you do not have a big enough boat to get out there to harvest it. That is what the whole political thing is over. The whole sports industry argued that if you bought a boat for $2,500, if you were a sport fisherman, there was an automatic multiplier of ten. If you were a commercial fisherman, your customers came down here, you walk in the shed and you bought a fish from me today for seventy-five cents a pound and that is all the farther that fish ever went. It is as though that fish never got processed and never got sold to a restaurant owner who cooked that fish, put it on a tray, and sold it for $9.95 a meal. That fish, the fish value of all the fish in the Great Lakes was based right here, at seventy-five cents a pound. When I send in my catch report at the end of the month it states that I caught 10,000 pounds of whitefish and that I was paid seventy-five cents a pound. According to the state, that fish never generated another cent. We all know better. I cannot eat 10,000 pounds of fish. I sold them to somebody. Half of that 10,000 pounds of fish went out of state. What kind of money do you want? Do you want other states' money to come back into Michigan to help the economy? But they still, even to their dying day, they would not add a multiplier, like two or three times because a lot of times the whitefish that was sold here originally for seventy-five cents was eventually sold at a market for as high as $4.75 a pound. So there was quite a mark-up in it. It was just political. But also, if you picked up a paper and you read this, unless you have seen it, what are you going to believe?

———————

"Coho" Bob Maynard worked as a commercial fisherman before beginning to offer charter boat fishing for recreational anglers. He was critical of the role of politics in fisheries management and policy.

I was born here in Pentwater on October 15, 1911. Other than three years in the service, I have lived here all my life and I have done quite a lot of fishing, although not so much the last year or two. My age has slowed me down a lot but I have been able to observe what has happened here, what it used to be and what it is today. I cannot help but notice the difference in viewpoints of the people who actually live here and participate and the opinions and the ideas that we get coming out of Lansing. Sometimes I think the right hand knoweth not what the left hand doeth as far as Lansing is concerned. We who live here often take an entirely different viewpoint. They seem to have the attitude that we are a little bit stupid, or our opinions do not mean much. But just for an example, the DNR has published reports during the last few years stating that the reason that the salmon population has gone down so much is because there was not enough food out there in Lake Michigan for them. But we who live along the lakeshore know that there are millions and millions and millions of alewife for the salmon to eat. The food base is definitely out there. So they gave the public the impression that there was not enough food. We cannot help but think they got up on the wrong side of the bed, so to speak. They just do not look at it the same way we do. We can see what is happening here, and they seem to get their information from some other source.

People at the head of things believe that the salvation is to stick with sport fishing and eliminate commercial fishing. So that is the way the powerful people in Lansing have decreed the rules. They want to stick with the sport fishing and eliminate the commercial fishing. And, of course, the Indians have their own rules and to a certain extent we have to abide by them according to the Treaty of 1836.

Donald Voight (Gills Rock, Wisconsin) maintained that the introduction of salmon by the State of Michigan further damaged native stocks of chubs and helped to drive commercial fishermen out of business.

Commercial fishermen could not take salmon. It was no good to the commercial fisherman, but I suppose this coho business brought a lot of money for sportsmen. When they first had this coho business in Michigan, you would be lifting chubs and the cohos would follow the chubs up in the nets. They would jump as high as your roller to try to get that chub. A lot of the chubs had teeth bites in them. The coho ate a lot. They were supposed to eat the alewife. They were not made for the lake. They were playing around with nature. Then we would come into the trout and the sports fishermen were the only ones who could catch them. They were selling them out of taverns and everything else. If we had one, they would hang us.

––––––––––––––

Third-generation fisherman Dennis Hickey (Baileys Harbor, Wisconsin) indicated that he and other commercial fishermen work consistently to influence policy despite the bias of both Wisconsin and Michigan toward sport fishing.

We have been really involved with the regulations all along. I think the biggest factor with regulations is the lake trout planting. All of the regulations that we have had over the years stem from concern about how fishing would affect the lake trout. Ten or fifteen years ago, there was a lot of conflict with sport and charter fishermen, particularly the charter fishermen. The sport and charter fishermen felt if there were any commercial fishermen, they would fish the lake out. They thought they were the new commercial fishery and were going to be the cat's meow. During the last five years, they have been going down the tubes. There is very little charter fishing left. A lot of the charter fishermen work for us because it is such a short season, and it costs so much to run the boats. Most of them have gas boats. They charge too much. It was a big novelty to catch those salmon at first and a lot of people were willing to take an expensive charter when they could fill coolers full of salmon and go home. They figured they would have their charter paid for with the dollars of fish that they caught.

Now they are not catching many salmon. The DNR cannot plant so many because the salmon exhausted the forage base. They have thinned the alewife out of the lake. There is not a whole lot of alewife population and the smelt population is going in the same direction. They are feeding pretty heavy on chubs now and we are concerned about that. Fortunately, now, we have got some biologists within the DNR who are willing to stand up to the sports groups and tell them we cannot keep planting at this pace. We have got to cut back. Just this last year, Michigan finally decided that they would cut back. That is a big breakthrough. But before this, the biologists were only interested in sport fishing. They thought everybody would be happy if they planted the fish in front of the biggest city where all your sportsmen were. The state will get all the money out of the license fees and everything will go great. Well, it did for a while, until they overused the alewife population, which was the original intent—to cut down on the alewife population by planting salmon. But then it actually got to the point where the salmon got BKD (bacterial kidney disease) because they did not have enough food. They got diseased from starving. Now you have got a different group of biologists in Michigan who have a better idea of how to manage the lake, so I think things are going to get a lot better along those lines.

Our biggest challenge is to regulate the exotics. You can regulate until you are blue in the face, but with all these exotics nobody knows for sure what is going to happen. When they do not know what to do, a lot of fisheries managers will turn around and say the first thing we have to do is stop the commercial fishermen. Not the sportsmen, because that involves too many license fees, too much money there. We need that. I think a lot of the younger biologists are getting a little different handle on sports fishing. In the past, the attitude was that a sport fisherman could not really damage the stocks. I think they have found out that with their modern electronics and fishing gear and the way that they pass information around, they can damage the stocks. You hear all your sport-fishing reports and within a matter of hours everybody is right there. They are going to have to watch the sport fisheries really close now. But exotics are going to affect them just like us.

As far as regulations, nobody knows where you can go with them. The regulations that we have now are a pretty good package as far as our whitefish fishery is concerned. The whitefish stocks, not only in Wisconsin but also throughout the Great Lakes, are probably better than ever in history. A lot of biologists were predicting that they would crash if you kept commercial fishing. We have size limits. We have mesh size limits. We have a closed season to let them spawn. You have got restricted areas that you cannot enter. You cannot go inside of a quarter mile of shore. You cannot come into the harbors. There are a lot of regulations that protect the fish. We cannot go beyond a certain depth with live entrapment gear because if you are lifting, the small ones would bloat and you would kill them. They are protected with the regulations that we have now. It is obviously showing because the stocks have been increasing even though we have been fishing our quota. The DNR sets the total quota.

Joel Peterson, who has been fishing out of Fairport, Michigan, his entire life, discussed how the introduction of exotic species by the Michigan DNR affected commercial fishing. He maintained that although the Garden Peninsula once had a reputation for renegade commercial fishermen, most harvested the resource in accordance with the law.

The DNR wanted strictly sports fishing. They wanted the whole lake strictly for sports fishing. They never really looked at the whole issue, what is the effect of cutting all the fishing out of the Great Lakes going to do? So they planted trout. Then they planted coho. The salmon were planted to help get rid of the alewives. The alewife makes up about ninety percent of the biological mass of the Great Lakes right now. It might be down a little bit now, but they are still there. So then we started planting these exotic species. We have got coho salmon, king salmon, German browns, and walleyes—all predators. Now they are worried about what we are going to feed them. We have got burbot, which is a "lawyer." All these fish eat other fish. It is like the big wheel. Your big wheel is going down the road real well and all of a sudden you say okay, let us stop fishing. Let us stop the commercial fishery. All of a sudden, the lakes start filling up with trash fish. So then you have to say well, "What are we going to do with these trash fish?" Well, let us introduce this fish.

The State of Michigan introduced salmon to the Great Lakes knowing they were eventually going to pass on the kidney disease that killed them off about eight, ten years ago. They knew it. It has been passed on to some of the whitefish, this kidney disease, and these educated people knew it was going to happen. They knew it when they did it. They do not look at the long run. That is the case with a lot of them, but they have got a job for the State of Michigan for thirty years. Then they can retire and walk away. And the minute they walk away, their whole attitude about fishing changes. We need some of these gill netters to get rid of some of this trash fish. It all goes back to politics and that is what the state is doing down there now, meeting with the tribe right now. I think the tribe's got their information in order right now. They know more about the fish stocks in the Great Lakes right now than the State of Michigan ever did.[68]

When they first started trying to regulate the production of whitefish in the bay here in 1965 a summer science camp was built over on Big Summer Island. College kids gathered research data over on the island. They would run three six-week courses in the summer. They rode my dad's boat and studied the fish population that was here. The State of Michigan used the data gathered there to try to put us out of business. I used to go to so many meetings in Lansing. A professor out of Stevens Point, Wisconsin, had his grad students up here studying recruitment in the fishery. They studied how many small fish were coming into the fishery, how many fish we were taking, and how many fish were sub-legal species. We scale sampled them, we aged them, and we sexed them. We tagged fish. We went to a meeting with the DNR and they sent a guy in. I was embarrassed for the guy who worked for the state. He came in with a little file. He started telling us what the fish stocks in all the Great Lakes were like. The guy from Stevens Point and his grad students had a file. He said this is a six-year study and it is inconclusive, but so far it looks like a stable fishery. The fishermen have been harvesting the same amount of fish for the last seven years in a row without any added effort, without trying any harder.

But if you work for the state there is to be no bending. This is the policy. And that is what it was. You were not allowed to think for yourself—if you started thinking for yourself, you were out of a job. Either you think my way or you do not play the game. We will get rid of you. The DNR had too narrow a vision. They just could not possibly believe that the lakes are big enough to be managed properly and that there is room for commercial and sport fishing. There is room for a guy to sit down here on the end of the dock and catch fish. When you say these fish stocks are going down, do not be too quick to say it is the commercial fisherman that is doing it. Most of the time, it is not. He might be a factor in it. You need to take into consideration the double-breasted cormorants, the zebra mussels, the pollutants, commercial fishing, and sports fishing. There are only fifty-two licensed commercial fishermen left in the State of Michigan. How many sportsmen are there? How many fish are you allowed as a sportsman to take? As a state-licensed commercial fisherman, I cannot take one lake trout. There is no commercial harvest of lake trout. The tribal fishermen can harvest lake trout in given areas under a tribal license. So I do not know. Where is the dividing line and where do you start and where do you stop?

You are looking at the political end of the fisheries. Years ago rather than trying to get the sportsmen and the commercial fishermen to work together the DNR wanted to pit them against each other. They said we were involved with a lot of poaching. I was licensed. I fished. All of a sudden you get a lot of people saying, "So this is the end of the Garden Peninsula. This is where it all happened." I said, "Do you really see any bad people here?" "No."[69]

Elaine Johnson (Door County, Wisconsin) wants the power of government and capital to be put to use for the benefit of the fishery resource and its harvesters and protectors.

I do not have much time for the DNR. They sit down there in their little silver castle, and they do not know what from what, but they think they can write all these regulations. For example, we have got to have an eighteen-inch square flag on a buoy. It rains and snows and freezes. The wind blows it into eighteen pieces. Along comes the *Barney Devine* or one of their patrol boats. They say, "Your buoy does not have a staff. Better write him up a citation." They do not make any allowances for the inclement weather.

The crew fishes thousands of pounds of fish. They measure fish on the boat and maybe you would get a sixteen-and-five-eighths-inch fish you thought was seventeen inches and threw it in there. But there would be very, very few undersized fish among 5–6,000 fish. I say this as a processor. If I went down there and bought an undersized fish, an illegal fish, and I came out with a little tiny fillet, do you think my restaurants would buy it? It is not marketable. It would be fruitless to begin with because your penalty is so great, and what are you going to do with them when you get ashore? I would not buy them and no other processor would. You have no place to go with them, so it would be really ridiculous to bring in an illegal undersized whitefish. Years ago if they happened to get two or three undersized fish you used to call them preacher's fish. They would give them to the preachers.

As soon as you take money and give it to the DNR or to our politicians, you wonder where they are going to put it. People think that your politicians are not working against you, and you can trust the DNR. I would not trust them with a damn nickel of mine. I agree that if the sport, Indian, and white commercial fishermen would put their money together on any of these problems, and we could trust the people we gave the money to, that would be the way to go. It is the damn money. The big money owns this government. It always has. They run everything. I am not against big money. People earn a dollar, good for them. I am happy for them. But damn it, do not ruin something I have doing it. That is what makes me mad. It is the big money that runs our government and gets by with a lot of things that you or I could not get by with. If you got money you can do pretty well what you damn please.

Bill Carlson of Leland is a fourth-generation fisherman who initially opposed the reorientation of Great Lakes fisheries toward sport fishing.

I thought the introduction of salmon was probably the single most important thing done in fisheries management for the Great Lakes. Howard Tanner is known as the father of the salmon fishery in the Great Lakes. There were a lot of other people involved too. When that whole concept came about it was necessary to do something. In 1967, ninety-eight percent of the biomass of Lake Michigan were alewives. There were so many alewives, they were taking up most of the room. The lake can only carry so much fish. If it was going to be alewives then something else had to give. The perch population was in absolute inverse proportion to the population of alewives. Now the alewife population is down some, or quite a bit, but the perch have not recovered and we do not know why. It may have something to do with the zebra mussels. I thought the salmon was a great introduction, not just for the quality of the lake but because it brought an economic boom to so many of the communities along the lake that were suffering because the commercial fishery had pretty much collapsed or been put out of business. It was a great economic return plus it brought some stability back to the forage base—predator to prey. A good healthy salmon fishery is still very important. We had a big alewife die-off in 1999 so the population of alewife still has a foothold here and it is an exotic species. It is not meant to be here.

When the new policies started in the late 1960s and early 1970s, I felt that I was the one that was being kicked out. Naturally, that would be my feeling. I thought it could have been handled differently. I thought it could have been handled better. I spent a lot of time fighting it, knowing eventually, I would lose. The highest economic return was for the sport fishery and that is how we do things in this country. That is why we just hauled 3,000 pounds of fish waste to the landfill instead of someplace that could have recovered it for fertilizer or food or whatever. It is an economic decision like everything else. It could have been handled differently but I am not going to spend any time telling you how it should have been done because that is old news.

———————

Alan Priest (Leland, Michigan) recalled the changes that took place in the Lake Michigan fishery during the 1970s as a result of the burgeoning alewife population. He was among those who interpreted the creation of a Great Lakes sport fishery as an alewife control measure rather than an economic development initiative.

During the 1970s, the smelt and the alewives were way overpopulated. That is why they brought in the salmon and the lake trout. I can remember I used to get off the boat at night, go home, take a shower and sit in a chair. My hand would just throb from picking those alewives and smelt. Alewife bones are sharp. If they sit in the nets a little while, when you get them out, your twine gets tangled and the bones get under your thumb and in your fingers. Smelt have teeth and when you grab them to clear their head from the net you are kind of hooking their teeth. In the wintertime, I used to take home a five-gallon bucket of smelt just about every other day to my dad. In the winter, that was just what I picked and threw in the bucket for my dad. Salmon and lake trout were introduced to eat alewives. Fisheries officials wanted the smelt in the lake for forage for the other fish. But salmon and the lake trout are not the only ones on the food chain that feed on alewife. Once in a while, we even have chubs come up with alewife in their mouth. Also, whitefish feed on them as well as brown trout, steelhead, and perch.

When they planted the salmon, they just exploded and went great guns. The charter boats out of here had the most success they ever had. They used to come in with two large coolers just full of salmon—each boat with two coolers. The heads would be hanging out one side and the tails hanging out the other. We used to fillet them down at the docks for the charter boats when they came in. We used to hate it when they came in with those great big salmon. The people crowded around and watched us fillet their fish for them. They would be asking all kinds of questions. The salmon fishing was big. Some of the coolers were holding eight or ten big salmon. Some of them were thirty pounds—a lot of them were twenty-five to thirty pounds. They were big fish. The salmon program helps the whole state—the restaurants, the hotels and bay stores and the people here. It does not particularly help me with chub fishing.

According to his wife, Joy, the late Ross Lang was always adapting his fishing skills and gear to accommodate changes in the fishery and state policy. He was determined to remain in fishing despite state efforts to drive him and other commercial fishermen out of business.

Ross had such love for fishing. I do not know of anyone that loved his or her job as much as he did. It was kind of refreshing to see that sort of thing. He did branch out in the fishing industry. He brought new things to the Great Lakes that were never brought here before as far as the seining and the whitefishing in this area were concerned. He was always looking for new ways to make things better. He was an innovator. He would read a lot. He read everything he could about commercial fishing, old and new. He tried out a lot of things. Many of them worked and many of them did not, but he gave it a try. He was a real engineer. When he died, I remember a brother-in-law, who is an engineer, said Ross was the best engineer he ever knew because he could fix anything when it came to fishing. He did all of his own work. When a wheel had to be changed on the boat and he could not afford to have it changed, he borrowed a wet suit from a friend and he went down in March and changed the wheel on the boat.

Sometimes the state will have you so strapped that you have to come up with something different. The commercial fisheries in this particular area of Michigan can only take chubs and whitefish. There are not as many fishermen left as there were in years past. When we first came here, there were probably seven or eight different boats here in Leland. Now there are two left. And that is the same with all the ports in the state. They were so regulated—all they can fish are chubs and the whitefish. Ross always used a particular term when he talked about lake trout and some of the fish that he was not allowed. They were sacred. Those were only for the sportsmen. He did not have anything against the sportsmen, nor did he resent the things that the Indians did when they came in. He never blamed them for that. He just went on his way and did what he could do for the fisheries in the state.

Chuck Jensen of South Haven discussed the effect of the DNR decision to create a sport fishery in Lake Michigan and how it helped to drive commercial fishermen out of business. He maintained that commercial fishermen lacked the political clout of sport-fishing interests. Many regulations are not, in his view, scientifically based.

There was not anything that was really that controversial until they decided to put the commercial fishermen out of business. Up until then, it was routine, with closed seasons and restrictions of the size of mesh. Our permit for fishing chubs allowed us to fish only so many feet of net. Before that, we were not restricted on how much linear footage of net we could use. There would probably be around twelve boxes, with 1,300 foot a box—that is three or four nets tied together and a gang of nets would be so many boxes.

It has just been one thing after the other with the introduction of the sports fishing for salmon. First, you had an overpopulation of alewives. Then the DNR wanted the alewives fished out. When they planted the salmon, they wanted the alewives kept in. Then the chub population varied so much, but then when it was good, they decided they did not want us to fish chubs because of the pesticide situation.[70] So that kind of wound everything up right there. We already could not fish perch and whitefish. This happened in the late 1960s and early 1970s. First, they cut out the whitefish because of the incidental catch of trout and salmon. Then they banned the whitefish and then later on, the perch from perch nets. The object of banning whitefish gill nets was because of the incidental catch of trout and salmon.[71]

We did not catch that many trout or salmon in our nets. Actually we did not have a chance to fish much after they restricted us. The DNR said if you brought up a trout in your chub net—this is in 180 foot of water and they are not going to live when they get up from the bottom—you have to throw that fish back in the water. You cannot bring it in. So we would throw a dead fish back in the water. We could not bring it in and have it for dinner. So that was one of the funny restrictions, but there were some incidental catches of trout and salmon.

The stocking of salmon did affect us because of the shutdown of the whitefish nets. We did not mind the stocking of the fish, but we did not want to be put out of business either. It was kind of a mixed feeling between the fishermen and the Steelheader Association. But like I say, they had a little more clout in Lansing than we did.

We had the Michigan Fish Producers Association and were fighting the Steelheader Association. We were fighting legislation and the sportsmen. We did not have enough numbers to have any effect. Claude VerDuin was the executive director or head of the Michigan Fish Producers Association for a number of years. I believe Roy Jensen of Escanaba was in the position of executive secretary. My dad went to Michigan Fish Producers meetings years before I did. The DNR would have speakers on different subjects. They would have a university speaker on certain subjects. Legislators would be there and biologists and so forth. So it was kind of mixed information. We would give our viewpoints and they would tell us what to do.

Claude VerDuin was an effective spokesperson. One thing we had to fight against were the restrictions on chub fishing. They were going to say you could not fish chubs inside of forty fathoms, or 240 feet of water. The people down this end of the lake said that is not too good for us, because as you come south from Holland it gets shallower. So for us to fish forty fathoms, we would probably have another hour's run. So we got it down to thirty fathoms south from Holland, and that helped out a lot. Forty fathoms is close to one-third or halfway out in the lake.

Finally, we were stopped from chub fishing from Grand Haven south because the chubs initially had too much pesticide in them. From Grand Haven north, the commercial fishermen were allowed to fish chubs. There is one particular line out there—this side has pesticides and this side does not. We were told at the last meeting I attended—which was quite a few years ago—that if the pesticide levels went down at this end of the lake, they would reissue permits for chub fishing. That is the last we ever heard. So evidently there are still more pesticides out there, but not north of Grand Haven.

We never did know why they allowed Wisconsin, Ohio, and Indiana commercial fishermen in during the middle to late 1960s. We were always restricted. Every port had a restriction of a fifty-mile radius they could fish. We could not take our tug and move to Muskegon or so forth. So for some reason they let nonresident fishermen come in from Ohio and Wisconsin. St. Joe and South Haven had quite a few tugs. They really fished the perch out for a couple years. I do not remember if their permits expired or the fish expired or what, but then they all went back to their ports more or less. A couple of Lake Erie boats stayed here.

It was kind of funny because they had these tugs in both these ports and they caught enormous amount of tonnage of perch for a couple years. So then, when the boats all left and it got back to normal fishing with a normal amount of fish the DNR said: "Well, they caught thousands and thousands of pounds last year, but they only caught a few thousand this year." But there was not the activity going on that there was in previous years.

––––––––––

Don Stiller, who began commercial fishing in 1942, recalled how commercial fishermen responded to the alewife population explosion and crash.

I would not say that the alewife chased the perch out but they competed with them. The volume of alewife was so great, it made it difficult to fish. The water was covered with them. When you set gill nets you either set them out of a box in open water or you spin them back. One fisherman will let the net run through his hand and the other fisherman holds a float line up as it goes over the stern. The alewives were so thick sometimes, you could hardly get the net in the water without picking up a bunch of dead alewives before it went to the bottom. In the early 1960s, you had to almost have a clothespin on your nose because of the sour and vinegar-like smell. There were windrows of alewives along the beach. People closed up their cottages and did not use them. Then, all of a sudden, after the big die-offs came, you did not see the alewife after that. When they first came, you could go down on the shore in the evening and you could hear kind of a roar. It sounded like a wind coming up. You could look out there and the whole surface of the water was shimmering as these alewives came ashore. They would come up from under the propeller of the boat. If you were towing a hunting skiff, they would jump right into the hunting skiff. Then they planted all these different varieties of salmon and trout and now they want to keep that forage base up so these sport fish have something to eat. And, of course, the sport fishing crowded us a little bit, quite a bit.

Sport fishing started up after they planted trout and salmon. But many years ago, when the perch fishing was good, they used to rent out rowboats. You would go out there and fill a five-gallon pail full of perch. In those years, nobody had big motors on their boats. They would probably have a little ten-horse kicker or something like that. They might not go out over a mile or a mile and a half out at the most. Now everybody has these big powerful boats, and they can go anywhere with them in any kind of weather.

Jack Cross (Charlevoix, Michigan) fished for more than forty years. He now operates a wholesale and retail fish operation.

During the 1960s and 1970s the state was trying to get us out of business. They did not want any commercial fishing and for a long time the legislators would not go along with them. They kept taking areas away from us and trying to cut us down but the fish were coming on stronger at that time and we were surviving it. When they put us out of the gill-net business, a lot of them got a payoff, which was very small. It was about ten cents on the dollar for what everything was worth. And a lot of the older fishermen did not want to go into the trap-net business because it was a big changeover, so they retired. We were younger then and we did it. But then they put us out of the trap-net business. It was a big changeover for us, too. We had never done that aspect of it.

When they started stocking salmon in Lake Michigan we looked at it commercially. When salmon were first put into the lakes, the commercial fishermen in Michigan could not take any of them. But the Canadian side could. The Canadians were taking the fish and bringing it back into Michigan. We were never allowed to take salmon. Before the salmon, they put the lake trout in. They let us take a certain percentage of them, a small percentage. When they were trying to get us out of business, they took the lake trout away from us and tried to narrow our fishing down to just whitefish and chubs. But we still had enough there to make a living and so we kept on. I do not personally see the salmon as a good fish for the Great Lakes because they take too many fish. They have got to eat their weight two or three times a day to survive and they do not just target one fish. They will take any fish that they can. I think it is something that the sportsmen like, I guess, because of size, but personally, if they are going to plant fish I would just keep it to the native fish of the Great Lakes.

I know all the fishermen personally. I have done business with them so much, I know their license number off the top of my head. If somebody comes along and wants to sell me fish, I would make them produce their license. They carry it in their pocket. It is like a driver's license. They would have to produce a license because I will not buy fish from somebody that I do not know. They have got some proof of identification. I have to make out reports of who I bought the fish from and how much fish. The white copy goes to the Michigan DNR, the state gets a yellow copy and then sends it to the tribe, a yellow copy goes to the person I buy the fish from, and I keep the pink copy. When the month is over, I put them all in an envelope and send them to the state. It is a daily transaction. Every day that we make a transaction, it is recorded and logged. So the state gets copies and we send them in every month so they know just what we are doing.

Chuck Jensen closed the family fishery in South Haven after nearly fifty years of business. He recalled the informal relations that existed between his father, Chris Jensen, and Capt. Charles Allers of the Michigan Department of Conservation's *Patrol Boat No. 1.*

In the early days they had the *Patrol Boat No. 1* which would cruise the lakes and check on illegal nets and so forth.[72] Everything was under control pretty well. Charles Allers was in command of the boat and might have been head of fisheries law enforcement division of the DNR or Conservation Department. The land officers kept a good eye on everything, too. They would come down once in a while and measure the nets. There was always a great debate over the mesh size as it was slack or stretched, wet or dry. The DNR had their rules and they enforced them pretty good.

Charlie Allers would come into port on *Patrol Boat No. 1.* He would come down to our fishery. He and my dad would talk and talk, and maybe argue a little bit about this and that. Then after a while, they would go up to the Elks and have a drink. That is the way they got along.

I think most all those old-time conservation officers on the patrol boats were mostly all ex-commercial fishermen. Melvin Plum is still living up in Charlevoix. He was on one of the smaller state boats. He worked with Jim McCash for Cross Fisheries years ago up in Charlevoix. Years ago, Melvin Plum and Jim McCash worked for Johnny Cross. They were all more or less connected in the fishing business—family wise or something. It takes one to know one. They know all the tricks.

There is this old story that either Roy Jensen or Claude VerDuin told. This is an old story. One time, years ago, they boarded a fish tug up north someplace and they were lifting illegal nets. And so they left one of the officers on board to go back in with them. So the crew put the officer up in the wheelhouse. And while he was in there they put all the fish overboard. They got in to port and there was no evidence. That was one of the stories.

Leon Voight (Gills Rock, Wisconsin) discussed the DNR's fishing policy and management style and was critical of the way the border dividing Lake Michigan between Wisconsin and Michigan was patrolled.

If a whitefish is a thumbnail short, the DNR will pinch you for it. They will take you down and book you. They can throw you in jail and fine you for it. They fine you by the pound if they find more. For a while there, they were really picky. They would come around measuring. Some fishermen went to court a few times because you can measure a fish and it can be exactly seventeen inches on the lake. By the time you get to the dock and you are dressing the fish, it could happen to be a quarter of an inch shorter because it shrunk with the ice. You put ice on them in the summertime, and after they die, the smaller ones will shrink. That is another reason why we like the heavier fish, the more meaty ones, because they do not shrink up.

We have been pinched for a small fish like that. They came in, dug through our fish one time about ten years ago, and they found twelve. I purposely had those fish lying on top of the box just so they could see those fish when they came down. There were six wardens. They jumped on the boat. They went up through that boat, down the bilge and everywhere looking for trout or something. Of course, they never found anything other than these small fish. The fish were skinny at that time and they had shrunk. There were a lot of small, skinny fish around and we got pinched for it.

About twenty years ago, you could keep a percentage of your incidental catch. You could keep ten percent of smaller whitefish you lifted. If you had 1,000 pounds, you could keep 100 pounds of smaller ones because they shrunk or something. There was a little leeway there. Then they took that away and started coming around pinching everybody. The fishermen were not used to doing it that way. They did not worry about having a small one in there. I think it was basically to help the wardens pinch you on something. That is basically what it was. It was just another one of their little niche things.

I know they patrol the line out in Lake Michigan. Here in the bay, they really patrol it. I do not know where they came up with these lines. As far as I am concerned, once you get three miles out or five miles out, it should be federal water just like it is in the ocean. I think you should be able to fish wherever you want as long as it is open water. These invisible lines that they put in these lakes are ridiculous. If your Loran happens to be off one day, all of a sudden you have a warden sitting alongside of you in a boat saying that you are in their side of the water and you get ticketed for it. The Michigan DNR actually came three-quarters of a mile into Wisconsin waters and took our nets. And there was no way I could fight that in court. These invisible lines are down in Marinette and Menominee. Michigan kept claiming more water and more water all the time. They kept moving lines on us and then they would not tell us about it. So they would come out and say: "This line has moved and you are in Michigan water."

Joel Peterson (Fairport, Michigan) discussed how fishermen regulate themselves through customary knowledge, occupational ethics, and the customary practice of returning legal-sized fish. The market also has a regulatory function.

Two gentlemen rode with me today. One said he would never have believed it. He said I dumped back twice as many fish as I took. We had about 1,700 pounds of fish today. I dumped at least 3,400 pounds back. A whitefish has to be seventeen inches long to be harvested. A lot of times if I do not think the fish is big enough even if he is seventeen inches, I will throw him back. Fishermen need to pay attention to what they are doing. We threw a lot of fish back over today that were long and skinny. Why should you try to market them? Let them fatten up. Two weeks down the road or a month down the road they could be twice that size. They could be worth something. Right now, all they are is a head and a tail and skin, so that's what we look at too.

We are run by the DNR. If you are a farmer, you are run under agriculture. Maybe fishing should be under agriculture also. Maybe we should treat these fish the same as a tree, as a renewable resource and harvest it appropriately. Most people say you are going to catch everything. How am I going to catch everything if my kid is going to be the fifth generation of fishermen? Now what does that tell you? Was there any planning? Did we try to catch all the fish that was out there? If they would have, it would never have gone past the first generation. We went from knowledge of fishing—from gill nets to pound nets to trap nets—and now all of a sudden, you find out that everything can probably be done if it is managed properly. The best you can do is take an educated guess of how many fish are in the Great Lakes and that is all it is. The state based its estimates on our catch report. There were twenty-one people that have a license to fish this area right here. We each produced annual harvests of one and a half million or two million pounds a year for the last twenty years. They found out we have a stable fishery. The State of Wisconsin had their fishermen on a quota. What was the sense of putting the quota on them before? The price of fish affects how many you harvest. If the price of fish gets down so low that you cannot sell them and make a profit, you are not going to harvest them, are you? So that is what went on there. It was mostly politics. That is all it is. It is the same with the negotiations with the tribes right now. If you ever stopped to realize it, we are the only food producers that are not governed by agriculture.

Brian Price of the Leelanau Conservancy, a former commercial fisherman, discussed the political and economic contexts of fisheries policy-making and implementation.

If I am licensed, the state sanctions me to fish and take a certain amount of the common resource. I provide a public service for which the market compensates me. The state is always going to have to sanction certain people to take from the lakes some of its bounty and others to take less, because you are always responding to these huge swings and transitions. You will never get this thing in sync. Will you ever then be able to say we are going to hammer out a policy that is completely fair to everybody? No, because when you get close to it, something else is going to happen and you are going to recede again.

There is a limited amount of fish, even if we were to assume this was a steady state system. There is a sustainable harvest of each of the species in that system, but we are not even close to having a steady state system. A sustainable harvest by definition is a limited amount of fish. Suppose I know exactly how much lake trout can be harvested from northern Lake Michigan for the next ten years. Then the question becomes who gets to take them? How much am I going to allocate as the treaty fishery for the Native Americans? They clearly have laid a claim that the court's backed up that they have a right to that resource in a certain amount.

How much am I going to allocate to a sport fishery that has got a lot of political clout and a lot of people having a lot of fun with it? They have certainly got a right to utilize that resource as well. They are the most broad-based group—anybody who buys a license, a boat, and a rod. How much am I going to allocate to the state-licensed commercial fishery if any? How good is my information? How much do I know about what fish are available and where they are located? How do I allocate it amongst the user groups?

We need good science, good public policy, and fair-minded, even-handed managers. We have not always had them. At various points in time, we never have any of those. Fisheries management has gotten a whole lot better, and more even-mannered, even-handed over the last twenty years. I think the science has improved, but it is always way behind. Maybe the experts could dispute that. I have been involved to some slight degree in fishery management authority meetings and so forth, and I know the kinds of numbers that they try to work with. It is never gonna be a precise thing.

I would like to see a day when there is a more cooperative relationship between the tribes, the state, and the commercial fishing industry. I think we have been moving that way for the past ten to twenty years. I hope the agreement that is being hammered out now will be a lot less rancorous than the consent agreement that was hammered out in 1985, and that no shots will be fired. If there is some sweeping vision that is available to change the ethic and the way that people use the resource, I am all ears. I am not aware of how we can depart from the model that we are still trying to refine.

We are struggling with a beast that is much bigger than we are. We will never quite understand it completely. Are we doing what is humanly possible to be responsible towards the resource? In general, yes. Are the parties involved acting in good faith? Yes, absolutely. Neither the white nor the Indian fishermen want to just take, take, take, take, and not give back. Are the managers doing their utmost to try to come up with fair and evenhanded policies? Yes, I think so. Are the tribes trying to be responsible in exercising their treaty rights? Yes, I think so. I have been on the outside of that situation and I have been on the inside of that situation to some degree, and I admire what they are doing. I happen to agree with their right to exercise those treaties.

From what I know and what I see, there will never be a time when everybody abides by all the regulations. Having said that, there is not flagrant violation of commercial fishing regulations on a massive basis enough to damage the resource. Some people believe that the catch reports are not even halfway accurate. They think that the Indians always lie about the catches. When I went to work for the tribe, I was surprised at just how honest and meticulous they were about keeping those reports. And I know that when I worked for them running a trap-net boat, we had nothing to lose by accurate reporting. The reports are going to be wrong when somebody from Grand Traverse Bay puts a hard quota on and you can only take 20,000 pounds of this type of fish. The guy goes out and takes that 20,000 pounds in the first month of the season. He has a lot of incentive to cheat because he knows the quota is ridiculous. If he knows the quota is ridiculous, he is going to lie about his catch. So there needs to be a better, more cooperative arrangement between the fishermen and the managers so that they get accurate information. Then there will be more confidence that the system works in terms of protecting the resource. Fishermen don't want to destroy the resource either. They know better than that.

I worked for Ross Lang who was a state-licensed commercial fisherman out of Leland, so I did not have to have a license. The license covers anybody employed by the licensee, and so I have never had a commercial fishing license of my own. If I wanted my own, I would have to buy it from somebody who has a license. This is a result of limited entry, where it is sort of like a liquor license; you cannot create another liquor license normally unless you know who to talk to. If I wanted to set up now in commercial fishing, I would have to go and buy a license from somebody who is not using his license anymore or was willing to sell it. I would have to ask the state if I could move the license to Leland in order to fish whitefish or wherever I wanted to go. The state would likely approve the transfer of the license. And they have been pretty good about it.

Steve Peterson has been fishing out of the Garden Peninsula his entire life. He grew up hearing stories of the conflict that took place in the area when a small number of local residents resisted Michigan DNR efforts to introduce the concept of limited-entry fishing.

The DNR has been not too bad, but back in the 1970s and early 1980s people who fished with their rowboats who could not get licenses had a lot of run-ins. They would fish at nighttime and stuff like that. There were only a few of them, but it only takes a couple bad apples to make everybody else look bad.[73] Now, you have to have your paper for however many pounds of fish you have caught. The paper has to go with the fish, so they could not even get rid of the fish even if they caught them. The DNR only shows up now and then. This area is not that bad, but downstate or Wisconsin they are always coming in and checking, checking constantly. Up here there are not as many sports fishermen like in the southern part. There are a lot more people who fish down that way. As soon as you come up north, there are not as many fishermen. For some reason, they stay down that way.

The season closes the whole month of November when whitefish are in spawning season. We can fish again in December. If it is a nice December, we will go back out. We usually get a good run in the spring. Then it slows down in the summertime when the water warms up. In the fall it cools back off again. The fish like cool water. They go deep in the summertime. Fishing has got a lot to do with the weather. If it is hot like that, the fish stay deeper, but if it is cold then it is not so bad. They like the cold water.

We go out every day where a lot of people only go out twice a week maybe. You have got to fish them. Today we threw back three times as many as we caught because they were too small. That is a good sign when you see the smaller ones. Salmon have started picking up during the last two years after a four-year decline because of the kidney disease. There were not many, so it was really hard to catch them. We fish a fifty-mile radius. It is trial and error. In the last few years, we have been trying new spots. We sell our fish to a fish buyer in Manistique named King. They do the shipping.

Rick Johnson was familiar with the particulars of the incident between game warden Don Euers and the LeClair family of Two Rivers, Wisconsin, which had taken place more than forty years earlier. On the whole, however, he maintained that relations with game wardens were far less antagonistic than they were before he entered the business in the 1970s.[74] He was pleased when the Wisconsin DNR sent its new wardens to meet with him and other commercial fishermen to learn about their gear and fishing methods and practices.

There are cases where the wardens have jumped on the boat and the fishermen locked up the doors and headed into a sea with the waves pounding like they were today. Obviously, that warden was up there scratching his toenails just trying to hang on. It is an old story. A warden did that and they took him off. I think it was in Two Rivers. They took him out and the warden shoved his jacket down the stovepipe to try to put out the engine, but they just kept going. The guy almost froze to death up there because his jacket was gone. That part of the fishing industry has gotten better. It is more of a business. Years ago, it was a way of life and a tradition, or heritage. There was something to being a fisherman. Events like that started over personality conflicts. Over the last ten or fifteen years it has gotten dramatically better.

Our relations with the wardens are a big concern. Last year was the first time in the history of the fishing industry there was a new class of fifteen or seventeen wardens. They actually called the fisheries up and asked if we would participate in some of their training. They brought them up to Baileys Harbor. We met with them and had open discussions. There were about five fishermen there. The new wardens asked all the questions they wanted. We tried to give them as many answers as we could. They saw the different aspects of the fishing industry including gill netting and trap netting and so forth. So that was a start right there. Obviously, most of those wardens are not going to be involved in the fishing industry. They are going to go all over the state. But it was a start. The instructor thought it was the best thing that he has ever gone through as far as training the wardens and getting them out to see commercial fishermen face to face. It gave the wardens a chance to see that they are real people. The fishermen are businessmen, family men, and church-going men. But it still is a concern. Hopefully the wardens are not going to all retire the same year and there will be a couple that will guide these younger guys through.

We had a couple of female fish biologists come along a few times. You do not see too many women in the DNR. I thought that they did a better job than some of the more experienced guys who were training them. They knew the ropes. They knew when to sit down and slack off. They were right on the job. They were out there on probably one of the roughest days I have ever been out and they hung tough. But you do not see many. I had a good friend that was trying to get into a full-time job for the DNR. She worked as a creel clerk for a couple of summers. She was just trying to make a living and stay involved in the department. She ended up having to quit because there were not any full-time jobs. It is a tough line to get into because of the lack of money in the department.

Kenneth Peterson (Fairport, Michigan) heard the Don Euers' story from the LeClairs.[75]

Pete LeClair might have been on with his dad, Joe, that day. There was some dispute over their gear or what they were taking. The DNR were going to climb right on his boat and gonna arrest him. He just shut the doors and away they went out in the lake. One of the DNR guys made the mistake of jumping on the top of the cab. He should have never done that, I guess, because they had her all buttoned up, and they took him to sea. He squealed to get in, but that is just hearsay, you know. Old Joe he told me the story one time himself. But that is why I say, it is just hearsay. He was a pretty good BS-er, old Joe. Maybe it was not quite that bad, but it was bad enough. They made the warden say he would not arrest them as long as they let him inside. He was getting cold. He got up behind the exhaust. He was on the stern of the boat. It was blowing that day and they were taking it right over the bow. They gave him a good ride. He was ready to get inside when they let him in.

Don Stiller, retired Wisconsin fisherman, reflected on the complexities of complying with regulations, especially those concerning fishing gear.

In the 1930s smelt came in the bay. Smelt net is less than an inch and a half or an inch and a half stretch. If you fish that net on the bottom you are going to catch quite a few perch because the perch tend to come up against the net and go to the bottom. So you had to fish them up off the bottom. You had to put dropper lines where each lead was so the net would come up eighteen inches off the bottom. They got pretty stringent on that and they made a few arrests on smelt nets. In fact, my father got a citation one time. He had the nets in the water and the warden come out and checked them. This was new at the time and fishermen did not know for sure what they were going to do about it and the warden said: "I do not know if they are legal or not." My father said: "I will take the nets out of the water." So he took them out of the water and he had them boxed in the garage and the warden came in the evening and he said: "Let me check those nets again." When he measured he said, "You are under arrest. The nets are illegal." They were not even in the water at the time. He did not pay a fine on it because he talked to a lawyer and he got the nets back. It was not too bad when we could fish different varieties of fish.

Another time there was a problem was in 1945 or 1946. In the winter prior to that there was a run of whitefish that came down into the south end of Green Bay. There was a seventeen-inch limit on them. Most were running sixteen and seven-eighths inches and they were in the net and when they came to the surface they were lost. Some fishermen brought the fish in because they thought it was wasteful to leave them there. Then they planted the trout and the walleyes. Years back, if you caught an occasional trout in the net, you never hesitated to bring it in rather than throw it away. I do not mean a lot of them, but maybe one or two. We never had too many problems with incidental catch or wardens. I did get cited one time in the wintertime when I was fishing through the ice in the slew, in a little tail slew. My brother was with me and we fished through the ice. We had six pounds of perch and we had to record them in this book. The book was right on the dash of my truck. We pulled up by my duck shack to put chains on the tires of my pickup truck so we could get out there. We had these fish in the pail. I heard the car coming. I thought it was my neighbor coming in and here it was the warden. Well, I had the book and I realized I had not recorded it. He came dashing over and wrote me up. He wanted a $408 fine. I am sure he realized that I was not trying to sneak the fish in. I would not have had them right in the open. But he checked me one time previous to that and I had four perch, and he said you get your book and write down two pounds. He said, "I could arrest you for one fish." So that is how strict they got.

"Coho" Bob Maynard, retired charter boat captain and commercial fisherman, maintained that people who opposed gill nets did not understand their use within the fishing community.

Y ou could put a four-foot-high piece of gill net out there forever—like a tennis net—and not fish out the lake. Some of the fish swim high and low depending on the time of year. Some of the fish you like to eat swim up near the surface, whereas at other times of the year, you may find them three to four foot from the bottom. The folks that live in the North Country, where the gill nets are used, have an entirely different opinion of them.

Lyle Teskie, former commercial fisherman turned charter boat operator, expressed the belief that the elimination of gill-net fishing ultimately contributed to the depletion of more commercially desirable fish stocks and a surge in the population of so-called rough fish.

I was a gill-net fisherman. I fished some trap nets, but I did not only do trap nets. I fished with my brother and my dad. In the past, there has been tension between commercial fishermen and sport fishermen. When the salmon fishing was at its best, there were sportsmen who politically tried to have the DNR curtail commercial fishing and stop the gill net from being used. In a way, the ban on gill nets contributed to the demise of the lake, too, because it killed off all the rough fish. The trap net does not kill off what we call garbage fish like carp and lawyer that eat other fish eggs. They are like a big vacuum cleaner. So when they stopped gill-net fishing up in the bay, the carp and lawyers really took off because the trap net does not kill them. When I commercially fished, there would be ten to twelve boats up there fishing gill nets every day, killing tons, literally tons and tons of garbage fish that eat other eggs. When they stopped gill-net fishing it led to a big demise in the other species. Now we are getting to where the fish actually hurt the fish. There was no predator on carp or lawyers. They just started eating more and more of the bass, the perch, whatever they could suck up.

So there are many things that have contributed to the lake's demise and basically it is man. It is either legislation or the debate between the sportsmen and the commercial fishermen. To appease the sportsmen the DNR stopped the gill netting and then, of course, the rough fish started eating more.

———

Kenneth Peterson, who fished off of Michigan's Garden Peninsula for more than forty years, recalled how Michigan's tight restrictions on gill netting limited the ability to fish under the ice for whitefish.

When we fished out of Fairport, we could fish gill nets under the ice. But then the DNR took the gill nets away from us, so we were licked there. We could not set gill nets under the ice anymore. Up here in the bay is the only place we set gill nets under the ice. And they took them away from us, so that was the end of that. They called them fish killing nets. The game fish like walleyes, trout, and whatnot, are not in the bay in the wintertime. You would get lawyers or suckers once in a while, and that was about it. It is just in recent years since they have been fishing trap nets that they get a trout now and then. They do not get any amount to speak of. They get more suckers and lawyers in trap nets, but you do not get many other game fish. I do not know why it is, there were never too many trout up in this bay. We used to get some little trout, over around the crib, over around Escanaba, in the steamboat channel. If you go up and down the bank, you get trout there once in a while. The trout stays more to the deep water.

We fished gill nets on the bay for the whitefish. There are better whitefish up in the bay here. We fished on the lake with trap nets for whitefish, too, but it was hit and miss. There were quite a few commercial fishermen who fished trap nets on the lake, too, but now that the Indians have got all the rights to fish on the lake, the white man cannot fish there. In other words, it is hell to be a white man. Before, nobody wanted to be an Indian. Now, they all want to be Indians.

———

Don Bell, Jr. of Mackinaw City noted that the combination of gill nets and trap nets gave fishermen greater economic flexibility.

When they banned gill nets in the 1970s it hurt. Those who could afford it went to trap nets. They got subsidized somehow or another and they went to trap nets. Trap netting is a seasonal fishery. Down here, you cannot fish trap nets through the ice in the winter. There is too much current through this area and we have big ships that go through here in the winter. Big Bay de Noc is secluded. When it freezes over, they fish traps through the ice and at times, do real well. If the winter is good and makes good ice in some of the bays down, the tribal members who can fish gill nets will fish them through the ice. It is a hell of a way to make a living, but they will do it. They go out in zero to ten-degree weather. If you get a little bit of a breeze, it gets pretty nippy out there. There are not many trees to hide behind. They can fish the gill nets year round, but they are not as select as traps. But in the last two or three years, more tribal members are switching over to trap nets from the gill nets. The way the law is written now among the tribes, if you are fishing traps, you cannot fish gill nets. You cannot fish them both at the same time. But if they tie their trap nets right off in the winter, they can fish gill nets through the ice in the winter and can still make a living. The bills keep coming in twelve months a year.

In this area, whitefish is our biggest product. We get a few trout, but not very many. Down in lower Lake Michigan, there are a lot of lake trout. Our guys up here, the tribal members, cannot go down there and fish. The Bay Mills and the Sault tribe cannot go down around Charlevoix; there is a line. They cannot go south of there—it is just for the Grand Traverse Band. There are not that many trout around here and the fishermen do not target them anyway because all they do is rip up their nets, unless they have heavy-duty nets instead of whitefish nets.

Don Stiller, a retired Wisconsin commercial fisherman, maintained that reports of the damage that abandoned gill nets do to the fishery were greatly exaggerated.

Sport fishing impacted us by almost putting us out of business completely at one time. This was when they first got big out in the lake. I do not think that they really wanted to get us out of business completely. But there are a lot of people who do not understand the commercial fishery. Some people are so naïve. They think that a net is a net—you drop it in the water and it is going to get filled up with everything, regardless of what size mesh it is. It is just going to clean everything out. Once in a while, you will read an article that says stray gill nets are all over the place. They say that stray gill nets fill up with fish and they sink to the bottom. The fish rot and then the net comes back up and starts fishing again. This is absolutely absurd because if the gill nets filled up with fish and they died, the net would come to the surface. When the fish rotted, it would be so tangled up and so messed up that it would never catch another fish. If you set a 240-foot net off the mouth of the river when fish were coming into the river, and you caught 100 pounds of suckers, they would have that net rolled up like a rope about as big around as your arm. It would not catch any more fish. Some people just do not understand the commercial fishery. They figure that commercial fishermen take everything out of the lake. But on the other hand, you do have fishermen out there that cheat, and that is not good either. They take illegal fish.

Washington Island-based commercial fisher Ken Koyen indicated that the Wisconsin DNR closely regulates the setting of gill nets.

The DNR tests with what they call graded mesh. Out of all the net methods used on the Great Lakes, the gill net is the most selective because it only catches what will fit in the mesh. The mesh for whitefish is four and one-half inches, stretched from corner to corner; a chub net is two and one-half inches. The DNR will start with one inch and then set so many feet of that size mesh, and then so many feet of the next size mesh and keep going up. That way, they can get the different year classes of fish. Obviously, a four-and-one-half-inch mesh will allow any small fish to go right through it.

The locality of the whitefish is in shallow water, closer to shore. But we are required to stay a quarter mile from the beach with the gill nets. Unfortunately, we have deep water just a little ways off the beach of the island, so there are very few areas that we can get up actually above eighty to ninety feet. The whitefish will feed on June bugs as soon as they start hatching. The fish will go to the surface and, of course, they will go in by the beach. But I cannot catch them.

Paul Goodman (Washington Island) discussed the obstacles he faced trying to remain in commercial fishing.

I was worried about the fishery shortly after I got back into it in 1975 when I saw that the equipment that we were using every day was going into the museum down the road. I am thinking—I could use that equipment. It is probably in better shape than the equipment that I am using. So I knew there was a problem because our equipment was in the museums already and here we are trying to make a living. You feel like you might be living in the Stone Age if you really think ahead on it.

I could see the push of law enforcement was heavier all the time. They were after us for really small things. You might be two fish over or two miles over. We had requirements and certain fish we could not keep. But when you are working with a large amount of fish and you are sorting, sometimes you would have a couple fish that were the wrong size in there. You would not even pay attention to it. The DNR would be waiting at the docks. Back in those days when they really were hitting hard, they would be waiting at the docks wearing camouflage. They were hiding in the brush and would come running out to the boats. We always felt like they were supposed to have permission and they claim they do not. The DNR claims to have more power than the state police. Actually, they claim they can come into your house and check your freezer without getting a search warrant. It sounds bizarre, but if you buy a fishing license it says on it that they are allowed to do these things. They actually feel like they have the right to enter private lands at any time. Nobody else is allowed to do that.

We were arrested a few times for undersize fish. Once we were fishing down toward Chambers Island. They had made a new rule that said that undersize had to be thrown overboard immediately. When we were fishing, we were throwing everything in the boxes. The little fish here and there are not going to make it anyway. So we are fishing along and all of a sudden, we got raided by a patrol boat. They were hollering they were going to come aboard. We were working. We scanned the fish and threw the little ones out. They arrested us right away. I had a crew with me that day and they arrested both of us. It went to court. We had to hire a lawyer. One time we actually had a warden say, "You know, we could break you just by having you go to court."

Leon Voight (Gills Rock, Wisconsin) observed that relations between commercial fishers and the DNR had improved.

The DNR is getting more open to listening to us. They know it is a hard living, so they are open to suggestions. Sometimes we have to bring them information. But if you go back about fifteen or twenty years ago, they just made their laws and you had to abide by them and that was it. They tried to make regulations favor the bigger fishermen more than the smaller ones. They tried to get the fishermen fighting against each other too. They did it for a while until everybody kind of got together. Now there are so many less fishermen. It seems like every year, more and more are dropping out of the business. They just cannot hang on or they have other businesses that they are running, too. It just gets too hard for them. The DNR worked the numbers out here in Wisconsin a few years back and they found that tourism-wise, the whitefish caught by commercial fishermen actually brought more money in than the sportsmen did. But they favor the sports fishery. There is no doubt about it.

We take biologists along. They try to ride with each boat at least twice a month. They come along, they take scale samples of the whitefish or chubs, whatever you are fishing, measure them, and they take and measure any trout and salmon that you catch because some of them are tagged. And ninety percent of the trout that are caught over on this side of the lake are all planted in Lower Michigan. For some reason, the trout that they plant here must go over there. I do not know because pretty much everything they get here comes from Michigan.

Some of the fishermen are close. I mean, everybody talks to each other. Some of them still do things the way they are not supposed to be done. Mostly, it is the bigger fishermen that get away with it. Smaller fisherman tries it, but he cannot and he gets nabbed for it. Of course, that was another reason for having more fishing quotas. Then they would not have to cheat on reports. But they are talking about new regulations for that too. But yes, everybody pretty much talks to everybody and I even talk to people in Michigan's Upper Peninsula. If you go to the meetings, they all get together and hash things out. Sure, there are arguments because one guy's fishing this and this guy is fishing that. They do not see eye to eye, but they all have the same regulations. I go to these meetings when they are close enough. I will go to them if they are in Sturgeon

Bay, or sometimes Green Bay. I have been to a few in Manitowoc. I do not travel all the
way to Madison.

––––––––––––

Ben Peterson holds a tribal fishing license from the Sault Ste. Marie Tribe of
Chippewa Indians and previously held a commercial fishing license from the State
of Michigan.

We are unique in the whole State of Michigan. We have a state license and we
have a tribal license. We have a state license authorized by the tribe. It is called
a joint venture. We are the only ones that I know of that have it. The tribe agreed to let
us try it, and the state agreed to let us try it and we have been using it, so we do not
know what the heck is going to become of it in the year 2000. We were going to fish
somewhere regardless, because I am a tribal fisherman. I am sure the tribe is going to
take care of us somehow. One of the boats we have since sold was bought from Jake
Ellefson. We actually bought his license. A long, long time back we did Jake a favor
and told him, if you ever want to sell your license, give us first chance and he did. He
remembered it and called back, so we bought his license.

In Rogers City, there is one state commercial fishing license; in Alpena, there is one
license; in Munising, there is one state license; in Marquette there is one state license;
and there are a couple down in Saginaw Bay. But in the whole UP, Fairport is it. We do
the only state-licensed fishing from here west, in a fifty-mile radius. Fifty miles puts
you down over by Cedar River and it is only twenty-five miles to the Wisconsin border,
so you got a real narrow strip. All the state commercial fishing licenses are almost all
combined right in this area. The Ruleau Brothers fish out of Cedar River. That is a pretty
good size operation there. Ruleau Brothers run a trawler and have got two trap-net
boats out of there.

Regulations are regulations. You live with them and try to do things by the book
and if you do something not by the book, you better not get caught doing it because
it is not worth risking your license over. I think the major thing hanging over our head
right now is the consent order in 2000. We have been here—my brother Joel and I been
both fishing together. We started with my father in the early part of the 1970s, around

1971 or 1972. We have gone through a million different changes and things. We have gone through the gill-net ban and into trap nets. They were afraid we were going to take all the fish out of the bay. We went through a quota for one or two years and they took it off because we could not even begin to take them. Most of the old-timers will tell you they have never seen a run of whitefish like this. It has never lasted this long. They used to be maybe five to eight years, or whatever, and then they would disappear for five or six years. This run has been going on since the late 1960s. There has been up years and down years. Who knows what the reason is? Maybe it is because we are getting pretty efficient and we are keeping this overpopulation problem down, but maybe that is a wives tale, too.

Way up in the tip of the bay up here where the fish spawn, we had a hot spot up there for about five years. Nobody caught on to where my brother Joe was catching fish. He would go up there and get ten, eleven, or twelve thousand pounds of fish in a day. They were running out of boxes and they had to put the fish in bins. We would go real early before everybody else would. They did not know where we were going.

Donald Voight (Gills Rock, Wisconsin) retired from fishing in 1985 after nearly forty years. He recalled how fisheries management had changed since the days when regulations were established directly by the state legislature

When we first started fishing, we were controlled by laws from the legislature. Now, the DNR comes with these rules and regulations and you do not know where you are. What good are the DNR regulations? They cannot make the fish grow. I would like to see fisheries management go back to the agriculture department. Agriculture used to be over the fisheries. We used to have a license from the agriculture department to do our fishing through the spawn.

Paul Goodman (Washington Island) is a third-generation fisherman of Icelandic descent. He discussed how state policy favored sport-fishing interests over commercial fishing interests.

I fished commercially pretty hard for quite a few years. Eventually there were a lot of regulations and there was the sport fishing. They started stocking sport fish and that started to make a little conflict of interest. They started stocking lake trout. We did not have any problem with salmon or anything back in those times, but it was lake trout. They started reintroducing the lake trout. Initially, we heard that through the lake trout program you were supposed to eventually be able to catch them commercially. The Indians and the sportsmen were supposed to get a percentage of them too, but that really was not in the cards. It seemed like it was more for the sport industry. This was firmed up when they started to find chemicals in the fish. They could not be sold commercially but you could fish them sport-wise. Fishing them commercially ended when you could not sell them because of chemicals. The fish picked up a lot of chemicals, mainly PCBs, because of the way they fed and their fat content.

Everybody thought that if the problem was ever cleaned up, they would be able to fish the lake trout commercially. But they are still not cleaned up enough to make them a commercial fish. Also, a lot of regulations were going on in the fishery. We were fishing gill nets at that time, and gill nets picked up a lot of lake trout as incidental catch. Then the DNR put a lot of regulations in because of the conflict with sport fishing. There was some black market fishery going on where people were selling lake trout. I guess you could call it a black market fishery if you are catching an illegal fish. Some of them were legal to an extent. For a while, they let you tag a certain size fish and sell it, but everybody was tagging more than that and selling them. Any time that you could make a dollar doing it and they are in your nets and they are ruining your gear, you were selling them. We really did not feel a conflict of interest in this area because there were not that many charter boats. There was only a couple and everybody was family. Everybody knew the guys who had the charter boats. They were not outside people.

Southern Lake Michigan was where the conflict was because you had people who did not know anything about the lake becoming charter captains and taking people fishing. They really were not fishermen or water-going people. They were mainly people interested in getting into a business and making some money because it looked pretty good. But in this area, you heard about the conflict and Department of Natural Resources pushed the point that there was a big conflict going on. But personally, I never ran into a problem where I had a conflict with anybody in all the years. But they said there was.

———————

Rick Johnson who has been commercial fishing out of Gills Rock, Wisconsin, since the 1970s, maintained that the DNR favored sport over commercial fishing interests. He expressed concern that sport-fishing interests would soon be successful in banning trawling and gill netting.

There is a definite bias toward sport fishing. The DNR keeps saying that there is not, but we make many trips to Madison. We have hired a lobbyist down in Madison to work for the fishery. You go to a legislator—this is the part of the process that just makes me sick—who says I agree with you guys, but how many votes can you give me? You say 100 or 200 maybe, if you figure in our wives. And then you have a sports group saying we have 100,000 members. Well, if you are looking to get reelected, that is fine, but to me, there is something to be said for doing the right thing.

Relations between sport and commercial fishermen have gotten better the last few years. There are sport fishermen on the Lake Michigan Task Force, and they are real nice guys, real down to earth, common sense guys. There are a few radical guys that go to Madison, scream bloody murder and these people listen to them. That makes it tough when you go before the legislature and try to do something. They also have some pull in the department. They obviously listen to them. So far, the rules have not come down. The sports-fishing interests have been in the background pushing for the last few years to ban gill nets. That has been one of their big issues. Trawling is another issue. Down in Two Rivers, trawling is a big industry. Right now, that is the main focus of the sport fishery—to get rid of those trawlers. They have kind of backed off on the gill nets for now. But I am afraid if and when they ever get the trawling ban the gill nets will be next. The State of Michigan obviously has banned them significantly unless you are Indian.

The reason they are against the gill nets is too much incidental kill. The trawling industry was big in harvesting alewife. Well actually, that is why they started in business—because there were so many alewife. When I was a kid, the shores were just lined with dead alewife. So these trawlers got in and caught the alewife and then sold them for pet food. I assume, looking at the size of their boats and their other equipment, that they made some good money at it. But now there's talk that the alewife have really declined and the salmon eat alewife almost exclusively. The sportsmen want all those alewife saved for the salmon and so all this is basically over a little stinking alewife.

A lot of the fighting between commercial fishermen and the DNR was done by the time I got into the fishing industry. There were a few problems the last year or two. I remember fishing down around Baileys Harbor. There is a line there and gill nets are not allowed to go south of this line. The guy I worked for said that we could go south of the line and so we did. Then the DNR came out and said you cannot go south of the line. So I remember yanking those nets out and heading for home. But most of that was done before I started fishing. I would say it has gotten better over the last ten years.

The working relationship between the fishermen and the DNR has gotten real good. The problems had a lot to do with the law enforcement. You had a bunch of new wardens who were just coming on board and thought that this was the way it is going to be, no questions asked. Now most of these wardens are getting real close to retirement now. Now it is different. They come down and ask how are you doing. They talk to you like a human being instead of just trying to force their way onto your boat on the lake. I am not going to let somebody on the boat if I do not know who he or she is, or if the conditions are not right to let him on the boat.

Joel Peterson, who fished the waters of Lake Michigan off the Garden Peninsula, discussed the variable nature of his relations with sport fishermen.

The next two months, June and July, we will have guys coming out here coho fishing. We had probably three weeks of excellent salmon fishing last year. We have got nets out there. We have got them marked. We told them where the nets were and what to do to avoid them. We told them as long as you do not call us names, we will probably give your downriggers back if you accidentally get them caught in the trap nets. Call us a bad name, you probably will not get them back. We will probably let them tie up here if they want to tie up here. We might let them park on our land near the dock. Most sports fishermen who have come here, nine out of ten of them are amazed that we even let them around the place. The sheds are never closed. They come here, they go in there, take their box of ice from the ice bin and leave $2 on the counter and walk away. I will come down here on a Monday morning and there will be money stashed all over the shed. They will write a little note: "I was here from Lansing" or "I was here from there, got a box of ice, thanks Joe, see ya." That is the way it is.

Neil Teskie (Gills Rock, Wisconsin) has been fishing since he returned home from college in 1971. He maintained that the committed fishermen do not knowingly break the law.

B ack in the 1970s it got a little tense with the DNR once in awhile. But the relationship has been a little better. Some of it is due to the fact that some of the troublemakers are not here anymore. They got caught going illegal activities and they booted them. They are out. The fishermen who are left are pretty serious about fishing and keeping it going. They attend the meetings and we talk with our representatives and we talk with the DNR. We try to work things out. Most of the regulations we ended up with are because of the people that jumped through the loopholes. As a matter of fact, the new task force that is creating this new reporting system is the result of fishermen who overharvested perch, bragged about it, and got caught doing it. They got caught and now the DNR wants a new reporting system. They want to tighten up the regulations and it was not even in our fishery. It was in the perch fishery. Sometimes it is as if they want to teach us some common sense by giving us another regulation. The bad guy or the troublemaker is gone—he is out of business and we are stuck with the regulation. I would say that we have numerous regulations because of those people.

The regulations are not such that I have never had a citation. I will be honest with you. I have had citations, but most of the time, it is because I got careless. It was not purposeful, willful going out and overharvesting. One time we were fishing under the ice and I ended up with a citation for too many undersized fish. We were not measuring that close. We had all kinds of fish. It was ten below zero and we were freezing. Anyway, I could make all kinds of excuses about it, but the bottom line is that I got careless. I always told them if you catch me coming in with a box of fish under the deck that is undersized, take me. But you are not going to catch me doing that. But some of these people are like that. I do not think that anybody that has any concern for the resource really knowingly violates the regulations. Out of 5,000 pounds of fish we caught today, I had a couple of fish that were in the box that when we got them to the shed they were a little undersized. They looked long enough. But that happens. It slips by you, but it is different than taking a bucket full and sticking them under the deck.

Ken Koyen (Washington Island) described the methods commercial fishermen employ to gain input into fisheries policy in Wisconsin.

I had a little bit to do with setting up the Northeast Wisconsin Commercial Fishing Association. We were part of that. I had something to do with the first quota increase. I wrote a few letters, made some phone calls and was very thankful to Hutchinson and Senator Alan Lasay. I wrote Lasee a letter. He called me at six o'clock in the morning to ask me if he could pass copies of it on. I think it helped. We got a 12,000-pound white-fish quota increase which we should of had years before. Now, I believe the DNR is worried the whitefish are eating themselves out of house and home, and there is not enough feed to sustain all the population, so they want it lowered. The small increase was just maybe three years or four years ago now—and it was a small increase. Now they are giving us a forty percent increase across the board to the entire state, the entire fishery.

Elaine Johnson expressed frustration with commercial fishermen who did not become involved in the process of fisheries management policy-making or did not review and support studies sponsored to help the fishery.

Fishermen can be an odd bunch. When I was secretary of the Wisconsin Fish Producers Association, they were going to shut down the chub fishery up here. We finally got the DNR to decide how many boxes you can set. The DNR did not want the chub population too low. They wanted them to replenish themselves. So that is why I made the suggestion that each fisherman in our district area fish with six boxes. Then we could have a study going on, an ongoing study of what was happening with six boxes or six gangs out there fishing. Then they monitored it and could see what we were doing, and at the same time we were testing grids. We would have to send in the chubs and they would be tested for contaminants. We would have to have three clean tests before the grid was clean and the chubs could be fished and sold. In fact, it was my suggestion that we just set six boxes each. That is all we will set. We cannot hurt anything, and then you sort of have a study going on. It was agreed with everybody, six boxes.

But some of the guys had to sneak in seven or eight boxes. They had to sneak them in so we really never got a decent study. It just prolonged the program that much longer. Why not go along with it? I could never figure that out. They were always out there to cut off their nose to spite their face. But the fishermen hurt themselves too sometimes. It gave them a living, not too great. Let us do a study that is true and honest and see how it is. There is really no easy solution. I think fishermen have to get out of their old tarpaper shacks and get into the real world. They have got real problems out there and you have to become an active part of it.

We love the fishermen. We have argued with them. We have cried with them. I have hated them. I have loved them. I have done everything that is humanly possible to do with them. We know a lot of fishermen from Michigan and from Wisconsin, a few from Minnesota and a few of the river fishermen. I got acquainted with them when I was secretary too. Because you are interested in them, they are interested in you. Chapter 29, the state statute that we fish under, intrigued me so much, I knew it by heart. Most of the administrative code I could recite at any time. So when we went to meetings there was lots of times that I could just quote something. So the fisherman says, "She might know something. We had better get next to her."

Rick Johnson, who began fishing out of Gills Rock, Wisconsin, in the 1970s, indicated that commercial fishermen fished under DNR limits as well as self-imposed limits.

We always try to stay away from any place where we have a lot of incidental catch. It not only rips our nets up, but it also reflects bad on you if you have a DNR employee along who jots down that you have X number of salmon that are dead or whatever. But there have been times that we have self-regulated ourselves. For instance, the whitefish quota was based on a five-year period. It was based on what you caught during that five-year period and the price at that time. For a couple of those summers, whitefish sold for about twenty cents a pound. My partner and I chose not to fish hard at that time. Why kill whitefish for twenty cents a pound? So we caught enough for our restaurant orders around here and let the rest swim. Other guys just pounded them. When it came down for an allocated quota, obviously they were rewarded for the production and we were penalized for our approach. But I guess in the long run, you have to do what you think is right. Sooner or later it works out.

It is pretty hard to manage fish stocks. We are pretty well managed by the size of the mesh that we can fish. It pretty much determines what size fish we are going to catch. We try to release juvenile lake trout, salmon, whitefish, or anything that comes in so they can live to swim another day. But there are not a lot of ways we can really affect management too much other than that. We have tried different ways of fishing nets. We were not the first as far as floating gill nets. In the fall here, we float six feet below the surface to catch the bigger fish. They are obviously worth more money on the market and have more roe. So we do different things like that to better manage the stocks. You also stay away from incidental catch that way.

Don Stiller, a retired Wisconsin fisherman who began fishing with his father in 1942, expressed the view that the DNR should allow commercial fisherman more leeway in fishing their quota and requiring undersized fish to be returned to the water dead or alive.

I was prompted to quit commercial fishing because we caught too many game fish in our last years, primarily walleyes. The law reads that you have to throw them over if they are alive. We could not bring them ashore. We could stay away from them for the most part, but every once in a while we could not. Well, I think we should have been able to use them. It is just against my religion, as it were, to throw those things back. But then I can see the DNR's point, too. They would say: "If you can keep them all you are going to fish them intentionally." At one time, you could take ten percent of illegal fish—say if you had 100 pounds of perch, ten percent could be a little bit undersize. But in later years, if they measured them and found one or two undersized fish, you were going to get cited for it. But with the amount of fishermen who were out there and did not want anybody to bring in an illegal fish.

When the quota system came in, we would get a letter. I would get a letter from the DNR stating that I was 100 pounds shy in my 3,700 pounds of fish. I would get a letter from the DNR office in Sturgeon Bay notifying me that when you make your last lift, any fish that you get over your quota must be returned to the water dead or alive. So in other words, if I had 100 pounds of fish coming and I would try to figure how many nets I could set so I would not catch over 100 pounds, but I might get more than that. If I got 250 pounds and I only had 100 pounds left, I would have to dump 150 pounds back, which is something that I could never see. They also had regulations that you had to take the fish out of the nets where you took the nets out of the water. You could not pick the fish out of the nets if you were tied to the dock. I could come in the river and not put a line on the dock, and stay out in the middle of the river and I would be okay. But as soon as I touched the dock, I was subject to getting a citation. Most of the wardens are good enough to realize that when you are fishing with a flat bottom boat and you go out and it is blowing hard, you are not going to sit there and take a chance on drowning to get the fish out of the nets. You have to bring them in. And you had to record your catch in a book. I would estimate that I had 150 pounds and then after the fish were weighed officially, you would put that weight in there. They wanted you to be within ten to fifteen pounds. You would use certain size boxes that held sixty-five or seventy pounds so you could come close. But regulations like that made it a little more difficult all the time.

Elaine Johnson, who has processed fish from Door County waters for more than forty years, maintained that the Wisconsin DNR's quotas on perch were so low that they effectively closed the fishery.

In Michigan and all the states, the Departments of Natural Resources felt that the sports people gave the best money back to the state. Probably, in some sense, they do. But all their fish are planted and have to be patrolled. The only fish that the fishermen have are wild fish, and they do not have most of those species anymore. They give such low quotas for perch. You cannot even start your engine with those kind of quotas. So no one that I know fishes it. The lake is shut off as far as perch fishing is concerned. They are allowed to catch whitefish and chubs.

Rick Johnson (Gills Rock, Wisconsin) discussed how the policy of limited entry and species quotas made individual licenses and quotas commodities that could be bought and sold on the market as long as DNR restrictions were met. Fishermen who already hold a license are typically interested in buying another's quota. Johnson and other Door County fishermen have bought the licenses of several other commercial fishers in order to reduce the competition.

The way Wisconsin is set up right now, there are, I believe, ninety-five licenses. There can never be more than ninety-five. That is the number. You never can get more than what there was the previous year. The only way you can get into fishing is to buy somebody else out, which is a good thing. If more people get interested, then the older guys have a chance to sell their rigs, and kind of get their retirement out of it. There were four or five guys down in Green Bay who sold their perch quotas at $7 a pound and they made a killing. Right now, you could buy those quotas for about $2 a pound, so it is certainly an advantage to me if more people get interested in it. But you still have to acquire a license. There are no more licenses. There are X number and that is it. And every year a couple licenses get dropped. Some guys got in trouble with the law and their licenses were revoked. They will not be re-issued. Two or three guys are retiring. This year, I know that there are four or five that are going to be dropped, so it will probably be close to ninety licenses in the state, and that is figuring all of Lake Michigan and southern Green Bay. That is not a lot of fishermen. To have a license you have to have a $5,000 investment, which is nothing. If you buy somebody out, you have to buy out more than that. You also have to have two years experience on a boat. So that is the big thing right now. If you wanted to start fishing tomorrow, you would have to work for somebody for two years, or keep it in their name and fish it that way.

But everybody has a quota so instead of buying another license, you could buy my quota. Why buy my license if you already have one? So the license gets dropped. I have three licenses for my rig and I really only need one. The Weborgs have five licenses and they really only need one. I have a license with a 33,000-pound quota and I have another license with a 33,000-pound quota and then another license with a 30,000 quota. I just had a forty percent increase in the quota. That is because the DNR thinks there are too many whitefish, and it is stunting their growth. A seventeen-inch whitefish should be about three years old, but they are five. So there is quite a bit of concern in the DNR that there are too many out there.

Neil Teskie (Gills Rock, Wisconsin) recalled how the target species for most Door County fishermen has been and remains whitefish. Chub was sought when whitefish stocks were down.

We fished whitefish most of the time. Chubs were not that prevalent and we just did not concentrate on them. I think 1979 was when I first started fishing chubs. We might have fished chubs a little bit before then off and on. I fished some chubs in around 1979 or 1980 when the whitefish fishing was a little slow. When we fished chubs, we started down at Two Rivers and we moved to Sheboygan. We actually rented a dock in the area of Sheboygan that they have redone. I actually rented one of those sheds from the city and it is still there.[76]

When we were fishing out of Two Rivers, the DNR had a quota period where every boat was allowed to catch 15,000 pounds. We had the *Betty* and my brother's boat, the *Falcon*, down there and we just about caught our 15,000 pounds. So we brought the *Gem* down. We had to have the boat in the immediate vicinity to fish the quota because we had another license on this boat. So we brought it down there, got together and traveled from Two Rivers to the Sheboygan Reef, which was six and a half hours one way. We used to leave at 1:30–2:00 in the morning. We had a compass and a radar and then time. That was it. So we would run down, find the buoy, and then we would lift the nets. We would get anywhere from 4,000 to 6,000 pounds to the lift.

One time it really blew hard and we could not go out. We went out the next day and it was real calm and when we went down there, we had over 10,000 pounds of chubs on the boat before we got in. Four of us picked fish for fourteen hours. We never moved away from that clearing table for fourteen hours. We picked forty-some boxes full of fish. Then we threw them on the front deck of the *Betty*. We had a bin up there and we threw them up there. When that ran out, we dropped them at our feet until we were standing knee deep in them. They were big fish at that time. They were really large chubs. It was unbelievable what we caught. We had 10,000 pounds. It took us four days from the time I left here until the time we had them in the cooler.

Leon Voight (Gills Rock, Wisconsin) discussed how the DNR policy of limited entry affects commercial fishermen.

To manage the whitefish fishery, our design is to let the smaller fish get away. Even if we get smaller fish of legal size we will throw them back in the water because we want the nicer fish for filleting. The markets like the bigger fish, so we just throw them back. They are the better spawners in the fall for producing more eggs. So management wise, we do that. In the past few years the DNR wardens have kind of let the pressure off of us because we have bigger quotas and can fish better and longer. With the regulations, they have put more paperwork on us. We have to fill out paperwork every day coming off the lake. We make sure it is filled out before we hit the dock. Sometimes they board us on the lake and check everything. We really do not have too many problems with them. In the last ten years we really have not seen much of them but they come around here every once in a while when they are not doing anything else.

We are regulated on the gear we can use, too. We are only allowed to put out so many feet according to our license. Each license holder can fish 12,000 feet of gill net, which is twelve boxes of nets. Years ago, eighteen to twenty years ago, we would fish twenty to twenty-five boxes of nets in the water. That was when there were not that many fish around. You had to fish a lot of gear. Now, with larger fish populations, we only fish five or six boxes, just enough to keep our orders going.

I can sell my quota to another fisherman for about twenty or thirty cents a pound then get it back the next year, or I can sell it to him permanently. I think nowadays, the going rate is like $3 a pound. If you want to go buy a 30,000-pound quota, most fishermen cannot really afford to come up with $90,000 to do it. I know there are a couple rigs for sale right now and they are just sitting because nobody can afford to buy them. But the DNR just gave us a forty percent increase, which helped us out a lot. A fisherman that has a rig for sale will probably end up selling his boat to the Indians up north and then sell his quota off a little at a time to certain fishermen who will actually buy it.

They can shut us down anytime they feel like it. The quota really is not ours. Every year, you have 100,000 pounds of quota. The DNR does not actually have to give you that quota. It is not yours. You do not own it. If they decide they are only going to give you a 50,000-pound quota, that is what they will give you. You do not know if you are going to get that quota or not. You always have that hanging over your head, too, you know. If you get pinched for some little violation, they can take your license away and there you sit without a license. That is why most everybody has two or more licenses just in case something like that happens. Then you can take your quota and transfer it onto the other license and still fish it.

There have been points where they almost shut the fishery down completely because somebody did something wrong. That has happened. But they have not really talked about backing off on the whitefish quotas. Right now they are still expanding them because the whitefish in Lake Michigan are just exploding in numbers. They are giving more quota out so that they can get those numbers down. They are afraid that there is not enough food in the lake for the whitefish to grow. Right now, the average whitefish grows to about seventeen inches in three years and that is legal size. If you have a warmer year where there is warmer water, they will grow even faster, yet you have to have the food there for them. They have been skinny, like they have not been eating enough. We will throw them back. A lot of times I will throw back legal size whitefish. They are so thin so we just toss them back in the water and let them fatten up.

When prices drop down, we will back off. We will take nets out of the water so we are not fishing so much gear because it does not pay to fish them when you do not get the money for them. We will do that. In the fall, come spawning time, we will take and pull our nets out five days early just so that those fish can go in and spawn. Other fishermen will do it. The trap netters will not do it. They fish right to the end because their quotas are so big that they take everything they can catch. But as for the smaller guys, you have to plan your year out more so you have enough quota to make it last from July 1st to July 1st. Right now, our quota is approximately 84,000 pounds.

The Weborgs' quota is about a half a million pounds now. They are the largest. With their increase, they have a half a million right now. They were at 365,000 and they were not even able to catch that, so I do not know how they are going to catch all this extra quota. Teskie is another one. He just got an extra 100,000 pounds. He is up to 300,000 now, and he could not catch the 200,000 he had before. But then again, you might have a year where the fish come right where you want them, and you will be able to fill those quotas. But it is kind of doubtful because you really have to fish hard to catch that much fish. We went from about 60,000 to 84,000 and we are working on the last of our increase right now. I figure probably in another two weeks, we will be done. Then we will just bring the boat over here to Gills Rock, paint it all up, and get it ready for summertime. Fix up anything broken, get it all ready to go, and then work on nets. We get our new quota on July 1. At this point, we have about two weeks for fixing up, unless the fish drop off, we do not catch as much as we plan on catching, and it takes us longer. It could happen that we go all the way to the end of this month, but I am hoping that we catch it in a couple weeks.

Daniel "Pete" LeClair (Two Rivers, Wisconsin) noted that the family fishery combines trawling with trap-net fishing for whitefish. LeClair opposes the DNR regulating the amount of time he can fish for his quota.

We use trap nets for whitefish in April and May. I think the nets have to be out by June 28 or something because sportsmen claim our nets are in the way and they do not have any place to fish, which is another crazy theory. We only use maybe three miles of shoreline north of Two Rivers. We only go out to about forty feet of water. That is the only area we fish in. The sportsmen can fish in between our nets with no problem, but they want the whole lakeshore from Door County all the way to the Illinois state line. This is the only area around us in Lake Michigan where we fish trap nets, except for one small operation out of Sheboygan. The sportsmen would not even give us that little area to fish our trap net. So I do not know how long this is going to continue. We just cannot put up with these regulations because we need more time to catch our whitefish quota.

If you have a spring where the water is cold and the whitefish do not come in, you miss two weeks of the whitefish fishing. In June the water temperature changes. The whitefish are here but we have to pull out because the sportsmen say we are in the way of their sport-fishing operation.

My kids started trap netting here five years ago. They fish in the summer months in shallow water. Our trap nets are set in about forty feet of water. In the spring they are usually set in around fifteen to twenty feet of water and later in the year, the whitefish move off into deeper water and then we go out to forty feet. But the spring season is very short so actually we cover very little area of the lake with our nets at that time. There are only two small operators and one big operator so it is not like the nets are set from Two Rivers all the way to Sheboygan or from Sheboygan to Sturgeon Bay. It is just one small area off of Two Rivers where the trap nets are set, but they will not even give us that small area. So we are not really expanding in that area. All we have left is the smelt fishery and the way it looks that is going to be gone within a year or two because we cannot continue under a five-and-one-half-month season. We need at least eleven months.

We used to be able to fish twelve months out of the year. You could fish whenever you could make a buck. There are times of the year when the forage fish separate and that's the time we like to fish, but the DNR closes the season at that time because we might catch a few alewife or chubs. These forage fish go where the water temperature is to their liking. Every year is different and it is hard to regulate by seasons. We like to go when the smelt are separated so that we do not have all the labor involved trying to sort the smelt out of the chubs or the alewife. You get 4,000 to 5,000 pounds and it takes you three hours to sort them—to get the smelt out. But you cannot afford the labor to sort them out. We can now fish for smelt from November 15 to April 20.

Our main fishing area is north of the harbor about ten miles away. If we went further, then we would get up near the nuclear plant where there are all big rocks. There are even rocks before that. This is the area my dad used to fish when he was in Kidville. In the Kidville area where my dad fished it is all nice sand there. But you get closer to the nuclear plant and it is all big rocks. You cannot fish there with pound nets, trap nets or gill nets or anything; it is just unfishable. Actually, all the way from there to Sturgeon Bay is rocks and shallow water.

I know this little area here. We were only allowed to fish in so many grids. Now, half of these grids are rocks or shipwrecks, so we can maybe only fish in half of it. We fished straight out of Two Rivers, ten miles north and maybe five miles out here in the middle of the lake south of Two Rivers. So, we are actually talking about an area about fifteen miles long and maybe four or five miles wide. That is all we have to fish in. Now, how can that little area—I do not care if you fished 365 days a year, twenty-four hours a day—determine what is in the rest of this lake? One percent of the lake, but we supposedly control the whole biomass of chubs, alewife, and smelt.

Rick Johnson (Gills Rock) has been fishing the Wisconsin waters of Lake Michigan for nearly thirty years. He discussed the process whereby the DNR required the fishermen to set their own quotas working through representative organizations. The process pitted fisherman against fisherman and created legal problems for him, which were ultimately resolved in his favor. Still, however, Johnson is glad the fishermen, not the DNR, set the quotas.

I am president of the Northeast Wisconsin Commercial Fishing Association. This is a group for the fishermen in northern Door County. We belong to the Wisconsin Commercial Fishing, Incorporated, which represents all Wisconsin commercial fishermen. I am chairman of the Lake Michigan Commercial Fishing Board. It is a board that is appointed by the governor. The task for this board is to basically allocate quotas. Besides allocating quotas, our job has been revised to including functioning as an advisory group to the big DNR board on commercial fishing issues.

We allocated whitefish quotas for all Wisconsin's Lake Michigan waters. The DNR sets the total quota and then it was up to the fishing board to set how much each fisherman got. If you want to see some fun, that was it. I cannot even remember how many meetings we had. It is like a nightmare. We would start at seven o'clock at night and go to two, three in the morning. We would come back two days later, and go through it all again. Every fisherman had a different formula regarding how he wanted the fish allocated. Everybody had lawyers there. It was terrible. Finally, the fishing board agreed on a plan. Everything we did was subject to DNR board approval. After we allocated the quotas, a group of fishermen from Two Rivers filed charges against myself and one other fisherman from Ellison Bay who was on this board with the Wisconsin State Ethics Board for violating the ethics law. This carries some pretty substantial fines.

All though the quota allocation process, we were told that the DNR would represent us—no problem. Well, that works fine as long as the whole fishing board is challenged with ethics violations. But they only challenged two individual members, so we were on our own to fight our own battles. It was thrown out before it even got to anything serious, but it is scary when you got five small kids at home and you are just getting your rig going. It was not an easy thing. I believe it was a $20,000 fine and five years in jail if you were found in violation, which we were not. But it was just a major, major headache for young guys that had gotten into the fishery. The quota was set based on your prior five-year catch history. So, for the young guys who only got into fishing the last two years, their quota was much smaller than the guy that had a five-year catch period. We were physically threatened. It was no fun task, I will tell you that.

Even with the problems, we felt it was better that we set the quotas. We did not feel the political pressure that the DNR feels. If somebody has got a legislator who is on their side, he is obviously going to lean on the DNR secretary. We did not have any of that outside influence. You can look at it that way. But at the time we felt like we were doing the DNR's dirty work. Everybody got pretty mad at us and the DNR sat in the background and let us take it all.

Neil Teskie (Gills Rock, Wisconsin) indicated that the quota system has made fishing a more reliable source of income. He has successfully combined fishing and work at his fruit farm and retail operation.

I am a major quota holder. I think that the quotas have made it stable for me. I can adjust my fishing times. I can take my fish when it is profitable. I can slow down in the summer when I need to take care of my orchards and I do not have to worry about beating the competition to the fish. So in some ways it has been good for me and in some ways it has been good for the fishery. There have been times in the fall of the year when our nets are just full of whitefish; we have released a lot of the legal ones because we do not have the means or the place to sell them. I have X number of pounds I can harvest. I am not going to take extra ones to sell cheap. I take the nicest ones out of the net and release the rest. There were years that I released as many as I harvested and they were all legal. This spring, I am harvesting everything that is legal because I have enough quota to work with. So in some ways it has been good for the fishery because we have been dumping back, not destroying, but releasing fish and turning them back and they get bigger. Then they come back to spawn. So quotas have been good and bad.

The downside of quotas is the fact that it takes two years to make an adjustment. Every two years the DNR re-evaluates the quotas. So there are not terrible downsides. I would never want us to do anything that would harm the fishery. I would like to always have as much quota as I have now. But if the need be, I can live through it—I am a survivor. That is one of the reasons why I have this orchard business going. I have seventeen percent of the whitefish harvest for this area, but if they reduce the quota to zero, seventeen percent of zero is zero fish. It is like the perch harvest. A lot of fishermen have tremendous percentages for perch in Lake Michigan, but the harvest is zero, so I kind of thought that maybe it might be nice to have something else going in case they reduce my quota. I do not think they will ever reduce the whitefish quota to zero, but I think that they might back it down someday and I will be able to survive.

Although critical of the way the Wisconsin DNR introduced limited entry and quotas, Elaine Johnson has accepted this management approach as one that will protect and enhance Lake Michigan fisheries. After forty years in the fishing business she limits her work to processing whitefish. She expressed frustration with the sport fishers' tendency to see commercial fishers as their opponents when they share the common goal of gaining influence in the fisheries policy-making and implementation process dominated by the Wisconsin DNR. Johnson helped to organize fishermen to fight for the survival of the Wisconsin commercial fishing industry.

The DNR decided that if they went into limited entry and quotas it would save the fishery. Well, fishermen are no different than all of us. There is a little greed in all of us and there is in a fisherman. Maybe this limited entry is not too bad an idea. So the fishermen went for limited entry, but they did not do it right. That is when I resigned. When setting quotas, some of the fellows had been in the fishery for quite a while. They went back ten years. Some were in the fishery only about four years, but they went back ten years. They took an average over those ten years and that was your quota. The guys that had been in the fishery for ten years were in pretty good shape. But these poor devils that were only in there two, three, and four years and had to take an average of ten, did not have much of a quota. They got the minimum, 45,000 pounds, which is not much. You got to have fish to keep the operation running.

With the quota we lost a lot of our fishermen, and sometimes maybe through our own greed, we lost ourselves. One DNR official said now that we have limited entries and quotas, the commercial fishery will boom, which it did. We have about 100 licensed now. Of those 100, maybe there will be three or four licenses in one family. They are now in the act of changing, taking out some old rules and putting in some new ones. But they better be damn sure they are not getting whipped again. If we really want to help secure the fishery, we would go along with some pretty stringent rulings. Well, by the time the rules came on the green sheet, they had taken the worst that we said and the worst of what they said. That is how the fishermen had a good-bye.

We had a lot of people who ice fished as a part-time occupation. Of course, we lost those guys right off the bat. They had to catch 13,500 pounds of fish to relicense themselves. The guys who fished in the wintertime could not relicense themselves because they had not caught the required amount of fish. They could have let these continue to ice fish. They never did any harm. The few fish that they caught did not amount to a pinch of baloney. All the ice fishermen put together never caught what a few big fishermen are catching now.

The fisheries have gotten so big they have had to increase their quotas. You have trap nets. Mark Weborg caught about 7,000 pounds of fish the other day. That is unheard of for a summer fishery even when we dropped down to 300 fishermen. Now, there are so few, so few. When law enforcement and fish management get together, they write up a bunch of rules and regulations and a green sheet is put on top to tell you a summation of what is in there. Sometimes we did not get that green sheet until the day of the meeting. When you came into the meeting, they handed it to you. You really were not prepared nor did you have any evidence collected earlier to say that this is not right. And you are supposed to have so much time, but they never did give you time.

We organized here. We had about 400 commercial fishermen, 411, I believe at that time. We banded together, and I really got the public behind us. We had association cards for people and they paid $2 to be an associate to the commercial fishermen. And with this $2 association card they would get ten percent off when they went down to the fishermen and bought a fish. It was an incentive for them to belong, but we needed their names. We would go on organized busloads to wherever the legislator was meeting. And, of course, we would have big banners on the side, you know, "Down with Bill

608" or whatever the issue was. We happened to have some good speakers in the fishery at that time. We flew down to Madison at least once a week. We were strong when we were united and had the public with us. So we kept our fishery for quite a few years.

I have seen a lot of changes in the regulations and the fisheries too. There was not always the abundance of whitefish. In the last seventeen to eighteen years we have had an unbelievable fishery. We have lifted 15 million pounds. We never had that kind of fishing around here.

Donald Voight (Gills Rock, Wisconsin) fished for nearly forty years in various Lake Michigan and Lake Superior communities in northern Wisconsin and Michigan. He is critical of the policy of using past catches to determine quotas. Voight also believes there are too many geographical restrictions on fishermen.

When we came back to Gills Rock we fished whitefish and then they opened up the chub season later on. I do not know what year they opened up the chubs here. I do not like that they allow chub fishing when they are spawning. That is just like having deer season open year around. We have fished mostly chubs out of Gills Rock. That is where we made most of our money. Then they put this quota business on according to what you caught, so we did not have much of a quota on whitefish. It was discrimination.

Indiana and Illinois have the southern end of Lake Michigan. Wisconsin has Green Bay to Marinette. Michigan has the whole Upper Peninsula and Lake Superior. Michigan's got Lake Huron and the whole works going around. Green Bay is a real breeding ground and some of these Michigan fishermen fish the bulk of it. That is not right. We carried a Wisconsin license and we bought a Michigan license so we could fish the Michigan waters in Green Bay. We even fished chubs in Michigan waters from here over to the Manitou Islands.

The DNR has probably changed their mind a little bit for the commercial fishermen. There have been a lot of commercial fishermen that have dropped out. There used to be a lot of boats here. At one time, years ago, there were twenty-some boats on Washington Island—just on the island. That is all there was to do.

In the years before the Wisconsin DNR established quotas for each species, commercial fishermen such as Daniel "Pete" LeClair of Two Rivers pursued different fish depending on their availability and marketability. LeClair recalled the investment he made when smelt stocks were plentiful.

The 1970s and 1980s were prosperous years. We were catching about 150 to 200,000 pounds a day. We had some real good years because you did not have much expense. Some of the years, we picked the smelt out when we had a good drag with lots of smelt in them. We picked the smelt out. At that time, we did not have smelt dressing machines. In the wintertime, if there were not much forage fish around, we would fish for smelt. We would get ten, twelve guys around a table and dress them all by hand. Soon, you could not get help—either they all got promoted or went to better jobs. Then we had to get automatic smelt dressing machines. We had to get a big sorting machine where it sorts the smelt to three different sizes. We got a smelt machine that was dressing seventy-five fish an hour and now we have a machine that dresses up to 175 fish an hour. So we really expanded into the smelt business. We got that going, but because of all the rules and regulations that started in 1991, it is being destroyed.

They gave us a good quota of smelt. But they do not give us time to fish it. They took our fishing time away because there are alewife out there. If they let us fish twelve months out of the year, we might catch some alewife and they have to save the alewife for the salmon and trout. But in 1994 and 1995, tons of them washed up on the beach and died on the bottom of the lake. So why did the salmon and trout fail to eat all these fish and make that fishing industry grow?

Since 1991, when they stopped us from taking any forage fish, sport fishing has gone down about fifty percent. So they did not gain anything. They destroyed our fishery plus they destroyed the sport fishery. So, what are the rules doing? They are not doing any good.

Paul Goodman, who has worked both as a commercial fisherman and as a charter boat operator, discussed the impact of changes in the perch fishery after the introduction of quotas.

Our big perch fishery is in Southern Green Bay and around Milwaukee and through those nearby ports. That is where they really catch perch. Those guys had rigs that were worth a lot of money. The whitefish fishermen have rigs and their boats are worth so much. They figure that potentially their fish are worth so much. They have a quota for 100,000 pounds they can put a price tag on it. That is how the perch fishery was until about three years ago, when all of a sudden the perch fishing collapsed and they could hardly catch a perch. They actually shut them down. The quota went to the point where they shut them down. Even the sport fishermen used to be able to catch fifty perch. Now you are allowed five. That is how poor the perch fishing went. So those operations that were worth some money could have sold. You would have sold it for some pretty good money and the next guy would have been out of business. That is just how it is. But now, those guys are sitting with perch rigs that are not worth anything because there is no fish to catch and there is no quota. Today things may look good, but what if there are no whitefish to catch? You may have a quota for 200,000 pounds of whitefish and your boats may be running. But if something happened like two bad years of spawn and the DNR was afraid that they had to bring the fishery back by changing the quota, and limiting you to 20,000 pounds, then you are in trouble.

They have always worked on buyout programs. Years ago, the Wisconsin DNR was looking at buyout programs because the State of Michigan had some buyout programs for fishermen. I think the State of Wisconsin figured the angles a little bit better. They figured out that there are ways to eliminate people without paying people. I am pretty certain that the people who were involved in the quota system probably calculated how it could happen. They knew the quota system was going to eliminate that many fishermen. I think some fishermen were enjoying that side's thinking. They were thinking it would help them to get rid of some fishermen because if there ever was a buyout, there would be fewer in the buyout program. I think they are still thinking that today. But I do not think that would happen because I did not see it happen to the perch fishermen. The whitefish fishermen think it would happen. But I do not think it would happen to the whitefish fishermen because some of the perch fishermen were pretty big. I do not think they would go retroactive and give those fishermen money as well.

Paul Goodman maintained that interest in the concept of limited-entry fishing came from within the ranks of organizations formed by the fishermen themselves. After limited entry and quotas were established, Goodman sold his quota and obtained a charter boat license.

We kept going in the fishery and whitefish fishing was good. We were also doing some chub fishing. Everything was going pretty well, but all of a sudden, about 1990, this idea came in to put quotas on the fish. There are a lot of fishermen that still blame the Department of Natural Resources. They say that they came up with this idea to put the quotas on and limit the amount of fishermen. I guess I do not see it that way. We had our own associations up here—the Northeast Wisconsin Commercial Fishing Association. In that association you had larger fishermen and smaller fishermen. There were a few fishermen trying to come in here from other states like Michigan. All of a sudden, you would see a few other fishermen trying to get in the area. There were people in our organizations who were looking at how to keep them from coming in this area. They wanted to limit entry because they did not want competition and the more competition you have the more your prices could go down.

It was difficult for me. I was a smaller fisherman at the time. There were a lot of small guys and then there were a handful of large rigs. The DNR found out they could not make rules that said you could not come from another state and get a fishing license because if you met the criteria you should be able to. Our guys figured out that if you have a quota and base it on a certain amount of years and allow fishermen to catch a percentage of the amount from those years, that will eliminate anybody else from coming in because there will be no quota for them. So what happened, certain years were picked, the four or five years prior in which you caught fish. Those years were picked and the amount of fish you caught and then you were given a percentage of the overall total from those years. The whole lakewide fishery was not divided up and each fisherman given a share. It was based on performance for a certain amount of years. In order to get a license during the following year, you had to catch 13,500 pounds in our area. They issued me a quota of 6,000 or 7,000 pounds. The next year they denied me a license because I could not meet the criteria for getting a license. And that happened to a lot of people. The smaller operations were done.

The quota system was not based on a biological reason. It was based more on politics. It was kind of a give-and-take thing with fishermen, trying to appease a situation where they did not want that many guys in the fishery. So a lot of fishermen were out of it. It was not biological. I met with biologists three weeks before and the fishery looked like it was in the best shape it had ever been in. Today, it is in really good shape as far as the stocks go. Whitefish production is really up, so it was not a biological issue. It was a political move. It is like big farmers and small farmers. People that were involved in the bigger operations were pushing the idea because it looked good to them. But some fishermen were afraid. They looked at a buyout program, but then the state got away from it—that would have been one way to do it, have a buyout of the smaller fishermen.

The state could have bought the smaller fishermen out, but instead, they were given quotas of a few thousand pounds of fish. You could sell your quota and get some money, but you could not get much money. I forget what I got for my quota. It was not much. If you were doing it for a livelihood, you might get $8,000 or $9,000 for it. You could sell your quota to another fisherman, so they could accumulate more. Your only way of staying in the fishery was to buy other small quotas and accumulate more. But when you're small, it is difficult to buy up everybody else's quota and keep right on going in business. So you figured you were pretty well done. That is the way it happened with the quota system. There are fishermen who say they had no idea that the quota was going to happen, but all the fishermen knew. The insiders knew quotas were the only way to eliminate people and it looked good for the bigger people in the fishery. Well, I got into charter fishing. I got a license to take people fishing and found out it was not too bad.

———————

Lyle Teskie discussed the introduction of limited-entry and quota fishing in Wisconsin and the role it played in getting him out of commercial fishing.

I think that commercial fishing has gotten the short end of the stick. I really do. Also, a few years ago, when there was 200 or so commercial fishermen, the DNR got involved and they were going to go with the quota system. They were going to get rid of some licenses. Actually, some of the bigger rigs in the commercial fishing industry went against the smaller rigs in the commercial fishing industry. The bigger rigs thought they would get these huge quotas. But low and behold, when it all came down, the DNR got rid of a lot of licenses but instead of all the quota being allocated to just a few of these huge commercial fishermen, the DNR said we are going to give a quota to everybody. So the little guys, even though they cannot fish, can sell their quotas. So the big rigs got stuck with less of a quota and the political thing there between the bigger fishermen and little fishermen did not work. I have resentment towards the sportsmen and the DNR over the politics. You do what you have to do. See, I knew the water. I knew the lake. I worked for my brother and I worked for another guy doing carpentry. I started an upholstery business and that was not enough to support my family so I had no other option. I could not get back into commercial fishing. I had to let my license go and you could not get one back, so I decided to be a charter boat captain.

Neil Teskie indicated that he had come to appreciate the work of the Wisconsin DNR in managing the Lake Michigan fisheries in its waters.

In the 1970s there was talk of banning gill nets. That is a pretty touchy issue for a guy that is married with kids. And that's all I know. I have a college education but I am not going back to that anymore. Everything I have done to this point has been to keep my fishing industry going. All my capital goes back into the rig, so when somebody starts talking about eliminating the fishermen, it gets pretty touchy. Banning a gill net is a touchy point. There was a lot of fighting and shouting. It was a learning experience. I do not think it was a bad experience for anybody. I think that there was a lot of misunderstanding on both sides. Most of us can sit down with the top sportfishing people in the state and talk. We do not necessarily agree, but we can talk and reach a compromise.

I think the Department of Natural Resources is proud of the fact that they have such a good commercial fishery in this state. Outside of the fact that we disagree on the way they manage sometimes, I do not think they do a bad job. There are times I do not think they know what they are talking about. They have kept the gill net in the state and we need the versatility of that tool, whereas Michigan has completely banned gill nets or made them so restrictive that they can hardly operate. In this area, we really need them because we have so much rocky bottom. You cannot fish trap nets at all times of the year. We are still allowed to fish chubs here. We have a good chub fishery. The whitefish stocks are healthy. Perch are done, but they have always been cyclical. I do not think its demise is anything to blame on one particular commercial fishery or sport fishery or environment. It is probably a combination of all the factors.[77]

Lyle Teskie recalled that conflict existed between commercial and sport fishermen, particularly when the former fished out beyond the line where Wisconsin waters ended and Michigan's jurisdiction began.

When I was commercial, we were hounded by DNR. We felt like criminals. If you go back, way back in time when I was young, we used to bring small fish up to the minister. We literally stopped that because we were too scared to get caught with a couple of fish. We stopped that because we felt that it was to the point where we would probably lose our livelihood or get a fine. And you know, sometimes, I guess you can say it is on both sides. It is like we pushed, and push came to shove. I did not push as much as some did. Some other guys antagonized people in the DNR. I have never hated a DNR person. It is just the idea that you are trying to make a living and constantly somebody is trying to make you feel like you are a criminal. It is not so much the legal or the illegal. It is when they look at you as criminals. I think things have changed somewhat. But now that I am a charter captain, I do not get bothered as much. They come down here and some are my relations. There are a lot of names we would call them and it is probably not right. They have children too. They have wives too. There is a good purpose to the DNR.

There was a lot more tension with the DNR when I was a commercial fisherman. We used to go across the line—we fished illegally across the line. And in a way, it was a game. We would go across in December, across the Michigan line, and the Michigan

DNR would kind of like play this game, too, and we would run our boats and they would chase us and we would get across the line and then they could not touch us. I did not do it a lot, but I did it a few times. I did it—not just for the game of it—but because there were no fish on this side. For some reason, fish would migrate and go up there and there are all these fish up there. It was just this line in the water and you just had to go half an hour beyond the line—the thrill of being in illegal waters. And we got caught and we got fined and rightfully so. We broke the law.

I got caught once; I never went over there enough for it to happen more. It was always the kind of thing—fish tugs are slow things. They move ten miles an hour and with helicopters and planes—the state had better equipment. We did not fish over there much. It was like, well, winter was coming. There was no fish on this side and it is a long winter because we did not fish on the ice. So you go up there and you get a couple lifts of 4,000 or 5,000 pounds, a couple of days work, and if you got away with it, it made January and February and March just a little better. But it was still illegal. I mean, we knew where the line was even though we did not have GPS or Loran at that time. We knew where the line was. We could tell within a quarter mile.

Mark Weborg, who has been fishing out of Gills Rock, Wisconsin, for more than thirty years, observed that during the past few decades the relations between commercial fishermen and the DNR have improved.

Our relationship with the DNR right now is quite good. We do not have too many problems. We have a general understanding. It was not that way for many years. We went all the way to federal court on some issues and finally got a positive ruling for us.[78] But it was very tense for quite a while. In fact, we had an out and out fight with them at one point. My crew and I ended up in jail, but we ended up winning that case. That is when we went to federal court. There are rules today that practically make it impossible to fish legally any day. The way the rules are written, if there was one fish there that was an eighth of an inch too short, they could confiscate today's whole lift of nearly 6,000 pounds. Years ago, there used to be a ten percent incidental catch allowance. Now there is no incidental catch allowance at all. But the federal judge ruled in our favor, saying there is no way the fishermen can fish under the rules you made for them. So certain changes were made. Since then, we have had a pretty decent relationship with the DNR.

Once we came in with about a ton of fish. It was a really blustery, nasty fall day. They wanted to start measuring all these fish when we hit the dock, and I said "no way." At that point, they were going to start grabbing fish. They came down with six wardens. It happened that I had two boats come in at the same time. I had six fishermen down there. Needless to say, six wardens do not have a chance against six commercial fishermen, even though they had guns. We did not care. My dad took one guy and held him right over the edge of the dock and said: "If you do anymore, I am going to drop you right in the water." A couple of other guys tried fighting a little bit, but they did not last long. We ended up putting the fish back on the boat and taking off with the boat. I stayed on the dock by myself. Of course, the police finally came and of course we are friends with the police. After this incident, the police understood what was going on. So I ended up in jail. Then the other guys came and joined me after they came in. But that did not last long, and we won that case. At that point, we already had two confiscations. They took our fish and we were never charged. We never saw the fish again. So we were not going to allow that to happen anymore. We had to take a stand. And we took a stand and we were glad we did. We paid a lot for it. It cost us a lot of money in court, but without that I do not know if we would even be fishing here today.

The DNR has a patrol boat. They look around once in a while. With eight fishermen fishing, it does not take much to patrol this area. They always tell us how much they spend to monitor our fishery, but there was one year when I never saw a warden. There is no illegal activity going on so there is nothing to look for. The only major concern they would have is if we took the small fish, but any fisherman with any smarts at all knows you cannot take the small fish because that is your future down the road and you would be eliminating it. So I would rather sacrifice a seagull than let it pick up a small whitefish that we threw overboard. That is illegal, but I would rather do that than see a small whitefish die.

Joel Peterson (Fairport, Michigan) has observed increased levels of collaboration between commercial fishermen and the DNR in recent years.

I think they have changed the regulations enough and they finally figured why bang your head against the wall. Let us try to work together, meet down in Lansing and see if we can hash this out. The DNR needs to see if the fishermen are seeing the same as they are. Maybe they are seeing worse than what we are seeing. We are only probably out there 200 days a year and their biologists or any of their law enforcement people are out there maybe two weeks if they are out there that long. So who has probably got the better knowledge of what is going on out there? When the black cormorants first starting showing up, I said "Hey man, we got a potential problem." They planted them suckers and reintroduced them into the Great Lakes. So now what are they doing? In the meantime, what are they doing to the fish population? What are they doing to the minnows along the beach, to the traps? Now they have even got smarter enough where they will swim around the trap nets. They are smart enough to know that is where them fish are. They are awesome fishing birds. But I decided that rather than fight let us try to find some common ground and try to solve these problems. Maybe they have finally decided there is room for both. There is room. If there is not enough room out here for sports fishermen and commercial fishermen, then we should pull the plug and drain her because there has got to be common ground someplace. Any time people cannot work together, it is a sad society then. Somebody is doing something wrong if government agencies cannot find common ground to work on.

I know I should be fishing. Hopefully, I will be fishing. Maybe we have kept our rig up a little bit better than anybody else because we have the idea that we were going to be fishing quite a while unless we are put out of business, We do not plan on quitting. I am on the Michigan Fish Producers Board and have been to Lansing numerous times. I have never met K. L. Cool, but I have met all kinds of people such as Jacob Eddy and all the guys down there. It was really neat for a little country bumpkin to go down there and really see how a lot of business got conducted—from six to eight over a martini. A lot of issues are cut and dried which I have no problem with as long as both parties know what they are talking about. And I think that is probably the way this country was founded. I just think some people are, you could say overprotective, but I do not think you can be overprotective. I think you can be cautious. You may be overcautious. You may be able to read all the bad factors into something. You could read as many things into a problem as you want to read into it. The thing is, how do we solve them?

It is a law in Michigan that you can only fish trap nets in ninety feet. Somewhere along the line we are going to have to pull the depth restriction off. We, as trap netters, are restricted to ninety feet because that is the law. There is one trawler that fishes on the Great Lakes that has been under a research permit for thirty years, and has no depth restriction on it. So here we are disadvantaged for having a license. He does have a license but it is in escrow to a research permit, so he has no depth requirement. So at certain times of year such as July, the fish go deep. Well right now, tribal licenses can fish from 110 feet. We are getting fish in the lake where the water is a little deeper, a little darker. I talked to the Indian biologists. I talked to the state biologists. They are all coming up with the same conclusion. These fish are moving deeper because of the light penetration. The zebra mussels are cleaning up the water, so the zebra mussels are probably doing their job a little too well and they are going to change the ecological balance of the whole lake. I mean, it has got its benefits because look out here at this water. Look at how clear and pretty it is. But you talk to the biologist, these fish do not like the light penetrating. So what is it doing? It is pushing the fish deeper. With our trap nets we can only go to ninety feet and if you set 120 feet you will catch fish, so what does that tell you?

Brian Price, who directs the Leelanau Conservancy, a land trust, recalled that in 1975 when he was working as a commercial fisherman, the fishermen agreed that the chub fishery had to be closed. He maintained that overfishing was not the cause for the crash of the chub population.

From 1973 until 1975, I worked on the *Frances Clark* with Fred Lang who was already probably about sixty at the time, and Ross Lang, his son, who would have been in his mid-thirties. I never even saw a large mesh gill net because we were very specialized at that time. There were three fishing operations; every one of them was restricted to just fishing for chubs. Not that many people liked to fish for chubs because it is hard work. The fish are small. It is a lot of picking, and the grounds are way out in the middle of the lake. At that point in time, the chub stock started to collapse. Neither we nor anyone else were catching a lot of fish. It was not fishing pressure that caused the Great Lakes chub population to crash. Nobody probably knows exactly what the cause was. We got into a situation where there were fewer and fewer chubs, and that was all we were licensed to catch. That is why I say the state needs to give fisherman flexibility.

Part of the reason for the crash was that females became heavily predominant in the population, perhaps up to 96 to 97 percent of all the fish out there. During the spawning season we would sell the chub roe, the eggs. We would screen them and process them, and put them in big buckets and sell them for caviar. We made more money on the caviar than we did on the fish, because they were all females. Something was stressing that population, but despite what anybody says, it was not the amount of fishing effort. Nevertheless, the fishery was closed which was the right response. Once again, somebody had to step in and do something. Closing the fishery is the only thing you could do at that point because you cannot change the ecology of the lake overnight.

––––––––––––––

Alan Priest described how a brush with the law changed his relationship with other fishermen and prompted him to temporarily get out of the business.

I had just started to run the boat in the late 1970s. I had been running the boat for just a couple years. Chub fishing was terrible. The fisherman who used to run the boat got out of it and went to carpenter work. So I started running the boat. He said, "Here, run the boat." He went out with me a couple times and I was on my own. When I was working with Ross and Fred, they did most of the lifting and setting and I did not know what was going on. I just went, picked fish, dressed fish, and got seasick. But then here is this boat thrown at me and I knew a little bit about where to go, but I did not know how to run the banks. But the boat was thrown at me and this was a year where there were just no chubs anywhere. You could not buy a chub. He said, "Either you catch some chubs or I am tying the boat up." And I said well, okay and I went and set a gang of nets. The buoys were in forty fathoms, but I went up to thirty-five to thirty-two fathoms, just to see if there were any chubs there. Well, they came like grapes. They were just thick. I fished there and fished there. The *Steelhead* went by me one day and they did not say anything. I was in about thirty-three fathoms of water. The next year, they pinched me.

Bill Carlson treated me like I was the worst person on earth, no good. I did wrong, but I went and found some chubs. I did not deliberately break the law. I did not go up into eighteen fathoms. I went above forty a little bit and I got pinched. I got up into a little shoal area—up to thirty—and the trout were there, but I was fishing chubs. So anyway, I was the worst person in Fishtown, so I got out of it for a while. I went to cut trees. I was a logger and I do not recommend it. Then I came down here and I said: "I want to get back into fishing." He said okay, so I have been fishing ever since.

Elaine Johnson's efforts to publicize how public policy and environmental issues affected Wisconsin's Great Lakes fishermen extended to the *Today Show*. Washington Island fisherman Steve Ellefson, who is now deceased, brought the famous news crew out on his fish tug along with a local newspaper reporter.[79]

In 1976 I contacted the *Today Show*. The roving reporter at the time was named Cunningham. I told him about the conflict that was going on in Michigan, Wisconsin, Illinois, Indiana, and all the states around the Great Lakes. I said, since this is the bicentennial year, why not come up and do a story on the commercial fisheries? So I got a letter from Cunningham saying he would be up. They made a date and came up. Keta Steebs, who writes for the *County Advocate*, said: "Elaine, I would give a million dollars if I could go with them over to the island." Steve Ellefson was over on Washington Island. I asked him if he could set nets so that no matter which way the wind blows, he could lift them in the lee of the wind and everything could be seen. He said he could. So anyway, the *Today Show* people came. Keta begged, begged, begged to go. So I went to Cunningham, and asked if he could please let her go. I said: "She is a local writer. She will stay out of the way. Can you let her go?" So they finally gave in and let her go.

I went down that morning and the boat came. And here comes Keta. She has got white pumps and hose on. She has got a real fine, wavy chiffon dress and a great big summer hat. She had this wig and long white gloves on. Keta thought she was really going to impress these New Yorkers. She went down the gangplank and got on the *Miss Judy*, Steve's boat, and away they went to the island. On Washington Island, they went all out for the celebrities. They smoked fish. They fried fish. They broiled fish. Every imaginable way they could serve fish, they had it, along with beer and bitters. They filled Keta up pretty good on fish and beer and bitters. Steve said at six o'clock the next morning, we were getting up and going fishing.

The next morning, here comes Keta ready to go fishing, dressed fit to kill. They went out there and Steve said when they got out there north of the island it was just a dead swell. He said you could not get away from it. Keta was down there by the lifter. Steve said: "Keta you have just got to go someplace else. You are in the wrong place here by this lifter. You will get all messy. You are in our way. Go up in the bow in the boat. Sit there."

Keta went up and sat on a little plank that ran across the bow. Of course, the bow would lift you, and you could fall. Steve said he was as busy as could be with those nets, so they would not tangle. There were many trout, which by law, had to be quickly returned to the water, dead or alive. If you do not do it, no matter what the weather conditions are, you are in violation. If you get two violations in three years, they take your license.

So anyway, Steve was clearing nets and he turned around and looked up in the bow in the boat, and there is Keta. She is ready to throw up. She is not going to make it. He said, "Keta Steebs, don't you dare throw up in my boat." He said that old wig had come around and was twisted. You could just see about an eye and a half. Steven said Keta looked at me with that one eye and she immediately took off one glove, and here it came. He said she vomited, filled that glove right up. The porthole was right there and she loosened the wing nut on the porthole, opened it, and threw the glove overboard. "There it went," Steve said, "it went by the lifter door and I could see that white thing going. We finished lifting and we reset our nets and headed for the dock."

Steve said that just before they got there Keta was really green, and a little white around her eyes. But he said that wig had almost covered her entire face, so just part of one eye was now showing. He said, "Keta, don't you dare throw up in *Miss Judy*. Don't you dare throw up." She looked at him for a moment and she peeled that other glove off, and threw it through the porthole again. It took three guys to get her off of that boat. She never asked to go on a rig again. But those kinds of things happen in the fishery.

One of the last remaining commercial fishermen in Washington Island, Ken Koyen maintained that the Wisconsin DNR was too tough regarding size limits.

O verall, the whole thing is set up to be able to write tickets, to control. I think there's more control than there need be. If you have a whitefish that is sixteen and seven-eighths inches long, you cannot keep it. It has got to be seventeen inches long. Even if that fish is dead, you have to throw it back. And if you throw it back, sure maybe a crab will eat it, but I would like to see a judge tell his grandson that caught a sixteen-and-seventh-eighths-inch fish to throw it back. I do not believe they would. Granted, if some guy has got a ton of short fish and none that are legal size, fine, give him a ticket. We got a ticket one time for thirteen undersized fish out of 3,400 pounds. Start handling 3,400 pounds of fish. They get to look a lot alike by the time you are done with them. Can you take the time and measure them all? I have it set right up where if you poke their nose in a corner, their tail has to come right to the edge of that tape. Otherwise, they go overboard.

Rick Johnson (Door County, Wisconsin), a fisherman for nearly thirty years, defended the honesty of most fishermen. He urged greater simplification in reporting techniques.

T he DNR sends observers, but that has gone down the last few years because of money. The DNR does not have enough money so they cannot afford to send riders along with us as much. When you sign up for a license, you agree to let the biologist go along with you. They ride probably seven, eight times a year, sometimes more. I would not agree with the statement that they need us because in their mind, they do not need us. I mean, they are getting a lot of free information from us, but they do not consider that anything. For instance, right now, we are going through a whole reworking of our laws. There is a commercial fishing task force. I am a member. The DNR does not consider that in-kind service to try and cut down on the license fees. They want to raise license fees to help them get more money, but we are saying what about this in-kind service?

The commercial fishing task force is a result of some things that have happened over the last five years. There have been two or three sting operations where fishermen have been caught illegally taking fish. A big one was down in the Milwaukee area where they took a considerable amount of perch, which is a very high-value fish. Another one was in Marinette. Again, they were taking perch and selling them for cash. The DNR set up a dummy company in Minnesota that would pay cash for the illegal fish. It has not been that many years since they gave us these reporting requirements. We have to fill out an estimate on the boat, and then fill in the actual pounds when we get it weighed. Then we have to report where and when we sold the fish. Well, then they found out that an estimate is just an estimate; it does not stand up in court. Then they also found out from their rules that illegal fish did not really mean illegal fish. If you ever saw the DNR code, it is just a jumbled mess. I mean, even the wardens themselves cannot understand it. If I do something wrong I expect to get a ticket, but I do not expect to get it three weeks later. The DNR—they might come three weeks, four weeks later and give you the ticket. It takes them that long to figure out from the code what you did wrong. I mean, it is stupidity.

They are talking about doing the reporting electronically now. There are a lot of good ideas. It will save us a lot of paperwork. The people who are going to cheat are going to cheat anyway. Unless there is a warden who makes an appearance every so often, those people are going to cheat. It is just human nature, I guess. It would be real simple just to have more law enforcement. We took a poll of the fishermen. Some fishermen did not see a warden for nine months. So the opportunity is there if you are looking to cheat.

There is somewhat of a black market for fish, especially for perch. Perch go for $5 or $6 a pound filleted. So if somebody can sell them, and obviously you have X number of pounds in your quota, if you can take an extra 3,000 pounds, that is a nice income for you. There is always somebody looking to sell them for a little less money. It is cash and it has been a problem. There are a few people. I would not say it is a major problem industrywide. Those who did it got caught, thank goodness. Unfortunately it puts a bad light on the rest of the commercial fishermen. The cover letter sent to us at the start of the task force basically said all commercial fishermen are liars and cheaters. Most of us took a great offense to that, because we pride ourselves in our honesty. For some of us, that is a real important part of our business.

Mark Weborg (Gills Rock, Wisconsin) regarded lobbying and keeping up with DNR regulations as essential aspects of commercial fishing.

The DNR is setting regulations in coordination with the fishermen. Right now we are going through a new rule package. There have been a couple instances where a few fishermen misrepresented their quota, and they caught them. But the DNR is under the understanding that it is happening statewide, which it is not. It is just your couple problem fishermen who want to stretch the limits. We have been working with a task force to try and come up with something we can live with and still be effective. It will be another six months or a year before anything is accomplished. I am taking part in it. We have four commercial fishermen on the committee. The biggest challenge in fishing is keeping up with the DNR. This changes and that changes, but we have got it now where most things have to go through the legislature. So you end up getting your lobbyist and it all costs money and takes a bite out of your profits. We have come to figure out that is all we can do. So we have fundraisers to raise money to try and stay in business.

Fishing in the years when it was more common for fishermen to hold a license in both Michigan and Wisconsin, Kenneth Peterson of Fairport had dealings with conservation law enforcement officials from both states.

The DNR in Wisconsin always treated me good. I could never complain about them. Of course, in Michigan nobody seemed to like them. They did not even want to see them come round. They could arrest you for almost anything if they wanted to, so I guess that is why they did not like to see them come around. Of course, we had state men that had just as much authority as their DNR, I think. They could have pinched us I suppose. They could have found a reason to do it. I was not doing everything 100 percent right. But I always thought in my mind they had a job to do and they were hired to do the job just like you or I. Everybody has got to live in this old world. So I tried to get along with them the best I could. You do not have to fall in love with them, but you got to try and get along with them anyway. When they get on you, they just hunt the hell right out of you in Michigan. But I guess it is just as bad in Wisconsin. It seems like if they do something in Wisconsin, Michigan follows. They do the same thing in Michigan.

"Coho" Bob Maynard, a former commercial fisherman, was critical of the lack of coordination between the various governmental bodies that regulate the fisheries.

I grew up in Pentwater, Michigan, and worked on the commercial fishing tugs. I saw how Wisconsin, Indiana, Illinois, and Michigan all had different ideas. For example, in Michigan, gill nets with a two-and-three-quarter-inch mesh are used for perch. Down in Indiana, they wanted perch so bad—they were so much in demand—they lowered the size of the mesh to two-and-one-half inches. As a result, they caught the small fish and by keeping the small ones it took more of them to make a pound. The various restaurants would buy every bit that they could catch. Over in Wisconsin, the alewives were taken by the ton for use as cat food and were sold for less than a penny a pound. That put down the population of alewife considerably.

Michigan made laws to outlaw gill nets per se with very few exceptions. These laws put many, many of the commercial fishermen totally out of business. The state paid off a few of them, but not many. You could not help but believe that they went at it wrong. Michigan had entirely different rules than Indiana, Illinois, and Wisconsin, but all are on Lake Michigan. Somehow, the federal and state people could not get their heads together on the same topic on the same lake when it came to governing the same fish. So we observed them all. The opinions that you get from folks like us are going to be considerably different than some of the ones that you might get from the people who are powerful down in Lansing.

Daniel "Pete" LeClair (Two Rivers, Wisconsin) maintained that during the 1990s, the DNR made policy changes reflecting the political clout of sport-fishing interests.

These are just selfish, greedy people. In my way of thinking, that is not the way you should manage a resource. It was never that way until 1991. Then they really socked it to us. I think it was because of the sport fishermen. The DNR knew better, but they just caved in to the pressure from the sports fishermen. I am sure lots people in the DNR agree this is the wrong way to go. We have local fish managers who agree but they cannot say anything. If they do, they will be transferred or lose their jobs. So they have to remain quiet. So it is really a political ballgame that has nothing to do with biological management of the resource. This is what is so frustrating—when it is so wrong and we know we are right, but you cannot get people to support you.

Wisconsin-based fisherman Don Stiller identified the organizations commercial fishermen formed to gain a greater influence in fishing-related legislation and public policy.

When the associations first came in there was a Southern Green Bay Perch Fishing Association that went up as far as Marinette. There was a Door County Commercial Fishermen's Association, a Southern Lake Michigan Commercial Fishermen's Association, and a Lake Superior association. All of these were separate. Fishermen are an odd bunch—hook-and-line fishermen and commercial fishermen both. At times, you would think that the people in Door County could care less what was happening to perch down here or the perch fishermen down here could care less what was happening to the whitefish fishermen up there. It is the same thing on Lake Michigan and the same thing on Lake Superior. But finally, they got the Wisconsin Commercial Fishermen's Association and all the associations got together and joined in on that. We had a lobbyist down in Madison that did a lot of good work for us. Before this, each association kind of looked out for their own particular business, although the Door County and the Southern Green Bay Association we used to have an astronomical bunch of people come to the meetings. I have seen them just jammed with people. We had a lot of good people that represented Green Bay. Jim Merrick and Mark Merrick were big fishermen and fought pretty hard for the fishermen in this area. Then there was Elaine Johnson up in Door County. She was really a good voice for that association up there.

Neil Teskie indicated that many of the commercial fishermen who are active with their own organizations are also members of the DNR's Lake Michigan Task Force.

I am on the Wisconsin Commercial Fishermen's Board. I go to the meetings. Charles Hendrickson of Baileys Harbor is the president. He is a fine president. When you are president or an officer, it means you are committed because it is not a paid position. I fished with him. He has fished with me. We fished partners. He fished the *Frances* for me before he had his own fishing operation. We had to kind of split ways when they went to quotas because there was not enough for two. So that is what happened there. He was fishing the *Frances* for me. I just had to say there is just not enough to operate the way we are operating because we were reduced on the amount that we could harvest. Charlie is on the task force and Rick Johnson is on the task force. The task force is a DNR board. The resources board appointed them to re-evaluate reporting and licensing—mostly reporting and landing of fish to close the loopholes. A lot of times, they would hand out the green sheet with all the regulations on it and you say: "What in the world were they thinking?" But if you have the task force and they have common sense, they will come up with something that will actually work. One of the rules was that we should have all the fish dressed before we leave the dock. In October, when the snowflakes are flying sometimes we are not going to stand down in that boat and dress that fish. We were just glad to get to shore with them and then get them up to the shed where we can turn on the heat.

They might make reporting easier and might eliminate some of the need for some of the personnel at the DNR. I will send in the catch report at the end of the month. But the task force only makes recommendations. The DNR passes the rules, so we never know what. They could refuse the recommendation but I think that things will work out. I have talked with Charlie Hendrickson. He seemed to think things were going along quite well. He said: "We are not going to get everything we want." We have to make some concessions and they are not going to get everything they want. The regulations really come out of the law enforcement division and they do not always approach it from the standpoint of the practicalities of fishing. But now it is out on the table and is being talked about. There are commercial fishermen, sport fishermen, wholesale license dealers, and some citizens at large on the board. It is an open forum. Anybody from the floor can have input.

As a youth, Neil Teskie (Gills Rock, Wisconsin) fished with his father and brother, Lyle, who is a charter boat operator.

There has always been friction between us and the recreational fishermen. Some recreational fishermen feel if they cannot catch a fish they have to blame somebody. At times commercial fishermen have been the scapegoats. But I get along well with them. My brother is a recreational sports fisherman and I know a lot of sport fishermen. There are people in the sport- fishing industry who do not want any commercial fishing, and there are people who do not care one way or the other and would support commercial fishing. So there are two camps on it. I would not say that the recreational fishermen are out to get me. I just say that the recreational fisherman has his priorities—what he thinks is important. I have what I think is important. Granted, the recreational industry has a lot of dollars that go into the state economy. There are about fifty families in the commercial fishing industry; we are not too big. We are not putting a lot of money in the state treasury, but we are providing a service that would not exist for most of the rest of the taxpayers of the state because you cannot catch a whitefish on a hook and line. If you do, it is rare. We compete for perch with sport fishermen, but I do not fish many perch. I have a 450-pound quota. I mean, I do not even mess around with it.

Bill Carlson (Leland, Michigan) maintained that fisheries management has becoming mired in politics to the peril of the resource.

Fisheries management was making some great strides in the late 1960s and 1970s because they were on a particular track. They were trying to get optimum yield from the fishery—the maximum sustainable yield from the fishery. The optimum yield concept is based on the most money for the resource. That is where the sport fishery took over. In recent years, fishery management has fallen way by the wayside. There still is some, but it is mostly concentrated on how many salmon can we plant here and have it be politically acceptable. How much do we have to plant for the Indians so that we can satisfy them? What does the sport fishery need? The trend or way of thinking is not: What can the forage base stand? What can we take out of the water and still maintain a viable fish population that may be able to continually maintain itself and the maximum sustainable yield? That thinking has kind of gone by because of all the political ramifications.

There are so many demands on the resource. The whole management thing, the whole conflict with the resource is, unfortunately, based on greed. The different factions want all they can get or all of it. The Indians want as much as they can get. The sport fishery wants all they can get. And I want my share, too. There is a greed factor and it is not based on sound management principles. If it were, the fellow that is fishing out of the harbor here and targeting lake trout would not be allowed to do it because lake trout are not self-sustaining. Almost 100 percent of the lake trout in the water are planted fish. If you want to have those fish begin to propagate, you have to have enough numbers of fish that are not infertile or sterile that can lay the eggs and reproduce. By taking those fish out of the water, you are just defeating the whole thing. A put-and-take fishery for the lake trout was not the intent of the Great Lakes Fishery Commission when they reintroduced it. The state is planting hundreds of thousands of lake trout for the sport fishery and the Indians to catch. I am not allowed to catch any so I do not become a factor in that particular case. Salmon is a put-and-take fishery also.

The Great Lakes Fishery Commission's idea was to re-establish lake trout in the lake, not create a put-and-take fishery. But they have had very little luck with natural reproduction. They might not have the necessary biomass—perhaps that could be the problem. It is a numbers thing. Maybe we do not have the numbers for lake trout to successfully reproduce. Of the millions of eggs being laid out there and fertilized, there are not enough to survive whatever mortality they face. I am talking biology and I am not a biologist. I am talking from my own experience and what I have been able to learn through courses that I have taken. The management of this resource does not make any sense to me. Management has become absolutely ridiculous because it is political. Politics dictate policy, not what is best for the environment or the species that live in the environment. It is just ridiculous. It is a laugh.

Chuck Jensen was employed in his family's South Haven fishery for many years before it closed in the early 1980s. He recalled the years before World War II when lake trout were raised in Michigan fish hatcheries in order to aid the regeneration of what was then a commercial species.

I n the early days before the sports fishery, the DNR tried to raise, plant, and reproduce trout only for the commercial fishery. They were not expecting the sports fishery at that time. So they were really working for us for a while as far as I know. But then they found out that they were not reproducing on their own. Then eventually, the salmon planting came along and the sports fishery came along and then they would not allow us to catch any trout anyway. The first plan was to restock the lake with trout but it did not work because they would not reproduce on their own. So the lake trout program did not help commercial fishing any.

Kenneth Peterson recalled the days when Garden Peninsula fishermen such as his father transported milk cans filled with fish fry out into the lake for planting for the Michigan Department of Conservation.

Y ears ago, they gave spawn permits, for trout mostly. I can remember when my dad fished for spawn. They used to come here and treat the spawn right in this area. Then they would put it in boxes with moss and everything and take it to the hatcheries. They would bring some of the fries back here. They would take them out in the lake here and dump them. My dad volunteered his boat to take them out there. They had the fry in milk cans with so many in the can and the water. When they would get out there and dump them over the stern right out of the cans. The fry my dad used to plant for the DNR were just little stinkers. He used to take them out here outside Point Detour and dump them over the stern.

Mark Weborg expressed frustration that despite federal stocking, the lake trout population had never recovered to the point that it could become a target species for commercial fishermen once again.

The lake trout were planted for the commercial fishermen because lamprey had taken all the lake trout out of the lake along with most of the whitefish. They planted them for our use but we never did get any use out of them. The sportsmen claimed them for their own. So there was a little disagreement back then. But then they introduced the salmon. Once they did that, they had no interest in the lake trout because fishing lake trout for sport is like pulling up a log. There is really not much fun in it whereas the salmon put up a pretty good fight. So since then, we have tried to communicate with the sport fishermen and explain how the nets are, where you can fish, and where they cannot fish. It has worked out real well. We really have no problems with the sport industry right now. The lake trout are still being planted year after year after year with no one getting any use out of them other than the Indians. The Indian fishery throughout the Great Lakes can take lake trout and sell them. At times, when the sportsmen cannot catch any other fish, then they will try for lake trout but it is really not a targeted sport species.

Dennis Hickey (Baileys Harbor, Wisconsin) is a commercial fisherman who assists state and federal fisheries officials in the effort to restore the lake trout fishery.

The Astroturf mats that are used to plant lake trout are a square bail. They are about three feet long, two feet wide, and two feet high. We started out making the frames of wood, then we went to wire, and then plastic or synthetic wood. They have worked pretty well. The Astroturf is the matting. We bought it. In fact, the fishermen paid for all the first matting. We cut it in squares. You lay down a square and pour the fertilized lake trout eggs on top of the matting. Then you tip another mat over and you lay it down on top of it, tip another one over and lay down another layer, like a sandwich. We put twelve of them in one bail and strap them together. We lowered them down with anchors and left them out there on the reefs—on the good, original spawning reefs. When they hatch out in the spring they are imprinted to these reefs. The eggs will hatch if they are

in the right waters, when the time is right for them and the water is at the right temperature. Then we went out and we trawled to look for some of them. We caught them.
They hatched. In fact, we pulled up mats at different times to see how they were pro-
gressing. The last time we pulled them up, we hit it right on the head. We set the mat
on the deck and all of a sudden it was just shimmering with little lake trout that had
hatched out of there. They were all over the deck. So it works. It was done about six miles
southeast of Baileys Harbor on a reef. We see live lake trout in our trapping nets. If we
see any that are not clipped we know that it had to come from somewhere, and those
hatched in the mats would not be clipped; everything that is planted has a clip.

––––––––––––––––

Paul Goodman maintained that lake trout do such damage to gill nets that commercial fishers feel they should be entitled to take whatever lakers they catch.

As the money got a little better some of the things got a little bit bigger. Rather
than allowing us just two lake trout, it was changed to 100 pounds—so it did get
bigger. There is no doubt that it got bigger. It was really hard for the fishermen around
here to justify returning a fish that swims into their net and it is dead and they are not
getting it. It was hard for them to justify just throwing it back in the water dead. It is
a marketable product, and it was really hard for these people. Plus, the lake trout were
really hard on the equipment—they are especially hard on the gill nets. Pretty good size
lake trout roll in the nets and tear them up. We were using large mesh nets—whitefish
gill nets—and they were tearing holes in the nets. They were the only thing that was
doing any damage to our equipment. So everybody was trying to recapture their damage and that was one way to do it—just send them down the road. But the ones that
got caught had too many fish. It looked bad. It looked bad for the industry because
people saw it. So I started charter fishing.

––––––––––––––––

Brian Price (Leelanau Convervancy) worked as a commercial fisherman for fifteen
years. He reflected on whether commercial fishermen should be permitted to fish for
lake trout.

343

When we get into the ethics of it all, and whether you should be fishing lake trout, it is not as cut and dried as it might seem. It is claimed that the commercial fishing industry destroyed the lake trout. This is probably not true. There were a lot of factors involved. Will the commercial fishery prevent the establishment of a naturally reproducing lake trout fishery? The fact of the matter is that the lake trout fishery is a put-and-take fishery. Every one of those fish except for a half percent or something, has a fin clip. They are put in the lake. They grow up and then it is a question of allocation, not ethics. It is not a question of ethics to catch and sell them and put them on the market, or to catch them with sport-fishing gear. It is a question of politics and allocation. It is not environmental at all. It is a good question—whose fish are those fish? The state is planting them, so it's up to the state to say whose fish they are. If they want them for the sport fishery, that is fine.

Whenever you have one subset of people that has rights and privileges that are different from some other subset of people, you are going to have problems. It is not specifically about lake trout. It is wrapped up in a lot of other cultural, racial, and environmental problems.

Most commercial fishermen do not want anything to do with lake trout. They are not a very good commercial fish species. They do not bring a high price. You would love to avoid them for the most part. Whitefish are much better tasting fish, most people would say. They are cleaner and have less contaminants. Lake trout is not a much-admired fish either by the sport fishermen or the commercial fishermen. They just happen to be native to the lakes. They can become very abundant, but right now, it is a put-and-take fishery. It would be nice to re-establish them but nobody knows why natural production has been a problem. There still is natural reproduction in Lake Superior. There are plenty of fish in Lake Superior that are not planted. But in Lake Michigan it has been twenty to thirty years since they decided to rehabilitate lake trout. They thought if they could get a critical mass of these fish in the lake, they would start to spawn. But they are not reproducing really at all.

The U.S. Fish and Wildlife Service thought that they had the wrong stock originally that were not adapted to the big lakes or perhaps they have not discovered where the spawning grounds were yet. They found the historical spawning grounds. I give them credit; they have really worked at this for twenty years. It is like a bad marriage. It has never worked out. They planted the fish out on the spawning grounds hoping that they would return. But lake trout are not salmon; they do not necessarily return. It is a pre-carious ecology and it always has been.

Most of the valued species in the Great Lakes for both commercial and sport fishing—the native fish—not only had lake spawning stocks that spawned on reefs out in the lake, but also, stream spawning stocks. It was critically important to maintain balance between these fish stocks because we know where, for instance, whitefish spawn in Grand Traverse Bay. We know pretty well by now and it is pretty easy to find them. The spawning stocks out in the lake are pretty exposed. One really nasty storm can take the eggs that were laid in November and due to hatch about 100 days later in March or early April, cover them with silt, blowing them into the rock crevices, and basically destroy a whole year's spawning reproducing on any one of those grounds. Ice gouges and other things result in wild fluctuations. You get a terrific spawning year when virtually everything happened right, and then you may not get another one of those for another four years or five years. The spawning stocks that ran up the rivers were in a much more controlled environment, and there was maybe not a lot by comparison in an average year. It was an insignificant amount of spawning reproduction from those places but it evened everything out. It kept some sort of balance. When the rivers were dammed up and the river mouths with saw mill waste and dust, we destroyed every one of those. There is no whitefish spawning in any river in Michigan. There is no lake trout spawning in any river in Michigan. There is no wonder; we have added even more uncertainty into the whole equation.

Alan Priest (Leland, Michigan) maintained that commercial fishermen were not interested in lake trout because there was little or no market for it. The lake trout restoration program was a disappointment for those who hoped to see the species become so plentiful that commercial fishing would be allowed.

I could never figure out why they make us throw back our incidental catch of dead lake trout. They could never give an answer really, but I am afraid that they think that we are going to start targeting that species of fish. There is no reason for us to target it. It is not a commercial fish and I do not want to deal with lake trout anyway. I am a chub fisherman. I do not care about lake trout. But to throw something back in the water that could be utilized and let it rot on the bottom, I do not understand that. It is the same thing with our menominee permit. Whenever we could fish menominees—June, July, and August was fine until they started planting the lake with lake trout. Then they stopped us from fishing for menominees. The rationale is that they go up into the shoals in the spring. Well they do, but when we start fishing them, they have gone back down to lower temperatures. We might incidentally catch a few lake trout here and there, but there are millions and millions of pounds of menominees over there in those islands and they will not be utilized. I am not saying go out and catch every one, just enough to smoke in the market or sell to Walters Fisheries in Ludington so he can smoke some. Or maybe filet them fresh—you have to do that with menominees. They are a real soft fish. Sell some fresh in the market and change the pace a little bit from fishing chubs all the time. I offered to take the DNR out—the guys on the *Steelhead*—to lift menominees for a couple weeks to show how many lake trout we would get. The lake trout were not just stocked for the sport fishery. When they first planted lake trout, the commercial fisheries were supposed to get a certain amount of them, but it never happened. They took everything away.

You can hardly make a living at chub fishing now because the price is so low and everything costs so much. It would help if we could split time and fish some menominees or even keep some incidental catch of lake trout. We have to fish below forty fathoms or 240 feet. You do not catch any lake trout to speak of at that depth. Once in a while we do, especially in the winter when there is no thermal climb and they are all over. They could be swimming the surface or swimming in 600 feet of water. But I just do not understand why we cannot take what is dead and utilize it.

It is a regulation that we cannot go above forty fathoms. The DNR figures that if we do, we would target the lake trout, which we cannot keep anyway. When it first started, we could take some of the lake trout. We had to tag them and pay the state back—I do not know how much it was, maybe ten cents a pound. Then they prohibited us from taking any trout. We just could not figure that out. I still cannot.

We have our fishing territory and they have taken some of our territory away such as Peterson's Park, Cathead Bay, and that area. In Lake Michigan, we can only go so far north. There is a boundary line. I think it is from the Northport Light to what we call Sixteen Fathom Shoals, about four miles north of North Manitou Island. There is a line that comes across there. That area is closed because it is a sanctuary for the lake trout breeding. They say they want to see if lake trout are going to breed on their own with no interference—no Indian nets and no chub nets in there. But the Indian trap-net boat can fish trap nets over there. Before Ross Lang died, he got permission to fish some trap nets over there. So there is no reason to have a sanctuary over there anymore.

Donald Voight began fishing with his father as a boy. He retired from fishing in 1985 after nearly forty years on the water.

M y dad told me it was in 1930 when they first saw the sea lamprey. It came in and the crew got excited. My dad did not know what the heck it was. He grabbed it and threw it out again.

Daniel "Pete" LeClair (Two Rivers, Wisconsin) indicated that the sea lamprey brought native stocks of lake trout and whitefish to the brink of extinction. The depletion of stocks forced commercial fishermen to largely end pound-net fishing and reduce gill netting in the 1950s.

W hen the lamprey arrived, it was an awful mess. The dead lake trout were two-feet thick on the bottom of the lake. When you would fish gill nets the lake trout would just rot and lay on the bottom. We never got a lot of our nets back because the leads on the bottom of our nets would sink through the decayed lake trout. When you tried to pull it up you would get your ropes back but your web would be gone. You could not pull it out of the dead, decaying lake trout on the bottom. That is how many lake trout were dead. Some of the nets we could not even get up. We had to leave them there. So it was a disaster to the pound-net fishery and the gill-net fishery. All that decayed mess of lake trout and whitefish. They killed the whole works all at one time. So they were some pretty tough years.

Brian Price, a former commercial fisher who now directs a nonprofit nature conservancy, recalled how fishing crew disliked the sea lamprey.

Wasn't this Ha...

When I first went to work on a Great Lakes gill-net tug, we were fishing chubs. We carried a machete on the boat stuck up into the rafters. There were two reasons why we had that machete. One, I have seen it used about twice when the weather just deteriorated so fast and got so nasty, you had to just chop the nets off and make like hell for home. Somebody would get mad, grab the machete, and say "That is enough; we are out of here." It is usually whoever saw the last big wave coming and did not like the look of it. The main reason it was originally on the boat was because the lampreys would hitch a ride on the back of the boat. You would see these eels stuck to the boat, trailing out behind it. Just out of frustration, and anger, you would go chop across the stern of the boat with that machete and just chop it off. The lamprey are just lurking; they are under control in the same way that crime is under control. Whether they have a great impact on fishing today depends on what area of the lake and the given fish stock.

Ben Peterson, who now fishes with a tribal fishing license, sees evidence that sea lamprey still take a toll on lake trout populations.

Almost every lake trout that I see fishing on the tribal side has a mark on them from the sea lampreys. You do not see any big lampreys anymore. When I see lampreys they are small, and I have only seen maybe four this year.

Based in Charlevoix, Michigan, Jack Cross is a former commercial fisherman. The Consent Order of 1985 closed much of the area fished by several generations of the Cross family. He now buys fish for his wholesale and retail operation from tribal fishers licensed by the Grand Traverse Band of Ottawa and Chippewa Indians.[80]

The Indians are regulated as to where they can fish, the type of gear they can fish, the time of year they can fish, and they are pretty strict with it. They are keeping track of their fishermen all the time. They are running up and down the roads and inspecting them. They inspect them on the lake to make sure they are all licensed. They have got their own court system and they punish fishermen if they are doing something wrong. They fine them and if they get too far out of line, they will take their tribal license away from them.

Reactions to the Consent Order were pretty hostile at first, particularly between sportsmen and the Indians. For a long time there was a lot of controversy, but it has kind of smoothed out now. There is a lot of room on the lakes. They did not realize it but it is a big lake. Some people were hostile to us because we kind of took the Indians in and gave them docks and bought their fish. For a few years a lot of people did not want us to be involved. The Indians work with us and we buy their fish. Some dock here and I go on the reservation and buy their fish. We work pretty well together and they stay with me pretty much. I have known most of them for a long time. Their fathers worked for my father. But even with all the struggles, my children are here with me. My son, my daughter, my son-in-law have worked with me. The Indians can bring me enough fish for us to keep going and make a good living at it. That is why we are still in it.

I do not know much about the treaty fishing issue, but I do not have any qualms with it. I think they have the right and, in fact, it was proven that they have the right to fish. The fish should be fished. It is no good without fishing it. Years ago, when they took areas away from us, the whitefish got so abundant in those areas, they were dying of old age. They were just dying off and that is no good either. That is a waste of a good natural resource and the lakes are one of the best natural resources we have in the state.[81]

Even back when my family fished, there were Native Americans fishing then, too. The tribal fishing issue did not just pop out of nothing. There were Native American fishermen who have worked with us since I was a little kid. Many of the Indians came off of Beaver Island and my dad came off of Beaver Island, so I kind of grew up with them. So I have known most of them from day one.

I pretty much work with the one tribe, the Grand Traverse Band out of Peshawbes-town. I do a lot of business with them and in turn I sell fish to the restaurants. We have a pretty good working relationship down there. I buy fish from Jim Raphael, Ed and Cindi John, and Skip Duhamel. I bought fish from Skip's dad—Art Duhamel. Skip and his dad were the same. They fought for their rights. Back when they were first coming into fishing, Skip's dad fought for their right to fish and Skip is that way too. He fought and got their right to dock at Northport.

Ben Peterson fishes out of Manistique, Michigan.

I am the tribal fishing member of the family. I fish out of Manistique. When I first moved over there in 1989, the Consent Agreement had already been signed in 1985. I waited for my son and nephew to get out of high school until I had a crew. The first year we fished over there, we fished trap nets, what the sport fishermen would like to see us fish. They were having a salmon derby at the same time as we were fishing. And somebody destroyed a $4,000 net on us and killed a lot of fish in the process. That was about the only run-in that we had. Otherwise, we get along together. We fish right out here near Summer Island, and they fish salmon there. I tell them where the nets are. We do not want to cause a problem. Sometimes some of the guys get tangled up in the net and we just tell them, we will give you the stuff back. It is no big thing. We had quite a few sports fishermen last summer.

"Coho" Bob Maynard of Pentwater discussed the politics of treaty fishing rights.

Judge Fox passed the rules that we must abide by; he took the side of the Indians and the Treaty of 1836 giving them permission to take enough fish to survive. That was the idea of the law at that time. Two hundred years ago, these were the native lands of the Indians. They lived by an entirely different set of rules than you and I. So, it becomes more complicated for that reason. The Indians themselves did not have the money to start up one of these. They are financed by someone in New York or somewhere who has a considerable amount of money to put in a thousand slot machines or things that cost a lot of money. It is the same way with the commercial Indian fishing. It takes a lot of money to get one of these commercial fishing boats and the proper trap or other kind of net. The average Native Indian does not have thousands and thousands of dollars to equip a boat like that.

Fourth-generation fisherman Mark Weborg discussed his relations with some of the tribal fishers who won the right to fish in the Michigan waters of Lake Michigan.

There is no Indian fishery in the State of Wisconsin other than up in Lake Superior. But there is an Indian fishery real close to us in Michigan's Upper Peninsula just north of here. By and large, the Indian fishery is really just a fly-by-night fishery. They go out and fish a day or two, go home and they drink that up. Once the money's gone, then they go out and fish again. But there are a number of good Indian fishermen that are in it and do real well. I have got several Indian fishermen friends up there and we communicate a lot and share thoughts and experiences and have a good time with them. Just this last month the judge ruled that the Oneida tribe—which is out of Green Bay—does not have the right to fish in Green Bay or Lake Michigan. So there are no Indian rights in the State of Wisconsin other than Lake Superior.

Bill Carlson (Leland, Michigan) maintained that the interests of the Grand Traverse Band of Ottawa and Chippewa Indians would be best served if they learned how to fish their areas at sustainable levels instead of seeking the legal means to expand their fishing areas.

The Indian fishery right now is being managed wrongly for the resource. Maybe not for the people, but in the long run, if you do not take care of the resource, you are not taking care of the people. The Indians have caught the fish in Grand Traverse Bay. That is why they are now fishing over here off Leland. When they catch them here, then they have to go somewhere else. So they are negotiating for more area to fish. They need more room, but they are running out of fish in these places. Now that is not fishery management. I am stating fact; it has nothing to do with whether I think the Indian fishery is good or not. It has to do with what is best for the resource. And what we are doing is making these people work themselves out of a job. It is not fair to them. And they are fighting like heck because either they do not believe it or they have real short-term gain in mind. The Bill Rastetters—their attorneys, make up things about fisheries and say why things are happening. He does not know. He is just trying to buy them more time, more area, or whatever. That is so shortsighted and so sad. It is so unfortunate.

Brian Price recalled that tribal fishing rights advocate Art Duhamel had a cordial relationship with many commercial fishermen. Some resented Michigan's efforts to put them out of business and they helped the tribal fishers get established.

A rt Duhamel was a great guy. I knew Art before he really started to fish. He was probably just back from Alaska where he had been a pipeline welder. He came back and was just starting to decide that he wanted to try fishing. He did not know anything and would ask questions. Ross Lang and I sold him nets. We would sell him rags and he knew they were rags, nets that we would not use anymore because they were too beat up. He was working out of a rowboat. I always liked Art; he was always a good guy. In the early 1970s or so the white commercial fishermen, the licensed ones, were so bitter. They really felt then they were going to be run out of business altogether. We had no problems whatsoever with helping Indian fishermen who had different rights than us. Now this may not be true anymore, but it was with Ross Lang, others, and me. Ross Lang was incapable of being obnoxiously competitive with anybody. His feeling was at least somebody will be fishing. Let us help these guys out, and then at least the state will not win entirely. That was the attitude back then. The state may get us out of business, but there will be somebody still out there fishing. Even if they are not my family, our people, there will be somebody.

I was unaware of any overt animosity or competitiveness between commercial fishermen of the white or Indian type. In fact, there was a lot of cooperation between them. The name-calling, animosity, vandalism, and other overt stuff, was the work of a very small minority of sport-fishing interests. But there was a much broader and more significant sort of resentment. There was concern about why I cannot do this if they can. I did not sign that treaty. It was not my deal. We still have to work with that.

The Native Americans have, for the most part, shown it is not the end of the world. The Native Americans are not unable or unwilling to regulate themselves through their own management. Some sport-fishing guys will still tell you they are unregulated. They are wrong. If it had become a nightmare situation and they were unregulated, the bottom line is the resource has to be protected. You would not see me coming to their defense. But it is a question once again of politics and allocation again. They have a right to a large part of the fishery.

Alan Priest maintained that tribal and nontribal fishers alike share a willingness to aid each other.

It seems like you are going along in life and all of a sudden—bang—something will happen. One night I was just getting home. My wife was at camp with the school and I was just getting home. I settled in and the phone rang. It was one of the Indians on a cell phone. He said their boat broke down out in front of the harbor here. I said, "Oh, piece of cake. I will come down and tow you in." Well, it did not happen that way. It was blowing from the northeast and they were about five miles out in the lake. We left the harbor and got to them. It was dark and it was blowing, but we were able to hook onto them and towed them in. It was just something that you do. I am not going to go away. Why cause problems? I am a very simple person. Simple is better in my book. Just work together. They wanted to try and pay me and I said no. All I ask is that someday if I break down that you will come and get me.

I just wish they would keep their equipment up a little bit better—keep the radios in better working order. That is one pet peeve with me. You hear things happening on the radio and you can help somebody. An Indian trap-net boat broke down out by Fox Island a week or two ago and I was coming home from Empire in a bad northeaster. We were rolling around and going into a head sea and we were pounding. If they had called me and wanted me to go up there—it would have taken us four hours to get there—I would have went up there and gotten them. They fish out of Peshawbestown. They are good fishermen. They are good people. You just have to deal with everybody. That is the way I look at it. My wife told one of the secretaries at work that I went out and helped an Indian boat and she said: "He did what?" Mary stuck up for me. She said: "You know, that's his profession. Those guys are there with him and they have to take care of each other."

Joy Lang (Leland, Michigan) observed how her late husband Ross willingly adapted himself to treaty rights fishing in the 1980s, just as he had accommodated himself to the planting of salmon in the 1960s and 1970s.

When they planted species from the West Coast it created a lot of problems for the commercial fisheries, although it did clean up the lakes. So you have to contend with both sides. When you have those situations you have to make the best of them and that is where Ross was always coming from. You find another way and just go from there. It is same with the Native Americans. He was often out there helping them because when you are out on a boat, you help other people. The few times he was called on, nobody else would go help them—so Ross would go out. Then he would have some of the sports fishermen upset with him for a short time because he was the kind of a person that would help anybody and they realized that. He never did get upset with the Native Americans. He always blamed the state for what happened to the Indians. The state went to the Indians and said we have this treaty, this is what you can do. So you cannot blame the Native Americans for pursuing it when it was put right in front of them, put on the plate in front of them. So he never blamed them. He said you have to work with them. They did not bother him in his work, not at all. He got along.

Leon Voight (Gills Rock, Wisconsin) indicated that Michigan tribes were unsuccessful in establishing treaty rights fishing in Lake Michigan outside of Michigan waters.

The Indians wanted to claim the water over here. They went to the court, the State Supreme Court, and lost their case because they are not native from this area. They did not like getting turned down like that. They were actually over here looking at docks to rent at the time that this was all brought up. I have never seen them since. The wider community did not really know anything about it because it was never published or anything. The only ones who really knew about it were the commercial fishermen and the sport fishery. The sportsmen did not want tribal fishing either because the Indians would be able to take their lake trout and salmon because they are not regulated for that. Of course, as for whitefish, they are not regulated as to size. They can take all they want. They can take a ten-inch fish if they feel like it. They do not have any regulations like that. They do not have quotas. They can fish all they want, which makes it bad for guys here who are regulated on our whitefish. They would be able to fish all they want and run as much gear as they want.

Chub fisherman Alan Priest, who has fished the waters of Lake Michigan from Leland since the early 1970s, would like access to other species and tribal fishing areas.

The Indian fishing has not affected me. It is not because I am just a chub fisherman and I do not go after lake trout. I am not a commercial sport fisherman—a charter boat owner. The Indians do not want to fish chubs. There's too much work in it. They want it quick and easy done. I would like to find a way to fish chubs over in the Grand Traverse Bay but I really do not know how to go about it. They are not utilizing that species over there.

A few Indians have fished chubs in the bay and they say they are real thick over there. Chubs take lots of effort. You just do not bring the chubs in and pack them on ice. You have to dress them and it takes a lot more time than if you catch an eight-pound lake trout where there is no effort and you are done. But I would like to talk to somebody to see if I could fish in the bay in the fall and winter when things quiet down and there is not so much boating and activity. I would have somebody go on the boat with me. I am not afraid to take people out. I would take the president out if he wanted to go—just to show what I do. I do not want to break any laws. I just want to make a living. Just have people leave me alone and let me do my business. That is why I get so mad about these guys, they will not let us fish menominees over there. Why not? Let them have some sportsmen go over there and see if they can catch some menominees. They might catch a few but not enough to relieve the pressure of so many menominees in that area of the lake. A menominee is a smaller whitefish. They call it a round whitefish. It is very good eating. In fact, if you clean them up, skin them, and then deep-fry them, they almost taste like perch. The species should be utilized. That's my gripe about it. Not to kill it, not to make it endangered or anything, just to utilize it a couple months out of the year. And not fish them very heavy, but for a change of pace.

I think the DNR should give us the incidental catch of lake trout. Why let that rot on the bottom? If they are alive and their gills are not bleeding, throw it back. If they are dead and usable, why not let us keep them? Let us do the same with the menominees. That's not asking for a lot. I cannot target lake trout. There is no way in the world. I do not want to target lake trout. To me, that is a sport fish that brings more revenue into the area. A lot of the people here are tourists. A lot of them are going to buy fish and eat at the restaurants. They go to the stores and the gas stations. Let the sport fishermen have that. I do not want any of that. But I will take those guys on the boat with me. I am willing to work with anybody. If they want me to work with the Indians I will—see what they can do, everybody get along. One thing I think they should do with the Indians—I understand they have some hatcheries and that they are restocking the lakes with salmon. But what about the lake trout? I do not see them putting anything back. They should be because the lake trout are not reproducing on their own. It is a proven fact. To get it to go, they have to restock and restock and restock. Put so much back for the state because it is a put-and-take fishery. There is not natural reproduction. That is what I think should happen.

NOTES

1. On the Great Lakes commercial fishing industry, see Margaret Beattie Bogue, *Fishing the Great Lakes: An Environmental History* (Madison: University of Wisconsin Press, 2000); Don Stiller, *A Multitude of Fishes* (Green Bay, Wisc.: Alt Publishing, 1998); A. B. McCullough, *The Commercial Fishery of the Canadian Great Lakes* (Ottawa, Canada: National Historic Parks and Sites/Canadian Park Service/Environment Canada, 1989); Tom Kuchenberg, *Reflections in a Tarnished Mirror: The Use and Abuse of the Great Lakes* (Sturgeon Bay, Wisc.: Golden Glow Publishing, 1978); Frank Prothero, *Men 'N Boats: Fisheries of the Great Lakes* (Port Stanley, Ontario: The Great Lakes Fisherman, n.d.); William Cashman, "The Rise and Fall of the Fishing Industry," *The Journal of Beaver Island History* 1 (1976): 69–87; Saralee R. Howard and Alan Moore, "Commercial Fishing in Michigan," *Great Lakes Informant* 3, no. 1 [n.d.]: 1–5; William Davenport Hulbert, "Fishermen of the Lakes," *Frank Leslie's Popular Monthly* 51, no. 2 (1901): 344–54; U.S. Department of Commerce, Bureau of Fisheries, *Fishing Industry of the Great Lakes*, by Walter Koelz, Bureau of Fisheries Document no. 1001 (Washington D.C.: Government Printing Office, 1926); John Van Oosten, "Michigan's Commercial Fisheries of the Great Lakes," *Michigan History Magazine* 22, no. 1 (1938): 3–39; David Johnson, "Commercial Fishing Its Past and Future," *Anchor News* (September-October 1981): 100–16; Robert Grunst, "Boats, Nets, and Rigs: Early Twentieth Century Commercial Fishing on Lake Michigan," *Michigan History Magazine* 77, no. 4 (1993): 42–45; Russell W. Brown, Mark Ebener, and Tom Gorenflo, "Great Lakes Commercial Fisheries: Historical Overview and Prognosis for the Future," in *Great Lakes Fisheries Policy and Management: A Binational Perspective*, ed. William W. Taylor and C. Paola Ferreri (East Lansing: Michigan State University Press, 1999), 307–54; H. J. Brinks, "Grand Haven Fishing," *Origins* 15, no. 2 (1997):

20–28; ; Clifford Ross Gearhart, *Pity the Poor Fish, Then Man* (Au Train, Mich.: Avery Color Studios, 1987); Russell Brown, "History of the Great Lakes Commercial Fishery," *Fishing For Solutions: Sustainability of Commercial Fishing in the Great Lakes, Great Lakes United Conference Proceedings* (December 1995): 19–40; Dennis Hickey, "U.S. Perspective on the Commercial Fishery," *Fishing For Solutions: Sustainability of Commercial Fishing in the Great Lakes, Conference Proceedings* (December 1995): 57–60.

On artistic interpretations of Great Lakes fishing, see: Leelanau Historical Museum, *Hans W. Anderson: His Life and Art* (Leland, Mich.: Leelanau Historical Museum, 1988).

2. On specific fishing communities, see Milwaukee: Prothero, *Men 'N Boats*, 72–73; "Lake Michigan Fishing in a Milwaukee Tug," *Atlantic Fisherman* 23, no. 3 (1942): 11; "Propose Jones Island Fishing Terminal," *Atlantic Fisherman* 28, no. 5 (1947): 18; "Lafond Moves to Baileys Harbor," *Atlantic Fisherman* 30, no. 6 (1949): 21; "Danger Area Designated," *National Fisherman* 35, no. 6 (1954): 18; Kahlenberg Brothers Co., "Interesting New Fish Tug *Frank Braeger* Launched," Bulletin no. 37 (Two Rivers, Wisc.: Kahlenberg Brothers Co., [n.d.]. Marinette: "To Construct Dock at Marinette," *Atlantic Fisherman* 28, no. 5 (1947): 18. Muskegon: "Whitefish Return to Muskegon Region," *Atlantic Fisherman* 28, no. 9 (1947): 14; "Begin Survey of Muskegon Fishing Conditions," *Atlantic Fisherman* 29, no. 4 (1948): 23. Escanaba: Gearhart, *Pity the Poor Fish*, 139–45; "Predict Good Future for Escanaba Fishing," *Atlantic Fisherman* 28, no. 11 (1947): 20; "Escanaba Fishermen Begin Winter Operations," *Atlantic Fisherman* 29, no. 1 (1948): 22; "Escanaba Smelt Catches Larger," *Atlantic Fisherman* 29, no. 3 (1948): 20; "Escanaba Fishermen Lose Nets" *Atlantic Fisherman* 29, no. 3 (1948): 20; "Escanaba Fishermen Ask for Harbor Space," *Atlantic Fisherman* 31, no. 6 (1950): 21; "Escanaba Fishermen Begin Taking Whitefish," *Atlantic Fisherman* 32, no. 4 (1951): 30; "Seeks Fishing Dock for Escanaba" *Atlantic Fisherman* 32, no. 6 (1951): 18; "Fishermen Injured in Tug Explosion," *Atlantic Fisherman* 32, no. 11 (1951): 20. Marquette: "To Build New Fish Plant at Marquette," *Atlantic Fisherman* 29, no. 3 (1948): 20; "New Fishermen with Marquette Fleet," *Atlantic Fisherman* 32, no. 10 (1951): 23. Racine: Prothero, *Men 'N Boats*, 70–71; "Gap in Racine Breakwater to be Closed," *Atlantic Fisherman* 29, no. 4 (1948): 23. Grand Haven: "Grand Haven Fishing Crew Interesting and Hardy Race of Men," *Muskegeon Chronicle*, 26 April 1930 (VerDuin Collection); "Naomikong Moves to Grand Haven," *Atlantic Fisherman* 29, no. 9 (1948): 23; "Hill Joins Grand Marais Fleet," *Atlantic Fisherman* 30, no. 6 (1949): 21; "New Gill Net Fishery," *Atlantic Fisherman* 32, no. 10 (1951): 23; "Tugs Change Hands," *Atlantic Fisherman* 32, no. 12 (1952): 36; H. J. Brinks, "Grand Haven Fishing," *Origins* 15, no. 2 (1997): 20–28. Ontonagon: "Ontonagon, Michigan—A Productive Lake Superior Fishing Port," *Atlantic Fisherman* 29, no. 10 (1948): 19; "Killorans Return to Ontonagon" *Atlantic Fisherman* 30, no.1 (1949): 28. Munising: " 'Roamer' Capsized," *Atlantic Fisherman* 30, no. 7 (1949): 23. Montague: "Chambers to Operate Out of Montague," *Atlantic Fisherman* 32, no. 8 (1951): 25. Frankfort: "Only Two Tugs Left in Fleet," *National Fisherman* 36, no. 6 (1955): 41; Kahlenberg Brothers Company, "Two New and Modern Boats," Bulletin no. 63 (Two Rivers, Wisc.: Kahlenberg Brothers, [n.d.]. Beaver Island: William Cashman linked the decline of fishing on Beaver Island to the Armistice Day storm of 1940, see: William Cashman, "The Rise and Fall of the Fishing Industry," *Journal of Beaver Island History* 1 (1976): 69–87; Francis E. Martin, "The Last Days of the Fishing Business," *Journal of Beaver Island History* 4 (1998): 191–211. Garden: R. J. Martin, "Garden Peninsula," *Michigan Conservation* 13, no. 5 (1944): 8. St. Joseph: Helen Spangenberg, "Four Generations of Family Wrest Living From Lake," *Michigan Conservation* 15, no. 1 (1946): 10–11. Two Rivers: Bouge, *Fishing the Great Lakes*, 83; Prothero, *Men 'N Boats*, 76–77; Ernest Swift, Madison, Wisconsin, to David LeClair, 4 November 1947, Records of the Wisconsin Fish Producers Association, Gold Meijer Library, University of Wisconsin-Milwaukee; Mary Ann Eggers, "The LeClairs," from "Fishing—The Oldest Industry in Two Rivers," Two Rivers, Wisconsin (27 March 1962). Leland: Prothero, *Men 'N Boats*, 89–90; "In the Mail Bag," *The Fisherman* 1, no. 3 (1932): 5. Green Bay: Don Stiller, *A Multitude of Fishes: A Century of Fishing on Green Bay* (Green Bay, Wisc.: Alt Publishing Co., 1998). Northport: Leelanau Historical Museum, *Hans W. Anderson: His Life and Art* (Leland, Mich.: Leelanau Historical Museum, 1988). St. Ignace: Kahlenberg Brothers Co., "*Irene* Added to Long List of Kahlenberg

Powered Tugs," Bulletin no. 42 (Two Rivers, Wisc.: Kahlenberg Brothers, [n.d.]). Waukegan: Prothero, *Men 'N Boats,* 86–69; Kahlenberg Brothers Company, "Kahlenbergs Power Bulk of Great Lakes Winter Fishing Fleet," Bulletin no. 51 (Two Rivers, Wisc.: Kahlenberg Brothers, [n.d.]. Port Washington: Kahlenberg Brothers Company, "Two New and Modern Boats," Bulletin no. 63 (Two Rivers, Wisc.: Kahlenberg Brothers, [n.d.].

3. On fishing, family, and ethnicity, see: Bogue, *Fishing the Great Lakes,* 74–88; Prothero, *Men 'N Boats,* 167–68; Howard Sivertson, *Once Upon an Isle: The Story of Fishing Families on Isle Royale* (Mount Horeb, Wisc.: Wisconsin Folk Museum, 1992); Stiller, *A Multitude of Fishes;* and "Veteran Fisheries Supervisor Retires," *Michigan Conservation* 15, no. 7 (1946): 12.

4. "Two Boats Change Ports," *Atlantic Fisherman* 30, no. 8 (1949): 23; "Munising Fishermen Buys New Tug," *Atlantic Fisherman* 32, no. 8 (1951): 25.

5. For more on methodological and interpretive issues regarding traditional ecological knowledge (TEK) and fisheries, see Gisli Palsson, "'Finding One's Sea Legs': Learning, the Process of Enskilment, and Integrating Fishers and Their Knowledge into Fisheries Management," in *Finding Our Sea Legs: Linking Fishery People and Their Knowledge with Science and Management,* ed. Barbara Neis and Lawrence Felt (St. John's, Newfoundland: Institute of Social and Economic Research, 2000), 25–40; Barbara Neis, Lawrence F. Felt, Richard L. Haedrich, and David C. Schneider, "An Interdisciplinary Method for Collecting and Integrating Fishers' Ecological Knowledge into Resource Management," in *Fishing Places, Fishing People: Traditions and Issues in Canadian Small-Scale Fisheries,* ed. Dianne Newell and Rosemary E. Ommer (Toronto: University of Toronto Press, 1999), 217–38.

6. "We Want the Right Regulations," *Atlantic Fisherman* 21, no. 4 (1940): 11; LaRue Wells and Alberton L. McLain, "Lake Michigan: Man's Effects on Native Fish Stocks and Other Biota," Technical Report no. 20 (Ann Arbor: Great Lakes Fishery Commission, January 1973).

7. For more on fishing and bad weather, see "Great Lakes Fishermen Suffer Net Losses," *Atlantic Fisherman* 28, no. 1 (1947): 20; "Windstorm Causes Big Losses," *Atlantic Fisherman* 29, no. 1 (1948): 22; "Lake Michigan Fishing Vessels at Green Bay Tied Up," *Atlantic Fisherman* 20, no. 7 (1939): 18; "Weather Conditions Cause Shortage of Fish," *Atlantic Fisherman* 20, no. 7 (1939): 18; "Ice Delays Open-Water Netting," *Atlantic Fisherman* 31, no. 4 (1950): 24; "Seasonal Weather Forecasts Would Aid Fishermen," *National Fisherman* 36, no. 6 (1955): 11–12. On winter fishing conditions see, Gearhart, *Pity the Poor Fish,* 76–90, 116–19; Stiller, *A Multitude of Fishes,* 1-2; Prothero, *Men 'N Boats,* 136–41; Winston Fleming, "Fishing Through the Ice in the Great Lakes," *Scientific American Monthly* 1 (January-June 1920): 143–44; P. C. Chamberlain, "Lake Huron: Fishing Boats Climb up on Top of Ice," *Atlantic Fisherman* 15, no. 2 (1934): 7; "Great Lakes Fishing Through Ice Becoming an Important Industry," *Atlantic Fisherman* 17, no. 1 (1936): 16; "Great Lakes Ice Hinders Fishing Operations," *Atlantic Fisherman* 29, no. 2 (1948): 25; "Whitefish Bay Netters Doing Well," *Atlantic Fisherman* 29, no. 2 (1948): 25; "Great Lakes Operators Ready for Winter Season," *Atlantic Fisherman* 29, no. 11 (1948): 19; "Ice Fishing on the Great Lakes," *Atlantic Fisherman* 30, no. 1 (1949): 19; "*Cheerio* Caught in Ice," *Atlantic Fisherman* 30, no. 1 (1949): 28; "Open Water Netting Almost Nil," *Atlantic Fisherman* 30, no. 2 (1949): 25; "Great Lakes Ice Fishermen Get Good Perch, Smelt Catches," *Atlantic Fisherman* 32, no. 2 (1951): 17; "Great Lakes Ice Fishing Season Gets Under Way" *National Fisherman* 36, no. 1 (1955): 18; "Snowmobiles Haul Nets and Gear," *National Fisherman* 36, no. 2 (1955): 37; "Winter Fishing on Lake Superior," *National Fisherman* 39, no. 2 (1958): 11; Kahlenberg Brothers Company, "Smashing Through," Bulletin no. 69 (Two Rivers, Wisc.: Kahlenberg Brothers, [n.d.]; Kahlenberg Brothers Company, "Kahlenberg Help Fishermen Defy Old Man Winter," booklet no. 45 (Two Rivers, Wisc.: Kahlenberg Brothers, [n.d.]).

8. "Fish Tugs Hold Race at Two Rivers," *The Fishing Gazette* 46, no. 9 (1929): 55; "Great Lakes Fishermen Hold Regatta Race," *Atlantic Fisherman* 27, no. 8 (1946): 31; "Fishing Boats Blessed," *Atlantic Fisherman* 31, no. 7 (1950): 27; "Sixth Annual Fleet Blessing," *National Fisherman* 35, no. 8 (1954): 24; "Fayette Fishing Fleet

Blessed," *National Fisherman* 36, no. 8 (1955): 26.

9. Women helped to increase or supplement fishing income, see "Women Slugging Nets," *Atlantic Fisherman* 23, no. 11 (1942): 15 and Bogue, *Fishing the Great Lakes*, 75–76.

10. The Smith family fishery provides a good example. See "Smiths Have Fished Great Lakes for 99 Years," *Atlantic Fisherman* 26, no. 8 (1945): 23; "Sells Interest in Fisheries Firm," *Atlantic Fisherman* 29, no. 2 (1948): 25; "Smith Brothers Celebrate Centennial," *Atlantic Fisherman* 29, no. 8 (1948): 28; "Smith Brothers Biggest Caviar Producer," *Atlantic Fisherman* 30, no. 4 (1949): 20.

11. Great Lakes fishermen sought numerous ways to improve the marketing of their fish. See "Fresh Fillets," *The Fisherman* 1, no. 1 (1931): 11; "Airplane Delivery," *Atlantic Fisherman* 20, no. 9 (1939): 17; "New Refrigeration Plant at St. Ignace," *Atlantic Fisherman* 21, no. 5 (1940): 19; "Fish Dealers' Committee Re-elected," *Atlantic Fisherman* 26, no. 1 (1945): 30; "Fish Institute Issues Poster," *Atlantic Fisherman* 26, no. 10 (1945): 34; "Big White Fish Shipment," *Atlantic Fisherman* 27, no. 10 (1946): 22; "Kavanaugh Has New Plant," *Atlantic Fisherman* 27, no. 10 (1946): 22; "Value of Michigan Catch Sets Record," *Atlantic Fisherman* 27, no. 11 (1946): 25; "Cooperative Advertising Program," *Atlantic Fisherman* 28, no. 6 (1947): 21; "New Fish Plant Attracting Tugs to Cedar River," *Atlantic Fisherman* 29, no. 5 (1948): 18; "Great Lakes Fish to be Flown to New York," *Atlantic Fisherman* 30, no. 7 (1949): 23; "Lake Michigan Fishermen Form Cooperative," *Atlantic Fisherman* 30, no. 9 (1949): 28; "Custom Packing for Fishermen," *Atlantic Fisherman* 31, no. 3 (1950): 23; "Fish Dealers Issue Recipe Booklet," *Atlantic Fisherman* 32, no. 2 (1951): 17; "Toronto Firm Sells Smoked Lampreys," *Atlantic Fisherman* 32, no. 8 (1951): 25; "Michigan to Observe Fish Week," *National Fisherman* 36, no. 1 (1955): 18; "Grover's Fisheries to Expand," *National Fisherman* 36, no. 2 (1955): 35; "Michigan Observes Fish Week," *National Fisherman* 36, no. 3 (1955): 23; "Great Lakes Dealers Sponsor Fish Month," *National Fisherman* 36, no. 8 (1955): 26; "Great Lakes Fishermen Want to Organize Cooperative," *National Fisherman* 36, no. 11 (1955): 27; "How to Improve Whitefish Quality," *National Fisherman* 36 no. 12 (1956): 41; Clarence Poel, "Ver Duins Promote Fresh Water Great Lakes Fish," *Grand Haven Tribune*, 29 March 1988; "Ludington Commercial Fisherman Hangs Up Nets," *The Great Lakes Fisherman* 24, no. 4 (1997): 17. On smoking fish, *see*: Gearhart, *Pity the Poor Fish*, 153–55.

12. Steve Nepszy, "To Catch a Fish: Commercial Fishing Methods on the Great Lakes," *Fishing For Solutions: Sustainability of Commercial Fishing in the Great Lakes, Great Lakes United Conference Proceedings* (December 1995): 41–52. On fishing gear and technology, *see*: Don Stiller, *A Multitude of Fishes*, 3–11; Gearhart, *Pity the Poor Fish*, 41–52; Prothero, *Men 'N Boats*, 141–60; "[Advertisement for] Pentwater Net Lifters," *The Fisherman* 1, no. 1 (1931): 15; " Fishermen Repairing Equipment," *Atlantic Fisherman* 27 no. 7 (1946): 26; U.S. Department of Commerce, Bureau of Fisheries, *Fishing Industry of the Great Lakes*, by Walter Koelz, Bureau of Fisheries Doc. no. 1001 (Washington, D.C.: Government Printing Office, 1926); Van Oosten, "Michigan's Commercial Fisheries," 5–23.

13. For more on how occupational identity among Great Lakes fishermen is expressed in oral narrative, see Timothy C. Lloyd and Patrick B. Mullen, *Lake Erie Fishermen: Work, Identity and Tradition* (Urbana: University of Illinois Press, 1990); Timothy Lloyd, "Fishermen in Court: Personal Narrative and Occupational Rights," in *"A Fully Accredited Ocean": Essays on the Great Lakes*, ed. Victoria Brehm (Ann Arbor: University of Michigan Press, 1998), 223–40. For more on how oral testimony has been used to interpret Great Lakes fishing boats and landscapes, see Janet C. Gilmore, "'We Made 'Em to Fit Our Purpose': The Northern Lake Michigan Fishing Skiff," in *Wisconsin Folklore*, ed. James P. Leary (Madison: University of Wisconsin Press, 1998), 457–75; Hawk Tolson, "The Boats That Were My Friends: The Fishing Craft of Isle Royale," in *"A Fully Accredited Ocean,"* 199–222; "The Story of the *Isle:* From Sailboat to Gas Boat," *Inland Seas: Quarterly Journal of the Great Lakes Historical Society* 51, no. 1 (1995): 20–30; Timothy Cochrane, "Commercial Fishermen and Isle Royale: A Folk Group's Unique Association with Place," in *Michigan Folklife Reader*, ed. C. Kurt Dewhurst and Yvonne R. Lockwood (East Lansing: Michigan State University Press, 1987), 89–105.

14. "P&H Hoist Used at Port Washington," *Atlantic Fisherman* 28, no. 10 (1947): 33; "Invents Herring Cleaning Machine," *Atlantic Fisherman* 28, no. 11 (1947): 20.

15. On Great Lakes fisheries production, see Prothero, *Men 'N Boats*, 129–32; "Perch Plentiful in Green Bay," *Atlantic Fisherman* 28, no. 6 (1947): 21; "Great Lakes Whitefish Are Plentiful in Green Bay," *Atlantic Fisherman* 28, no. 10 (1947): 33; "Great Lakes Fisheries Production Increases," *Atlantic Fisherman* 29, no. 7 (1948): 18; "Great Lakes Fishermen Foresee Better Fall Production," *Atlantic Fisherman* 29, no. 9 (1948): 23; "Great Lakes Whitefish Catches Good During Fall Season," *Atlantic Fisherman* 29, no. 10 (1948): 23; "Advances Theories on Over Fishing," *Atlantic Fisherman* 29, no. 10 (1948): 23; "Great Lakes Whitefish Yield Shows Strong Comeback," *Atlantic Fisherman* 30, no. 1 (1949): 28; "Great Lakes Production Shows Improvement," *Atlantic Fisherman* 30, no. 4 (1949): 19; "Superior Whitefish Hauls Fair to Good," *Atlantic Fisherman* 30, no. 4 (1949): 19; "Great Lakes Whitefish Catches Sizable," *Atlantic Fisherman* 30, no. 4 (1949): 20; "Great Lakes Fishermen Making Good Catches in Superior," *Atlantic Fisherman* 30, no. 6 (1949): 21; "Production Generally Good," *Atlantic Fisherman* 30, no. 7 (1949): 23; "Michigan Whitefish Catches Normal," *Atlantic Fisherman* 30, no. 7 (1949): 23; "Great Lakes Whitefish Stabilize Production," *Atlantic* 30, no. 8 (1949): 23; "Great Lakes Mixed Fish Catches Above Average," *Atlantic Fisherman* 30, no. 9 (1949): 28; "Lake Superior Trout, Whitefish Takes Good," *Atlantic Fisherman* 30, no. 10 (1949): 26; "Lake Huron Whitefish Production Good," *Atlantic Fisherman* 30, no. 12 (1950): 22; "Chub, Yellow Pike, Smelt Takes Up," *Atlantic Fisherman* 31, no. 2 (1950): 22; "Wisconsin Fish Catch for 1949," *Atlantic Fisherman* 31, no. 2 (1950): 22; "Great Lakes Fishermen Make Good Perch, Smelt Catches," *Atlantic Fisherman* 31, no. 3 (1950): 23; "Michigan Production Shows Increase," *Atlantic Fisherman* 31, no. 4 (1950): 24; "Perch Plentiful in Lake Michigan," *Atlantic Fisherman* 31, no. 5 (1950): 28; "Great Lakes Fishermen Getting Good Returns from Trolling," *Atlantic Fisherman* 31, no. 7 (1950): 27; "Great Lakes Fish Landings Improve During September," *Atlantic Fisherman* 31, no. 9 (1950): 21; "Lake Michigan Chub and Perch Catches Good," *Atlantic Fisherman* 31, no. 9 (1950): 21; "Fisheries of the Great Lakes Waters," *Atlantic Fisherman* 31, no. 11 (1950): 14; "Lake Superior Whitefish Yields Fair," *Atlantic Fisherman* 31, no. 12 (1951): 22; "Michigan Fish Production," *Atlantic Fisherman* 31, no. 12 (1951): 22; "Great Lakes Fishermen Making Good Catches in Open Waters," *Atlantic Fisherman* 32, no. 1 (1951): 22; "Lake Michigan Pike Catch Sets Record," *Atlantic Fisherman* 32, no. 2 (1951): 17; "Great Lakes Open-Water Netting Begins Early," *Atlantic Fisherman* 32, no. 3 (1951): 21; "Great Lakes Trout, Whitefish Hauls Best in Recent Years," *Atlantic Fisherman* 32, no. 6 (1951): 18; "Lake Superior Catches Better," *Atlantic Fisherman* 32, no. 6 (1951): 18; "Green Bay Whitefish, Perch Catches Good," *Atlantic Fisherman* 32, no. 6 (1951): 18; "Michigan Catch Increases," *Atlantic Fisherman* 32, no. 7 (1951): 24; "Wisconsin Fish Production for 1950," *Atlantic Fisherman* 32, no. 8 (1951): 25; "Great Lakes Catches Improve as Fall Season Gets Underway," *Atlantic Fisherman* 32, no. 9 (1951): 48; "Great Lakes Fishermen Have Good Lake Trout Catches," *Atlantic Fisherman* 32, no. 10 (1951): 22; "Supplies of Freshwater Fish Moderate," *Atlantic Fisherman* 32, no. 10 (1951): 22; "Great Lakes Herring Fishermen Hampered by Wintry Weather," *Atlantic Fisherman* 32, no. 11 (1951): 20; "Great Lakes Fishermen Make Record Herring Landings," *Atlantic Fisherman* 32, no. 12 (1952): 36; "September-October Landings," *Atlantic Fisherman* 32, no. 12 (1952): 36; "Great Lakes Fishermen Are Making Good Spring Catches," *National Fisherman* 35, no. 5 (1954): 32; "Great Lakes Fishermen Are Making Good Perch Catches," *National Fisherman* 35, no. 6 (1954): 18; "Fish Yields Improve with Approach of Fall," *National Fisherman* 35, no. 8 (1954): 24; "Great Lakes Fishermen Expect Good Herring Season," *National Fisherman* 35, no. 9 (1954): 18; "Michigan Fish Production Down," *National Fisherman* 35, no. 9 (1954): 18; "Great Lakes Fishermen Making Good Herring, Pike Hauls," *National Fisherman* 35, no. 10 (1954): 18; "Great Lakes Fishermen Are Having Average Fall Season," *National Fisherman* 35, no. 11 (1954): 22; "Great Lakes Fishermen Having Exceptional Smelt Season," *National Fisherman* 36, no. 2 (1955): 34; "Great Lakes Fishermen Making Profitable Spring Catches," *National Fisherman* 36, no. 3 (1955): 23; "Good Chub and Perch Take on Lake Michigan," *National Fisherman* 36, no. 3 (1955): 23; "Great Lakes Smelt Run Reaches Its Peak," *National Fisherman* 36, no. 4 (1955): 28; "Fish

Production Shows Increase in 1954," *National Fisherman* 36, no. 4 (1955): 29; "Great Lakes Fishermen Are Making Good Spring Catches," *National Fisherman* 36, no. 5 (1955): 16; "Taking Trout, Whitefish off Apostle Islands," *National Fisherman* 36, no. 5 (1955): 16; "Great Lakes Fishermen are Making Good Walleye Hauls," *National Fisherman* 36, no. 6 (1955): 40; "Great Lakes Trap Netters Getting Excellent Hauls," *National Fisherman* 36, no. 7 (1955): 24; "Lake Michigan Producers Doing Well," *National Fisherman* 36, no. 7 (1955): 24; "Fall Season Brings Improved Catches," *National Fisherman* 36, no. 8 (1955): 26; "Herring Yields Improving," *National Fisherman* 36, no. 9 (1955): 20; "Great Lakes Fishermen Making Good Perch, Herring Catches," *National Fisherman* 36, no. 10 (1955): 31; "Enjoying Profitable Fishing," *National Fisherman* 36, no. 11 (1955): 27; "Frigid Weather Cuts Production," *National Fisherman* 36, no. 12 (1956): 40–41; "Fishermen Enjoying Good Smelt Season," *National Fisherman* 39, no. 1 (1958): 27; "Great Lakes Show Improved Trout, Herring Catches," *National Fisherman* 39, no. 4 (1958): 27; "Catches of Lake Trout Show Improvement," *National Fisherman* 39, no. 7 (1958): 11; "Wisconsin Expects Good Perch Catches," *National Fisherman* 39, no. 7 (1958): 11; "Great Lakes Fishermen See Better Trout Catch," *National Fisherman* 39, no. 8 (1958): 26; "Fishermen Get Good Chub Takes," *National Fisherman* 39, no. 12 (1959): 26; Walter R. Crowe, Profile of an Industry," *Michigan Conservation* 36, no. 2 (1968): 18–22; John A. Scott, "A Historical Review of the Productivity and Regulation of Michigan's Commercial Fisheries, 1870-1970," in *Michigan Fisheries Centennial Report, 1873–1973* (Lansing, Mich: Michigan DNR, Fisheries Division, April 1974), 75–82; Norman S. Baldwin, Robert W. Saalfeld, Margaret A Ross, and Howard J. Buettner, *Commercial Fish Production in the Great Lakes 1867–1977*, Technical Report no. 3 (Ann Arbor: Great Lakes Fishery Commission, September 1979); Kuchenberg, *Reflections in a Tarnished Mirror*, 34–38. On herring, see "Great Lakes: Boat Yards Having Exceptionally Busy Season," *Atlantic Fisherman* 18, no. 9 (1937): 16; "Great Lakes Fishermen Take Delivery of Many New Fishing Vessels," *Atlantic Fisherman* 19, no. 3 (1938): 12; "Lake Herring Sets Record," *Atlantic Fisherman* 22, no. 11 (1941): 13; "Record Catch of Herring," *Atlantic Fisherman* 22, no. 12 (1942): 15; "Wisconsin Herring Fillet Production Expanding," *Atlantic Fisherman* 23, no. 11 (1942): 15; "Cousin of the Whitefish," *Michigan Conservation* 13, no. 4 (1944): 4; "Large Herring Catch," *Atlantic Fisherman* 26, no. 1 (1945): 30; "*Collier's* Features Great Lakes Herring," *Atlantic Fisherman* 26, no. 1 (1945): 30; "Preparing Herring Size Limit Bill," *Atlantic Fisherman* 26, no. 2 (1945): 28; "Size Limit Placed on Herring," *Atlantic Fisherman* 26, no. 5 (1945): 28; "Herring Run Starts," *Atlantic Fisherman* 26, no. 10 (1945): 34; "Big Cornucopia Herring Catch," *Atlantic Fisherman* 26, no. 12 (1946): 24; "Making Good Herring Catches," *Atlantic Fisherman* 27, no. 1 (1946): 29; "Herring Run Underway," *Atlantic Fisherman* 27, no. 10 (1946): 22; "Make Bigger Herring Catches," *Atlantic Fisherman* 27, no. 11 (1946): 25; "Great Lakes Herring Run Is of Record Volume," *Atlantic Fisherman* 27, no. 12 (1947): 26; "Marquette Fishermen Catching Herring," *Atlantic Fisherman* 28, no. 1 (1947): 20; "Great Lakes Herring Run Sizable Though Late," *Atlantic Fisherman* 28, no. 11 (1947): 20; "Green Bay Herring Run Fair," *Atlantic Fisherman* 28, no. 12 (1948): 51; "Great Lakes Fisherman to Open Mullet Cannery" *Atlantic Fisherman* 29, no. 6 (1948): 25; "Great Lakes Herring Run One of Best in History," *Atlantic Fisherman* 29, no. 12 (1949): 36; "Herring Harvest Expected to Be Sizable," *Atlantic Fisherman* 30, no. 11 (1949): 30; "Escanaba Herring Run Ends," *Atlantic Fisherman* 30, no. 12 (1950): 22; "Great Lakes Herring Netters Anticipate Record Hauls," *Atlantic Fisherman* 31, no. 11 (1950): 27; "Great Lakes Fishermen Make Good Herring Catches," *Atlantic Fisherman* 31, no. 12 (1951): 22; "Herring Production Shows Gain," *Atlantic Fisherman* 32, no. 1 (1951): 22; "Saginaw Bay Herring Netters Break Ice," *Atlantic Fisherman* 32, no. 11 (1951): 20; "Discuss Herring Price," *National Fisherman* 35, no. 11 (1954): 22; "Herring Attacked by Lampreys," *National Fisherman* 36, no. 1 (1955): 18; "Green Bay Herring Run Reaches Peak," *National Fisherman* 36, no. 12 (1956): 41. On minnows, see "Minnow's Return Brings Food Fish," *Atlantic Fisherman* 29, no. 9 (1948): 23.

On smelt, see Kuchenberg, *Reflections in a Tarnished Mirror*, 68–71; Gearhart, *Pity the Poor Fish*, 46, 52, 89–90, 99, 101–15, 130, 134; F.J. Bjerg, "Winter Smelt Fisheries on the Great Lakes," *The Fishing Gazette* 52, no. 13 (1935): 10, 37; "Catch of Smelt Exceeds Trout," *Atlantic Fisherman* 17, no. 7 (1936); "Smelt Market

Glutted," *Atlantic Fisherman* 18, no. 2 (1937): 20; "Wisconsin Fishermen Report Heavy Catches of Smelt," *Atlantic Fisherman* 20, no. 4 (1939): 18; "Smelt Runs Are Problem for Commercial Fishermen," *Atlantic Fisherman* 21, no. 1 (1940): 9, "Survey of Smelt Situation," *Atlantic Fisherman* 21, no. 9 (1940): 17; "Escanaba Smelt Harvest," *Atlantic Fisherman* 22 no. 3 (1941): 18; "Smelt Group Plans Large Herring Pack," *Atlantic Fisherman* 22, no. 10 (1941): 10; "Great Lakes Predict Largest Smelt Catch in History," *Atlantic Fisherman* 22, no. 12 (1942): 15; "Great Lakes Smelt Production of Interest to Government," *Atlantic Fisherman* 23, no. 3 (1942): 19; "Jamboree," *Atlantic Fisherman* 23, no. 3 (1942): 19; "Great Lakes Smelt to be Canned," *Atlantic Fisherman* 23, no. 4 (1942): 22; "A Fish Mystery," *Business Week*, 20 March 1943, 42–46; John Van Oosten, "The Great Smelt Mystery," *Michigan Conservation* 13, no. 6 (1944): 8; "Great Lakes Smelt Fishery Staging Comeback," *Atlantic Fisherman* 26, no. 3 (1945): 34; "Make Fair Smelt Catches," *Atlantic Fisherman* 26, no. 4 (1945): 38; "Smelt Runs Returning to Different Places," *Atlantic Fisherman* 26, no. 6 (1945): 28; "Smelt May be Staging a Comeback," *Atlantic Fisherman* 26, no. 11 (1945): 38; "Return of Smelt Not Unmixed Blessing," *Atlantic Fisherman* 26, no. 12 (1946): 24; "Smelt Making Comeback at Escanaba," *Atlantic Fisherman* 28, no. 1 (1947): 20; "Great Lakes Having Big Smelt Run," *Atlantic Fisherman* 28, no. 3 (1947): 26; "Smelt Numerous in Several Locations," *Atlantic Fisherman* 28, no. 4 (1947): 8; "Great Lakes Smelt Fishermen Making Large Hauls," *Atlantic Fisherman* 29, no. 4 (1948): 23; "Lake Michigan Smelt Take Shows Increase," *Atlantic Fisherman* 29, no. 6 (1948): 25; "Making Good Smelt Catches in Green Bay," *Atlantic Fisherman* 31, no. 2 (1950): 22; "Great Lakes Smelt Catches Largest in Several Years," *Atlantic Fisherman* 31, no. 5 (1950): 28; "Lake Smelt Canned as Cat Food," *Atlantic Fisherman* 31, no. 6 (1950): 21; "Fungus Causes Death to Smelt," *Atlantic Fisherman* 31, no. 7 (1950): 27; "Big Smelt Run Expected," *Atlantic Fisherman* 32, no. 3 (1951): 21; "Great Lakes Smelt Yields Best in Many Years," *Atlantic Fisherman* 32, no. 4 (1951): 30; "Contends Smelt Is Menace," *Atlantic Fisherman* 32, no. 11 (1951): 20; Ted Bentz, "Catching Great Lakes Smelt Through the Ice," *National Fisherman* 36, no. 2 (1955): 33–34; "State Buys Escanaba Smelt," *National Fisherman* 36, no. 3 (1955): 23; Bea Noye, "Smelt Run on Cold Creek," *Michigan Natural Resources* 39, no. 2 (1970): 14–17; W. C. Latta, *Michigan Fisheries Centennial Report, 1873–1973* (Lansing, Mich.: Michigan DNR, Fisheries Division, April 1974), 90–91. On sturgeon, see Kuchenberg, *Reflections in a Tarnished Mirror*, 35; Gearhart, *Pity the Poor Fish*, 113; "Sturgeon Now a Commercial Fish," *Atlantic Fisherman* 32, no. 7 (1951): 24; "Spawning Sturgeon Being Protected," *National Fisherman* 36, no. 5 (1955): 16; Horace Loftin, "Nature Ramblings," *Science News Letter* 70 (6 October 1956): 224; "The Lake Sturgeon," *Michigan Conservation* 29, no. 1 (1960): 15-16; Wayne H. Tody, "Whitefish, Sturgeon, and the Early Michigan Commercial Fishery," in *Michigan Fisheries Centennial Report, 1873–1973* (Lansing, Mich.: Michigan DNR, Fisheries Division, April 1974), 51–56; Ned E. Folgle, "Michigan's Oldest Fish," *Michigan Natural Resources* 44, no. 2 (1975): 32–33; Larry Dame, "Michigan's Legacy Fish," *Michigan Out of Doors* (February 2000): 30–33. On rough fish, see "Removing of Fish," *The Fishing Gazette* 32, no. 2 (9 January 1915); "Great Lakes: Conservation Bill Is Signed," *The Fishing Gazette* 54, no. 5 (1937): 50; "Rough Fish Fund," *Atlantic Fisherman* 22, no. 7 (1941): 18; "Big Rough Fish Hauls," *Atlantic Fisherman* 28, no. 11 (1947): 20; "Signs Lake Boundary Compact," *Atlantic Fisherman* 29, no. 2 (1948): 25; "Great Lakes to Test Chemicals on Undesired Fish," *National Fisherman* 39, no. 7 (1958): 11.

16. Prothero, *Men 'N Boats*, 168; "Booth Fisheries Closing its Green Bay Branch," 19, no. 5 (1938): 12; "Booth Fisheries Shows Profit," *Atlantic Fisherman*, 21, no. 7 (1940): 18; "Rackstraw Buys Booth Fisheries Plant," *Atlantic Fisherman* 28, no. 6 (1947): 21.

17. Jean L. Manore and John J. Van West, "'The Water and the Life': Family, Work, and Trade in the Commercial Poundnet Fisheries of Grand Bend, Ontario, 1890–1955," *Fishing Places, Fishing People: Traditions and Issues in Canadian Small-Scale Fisheries*, ed. Dianne Newell and Rosemary E. Ommer (Toronto: University of Toronto Press, 1999): 55–79.

18. On pound-net fishing, see "Lake and River Fisheries," *The Fishing Gazette* 22, no. 8 (1915): 236; Kuchenberg, *Reflections in a Tarnished Mirror*, 39; "Lake and River Fisheries," *The Fishing Gazette* 22, no. 10 (1915): 300; "New Regulations and Legislation Seek to Improve Lake Fisheries," *The Fishing Gazette* 54, no. 8 (1937): 34.

19. Ludwig Kumlien, "The Fisheries of the Great Lakes," in *The Fisheries and Fishery Industries of the United States, Section V-Vol. 1: History and Methods of the Fisheries*, comp. George Brown Goode (Washington, D.C.: Government Printing Office, 1887), 761.

20. Kumlien, "The Fisheries of the Great Lakes," 761.

21. On the history of the Mackinaw boat, see J. W. Collins, "Vessels and Boats Employed in the Fisheries of the Great Lakes," U.S. Commission of Fish and Fisheries, *Report of the Commissioner for 1887* (Washington, D.C.: Government Printing Office, 1891), 19–29; Owen S. Cecil, "The Mackinaw Boat," *Wooden Boat* 158 (February 2001): 60–69; Howard I. Chapelle, *American Small Sailing Craft: Their Design, Development, and Construction* (New York and London: W.W. Norton, 1951), 180–84; *Truscott Boat Building Co. Catalog* (St. Joseph, Mich.: Truscott Boat Building Co., 1900), 3, Michigan Maritime Museum Collection, South Haven, Michigan.

22. On steam and diesel tugs, see "She's ... In!," *The Fishing Gazette* 48, no. 13 (1931): 13; "Great Lakes Fish Tug Has Dual Engine Drive," *Atlantic Fisherman* 26, no. 9 (1945): 27; "42 ft. Steel Fishing Tug Has New Features," *Atlantic Fisherman* 26, no. 10 (1945): 40; "Gill Netter 'Sir Knight' Added to Michigan Fleet," *Atlantic Fisherman* 26, no. 12 (1946); "[advertisement for] Kermath Manufacturing Co.," *Atlantic Fisherman* 27, no. 2 (1946): 6; "Penguin Joins Milwaukee Fleet," *Atlantic Fisherman* 27, no. 5 (1946): 31; " 'Fair Lady' Has Conveyor System," *Atlantic Fisherman* 27, no. 12 (1947): 26; "*Intruder* Joins Pentwater Fleet," *Atlantic Fisherman* 29, no. 5 (1948): 18; "Two Tugs Get Radiotelephone Equipment," *Atlantic Fisherman* 29, no. 6 (1948): 25; "New Gill Netter 'Eagle II,'" *Atlantic Fisherman* 29, no. 9 (1948): 23; "Great Lakes Production Reported Fairly Good. Some Areas Show Drop," *The Fishing Gazette Annual Review* 65, no. 12 (1948): 278; "Complete New Reel Shed," *Atlantic Fisherman* 30, no. 1 (1949): 28; "Three Fish Tugs Change Hands," *Atlantic Fisherman* 30, no. 1 (1949): 28; "Fairport Tug 'M&R' Repowered," *Atlantic Fisherman* 30, no. 6 (1949): 21; "Several Port Washington Tugs Move," *Atlantic Fisherman* 29, no. 5 (1948): 18; "Good Chub Yields in Michigan," *Atlantic Fisherman* 32, no. 12 (1952): 36; "New Gill-Netting Boats Prove Highly Successful," *The Fishing Gazette* 37, no. 2 (1920): 56; "Pioneer Fishing Tug Still Leading," *The Fisherman* 1, no. 1 (1931): 9–10; "Bolinders for New Great Lakes Boat," *Atlantic Fisherman* 16, no. 2 (1935): 27; "Budas in Two New Great Lakes Boats," *Atlantic Fisherman* 16, no. 4 (1935): 27; Robert Grunst, "Degrees of Heat: The *Leona G.*" *Anchor News* 15, no. 1 (1984): 4; Robert C. Grunst, "Farsighted Designs: The Fish Tug *Johanna* and Trends in the Upper Great Lakes Fishery," *Inland Seas: The Quarterly Journal of the Great Lakes Historical Society* 53, no. 2 (1997): 97–108; "Oil Engine Makes Great Cut in Operation Costs," *The Fishing Gazette* 40, no. 2 (1923): 21; "'*H.J. Dornbos*' to be Scrapped," *Atlantic Fisherman* 27, no. 12 (1947): 26; Robert C. Grunst, "The *Swan*, the *Elk*, and the *Shark*," *Inland Seas: The Quarterly Journal of the Great Lakes Historical Society* 50, no. 1 (1994): 32–38.

    On the Kahlenberg Brothers Company, see Scottie Dayton, "Kahlenberg Brothers Built Engines for Some of the Toughest Boats in the World," *Wisconsin New Month Magazine* 41, no. 2 (1997): 4- 7; Michael Csenger, "Big Bad Blows," *Landland Boating* (August 1998): 56–58; George Wakefield, "Your Grandfather's Diesel," *Inland Seas: Quarterly Journal of the Great Lakes Historical Society* 50, no. 1 (1994): 14–16; "Kahlenberg Brothers Company, A Brief History" (Two Rivers, Wisc.: Kahlenberg Brothers, [n.d.]; Kahlenberg Brothers Company, *Kahlenberg Marine Diesel Model C Series* (Two Rivers, Wisc.: Kahlenberg Brothers, [n.d.]); Kahlenberg Brothers Company, "Smashing Through," Bulletin no. 69 (Two Rivers, Wisc.: Kahlenberg Brothers, [n.d.]); Kahlenberg Brothers Company, "Scottish Design, Canadian Built and Kahlenberg Powered," Bulletin no. 66 (Two Rivers, Wisc.: Kahlenberg Brothers, [n.d.]); Kahlenberg Brothers Company, "*Patty Nolan*: A New Kahlenberg Powered Tug," Bulletin no. 41 (Two Rivers, Wisc.: Kahlenberg Brothers, [n.d.]); Kahlenberg Brothers Company, "Motteurs Marins A Huile Lourde Kahlenberg," Prospectus no. 15 (Two Rivers, Wisc.: Kahlenberg Brothers, [n.d.]); Kahlenberg Brothers Co., "Interesting New Fish Tug *Frank Braeger* Launched," Bulletin no. 37 (Two Rivers, Wisc.: Kahlenberg Brothers, [n.d.]); Kahlenberg Brothers Company, "Kahlenberg Help Fishermen Defy Old Man Winter," Booklet no. 45 (Two

Rivers, Wisc.: Kahlenberg Brothers, [n.d.]); Kahlenberg Brothers Company, "Kahlenbergs Power Bulk of Great Lakes Winter Fishing Fleet," Bulletin no. 51 (Two Rivers, Wisc.: Kahlenberg Brothers, [n.d.]); Kahlenberg Brothers Company, "Two New and Modern Boats," Bulletin no. 63 (Two Rivers, Wisc.: Kahlenberg Brothers, [n.d.]); Kahlenberg Brothers Company, "A Low Repair Cost Operating Record," Bulletin no. 58 (Two Rivers, Wisc.: Kahlenberg Brothers, [n.d.]); Kahlenberg Brothers Company, "*Bossler Brothers* New Fishing Boat Recently Launched," Bulletin no. 72 (Two Rivers, Wisc.: Kahlenberg Brothers, [n.d.]); Kahlenberg Brothers Company, "New Great Lakes Fish Tug Now in Service," Bulletin no. 56 (Two Rivers, Wisc.: Kahlenberg Brothers, [n.d.]). On setting nets from the air, see "To Use Airplane in Fishing Operations," *Atlantic Fisherman* 29, no. 5 (1948): 18.

For more on the personal experience of working on fish tugs in the early-twentieth century, see Charles R. Hoskins and George P. Wakefield, "A Great Lakes Fisherman," *Inland Seas: The Quarterly Journal of the Great Lakes Historical Society* 35, no. 4 (1979): 250–57; [part II] 36, no. 1 (1980): 22–28; [part III] 36, no. 2 (1980): 103–10; George P. Wakefield, "A Real Live Steamer: A Fish Tug's Engine Room," *Inland Seas: Quarterly Journal of the Great Lakes Historical Society* 48, no. 1 (1992), 41–48; George P. Wakefield, "Fish Tug Engineer," *Inland Seas: Quarterly Journal of the Great Lakes Historical Society* 50, no. 2 (1994), 97–103. For more on the broader economic/environmental context of fish tug use, see Bogue, *Fishing the Great Lakes*, 44–58, 253–78; Prothero, *Men 'N Boats*, 143–44. For more on shipyards that specialized in fish tugs, see *Peterson Builders: Fifty Years of Shipbuilding Excellence, 1933–1983* (Sturgeon Bay, Wisc.: Peterson Builders, 1983).

23. On chub fishing, see Kuchenberg, *Reflections in a Tarnished Mirror*, 146; B.A. Griffen, "Great Lakes Activities," *The Fishing Gazette* 54, no. 10 (1937): 100; "Wisconsin: Ruling May Put End to Chub Fishing," *Atlantic Fisherman* 19, no. 5 (1938): 12; "Wisconsin Reaffirms Old Chub Net Mesh Ruling," *Atlantic Fisherman* 20, no. 9 (1939): 17; "Lake Michigan Chub Take Shows Increase," *Atlantic Fisherman* 30, no. 11 (1949): 30; "Seek More Liberal Chub Regulations," *National Fisherman* 36, no. 4 (1955): 29; "Adson Casey, Commercial Fisherman," *Michigan Conservation* 24, no. 4 (1955): 15–18; "May Allow Deeper Gill Nets for Chubs," *National Fisherman* 36, no. 9 (1955): 20; "Chub Fishing Good," *National Fisherman* 39, no. 3 (1958): 29; W.F. Carbine, "One Answer for a Fishery," *Michigan Conservation* 29, no. 4 (1960): 25–27. On carp fishing in Wisconsin, see Stiller, *A Multitude of Fishes*; "Lake and River Fisheries," *The Fishing Gazette* 36, no. 3 (1919): 72; "Want Permit to Fish Carp," *Atlantic Fisherman* 19, no. 3 (1938): 12; "Carp Fishing Granted," *Atlantic Fisherman* 19, no. 4 (1938): 12; "Wisconsin Finds New Market for Carp," *Atlantic Fisherman* 20, no. 5 (1939): 11; "Carp Comes Into Its Own in Wisconsin," *Atlantic Fisherman* 21, no. 5 (1940): 19; "Claim Commercial Fishermen Dump Fish," *Atlantic Fisherman* 21, no. 12 (1941): 17; "Wisconsin Carp Haul Over 11,000,000 lbs.," *Atlantic Fisherman* 22, no. 12 (1942): 15; "Carp for Human Consumption," *Atlantic Fisherman* 26, no. 2 (1945): 28.

24. "New Trap Netters for Brown Fisheries," *Atlantic Fisherman* 29, no. 4 (1948): 23; "Changes in the Fleet," *Atlantic Fisherman* 29, no. 7 (1948): 18; "Trap Boats Launched," *Atlantic Fisherman* 30, no. 8 (1949): 23; "Brown Establishes Grand Haven Branch," *Atlantic Fisherman* 32, no. 12 (1952): 36; Kuchenberg, *Reflections in a Tarnished Mirror*, 33. On the replacement of a gill-net tug by a trap-net boat, see "Has Narrow Escape," *Atlantic Fisherman* 31, no. 7 (1950): 27.

25. "Michigan Moves One Step Closer to Ban on Gill Nets," *The Fisherman* 25, no. 2 (1973): 1; "Michigan Rules for 1974 Undergoing Additional Changes," *The Fisherman* 26 (January 1974): 1,4; "Officials of Michigan DNR and Attorney General's Office Working on Plan to Compensate Fishermen," *The Fisherman* 28, no. 1 (1976): 5; "Michigan DNR Commission Approves Plan to Ban Use of Small Meshed Gill Nets in Lake Michigan," *The Fisherman* 28, no. 4 (1976): 15; "Fishermen Oppose Gill Net Rule," *The Fisherman* 29, no. 8 (1977): 8; John Carr, "A Positive Analysis of a Negative Report," *The Fisherman* 30, no. 1 (1978); Prothero, *Men 'N Boats*, 93, 133–34.

26. On conflict between commercial fishermen and promoters of tourism, see "Bays de Noc to Remain Open,"

Atlantic Fisherman 30, no. 12 (1950): 22; "Against Reefing of Gill Nets," *Atlantic Fisherman* 31, no. 4 (1950): 24.

27. "Lake and River Fisheries," *The Fishing Gazette* 22, no. 6 (1915): 172; "Lake and River Fisheries," *The Fishing Gazette* 22, no. 11 (1915): 332; "Lake and River Fisheries," *The Fishing Gazette* 22, no. 15 (1915): 460; David Le Clair, "Right or Might in the Fishing Industry?" *The Fishing Gazette* 38, no. 9 (1921): 49–51. On criticism of LeClair's proposal, see "Lake and River Fisheries," *The Fishing Gazette* 22, no. 17 (1915): 517. Fishermen such as J.S. Gagnon of Racine, Wisconsin, who were convinced that fishing would improve if each of the states bordering Lake Michigan enacted uniform closed season laws, supported LeClair. See "Lake and River Fisheries," *The Fishing Gazette* 22, no. 9 (1915): 268.

28. "Wisconsin Advisory Board Formed," *The Fishing Gazette* 54, no. 11 (1937): 36; David LeClair, "Facts Concerning the History of the Fishing Industry in Two Rivers, Wisconsin" (Two Rivers, Wisc.: David LeClair, 1945). On fishing during spawning season, see "Commercial Fish Material: Spawn Taking Records—Lake Trout and Whitefish, 1927–1930," State Archives of Michigan, Michigan Historical Center, Lansing, Michigan, 75–34, Box 14, File 1; Bogue, *Fishing the Great Lakes*, 93, 152, 176–77; "Why the Extra Eight Days," *The Fisherman* 1, no. 1 (1931): 6; "The Fisherman Is Different," *Michigan Conservation* 5, no. 1 (1935): 2; "Spawn Fishing of Past Judged Economically Unsound and Wasteful; Authorities in Favor of Closed Seasons," *Michigan Conservation* 6, no. 3 (1936): 6; "Great Lakes: Fishermen to Meet to Write New Rules for Industry," *Atlantic Fisherman* 18, no. 9 (1937): 14; "Wisconsin Fishermen to Meet," *The Fishing Gazette* 54, no. 12 (1937): 23; "Great Lakes: Record Catches Reported," *The Fishing Gazette* 54, no. 13 (1937): 40; "Name Advisory Committee," *Atlantic Fisherman* 19, no. 6 (1938): 16; "Wisconsin Fishermen Ask Changes in the State Fishing Laws," *Atlantic Fisherman* 20, no. 2 (1939): 11; "New Fishermen's Committee Set Up," *Atlantic Fisherman* 20, no. 2 (1939): 14; " Want Commercial Fisherman for Commission," *Atlantic Fisherman* 20, no. 8 (1939): 12; "Retired Peninsula Fisherman Dies, " *Atlantic Fisherman* 21, no. 9 (1940): 17; "Views of Wisconsin Fishermen," *Atlantic Fisherman* 22, no. 9 (1941): 16; "Favor Longer Closed Seasons," *Atlantic Fisherman* 27, no. 9 (1946): 22; "Seek Action on Pollution," *Atlantic Fisherman* 28, no. 3 (1947): 26; "Committee Named to Advise on Fisheries Laws," *Atlantic Fisherman* 32, no. 9 (1951): 48. Michigan stopped granting permits to fish during spawning season to collect eggs for the hatcheries in 1933 despite the protests of commercial fishing interests and fishermen were required to take and save all eggs from spawning fish even before the closed season. See Michigan Department of Conservation, Office of Information and Education, *1921–1946: Twenty-Five Years of Conservation in Michigan* (Lansing, Mich.: Michigan Department of Conservation, Office of Information and Education, 1960), 14.

29. Commercial fisherman George Clark was a member of Michigan's first fishery commission. *See: Michigan Fisheries Centennial Report, 1873–1973*, (Lansing, Mich.: Michigan DNR, Fisheries Division, April 1974), 9.

30. Everett LaFond, "Practical Conservation," *The Fishing Gazette* 54, no. 3 (1937): 9, 38; "The Great Lakes: Regulation Advocated by Commercial Men," *The Fishing Gazette* 54, no. 4 (1937): 35; "The Great Lakes Fisheries: Fisheries Bill Delay Reported," *The Fishing Gazette* 54, no. 6 (1937): 30; "Wisconsin Fishermen Re-elected," *Atlantic Fisherman* 22, no. 3 (1941): 18; "Seek Change in Fisheries Control," *Atlantic Fisherman* 28, no. 4 (1947): 28. On elected officials who represented commercial fishing interests, *see*: "Great Lakes: Proposed Changes in Fishing Laws Outlined," *Atlantic Fisherman* 18, no. 2 (1937): 20; "Wisconsin Fishermen Want Different Supervision of Fisheries," *Atlantic Fisherman* 22, no. 1 (1941): 9; "Wisconsin Fishermen Appeal to Governor," *Atlantic Fisherman* 22, no. 1 (1941): 9; "Seek Conference on Great Lakes Fishing," *Atlantic Fisherman* 26, no. 3 (1945): 34; "Mackinac Breakwater," *Atlantic Fisherman* 26, no. 5 (1945): 28; "Control of Outlying Waters," *Atlantic Fisherman* 30, no. 3 (1949): 25; "Net Bill Veto Arouses Fisherman," *Atlantic Fisherman* 30, no. 8 (1949): 23; "Asks Planting of Walleyes," *National Fisherman* 35, no. 5 (1954): 32. On the Wisconsin Commercial Fishermen's Association, see "Wisconsin Fishermen Seek New Open Seasons," *Atlantic Fisherman* 16, no. 8 (1935): 22; "Wisconsin Fishermen Reorganize," *The Fishing Gazette* 55, no. 2 (1938): 26; "Wisconsin Fishermen Hold Meeting," *The Fishing Gazette* 55, no. 7 (1938): 30; "Wisconsin Fishermen Re-elect all Officers," *The Fishing Gazette* 57, no. 1 (1940): 40.

31. "Wisconsin Fishermen Organize," *Atlantic Fisherman* 16, no. 12 (1936); "Wisconsin Fishermen Protest Shortening of Closed Season," *Atlantic Fisherman* 17, no. 10 (1936): 13; "Wisconsin Fishermen Hold Annual Meeting," *Atlantic Fisherman* 17, no. 12 (1937): 14; "Wisconsin Fishermen Organize," *Atlantic Fisherman* 19, no. 2 (1938): 14; "Wisconsin: Green Bay Fishermen Form Protective Union," *Atlantic Fisherman* 19, no. 6 (1938): 16; "Wisconsin Conservation Association Favors Larger Size Mesh Nets," *Atlantic Fisherman* 20, no. 10 (1939): 8; "Favor Fishing During Closed Season," *Atlantic Fisherman* 28, no. 5 (1947): 18; Ernest Swift, Madison, Wisconsin, to David LeClair, Two Rivers, Wisconsin, 4 November 1947; "Producers Ask Changes in Regulation," *Atlantic Fisherman* 29, no. 9 (1948): 23; "Fishermen Seek Changes in Laws," *Atlantic Fisherman* 31, no. 5 (1950): 28. On the Michigan Fish Producers Association, see "Michigan Fishermen's Association Council Is Organized," *Atlantic Fisherman* 21, no. 9 (1940): 17; "Great Lake Fisheries Work on Problems" *The Fishing Gazette* 62, no. 6 (1945): 114; "Fish Producers Oppose International Commission," *Atlantic Fisherman* 26, no. 11 (1945): 38; "Favor Reduction in Net Size," *Atlantic Fisherman* 27, no. 11 (1946): 25; "Producers Association Reorganized," *Atlantic Fisherman* 28, no. 1 (1947): 20; "Two Producers Organizations Affiliate," *Atlantic Fisherman* 28, no. 3 (1947): 26; "Consider Closer Inspection of Food Fish," *Atlantic Fisherman* 29, no. 2 (1948): 25; "Ask Ban on Commercial Walleye Trolling," *Atlantic Fisherman* 29, no. 8 (1948): 28; "Trout Catch Less Due to Lampreys," *Atlantic Fisherman* 30, no. 1 (1949): 28; "Legislative Program of Producers Association," *Atlantic Fisherman* 30, no. 3 (1949): 25; "Want Life Saving Equipment," *Atlantic Fisherman* 31, no. 5 (1950): 28; "Fish Producers Hold Annual Convention," *Atlantic Fisherman* 32, no. 2 (1951): 17; "Fish Producers Association Meet," *National Fisherman* 35, no. 9 (1954): 18; John Swartley, "Battle Lines Drawn Here for Gill Net Debate," *Petoskey News Review*, 9 August 1973; "Fish Boycott to Stay Over Ban on Gill Nets," *Petoskey News Review*, 23 August 1973; John Swartley, " First it Was Beef, Now Fish Short on Menus," *Petoskey News Review*, 28 August 1973; "Phony Blackmail Charged by DNR in Fish Boycott," *North Woods Call*, 29 August 1973; "Michigan Task Force Studies Needs of Rural Areas and Small Communities," *The Fisherman* 34, no. 3 (1982): 3, 8, 17. On the West Michigan Commercial Fishermen's Association, see "Lower Michigan Fishermen Draft Law Program," *Atlantic Fisherman* 18 no. 1 (1937): 13. On the Wisconsin Fish Producers Association, *see* "Wisconsin Fish Producers Hold Convention," *Atlantic Fisherman* 28, no. 10 (1947): 33; "Wisconsin Producers Ask Law Changes," *Atlantic Fisherman* 30, no. 4 (1949): 19; "Wisconsin Fish Producers Hold Elections," *Atlantic Fisherman* 31, no. 9 (1950): 21; "McDonald Heads Wisconsin Producers Association," *Atlantic Fisherman* 32, no. 3 (1951): 21. See also "Association Seeks Smaller Mesh Size," *Atlantic Fisherman* 28, no. 1 (1947): 20; "Straits Commercial Fish Association Formed," *Atlantic Fisherman* 28, no. 4 (1947): 28; "Wisconsin Fishermen Form Association," *Atlantic Fisherman* 28, no. 9 (1947): 14; "Fisheries Association Elects Officers," *Atlantic Fisherman* 29, no. 1 (1948): 22; "Two Fishermen's Associations Hold Meeting," *Atlantic Fisherman* 29, no. 7 (1948): 18; "Greater Fish Hatching Activity Favored," *Atlantic Fisherman* 29, no. 10 (1948): 23; "Want Restrictions on Walleye Fishing," *Atlantic Fisherman* 31, no 11 (1950): 27; "Seek Net-Free Trolling Areas," *Atlantic Fisherman* 31, no 12 (1951): 22; "Great Lakes Producers See Need for More Hatcheries," *National Fisherman* 36, no. 12 (1956): 40.

32. "Great Lakes Have New Fishermen's Association," *Atlantic Fisherman* 21, no. 1 (1940): 9.

33. On commercial fishing support for federal regulation and the Great Lakes Fisheries Commission, see Bogue, *Fishing the Great Lakes*, 105; "Lake and River Fisheries," *The Fishing Gazette* 36, no. 13 (1919): 292; "Fish Hearings Planned," *Atlantic Fisherman* 26, no. 1 (1945): 30; "Great Lakes Fishermen Confer With Congressional Group," *Atlantic Fisherman* 26, no. 2 (1945): 28; "Fishery Commission Elects Chairman," *National Fisherman* 39, no. 12 (1959): 26.

34. On Claude Ver Duin, see Kuchenberg, *Reflections in a Tarnished Mirror*, 145–47; "Former Grand Haven Mayor Dies at 82," *Grand Haven Tribune*, 9 November 1990; and Robert Ver Duin, "A Tribute to Claude Ver Duin," *The Fisherman* [1990] p. 3, 10; Ray Voss, "State Adopts Strict Commercial Fishing Rules," *Grand*

Rapids Press, 8 November 1969; Clarence Poel, Claude Ver Duin Spokesman for Fisherman 50 Years," *Grand Haven Tribune*, 6 March 1981; Clarence Poel, "Ver Duins Promote Fresh Water Great Lakes Fish," *Grand Haven Tribune*, 29 March 1988. Ver Duin also served on the Marine Fishery Advisory Committee. See Elliot L. Richardson to Claude Ver Duin, 14 October 1976, from the Claude Ver Duin papers in the possession of William Ver Duin, Grand Haven, Michigan; "Grand Haven Man Appointed to Top Level Fisheries Committee," *Grand Haven Tribune*, 30 October 1976.

35. "Editorial Comment: Our Own Magazine," *The Fisherman* 1, no. 1 (1931): 7; Claude Ver Duin, "Gill Nets Not 'Killers,' Fisheries Council Official Says," *The Fisherman* 25, no. 1 (1972): 7; Robert Ver Duin, "Condemned Gill Net Pleads 'Not Guilty,'" *The Fisherman* 26, no. 1 (1974): 1; also Robert Ver Duin, "I am a Gill Net," *The Fisherman* 27, no. 2 (1975): 1; "Michigan Task Force Studies Needs of Rural Areas and Small Communities," *The Fisherman* 34, no. 2 (1982): 5, 10.

36. "Lake and River Fisheries," *The Fishing Gazette* 32, no. 18 (1915): 582.

37. On the efforts of the Michigan Fish Producers Association to assist commercial fishermen, see Bill Scarbrough, "From Your Secretary-Treasurer," *Commercial Fisheries News* (January 1986). On Wisconsin efforts to aid fishermen, see "Wisconsin Fishermen Hold Huge Annual Convention," *The Fishing Gazette* 46, no. 7 (1929): 43; "Conservation Laws Discussed," *Atlantic Fisherman* 27, no. 6 (1946): 27.

38. Fishermen rejected the claims that they were primarily responsible for the demise of fishery. See Prothero, *Men 'N Boats*, 164–66; "Plan to Outlaw Gill Nets Brings Tempered Rebuttal," *Charlevoix Courier*, 6 September 1967; "Commercial Fishermen Leery of New State Plan," *Charlevoix Courier*, 13 December 1967; "Letters: Whitefish Take," 26 January 1970, Garden Peninsula Historical Society (GPHS) scrapbook; "Fishing Policies," *Escanaba Daily Press*, 6 April 1970; "Fishermen Protest DNR's New Controls at Hearing," 28 October 1970, GPHS scrapbook; "Governor Asked to Help Save State's Fishing Industry," 11 November 1970, GPHS scrapbook; "DNR Commission to Hear Fishermen," 12 April 1971, GPHS scrapbook; "State's Commercial Fishermen Are Threatened by DNR Fishery Controls," *Northland Press*, 26 July 1973; "Net Ban Phase Mistake," 12 April 1974, GPHS scrapbook. Martin Glass, "Commercial Fisherman Loses License for not Fishing Enough," *National Enquirer*,[n.d., 1973], GPHS scrapbook). See also Bogue, *Fishing the Great Lakes*, 3; Gearhart, *Pity the Poor Fish*, 204; Martin, "The Last Days of the Fishing Business," 191–211; Kuchenberg, *Reflections in a Tarnished Mirror*, 18, 205.

39. On commercial and sport fishing see Prothero, *Men 'N Boats*, 162–63; "Activities on the Great Lakes," *The Fishing Gazette* 53, no. 4 (1936): 27; "Fishermen Vindicated," *Atlantic Fisherman* 23, no. 4 (1942): 22; "Delta County Walleye Group Meets," *Atlantic Fisherman* 32, no. 9 (1951): 49; "Want Limit on Number of Nets per Fishing Tug," *National Fisherman* 36, no. 9 (1955): 20; "Sportsmen Support State's Fish Plan," 24 February 1971, GPHS scrapbook; Paul L. Dorweiler, *Great Lakes Trout and Salmon Fishing* (Coon Rapids, Minn.: Paul Lawrence and Associates, 1982); Gearhart, *Pity the Poor Fish*, 148; Martin, "The Last Days of the Fishing Business," 204; "Commercial Fishermen vs. Sport Fishermen," *Atlantic Fisherman* 20, no. 10 (1939): 8; "Marking of Nets Recommended," *Atlantic Fisherman* 29, no. 7 (1948): 18; "Seek Commercial Ban on Brown Trout," *National Fisherman* 36, no. 8 (1955): 26; Bob Gwizdz, "Group Trying to Limit Commercial Fishing," *Kalamazoo Gazette*, 7 October 2000.

40. Gearhart, *Pity the Poor Fish*, 71; "Ryan Says He Will Advocate Compensation for Fishermen," 6 August 1974, GPHS scrapbook; "DNR Restrictions put Fishermen in Line for Payment," 5 October 1970, GPHS scrapbook; "Ruppe Testifies for U.S. Funds for Fishermen," [n.d.] GPHS scrapbook.

41. "'Just Leave us Alone!' The Garden Peninsula vs. the State of Michigan," *The Magazine of the Detroit News*, 17 October 1981, GPHS scrapbook. On earlier friction between commercial fishermen and the state, see Gearhart, *Pity the Poor Fish*, 112–15, 175; "Great Lakes Fishermen Protest Net Seizures," *Atlantic Fisherman* 27, no. 1 (1946): 29; "Nine Face Charges in Fishing Incident"[unidentified newspaper clipping] [n.d], 1970, GPHS scrapbook; "Jensen Assures Cooperation" [unidentified newspaper clipping], 1 May 1976, GPHS scrapbook; "DNR Shooting on Garden," 6 May 1976, GPHS scrapbook; "The Folks of Michigan's Garden

Peninsula Don't Think Themselves as Renegades..." [unidentified newspaper clipping] [n.d] 1982, GPHS scrapbook. On Michigan DNR hostility to commercial fishing see Kuchenberg, *Reflections in a Tarnished Mirror*, 102–3, 202–7 and Prothero, *Men 'N Boats*, 164–66.

42. "Fishing for Everyone, DNR Aim, Says Long" [unidentified newspaper clipping], 11 September 1973, GPHS scrapbook.

43. Paul Thompson with Tony Wailey and Trevor Lummis, *Living the Fishing* (London: Routledge & Kegan Paul, 1983).

44. Prothero, *Men 'N Boats*, 82.

45. On Joseph LeClair (father of Daniel Peter), see "State's Right to Inspect Tugs Upheld," *Atlantic Fisherman* 29, no. 3 (1948): 20.

46. On the Weborg family, see "The News in Review," *The Fisherman* 29, no. 2 (1977): 6; "Hearing Examiner Rules in Favor of Wisconsin Fisherman," *The Fisherman* 33, no. 3 (1981): 15; "Judge Rules that Fishing Vessels Are Subject to Property Tax," *The Fisherman* 33, no. 9 (1981): 6; Prothero, *Men 'N Boats*, 79.

47. On the Carlson family, see Rita Hadra Rusco, *North Manitou Island Between Sunrise and Sunset* (n.l., 1991), 61–69; Prothero, *Men'N Boats*, 89; "Fishermen Preparing for Fall Run," *Atlantic Fisherman* 28, no. 7 (1947): 26; "Great Lakes Fishermen Begin Open Water Operations," *Atlantic Fisherman* 29, no. 3 (1948): 20; Tom Fox, "Fisherman's Life Fading on the Lake's," *Detroit Free Press* [1973], from the Michigan Department of Natural Resources Charlevoix Research Station scrapbooks [hereafter, CRSS]; Grand Traverse Area Sportsfishing Association, "The Treaty of 1836 and the Fishing Case," 17 February 1976, CRSS; Suzy Averill, "Leelanau's Dying Industry," *The Weekender*, 30 April 1970; Marsha Robinson, "Commercial Fishermen Struggle On," *Petoskey News Review*, 9 April 1975; Tom Dammann, "Big Lake Fishing Permit Lottery 'More a Funeral,'" *Grand Rapids Press*, 20 April 1975; Bob Campbell, "Tainted Catch," *Detroit Free Press*, 24 August 1986.

48. On the late Ross Lang, see Amy Hubbell, "Pioneer Leland Fisherman Fondly Remembered," *The Leelanau Enterprise*, 30 April 1998 and Dennis Knickerbocker, "Tangled Issues: Tribes Improve Relations by Switching to Trap Nets," *Lansing State Journal*, 24 October 1989; Prothero, *Men 'N Boats*, 89.

49. On Don Bell, see Gearhart, *Pity the Poor Fish*, 143–52; Prothero, *Men 'N Boats*, 170.

50. "Hold Up Zone Plan, Fishermen Ask DNR" [unidentified newspaper clipping], 17 January 1970, GPHS scrapbook.

51. "Successful Fish Market Built on Simple Policy," *The Fisherman* 30, no. 5 (1978): 5, 12; "Historic Fishery Building to Serve as Museum Annex," *The Ship's Lamp: Newsletter of the Michigan Maritime Museum* 17, no. 4 (1999): 7.

52. "Alewife Decrease Feared by Many," *Milwaukee Sentinel*, 23 May 1984

53. "National Fisheries Institute Asks for Change in the Compensation Act," *The Fisherman* 29, no. 8 (1977); "Relocated Fish Company Provides Boat Service for Tourists," *The Fisherman* 15, no. 8 (1947): 6; "Great Lake Reports," *Atlantic Fisherman* 14, no. 2 (1933): 13; "Move to Lake Huron," *Atlantic Fisherman* 20, no. 9 (1939): 17; Mike Ready, "Living Off the Lake," *Northland Press*, 22 June 1972; Mike Ready, "Fishermen Being Forced to Switch or Quit; DNR Fears Lake Michigan is Being Fished Out," *Charlevoix County Press*, 30 January 1975; Tom Dammann, "Big Lake Fishing Permit Lottery 'More a Funeral,'" *Grand Rapids Press*, 20 April 1975.

54. "Sorry No Fish Today," [Placard produced by John and Bonnie Stelmaszek] GPHS scrapbook.

55. On Terry Buckler, see Gordon Charles, "New Netting Methods Prove 'Spectacular,'" *Traverse City Record Eagle*, 19 June 1977; Prothero, *Men 'N Boats*, 89.

56. "Great Lakes: Spring Activities Reported," *The Fishing Gazette* 55, no. 4 (1938): 36.

57. Gordon Charles, "New Netting Methods Prove 'Spectacular,'" *Traverse City Record Eagle*, 19 June 1977; Mary Paden, "Purse Seining in Lake Michigan," *Michigan Out-of-Doors* 31, no. 9 (1977): 42–43, 78, 80.

58. Thomas M. Kelly, *Purse Seining on the Great Lakes: Catches, Effort, and Problems* (Ann Arbor: Michigan Sea Grant Publications Office, September 1979); Michigan Sea Grant, *The Michigan Purse Seining Demonstration Project* (Ann Arbor, Mich.: Michigan Sea Grant MICHU-SG-78–103); Thomas M. Kelly, *Purse Seining on the*

Great Lakes: Vessels, Gear, and Operation (Ann Arbor: Michigan Sea Grant Program Publications Office, January 1979).

59. Claude Ver Duin, "Comments and Observation," *The Fisherman* 28, no. 7 (1976): 2.

60. "*H. J. Dornbos* Damaged by Fire," *Atlantic Fisherman* 30, no. 4 (1949): 19.

61. Gordon Charles, "New Netting Methods Prove 'Spectacular,'" *Traverse City Record Eagle*, 19 June 1977.

62. "*Jackie C.* a Modern Gill Netter," *Atlantic Fisherman* 18, no. 2 (1937): 20.

63. Kuchenberg, *Reflections in a Tarnished Mirror*, 27; "Inland Lake Trawling," *National Fisherman* 39, no. 1 (1958): 28; Prothero, *Men 'N Boats*, 134–35.

64. Tom Dammann, "Big Lake Fishing Permit Lottery 'More a Funeral,'" *Grand Rapids Press*, 20 April 1975.

65. Gordon Charles, "Astroturf Helps to Develop Lake Trout," *Traverse City Record Eagle*, 23 November 1997.

66. "More Fishermen Paid off in Michigan," *The Fisherman* 28, no. 8 (1976): 5. On the Buckler family fishing operation, see "In the Mail Bag," *The Fisherman* 1, no. 3 (1932): 5; "The News in Review," *The Fisherman*, 16, no. 2 (1948): 12.

67. "Michigan Begins Compensating Gill Net Fishermen," *The Fisherman* 28, no. 5 (1976): 3; "Michigan Pays Herring Fisherman to Give up Gillnets," *The Fisherman* 31, no. 8 (1979): 18.

68. Joel Peterson has a copy of a January 1986 *Commercial Fisheries News* containing a letter from then-director of the Michigan Department of Natural Resources, Ronald O. Skoog, assuring fishermen that the state intended to assist them through their economic transition. See Ronald O. Skoog, "The Commercial Fisherman's Life Seems Destined to be One of Uncertainty," *Commercial Fisheries News*, no. 8 (January 1986): unpaged, copy in possession of Joel Peterson.

69. Roy A. Jensen, "Unknown Gunman Fires on Fisheries Patrol Boat as it Prepares to Lift Gill Nets Set in Restricted Area," *The Fisherman* 28, no. 5 (1976): 9.

70. An increase in pesticide levels was detected by the Michigan DNR in the spring of 1979. See "Chub Fishery Hampered by Presence of Dieldrin," *The Fisherman* 31, no. 8 (1979): 18.

71. On the state's buyout of Michigan fishermen, see "Michigan begins Compensating Gill Net Fishermen," *The Fisherman* 28, no. 5 1976): 3–4; and "More Fishermen Paid Off in Michigan," *The Fisherman* 28, no. 8,9 (1976): 5, 5

72. "New Patrol Boat for Fish Commission in Michigan," *The Fishing Gazette* 46, no. 10 (1929): 63; "Michigan Patrol Boat Covers Wide Area," *Atlantic Fisherman* 27, no. 6 (1946): 27.

73. "Fishermen, Officers Clash at Fairport" [unidentified newspaper clipping], 1 April 1970, GPHS scrapbook; "Five Plead Innocent to Fairport Counts," 7 April 1970, GPHS scrapbook; "Charges Dismissed Against Fishermen" [unidentified newspaper clipping], 13 May 1970, GPHS scrapbook; "DNR Clashes with Fishermen, Three Garden Area men Arrested" [unidentified newspaper clipping], 17 April 1975, GPHS scrapbook.

74. "Great Lakes Fishermen Come to Blows," *Atlantic Fisherman* 21, no. 12 (1941): 17.

75. Compare retired game warden Jim Chizek's account of the incident. See Jim Chizek, *Protectors of the Outdoors: True Stories from the Frontline of Conservation Enforcement* (Lodi, Wisc.: Flambeau River Publishing-White Leopard Press, 1999), 67–78.

76. "Chub Assessment Program for Lake Michigan Increased by Wisconsin DNR," *The Fisherman* 29, no. 3 (1979): 9

77. "Fishermen Awarded Prizes for Cooperating in Tag, Release and Recovery Research," *The Fisherman* 34, no. 2 (1982): 3.

78. For an account of the dispute between the Weborgs and the Wisconsin DNR, see "Hearing Examiner Rules in Favor of Wisconsin Fisherman," *The Fisherman* 33, no. 3 (1981): 15 and "Judge Rules that Fishing Vessels Are Subject to Tax Property," *The Fisherman* 33, no. 9 (1981): 6.

79. According to published reports, this event actually occurred in 1975. See: "Scenes and Comments on Wisconsin's Commercial Fisheries, scheduled for Nov. 21 *Today Show*," *The Fisherman*, 27, no. 7 (1975): 10.

80. Other fishermen such as Francis Martin formed partnerships with Native Americans. See Martin, "The Last Days of the Fishing Business," 209–10; Mark E. Dixon, "Indian Netters Reap Large Trout Catch at Charlevoix," *Petoskey News Review*, 10 August 1977; Mike Ready, "Gill Netting to Double in Grand Traverse Bay," *Traverse City Record Eagle*, 26 July 1979.

81. "Michigan Supreme Court Rules in Favor of Indians in Commercial Fishing Dispute," *The Fisherman* 29, no. 1 (1977): 5; "Settlement of Indian Fishing Controversy is Costly for Non-Indian Fishermen," *The Fisherman* 35 (1985): 3, 17.

3

Sport-Fishing Claims

A Cultivated Lake and Its Recreational Bounty

L
AKE MICHIGAN'S SPORT FISHERIES—noteworthy for the recent popularity of the region's salmon sport fishery—owe their historical development to American society's cultural desire to use natural resources in a manner that is distinctly recreational or leisure-oriented.[1] This legacy dates to America's industrial and urban transformation in the mid-nineteenth century. During this time, Americans began to partially shift their worldview away from dominating nature to seeing it as a source of meditation, spiritual renewal, physical rejuvenation, character development and, most tellingly, an experience that was the bedrock of the nation's consciousness. In a longstanding tradition that is both cultural and ecological, the recreational use of natural resources such as fish became, and continues to be, a qualitative benchmark of the "good life" in American society.[2] Informed by this tradition, the oral histories that follow have a mythic quality that links this sentiment to the modern origins of Lake Michigan's sport fishing community. Most of these informants personally witnessed the sweeping transformations that sport fishing and its management policies brought to the use of the lake's fish and its shoreline—an experience that only reinforces the mythic tone of their narratives. By the close of the twentieth century, sport fishers could cast their eyes over the resource with self-assurance; Lake Michigan's fish were their cultural patrimony and fishing the lake's waters a ritual that regionally authenticated a pastime deeply engrained in the American national character.[3]

The cultural antecedents that gave rise to sport fishing's popularity in the nineteenth century, and its striking ascendancy throughout the twentieth century, are an instructive lesson in how a democratized, mass-consumed leisure activity expressed society's changing relationships with nature or the environment. The efforts of antebellum Americans to more concertedly promote English sport fishing traditions reflected their desire to uniquely define national heritage without preempting the recent memory of the nation's founders or possibly violating an egalitarian ethos that, in ideal terms, would celebrate the commonweal and not individual personalities.[4] Mid-nineteenth-century America countered these vexing dilemmas by finding unanimity around an ostensibly inclusive, and nationally distinct, historical touchstone: the influence of the American natural environment.[5] Henry David Thoreau and Ralph Waldo Emerson provided a classical voice for these sentiments while, on a broader cultural plain, a popular fascination with the continent's natural environments increasingly contributed to a historical sense of place.

Amidst these cultural sentiments, it was not long before the "fish story" became a well-established genre of American folk and popular culture, and sport or leisure fishing the subject matter of a broad spectrum of American writing. Mark Twain, Ernest Hemingway, and Zane Grey are among the most conspicuous founders of this writing tradition, but they were accompanied by a seemingly endless list of authors who used sport fishing in popular novels, prescriptive/self-improvement anthologies, travel writing, and numerous serial publications. While Hemingway is frequently noted for his connections to fishing in northern Michigan, over the past century numerous writers—such as Robert Traver, Ben East, Jim Harrison, Jerry Dennis, Jan Zita Grover, Kathleen Stocking, and David N. Cassuto—have claimed Great Lakes sport fishing as a source of inspiration and cultural commentary.[6] Along with writers, well-known visual artists such as Winslow Homer and Thomas Eakins further legitimated the cultural standing of fishing and outdoor life in American society by making these activities a focus of their work.[7] Historically, a tradition of visual artists has complemented the cultural and ecological temperament of Great Lakes sport fishing. These works have ranged from the late-nineteenth/early-twentieth-century documentary photography of George Shiras III to the contemporary etchings of Ladislav Hanka.[8]

While a cadre of America's native-born elites were preoccupied with articulating a national identity shaped by the country's natural resources, an equally zealous

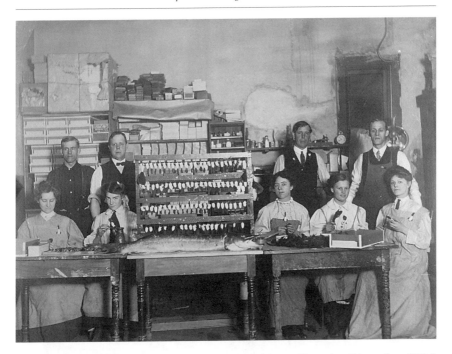

W. J. Jamison Company, c. 1910. Women produced fishing tackle at the Chicago-based W. J. Jamison Company. While such companies promoted their products by emphasizing the region's sport fishing opportunities, most Midwest tackle companies did not produce gear specially for use in the Great Lakes until after salmon stocking began in the late 1960s. Courtesy of William Cullerton, Jr.

contingent of commercial interests saw financial promise in a burgeoning outdoor recreation industry. By the early twentieth century, with Thoreau's portraits of fishing scenes firmly in mind,[9] sport-fishing advocates combined transcendentalism's devotional oeuvre to the outdoors with practical social, economic, and ecological concerns. Sport fishers argued that their pastime restored the spirit and mitigated industrialization's harsh societal effects. Responding to antimodernism's contemporary cultural criticism and outright nostalgic sentiment, sport fishing was also touted as one gesture that could help maintain the "nature" or, more hyperbolically presented, "frontier" experience deemed so essential to America's ethos. The stakes became even higher as industrialization threatened the sport fisher's quarry, and with it, the anticipated ethical, cultural, and civic benefit of the activity itself.

Perch fishing on Lake Michigan has been a popular past time for men and women for over a century at the pier in South Haven, Michigan. Courtesy of Michigan United Conservation Clubs.

In quintessential American fashion, this legacy stemmed from a diverse cross section of cultural and economic interests that found common cause in what became "the sporting life." Americans selectively chose certain nature-oriented activities, principally fishing, hunting, and camping, and made them into consumer activities that became the hallmarks of the American outdoor movement; albeit with presumably lofty goals consistent with the country's "Arcadian myth."[10] Lake Michigan's sport fishery became one among many regional manifestations of this sentiment. Recreational fishing's wide support across social and gender lines not only broadened its function in shaping the American cultural scene, but also heightened its economic importance. Not surprisingly, as American sport fishing aspired to be a counterpoint to certain modernizing forces, its cultural ascendance put it in the paradoxical position of becoming a modern industry with an increasingly corporate outlook. These developments were as much in evidence along the shores of Lake Michigan as they were anywhere else in the country. The Grand Rapids and Indiana Railway (known as "The Fishing Line") and the Chicago and Northwestern Line specialized in getting anglers to fishing locations along Lake Michigan's eastern and western shores.[11] Steamship service from Chicago and Milwaukee made it possible for wage earners and their families to travel to southwest Michigan's lakeshore towns spanning from St. Joseph to Ludington, where they enjoyed perch fishing from jetties or rented skiffs.[12] Wealthier sport fishers were among those who invested in the upscale resort communities of Traverse City, Charlevoix, Petoskey, and Harbor Springs on the northwest shores of Michigan's Lower Peninsula or Wisconsin's Door Peninsula.

Sport fishing's popularity in the Great Lakes region grew steadily throughout the early twentieth century. Fishing tackle companies, including nationally known

The Shakespeare Company and other leading fishing tackle manufacturers quickly responded to the growing demand for sport fishing gear suitable for fishing salmon from the Great Lakes. During the 1920s, company founder William Shakespeare of Kalamazoo. Michigan, a supporter of the Izaak Walton League of America, helped raise funds for improvements at the State of Michigan's Wolf Lake Fish Hatchery. Courtesy of Kalamazoo Public Library.

The *Shirley* was a trap-net boat that was converted to a party boat for perch anglers. As the commercial fisheries of the Great Lakes struggled in the post-World War II era, such adaptations became emblematic of the shifting priorities and ecological realities that confronted Lake Michigan's fish-using constituencies. Courtesy of Michael J. Chiarappa.

firms such as Shakespeare and Heddon that were based in the Lake Michigan watershed, promoted wildlife conservation and were instrumental in the founding of the Izaak Walton League of America in 1922.[13] When automobiles became the preferred mode of travel to fishing locales, oil companies issued maps providing directions. It was not long before calendars, brochures, and other commercially oriented promotional material began featuring Great Lakes sport fishing scenes. Some of these materials included images of American Indians to provide a measure of historical and regional authenticity to the act of sport fishing.[14]

Combining the American gospel of wealth with the recreational consumption of natural resources, sport fishing in Michigan and Wisconsin, mainly inland fishing, became a profitable commercial enterprise that fostered an unparalleled coalition among tackle companies, the tourist industry, fishing guides, conservation groups, and government. The formation of the influential Michigan United Conservation Clubs (MUCC) in 1937 signaled just how high the stakes had risen. The establishment of MUCC was an indication that sport-fishing interests reaped

Michigan Governor G. Mennen Williams (right) greeting executive secretary Harry Gaines of the Michigan United Conservation Clubs (MUCC). As the state's foremost wildlife conservation organization, MUCC enthusiastically embraced the enhancement of Lake Michigan's sport fisheries during the second half of the twentieth century. In the 1970s, it would mount concerted campaigns against the use of gill nets and the re-assertion of tribal fishing rights. Courtesy of Michigan United Conservation Clubs.

both commercial and ecological dividends from progressive management schemes that influenced the organization of the Michigan and Wisconsin Conservation Commissions and the U.S. Bureau of Fisheries Great Lakes Fishery Investigations in the 1920s.[15] With sport fishing so culturally and economically enshrined, the stage was set for a new chapter to unfold on Lake Michigan after World War II.

Today, sport fishing is a highly visible part of the Lake Michigan scene, but few recognize the historical developments behind its ascendance. This is not to imply that sport fishers do not have a sense of the history or tradition of their activity. For many sport fishers, going onto Lake Michigan—or to its shores or nearby tributaries—is a calendar ritual deeply rooted in many life histories. Not only the substance of personal memory, group participation among families, fishing clubs, and communities gives Lake Michigan sport fishers a collective memory that ultimately serves as the basis of both folk and institutional history. The past, and its current interpretation, is the basis upon which sport fishers culturally construct their claim to the resource. Fundamentally, sport fishing is a historically minded activity, one in

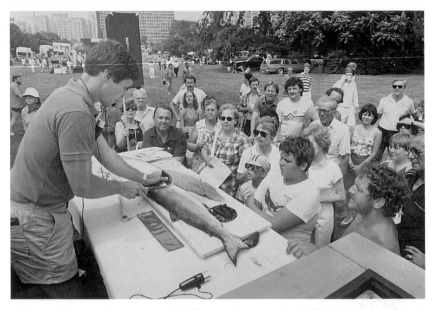

William Cullerton, Jr. demonstrates fish filleting techniques to on-lookers in Chicago's Lincoln Park in 1980. Such events helped promote salmon and other sport fishing in Lake Michigan. Courtesy of William Cullerton, Jr.

which relationships are forged with the environment and this particular resource over the course of many angling hours. Past success and failure is duly noted and informs future activity; all details enter the fisher's personal record and, as tradition shows, some will enter the sport-fishing community's collective historical record in oral or written form.

The eleven people who were interviewed about the management of Lake Michigan sport fisheries includes anglers who had been fishing long enough to remember when the majority of recreational fishermen in the states bordering Lake Michigan focused their attention primarily on inland lakes, rivers, and streams. Fishermen who were born in the 1920s and 1930s, and have fished for more than fifty years, recall that Lake Michigan's sport fisheries claimed little of their time before the stocking of salmon in the 1960s. They note that lakeshore towns offering good fishing piers and handy boat liveries were lively during perch season, but rarely attracted the angler's attention at other times of the year. The summer months offered fishermen the opportunity to get out on the open water on one of a handful of "deep sea" fishing boats that operated out of northern Lake Michigan and Lake Superior ports. In the fall, when cooler temperatures arrived, steelhead fishing attracted a small, but devoted following to Lake Michigan's tributary rivers and streams.

Some sport fishers who had never fished Lake Michigan's waters prior to the stocking of salmon or who scarcely remember a time when the lake's waters did not teem with this species, were invited to offer their viewpoints on Lake Michigan fisheries management. For instance, downriggers and other equipment used in Great Lakes sport fishing were already in use when Scott Anderson became a charter boat captain. Other sport fishers interviewed as part of this oral history project were involved in the process of making or designing tackle that would help them catch fish in deep water. Anderson discussed the set of circumstances that compelled him to become a charter boat operator.[16] Others such as Bob "Coho" Maynard, Paul

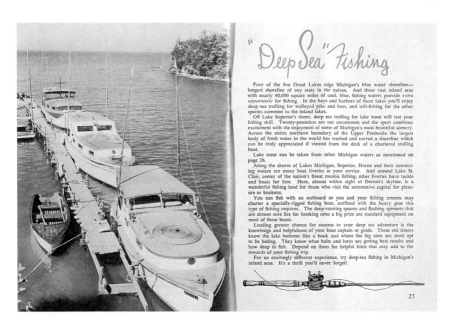

"Deep Sea" fishing was promoted by Michigan tourism officials during the 1930s and 1940s in an attempt to shift some of the recreational anglers' interests from inland lakes and streams to the Great Lakes. Despite these efforts, sport fishing on the Great Lakes was not widely popular until the late 1960s when Michigan and later, Wisconsin began stocking salmon. Courtesy of the Michigan Tourist Bureau.

M. Goodman, and Lyle Teskie became charter boat captains as part of an economic strategy to counter the economic, environmental, and policy changes they faced as commercial fishermen. Given their background, it is hardly surprising that Maynard, Goodman, and Teskie express empathy for the commercial fishermen.

Overall sport-fishing attitudes toward commercial fishermen have mellowed as their ranks have thinned and they have lost the political clout they once enjoyed. Today, the disagreement that exists between sport and Euro-American commercial fishers hardly resembles the animosity that existed in the late 1960s and early 1970s when sport-fishing interests insisted that the DNR prohibit gill-net use. When the Fox decision upheld treaty rights fishing in 1979, sport fishers only became more entrenched in their opposition to the commercial fishing activities of Lake Michigan's tribes. Although the federal courts have directed Consent Agreements in 1985 and 2000 to ameliorate these tensions—by creating coordinated regulation, research, and allocation schemes between the State of Michigan and the tribes— many sport fishers continue to be suspect of any commercial use of Great Lakes species. Going beyond their strained relations with the tribal fishery, contemporary sport fishers are also confronting internal squabbles that are firmly rooted in the recent history of their endeavor. These sport-fishing interests are currently divided in their view of how the Michigan Department of Natural Resources should respond to the decline in salmon fishing.[17]

Since the early 1980s, the only challenge to sport-fishing dominance of the policy-making and implementation process is from the Indian tribes whose treaty fishing rights have been upheld in U.S. federal court in spite of significant opposition from the State of Michigan. Some sport fishermen and sport-fishing organizations have been particularly active in the negotiations for the Consent Agreements of 1985 and 2000. This constituency is divided over the issue of the tribes' right to self-regulation of their fisheries. The Grand Traverse Area Sport Fishing Association has been particularly outspoken against the fisheries management policies of the Grand Traverse Band of Ottawa and Chippewa Indians—particularly the licensing of gill-net fishing.

Not limiting their protests solely to tribal fisheries management in treaty waters, sport-fishing interests also clash with the Michigan and Wisconsin Departments of Natural Resources over specific management issues or regulatory

A poor salmon fishing season in 1995 sent sports fishermen and charter boat operators searching for causes. Grand Traverse Band of Ottawa and Chippewa Indians commercial fishing
license holder Skip Duhamel, son of treaty rights fishing activist Art Duhamel, was identified
as responsible in a *Traverse City Record Eagle* political cartoon by Gene Hibbard. Courtesy of
Traverse City Record Eagle.

procedures. For example, salmon fishing has become so culturally entrenched over
the past thirty years within the Lake Michigan sport-fishing community that many
of its members have been outspoken in their opposition to annual reductions in
the number of salmon planted. Most sport fishermen, however, revel in their amicable relations with the departments that have jurisdiction over Lake Michigan's
fisheries resources and favorably acknowledge the recent history of both DNRs in
managing the lake to encourage sport fishing. Considering Pacific salmon's mythic
status in the creation of Lake Michigan's modern sport fishery, such sentiment is
hardly surprising.

The demure origins of Lake Michigan's sport fishery could hardly foretell its
transformation from a scarcely noted local and regional activity in the nineteenth
century to one that captured national attention by the late 1960s. In the middle of
the nineteenth century, the natural bounty of the Great Lakes region—iron ore,

timber and, of course, fish—drew the attention of financial capital. This "devouring" temperament transformed the Great Lakes into America's most industrialized seas.[18] But the commercial bustle on inland seas did not prevent another sector of American society from seeing additional possibilities in its teeming waters. Some native-born American elites, less intent on direct commercial utilization of the Great Lakes, saw the region as an angling paradise; an environmental context whose outdoor activities could contribute to unifying American society around its natural heritage.

Prominent nineteenth-century angling writers, most notably Robert Barnwell Roosevelt and Thaddeus Norris, brought the open-water, sport-fishing opportunities of the Great Lakes to the attention of thousands of readers.[19] As sportsmen, they primarily enticed their angling audience with the prospect of placing an artificial fly on one of the region's many bountiful streams. But Roosevelt, Norris, and others also made sure to describe the "sporting" qualities of the fish that inhabited Lake Michigan. They conceded that certain Great Lakes species, such as lake trout, were hardly spectacular sport fish, but such circumstances were duly mitigated by the sublime surroundings of the "big lake." Influential in the founding of the American Fish Culturalists' Association (later the American Fisheries Society), the activism of the two conservationists undoubtedly helped to convince Spencer Fullerton Baird to channel research resources and political capital toward the Great Lakes when he became head of the U.S. Fish Commission in 1871.[20] It was not long before a number of this era's best known fisheries researchers—George Brown Goode, David Starr Jordan, Barton W. Evermann—were giving Lake Michigan species due attention in published works directed toward a sport fishing audience.[21]

During the late-nineteenth and early-twentieth centuries, literary notice, scientific study, and other early and rarely noted actions helped to create a sense of identity for Lake Michigan's sport fishery and, in the process, made it a political issue. This action signaled a more transcendent development that was occurring at regional venues throughout the United States; Lake Michigan's sport fishers and their fellow stakeholders were being initiated into a political debate over how fisheries resources were going to be culturally and economically utilized.

The work of late-nineteenth/early-twentieth-century sport and travel writers, scientists, and anglers to further the political influence of sport fishing was auspicious in terms of its long-term implications. In the immediate context, however, these steps only gradually motivated the political activism of Lake Michigan's open-water, sport-fishing interests. A number of factors contributed to the deferral of a more overt political consciousness on the part of Lake Michigan's sport-fishing community. For many, the rallying cry of conservation had yet to be heard; concern over environmental degradation and resource depletion were blurred by a national ethos of limitless frontiers. But of more tangible concern, at least until after World War II, were strikingly practical considerations that worked against high-volume participation in a "big lake" sport fishery and a political voice to advance its interests.[22]

Lake Michigan's early sport fishery was, of necessity, essentially a shoreline activity. The occasional photograph or picture postcard shows an angler holding a lake trout, but scenes featuring jetties congested with leisurely fishers pursuing the delectable yellow perch predominate. Lacking today's technology and amenities, weather conditions and sheer scale made Lake Michigan inhospitable to fishermen who ventured out in small craft. At the time that its open waters were most inviting, its most prized sport fish—the lake trout—was frequently at depths that were ineffectively broached by available tackle or sport-fishing boats. Catching lake trout was often compared to lifting a dull, dead weight from the lake's bottom and perch fishing—stunningly egalitarian in the flocks it attracted to Lake Michigan's shores—may have been seen as too ordinary to evoke more sweeping boosterism from those familiar with leisure fishing opportunity. Failing to receive sustained applause for their sporting qualities, these species, along with others, did not politically galvanize a distinct Lake Michigan sport-fishing base throughout the first half of the twentieth century.

The limits imposed by nature, technology, and the configuration of the recreational economy diluted the political impact of sport-fishing interests. The efforts of Lake Michigan's sport fishery advocates to strengthen their claim as resource users and to gain more political clout were complicated by the tendency of Lake Michigan states to informally forfeit much of their management effort to the federal government. These states chose to focus on inland streams and lakes, and allowed federal agencies considerable breadth in overseeing Lake Michigan's fisheries resources, principally for the benefit of the commercial fishing industry. Two world wars and the Great Depression further delayed the development of a politically charged recreational fishery on Lake Michigan.[23]

The call for organizational action among fishermen came from the Michigan Department of Conservation immediately following World War II. This department advised the state's sport fishers that their interests would best be served if they joined a sportsmen's club. On its face, such sentiment seems a natural call for parties mutually concerned with fisheries resources. But perhaps more telling, acknowledging that sportsmen's groups were instrumental in the movement against water pollution and a host of other natural resource issues, the Department of Conservation conceded the highly political dimensions of its stewardship enterprise and how they might handle the future use of fisheries resources. As if to ease this burden and open the possibility for new fisheries, the department invoked the collective burden of the public trust doctrine in the most unabashed terms in 1948:

> The Department is an agent of the public; its reason for being is to serve the public. Fish and game belong to the public. Certainly, if the Department is to serve the public's best interests in the protecting of fish and game supplies, it should have the support of the public; at least, the support of that section of the public—fishermen and hunters—who are most concerned about the adequacy of fish and game supplies and their perpetuation.[24]

Michigan's conservation officials had a longstanding relationship with sport fishers, but such strongly worded affirmations foretold an emerging trend. The Michigan Department of Conservation would give sport-fishing interests a role in the policy-making and implementation process, but only if they organized and actively sought public funds and support for it. Eager to see sportsmen involved in determining the use and allocation of Michigan's fisheries resources, the Michigan Outdoor Writers Association urged veterans of the military and the industrial home front of World War II to respond to the allure of Great Lakes outdoor life. For anglers, their desires ran headlong into the bleaker side of the region's fishing sector at mid-century—polluted waters, a commercial fishing industry crippled by years of ineffectual policy and desperate overfishing, and the devastation wrought by the sea lamprey. This context fostered the mechanisms by which state government and sport-fishing constituencies took the first steps that ultimately led to the transformation of Lake Michigan's fisheries.

On the docks in Milwaukee, a fisherman's dream comes true as he lands a salmon from Lake Michigan. During the late 1960s and early 1970s, when the forage base was abundant, all doubts as to whether salmon would flourish in the fresh water of the Great Lakes were laid to rest. Courtesy of the State Historical Society of Wisconsin, WHi (X3) 50109.

Interest in sport fishing rose steadily after World War II, fueled by state efforts to promote outdoor recreation economies as well as federal assistance from the Dingell-Johnson Act. Around the shores of Lake Michigan, enthusiasm for sport fishing was on the slow, but steady, rise. Interest in sport fishing on the lake was promoted by MUCC, whose political influence increased from the time of its founding in 1937, and by one of America's deans of sport-fishing writing, Ben East.[25] For its part the State of Michigan, borrowing an ocean-coast term, began encouraging readers of its tour guide and map to take advantage of "deep-sea fishing" on its Great Lakes waters and utilize the Mackinac Bridge, completed in 1957, to reach pristine fishing waters in the Upper Peninsula.

Despite public and private efforts to build interest in Lake Michigan's sport fisheries, there was only limited interest in perch, lake trout, and other species. The explosion of the alewife population, which left the shores of Lake Michigan littered with piles of dead fish, further complicated efforts to attract and organize anglers. In the early 1960s, functioning in a context in which sea lamprey predation and alewife severely disrupted the biomass of Lake Michigan, Michigan Department of

Coho fever brought overwhelming numbers of salmon fishermen to public boat launches and lakeshore parks on Lake Michigan in 1970. Three years earlier the need for greater attention to safety was underscored by the deaths of seven salmon anglers in a November 1967 storm. Photograph by Norm Brown.

Conservation director Ralph MacMullan recognized that dramatic measures needed to be taken if a sport fishery was going to have any serious future prospects. MacMullan hired Howard Tanner—a fisheries scientist with a Ph.D. from Michigan State University—as his Fisheries Division chief in 1964 and urged him to take bold steps. Having researched the feasibility of introducing Pacific salmon into the Great Lakes while on the faculty of Colorado State University, Tanner was convinced that this measure was the key to a prosperous sport fishery on Lake Michigan. The successful introduction of this species was, in the short run, nothing less than revolutionary. It was a professional milestone for Michigan-native Tanner and a political triumph for the Department of Conservation. Capitalizing on the groundswell of political support, the DNR utilized the salmon fishery to create a vast and unprecedented network of alliances among sport-fishing organizations, tackle companies, recreational boat manufacturers, and tourism interests. It popularized recreational fishing on Lake Michigan beyond most people's expectations and beyond even its own estimates. As the following narratives indicate, the state assisted these sport-fishing interests at every step and radically redefined the politics of fishing on Lake Michigan.[26]

The establishment of a successful recreational fishery for Pacific salmon in Lake Michigan in the late 1960s generated so much excitement that, in hindsight, it evoked unprecedented political passion and activism among the region's angling community. The strident positions of Lake Michigan's angling community were fostered through a privileged relationship with state government. At the urging of state government, both statewide and local organizations were established to advocate the recreational use of Lake Michigan's fisheries resources. Oral history reveals that this slanted political coalition often defied the impartial spirit of the public trust doctrine; in fact, sport fishers consistently recount their compatible relationship with state government—a merging of sympathetic agendas that literally blurred the institutional boundaries that separated the groups. Even though the restructured Michigan Department of

Frankfort, Michigan, was one of the many lakeshore towns that experienced an economic bonanza from sport fishing during the late 1960s and the early 1970s after salmon were introduced to Lake Michigan. Photograph by Norm Brown.

Sport fishing organizations opposed the use of gill nets in Lake Michigan and claimed that commercial fishermen, particularly those who used gill nets, posed an economic and ecological threat to their fishery. Courtesy of the Michigan Department of Natural Resources, Great Lakes Fishery Research Station.

Conservation, and its successor agency, the Department of Natural Resources, had the power to allocate Lake Michigan's fisheries resources principally for recreational use, it was clearly emboldened by the tremendous political support it came to enjoy from every constituency connected to sport fishing.[27] The formation of Michigan Steelheaders, primarily by West Michigan residents, revealed a new vanguard of politically organized sport fishers whose eyes were firmly fixed on Lake Michigan's recreational bounty.[28] Following its organizational meeting in March, 1967, the Michigan Steelheaders acknowledged its determination to become "better informed" so its members could "act on important matters such as impending state legislation."[29]

Within this political atmosphere, the Michigan DNR moved forward on restricting commercial fishing licenses, limiting areas that could be commercially

FISHERMEN

Your License and Tax Dollars Financed this 1200 lb. Lake Trout Catch for

GILL NETTERS

at Torch Lake Village on 9-14-78

HELP US STOP GILL NETTING
JOIN THE S.G.N. ASSOCIATION

Stop Gill Netting Now (SGN) was the most adversarial organization created by Lake Michigan sports fishermen who opposed treaty rights fishing during the late 1970s and early 1980s. Posters, newsletters and a newspaper were published by SGN to recruit members and influence public opinion. Courtesy of the Michigan Department of Natural Resources, Great Lakes Fishery Research Station.

fished, and curtailing or outright banning the use of gill nets and the practice of snagging.[30] Lake Michigan sport fishing continued to prosper into the 1970s, when its political activism became even more focused on the elimination of gill nets and a limited commercial fishery. These efforts peaked when Native Americans asserted the retention of commercial fishing privileges under nineteenth-century treaties with the federal government. Although these rights were judicially affirmed, the movement to reclaim treaty fishing rights unleashed a variety of sport-fishing reactions, most of which were negative. The complexion of these efforts varied from the traditional role played by the well-established MUCC and the more recently empowered Michigan Steelheaders to local groups such as the Grand Traverse Sport Fishing Association and the more militant activism espoused by Stop Gill Netting Now (SGN).[31]

By the close of the twentieth century, Lake Michigan's sport-fishing community emerged with a cultural and political identity that bore the marks both of its earliest antecedents and of its most recent past. Perhaps because it had less territorial water

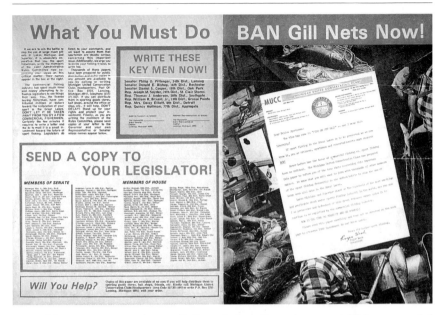

Sports fishing opposition to the use of gill nets by state-licensed commercial fishermen was led by the state's largest conservation organization, the Michigan United Conservation Clubs (MUCC). Courtesy of the Michigan United Conservation Clubs.

at stake, the State of Wisconsin did not favor sport fishing at the expense of commercial fishing to the degree exercised by the State of Michigan. This in no way understates the formidable rise of Wisconsin's Lake Michigan sport-fishing community and its ability to influence state policy. Sport-fishing organizations from every Lake Michigan state parlayed their political stature into working cooperatively with state agencies on stock assessment, hatchery projects, and educational programs.[32] Sport-fishing interests also gained far more officious standing on governing bodies that dictated the course of fisheries management on Lake Michigan, particularly the Great Lakes Fishery Commission and numerous state-sanctioned advisory boards and task forces. When Lake Michigan's sport-fishing community became an official party in the 1985 and 2000 Federal Consent Agreements to allocate the lake's fisheries resources between Native American and state-licensed users, it was a profound indication of how far it had come in making this freshwater basin the most politicized of the Great Lakes.[33]

The regional sentiment that is expressed in the following oral histories was

Great Lakes Steelheader

M.S.S.F.A
Box 147
Paw Paw, Mich. 49079

BULK RATE
U.S. Postage Paid
Paw Paw, MI.

Non-Profit
PERMIT NO. 94

MYRL KELLER
GREAT LAKES FISH STATION
CHARLEVOIX, MI 49720

THE VOICE OF THE MICHIGAN STEELHEADERS

VOLUME THREE   SEPTEMBER, 1979   NUMBER 9

GRAND TRAVERSE BAY "BOAT–IN"

Largest Great Lakes Sportsfishing Fleet to Assemble in Demonstration Against Threat Posed by Gill Nets

The largest sportsfishing fleet ever assembled on Lake Michigan will troll Grand Traverse Bay Friday, Sept. 28 in a demonstration of concern for the future of Great Lakes fishing.

The massive "Boat-In" organized by the Michigan Steelhead and Salmon Fishermen's Association will bring some 5,000

on the Great Lakes the gill netters move in," he said.

Boat-In Chairman Richard Swan, a Claire, Mich. fishing guide, said he expects the south end of West Grand Traverse Bay will be "filled to capacity" Sept. 28 by fishing boats from Michigan

and Wisconsin. After the noon assembly of boats, sportsfishermen will follow a "catch and release" policy during the afternoon to demonstrate their concern for the wise use of natural resources, he said.

A special press briefing is

scheduled for 1 p.m. with John Spencer, a member of the Great Lakes Fishery Commission and the Governor's Great Lakes Advisory Committee; John Scott, Chief of Fisheries, Michigan Department of Natural Resources; Tom Washington, Executive Di-

rector, Michigan United Conservation Clubs; and Andy Pelt, Executive Director, Michigan Steelhead and Salmon Fishermens Association.

A rally for Boat-In participants Friday evening will feature special briefings by Scott and Pelt.

A demonstration in opposition to the use of gill nets by state-licensed commercial fishermen was organized by the Michigan Steelheaders in September 1979. Traverse City, Michigan, was the center of sport fishing opposition to the gill nets. Courtesy of the Michigan Steelheaders.

forged within a distinct context that fueled the creation of Lake Michigan's modern sport fishery. In the 1950s and 1960s, Lake Michigan suffered from industrial pollution, sea lamprey predation, over-propagation of alewife, and years of ineffectual commercial fishing policy. Invoking oral history to justify their use and management priorities, sport fishers see their activity as having rescued Lake Michigan's fisheries. These personal and collective memories trace the genesis of Lake Michigan sport fishing to the changing face of America's environmental politics in the late 1960s and act as an expression of a charter to alleviate Lake Michigan's afflictions. Equipped with this perspective, anglers fuse their activity's standing in American popular culture with its financial success in the Great Lakes region to create narratives with a decidedly mythic tone. The roots of this oral historical tradition start with the community's zealous response to the first ritual ascents of immature jack salmon in 1966, and mature salmon in 1967, at the entrances to Lake Michigan's

The opening day of salmon fishing during the late 1960s and early 1970s brought scores of anglers to the Lake Michigan's tributaries and inlets. In the early years of the "coho craze" many lakeshore towns were woefully unprepared for the onslaught of fishermen. Courtesy of the Great Lakes Fishery Commission.

tributaries. The mythological dimension of this oral tradition is accentuated by ongoing accounts of the frenzied atmosphere that accompanied the newly invented sport fishery. Adding melodrama to their fishery's triumphant birth, these narratives specifically describe inexperienced "deep-sea" anglers dying on Lake Michigan's open water in boats ill-suited to the task while others fought for limited space at crowded lakeshore and tributary sites.

Seeking to affirm their providential view of the successful introduction of salmon to Lake Michigan, sport fishers orally chronicle the research, physical improvements, and custodial measures they took to further this recreational tradition. Most of these fishers had very little experience actually fishing on Lake Michigan prior to the 1960s. Not only did they have to learn how to fish for recently introduced Pacific salmon, but they also had to educate themselves in the systematic development of tackle and the adoption of larger open-water boats. Citing a larger developmental dividend from these efforts, they describe themselves as agents in a context that encouraged the exploration of new, open-water sport fisheries for native

Great Lakes stocks. Sport fishers readily remark that these changes contributed to the transformation of Lake Michigan's shoreline; indeed, the building of marinas and boat-launching facilities for the sport fishery were principal catalysts in making Lake Michigan's cultural landscape increasingly leisure-oriented in the 1970s and 1980s. These tangible changes—particularly in a region experiencing the effects of industrial lag—convinced sport fishers that each new stage of their activity was a locally derived contribution to the progressive-minded, efficient use of Lake Michigan's natural resources.

1. BEYOND ALL EXPECTATIONS: THE CULTURAL BIRTH OF LAKE MICHIGAN'S SPORT-FISHING COMMUNITY

Holland native Gordon Zuverink recalled how his interest in fishing was a result of both family and community ties. He refers to the modest scale of sport fishing on Lake Michigan prior to the 1960s.

I was born in Holland, Michigan, on November 9, 1920. I came from a rather large family. We were all fishermen, including my father, who introduced me to fishing when I was a little kid. My father and older brother loved to go out fishing on the pier at Holland State Park. So my first introduction to fishing was to take me out to the pier and tie a rope around my waist and tie it to the pier and stick a cane pole in my hand and I would be fishing. I am one of five boys. We all fished during our life, but I am the one that stuck with it through my whole career.

When I was in my teens we would fish on Lake Macatawa and catch blue gills and large mouth bass. Lake Macatawa was so clear you could see two, three feet down. It had lily pads growing on it. Our family had picnics in the summertime at Pine Bay Camp where there were rental boats, wooden rowboats. We would rent a boat and fish blue gills in the lily pads. I have never forgotten the clarity of the water in Black Lake, as it was known at that time. Now, you cannot see six inches into the water, thanks to industry and progress.

Perch fishing was a hot item at that time. Generally in the spring, Decoration Day (Memorial Day) was historically the start of perch fishing on the pier at Holland State

393

Gordon Zuverink is a sport fisherman from Holland, Michigan, who has actively supported the enhancement of Lake Michigan's sport fisheries by the Michigan DNR since the 1960s. Zuverink has served on the Lake Michigan Advisory Committee to the Great Lakes Fishery Commission. Interview, 31 July 1999. Photograph by Michael J. Chiarappa.

Park. And Fourth of July was generally the end of it. And perch fishing was great at that time. It was almost wiped out during the 1950s. We were quite adept at catching cisco while fishing for perch. And there were lots of them out there. The cisco was really a sport fish, and really a lot of fun to catch. They were much larger than perch, of course. The cisco came in late June, just prior to Fourth of July.

Kevin Naze noted how his work in journalism got him involved in working as a fishing guide and on charter boats. He is part of an influential journalistic tradition that has promoted Lake Michigan's modern sport fishery since the 1960s.

I write for the Green Bay *Press Gazette*, Door County *Advocate*, and the Kewaunee County papers and edit a site called fishwisconsin.com on the Internet so you can look up stories on there. I write for different magazines in Wisconsin and the Midwest. I am a fishing guide in the streams and on the ice as opposed to a charter captain. I am not a charter boat captain. A charter boat captain takes them out in the boats. I

Kevin Naze, a native of Wisconsin's Door County, is a journalist, fishing guide, and charter boat crew member. Interview 1 June 1999. Photograph courtesy of the Great Lakes Center for Maritime Studies.

work at a charter business in Algoma. We have three boats and probably take out about 300 to 400 trips a year, so I have a pretty good knowledge of the charter business. I grew up in Algoma. I fished the lake (Lake Michigan) as long as I can remember. Out on the lake you go for lake trout, brown trout, and chinooks. The streams have runs of salmon and steelhead.

I was a writer first. I started writing in high school. We had a class in photojournalism where we had to get pictures published in the local paper, so I started a column twenty years ago this year, back when I was a junior in high school. It's hard to believe, but I have been writing for the local Algoma paper, a little weekly, for twenty years now. And it kind of branched from there. I worked full time as a sports editor in Algoma for seven years. In 1988, I went full-time freelance because I was selling enough of my work in different markets. I liked the opportunity to be able to sell to whoever I wanted and to be able to resell different stories to different markets that are non-competing. It has expanded even more with the Internet. Now, I write an outdoor column for a newspaper out in Oregon. I have never even been to Oregon, but through research on the Internet and phone calls I can write a column for it. The fishwisconsin Internet site is fishwisconsin—all one word, all lower case, no dashes. They did not buy all the domains they should have, so sometimes people tell me they looked it up and could not find it.

I write once a week for Algoma, twice for Door County, and three times for Green Bay each week. The column in Oregon is weekly. I either put in one of my own feature articles or somebody else's that I edit plus listing weekly fishing reports in the fishwisconsin site. So it is pretty much a constant process. You try to keep track of what is hot, such as if somebody catches a state record fish, which has happened four times since 1994. Here in Sturgeon Bay, there was a 44.92-pound chinook. These numbers are in my head because luckily, I was the first person up there and got the exclusive story and photos. I sell them all over the country basically. Boating magazines out in New York want state record fish photos, so it is kind of neat for me. There were two record holders in Algoma. In 1997 a woman from Minnesota caught a 27.11-pound rainbow trout, otherwise known as the steelhead, and in 1996 a gentleman from Minnesota caught a 35.11-pound brown trout, which beat an eighteen-year-old state record. Twenty-five days later, my neighbor caught a 35.12-pound brown trout. He beats him by a hundredth of a pound. So today with the digital accuracy they gave this other guy the new record and the poor guy that broke an eighteen-year-old record had a record for about twenty-five days, so that is kind of interesting. I mean, those are hot stories obviously, state record stories, but the cormorant issue is pretty big right now.

To me, it is a world-class fishery. You would have to go to Alaska or British Columbia to find fishing like we have in Lake Michigan. We are pretty fortunate. There are a lot of people who live right here and take it for granted. Working at a charter business, I see people who drive nonstop all night, eight, ten, or twelve hours to come here. They cannot wait to get here to fish. In the middle of summer the boat ramps will be just backlogged for a half an hour and you have to wait in line to get in. People are excited about it. A lot of the locals wonder what all the hullabaloo is about but once they get out there and try it, they are pretty excited themselves.

Scott Anderson is a charter boat operator who works out of Leland. He began sport fishing as a youth with his family. Anderson has been in the charter boat business for sixteen years and his oral testimony sheds insight on how midwesterners adopted "deep-sea" fishing methods on the Great Lakes.

Scott Anderson is a charterboat operator from Traverse City, Michigan. His boat, the *Farfetched*, operates out of Leland, Michigan and is one of the most active chartering services in northwest Michigan. Scott Anderson was interviewed on May 26, 1999. Photograph by Michael J. Chiarappa.

I got started in the fishing business when I bought a boat that I could not afford. Actually, when I was nine years old I caught a sailfish. My parents used to vacation in Florida, and I loved big-boat fishing. Through some moves I ended up in Wisconsin and a friend of mine said, "Hey, you want to go fishing?" I said, "I cannot go fishing. I play golf." Finally, he convinced me to go with him. It was big-boat fishing. Eventually, he and I bought a boat together. I thought it would be nice if I could take some friends out and make a little money at this. So I went out, got my captain's license, and moved to Traverse City. The captain who was running the old *Farfetched* developed cancer. He ran an ad for a captain. I answered the ad. I ended up buying the *Farfetched*. It was in 1983 that I came to Leland. So, I have been here sixteen years.

Richard Stevenson recently became a licensed charter boat operator. He has been a crew member on both commercial and charter sport-fishing boats.

My grandpa worked for the Wisconsin DNR when they first started planting lake trout in Lake Michigan. He was one of the pioneers out there. He took me out

Richard Stevenson is a charter
boat operator who fishes out of
Sturgeon Bay, Wisconsin. Interview, 31 May 1999. Photograph by
Matthew Anderson.

when I was real young and I started learning how to catch them. We caught a lot of fish.
I got real interested in it. I fished commercially out of Key Largo, Florida, a few years
ago for yellow tail tuna, grouper, and whatever else came along. We did not use nets.
Actually, we caught them all on rod and reel. We anchored and bottom fished. It was a
lot of fun actually. It sounds like a lot of fun, just catching fish all day, but we did it a
little different. We used heavy line type drags and we cranked those fish in pretty fast.
Your arms got pretty sore by the end of the day. I have worked fifteen hours to eighteen hours out here in Lake Michigan and I worked eight hours in Florida and I would be
way more tired after eight hours in Florida than fifteen hours out in Lake Michigan.

Over the past twelve years, I have worked for most of the charter boat captains
around Sturgeon Bay. Now, I have a captain's license myself and I am ready to give it
a shot. The test you have to take to get your charter boat operator's license is the hardest test anybody could ever take in their life. I think anybody who wants to do any
guiding of any kind should take it. Even if they are just out guiding ice fishing and
you are not operating a vessel, the law is you have to have a captain's license. I tried
getting a license for guiding for ice fishing. The DNR will send you a guide license, but

you have to have your captain's license number on it. Your captain's license, that is federal. Your guiding license comes from the state.

"Coho" Bob Maynard discussed how he worked briefly in commercial fishing before becoming affiliated with sport fishing through charter boats and the operation of a tackle shop.

I worked on the fish tug *Peggy Marie*. That was one of the last ones owned by Stover and Misenheimer. They have since passed away, of course. At one time, there were seven commercial tugs out of Pentwater alone. Then it got down to three, and then it got down to none. I only worked in commercial fishing a couple years, but my younger brother did it for many years. When he was just a little fellow, he would go down and learn how to mend the nets. It was quite a trick to know how to mend them. He learned that at a very young age, and found himself being very useful. He made several dollars that way doing odd jobs. We who lived here and more or less grew up with commercial fishing, had a lot of respect for the people that did it—the long hours of work and the risky business and all of the dangers that go with it. We did it because everybody else was and you could make a little money. The other kids around town were doing the same job. It gave me an opportunity to make a little money during the Depression years.

I helped out a little bit on a charter boat, but I did not work on one as a steady job. It required quite an investment to be a charter boat fisherman, including all the various licenses and permits. You have to pay to keep your boat someplace. You got a lot of money tied up and you may not get any money back in charter boat fishing.

A lady reporter came up here and we went out on a boat and caught a nice bunch of salmon. She took some pictures and said she would send us some pictures. At that time, my kid brother was working in the post office and she apparently had forgotten my last name. So she just sent the pictures along and she put "Coho Bob, Pentwater." Everyone got a kick out of that at the time and the word got around and we showed the pictures around and everyone started calling me "Coho Bob"—making a joke and the name stuck with me. But I have been affiliated with the fishing so closely and for so long that it just seemed to fit right in.

Lyn Ray is a native of the Grand Traverse Bay area and former president of the Grand Traverse Area Sport Fishing Association. He is a charter boat captain whose family members previously worked in the commercial fishing industry. Interview, 26 May 1999. Photograph-Great Lakes Center for Maritime Studies.

A longtime resident of the Traverse City-Leelanau Peninsula area, Lyn Ray is a Great Lakes fisherman who, prior to becoming a charter boat captain, was involved in commercial fishing.

I am a native of the Grand Traverse area. My mother and dad were schoolteachers. I had an uncle who was a commercial fisherman on Lake Michigan out of Omena. My dad was a teacher in the winter, and then worked with my uncle on the fish tugs in the summer, so I was exposed to it at a really young age. I was out with him about forty-five or fifty years ago. I got into chartering in the early 1970s. I was a sales representative for Big Jon, the company that makes the downrigger. I went around to boat shows in Florida and Chicago and Detroit. Then I decided to get my own captain's license and get into the business myself. I have been in business now for twenty-six years.

Roy Holmquist has been sport fishing since he was a boy. During the 1940s, he began fishing competitively by entering sport fishing contests for brown trout. Holmquist moved to Wisconsin's Door County in the 1960s and has actively promoted the region's sport fisheries. Now retired, Holmquist occasionally works on charterboats. Interview, 2 June 1999. Photograph courtesy of the Great Lakes Center for Maritime Studies.

Roy Holmquist recalled how he became involved in sport fishing in Wisconsin's Door Peninsula. He notes how sport fishing's popularity rose conspicuously during the 1970s and 1980s.

I was born in Illinois. One of my buddies came up here in the early 1960s. We had always fished in Illinois and when he came up here, he said: "You will never believe it. I was over at Baileys Harbor and there was a big black spot out there with nothing but brown trout." He said they averaged six pounds and I did not believe him because fishermen have a little tendency to prevaricate once in a while, especially when they catch something. He finally talked us into coming up. My wife and I came up and did a little fishing with him. We could not believe how great the fishing was up here. We had browns in close to shore and we had shore-run rainbow. It was great and we are trying to get it back again. We have been working with the DNR on that deal. The king salmon were mostly in Sturgeon Bay. We caught a lot of king salmon fishing out of there and it was just great fishing. But over the years, it has gone down. Maybe it is the zebra mussels and the cormorants. I think they have been taking a lot of our baby fish.

According to people from Lake Erie, the zebra mussels are helping because the weeds are growing and the fish have more places to hide. So far, that has not happened for us. So it is one of those things. Good old mother nature, you know. When you talk to some of the old-timers up here who have fished forever, they say the fishing runs in cycles. We are hoping that is what is happening now.

The first place that we fished in Door County was Baileys Harbor—right where Nelson's Store is. That is where my buddy had seen all the brown trout—right out in front and we used to fish there. We used to fish off the Baileys Harbor Yacht Club pier for rainbows—some beautiful rainbows. The first couple times we saw it we could not believe it. We used the fish spawn and we would take corn and chum a little bit and then throw out the spawn and all of a sudden bang, you would have a rainbow. It was fabulous fishing. It was just great. We used to stay at Nelson's in a little motel unit connected to the hardware store. We stayed there for years. That was our spot. We could leave our boat there and get back out and go fishing if we wanted to in the lake. We used to get lakers and salmon out in the lake and, of course, brown trout and occasional rainbow, too. We had that shore run rainbow which was really great. Now, we are working with the DNR to try to get that back again.

In the early 1970s, this area was not that well known for sport fishing. It was very quiet. It was just by accident that my friend found a place up here and saw the browns. Little by little, the word gets around. Most people stopped at Sturgeon Bay and they never came up this far. My buddy found it by accident and boy, we just were in heaven, you know. Every harbor had browns in it. You had them in Egg Harbor, you had them in Fish Creek, Ephraim, Sister Bay, and Ellison Bay. In fact, it was a big deal for us to come from Baileys Harbor up to Ellison Bay to fish because we had all the fish right down there. But mostly, we came up here for the salmon because the salmon used to hang out right here on Porcupine Bay. There are a couple of nice reefs and they just used to hang in there and we used to come and fish. You would start at five o'clock in the morning and by ten o'clock you would have ten salmon, no problem, and big fish. They ran from eighteen to twenty-eight pounds. It was just fabulous fishing.

I helped a couple times with the charter people when they were short of help. Most of the time we just came up here strictly for sport. I did not really help anybody until we came up here and were retired. We also fished the brown trout tournaments. I think

1945 was the year I won it. The fish is up on the wall. It was twenty-one and a half pounds. It was a $2,000 fish. It is a female brown trout. My wife caught one that was eighteen pounds and I caught another that was nineteen pounds. We caught these fish way back when we first started fishing. In fact, both of them came from Baileys Harbor. The big guy came off a little reef off of Ephraim. This year we fished in the tournament and came in tenth. The biggest fish we got was just a twelve and a half pounder. We trolled twenty-seven miles for two fish. At least we took tenth place, so that was nice. We got our money back for the tournament. The brown trout tournament is run out of Baileys Harbor. It seems to carry just about the same amount of people every year. When they first started there were not that many people. Since about the early 1990s it has been about the same bunch all the way through—something like 450 people. Normally, it is a three-day tournament. This year it was four days.

My boat has four electric downriggers. I also have a temperature gauge on there that goes down with the downrigger ball to tell you the temperature and the speed down there so you control your fishing. Some days the fish want the bait moving at two miles an hour and the next day it might be three. Sometimes, with our currents out here, if you go through Death's Door, you go one way with the current and your lure is actually going five miles an hour. You come back the other way and it is going half a mile an hour. So it really helps to have equipment to gauge conditions so you have the lure working perfectly. A couple times we have gone over there by Death's Door and there might have been eighty boats trolling through the center. Now, in the last few years, the salmon fishing has not been that great. You do not see quite that many boats anymore. In fact, now, if you see fifteen boats you see a lot. But, of course, the charter fishermen still work it.

The fishing is not quite as easy as it was years ago. Years ago, you would put your lures down and eventually there were so many fish you got them. I have gone through Death's Door when we first starting fishing with the downrigger cables and the downrigger cables were actually hitting fish. You could see them vibrate and mark them on the locator. But there are not quite as many now. I do not know if they have changed their habits or what they are eating or if they are following bait fish someplace. It is still up in the air and we are wondering about it. But again, there are times when fishermen go out there and hit a bunch of them. When we have fished the ship canal in

Sturgeon Bay a couple times with the four downriggers, we have had four kings on at one time. It is like a fire drill with everybody running around doing this and that. Lines are getting tangled and people are getting hit with the net.

It used to be a big deal if we would take a run over and fish at Washington Island. Years ago, I had a friend of mine that used to fish there. We used to take the ferry across to Washington Island and fished off of Rock Island and Washington Island. It seemed like you got bigger salmon over there. It was amazing. You would fish in the morning and catch ten fish. That was fantastic fishing.

Our main fishing is done in good old Lake Michigan. The small-mouthed bass fishing was real good last year and in 1999 I have just fished it once. The water is down about two and a half feet and it is so clear where we fish. I have watched fish come up with my four-pound test and all of a sudden they will back off, which we never had before. The DNR has raised the size limit this year to fourteen inches which is good because years ago, they did not have a size limit on them. I would see people keep little bass, which was a crime. There is no meat on a fish that size, and small-mouthed bass are a tremendous fighter. They are a picnic when you get them on.

Years ago, we used to fish off of Anderson Dock in Ephraim for small-mouthed. That was our main small-mouth bass dock and we used to fish there. If you caught a big female—say four and a half or five pounds in the spring—we always used to throw them back. One day my buddy and I caught three of them in a row and there was a guy that was fishing there and he saw us throwing the fish back. He said, "How big do they have to be here before you keep them?" We had to explain to him what we were doing. He said he thought he was in real trouble because he had never caught a fish that size. I am little bit against the bass tournaments up here. They have them in the springtime of the year when it's spawning time. I wish they could just push them off until the fish get done spawning and give them a chance. I had a friend that was down there about four years ago after one of the tournaments and he said he could not believe how many dead bass he had seen. I said, "Well, did you tell people about it?" He said, "Yes, but they do not pay any attention to me." It just does not seem right to me to catch them when they are spawning. Then they keep them in the live wells and weigh them and then throw them in another pond. Something has to be happening to those fish. But that is my own personal opinion. Now I know people in town love it because it brings up all these people for their lodging and meals and bait and tackle

Since 1983, Don Nichols has operated the perch fishing party boats that attract hundreds of anglers to South Haven, Michigan, each season. Nichols first became involved in charter boat fishing in the 1970s. Interview 21 May 1999. Photograph by Michael J. Chiarappa.

and everything else. Of course, a lot of the local fishermen feel the same way but I do not know how we can stop it.

Party boat company operator and captain Don Nichols acknowledged how the stocking of salmon and other game fish in the Great Lakes helped to create the charter boat and party boat business on Lake Michigan. Nichols learned the business in Florida and got a great deal of on-the-job training.

Y ou can make a living running a party boat because you carry the volume of people and there is more money involved. I had to learn the party boat business. I went down to Florida. At the first party boat dock I came to, I told the owner what I wanted to do up here in Lake Michigan. So I was not any competition to them. They are pretty tight down there. He taught me a lot of things I still use today. There was no one up here charter fishing; I had nobody. I was in my early twenties. I had two fishing poles, two baits, and two reels borrowed from my father-in-law. I was working at a marina up the river here. The guy I worked for, the owner of the marina, was the type of guy that made sure that if there was a buck to be made, he would either make it or whoever was working for him would make it.

Apparently, somebody came to the marina and said they wanted to charter a boat to go fishing. Well in those days, the salmon program was planted in one river up north, the Platte. There was a spring run that went by as they migrated north for the fall, but it only lasted two weeks. But we did not know that in those days. I think I charged him $50, and we went out. We trolled all day and never even had a strike.

As you worked you learned more. Back when I first started, I was sitting at the dock and a boat pulled in across the way. It had lettering all over it; it was a Shakespeare-sponsored charter boat. So I ran over and introduced myself. The captain was really friendly and nice. In fact, he even gave me some free tackle. He asked me about the number of passengers permitted with my charter license. I said, "License?" and he pointed to his Coast Guard license on the wall. And I said, "Oh, we have to have one of those?" That is how green everybody was around here. I said, "How do you do that?" And he told me I had to pass a test with the Coast Guard. So I went over to Chicago. I remember it took them an hour to find the test. It was an essay test, of all things, that is how old the system was. So I wrote down what I thought based on the rules of the road and a few other things. The commander called me in after I finished. He had my test there with all these red marks all over it. I had been to high school. I knew what the red marks meant. And he said, " Well, I just want to know why you answered it this way." So I explained and he passed me and I got my license.

Well then, now I am a full-fledged legal charter boat captain. So I quit my job at the marina—a mistake. I sat around for a few weeks waiting for all these people to come around. Well, I was told that the fish migrate; I knew nothing about salmon fishing, hardly any fishing. So a good friend of mine, a schoolteacher who got his license at the same time, we drove up north. We ended up in Montague and Whitehall. It looked like boom city. There were all these charter boats and the fishing was fantastic. So we came home and decided that is where we should take our boats. So a couple weeks later, we got up there. There were no boats. They were all gone. The next thing we know, the fish had migrated out of there. Manistee was now the big boomtown. When we got there, that was the end of the run as far as going any further north except up to the Platte and that's where it all started. That was a real boomtown.

After what happened in Manistee, we still had a spring fishery down here but it was short-lived. If you were going to be in the charter boat business, you had to follow the fish, which meant being away from home and working your way up the coast and all this. A lot of municipalities wanted to get fish planted. So rather than plant six million fish in two rivers, eight or nine million fish were planted in thirty rivers, with the expectation that we can all stay home in our own port. The system has worked pretty successfully and that is why you do not have the roving charter boats anymore. The roving charter boat business only lasted three, four, or five years before the DNR started planting in all the rivers. We used to get 250,000 or 300,000 fingerlings for the Black River, which gave us a nice spring fishery and a good fall fishery.

I got a charge out of being the first charter boat captain in South Haven. I was the first one to bring trolling boats and the party boats here. They had party boats like this in Saginaw Bay for many years prior to this, which, I guess, have all but died out now. I went to Florida and the East Coast to learn everything. There, you are talking three, four generations of party boat fishing. In fact, I bought my first boat in New York, on Sheepshead Bay. The only reason I bought it there was that it was the closest place to South Haven that would have enough boats and one possibly for sale. My father was going in as a partner with me. My father was a very stern person and he lived through the Depression and reminded all of us—through our growing years—of the Depression.

Scott Anderson began operating a charter boat fishing business in Leland sixteen years ago. He indicated that part of his job is to ensure that all of his customers have licenses and obey Michigan's fishing regulations. He must also comply with U.S. Coast Guard rules and regulations.

The DNR enforces the size limit. It all comes out in the management guide you get when you buy a license. I buy my own license once a year. I think it was $31 for myself for the entire year. Most people can buy a one-day license, which runs somewhere between $5 and $6. They have got a refuge just northwest of us which is called the South Fox refuge. Trout and salmon season begins the last Saturday in April. Lake trout have to be eight inches in the streams and sixteen inches in the lake. The DNR guide book has pictures of the fish. Needless to say, when we are out fishing, it is up to us to make sure that we meet those standards because we do not know whether or not that DNR officer is going to be sitting waiting for us to check our catch. We do everything we can right now to limit the number of fish people take. I do not take my limit when I go unless somebody does or can use the fish.

The boat itself is inspected every two years. There are two different inspections. There is a topside inspection where we look at safety equipment and make sure all the things work. Every six years there is a hull inspection, which is an inspection in which they check all the through-hole fittings. They actually climb around in the bilges and really take a hard look at the boat. Plus, in addition to that, you have to have your licenses and your things posted. You have to have your radio license. If you have got radar, you have got your radar license. There is an emergency procedure checklist.

Charter boat captain Lynn Ray indicated that some of his responsibilities are to ensure that those fishing on his boat hold appropriate licenses and obey DNR fishing regulations.

I have quite a good local business, but I built up a clientele that comes from Detroit, Grand Rapids, Chicago, Ohio, and from all over the country. Probably ten percent is local and ninety percent of the customers are tourists or people on vacation. It seems like everybody wants the salmon, mostly because of the size and the fight. The way the bays are situated and located this far north, our salmon fishery does not start until the end of August and runs through September. But the rest of the time we have lake trout which is our mainstay fish, and brown and rainbow trout. There is also a whitefish, perch and bass fishery in the bays, but there is not too much chartering done for those species.

Some of the customers are great fishermen. But a lot of them are just families here on vacation. Some have been fishing with me for a while. The other day, a guy who looked like he was about thirty, he had a boy that was ten with him and he said, "I had to bring him up and take him fishing with you because that's what my dad did for me when I was ten."

I have three trips available, a four-hour trip six until ten, or seven until eleven and noon until four, or one until five. Then I have a 5:30 till 9:30. Those are available because a lot of people have conventions. They have got meetings all day. They can go in the evening or they get off in the afternoon and they have meetings in the morning. During the spring, I do not offer all three, but I do in June, July, and August. After that, there is not enough daylight.

We have a twenty-inch size limit on lake trout and ten inches on everything else. We return a lot of lake trout and are very strict on the limits. The DNR is quite often there to check us and even if they were not, that is something we are staunch about. Everybody has to have a license if they go on a boat. We write licenses at the dock. We are a licensed agent, so we write one-day, six-hour licenses for the state. My secretary is bonded by the state to write them.

Operating a charter boat business out of Leland, Michigan, for sixteen years, Scott Anderson reflected on the demands and rewards of the operation.

Surprisingly, we get clientele from everywhere. I have had people from France and England. I had people from Russia last year. There is a big Ohio contingent up here because the way the railroads used to run from Cincinnati-Detroit-Traverse City. So still, one of my biggest zip codes is Cincinnati in my mailing. So we deal locally and we deal internationally. A lot of Germans were around here last weekend. I do not know whether there was a bus tour or something, but a lot of people were walking around here speaking German.

Everybody thinks this is an easy job. They say, "Ah, you go fishing every day." But it is not an easy job. What is the hardest part of the job? I have been asked that question before. I have a simple answer. It takes a little while. I leave the house somewhere between quarter to six and six o'clock in the morning. Last year, I had one day off in seventy-two days. It is a seven-day-a-week job. I did not have trips every day, but I was busy. I get down here about twenty after six o'clock. There is a cooler on my boat and there are people standing on the dock. Some of the people on the dock have not slept all night. They have been thinking about this trip ever since they booked it. Now maybe it was only yesterday, but I have got commitments all the way into September right now and I have got a lot of trips in June. Now these people are thinking, man, I cannot wait to get to Traverse City, get to Leland on June 20th. I am going to go fishing.

I am so excited and so where are the fish? They are four feet off the dock with an adrenaline rush and I am trying to drink my second cup of coffee. What do you have to do? You have to go and meet them. You have got to go right up there. It does not make any difference what is going on. You have to start the show right then. It is just a matter of getting things ready and things like that.

I can remember going out when I was kid. The engine started and I remember flying on to that boat. So they get on the boat and you start out. The whole trip is just a major adrenaline rush for these people. You stop the engines; people are still excited. You start catching fish. Now we are getting into a little bit of a routine. The questions are not one every thirty seconds; they are one every two minutes. I love how people switch places and join me on the bridge. I will get the same ten questions from seven or six different people. Anyway, that is part of the job. So then you go through your trip, you catch your fish, and on the way in, people just bottom out. They just zone out. They have been on a high for who knows how long and now it is over. They have had a good time.

So you come in, back into your slip. What's on the dock? Another cooler. People are hopping on the boat before the other ones are off. "What did you catch?" "Show us! Show us! Where are they?" Your lunchtime lasts about twenty minutes and you quickly have a sandwich because these people are sitting on your boat ready to go. So from 6:30 in the morning until 6:15, 6:30 at night when you are saying good-bye, you are on a twelve-hour high with these people and you have to take care of them. That is eighty-four hours a week when you do it times seven. That is the toughest part of the job. The toughest part of the job is going with the people when they want to be out, staying with the people through the highs and lows of what is going on.

Kids are cool. You put them in a chair, put it down by the back deck, the put the rod in the gambrel housing, put the rod up next, and that kid can crank all day long and not have mom or dad help. The kids' faces are just phenomenal. That is the coolest. I also enjoy the people who I have had with me for many, many years that are now friends. We will go to lunch with them or something like that. But kids are the coolest. There is a kid that I taught to ski when he was five years old. He and his dad still fish with me and he just turned seventeen.

I think there are thirteen charter boat captains in Leland. If you asked each one of them, "What's the purpose of your business?" I would guess that they would say, "The purpose of my business is to entertain my guests." If the fish are biting, it is easy. If the fish are not biting, guess what? It is quarters behind the ears and I start doing a dance step on the back deck. That is part of it. I got toys for the kids. You want a drink of beer on this boat? The beer flag has to go up. Fish are not biting, try this one. If you cannot catch the big ones, maybe you can catch some bass. So my business is entertainment. My business is not catching fish. I try to keep the guests involved. I teach skiing in the winter. If it is rough, I do ski lessons on the back deck of the boat because a lot of the similarities of standing on a moving deck are like what you would get on a ski hill. I have people setting lines. I just do whatever I can. We have got to entertain people.

Richard Stevenson discussed the difficulties in starting a successful charter boat business. He combines shipyard labor with work as a guide for other charter boat captains. Newly licensed as a charter boat captain by the U.S. Coast Guard, he takes customers out on his own boat whenever possible.

I work for Rowland Salvage. I used to build these big boats. Now I repair them for Rowland Salvage. I do a little guiding on the side. I have two kids. I cannot guide full time yet. I will probably do it for some of these captains on weekends when they have other things to do. A lot of the captains, like Fritz Peterson, fish bass tournaments and walleye tournaments. When Fritz Peterson fishes the walleye tournament, he needs somebody to run his boat. I am basically a part-timer right now.

As a guide, it is my job to know where to fish and what they are going to bite on. I make sure the customers are happy. A good guide always keeps his customers happy because lord knows that fish do not bite every day. If they are not biting, I can tell a lot of jokes. I have learned several jokes on these charter boats in the past twelve years. There is not really much you can do, just pray to God that something is going to hit that line. I just keep a smile, always having a positive attitude to keep everybody in a positive attitude.

The charter business has been growing quite rapidly. In the past twenty years it has probably tripled if not quadrupled. There were not that many fishermen around when I first started fishing. They planted salmon on that lake about thirty years ago

411

and that is when it pretty much started. The fishing was good just about everywhere thirty years ago. Sturgeon Bay really was not that popular of a spot.

Fishing was just a whole lot better twenty years ago. You could make a living guiding and now you cannot. I have to have two jobs. Lot of the captains around here have two jobs. They had this big PCB scare in the mid to late 1980s. It was a problem. It was a mess out there. They have cleaned things up a lot since then. But even back then, I do not think the fish were as bad as people made them sound. I think they said if you had a pound of fish a day for the rest of your life, you were going to die. That makes a whole lot of sense to me. My grandpa fished out there through the bad years when they planted fish out there. He died because he had glaucoma. He lived seventy-seven years. He was almost eighty when he died. It had nothing to do with any PCBs.

A lot of the pollution comes out of Green Bay and larger cities around here. These fish, there is nothing wrong with these fish. If you take a chicken and you grind it up the same way they grind these fish—head and everything—you will have just as many, if not more PCBs, in a chicken that you go buy at any supermarket as you have in these fish out here. It is just nothing but aiming at our fishing economy that we had going here. Notice I said "had." It kind of fell apart. Charter boats, we probably got twenty-five percent of the boats running charters out here now full time, probably twenty percent full time, as we did ten years ago. It has gone down big time. People do not want to fish any more.

Last year, we had eleven charter boats. We were one boat short, so we hired a captain out of Green Bay and I went with him. I was working for Jerry Cefalu at the time. His kid worked half a week and I worked the other half a week. There are probably only ten charters who are recognizable. There are some small ones and there's some bootlegging going around, too, but I would imagine that it is pretty hush-hush. They do not talk on the radio or anything like that too much. There are probably ten of them around.

The customers are mostly from corporations and people with a lot of money. You do not see too many middle or lower class people anymore running around out there because for one, society seems to be getting tight again. And a lot of people, especially middle class, they buy their own boats and do their own fishing. And you got all these TV shows and magazines and people read that information in their spare time and turn into instant fisherman and go fishing.

Most captains do not charge enough. A good size boat for trolling for salmon out in the lake, one that you can actually go out and fish in the waves with—a boat ranging between thirty-two and thirty-eight feet—runs between $400 and $500 a trip for six hours. They should be getting more because what people do not realize is that it probably costs $4,000–$5,000 a year just in docking. You have to pay for docking in the summer and storage in the wintertime. Dry-docking gets very expensive. You have to pay for your fuel. They probably burn fifty to sixty gallons of fuel a trip depending on the vessel and motors. And there is a lot of equipment, especially out here with all the competition with the sport fishermen and the other fishermen. They got sport shops selling lures and giving them tips on a marine band radio. They have got to buy a lot of lures. It gets pretty expensive. You probably spend $300 to $500 on new lures and it adds up. It takes a trip right there to pay for the lures. If a charter boat runs 100 trips a year, that is pretty good, because the business is going down. When the business goes down, you run less trips, and you make less per trip because your expenses are supposed to be spread out over the year's course, usually 150–200 trips. Fifteen years ago they charged $300 to $350 a trip and they did not even start raising prices until about five years ago. Then they went up a lot, which they should have, but they were afraid to raise their prices because of business falling.

Still, everybody wants to be a charter captain. We try to get along out there. It is not easy. There is a lot of back stabbing going on out there, but I think that is how it is been forever. When you get these guys you spend 100 hours a week out there and that is all they do. They are sitting out there. They get on the radio and they might get antsy or something. You have to watch what you say out there, because they will shoot you down and they will all group up on you and they wait for somebody to pick on, especially the new guys. We do not care for them too much and there's a little hostility between the new captains and people who been out there twenty years. A lot of these captains, we just lost one this year, he had been out there for thirty years. He is done for a year or forever, I guess. He retired but not by choice.

The charter boat captains used to be able to live off whatever they made in the summer. They charged the same amount, but they ran an extra fifty to seventy-five trips a year. They made more per trip because of it, because their overhead was already paid off after so many trips. So actually you make more if you run about seventy-five trips. Like one year you think your income would be half of 150 trips but it is not, 150 trips is like three times as much as seventy-five. You used to be able to make enough money where it would last you all winter and now, you have to have two jobs. Some guide through the ice. There are not many people who want a guide through the ice. There really are not that many ice fishermen around. A lot of them do not really need a guide to go ice fishing. You need a buoy. You go out there in your car and you pay $36 for an auger. It costs you $200 for a charter or you can buy your own equipment for $200 and drop your own pole. If you are a fisherman, you are a fisherman. You know how to catch a fish. If you want to go out on Lake Michigan, it is a lot cheaper to spend $400-$500 than try a boat yourself and do this because it is going to cost you money just to do it in the first place at your own expense. So that's why it is so hard to guide through the ice for perch fishing. People do not want to pay any money to do that when they can just do it themselves.

Boats follow you around so we pretty much stick to our reef out here. It is a pretty popular reef called the Bate Reef. People come from all over the country to fish that reef especially during the Door-Kewaunee County salmon tournament. The reef has the highest concentration of salmon in Lake Michigan. We had 2,000 fishermen in that tournament and usually three or four of the top ten places are caught off of that reef. You put two or three hired boats on that reef and they can be just bumper to bumper on there. It is only a two-mile reef. It goes from forty foot down to 100 foot and salmon like that. They get a lot of lake trout on there. There are a lot of fish on there. You go across that reef and there are always fish on your graph. But I have my own little spot because I do not like that—I am not a follower. I do not want to deal with it. I like to stay incognito and go far out. I found a pretty good spot myself. It does not have as high a concentration, but then there are not as many people fishing either which actually gives me an advantage and I will catch more fish on there because of it.

Formerly of the Michigan DNR and the Michigan Bureau of Tourism, Stan Lievense discussed how he adapted gear to suit the unique nature of salmon fishing in the Great Lakes.

There is stream fishing for chinook salmon. I did a first there. I met with a fisherman from the state of Washington who moved to Michigan. I was looking ahead trying to answer problems that might occur and I said, "These salmon are going to small streams. What do you do in the state of Washington if you get a big salmon on your line in one of these small streams?" It meanders all over the place, you know, winding here, there, and everywhere. He said, "You cannot land them so I just cut the line." That is what they did. No way would I ever cut my line, so I reasoned that there has to be a string with which you can hold him, so I designed a whole new fishery. Chinook like a fly. If you keep poking it in their nose when they are up at spawning time, they get aggravated and they will grab the darn thing. What I do is I marry the line to the handle, and do not give them an inch of line. The rod is pulled right down. So I finally learned, if I put the butt in my belly button, then I have leverage and he does not have any place to go. So this is what happened. He is throwing water all over the place and it is a very exciting type of fishery. From that, I learned what lines to use. It took twenty-pound test monofilament line to hold a twenty-pound test salmon or less, thirty-pound test monofilament to land a thirty pounder my way. And then a year or two later, I was honored to find out that I had been selected to the Fishing Hall of Fame.

As with most members of Lake Michigan's sport-fishing community, party boat operator Don Nichols (South Haven, Michigan) recalled the need to learn how to fish for salmon in the Great Lakes.

During the first rush of salmon, saltwater techniques and baits and everything were tried. It did not work real well and so it was a learning process. We were trolling on the top twenty-foot column of water and the fish are down eighty to ninety feet. So we invented the downrigger, which is now used on the coast and in Florida. We invented downriggers as a way to get your bait down deep, but still have the sport of just bringing fish up, not ten tons of lead. As far as where the salmon migrated to, that we knew because it was where the state had planted some three or four million. But when it was over, it was done. Coho salmon is a three-year fish. He will spend half that lifetime in the hatchery, and then the other half out on the lake. That last summer is when he puts on his weight and gets quite large. In those days, we never caught a fish less than twenty-two pounds. If you caught a twenty-two pound coho now, you would be famous. But that is just how much forage food there was out there. There did not seem to be any competition at all. Our lake trout fishery was real slow then because of the lamprey eel, over-harvesting, and other factors. The salmon had the whole reign of the lake and with all that food, it was quite a deal.

———————

Lyle Teskie (Gills Rock, Wisconsin) recalled making the transition from commercial fishing to charter boat operator. Although not frequently acknowledged, this occurrence sheds important insight on how individuals have negotiated dual membership in these tradition-bound occupations.

I became a charter boat captain because I left commercial fishing due to the new, advanced gear. There are two types of fishermen. There is one type of fisherman who is a gill-net fisherman—an older type of gear, more hard to work. You could not catch as much fish with it, and so the price of fish stayed up. I am talking about technology. Then, DNR allowed the trap net to come into the lake. They caught twenty times more fish. The price fell down to nothing. You caught 100,000 pounds of fish in a year and got $1-$1.25 a pound. Two people could live off of half that amount because you could split it—half for the fishermen and throw half at the rig. But after the trap nets were reintroduced, it was not three or four years before there were too many fish on the market. Now we got like forty cents a pound on 100,000 pounds of fish—$40,000. Throw twenty at the rig or sometimes thirty, and two fishermen could not live off of it. There were other things like the weather patterns. But I do not think you can just point your finger at one person. I know the DNR likes to blame the commercial fishermen for its problems. I do not like the bureaucracy because it is not governed by anybody. I do not personally have anything against the DNR other than what they do is almost for show, almost political. And that is the sad part. I made—I think it was $10,000 one year and $7,500 the next year. My accountant said, "Lyle, get out of business." So I did. I remember the day I let the boat go. It was like a divorce. That's how I felt when the boat left. But I had to do something. I had a family to support.

I guess you learn from being on both sides—commercial and sport. I suppose you would have to say there was a certain amount of desertion, but my family are reasonable thinking people. They knew the situation. They knew that I was not making a living. They knew that I had to do something else. My brother, Neil, is a commercial

Lyle Teskie is a native of Door County, Wisconsin who started commercial fishing with his father and brother, Neil Teskie, when he was a boy. No longer a commercial fisherman, Teskie now operates a charter boat and cottage rental service. Interview, 4 June 1999. Photograph courtesy of the Great Lakes Center for Maritime Studies.

fisherman. I have my charter boat right next to him. People get off the dock and buy fish from him if they do not catch any with me. It is one of those things. It is a unique situation. If everyone could get together like that and manage the lake, but the sad part is that I have a feeling that it is too late for the sport fishing to recover. I may lose my charter fishing business. I will lose the entire income in the charter business. I will lose the income during the month of July when the fish are out here and we rent slips to sport fishermen. But I will do something else.

I cannot get on the boat and honestly tell people that things are really great knowing the way they are. I do not want to come across as like I am the most truthful person, but I cannot do it because it is like you are on a boat and you start lying to people. People are not stupid. They have heard it at the restaurant. Now you tell them something different. They will hear it on the radio. It happened to me one time when I was telling everyone how great it was and somebody said, "No, it was horrible. It was horrible." And from that time on, I decided to tell the truth. It's one of those things. But I tell them the truth. They should know the truth. Why not?

Paul Goodman (Ellison Bay and Washington Island, Wisconsin) was a commercial fisherman and in the 1990s became a charter boat operator.

When I am doing charters, I am mainly targeting salmon. There are fishermen in the Sturgeon Bay area who target salmon, but they also target lake trout. It is a little harder to fish lake trout in this area than it is further south. There is not much in the bay. Years ago, when they first started stocking, the bay was just crawling with lake trout. It was pretty easy because the bottom's muddy and flat out there. But they stopped putting them in the bay because they were getting in the gill nets and we were fishing them in the bay. So then they started stocking them in the lake. Now, the lake side up here has a lot of rocky area so it is harder. You have to fish the bottom for them, so it is harder to fish them. If we were really pushed into it, we could probably do it. We could probably figure out ways to catch them. But fortunately, we have had the salmon—people hear the word salmon and they love to fish for them. It is the fish of choice. I have fishermen that fish other places for lake trout and they say it is like pulling an old boot off the bottom. And then they get a salmon on the run it is so exciting—that is the thrill for them. Chinook salmon is the fish of choice here.[34] Our season for charters is usually mid-June through the beginning of October. But July and August are our best months and then it is fringe on the other end. To make enough money to make a living is a little bit tricky.

We have lost a lot of people in chartering because fishing did go downhill in the charter industry over the years. It was so good. It was so good that people that did not even know how to fish could throw a line in the water and catch fish because they were really stocking heavy. You could throw a line in and not even know which end of the rod you were standing on and catch a fish. I mean, that is how good it was. And the boat traffic here was terrible. All the magazines had it as the best fishing pond in the world, and everybody was coming here and you could hardly stand the boat traffic. Then fishing went downhill a little bit and a lot of people who were bringing their own boats quit coming, which was okay. Bring back some sanity to the fishing—where you did not catch a fish every two minutes, but you would catch a fish once in a while.

We just have to keep hoping that nothing really throws it off. There are a lot of people who think we are going to be done charter fishing in two years. I have heard that for five years. It could keep on going for quite a while. It is a pretty big industry for the state. Even the Department of Natural Resources itself is kind of an industry. If they are not selling licenses to do things, they are not keeping their jobs. A lot of guys would be out of work in their industries if all this natural resource business was not going on. You can see it on the land around here. They promote deer hunting. Now they are stocking turkeys. We got turkeys in this area. That is all big money for them. It keeps a lot of their programs going. It keeps a lot of people employed and I do not think they are going to want to let go of the fishery.

Years ago, fishing, even pan fishing, was a big draw for people here. But our motels are not promoting fishing like they used to, because they do not really need the people. They have got them coming for the other things and would rather not have a cooler full of fish sitting in a motel room. You can see that tourism has changed. I know the resorts have all changed. They will keep brochures in there about fishing, but they do not care to advertise in the magazines promoting fishing because they are going to fill up—it does not take fishermen anymore.[35] We are just lucky that some of the people that come up to the Door Peninsula still like to fish.

We have had pretty good growth here. Our land values are up. If you bought land quite a while back, you are actually worth something. You may not have any money, but you got a piece of land that's worth something, so it makes a difference. There is no doubt it makes a difference. The growth here has been good that way. Even the people that come up here from the city do not want to see the growth, but if it was not to this point, they would not even be here. They would not be coming to an area that has nothing. People are kind of funny. They all come up here and say they want to be in the peace and quiet. But if you go to Sister Bay and north—tourism is like fifty percent of Sister Bay and Ephraim, because people want to go where there's something going on with people. All these people that want to be up in the north woods. There are a few trees and water sports, boat rides, a theater, and good restaurants, which they all like nowadays. When you are on the water—when you are commercial fishing—when you are on the water all the time you do not even see it happening. It can happen all around you. People from all over the place have T-shirt shops and little restaurants and all of a sudden, they are the ones that have really made the big living around here and they have only been here ten years or twelve years.

Holland's Gordon Zuverink recalled that, in spite of the euphoria that surrounded the early years of the coho salmon fishery, many sport fishers had neither the equipment, boats, or knowledge to safely fish the open waters of Lake Michigan.

After the first fall when the coho first came back the next year, that is when we started taking my buddy's boat out in Lake Michigan. Not very deep, but when the fish came near shore. That was primarily in August when they would start coming in closer and primarily out in the Manistee area, of course. That is where they honed in on it and so we chased salmon out there like everyone else did with primitive equipment. We used a pretty good sturdy rod and lures of some kind that would go down a ways and get these fish. We did not have the knowledge of going down to catch at the lower depths of fifty to sixty feet, other than putting a hunk of lead on the line and letting it go down there. Then, of course, that brought about the advent of the downriggers. Fishermen would figure out a way to get down there. If a pound of lead would not do it, they would put a pound and a half on to get down there. Mostly they tore the equipment up because they were so big at that time.

I recall that Saturday when the big storm hit in Manistee when I believe, seven fishermen drowned and many boats were capsized. The following day, Sunday, we were up there and went to Manistee and looked over the devastation. There were boats beached on the shore full of sand and water. I saw tow trucks trying to pull them out of there. There was so much sand in the boats they would pull them to pieces. We drove to Bear Lake and Bear Creek—off the Big Manistee River. And at the first bridge we drove across, there were fishermen lined on both sides of the stream just chasing these fish that were congregated in front of them. That is when they had altercations with the DNR. Guys were snagging fish, and the DNR was trying to arrest them. Fishermen would get into fights with the DNR. It was a nasty, nasty time.

Party boat captain Don Nichols discussed how the decline of heavy industry and increased awareness of pollution coincided with efforts to create a sport fishery and redevelop the lakeshore for recreational use.

During the 1950s–1960s, the Black River and many rivers were the backdoors to industry. The lakes and the rivers were where you threw your refrigerator when you were done with it. The beginning of recognizing big-time pollution was in the middle 1960s. They started mandating that every community along all the Great Lakes start cleaning up their sewage facilities. As a child in South Haven, I would see three or four recreational boats go fishing on a weekend. Two weekends ago, we had a thousand boats out here. During the week we have two or three hundred boats. Now we have a recreational fishery and with recreation, you are going to start to see how pretty river is. Soon it is let us remove that, and put in a condominium or something. All of these things—recognition of pollution, the decline of industry and the growth of recreational boating all formed together in the 1960s.were kind of forming together.It all just kind of worked together in my lifetime and here we are. Yachts are everywhere. I think we had something like eighty or ninety slips in this harbor back in the 1960s. We now have 2,800 and the harbor has not gotten any bigger. It just got a little more congested.

We have always had recreational fishermen and they have always had their small boats. We always had a perch fishery that was up and down. In the 1960s it was way down. It started bouncing back when they got a control on the alewives, because the alewife and the perch compete for the same areas. When that happened, you had more boats. I do not know whether alewife control also spurred recreational boating, not just fishing, because all of a sudden, we were starting to get a lot of yachts. We were starting to get yacht clubs. We were starting to get sailboats. The water became a real playground, which it was not prior to that time.

Fishing may have helped spur that along because of demand for more boats. Most of your fishing boats in those days were inland fishing boats. They were not the best thing to have out here in the lake. Companies started building fishing boats, big lake boats called coho boats, so you could go out and enjoy the sport in a safer boat than what we had in the beginning. So all of that, the boat companies and everything else, started spurring this and when you see somebody having fun on the water as a recreational use, then fun can also be living on the water. So it all kind of grew together. There was an instant there in 1973, when the energy crisis was on. All of a sudden all the yachts were replaced with sailboats. We had about an eight- or nine-year period there when everybody owned a sailboat. Even the fishermen were sailing out there. But it is kind of going back to more powerboats now. But it is not just South Haven. It is everywhere.

Sport fisherman Gordon Zuverink recalled how the early years of the salmon program completely reshaped attitudes toward sport fishing on the Great Lakes.

When Pacific salmon were introduced by Howard Tanner, why that produced a fantastic fishery. I was in on the start of it. I remember my fishing buddy, Gene Groters from Holland, had a cabin at Peacock, right on the Little Manistee River. In the spring of 1966 the coho were first planted in the Big Manistee River and Bear Creek. In the fall we heard they were catching some coho, so we made a few trips up on the Bear Creek. That was where I caught my first coho jack. He was not a mature fish. I caught him on a Mepps spinner. I will never forget it. There was a start of a fishery and it was probably fifteen to sixteen inches long and that was the first run of jacks that came out of Lake Michigan.

The following fall 1967, we had the big ones, fifteen to seventeen pounds. We really got into it on the Big Manistee River at that time. You would stand shoulder to shoulder among the fishermen catching, getting a hold of these big coho, and they were large at that time. That was really fun. When the run first started that fall, I will never forget it. It was a Sunday. My wife and I were up at Gene's cabin and we took his boat out and launched it at the mouth of Bear Creek and the Big Manistee, and we were fishing for steelhead. We were fishing on a favorite gravel run of ours, what was eventually known as "farmer's yard" where the big fish, where the big coho came in. And we were anchored and fishing this gravel run and all of a sudden we heard some commotion downstream and there was a bunch of fish porpoising coming up the river. The river was alive with fish and they stopped right in the run where we were fishing because that was a favorite holding spot for them. We thought we died and went to heaven. The fish were jumping all over the place and we never did land one. We did not have strong enough equipment to hold them, but we would get a hold of them and they would jump and fly around and break our line off. But that was the first run that came into the Big Manistee River and that was the start of it and Gene Groters and I were sitting right in the middle of it.

Coho were put in in 1967 and 1968. I believe we had the first run of coho and then a year or two later, they put in chinook. It was three years before chinook really came back in great numbers at Tippy Dam, so it had to be the early 1970s. We would not go fishing until dark, and we would get back to the cabin at twelve or one o'clock, and have three or four of these big monsters with us. And of course, that is when our equipment got stronger, the rods got stiffer, and the line got stronger. Using our ingenuity of various terminal tackle—tying yarn on a hook along with the crawler and then cutting rubber crawlers in half did the trick. In the late 1960s, I built my own cottage up north. We always looked forward to Friday night when my wife and I could run up to the cottage on Little Bass Lake, which was north of Scottville, and east of Free Soil. We spent all our free time up at that cabin because we were chasing fish.

We also had surf fishing at that time at Ludington. The big chinook would look for the mouth of the Big Sable River where they were born to go up and spawn. So the fish would be migrating back and forth in the surf out at the state park. We would throw spinners out there and catch salmon and stand out in the waves in our waders. I remember several times when I was standing out there and a whole school of chinook came right at me. Mostly, I fished on the north side and they were coming from the north to the south and looking for the mouth of the river and they were all around me, behind me, in front of me, and around my boots, bumping into my boots—big chinook salmon. I saw the same thing at the Platte River with coho, fishing out in the surf when the coho are looking for the mouth of the Platte River. I was standing out there on the sandbar fishing and here comes a whole school of coho behind me, between me and the shore, and they are going to run up the mouth of the river. These were some fantastic experiences, I will tell you.

Party boat operator Don Nichols noted that his job required a thorough, up-to-date knowledge of the ecology, culture, and history of Great Lakes fisheries. More important, in applying this knowledge, he sees a role for himself in protecting the fishery.

During the 1960s, the federal government was working on trying to bring back the lake trout, a native fish. The state worked on that too, but the federal end of it was bigger because that was the last big commercial fish that the commercial gill nets took along with whitefish. The lake trout made a pretty good recovery, but not as well as they would like. It could be because they are not natural. They are raised in the hatchery. They spawn differently now than they did naturally, so there are a lot of different factors. And they are learning things all the time, the state is, and I try to stay up on what I can, not so much the game fish anymore because my business is perch, and we have had some problems with that, so I pretty well stay up on that information.

At the time, I wanted fifty perch per day. There was no limit and then they went to 100. Fishing is about eighty percent psychological; the rest is the fish, the fun, and the hype. I have to play that psychological game out here. I have seen it where you go out there and the guys were really into the fish. When he starts getting over fifty, he is getting as frenzied as the fish are. And then when the trip's over and we go in, the fisherman says, "Oh my goodness, what am I going to do with all these fish?" I have seen that time and time again. Yet, if you put a limit on there, a limit that if he goes home with—right now it is thirty-five perch—that is more than a meal, but the idea of a limit is that he has accomplished something. I do not care if it took him four hours, one hour, or two. Wow, I hit a limit. This spring (1999) we were getting limit catches out there and everybody was ecstatic. Then, once in a while, somebody points out and says, "You know, that's still not a lot of fish—not like we used to get." Four thousand, eight hundred was the best I ever did out here on one day. Now, 1,000 fish—everybody has got their limit. It is the psychological part of it to a fisherman. Yes, I was an advocate for limits way back just to cut out the waste and give an accomplishment to the fishermen that I am entertaining. That is what I am in, I am in the entertainment business here. The fishing is second.

It is not against the law, but we do not allow sorting of fish on our boats when we are out in water over fifty feet deep. Now, your spring fishery, which is our best fishery, that is our most consistently good catches. You catch some small fish and you catch some big fish. When they come up from that depth at that speed, their air bladder explodes and you see little boats out there, old-timers wanting that big perch, can only get thirty-five, so he is sorting, throwing the little ones back. You can go out there and get your limit with a net just for the little fish flopping around on the surface. If we try to say something on the public address system, we just get some rude remark back because it is not illegal. So now we try to educate. Now, down in Florida, they put a lot of restrictions on bottom fish, on size and everything. But again, you bring a fish up from that depth and that air bladder, you puncture that air bladder and he's got a ninety percent chance of making it. That will heal and he can get back down to the depth he came from. So we try to educate people. We do not allow any sorting on here, but little boats that are alongside us, we will say, at least puncture the air bladder. So that is a conservation thing that we do on here.

Perch are just too valuable. I have never had a person on here yet that said, "I am just here to fish. Give my fish away." They want the fish. Perch are the lobster of the Great Lakes and it was seventeen dollars a pound at one time here a couple years ago. It is a valuable fish and I do not think anybody, even nonfish eaters, does not like to eat perch. When I started out, the state had a little thing written on the beer can, please puncture and make sure it sinks totally. Everybody threw their trash over the side including candy wrappers and what have you. Once in a while, I will have an old-timer on here that still does things the old way. We are polite about it, but we are firm about it too. We abide by the law. You do not go over your limit. You do not do this; you do not do that. Under the law, our sewage systems are contained on the boat—you have to bring it back to the dock to pump it off. Come a long ways from—I used to be embarrassed out there—go flush a john, it just went right out the side of the boat.

Everybody who is a nonfisherman will take a look at the fish and bring it up and say, "Oh my gosh, look at the tongue sticking out." But it is his air bladder and it is pumped up. There is a lot of pressure down there at sixty-five feet and so you bring him up and it just expands. And the first thing he does is vomit and then the air bladder comes right up the mouth. Well, there is no way that he can reduce that air bladder to go back down. It is not like a puffer fish in the ocean. But, if you puncture the air bladder, the air comes out just like a balloon and then he can get back down. The biologists tell me that it will heal. Now, if you are in fifty feet of water or less, you do not usually have that kind of problem. Then I do not mind. People want to throw the little ones back and just keep big ones, that is fine. But if the fish is not going to make it, then you are going to keep it.

We have two types of fishermen. One is a professional. He wants meat. He does not care how rough or cold it is. He does not care about the weather. He does not care about anything but catching a lot of fish. That is what we run into in the early part of the season. We also have the tourist fishermen. They walk by our little sidewalk sign and say, spur of the moment, "Golly that looks like fun. Let's do it." They do not need a lot of fish. They just are going for the experience like a Grandpa taking his kid for the first time to catch his first fish. So that is basically it—otherwise fishermen are made up of every kind of walk of life that you can think of. I can see the guy walking down the ramp and I will tell you number one, if he will he get sick or not, and number two, if is he going to be a hard one to please or a happy one to please. After a while, you just pick this up because we run 9,000 to 10,000 people a year. There are fishermen from all walks of life. It is not just one type of person. But those are the basic groups that we have. The professional brings his own equipment. He is going to fish hard. The tourists take one of our rental rods and beat it to death.

If somebody is going on their first trip, you can be aware of that and not treat them like some ignorant fisherman and teach him. Now he has to want to learn, too. Fishermen are funny that way. Either they want to learn or they do not want to hear a thing. If they have their own theories, that's fine, but if they want to learn, I will teach them what I know. And yes, I find people that are interested in this particular sport. They want to learn and they do understand the resource—all my steady customers, which makes up about forty percent of our business. These are weekly customers, come every week. They are just about as aware of everything as I am. I am, as you can see, a talker, so they want to listen, they want to learn and I will tell them. I think I have four customers left that date back to 1975; we call them originals. In 1973 or 1974, that is when I started party boat fishing. Prior to that, it was trolling. I still have a couple originals. They are like family. I have had people get on here and have such a good time they come every week until they burn out.

You have to like people to be in this business. You have got to really like them, because there is going to be the ones that stress you out, the ones that put the pressure on, and the ones that you cannot please. I have had them call me up and say, "I am bedridden now but I would like to go one more time." I say, "If you get here, we will load you on." I have had people come down that were told they had six months to live, three months to live, heart failures, cancer, and said they were going to spend the rest of their feeling good days going fishing with me.

————————

Scott Anderson, a sixteen-year veteran of the charter boat fishing business, commented on the economic shortfall created by declining salmon stocks.

There is a decline in the charter operations as a result of the loss of salmon. When salmon fishing came on, so did charter boat operations. As salmon fishing declined, charter boat operations did too. It should be in the public record. The DNR has all those records. I am going to say I guess there were 1,100 charters on the Lake Michigan side at one time. It might be down to 800 now. And that is partly a result of the demise of the salmon fishery. A whole bunch of things have affected it. The reason they were put in was to control the alewife. Back in the 1960s, we had three-foot piles of stinking fish along the shore that killed the tourist industry in Michigan. So they put the salmon in. They started with coho, then put chinook. Now we developed a salmon fishery because they were only a four-year or a two-year-old fish, which was great. They come up to spawn, people catch them. They give a big fight and are lots of fun to catch. Then the forage base started to decline. That is one of the reasons. The reason the forage base declined was because there were people in Wisconsin waters netting what they call the biomass for cat food. They were taking billions of pounds of alewife and smelt for cat food in huge nets. So that was one reason. The second reason is that fish started to get bacterial kidney disease. So we were starting to see die-offs of fish because of bacterial kidney disease.[36] We got into a situation where they started to reduce the plants because there was some natural reproduction occurring in some streams. So they started reducing that. We had our friends putting gill nets in waters. Needless to say, the number of charter boats dictated the number of salmon caught. There were a lot of charter boats, a lot of salmon caught, and that was part of it. There were a lot of articles done back in the early 1990s about the demise of the salmon fishery, what happened to it, and why it happened. We are just right now starting to see it pick up just a little bit.

Last year was not as good as the year before but compared to three years ago, but we are doing a lot better. That is good news. Now if the treaty says they can net salmon, that's bad news. They have given the opportunity to the tribes to have the weirs in Traverse City.

The weir is in a fake creek on the Boardman River. That's the best way to describe it. They put a block in the river and they put this staircase down into the water. The fish jump. Salmon jump up and they are caught in runways and harvested. It was put in as part of the agreement. They needed a spot to harvest the eggs. The fish ladder also gets the salmon into the bays. They wanted salmon fishing in the bays. From the time I got here up through 1992, Leland was the number one salmon port in the state of Michigan. Leland was a little tiny port with very little activity. Then we started losing our salmon fishing. Leland used to be in the top five in catches per hour, in other words, fish caught per hour.

Sport-fishing writer and fishing guide Kevin Naze (Door County, Wisconsin) discussed changes in the local salmon fishery. His narrative also reveals how journalists participate in the boosterism that surrounds Lake Michigan's sport fishery.

Most people would agree that the mid-1980s was probably the heyday of Lake Michigan salmon fishing. After they collapsed, people needed something else to look forward to, so they started exploring the lake and they started roaming the mid-lake area, ten to twenty miles offshore or better. And they started finding these steelhead that the Wisconsin DNR began stocking in 1984, I believe, including the skomania strain and Chambers Creek. These fish preferred to roam the whole lake and feed near the surface. And they are an exciting fishery because when you hook one, they jump four or five or six times. If they come off a wave, they are six feet in the air sometimes. It is really neat. People just get really pumped up to see that the first time. A lake trout will sit and dog you on the bottom and tire your forearms out. You feel like you are lifting up a ten-pound weight. Salmon will zip out so much line you wonder if you are going to run out of line. All of a sudden, he stops, and you have got to reel in as fast as you can. A rainbow will just jump and jump and jump and it is pretty exciting, pretty intense to watch them. Sometimes they literally jump themselves to death and come back on the surface just across the top, you are reeling as fast as you can and they are just coming in at the end. That is as good as it has ever been.

With the exception of last year, the mid-1990s to 1997 was the best catch per angler hour in charter boat history. In other words, if there are six guys on a boat fishing six hours, that's thirty-six angler hours, let us just say. And they are averaging around, I think it was around .4 to .5 fish per angler hours. So it figured out to, if you multiply it all together, it is around fifteen fish a trip or something like that which is not that bad, better than even in the heyday of the 1980s. But I think the size of the salmon maybe was better in the 1980s—for overall numbers. The number of twenty-pound salmon was better in the 1980s. During the early to mid-1990s, after salmon crashed and there were fewer of them, the remaining ones got bigger.

The Door-Kewaunee salmon tournament is nine days every summer, at the end of July through early August. I believe it was around 1994 or 1995, we had fifteen salmon over thirty pounds registered in that nine-day period and that was a record. And the next year, it was about thirteen. In recent years, it has been only three or four again. But in the 1980s, some years it was twenty-six pounds, twenty-eight pounds, and twenty-nine pounds, that won the whole tournament. The size has gotten bigger as the numbers have gone down. The chance for a trophy is even better than ever as evidenced by a sixteen-year-old kid going out on his first charter ever in 1994 and comes back with a 44.92-pound salmon. The stories that are out there, the untold stories—that is the neat thing to me as a reporter. For example, that kid with the salmon, they weighed that fish at Max Sports Shop at 44.4 pounds. They called me up in Algoma. I was laying in bed because we had a thunderstorm in Algoma. Otherwise, I would have been on the lake fishing myself. So I zip all the way up here. Hey, let us take that fish over by the boat and get some pictures. So we got some pictures and all of sudden we get a call on the cell phone. Get that fish back here. The DNR has to be here at the weigh-in to make it official. So here this fish had been dripping blood and crap. We know it has lost some weight and the old record was forty-three pounds or something. So we thought, oh my gosh, what if it lost all that water weight. So we stick a hose down its throat and fill it up with water and stick it in the cooler filled with water and make sure it's soaking up water, all the water it lost. We bring it back and it weighs a half-pound more than it did. So there is an untold story that has never been written, so I get to see some things that just are better left unsaid, I guess.

The sixteen-year-old kid who caught the fish got up in the middle of the night, around one o'clock in the morning. They were from Oconto. He did not want to come over. His dad said, "Come on, we are going fishing." "Oh man, I want to sleep." You know how it is when you are a high schooler. So they drive over and they draw cards. He is the first one drawn. They just head out on the boat five to five and around first line, second line in, that fish went off and they handed him the rod and he fought it for about twenty-five minutes and he told the captain, "You got a line cutter? I cannot take this in. I am so sore." He was just fed up. And all of a sudden, the fish came to the boat and he saw the size of it. The captain was never going to cut the line anyway, but he was teasing him with the nail clippers. The kid was saying, "Get out of here, get out of here." Then the fish took out line again and about twenty minutes later, he has himself a state record. The kid went from really being exhausted to being exhilarated when he saw the beauty of that fish and its size.

Paul Goodman (Ellison Bay and Washington Island, Wisconsin) began working on the water as a commercial fisherman and later became a charter boat operator. His dual affiliations with both fisheries allow him to offer some alternative viewpoints on the culture of sport fishing in northern Lake Michigan.

If the commercial fishermen needed help and somebody to stand up for them in northern Lake Michigan—because it looks like there's a conflict with the sport fishery in the south end of the lake—the sport fishermen in northern Lake Michigan would do it. I am sure that it would happen. I have already had commercial fishing people approach me and say, "Could you get your club president to put in a good word for us when he is talking to the DNR?" Yes, we can. And why not? You like to see fishermen making a living. I have my foot in both worlds. I am dealing with the sport men and I am dealing with the commercial fishermen, so I want to see them both survive. You got two industries that may be dying and you are trying to keep them both going.

When I started charter fishing, I put a lot of stress on myself because you have to catch this fish and you have to do this and that. You realize that it is not just the catching of the fish. You are on the water and people are enjoying it and they are on vacation and you catch some fish. You do not have to go out and kill a bunch of fish. I do not even put a picture of a fish on my brochure for that reason. I see some pictures and they have a rack of twenty or thirty fish and I am thinking I am not going to catch twenty or thirty fish every time and these people really do not need twenty or thirty fish. If they catch a couple fish or have a good time, it is okay. They might do real well. They might have twenty or thirty fish, but I really do not like to take meat hunters fishing because charter fishing is a sport thing. If they want to commercial fish, they should come down to the fish market, buy a bunch of fish, and then take the ferry for a boat ride. But if they are serious about having a good time and catching some fish, that is the way I look at it. It is more of an entertainment thing. Any time that you are playing and you can afford to go out and buy your dinner, I think it is a sport. I think it changes.

Some people do catch and release. Some people call that playing with your food, but it is good sport. I do not think that they should take it so serious that they want to fill their freezers up. Some people do and I have kind of eliminated that in my fishery.

I rescheduled myself to start at like nine o'clock in the morning, so I eliminate some of that problem right away. I get people that like to go fishing. It is a sport and they are having a nice day. They take a lunch along. I do not promote killing a bunch of fish. That's the personal way I manage the resource and it is the way that I manage to be with the kind of people I like to be with. I also consider it good business practice because if the fishing goes downhill at all—which it did for a few years—my people were still coming back. They are still going to catch some fish.

---

2. THE MOST POLITICAL LAKE: SPORT FISHERS FIND A VOICE

Sport fisher Gordon Zuverink recalled that prior to the stocking of salmon, there was little interest in fishing on the lake beyond the perch and the steelhead fisheries.[37]

Lake Michigan fishing for me did not start until Pacific salmon were put in. Other than shore fishing, I did not do any boat fishing on Lake Michigan until the late 1960s and early 1970s when the Pacific salmon were introduced. We chased steelhead in the streams, but there were not many of these migratory trout. In fact, probably in the late 1950s and early 1960s we started taking vacations in the spring and fall at Grand Marais and the Big Two Hearted River. That is where I caught my first big steelhead in the Big Two Hearted. They reside in Lake Superior, but in the spring and fall they would make their runs into the Big Two Hearted River which was probably the most commonly known fish stream up there. And we fished some of the smaller streams off of Lake Michigan. But that is the only place we could really catch any steelhead. As the years progressed, they became more numerous there in the Big Two Hearted River. I spent time in the Upper Peninsula with my father-in-law fishing the Fox River, but those are the two rivers in the Upper Peninsula that really caught my attention—the Fox at Seney just south of Grand Marais, and the Big Two Hearted.

I also fished for steelhead in the Big Two Hearted River with a fishing buddy of mine. The steelhead started showing up in the Big Manistee from Tippy Dam on down. My fishing buddy had a riverboat at that time. We would chase steelhead on the Big

Manistee primarily from Tippy Dam down to the mouth of Bear Creek. If you went up there for a weekend and caught one or two steelhead, you had a great time. That is when I almost gave up on the stream fishing, the little fish, and chased the migratory fish. They were almost extinct. I read stories, history prior to the collapse of the fishery, where guys would go out and catch ten or twelve steelhead, take them home in a gunny sack off of the Big Manistee. Then it collapsed like everything did when the sea lamprey reached Lake Michigan. They killed off everything left by industrial pollution and some overfishing with gill nets.

Gordon Zuverink recalls how Michigan Steelheaders was promoted involvement in the policy making process of the Michigan DNR to build political and public support for sport fishing. He illuminates the historical relationship that developed between these two Lake Michigan fisheries stakeholders.[38]

The Steelheaders were instrumental in forming a committee. We kept pressing the DNR saying that we should have some citizen input into DNR affairs and the things that DNR was going to do. So we were instrumental in saying that this task force should be formed. It was called the Lake Michigan Task Force. Now it is called the Lake Michigan Advisory Committee and Lake Huron Advisory Committee and Lake Erie Advisory Committee. They have three now. It started with the Lake Michigan Task Force. We would meet probably every six weeks and DNR personnel would be there to tell us what their plans were and they would answer our questions. We would bring issues to them, things that needed attention, and it was a very good working committee. That is why they decided to add a Lake Huron and a Lake Erie task force also. I sit on the Lake Michigan Advisory Committee. It is good for the sport fishermen's interests. It is a way to let the DNR know about sport fishermen's problems and interests. If someone is a fishery biologist, he may have a one-track mind. We have to give him the end users' thoughts on how best to do these things, whether something will work or will not work, or is in the best interests of sport fishing. After all, that is why these fish are put in there, for our use, for sport fishing use. The salmon were originally put in not for a sport fishery but to get rid of the alewife and it worked, but it provided a world-class fishery.

Norm Spring, a life long sport fisherman from Grand Haven, Michigan, was a founding member of Michigan Steelheaders, a leading sport fishing organization. Interview, 28 June 1999. Photograph by Michael J. Chiarappa.

Norm Spring of Grand Haven recalls that in 1967, Stan Lievense of the Michigan DNR (formerly the Michigan Department of Conservation) played a leading role in helping sport fishermen create the politically active organization known today as Michigan Steelheaders.

I have always been active in hunting and fishing. My father got me started in it when I was a young fellow. I have never lost interest in either hunting or fishing, but particularly fishing over the years. We arrived in Grand Haven, my family and I, in 1961 and I began teaching in the local school system. I joined the North Ottawa Rod and Gun Club the very first year that I was in Grand Haven. I was in other organizations in other communities as well. I was up in Sebewaing prior to that, and I was down in Oxford prior to that. I always got involved in outdoor activities of one sort or another and mostly hunting and fishing. But when I joined the North Ottawa Rod and Gun Club in Grand Haven, it expanded into other things and these other areas came up and are interrelated.

433

When we moved to Grand Haven, a lot of us felt that there was not much fishing going on in Grand Haven. We thought that perhaps we ought to do something about promoting fishing to a bigger extent than it already had been. And so we decided to form a fishing organization and we eventually named it Michigan Steelheaders. And a fellow who was very active in this formation of the Michigan Steelheaders was a friend of mine that worked for the DNR as a biologist, Mr. Stan Lievense. He was still living up in Traverse City at this point and from the DNR's area of expertise, he was able to help us a great deal in forming this organization. The very first meeting we called was in Grand Rapids in April 1967. The meeting was called by sending letters out to known fishermen around the state of Michigan and advertising in the newspaper that we were going to form this fishing organization. We met in the museum in Grand Rapids. And according to some of the news reporters who showed up at the time, they estimated that there were over 500 people who showed up for that very first meeting. Well, we elected a president. I happened to be elected as the very first president and Ron McCandlis was elected as the secretary. We formed a board of directors whom we appointed and started meeting in the different towns for directors' meetings. Then we had annual meetings throughout the state of Michigan and we ended up by traveling to about seventeen different communities around the state of Michigan in the springtime, calling these meetings "Coho Salmonars." Well, eventually to make a long story short of this organization, we ended up with a lot of different organizations that were affiliated with the state of Michigan and the Michigan Steelheaders. They are all local Steelheader groups and now it is a pretty good size organization.

Our primary purpose in forming this organization was to have a better voice in the fishing in Michigan and, as you well know, back in the early 1960s coho was planted and that developed into history now. We have had a lot of say-so in a variety of different matters in how we fish, the numbers of fish that were taken, and the planting of different fish. I must say, it has turned out to be a pretty good fishery for the sport fishermen in Michigan.

As a fish biologist, Stan Lievense had a keen interest in all aspects of fishing. He was just a member of the fishery part of the DNR, but was able to help our group considerably in making appropriate contacts with other fishermen and finding facilities for us to use and at least that got us started. Of course the DNR had ideas that the average fisherman probably would not think of, so we shared information and worked together as two groups of people that were interested in the same thing, sport fishing. Well, in reality it was a little bit the other way around. Stan Lievense and some of the people he worked with felt that it would be a good idea to have a fishing organization. Stan happened to be a good friend of mine and he knew that I was a fisherman and he actually approached me and we talked about that collectively. And so I would say that Stan was more the impetus in forming this organization. He encouraged me.

Michigan Steelheaders is the largest sport-fishing group that exists in the state of Michigan—oh, absolutely. There are several chapters of the Steelheaders and several different communities have their own chapter with several that have maybe 100 or 200 people or more involved in just that local community. So it is probably the most, the largest fishing organization in the state. There are some derivatives from the Steelheaders. Some have broken away and call their chapter something else. But nevertheless, a lot of it started with the Steelheaders. I do not want to take anything away from any organization, but I would say that the Steelheaders probably are still the strongest. The MUCC has had other fisheries interests and committees, but never anything like the Steelheaders. I would say within the rubric of MUCC, the Steelheaders have the most extensive network in my opinion. The Michigan Steelheaders was interested in all species of fish in Michigan as far as sport fishing is concerned, not just salmon. The steelhead is just for a namesake, the steelhead seemed to be the most desirable kind of a fish in Michigan because it is an anadromous fish. It goes up in the stream to spawn and goes back out on the big lake. It is a strong fish and it lives longer than the salmon does which dies after it spawns. But the Michigan Steelheaders are interested in all species of fish.

Charter boat captain Lynn Ray is a member of the DNR's Lake Michigan Task Force, a policy-making advisory committee, and served as president of the Grand Traverse Area Sport Fishing Association.[39]

I know most of the local DNR officials. They inspect our boats and we see them around. I cannot say that I have actually had any problem with any of them. Some are friendlier than others, but I am very happy with most of them. I am on the DNR Fish Advisory

Council for Lake Michigan. We are an advisory council for the DNR, but it does not have anything to do with the officers. It is called the Lake Michigan Task Force.

The Lake Michigan Task Force started when we had a real problem with the fish population in Grand Traverse Bay. The Indians had their nets across there. They came down in here for a few years and just about eliminated the fishing. So they are trying to build it back up and it is coming back. We are getting along with them. This was in the early 1980s to about 1985. If you went out there and saw four or five fish you were excited. They were catching lake trout and that is our mainstay here in the bays. I am not totally against Native American fishing. There is a commercial fishery out there, especially out on the big lake, and if anybody is going to be allowed to take them, I think they should be. The gill net is my real problem because it just kills everything. Anything that gets in it is dead.

With the trap net, the fishermen can return sports fish like lake trout. They can keep their whitefish and the commercial species. On the big lake in the deep water, they catch chubs and can use gill nets deep. They do not hurt the other fish. We used to get all upset about it and we realized that it is a treaty. We have got to recognize it and work together. That is the issue right now, support their fishery, give them the fishery, and try to keep one for the sport fishermen too. That is why I got involved. I was president of the sport fishing association for four years. Brian Springstead is now president. I resigned a couple years ago. It just got to be too much. But what they are trying to do—on the bays here—small boats can get out there. People come up on vacation and they can all go fishing. I remember when I used to see seventy or eighty boats out here on the bays when the fishing was good. You would go down to Frankfort or Leland and they have six-foot waves. That involves getting out in the big boats and charter boats and guys will not take a chance on it. That is why I thought these bays should be preserved for the sport fishermen. More people could get out and more people can utilize it. Not everybody can afford a forty-foot boat.

The Lake Michigan Task Force does not really do much with the Native American issue. It deals more with size limits. They went to a twenty-four-inch limit on lake trout in Grand Traverse Bay. The size on the lake trout in Lake Michigan is ten inches. The legal size on lake trout in Grand Traverse Bay was twenty-four inches because our population of lake trout was down so low. After about three years, it was killing our business. Then they came out with fish advisories as far as eating fish. Do not eat any fish over twenty-four inches, but you cannot keep lake trout until they are twenty-four inches. It was contradictory. Everybody that got on the boat would ask, "Can we eat these fish if they are over twenty-four inches?" That really caused a lot of problems, so we got the task force to reduce the lake trout limit size to twenty inches in the bays. Now I think it should be twenty all over. I would like to see them go statewide with that rule. But we did get it down to twenty inches and it has helped our catches. It makes people happy. Take a three-year-old kid out who has never caught anything bigger than a blue gill and get him a four-and-a-half-pound lake trout. Then you had to say, "Well, that's not big enough so you have to throw it back." You would almost rather he did not catch it than take it away from him. But twenty inches is feasible.

The Grand Traverse Area Sport Fishing Association has a big annual meeting. We have a membership now of about 700. We had it up to 1,000 or so. As a matter of fact, we had 1,100 at one time but then after the treaty issue was over, the guys faded off. This year, due to the consent order, it will be way up again. We have an annual meeting and a lot of the fishing companies and boat companies donate prizes. We have a large raffle and a big dinner. We take some of that money and put it towards the ponds kids fish in during the Cherry Festival Parade. In 1999 we had two or three fishponds because they went over so big. That is one of the things we would rather be doing with our money than spending it on attorneys. I just hate to guess how much. It used to be over $100,000 a year for our attorneys. We would rather be putting that money back into fishing, but we just do not have it. We do the fishpond and we are probably going to try to do a senior citizen fish trip, where guys in the association take some people out fishing. They would probably do a lot more if we did not have all those attorney fees.

Most of our membership is not local. They are from all over the state and from Wisconsin and so forth. When there are no issues, the membership fades. But now that the Native Americans are asking for more fishing area from Leland down to Arcadia during the last year, all of a sudden the guys from Frankfort are saying, "Oh-oh." They run right back in and join the association. So that is why our numbers fluctuate, depending upon the issues. They have been asking to go down to Arcadia for the last couple years and the judge has turned them down because that was not in the original agreement—it was just to Leland. The Indians say they are running out of fish and we wonder why. By asking to expand their area means they are taking too many fish.

It is a black-and-white issue to me. If you gave me a certain area and say I can do anything I want there and then I say I need more, they are going to say you have not been taking care of what you got. That is basically what has happened. They are talking about doing some fish planting now. The state and the feds do all the planting. Tribes do not have any hatcheries and do not have anything else.

During the renegotiation of the 1985 Consent Agreement, Scott Anderson, a charter boat operator out of Leland, maintained that sport fishing—particularly charter boat interests—would organize in opposition to the expansion of tribal fishing areas if they realized the extent to which it could threaten their livelihood.

The Grand Traverse Area Sport Fishing Association is the only organization right now that is really involved with this negotiation process. As charter boat operators, we should be educating our clientele about what could happen. The problem we have is that it is only the Traverse City and Hammond Bay people that see and hear about tribal fishing every day. Frankfort does not see it because they are forty miles south. Onekama does not see it, but there is a group down there that is supportive. We get no support from Ludington.

If a tribal fisherman was coming in to Manistee harbor every day with ten tubs of lake trout, three tubs of salmon, and a tub of brown trout, all of a sudden they would know what is going on. When the Consent Order Agreement is renewed, I think they will have tribal fishing down there and all of a sudden, before they realize it, they will see what has happened. We will see what the new 2000 Consent Order Agreement will bring. I have hopes. Of course, when the 1985 agreement was signed there was a stipulation in there about trap netting only. That did not work. We provided boats and that did not work and we ended up right back where we are. But it will be interesting to see what the agreement gives us.

Sport fisherman Stan Lievense continued to promote sport fishing on the Great Lakes even after he left his position with the Michigan DNR. His commentary illuminates the economic interests that link government, tourism, and sport fishing.

After working with the DNR fish division I got a job with the Michigan Tourist Bureau. I was very disturbed that our tourist bureau was not putting more effort into promoting the salmon fishery. I had a meeting with a state senator and I gave him my view. I said, "I think it is shameful that they do not have a natural resources man." He said, "I think that's a good idea. I will get you a meeting before the tourist commission." I told them what they should do. They should have every fisherman promoting Michigan fishing, period. The way I worked it, I had to be the originator of all the contacts. I would invite outdoor writers to have a Michigan fishing experience. The tourist bureau would come up with some of the expenses for the outdoor writers. So I had outdoor writers coming from all over, especially from the Midwest, and even further. They spent a couple days with me and I would take them for a facet of Michigan sport fishing. So we got lots of promotion and that allowed me to buy a boat and twin outboard motors and depth sounders and all the gear necessary so I could be a modern fisherman. Along with this was a lot of speaking and radio work. In fact, I found a good technique. I noticed some of the other office staff had interns at no expense to the state. I got a student intern and I let her take over my radio program. She called around for reports from key fishermen around the state and then made up a fishing summary for the weekend. She did a beautiful job on the radio program, talking about fishing conditions around the state.

I would like to think tourism increased because of our efforts. The director of the tourist bureau at that time turned out to be a man who was an avid fisherman. He was very much interested in my job and saw the importance of it. But he knew—since I got my job through a state senator—that I could leave as fast. So he had my secretary keep an account of all the promotional outcomes from my speaking, my doings and so forth, and I have got that to this day as examples of how they used the information I gave them. She would search the newspapers. In the Lansing office, they got copies of all the newspapers. She would go through them and find a fishing article about the catch of fish here or there and keep it. Then, with that, point out how I was involved with that to prove that I was really making a contribution. They liked what they got and they gave me a permanent job and, believe it or not, when I retired, they abandoned the job. It is vacant to this day. I worked there until 1980.

My best job was my promotion of Michigan salmon fishing. It opened the door and enlightened a lot of people regarding its new potential. I can remember in my younger days, I just looked at the West Coast and saw all these salmon being caught and boy, I vowed someday I would get out and catch some of those big fish. So I realized how important it was. You must realize how Michigan gambled. Nobody had ever taken a saltwater fish like that—that has part of its life cycle in freshwater—and placed it in a total freshwater environment. Many would say, "It will not work, it will not work." So it was amazing that they survived very well. They did not need the saltwater. This was a big advancement.

I did a lot of photography. I took the travel bureau photographer with me a lot so we could advance the fishing pictures to the magazines. They were mostly of fish caught, showing what was available, what was possible. I covered the whole state, so I was involved in Lake Superior, Lake Michigan, Lake Huron, Lake Erie, but only from the promotional standpoint. It was a nice career move. I had a lot of contact with outdoor writers and they called me the "coho ambassador."

I invited a writer from the *Chicago Tribune* to go charter fishing out of southern Michigan waters. I had a charter boat skipper who would volunteer. The writer caught a grand slam—every one of the trout species—that is, lake trout, coho salmon, chinook salmon, brown trout, steelhead, in one afternoon of fishing.

I was very proud of the information we distributed. The DNR would plant fish every year but the fishermen never got that information. We told them when the fish would be catchable. We listed the dates of all of the plantings of trout and salmon in the Great Lakes and/or tributaries and what matured in a particular year for all the counties of the state. We distributed tons of brochures. I would send a whole pack of them to Michigan Steelhead meetings. They could call me for information. I helped very much in making a fishing map of southeastern Michigan. One brochure is on catching a fall run chinook salmon. In 1976 I started a charter boat directory of all the charter boats.

I wanted people to look at all the water we have got. We have got an excess of sport-fishing opportunities and we were not utilizing them all. I do not think there is enough publicity, especially in the Great Lakes waters where it does not hurt if you mention the specific water a lot. Maybe I will take that back in a few years, because Little Bay de Noc has been getting a lot of promotion and in June, it is overfished. The fishermen are just solid over there.

Sport fisherman Gordon Zuverink of Holland saw the alewife as a political problem. The alewife crisis helped channel more money toward state efforts to create a sport fishery in the Great Lakes.

You ask Howard Tanner, the guy that came up with the idea, he will tell you we had to get rid of the alewife. The alewife were a foot deep out on the beach here. I went through that living here. You would get within three miles of the Holland State Park in June and you could not stand the smell of the rotting alewife on the beach. The prevailing west wind blew the fish up on the beach. The state park employees were obsessed with trying to get rid of the dead alewives. Daily, they would have to clean the beaches from these alewives and it worked. Now we are concerned with not enough alewife to feed the salmon. There is not enough forage base for the predator fish to feed on. We are trying to get a balance on that and last year they decided that we better cut back on the chinook plant. They are the biggest consumer of alewife, and alewife are becoming seriously short, which I do not believe now, because people are still complaining about the dead alewife out here. So it remains to be seen whether that was the right thing to do or not. In the spring of 1999 the DNR did curtail their chinook plants in Lake Michigan from 6 million down to 3 million or 3.5 million, drastically cut it between all four states involved. So three years from now, we are going to find out whether it was the right thing to do or not, whether our fishery is shot.

———————

South Haven–based Don Nichols recalled the impact of the salmon-stocking program on both the DNR and the commercial fishery.

The salmon came from saltwater to strictly freshwater. The whole idea of introducing the salmon was to try to clean up the alewife population. I can remember when I was out boating, the alewife were inches thick on the water for miles; it was just the biggest die-off you could ever imagine. Front-end loaders were on the beach, constantly digging holes and burying them. So that was the reason the salmon were planted here.

The Department of Natural Resources exploded with the salmon program. They were going to do something that had never been done. How big could it be or how disastrous could it be? I remember Mr. Howard Tanner, who was the forerunner of let us put the salmon out there. We have to do something with these alewives. It was his success story. And recreational sport-fishing dollars are in the billions now. There are a lot of states around Lake Michigan that are very envious of Michigan having the foresight to do something back then. As soon as they saw that recreational fishing is where the money is, that commercial fishing was dying anyway, they slowly put those folks out of business. They had good reasons for what they did. The fishery was in bad shape. I think at that time chubs were about the only thing that was sellable or notable. And then, at the end, just to get the gill net out of here, the DNR said you cannot ship them. You can go catch them, but you cannot ship them—too many PCBs. I have got very close friends long since retired who were commercial fishermen; it is a tough life. Commercial fishing was not where the dollar was and Michigan needed that. The state had that beautiful research boat, The Steelhead, built at that time and stepped in there. The DNR stepped up their research to the point where the feds have kind of slacked off now, for budget reasons.

The commercial fishermen I knew at that time were from families that had fished the lake for three and four generations. That is all they knew, and they were very respected in many ways. They are out there battling elements. They are not making a great living and are supplying a food source to the public. It just seemed like the general tune the state picked up on was that these guys are bad. There is hardly any fish left and they are taking what is left. When the DNR started imposing rules and regulations, the commercial fisherman saw the handwriting on the wall. Why should I be resourceful? In the past, they policed themselves and did an excellent job. I have listened to stories of the old-timers saying that when we saw this fishery in a little bit of trouble, we quit fishing it. We would actually take our tugs and go fifty to one hundred miles up the lake and fish there until it would come back. So they policed themselves. But those last couple years when they knew that they were going to be out of business, what the heck, let us go for it. Not all of them, but some of them did. So that added fuel for the public saying, "Yeah, they are out there, and now we throw in the Indian deal." All that came across.

Lyle Teskie is a former commercial fisherman who now operates a charter boat service. He commented on the work of the Wisconsin DNR in managing Lake Michigan fisheries.

I think the lake has been mismanaged. I think technology has hurt. Conservation has turned into a political thing. I have my own opinions and everybody else has their own, but the things that you see when you live on the lake make you wonder, what are we doing? The DNR has got to the point where they are more into the politics whether it is commercial fishing or sport fishing. Commercial fishing is fighting against the sport fishing and they are having meetings about it. This battle has been going on for years. What is really damaging the lake is falling through the cracks. You could blame the DNR strictly, but I would not do that. There are certain things that the DNR has done that I will never understand. They allowed the trap net to come back into Lake Michigan and Green Bay in the 1950s. They let it in for about four or five years and it took the population of the whitefish down so drastically, they outlawed it. Why did they introduce the trap net back into the lake again in the 1970s?[40]

It is difficult making a living in anything related to fishing. It is slow strangulation. As a matter of fact, for years, we just wished the DNR would just stop planting fish entirely and just get it over with. Do not slowly strangle us to death. Just tell us it is illegal. Do me a favor. Do not just taunt me. Do not keep planting less fish. Do not keep saying in the paper that they are horrible to eat. I had fish tonight. We caught a brown trout here on Saturday afternoon and ate it tonight. I understand the fish are bad in certain areas I will not eat them. But fish is still good for you. It all depends on where you are eating it. I am not here to take any heads off, but I am looking at a couple years as far as fishing goes.

I gave up the political thing because when I was in commercial fishing, we used to go to these meetings in Green Bay and fight for our livelihood. I fell asleep and almost went into the ditch one night when I was coming back from a meeting. My first child was only about a year old. I said to myself, "I will be darned if I am going to lose my life going back and forth to these meetings fighting with the bureaucracy that I cannot win against." But that is one of the sad things that happens when political things get involved. I think you have to almost consider that the DNR has no choice. People scream. Sportsmen scream, "We want this." Commercial fishermen scream, "We want this." And the environmentalists say, "We want this bird in the lake." And when the gear starts turning, maybe they will have the power to stop it. Maybe they do not. But as far as introducing something into a lake that would be hazardous to it, that makes me think less fondly of them.

Every time my brother, who is a commercial fisherman, turns around, there is some new regulation. There are quotas. I could be totally wrong as far as what the DNR has done as far as juggling sportsmen against commercial and commercial against sportsmen and at the same time getting what they want out of it. I do not understand the DNR because they are not accountable to anybody. Anything that is not accountable to somebody leaves too big of a door for something to go haywire. They appoint their own people. They basically can do what they want.

I do not like the DNR law enforcement. They go around and arrest people with guns on. Granted, there are the lunatics out there, but it is as though they teach the warden to assume everyone is a suspect. They assume everyone is doing something wrong. I understand the reason they are always checking the fishermen out, but it is only fish. They should not be walking around with guns.

Sportswriter and fishing guide Kevin Naze acknowledged that Lake Michigan sport fishermen place a significant demand on fisheries resources.

The bass and walleye tournaments are regulated but not enough to protect the spawning fish. If their nest is right here, they intensely guard it. You can catch one fish twenty times in a row. If you catch him and throw him back, he is going to swim back there. You can catch him again and again. That is what is happening in these fishing tournaments. It is almost like tormenting the fish. The tournaments are getting to be pretty high stakes things, which encourages people. They can run forty miles sometimes. They are allowed to fish the whole of Green Bay for fish. Sure, it is catch and release and out of 1,500 fish, they claim only five. But how many of them are stressed afterwards from all that driving and throwing them back in the bay? I do not like to see people profiting off of the resource. I do not mind a salmon or trout tournament because it is total luck. You go out there, it is a huge lake, whereas bass and walleye are in specific spots in the bay, a bay that is populated with swimmers, jet skiers, and mom and pops sitting there with a bobber. The tournament fishermen are roaring by in these 200-horse Mercury engines, throwing their wake on them. It is getting to be so crowded on the bay already; they are going to have to do something. People have to be more considerate of each other, I guess. But on Lake Michigan, we have not had a problem.

Around 14 million trout and salmon are stocked by the four states every year. They swim the whole lake. When I catch some tagged fish some years, I turn them over to Paul Peters at the DNR in Sturgeon Bay. If they are hatchery-raised and have a missing adipose fin, chances are they have this little micro-tag in their snout imprinted with data saying "Sturgeon Bay '94" or whatever. So I cut off the head, bring it to the DNR and they run it through a metal detector or whatever. They keep doing it until they get down to a little chunk of flesh. Then they dig out this tag and put it under a microscope and read it. Every one I caught off Algoma—about five a year throughout the 1990s—had been a Michigan-stocked fish. They roam the whole lake. The salmon do not stay where the DNR stock. The only time it really helps is when it is spawning time. They got this natural imprinting where they come back, ninety-five percent or better come back to the river where they were stocked. This was found through the DNR's tagging studies. They take eggs here in Sturgeon Bay out of a place called Strawberry Creek. They take eggs at the Kewaunee River, and Root River at Racine. They match a fish up to their list and check where it was stocked and so forth. They are finding that amazingly, they may travel over the whole lake. Some of the salmon in a particular year class, for example, were caught at Ludington. Yet a month later, they are back here at Sturgeon Bay. How they know how to do it is one of the mysteries of nature or God. It is just amazing.

Charter boat operator Don Nichols expressed the view that state cooperation has brought mixed results with regard to the perch fishery.

We have a perch problem. We had it in the 1980s and we had it in the 1960s. And we are just getting over it now. There was a problem. But the press got a hold of this, and just about ruined my business by reporting that perch are going to be extinct. I went to a seminar in Chicago and heard a student biologist who was dependent on grant money and I am sure, aware if you can blow the whistle loud enough, the grant money comes rolling in. She painted this perch problem just black. I even told her I have got some theories of my own why it is down right now. But the press ran with it. The head of all the agencies in the Department of Natural Resources and all four states, they all ran with it, saying that we have a serious problem here. We have got to get out there and find out what it is. Meanwhile, let us close the fishery or cut it right down to nothing. In Michigan, we are sitting here saying, "Wait a minute. Our perch fishery is not that unhealthy. We have not had commercial fishing since 1965." So they are trying to figure out a way to go that is not so drastic. On the other hand, Michigan has ninety-nine percent of the watershed, so all your planted game fish are basically Michigan. But they are a migratory fish, so what do they do? They start off at the bottom of the lake. They like the cooler water. The prevailing winds come across the lake, so the other side of the lake is cooler than our side. So the fish go up that side and their recreational and commercial fishermen are harvesting our salmon, steelhead, trout, and everything else.

Michigan is on its hands and knees begging the other states to go in a coalition deal and manage the lake together. And the other three are saying, "That's all right. You guys keep planting fish and we will keep harvesting." They finally got together on it, and then shortly after that started on this perch problem. So there was a political endto the issue. We have to work both ways. These were different comments made by head people sitting around the table having coffee. They were not public comments. So they went along with the June closure. That is what crippled us the most. And then came the limits, although we have no problem with the limits. In fact, I fought for perch limits for years because there was too much waste.

Holland-based sport fisher Gordon Zuverink discussed the promotion of sport-fishing interests. He illuminates the role that sport fishers play in publicizing various issues.

I do a little bit of outdoor writing when the spirit moves me and a topic comes up that needs publicizing. I do not write fiction. I do editorials in the local *Centennial*. We print letters to the editor and when somebody starts taking a stand that grinds me why, I have to answer it when it has to do with fishing. For instance, in Port Sheldon they are supposed to put piers and boardwalks and parking areas there with part of the money from the Consumers Power fisheries settlement. The cottage owners association fought this proposal tooth and nail. They had published several articles in the local *Centennial* opposing spending money on a place that has no fishery. I have been arguing with these people verbally, personally, nose to nose. Two different guys had written articles saying there was not a fishery at the mouth of the Port River, so I could not stand it. I had to answer it. I wrote a rather lengthy letter to the editor and they printed it. It eventually was in our local newspaper too. One of our guys from the Michigan Steel-headers sent that article to the state, and they published it in the *Steelheader News*. That is the type of writing I do.

One time I was intrigued with a pamphlet that came up from the Great Lakes Fishery Commission about exotic species introduced into the Great Lakes. With the per-mission of Randy Eshenroder, the chief biologist of the Great Lakes Fishery Commission, I did a summary of it and it was published. I summarized it primarily for those who did not realize that when they planted chinook salmon, Pacific salmon into the Great Lakes in the 1960s, it was not the first time. It was done before way back when and it did not take. Salmon were planted in the late 1800s and it was a trial that did not take. Pink salmon were first introduced accidentally; they were not planted. Someone dumped a few buckets full of pink salmon in Canada on northern Lake Superior just to get rid of them out of a hatchery. They had raised some sampling, and that exploded into lots of pink salmon in Lake Superior. That was just an inadvertent dumping of pink salmon. Since I wrote that article, there have been a lot more exotic species come into the lake. I wrote that before the water flea, zebra mussel, gobies, and river ruff were discovered. The boats are bringing in exotic species. Most of them are not good for the fishery, not good for the lake.

Don Nichols discussed the negative impact of politics in fisheries policy, but noted that he and all fishermen benefited from DNR-sponsored research.

The DNR are human. They are just like us. They study different parts to get the job that they have and they have made some big blunders, some they do not even want to talk about. I just dug up one the other day. I thought smelt was a native fish to the Great Lakes and it is not. It was—they say accidentally—introduced by the DNR. It wiped out four species of herring, which was a big commercial fishery at the turn of the century. The DNR has the field guys, we have the biologists, we have the hatchery runners, and then we switch over here to the political side. The political side is usually made up of those guys that have been there long enough to work up and wanted to be on the political side. And there you can see night and day.

I was fortunate enough to be close to Wolf Lake Hatchery and James Copeland, the gentleman who just retired from there a few years ago after thirty years. Copeland was an avid perch fisherman. He would share everything, all the information. What I had to share back were daily records going back thirty years. I have got a high school education. I am not a biologist and I would have a rough time arguing with one. But Jim Copeland said, "Stand on your records; they mean something." The DNR had their little research. At that time, the feds were still into the research. Their boat was kept right up here in Saugatuck. She would make cruises to sample perch and the game fish—mainly the native fish, the lake trout and the perch. They would moor alongside my boat because I had the only place in town that was big enough to handle them and have facilities. So, I would get to spend the evening and maybe the next day with one of the biologists on board observing whatever they were studying. I just soaked up everything I could. I have great admiration for all of those folks. On the political end, you do what you have to do. I understand that part, too. That is a very important part, not a part that I would want.

———

Sport fisherman Gordon Zuverink has served on the advisory committee to the Great Lakes Fishery Commission for more than two decades. In this role, he describes how sport-fishing interests accumulated political power over the second half of the twentieth century.

I have been a member of the Great Lakes Fishery Commission Advisory Committee since 1980. In 2000, it will be twenty years. I was nominated by the Michigan DNR, but the governor has to okay my nomination before it can go to the Great Lakes Fishery Commission. The advisory committee has annual meetings, alternating between Canada and the U.S. The researchers and the biologists make their annual reports and we sit in on all these two-day meetings and soak up all the information that they have to offer. This is where decisions are made. Our advisory committee is there to advise the commissioners. We provide citizen input.

There were low points when I first got on the committee. Claude VerDuin, a commercial fisherman from Grand Haven, was one of the commissioners. When we started up the advisory committee, it had been defunct for many years. It was authorized under the Convention of the Great Lakes Fisheries in 1955, but the advisory committee was never really organized until 1978, 1979, and 1980, when they started organizing again. I remember when we came on, Claude said at the annual meeting, "Now you guys sit in the back row there and just listen. You are not here to speak, just listen."

Today, we sit in the front tables and we are a power. It is interesting to me that when we have a presentation, the chairman of the commission says after it: "Are there any questions from the commissioners? Are there any questions from the advisors? Any questions from the audience?" It makes me feel good to know we are an important entity, and we are. We do lobbying for the Great Lakes Fishery Commission. We can convince our legislators that we need more funding for the sea lamprey program and we have a pretty good function there.

The researchers, biologists, and the agencies—the Michigan DNR and all the neighboring states' DNR agencies participate. They provide testimony to the four commissioners from the U.S. and four from Canada. The commissioners control everything on the Great Lakes, primarily the sea lamprey eradication and the restoration of lake trout. The Great Lakes Fishery Commission was organized originally to bring back the lake trout and eradicate the sea lamprey. This work involves the commission in issues relating to water quality, control of exotic species, control of ballast water, and the balance of the various species in the five Great Lakes. Their primary goal was to get the lake trout rehabilitated. They have tried hard to get self-sustaining, natural reproduction of lake trout and they cannot get it. So it is an ongoing effort to try and get natural reproduction of lake trout. For some reason or another, the hatchery-raised lake trout do not naturally reproduce out there. It is a put-and-take fishery. And then, of course, we have the Native Americans. We must try to appease them and try to create enough fish out there for them to maintain their commercial fishery. That is all part of it. Their representatives, the treaty Indians representatives, sit on the boards also. I was chairman of the advisory committee a couple years ago and I am vice chairman now.

I have been vice chairman for the last couple of years. It is been very interesting, very interesting. It is time-consuming, but I enjoy it.

I was appointed to represent the public-at-large (PAL) on the advisory committee. Dennis Grinold, who was put on just a few years ago, represents the sport fishery. I was instrumental in getting him nominated. And we have a commercial fisherman on the advisory committee. There are three members on the advisory committee—sport, commercial, public-at-large—for each lake that borders Michigan. So Michigan has three for Lake Michigan, three for Lake Superior, three for Lake Huron, and three for Lake Erie. Wisconsin has three for Lake Superior and three for Lake Michigan. Illinois and Indiana just have Lake Michigan. In New York, you have people on Lake Ontario and Ohio and Michigan for Lake Erie, and Pennsylvania representatives are on for Lake Erie.

Lake Michigan is the only lake that is not bordered by Canada, so we do not have any advisors for Canada. The other lakes have advisors from Canada. With twenty percent or about one-fifth of the world's freshwater, I do not have to tell you, it is a big basin and requires lots of attention.

The Great Lakes Basin has got eight Great Lakes states, out of fifty states. When it comes time to put some pork in the bills, we want our share. We have to convince the other forty-two states that we need it badly. So that is where legislation is involved. We try to get our fair share of the piece of the national budget—primarily for sea lamprey control. We are constantly working on the national budget. In fact, we got an issue right now. There was an extra million dollars in there for the sea lamprey program. Now, I was just told that they are trying to strike out the million dollars and we must have it in there. It is part of an amendment on a bill. We need all the money we can get because we have a serious problem on the St. Mary's River. That is the nursery of the sea lamprey; it produces more sea lamprey than any other source on the Great Lakes.

Richard Stevenson discussed the changes in sport fishing in the twelve years he has been involved in charter boat fishing.

We troll for salmon and trout. When I first started, fishing was real good out here. You really did not even have to know what you were doing. You could throw a door hinge out there with hooks on it and catch salmon. There were plenty to be caught. The salmon population increased very rapidly. They were a lot bigger too; you did not see too many of these two or three pounders like you see now. A lot of that has to do with what they are eating. We used to have a big problem with alewives, which is why they introduced salmon out here in the first place. They started trawling, which is basically dragging a net behind a boat, and they started catching all these alewives. The trawlers did a real good number on the alewives. Now, there are not as many alewives around. You used to see them lying on the beach, sometimes stacked three foot high. They stunk up the whole place. The planting of the salmon definitely brought this county a lot of money. You get a lot of tourists coming up to fish for them. It gave people jobs. But there were too many alewives around. I remember walking on the beaches. You would see the alewife lying all over and it did stink.

The DNR regulations have not really changed much over the years, not since I have been involved. You are allowed two lake trout. You are allowed five fish overall. I believe that is how it has been for as long as I have fished out there. I think that is a pretty fair bag limit. They opened up a reserve here for us for the lake trout. They are letting us go in there and fish now. We have been catching a lot of lake trout and they are a lot bigger. We could not fish in that area for probably fifteen years. They opened it up a few years ago.

We have questions about what the DNR is doing with the perch out there. They allow five perch. They cut the limit down. Maybe it is a good thing. I do not know. I really do not fish perch out on Lake Michigan, but I fish them all year in Green Bay. They cut that limit from fifty to twenty-five because the population went down. I blame that on the bass because I noticed the bass population's gone up quite a bit since that perch population went down. I think, maybe, a bass is a lot more aggressive than a perch and they kind of feed pretty much on the same stuff in there. Bass are sucking up all the food from the perch. There is a five fish bag limit on bass. I think the reason they changed the minimum size from twelve inches to fourteen inches is to get a lot of tourists who like to fish bass. They get pretty high revenues from bass. I do not think it has anything to do with a minimum population. I think it is just their pocketbook. The bass are screwing up a lot of other fish around here.

The DNR definitely has way too much jurisdiction. It should be limited a lot. They can walk right into your house without a permit and check your freezer to make sure you do not have too many fish in there. If they want to, they can pull you over and do whatever they want. They can sit there and go through all your stuff on your boat, your vessel or whatever. They are not very nice people either. If they pull you over, they are going to give you a ticket for something. I think that should change. They should have the same jurisdiction as a police officer. We do not really care for them that much. I am not speaking for myself either. I speak for a lot of fishermen around here. I do not hear too many good things about them. Enforcement depends on the mood they want to be in, especially in the month that they have to have their quotas in or whatever. Sometimes, they are just trying to pull a fat one on you and take more money from you. There are some undercover wardens. I know one that is undercover. If there is one, there are probably two. There are probably three or four other ones around here and more up in Door County. I imagine they probably switch around. They do not want you to recognize them all. They like to be sneaky.

I had a game warden come up to me one day. I had caught a small northern pike. Small northern sometimes get stripes on them with the spots. He said the fish was a muskie because of the stripes. I said, "This fish is not a muskie because of the spots." We are arguing about this fish and finally he had to go ask somebody else, another game warden. He says, "Oh yeah, that's a northern." These guys go to school and get paid all this money, and here they cannot even tell the difference between a muskie and a northern. I was about seventeen years old at the time and I knew the difference.

Roy Holmquist discussed how sport-fishing advocates collaborate with the DNR in the interest of fishing and tourism. He also points out that relations between sport and commercial fishers are not always contentious.

Fishing ties in with tourism. I was president of Project Fish for six years. There is a one-time fee of fifteen dollars to get in the club. We have people that have entered from all over. It is just amazing all the different people that you get to meet while you are fishing. They want to know about what is happening up here. So we get them in the club and let them know. Project Fish is a group of sport fishers who help keep up the stocks. The DNR has recognized us with a little plaque on the wall for our donations. We run two benefits a year. We have walleye fries. All the money we make is usually donated back to the DNR for the stocking program. We are holding the money now for the shore run rainbow because we have really been pushing it. The DNR is working on two different strains that are going to be shore run rainbow, so we are hoping that it is going to go.

We have a good working relationship with the DNR. They really are good. You know, if it was not for the DNR, we would be sunk up here. We have been getting that one strain of brown trout from Michigan. The DNR was saving money instead of shipping the ones from Wild Rose up here. They got the ones from Michigan which have a shorter haul. I talked to Mike Toneys, the DNR man for Door County fisheries. He said, "Do not worry, Roy—you will be getting Wild Rose strain again." He said it was a mistake getting the fish from Michigan. It was penny wise and dollar foolish. We talk to the DNR and they are great. I am really impressed with our DNR up here. They really try to help you.

Every once in a while, the DNR has a meeting with the commercial fishermen to talk about quotas. They always call one of us from the club to come over and offer our input to see if the nets are hurting our salmon or if there is any incidental catch of other sport fish. I always go over there and I stick up for the commercial fishermen. They are not hurting us a bit. So there are no problems. But every time they have a meeting, they call the sportsmen and they have them come down to see if there is anything that is bothering them. We have gotten along great with the commercial fishermen. The commercial fishermen let us know if they see things that would benefit us. They tell us about big schools of marked fish up on the top water. Even our charter boat fishermen are great—if you call them on the radio to find out what is going on and what the fish are hitting on and their depth.

I get what they call a patron license, which covers everything. It has got all your stamps, your hunting and fishing—pheasant hunting and deer hunting. It costs about $125 now. But actually, if you figure out all your licenses, you are actually saving money. They also give you a park sticker and if you figured out the total cost it would be about $200. It is a good deal. If I am not mistaken, I think there is a Pittman-Robertson deal where they got a tax on their sporting goods which goes toward maintaining resources.

Charter boat operator Don Nichols reflected on the role of politics in fisheries policy on the Great Lakes.

I was contacted about a perch seminar and I attended. I noticed when I was asked a question—because they knew I was in this business—somebody in the back row would stand up and say close down the perch fishery for five years. And I thought, well, you are a little radical on this. Some of the ideas were kind of off the wall. So I would just be quiet. I thought, what can come of this? I had no idea. I talked to other guys who were in different rooms and they said, "Yeah, we had some idiot in the back row that got up and said close it down." So anyway, when analyzing what became of this meeting, the next thing they were doing was an emergency shutdown for the month of June. It is ironic because it happened to be when perch are spawning. The general public thought it was good to close the perch fishery for spawning. But no, they did not close it for spawning; they closed it to take a month's pressure off the fishery. I said, "How about I give you the month of January, February, or one of the six months out of the year we are not fishing anyway?" They went ahead and closed the perch fishery because a little organization called Perch America, made up of 200 fishermen, sent out a newsletter saying you have to go to this seminar and stand up and tell them to close it down.

There was a woman who did a perch study and then stood up in front of 350 people and painted this black picture and nobody could refute it. Nobody had any data. The federal government did perch studies yearly. They would go from Saugatuck, all the way around the bottom end of the lake and up the other side. Then they wrote the data down, analyzed it, and put it in booklet form. They quit doing that in 1983 because they said we have seen the perch fishery up and down. It bounces back and it has got different cycles and so we are going to spend our money on other things due to the budget. And the state never really did any perch studies. All I have are my records and I already knew that there were cycles in the perch fishery. It was cast in stone at that meeting that we were going to use the month of June for a closure. I had no problem with cutting the limit from fifty down to thirty-five. But I knew what it would do to this business. I knew it would hurt the community, but I had no idea how big it would be. So the community got behind me and we lobbied that whole summer and got June opened back up the following year. There is still a closure in the other states and they still had very low limits and absolutely no commercial fishing. Wisconsin does their commercial fishing for perch in Green Bay, so they were not worried about shutting it down in Lake Michigan. And that is a good viable fishery up there. So they are doing studies now, not as much as I would like to see.

Unfortunately, in 1980 I had just purchased a much larger vessel than this (the *Captain Nichols*), much more boat than I should have had, but the deal was right. But I had a lousy perch year in 1980. I was so wrapped up in the boat that I was not paying attention to the fishing. Then in 1981 and 1982, I was not fishing at all. I was building this boat in the large building over there. My avid perch fishermen friends that were retirees were always out there, every day. They would come over and they were serious saying the perch are gone. Why are you spending this money and this time building this boat? Jokingly, I just told them that they were not catching fish because they did not have me out there. I kept no records then and the state kept sparse records. So they dug them out for me. I went through them and sure enough, we had a real down time period. There was no big press about it. Nobody seemed to be interested. That was basically about the time the federal government had quit researching perch, too. And because there is no commercial fishery up here, it was just a small recreational fishery, what's the big news? Then, in 1983 when I launched this boat, all of a sudden we were getting back into fish. Not real great, but they are all about six inches or seven inches. Prior to that, when I quit from 1979 to 1980, there were just large fish. So these are all things that I had assumed in my thinking. In 1994–95 there was nothing but large perch. Then all of a sudden, it is down to nothing. This year, we started out on a good note and they were small fish. So I am seeing a cycle and it is just a matter of convincing the person with the Ph.D. But we are working together.

When our perch fishery was in a slow period, I wanted to spend all my time working on that. And I have got some great theories. Some of them held up as long as ten years and then they went right out the window. The habitat and their food and what they eat have changed. The first fifteen years I was in business, it was strictly crayfish. Guys would bring minnows but you could not catch a perch on a minnow. Then it started to switch fifty–fifty and now it is mainly minnow and wigglers. There are a lot of changes going on. I am a firm believer, regardless of what we all do, Mother Nature is going take care of us. She takes a lot of time to do it, a lot of time.

Lyle Teskie is a charter boat operator from Gills Rock, Wisconsin. He indicated that since he became a charter boat captain, he has experienced less conflict with the DNR. As a former commercial fisherman, he can readily see how one's relationship with the DNR varies based on resource user's methods and clients.

I have not had any problems with the DNR since I became a charter boat captain. The last time they stopped me, they showed up way out in the middle of the lake. I am way out with a bunch of guys, fifteen miles out, cannot see anything, and here comes the boat and it is the DNR. I do not personally have anything against them. They are people too. But I show them the licenses and treat them with respect and they treat me with respect. They know me. And if something is not right, something is not right. I mean, it is not like I have illegal fish on board. I mean, it is kind of funny because there are so few fish as far as charter fishing is concerned. It is like, how could you have any illegal fish? You could have undersize ones but they usually do not bite. But the DNR shows up. They show up now and then and some guys give them more of a hard time. I have learned a lesson in the past and it is not worth it. Your customers are there. You could yell and scream and give them a hard time. Your customers want to get on with fishing and they are polite.

Sport-fishing writer and fishing guide Kevin Naze discussed DNR policy toward commercial and sport fishermen. He alludes to his role as a journalist and the manner in which it affects Lake Michigan sport fishing's political and conservation issues.

The commercials up here cannot target any of our sport fish other than yellow perch. They are allowed perch, whitefish, chubs and those kinds of fish. The trout and salmon that you buy in the local markets are all shipped from Canada and Alaska. No commercial fishery is allowed for Great Lakes trout or salmon other than for the Indians. In the old days, there was a lake trout commercial fishery. Historically, in the 1930s, 1940s, and 1950s, overfishing by commercials combined with predation by sea lamprey virtually wiped out lake trout. They had to be restocked in the 1960s. I am friends with some of the commercials. They have argued the point for years that they are always too tightly regulated, but they have the equipment that can really devastate a fishery in no time at all, especially in shallower water. The nets do not regulate themselves. They will gill net a trout or a salmon or whatever. So we have to be careful where we allow them to fish. I do not want to see the commercial fishermen put out of existence. I love eating whitefish, chubs, and all those fish, and I think the DNR has a good handle on them. Their quota system is fair and the quotas are reviewed constantly. If the population goes up, they are given a little more.

As far as the sport fishermen in Wisconsin go, our fishery is almost strictly a put-and-take fishery. This means the state uses our license money to raise fish in the hatchery and stock them in lakes and streams. They grow, we catch them, and harvest them. Catch and release is not so important here, because our fish do not spawn successfully on their own. Our Wisconsin streams are silted from farmland runoff and so forth. There is some natural reproduction but very little because the fish need this natural bubbling spring-fed water with rocks and slow temperature increase. Our streams may be muddy, or there is a quick increase in temperature, or the eggs may be covered with silt during a big storm. We are allowed to take five fish a day. Only two can be lake trout. So you could take, for example, two rainbows, a salmon, and two lake trout for your five-fish bag.

As far as the future of the sport fishery goes, I would hope it just continues to produce good action, consistent action, and an occasional record to spark the interest, to get newcomers to the sport. Walleyes, bass, and pan fish on the inland lakes are probably ten times more popular. But once people come out and try the big lake, they find out they do not have to be intimidated, even if they have a small boat. For years, I fished out of a sixteen-foot boat out on Lake Michigan. And if you watch the weather forecasts, you can do it with no problem. I fished sometimes in 200–300 feet of water ten miles out. But if you knew it was going to be a calm day and the winds were not supposed to pick up until the middle of the afternoon, just fish for a few hours in the morning and head back in. I have an eighteen-footer right now and I have full confidence in it. There is a good camaraderie among the anglers. You have marine radios and if bad weather is coming, somebody hops on: "Hey guys, there is a storm in Green Bay. It is really moving fast. We might want to head out of here." And everybody heads out. So people pretty much share information out there except during the tournaments. They are a little more secretive if they find a hot spot or something. But I think it has got a really bright future because people really have to travel to British Columbia, Canada, or Alaska, to find any of this kind of fishing. The West Coast fisheries out of Oregon and Washington are fading. Their native runs are being wiped out by who knows what—dams, siltation of their streams, urban runoff, and all kinds of problems. They have cormorants and terns and gulls that are predating on the small stocks of salmon and trout, too, so there is a lot of ongoing stories that are going to be happening and to keep an eye on. There is always something to get people fired up.

If you involve the people, the readers like it more. I try to involve the people in my stories rather than just writing what I call "Me and Joe" stories, like me and Joe went fishing and we caught five fish, here is how we did it. I do not get into that as much as I do the educational issues. I feature stories on the sea lamprey and its life history and what it has done and where it is going. The sea lamprey is a big ongoing story right now because they finally got to treat the St. Mary's River last year which is the biggest producer of sea lampreys anywhere. They finally figured out a way of treating it, so hopefully the lampreys will get reduced. And we found a lot of scarring in the last couple years, more than ever, on the trout and salmon and so we are a little bit leery that they could really take hold if they are not gotten under control. It is a constant political fight to get the funds just to fight it. Canada kicks in, I think a third or so and U.S. is around two-thirds based on land area on the water. This is something you have to make people aware of every year. Call your senators and representatives and tell them why this is important. People need to get involved in the fishery and need to be educated about it and then they will appreciate it more.

Norm Spring, the first president of the Michigan Steelheaders, expressed the widely held sport-fisher's view that gill nets are harmful to the fishery.

Obviously, we did some promoting of sport fishing primarily to the disadvantage of the commercial fishermen because we were always opposed to gill netting because gill netting targets no particular fish. It just kills anything that swims into it and, of course, a lot of fish are wasted that way. And if the nets are not picked up then, of course, all the fish are wasted. But we felt that gill netting ought to be banned. In the early 1970s, we had statewide meetings and decided that gill nets should be banned and commercial fishermen should switch over to trap netting. Less commercial gill netting advanced sport fishing even further. Eventually, the Indian treaties were asserted and it started all over again when the Indians developed a commercial fishery with the gill nets. The gill-net fishery is still going on today and there is a lot of controversy involved in it.⁴¹

The trap-net fishery is much more practical because the fish that are targeted are kept and the others are released. That way, you do not waste so many fish. The gill net is very impractical because when you leave nets in the water and you cannot get to them because of storms, then there is a whole series of fish that die. If the nets get taken away by storms and are released in some way, then the nets are just floating around on the bottom—they keep fishing all by themselves. The fish swim into them and they get caught and die and rot and more fish swim into them. So they fish literally forever.

Don Nichols discussed why the Michigan DNR supported a ban on gill nets. Along with other sport fishers, he recognizes that harvesting methods shape a complex political and economic debate among all fisheries stakeholders on Lake Michigan.

The state wanted the gill net gone, number one, because it is a marvelous way of taking all fish. Number two, it fishes around the clock. It is not like hook and line. And number three, it was interfering with the great new salmon and game fish program because the net would take that too, accidentally, but it still would take it. So they just wanted that net gone. All you have to do is close the fishery down because the fishery was in trouble and it was, and a guy is not going to last sitting at the dock. In 1965, that was the last of the commercial fishing for perch in Michigan. In the early 1970s, the DNR stopped commercial fishing for chubs. Indiana kept right on going. Illinois kept right on going. Eight or nine years ago, they too wanted to get rid of the gill net. Illinois required that the net be three feet off the bottom rather than nine, so as to not take the bigger fish—they would not get caught in there. They were just going for perch, the only commodity that the two states had. The Indiana DNR ended the use of the gill net, but you can still go out and net with a trap net, gear that is five times more expensive and it is hard to put in. A storm can wipe you out. But the state said that is what you are going to fish with, thinking that most guys would get out of business. Well, a few of them stayed in there, and the comical part of it was it did not take them but two years to figure out how to work a trap net very successfully. You can see it right in the catch quotas. And so they just started right back up. The problem with a trap net is that can become a navigational hazard. If you have eighty-eight miles of coastline and thirty-seven miles or so of net, the recreational boater is not even going to go out and attempt to fish. And so what is he do? It is just as easy for him to come to Michigan. So they lost their recreational dollar totally. Now what do you do? We cannot change gear again.

Richard Stevenson (Sturgeon Bay, Wisconsin) wants a greater portion of Lake Michigan to be under the jurisdiction of the State of Wisconsin.

I do not know if it is the DNR or who makes these regulations, but there is a boundary out there. Wisconsin has got about twenty miles out, but it is seventy-five miles across. Wisconsin should get half. Instead, Michigan gets three-quarters of the lake. I do not think that is fair. Sometimes the fish are out twenty-five miles. We cannot go out there and get them. I remember there was one captain who got nailed big time. He got nailed for guiding without a Michigan license. His customers got fined for fishing without a Michigan fishing license, so he ended up with a couple thousand dollars in fines just because he was a couple miles over that border. He did not know. I mean, how can you blame him? Everybody knows it is seventy to seventy-five miles across. You automatically figure you can go at least thirty miles across the inland. I think he was twenty-five or twenty-six miles out and they fined him pretty good.

Kevin Naze discussed the organizations that sports fishermen created to influence the policy-making process. Convinced that sport fishing creates a greater economic return, he sees its interests as paramount to those of commercial fishing interests. As a journalist, he shows the influential partnerships that have been forged between the DNR, the sport-fishing community, and the press.

There are many sport-fishing organizations—the Great Lakes Sport Fishing Council, the Great Lakes Federation of Fishing Clubs, the Algoma-Kewaunee Area Great Lakes Sport Fishermen and the Green Bay Great Lakes Sport Fishermen, Northeast Wisconsin, and Salmon Unlimited of Racine. All these different sport clubs are kind of together in the Wisconsin Federation of Great Lakes Sport Fishermen. They have somebody as a lobbyist or maybe the term is not lobbyist. I do not know if they have a full-time lobbyist. They probably have people that are dedicated and concerned about the fishery who attend meetings. For three years, I was president of a local group and went to all these meetings. It gets very tiring, fighting, but, thank God, there are some people who represent sport-fishing interests, because the commercial interests are always there. They are always looking for the extra way to make a buck. We are trying to protect the sport fishery as a whole because the commercial fishery, while it does bring in a lot of dollars, is mainly for the individuals that work for them. There is a big impact from the commercials that fish perch. People do go and eat and they help a lot of restaurants and so forth. There is definitely an economic impact from the people who want to come to the fish fries.

There is a lack of trust because there have been so many arrests through the years of commercials getting caught overharvesting. There are some real good commercials. I think most of them up here in Door County and in Algoma have never been caught of any wrongdoing, but there is a lot of fishy business going on down south and around Marinette where people have been caught. How many times did they do it before they were caught with too many pounds of perch or selling to restaurants without reporting and so forth? So the economic impact of the sport fishery is far greater because it fills the hotels, it fills the restaurants and the bait shops. It is incredible. Even to a little town like Algoma, with 3,000 people, sport fishing probably brings in multimillions in the summer months. In one day, there might be 100 to 200 private boats that have come there from Green Bay, Minneapolis/St. Paul, and all over Minnesota. Most of our charter fishery, about two-thirds, is Minnesota customers because it is a straight five-hour shot across the state, through the middle of the state. The fishermen stay at the campgrounds and the hotels. They go out to eat and go to the supermarkets. It really revives the small towns. Otherwise, without an interstate going by, we are thirty miles from the interstate, we might slowly die. If this lake ever dies, the small towns are going to probably go with it.

Commercial fishing and sport fishing could coexist if the commercials lobby for what they want, but yet be realistic and do not be selfish. They have to keep in mind the good of the fishery. If they are truly sincere that they do not think they will hurt the fishery in any way and if the DNR agrees with them, fine. Sport fishermen do not harvest whitefish; we do not harvest chubs. The yellow perch is tricky because that attracts people year around on the bay in Lake Michigan. We finally got them to close down the sport fishery at our sport fishers' request. You would never have seen the commercials go and ask for a closed season. But we went and we said the perch are hurting in recent years. We want the spawning season closed for two months. The DNR did it. For the last two years, from the middle of March to middle of May, perch fishing is off-limits. There was a time when they came into every bay and just spawned in droves and you could catch your limit easy. And people were pulling out all these egg-laying females. The DNR argued, "Well, it is only five percent of the year's harvest." But our argument was it is the prime, the big adults. They finally relinquished.

The DNR and the U.S. Fish and Wildlife Service do not ever like to admit they are wrong. We told them for ten years that the lake trout experiment between Algoma and Sturgeon Bay was not working. About ten years later, they finally agreed. It used to be refuge and we could not fish in it. We lost all that water for charter fishing. It has been open for years now. It is our honey hole until the rainbows and salmon start. Right now, only lake trout are biting out there for us and our customers are happy to catch something, so at least we are allowed to go up into this spot between Algoma and Sturgeon Bay and bottom bounce and catch these big lake trout. I think there is definitely room for both commercial and sport fishing out on the lake.

The perch is the only one they have to watch closely. Right now, they shut down the commercial fishery on Lake Michigan for perch out of Wisconsin. I am pretty sure it is the same in the other states, too. And the angler limit is only five a day, which is practically nothing. But until they show signs of rebounding, which they may never do, they may find it was the zebra mussels or the alewives or some exotic that has really influenced things and changed the whole ecosystem. It is a big lake and nobody can really say they know how to manage it totally. They are just using their best educated guesses and learning by experience as they go.

I am glad that we have had the DNR and the Fish and Wildlife Service. There are a lot of people who curse them, including a lot of sport fishermen. They like the old

bumper stickers that the DNR is "Damn Near Russia." They also think the fisheries managers are overpaid and drive around in new vehicles. I do not see it that way at all.
Every one of them that I know, including the warden that I am going to be meeting up
with soon, loves hunting and fishing as much or more than any of us. He just does not
have the time to do it. He is busy protecting the resources. The fish managers like Mike
Toneys and Paul Peters, love to get out on the lake themselves. Why would they want
to do anything to hurt the lake? Yet some of these people think the DNR is out to hurt
us, hurt the sport fishery. I do not know why they think that way.

Leland-based charter boat operator Scott Anderson indicated that he and other charter boat captains maintain friendly relations with Michigan DNR conservation law
enforcement officials. Such amicable relations are indicative of the mutual political
and economic interests of the state government and sport-fishing industry—a development attributable to the phenomenal rise of tourism in the twentieth century.

The DNR does not have enough people to enforce the regulations they have. We have
one conservation officer that does everything from inspecting charter boats to
checking out turkey hunters. Just doing that in Leelanau County would be a full-time
job, but I think his territory is even bigger than that. He does not have enough time to
do what he is assigned to do. As far as regulations go, I look at it this way—if I have a
family of four on board and I catch eight lake trout, that is more fish than those people will ever use. I try to make sure that if we can use them, let us keep them. If we
cannot use them, let us try to save them. We will keep what we need. The worst thing
is when people get on the boat, catch fish, and then say we do not want the fish.

I have never been inspected on the lake by the DNR in sixteen years. One time I
came out and the guy was inspecting a boat. That does not mean they have not been
out looking, because they have looked at other boats, but they have not checked me.
And so we pulled in and he came over and said, "Hi Scott, how are you doing?" We
know these guys. We are side by side a lot. He said, "How did you guys do?" And, of
course, my people open the cooler and they show them the fish. And he says, "Okay,
just wanted to check. Looks like you got a nice catch. Can I see your licenses?" That
was the one time I was checked.

The conservation officers have to do inland lakes, too. There are many inland lakes in just Leelanau County and then you have Lake Michigan. There is about sixty-five miles of Lake Michigan shoreline in Leelanau County. It is impossible for them to do it. The guy that we have is really great. His name is Mike Borkovich. He will come down and say, "How is it going? Is everything all right?" He respects us and knows that we are going to take care of what we need to do to take care of business. He trusts us. The charter boat captains in Leland have a very, very good relationship with him. What the wardens do is phenomenal and tough. It is a tough and thankless job. They do lots of stuff we do not see.

Richard Stevenson of Sturgeon Bay recalled an incident where it was assumed that the presence of a group of Wisconsin game wardens meant that a local charter boat captain was accused of breaking the law.

Jerry Cefalu is probably one of the most respected captains out here. He has fished and guided on Lake Michigan since they planted out there. He is a real clever guy and every once in a while, he twists the rules and gets away with a lot. He is pretty clever. He is a friend of one of the game wardens around here. His friend called him and told him he had a couple new recruits and would he help give these guys an idea what to look for if they go out on that lake and check people? Jerry figured there would be maybe five or six new wardens. There was about twenty-five or thirty of them. They surrounded his boat, fully dressed with their .45s on the side. This other charter captain, Dave Peterson, drives over by his boat. He looked and thought, oh no, they got him. Oh wow, they really got him. So he takes off. And then this other guy comes and the same thing happens. Soon everyone thinks Jerry got busted big time. They really got him. And he was just trying to explain to these guys what to look for out there. It was pretty funny. They must have been the new wardens for all of Wisconsin, because I do not think we need thirty game wardens around here.

Gordon Zuverink, a sports fisherman from Holland, discussed how local fishing clubs aided the DNR in its effort to create a sport fishery on Lake Michigan.

I am a life member of the Holland Fish and Game Club.[42] I guess that maybe we are more localized, of course, and we do not do a lot of lobbying and legislating like the Steelheaders do. Through the Holland Fish and Game Club, I was primarily responsible for getting a plant of chinook in Holland. We did not have chinook planted in Holland prior to 1989. Starting in 1987, I began pressing the DNR with the help of some of my legislators, convincing them that we should have a plant of chinook salmon in Holland. This way, we could get these fish congregated outside the Holland pier when they wanted to run up into Black River. Finally, I won my case. I met with Mike Moore, one of the guys that was pretty high up in the DNR, and he finally relented, and said we will get you a plant. It was not until 1989, but we did get a plant of 100,000 chinook and have had it ever since.

The first plants we had were planted in the ponds at Holland Fish and Game Club. I was in charge of getting the various guys together to feed these fish three times a day, take water temperatures, and watch them and wait for them to smolt. Once they reached the smolting stage, the pond could be emptied. It had boards in it, and so we would start removing the boards and letting these fish go downstream and ultimately get them all washed down into Lake Michigan. That was very interesting. There was cooperation between the Holland Steelheaders and the Holland Fish and Game Club at that time. Eventually, we had to dispense with planting fish in that pond because the pond is what the DNR calls a warm-water fishery and salmon and steelhead are cold-water species. We would get the fish around the first of April. Then, around the first of May, sometimes a week or so later, we would have to hold them until the smolt. When the weather warmed up, we were concerned with the water getting too warm to hold the fish. A couple of times we had to let them go early because the water warmed up and they started dying. So that is why we had to monitor this very closely and it was a big job to get a successful plant. So then the DNR said we cannot take the chance anymore. We do not want to lose 100,000 chinook. We cannot take the chance, so we will just dump your fish right into the channel at the State Park. So that is where they make our plants now. They put them right in the channel, but they hold them in the hatchery longer. They hold them in the hatchery until they get to what they call the smolting stage and then they dump them in here. They only hang around a couple days and then they swim out into Lake Michigan and do their feeding and growing. There used to be good cooperation between the Fish and Game Club and the Steelheaders.

The DNR was already using four ponds that emptied into the Black River for raising walleye. The shallowest pond was used for raising minnows for feeding walleye. They had a very successful walleye program here. Lake Macatawa is one of the places that they seine and shock brood stock walleye, take the eggs, and hatch them in the hatchery. Then, when they are hatched out, then they bring them to the ponds at Fish and Game Club, and raise them until they are to a point where they can start taking them out and planting them in the Muskegon Lake and Lake Macatawa and various lakes. So this is kind of a pretty well organized fishery station here. This cooperative effort has gone on for years. That is why the ponds were put in there originally, so that we could assist the DNR in raising some walleye. And they raised catfish in there at various times. I do not know what other species they used but they have been used for various purposes. It is a pretty important tool for the DNR.

"Coho" Bob Maynard, who operates a fishing tackle shop in Pentwater, Michigan, regarded the snagging controversy as one of the unintended results of the Michigan DNR's Great Lakes salmon stocking program.

The DNR has good intentions but sometimes the way they go at it seems to be just opposite of what the rest of the people think. You will find that the average person is glad to cooperate with the policies that come out of Lansing. For example, a few years ago it was considered legal to snag a fish as they went up the river to spawn. Then they found out that it was not the right thing to do. Apparently, the opinions were so different. Then snagging became illegal and the fines they had were considerable. A company over here, processed thousands of tons of spawning salmon for less than a penny a pound. The public was not allowed to take them as they proceeded up the river to spawn in October. Yet the DNR was selling them by the ton for less than a penny a pound. That policy left a bad taste in many people's mouths.

Sport fisher Roy Holmquist of Ellison Bay, Wisconsin, recalled when the DNR permitted snagging.

W e used to have snagging for salmon and brown trout. In fact, that is what we used to do when we first came up here. Then it was eliminated. Now there are still people, if they see a bunch of fish and they do not know how to catch them, right away they want to start snagging them. The DNR catches quite a few of them and it is a pretty hefty fine, which is only right. Actually they are stealing our fish instead of catching them legally because it is awfully easy to snag fish when there is so many of them. I have seen guys with a little lure and a hook and you know darn right that the lure is not working especially when you pull a fish in backwards. They have thirty-pound test line as well.

Kevin Naze, a Door County, Wisconsin, sport-fishing writer, fishing guide, and charter boat crewmember, discussed how sport fishermen organized in opposition to snagging.

R oy Berres from the Northeast Wisconsin Great Lakes Sport Fishermen's Club helped get us started. I started in a club called the Algoma-Kewaunee Great Lakes Sport Fishermen back in 1985. In 1986 we helped get rid of snagging of salmon. It went to a statewide vote. We accumulated like 1,200 signatures. There is a case where the sport fishing community took an active role in what they thought was the correct ethical behavior for fishing. They did not like snagging from a standpoint that it was teaching kids the wrong way of fishing. Sure, the salmon are coming in to die, but you do not have to snag them. They will bite regular baits, not near as good as catching them snagging, but the people will still come for the fish, even if there is not snagging. And if they are snagging on the side, so be it, but we cannot have these ugly big two-ounce leaded trammel hooks flying all around. People were getting hooked in the ears, head, and shoulders. They were arm to arm on opening day. It was dangerous out there. People came in droves from Iowa. They trampled the banks and left litter and line on the bank. It was just a free-for-all frenzy. Then they started selling the eggs for a buck a pound. One female has about five pounds of eggs in her belly, so for five bucks, a fish was gutted for the eggs and the carcass was thrown on the beach. It was really god-ugly, so we started the effort to ban snagging.

Holland's Gordon Zuverink recalled the emergence of the snagging controversy after salmon planting took place.

We had what we called the "farmers yard," a particular hole on the Manistee River just below the mouth of the Bear Creek where all the coho were holing up and gathering before they went into the Bear Creek. Fishermen lined up along the banks. We used to park on the "farmers yard" for a dollar and there were cars all lined up in his "back forty." He had made a parking lot out of that. And then you would walk down to the stream from there and you could fish. Well, guys were pretty much shoulder-to-shoulder fishing and casting. They were casting with lures and crawlers and live bait and whatnot. A guy right near me seemed to have a fish on his line all the time. He would land a fish and then he would put it on the string and then he would stand back and smoke a cigarette. I thought I had to find out what he was fishing with. I asked him and he said, "I will show you." He opened a box of hooks and it was treble hooks. He said, "I just tie this treble hook on here." In fact, he tied two of them on. He said: "I put a bell sinker below that and I throw it out there until I feel a fish hit it and then I jerk into him. That is the way I catch these fish." Well, he was snagging them and there were not any DNR personnel around to stop that. He would get one almost every cast. Occasionally, we would hook one by the fin when we were fishing with spawn bags or crawlers or if we were fishing with a spinner, occasionally we would foul one up. But most of the time, you would catch them by the mouth. But his were all snagged. They were in there so thick that you could not help but foul hook a fish on occasion, and quite often, they were foul-hooked. But it was not easy to land a foul-hooked fish unless you were really rigged for it because they were just too strong when you are not pulling them in by the mouth. But that was my first glimpse at snagging. Of course, then it escalated into a real fiasco, just a terrible, disgusting way to fish.

There were also some snaggers down at the Big Manistee River. I was standing right next to a guy who was snagging. I saw his rig and all of a sudden a guy came over, in plain clothes, and jumped over and grabbed the guy's rod and tried to hold his equipment because he was fishing with illegal equipment. In the ensuing scuffle, the guy's rod broke and what really ticked off these fishermen was the fact that it was a plainclothes DNR man. There was another one there too, and they started fighting on the bank. The fishermen were trying to throw these guys, the DNR men, into the river. It was bad. It was terrible. After the incident, these fishermen were issued a citation—then one of them started coming around and taking names of people who would be witnesses to the fact that the DNR man broke his pole and he asked me for my name. I said I would not defend that guy for snagging.

You could not snag a steelhead or brown trout. It was illegal to keep a steelhead or brown trout that was foul-hooked. It was only permitted for salmon because the reasoning was that they were going to die anyway and the DNR's got a mess on their hands with all these dead fish in the river. That is why the DNR relented and said, "Let's let them take them out." There were some restrictions. The first restrictions were the hook size and then the number of hooks on a line and where the lead was placed.

We had two factions, the true sport fishermen and the sport fishermen who had deteriorated into illegal fishing. And, of course, I do not know why, but most of them were from Indiana. Perhaps they were not accustomed to being patient enough to wait for the fish to hit or to lure the fish into striking. They had to snag these fish and, of course, the DNR finally relented and made it legal which was a horrible thing to do.

The good fishermen did not go to Tippy Dam anymore. The sport fishermen did not go there because you could not fish. I tried it. You could not get your line out there and get a good drift through there without getting jerked back in by one of these snaggers, so we just did not fish there. We would go and watch the activity, but we never fished there. We would go downstream where there were not any snaggers and do our fishing. The Big Sable River, a short stream running to Hamlin Lake at the State Park in Ludington, got a serious plant of chinook shortly after they were introduced. We had a good run of fish in there, but that was when snagging was declared legal. They had fishing periods and you had to fish by permit and get a badge at the office that allowed you to fish half a day. We did not even go there and apply for a permit.

My son-in-law, two grandsons, and I were up at the cottage watching these guys snag. On this picnic table there were some spark plugs they used for a weight. This guy was throwing out and jerking. I noticed he had a spark plug on for weight. He did not have any lead with him and he had to drive a hook above it. Finally, he said, "I cannot seem to get them." I said, "Maybe they are not biting on spark plugs today." We left because I was afraid I was going to get into an altercation with him. My son-in-law never forgot that. To this day, every once in a while he will say, "I guess they are not biting on Champions today."

_____

Sport fisherman Gordon Zuverink described the equipment used by fishermen who snagged salmon and the impact of the practice both on the environment and sportsmanship.

A "silver spider" was a hunk of lead molded onto a big treble hook. They were sold in bait stores. The "silver spider." I wish I had a picture of the bait and tackle stores. That was the prime lure to see in those days. The counter was just loaded with them. The bait stores made these things themselves. They had molds that would hold the treble hook and they would pour the molten lead into it and let it dry and pull it out of there, let it cool down and pull it out of there. They would dump out a dozen of them at a time. That would be called the down years, I think.

At Tippy Dam, fishermen were on both sides of the river, shoulder to shoulder, throwing these silver spiders out there and hooking onto a snag and breaking their line. What a mess they had in those deep holes, those holding holes at Tippy Dam! Annually, they would have a river cleanup. Consumers Power would cooperate and close down as much as they could, so that the river would drop and they could get into the water with some diving equipment and clean it out. They had, at one time, a ball of monofilament line almost as big as an automobile that they pulled out of that river, line that had hooked onto logs. And they would pull out hundreds of pounds of lead that was down into that stream. It was just a horrible mess. And their equipment got so big they had short four-foot rods, stiff rods, and fifty- and eighty-pound test monofilament line and they would even break those big rods occasionally when they would try to force a fish in. They were not playing the fish. They would snag it and just start reeling in and dragging the fish to shore. It was not sport anymore. It was meat— that was what they were after. People that were not there just do not know what a deplorable situation it was. I tried what they referred to as the "Newaygo twitch" because it happened in the Muskegon River. It was cast out and jerk, jerk, jerk and reel, jerk and reel, until all of a sudden you would lay the hook into some flesh and then the battle would be on. I tried it, and thought this is a horrible way to fish. It was also tiring. Your arm would get so tired. Fishermen would have to take a ten- or fifteen-minute break and rest their arm it was so tiring to jerk constantly. They did not just throw it out there and wait for the fish to run into it. They were jerking constantly.

It was a sorry sight to see on the banks of the Big Manistee at Tippy Dam, both sides lined with fishermen and all the rods jerking, jerking, jerking. Then somebody would hook a fish and he would get tangled up in everybody else's line and they would have four or five guys all tangled up into one fish. As soon as the fish was hooked, he would head the other way and start to the other side of the river so now you would get two fishermen on the other side of the river hooked into the same fish you had. Now, everybody was arguing whose fish it was, so they are all pulling against each other. It was, I can tell you, a nasty situation.

Gordon Zuverink maintained that the Michigan Steelheaders played a major role in convincing the Michigan DNR to ban snagging.

After snagging had been made legal, the Michigan Steelheaders fought and fought so hard to cease the snagging bit and just do away with it. The state park at Ludington was just full of campers in the fall because it was a hot spot for snagging. All these fish ran up against the dam and there was no place to go and there was just women, kids, men, everybody standing there snagging. They did have one year, which I was quite excited about, when we first started pressing the DNR to make snagging illegal. The DNR agreed the fish could be made to bite, so they tried to alternate snagging and sport-fishing days. On our days, I would go there and I would get a badge from the state park office, an instructor's badge. I would fish legally with legal terminal equipment and fish with spawn bags or crawlers and I would occasionally land a fish. I fished with smaller hooks. I can remember one time a guy said, "I cannot believe that little hook you got in that fish. How did you ever land a fish with that small hook?" I said, "It does not take much. Just do not jerk him in. Play the fish like you are supposed to, as a sports fisherman."

At Ludington, on the Big Sable River, the DNR wanted to see if snaggers could be convinced that you did not have to snag to catch fish. That is where the members of the Steelheaders organization were supposed to come there as instructors. In fact, as I recall we had to show our membership card and we had it as an instructor badge. That is what we wore, and we were the only ones that were supposed to be fishing on those days and that was wonderful. All the snaggers were sitting on the bank watching us and they could not fish. It was an easy situation to handle there because you only had a half a mile of stream from the mouth of Lake Michigan to the dam below Silver Lake.

You did not have to snag to catch the salmon in the fall because they kept saying they are done feeding. Once they enter the streams, they are done feeding. But that does not mean that you cannot entice them into striking. We had good success and those were great days. I remember those off days. I could not wait to get out there on the off days on our legal fishing—good fishing days—to get up there and have all these fish out in front of you. There were not a lot of fishermen because you had to have an instructor's badge in order to fish and the DNR was patrolling the river at that time. But it was a very enjoyable time.

The Steelheaders did convert some of these people into the proper way of fishing. Then we found that a lot of these snaggers were snagging on snag days and would fish with proper terminal tackle on the days when snagging was illegal. That was a step in the right direction and finally they made snagging illegal and it all eventually ended. Occasionally, there is still some snagging going on. I notice at Tippy Dam when I fish in the fall that guys will quite often foul-hook a chinook or coho salmon and land them sometimes. They will land them and put them on their stringer and occasionally, if the DNR is there and spots it, they will issue them a citation to convince them that it is not the way to fish. But the Michigan Steelheaders were primarily the reason for the DNR to desist, to stop the snagging because we were sport fishing.

Kevin Naze regarded commercial trawling operations as inconsistent with what he sees as the larger economic return from sport fishing.

There have been some ugly confrontations centered around Manitowoc and Two Rivers. I hate to target one area, but if you go down there, you will find that out. They have some trawlers there that definitely target certain species like smelt, for example. It is one of the few areas in the lake where they have good success with trawling. The DNR allowed them to trawl for millions of pounds of alewife each year. They sold the alewife for pennies a pound for cat food and so forth. Sports-fishing groups were concerned about this throughout the 1980s. We finally went to the DNR and said, "We need this fish." Then the collapse of the salmon came and that really helped. There are a lot of people who do not trust each other down in that neck of the woods. They do not know if they are really reporting all their smelt harvests each year or if the sport fishermen are asking for too much. It goes both ways.

The commercials cry, "It is our livelihood and this is X amount of generations that have been fishing." It is a hard business to be in. I would not want to do it. You have got expenses and equipment. That lake can be a monster some days. I live a mile from the lake and I get to pick and choose the days that I go out. I go out for fun in my own eighteen-foot boat. These guys have got to go out hell or high water. They go out in driving rainstorms, thunderstorms, eight-foot seas, all to tend their nets and get the fresh catch. In Manitowoc and Two Rivers, there are some good guys down at the Susie-Q Fish Market. They do not get along with the Manitowoc-Two Rivers sport fishermen that much. It goes both ways.

Last year, the LeClairs asked for a higher smelt quota. One of the LeClair girls gave a real good presentation on what the family business means to her. So I wrote a big spread on the need to keep the family business. The next day, I wrote the sport-fishing side. The smelt are down, so why kick them when they are down? Let the smelt recover first and then we will give you a bigger quota if they can show that the population is coming up. Your livelihood is in jeopardy, yes. They have ten employees or whatever. But we are talking about a multibillion dollar sport-fishing industry that attracts 50,000 charter participants each year and hundreds of thousands of private boaters, not to mention shore fishermen and stream fishermen. So they are always crying for their individual business, which is very important, but you have got to look at the lake as a whole to see how it is going to affect everyone. I think the commercials are going to be gradually run right out of business. I can see it happening because the good of the lake has to come first. I hope it does not happen that way because they and the history of the lake are important. Hopefully, there will always be room for both.

———————

Lyn Ray regarded the planting of walleyes by the Grand Traverse Band of Ottawa and Chippewa as evidence of the lack of coordination among the three parties involved in the regulation of Lake Michigan fisheries—the tribes, the Michigan DNR, and the U.S. Fish and Wildlife Service. He maintained that in exchange for allowing the tribes to establish casinos, the Indians should give concessions to the Michigan DNR and sport-fishing interests.

The lake trout are all planted by the sportsmen's dollars. The state has two lake trout hatcheries. The other ones are for browns and rainbows. Salmon—the big thing is the salmon. The Feds have the big lake trout hatcheries. So federal dollars are what's planting the lake trout. The Indians planted 40,000 walleyes last year, but DNR asked them not to. They did not want them introduced into these waters. The Indians went ahead—and that's why I say there's no communication here with the DNR. I am a member of the Elk Rapids Sportsmen's Club and we wanted to plant walleyes. We will buy walleyes and put them in. We went to the DNR and the DNR said no, definitely no, because they did not think the habitat was right. You cannot do it. If you do it, we will fine you. So last year the Native Americans decided they wanted to plant walleyes because they are really marketable. Everybody wants walleyes to eat, so if they could get a walleye fishery out there like they got in Lake Erie, it would be a real smart thing for them to do. But the DNR said no. We do not want to screw up the ecology and what fishery we got going. So they went in Suttons Bay and dumped 40,000 of them anyway.

Well, you want to know the truth, if they open it up at Manistee and Ludington, you are going to see boats sinking and people getting shot. I have no doubt in my mind. I would bet money on it. Because the fishermen down there, that's their living. In those towns, that's their life. They have already had a couple incidents down there and they were not bad. I think that is why the judge has not opened it up down there. I think there should be a fishery down there, but it should be way out. But I am not even sure those guys would accept that. Now the guys at the Manistee Fishing Association told me that they sat down with the tribe, the Little River Band of Odawa. They said help us with the town to get a casino and we will not commercial fish. I said, "Do not believe everything they tell you." Well, they helped them get their casino but now there's three or four that want to fish.

But I really believe that if the Indians are allowed to fish around Manistee, it will be like it was here when it all started. They were flattening tires. It got to be pretty heated in the Traverse City area. The Native Americans were carrying loaded shotguns, so they were aware of what might happen. So I hope that we do not see that happen because that is not going to do anybody any good. I have known local guys who just cannot understand it. It does not make sense to them. The older guys who have worked, retired, and want to go fishing just do not understand how they can come along and be able to do the things they can do and that they cannot. When I was president, I had a lady call me because her husband had his gun all loaded. She said he was going to go shoot the Indians and go to jail for the rest of his life. You have to do something. It was that bad.

It is terrible that you cannot just talk about fishing without getting into Indian issues. I just wish it could get worked out. There's a commercial fishery out there in Lake Michigan. Let it be utilized. But do not clean out areas. Do zone fishing. Let the Indians fish down south for a month, then move up for a month, and here for a month, and at least keep the fishery alive in some places. Of course, they are telling the sportsmen not to worry about it because after another five years, no one is going to want to do it. To the young guys coming up, fishing is too much work. They can go to the casino. It is a really tough way to make a living. Of course, they are making an awful good living. We are making it easy for them by planting the fish. I would like to see the governor step in and say, "Okay, if you want casinos, then quit gill netting." The gill netting has to stop. Now the trap netting, I do not have as much of a problem with that.

Charter boat operator Scott Anderson supports limits on tribal use of gill nets in Lake Michigan. Anderson discussed allegations made by tribal fisher Skip Duhamel that he and several other charter boat operators took his nets. His apprehension about the renegotiation of the 1985 Consent Agreement stemmed, in part, from media reports that the Grand Traverse Band would seek an expansion of tribal fishing areas. His commentary embodies the sport-fishing community's longstanding antipathy toward tribal fishing and gill netting and exemplifies why these issues are such enduring themes in this group's oral tradition.

Two years ago or three years ago a net went adrift. And it was sometime in May. Probably, middle of June, we get a call from one of the charter boats. The captain said, "I got into something. It has got all my down riggers. I cannot move. I cannot believe the oil slick that is on the water." The guy had to cut his downrigger wire because it was so entangled. This net was set up off the clay banks up here, four and a half miles out in the lake. That day four charter boats got into that net. I was one of them. Fortunately, I only had one downrigger get into it. I must have gotten hold of a tail end; I did not get the middle. I got the net up where it was probably fifteen to twenty feet down before I had to cut my downrigger. There were many rotten fish in it. The stench from the dead fish turned your stomach. It was terrible. We were accused of taking that net but it was found floating out in one of our prime lake trout areas. Skip Duhamel thinks we are against him. I do not know of anyone around here that would do that. Back, pre-1985, there were some pretty hard core, standup people around here. But once we got the 1985 Consent Order, our end settled down. We had something we could live with.

Back in 1985, I was just getting started here, so I did not have much clientele. The tensions between the tribal community and the sport-fishing community were really, really tough. And there were some concessions made by the tribal people. There were concessions we made. We went from a five-fish limit on lake trout down to two. There was a slight increase, if I remember right, in license fees for one-day people to help cover some of the expense. Grand Traverse Bay went to a different size limit to try to encourage the growth of the smaller fish. We have actually been out with a DNR officer and have seen the fact that the nets were laid lower than the 45th parallel. Not that much, but they were south of the 45th. The tribal community elected not to do anything. The gill net kills all species—salmon, trout, brown, steelhead, or anything that goes into the net. Occasionally there are burbot, which are freshwater cod. The Indian throws those away because there is no market at all.

If in ten years, my kid wanted to take over my business, we might have to take another look at it. I have major concerns with this new agreement. I have major concerns. There is competition for the resource. And it is not that there is not enough resource right now. It goes back to what are we going to do ten years from now. As tribal history goes, I understand that the Indians would move into an area and as the resources were depleted and it was more difficult to do what they needed to, they would move. So are they going to continue to bleed the resource? I go back to my concerns with the new agreement. A year ago they published some of the things that they were looking for.

The sports fishermen are really coming quite a ways to meet the tribes as far as compromise goes. There's a different judge now. Judge Fox is no longer going to be presiding. Is there a different feeling or maybe a hope that at least things will stay the way they are and more concessions will not be made? If we could stay where we are, we would be all right. We need to somehow predicate catch limits equally to sport fishermen to tribal. I do not what that is, but we need some kind of system to manage where it is. How we enforce it, how it is done, I cannot tell you. But we cannot continue to take 3,000 pounds of lake trout a day at times out of an area and expect it to continue to survive. If all fifteen charter boats went out every day, twice a day, we might catch 3,000 pounds of fish. We do not because our fish weigh about four or five pounds. Let us hope that the groups that are together look at ways of managing the resource. One of the demands that the tribe made back a year ago was that they wanted fishing over Lake Michigan, all the way down to the Indiana line. We are here every day and we see what is being taken. The people south of the 45th parallel do not see it.

When your granddaddy's daddy, granddaddy's uncle sat down across the table and wrote this agreement, they had a vision of what they were signing. The big word that constantly comes up is a word called subsistence. What was subsistence in 1836 and what is subsistence in 1999? Subsistence in 1836 was the fact that the tribe had to take care of their tribal members and provide food. So now I say to people that are on board my boat, I say back when our forefathers signed that, there was the intent of the law and the word of the law. The intent of the law by our forefathers was to provide food for the family and the tribal members. What's now the word of the law is commercial fishing because subsistence provides income, or income is subsistence. It is very much a play on words. Somebody needs to sit there and say let us define subsistence in 1999 terms.

The judge should say let's take a real look at this treaty and let's get the lawyers out of here who are saying the word THE is "the." At the O. J. Simpson trial they nittygrittied every word. They should ask what did the treaty mean back when it was signed. Here is what the treaty meant and this is what the treaty should mean in 1999. That is the nuts and bolts of the whole thing. The tribes are doing very well in the casino. They

477

get a very, very nice return. Their lands are tax-free. They pay no personal income tax. Their health insurance is provided. The cost of the negotiation is being paid by U.S. tax dollars. So as I understand it, we pay the lawyer to fight us.

Charter boat captain Lyn Ray of Traverse City acknowledged that in Grand Traverse Bay, the sport fishery was dependent on the lake trout, a put-and-take fishery. Salmon fishing was limited to a few weeks in the late summer and early fall. Ray has testified on behalf of the Michigan DNR as a representative of sport-fishing interests in the Grand Traverse Bay area. When the 1985 Consent Agreement was being renegotiated in anticipation of its 2000 expiration, he spoke in favor of reducing tribal fishing rights.

I think the federal government is finally realizing that the natural reproduction of lake trout is about one to two percent. We have a different strain of lake trout than were here when the lampreys came in during the 1940s. They just about eliminated the original mackinaw, the old mackinaw lake trout. And it is either this new lake trout strain that we planted or, of course, there are so many different theories on it. They say the spawning grounds are covered with stuff. They have laid down artificial reefs for spawning and that refuge zone I was talking about up north, they plant like 2 or 3 million fish in that, trying to get natural reproduction. Now as far as I know, it is one or two percent. So the lake trout fishery in Lake Michigan, all the lakes, is probably put-and-take. I mean, they have to plant millions of them every year or you do not have a naturally reproducing fishery. That is what it amounts to.

Coming back now, lake trout are very slow growing—about a pound a year. If you catch a four-pound fish, he is probably around four years old. The creel census guy takes scale samples and measures and weighs them. He is there about every time we come in. The planted lake trout have a fin clip. They can tell where they were planted, when they were planted, how big they have grown, and everything else. In recent years, we had a couple of lake trout that were about fifteen or sixteen pounds and they were about seventeen years old. For lake trout, you have got to keep planting them every year and get the numbers way up there. Chinook salmon live for four years and die. The coho salmon live three years. The DNR can adjust the stocking pretty easily with a three- or four-year program. The lake trout are slow growing, so it is hard. They have got to look at the big picture and say where is it going to be ten years from now by their planting this year. With salmon, they plant them one year and they are pretty good size by the second year and by the fourth year they are huge. Lake trout is our mainstay fishery up here yet, anyway we look at it.

I would like to have something more uniform as far as the Native Americans and their catches and the enforcement on it. I do not believe there has been enough checking on it. They pretty much do what they want to do. Their catch of lake trout is limited to twenty-five percent. After that, they are supposed to move. I do not believe they do.

Skip Duhamel once came up to me and wanted to talk because the negotiations were coming up. He did not want the other tribes in here. He came up and introduced himself and said, "We have to get together and help each other." And I said, "Well Skip, I have been telling you that for years." He did not want the other tribes coming down to Traverse City. The Grand Traverse Bay band does not want the Manistee band coming to Traverse netting in their bays. They want to keep it for themselves, so the bands kind of fight a little bit between themselves over zones.

What they are trying to do is allocate fifty percent of the fish to the sports fishermen and fifty percent to the commercial fishermen. Well, you are talking thousands of sports fishermen, hundreds of thousands probably, and you are talking about three families on the other side, which does not quite seem fair. I sat in on the early negotiations back in 1985 when I was used as an expert witness on the fish stocks. I sat through these meetings and we were struggling to pay our attorney. We would walk into court and there would be four or five attorneys on the other side and we were paying for them. It was our federal tax dollars that are paying for them. And you are sitting there saying, "What am I doing, we are just beating our head against the wall."

The judges have taken a very liberal look at it. Judge Fox was the one that really put the monkey wrench in things for the state as far as I am concerned. Judge Enslen is better, a lot better, than Fox was but once you get a precedent set it is so tough to change it. I told him when I say the pledge of allegiance I have real trouble when I get to this one nation under God because I am not sure if I am in the Ottawa nation or the Cherokee nation or the Sioux nation. We are not supposed to have the nations inside of nations and that's just what we have. I mean, you have created a super citizen. They have got rights—they have got gambling rights. They do not have to pay taxes. Do not pay taxes on their cigarettes or gas. We are all supposed to be equal. It is hard to teach your kids that we are all equal when they go to school with a Native American who gets free college, any state college, and plus gets paid for going and we are paying for it. Anymore, It is just hard to tell kids that everything's equal. Well, it sure is not if you are a Native American. You get so much money. Right now, I do not know what it was, but they all got like $11,000 or $12,000 for every member of their family from the casinos. We are not all equal.

I was down in Judge Fox's court. I saw him. He was elderly, long-haired, and real liberal. I saw him sit back in his chair one day, put his feet up on the desk, and he had on a black robe with black tennis shoes. That impressed me right away. It was like the court did not really mean a thing to him. He did not look like he paid attention about half the time. He just basically gave them everything they wanted. He did not go by the treaty. There are so many things in those treaties. It is like they have gone through and picked out what they wanted. There were all kinds of things you could preserve. Well, they kind of go through and say: "Well, we did not mean that or maybe the chief was drunk when they signed that." They just kind of go through these treaties and pick out what they want. And this whole fishing issue with subsistence, it said right in the treaty they can go fish for themselves to provide their family with food. It did not mean commercially. They did not know what a commercial fishery was. They did not have a clue. It was never meant to be commercial fishery. It was meant for subsistence. It says right in the treaty, subsistence, subsistence, but the judge says, "Well, I am saying they can go catch those fish and sell them and that makes it subsistence."

Scott Anderson, a charter boat operator from Leland, indicated that as the population of salmon diminished in the mid-1980s, sport-fishing boats focused more and more on lake trout.

The lake trout population of Lake Superior is now self-sustaining. Needless to say, that is the goal of the DNR and the U.S. Fish and Wildlife Service, who actually govern a lot of what goes on with the lake trout here. It is not just the Michigan DNR. The ultimate goal is to make a self-sustaining lake trout population and that is why they

480

have the refuges outlined as a nonfishing area. In the mid-1980s, we were salmon fishing. We never looked at lake trout. My wife and I would come down at 5 o'clock on Saturday or Sunday, go out to a place we call First Bank, fish for twenty minutes, have a little cheese and some beverage in the back of the boat. Then we would come back in, hang ten fish up, and wait for the people to walk by. That is how I got my business started. In the mid-1980s I could say to my wife, "Go out there to where it gets deep, put some lines down, I will come back in an hour, and we will meet." And she caught fish. There were that many salmon available. And we did not catch lake trout, only infrequently when we were fishing for salmon. We did fish lake trout in the early season, but our salmon fishing would start sometime during the second week of June, third week of June, and that really took us all through the year.

As the fisheries changed, as the salmon fishing died off, we had to redirect our attention to something that we could put on the boat for people to catch. So we started fishing lake trout. By about 1992 or 1993, we were doing more lake trout fishing than salmon fishing. There are a lot of lake trout out there. We are very, very successful at getting them. I do not want to say lake trout are a dumber fish as far as catching them, but they are not hard to catch. If you see them, you can usually get them, and that is good for our clientele. They want the box. They have a smell to it other than ice. So that is what we do.

Trap nets get your high-priced fish. That is simple. They leave the sport fish for what they were intended for. Salmon were not intended to fill somebody's nets. Salmon were meant to come in here to kill off the alewife and provide a sport fishery for the Great Lakes. You can ask Howard Tanner that. You can go back to when they put them in here in the mid-to late 1960s. You can go back to fishing with fourteen-foot rowboats with people rowing to troll and handmade downriggers and everything else. Do we quit planting them if they are not there? I do not know how many lake trout they are really planting in Lake Michigan right now, but I bet the number is huge. They come down here, put them in the boats and take them out to the South Fox refuge. They do not just come to the edge of the water and dump them here. They are physically taking them out into a location where they are protected and hopefully, they will come back there to spawn.

481

Kevin Naze (Door County, Wisconsin) maintained that commercial fishermen should be allowed to fish for lake trout in Wisconsin waters where they are abundant and not sought by sport fishers.

Fishermen in Wisconsin are limited to two lake trout because the U.S. Fish and Wildlife Service is trying to get the lake trout to naturally reproduce on its own again. They are a native fish to the lake but they are struggling to reproduce. Some people think it is the PCBs. I disagree, because the commercial fishermen have cooperated, gone out there with their nets, and netted lake trout. They take the sperm, they take the eggs, mix them together, and bring them to the hatchery. They put the fertilized eggs in an Astroturf sandwich they call it, out on a historic spawning reef in a hundred feet of water off Jacksonport. They go down there with underwater cameras and they document the egg hatching. Some fry are coming out of there swimming. There is a hatch. But they are finding the empty eggs too. I think it has been bred out of the lake trout possibly. For years, they have been held in these six-foot deep brood stock pens in a hatchery or something. Who knows how Mother Nature works? But for some reason, the lake trout that are supposed to be spawning in a hundred feet of water come to Algoma every fall. They are spawning along the pier and their eggs are getting uselessly washed up in the surf. So there is one reef down south between Milwaukee and Port Washington where they are hoping—they think it is the last chance for natural reproduction. If it does not happen soon, I think they will abandon this two-fish limit and everything else. But they are trying everything. They are trying different strains from Canada and all over. They want to have a native fish. That is part of what the feds have to do to re-establish native fish and wildlife in areas where they were taken out by man or sea lamprey.

The lake trout are not targeted heavily because they are not a real sporty fish. I like lake trout. The smaller ones are great on the grill or for boils. I would not eat a big one because it has been in the lake ten to twenty years, and if you believe in the contaminant stuff, those are the kind that are going to accumulate the PCBs and so forth. For some reason, the lake trout are moving into shallow water in the fall to spawn, which is not where they are supposed to be. They are supposed to be out in eighty, ninety, or one hundred feet of water, spawning on these deep gravel bottoms in the rocks, letting their eggs get trapped in the rocks so they are not blowing all over. So until they can get that fixed, they have shown no significant natural reproduction in the last fifteen to twenty years. The rainbow trout and the chinook salmon on the Michigan side are showing reproduction because your rivers are maybe more wild or whatever. I think Michigan estimates that one out of every three chinooks are now naturally reproduced.

If lake trout abundance stays high and if sport angler interest stays low for the lake trout, I would not mind allowing the commercials to take some of the lake trout because there are plenty to go around for everybody. I know they want to be able to fish for lake trout. They have cooperated in the past. They have used their equipment to net these lake trout out on these deep reefs and let the DNR tag them and they have put down those Astroturf sandwiches. So why not let them enjoy some of it too? Historically, they were allowed some lake trout. I think if they can prove that there are areas that have high abundance of lake trout with very little targeting by the sport fishery, the DNR should definitely let them take those areas. For example, up near Jacksonport, where nobody bumps the bottom for lake trout like we do between Algoma and Sturgeon Bay. They fish lake trout hard when nothing else is biting. From Sturgeon Bay north there is very little targeting of lake trout, so why not let the commercial fishermen take some of them?

––––––––––––

"Coho" Bob Maynard (Pentwater, Michigan) recalled efforts to get the state involved in the sea lamprey problem.

The lamprey eel and all these newer items that have happened in more recent years are the real culprits. Forty to fifty years ago, it did not do us any good to take samples of lamprey eel in a glass jar with formaldehyde to the people in Lansing and the people in Ann Arbor, the powerful people. They did not believe us or for one reason or another. They did not do much to help us. There is where your trouble is, the lamprey eel and similar things.

––––––––––––

Sport fisher Roy Holmquist (Ellison Bay, Wisconsin) discussed the effects of the sea lamprey on sport species.

L ast year, I did catch fish that actually had lamprey marks again. I think they cut down a little bit on the lamprey program. In fact, we went over to Michigan to fish for salmon on the Manistee River and they had poisoned it for lampreys and I could not believe the amount of lampreys. They were little. I guess it was the baby ones that they killed but it was just amazing how many lampreys were in there. See, when we fished back home in Illinois, we very seldom had that problem because it was mostly cohos, not too many kings or lake trout. Evidently, the lampreys never got on the cohos. But when we came up here, we started seeing fish with the marks on them. Even last year, I caught two fish that had lampreys hanging on them. In the fall of 1998, I saw a brown trout swimming around with a lamprey hanging on him. That was another deal that came in through the ship canal—another ocean-going species that took over—just like the zebra mussels and the gobies.

NOTES

1. On sport fishing in Lake Michigan, see LaRue Wells and Alberton L. McLain, "Lake Michigan: Man's Effects on Native Fish Stocks and Other Biota," Technical Report no. 20 (Ann Arbor: Great Lakes Fishery Commission, January 1973), 8–10. On learning how to fish for salmon and other sport fish in Lake Michigan, see Hank Babbitt and Dave Kitz, *Catching Coho: The Complete Guide to Freshwater Cohos Salmon Fishing* (Ann Arbor: Sports World Publishing Company, 1968); Byron Dalrymple, "Neglected Fishing Bonanza," *Field and Stream* 60 (August 1955): 36–39, 100–1; Jerry Chiappetta, "Where the Fish Are," *Field and Stream* 70, (May 1965): 16–18; Jerry Chiappetta, "Big Steelhead Are Back," *Field and Stream* 70 (April 1966): 47–49, 177–81; Jerry Chiappetta, "Salmon Succeed in Great Lakes," *Field and Stream* 71 (December 1966): 10–15; Michigan Tourist Council, "Coho, Chinook, and Steelhead in Michigan" (Lansing, Mich: Michigan Tourist Council, 1967); "Steelhead Fishermen Get Organized, Name Officers," *Grand Rapids Press,* 1 April 1967; Ray Voss, "Sport Fishing Club Formed in State," *Muskegon Chronicle,* 1 April 1967; A.J. McClane, "Where East Meets West," *Field and Stream* 71 (April 1967): 78–80, 89–92; John O. Cartier, "Spring Specktacular," *Outdoor Life* 139 (May 1967): 76–78, 118–21; Russell McKee, "Fishstory," *Michigan Conservation* 36, no. 6 (1967): 2–8; Jerry Chiappetta, "The Coho Craze in Michigan," *Field and Stream* 72 (January 1968): 42–43, 103–5, 113; Jerry Chiappetta, "Great Lakes Salmon," *Field and Stream* 72 (March 1968): 62–63, 92–94; Keith Wilson, "80 Snug Harbors," *Michigan Natural Resources* 38, no. 2 (1969): 25–28; Vlad Evanoff, "The Coho Catches On," *Motor Boating* 124 (October 1969): 63, 107; Henry F. Zeman, "Surf Fishing, Michigan's Newest Sport," *Field and Stream* 74 (February 1970): 150–61; Victor R. Patrick, "Salmon Water Patrol," *Michigan Natural Resources* 39, no. 5 (1970): 16–19; A.J. McClane, "Salmon Potpourri," *Field and Stream* 75 (December 1970): 88–90; "Tips for Tackling Chinook," *Michigan Natural Resources* 40, no. 3 (1971): 29; Dave Otto, "Up the Down Lakers," *Outdoor Life* 148 (July 1971): 56, 76, 78, 80; Stanley J. Lievense, "Light, Color and Fish Vision," *Michigan Natural Resources* 40, no. 4 (1971): 24–25; Ken Heuser, "Rainbows over Lake Michigan," *Field and Stream* 76 (February 1972): 75, 24 ; Richard J. Enger, "Grand Traverse Bay: Melting Pot for Game Fish," *Field and Stream* 78 (April 1974): 182–88; Stanley J.

Lievense, "Michigan's Forgotten Fishing," *Michigan Natural Resources* 43, no. 5 (1974): 10–13; John O. Carter, "Chinook: Mystery Heavyweight of the Great Lakes," *Outdoor Life* 157 (May 1976): 78–79, 146, 148–51; Russ Fimbinger, "Salmon Bonanza," *Michigan Natural Resources* 54, no. 4 (July–August 1985): 39–43; Ken Schultz, "Great Lakes Fall Salmon," *Field and Stream* 90 (September 1985): 42–44; Jack D. Bails, "Waters of Change," *Michigan Natural Resources* 55, no. 3 (May–June 1986): 45–55.

On fishing in an urban landscape, see Jan Zita Grover, *Northern Waters* (St. Paul: Graywolf Press, 1999), 142–57

2. For more on outdoor life in American culture, see Peter J. Schmitt, *Back to Nature: The Arcadian Myth in Urban America* (Baltimore: Johns Hopkins University Press, 1990). For more on the broader context that fueled America's interest in outdoor activity and the cultural construction of nature as a rejuvenating concept, see T. J. Jackson Lears, *No Place of Grace: Antimodernism and the Transformation of American Culture, 1880–1920* (New York: Pantheon Books, 1981); Yi-Fu Tuan, *The Good Life* (Madison: University of Wisconsin Press, 1986); *Topophilia: A Study of Environmental Perception, Attitudes, and Values* (New York: Columbia University Press, 1974), 92–112.

3. "Alas, Rockford Fisherman's 'Record' Chinook is Unofficial," *Grand Rapids Press*, 4 October 1969.

4. John F. Reiger, *American Sportsmen and the Origins of Conservation* (New York: Winchester Press, 1975), 25–49.

5. Michael G. Kammen, *Mystic Chords of Memory: The Transformation of Tradition in American Culture* (New York: Knopf, 1991), 40–61; For more on how Euro-Americans fused this sentiment and notions of American authenticity with the appropriation of Native American culture and recreational fishing, see Philip J. Deloria, *Playing Indian* (New Haven: Yale University Press, 1998), 95–153.

6. Ernest Hemingway, *The Nick Adams Stories* (New York: Scribner, 1972); Robert Traver, *Trout Madness* (New York: St. Martin's Press, 1960); Ben East, "Trout from a Roadless River," in *Outdoor Life's Anthology of Fishing Adventures: The World's Best Stories of Fishing Adventures* (New York: Popular Science Publishing, 1945), 104–110; Jim Harrison, *Just Before Dark: Collected Nonfiction* (Boston: Houghton Mifflin/Seymour Lawrence, 1991); Jerry Dennis, *A Place on the Water: An Angler's Reflections on Home* (New York: St. Martin's Griffin, 1993); *The River Home: An Angler's Explorations* (New York: Thomas Dunne Books/St. Martin's Griffin, 1998); Jan Zita Grover, *Northern Waters;* Kathleen Stocking, "Listening for the First Smelt Run," in *Michigan Seasons,* ed. Ted J. Rulseh (Waukesha, Wisc.: The Cabin Bookshelf, 1997), 11–15; David N. Cassuto, *Cold Running River* (Ann Arbor: University of Michigan Press, 1994), 29–47.

For more on the cultural and environmental factors that influenced Hemingway's Michigan/Great Lakes fishing-related writing, see Robert O. Stephens, *Hemingway's Nonfiction: The Public Voice* (Chapel Hill: University of North Carolina Press, 1968), 151–79; Frederic J. Svoboda, "False Wilderness: Northern Michigan as Created in the Nick Adams Stories," in *Hemingway: Up in Michigan Perspectives,* ed. Frederic J. Svoboda and Joseph J. Waldmeir (East Lansing: Michigan State University Press, 1995), 15–22; Joseph M. Flora, *Hemingway's Nick Adams* (Baton Rouge: Louisiana State University Press, 1992), 1–25, 145–75; Susan F. Beegel, "Eye and Heart: Hemingway's Education as a Naturalist," in *A Historical Guide to Ernest Hemingway,* ed. Linda Wagner-Martin (New York: Oxford University Press, 2000), 53–92; James R. Mellow, *Hemingway: A Life Without Consequences* (Reading, Mass.: Addison-Wesley Publishing, 1993), 12–15, 23, 28–33; Constance Cappel Montgomery, *Hemingway in Michigan* (New York: Fleet Publishing, 1966), 11–18, 141–58. On Traver, see Dixie Franklin, "Ever the Fisherman," *Michigan Natural Resources Magazine* 57, no. 2 (1988): 4–13.

7. David Tatham, *Fishing in the North Woods: Winslow Homer* (Boston: Museum of Fine Arts, 1995); Nicolai Cikovsky Jr. and Franklin Kelly, *Winslow Homer* (New Haven: Yale University Press, 1995); William Innes Homer, *Thomas Eakins: His Life and Art* (New York: Abbeville Press Publishers, 1992); Gordon Hendricks, *The Life and Work of Thomas Eakins* (New York: Grossman Publishers, 1974); Martin A. Berger, "Painting Victorian Manhood," in *Thomas Eakins: The Rowing Pictures,* ed. Helen A. Cooper (New Haven: Yale University Press, 1996), 102–23; Ben C. Robinson, "Emerson Hough's Wild Waters," *Forest and Stream* 93, no. 8 (1923): 432–33, 463–67.

8. George Shiras III, *Hunting Wild Life with Camera and Flashlight: A Record of Sixty-Five Years' Visits to the Woods and Waters of North America, Volume One* (Washington, D.C.: National Geographic Society, 1935), 377–96; T. L. Hankinson, "Results of the Shiras Expeditions to Whitefish Point, Michigan: Fishes," in *Michigan Geological and Biological Survey, 1915: Miscellaneous Papers on the Zoology of Michigan, Publication 20, Biological Series 4* (Lansing, Mich.: Wynkoop Hallenbeck Crawford Co., 1916), 111–70; Mike Sajna, "George Shiras III: Father of Wildlife Photography," *Michigan Natural Resources Magazine* 59, no. 6 (1990), 4–13; Ladislav Hanka, *Etchings by Ladislav Hanka* (Kalamazoo, Mich.: 1998).

9. See references to fishing in Henry David Thoreau, *Walden; or Life in the Woods; On the Duty of Civil Disobedience* (New York: Holt, Rinehart and Winston, 1966); *A Week on the Concord and Merrimack Rivers* (Princeton, N.J.: Princeton University Press, 1983).

10. Schmitt, *Back to Nature*.

11. A comparable situation in which railroads promoted outdoor, sporting activities is presented in Dona Brown, *Inventing New England: Regional Tourism in the Nineteenth Century* (Washington, D.C.: Smithsonian Institution Press, 1995). See also Robert Barnwell Roosevelt, *Superior Fishing: The Striped Bass, Trout, and Black Bass of the Northern States* (St. Paul: Minnesota Historical Society Press, 1985), 185.

12. Robert Page Lincoln, "Angling for the Perch," *Forest and Stream* 93, no. 6 (1923): 304, 328, 330, 332.

13. Dr. William A. Bruette, "The Izaak Walton League Convention," *Forest and Stream* 96, no. 6 (1926): 327–30. A treatment of the early history of the Izaak Walton League is provided in Philip V. Scarpino, *Great River: An Environmental History of the Upper Mississippi, 1890–1950* (Columbia: University of Missouri Press, 1985), 114–50. For more on the Izaak Walton League's role in commercializing outdoor activity see James Kates, *Planning a Wilderness: Regenerating the Great Lakes Cutover Region* (Minneapolis: University of Minnesota Press, 2001), 103–8.

14. Deloria, *Playing Indian*, 95–153.

15. Ben East, "Is the Grayling Doomed," *Forest and Stream* 100, no. 5 (1930): 340–41, 366–69; "MUCC's Annual Meeting, November 8–10," *Michigan Conservation* 9, no. 12 (1940): 3, 10

16. For more on charter boat operation, see Jerry Chiappetta, "Coho—Fish of Surplus," *Field and Stream* 73 (December 1968): 42–45, 82–84; John A. Scott, "Great! Lakers are Back," *Michigan Natural Resources* 40, no. 3 (1971): 26–27; "Jim Bennett, Savvy Great Lakes Pro," *North Woods Call*, 18 July 1973; "Michigan's Great Lakes Perch Fishing Areas," *Michigan Natural Resources* 45, no. 3 (1976): 25; Russell McKee, "Winning Ways for Deep Water Anglers," *Michigan Natural Resources* 53, no. 3 (1984): 47–51; Jean White, "Lake Michigan Fishing: No Shore Thing," *Saturday Evening Post* 261 (September 1989): 86–87; Gerald P. Rakoczy and Richard D. Rogers, "Charter Boat Catch and Effort from the Michigan Waters of the Great Lakes, 1989," presented at *Regional Charter Boat Workshops* (winter 1990); John Block, "Finlander Expands, Relocates in Ludington," *Kalamazoo Gazette*, n.d.

17. "Fishing For Anglers," *Milwaukee Sentinel*, 18 December 1990.

18. Webb Waldron, *We Explore the Great Lakes* (New York: Century Co., 1923), 21.

19. Roosevelt, *Superior Fishing*, 12, 15, 17, 21, 41, 46–48, 62–63, 129, 131; Thaddeus Norris, *The American Angler's Book: Embracing the Natural History of Sporting Fish and the Art of Taking Them* (Philadelphia: E. H. Butler and Co., 1865), 27–36, 202–5, 250–58, 269–71; *American Fish Culture: Embracing all the Details of Artificial Breeding and Rearing of Trout; The Culture of Salmon, Shad and Other Fishes* (Philadelphia: Porter and Coates, 1868).

20. Reiger, *American Sportsmen and the Origins of Conservation*, 25–56. See also Dean Conrad Allard Jr., *Spencer Fullerton Baird and the U.S. Fish Commission* (New York: Arno Press, 1978) and E. F. Rivinus and E. M. Youssef, *Spencer Baird of the Smithsonian Institution* (Washington, D.C.: Smithsonian Institution Press, 1992).

21. G. Brown Goode, *American Fishes: A Popular Treatise upon the Game and Food Fishes of North America* (New York: W. A. Houghton, 1888); David Starr Jordan, *American Food and Game Fishes* (New York: Doubleday, Page and Co., 1902). For more on the early outreach activities of North American fisheries scientists, see Christine M. Moffitt, *Reflections: A Photographic History of Fisheries and the American Fisheries Society in North America*

(Bethesda, Md.: American Fisheries Society, 2001), 5–18.

22. "Letters to the Press: DNR Policies," 13 January 1970, Garden Peninsula Historical Society scrapbook [hereafter GPHS scrapbook]; Kevin Clark, "Close Monitoring by the DNR Is Called For," *Traverse City Record Eagle*, 7 March 1998; Norm Spring [Address to Michigan Conservation Commission], Grand Haven, Mich., 10 August 1967, original in the possession of Norm Spring, Grand Haven, Michigan; Kevin Clark, "Letter From the Editor, Making Heads or Tails Out of It All," *Grand Traverse Fishing Association Newsletter* 1, no. 1 (1998): 2.

On Glen Sheppard and the *North Woods Call*, see Robert Doherty, *Disputed Waters: Native Americans and the Great Lakes Fishery* (Lexington: University of Kentucky Press, 1990), 78–79

23. On hatcheries, see Margaret Beattie Bogue, *Fishing the Great Lakes: An Environmental History* (Madison: University of Wisconsin, 2000), 184–87; Norm Spring [Letter from Michigan Steelheaders President], *The Fish Line* 1, no. 1 (6 May 1967); Diane Conners, "Court Won't Hear Gill-Net Dispute Until December," *Traverse City Record Eagle*, 28 August 1997; Steve Kellman, "McManus: Trust Should Repair Fish Hatcheries," *Traverse City Record Eagle*, 15 October 1997; Bob Gwizdz, "Group Trying to Limit Commercial Fishing," *Kalamazoo Gazette*, 7 October 2000.

24. *Michigan Conservation* 17, no. 4 (1948): 1.

25. On MUCC, see Clifford Ross Gearhart, *Pity the Poor Fish Then Man* (Au Train, Mich.: Avery Color Studios, 1987), 202–4; Tom Kuchenberg, *Reflections in a Tarnished Mirror: The Use and Abuse of the Great Lakes* (Sturgeon Bay, Wisc.: Golden Glow Publishing, 1978), 123–25; Doherty, *Disputed Waters*, 103–9; "Legislative Recommendations," *Michigan Conservation* 11, no. 7 (1942): 6; "Ban Proposed on Lake Trout Netting," (Photo) *Grand Rapids Press*, 30 June 1958; "Statement of Thomas L. Washington on Behalf of the MUCC" [Presented before the House Subcommittee on Fisheries and Wildlife Conservation, 6 June 1980, Traverse City, Mich.], Michigan DNR File, Michigan State Archives, box 8, Lansing, Mich.; "Ban Gill Nets Now" (Lansing, Mich.: Michigan United Conservation Clubs, n.d.); Bill O'Brien, "Mutual Respect Urged in Fishing Talks," *Traverse City Record Eagle*, 24 March 1999.

The Michigan Steelheaders demanded a "paramount position" over fishing from the Michigan DNR. See "Minutes of Michigan Steelheaders Association Meeting, 2 June 1967," Baldwin, Michigan, Norm Spring, Grand Haven, Mich.; For more on the Steelheaders, see "Letter from Norm Spring to Michigan Fisherman [n.d.], original in the possession of Norm Spring, Grand Haven, Michigan; Norm Spring, "Dear Fellow Fishermen," *The Fish Line* 1, no. 1 (6 May 1967): 1; Stan Lievense, Lansing, to Norm Spring, Grand Haven, 13 March 1967, original in the possession of Norm Spring, Grand Haven, Michigan. On Norm Spring, see "Steelhead Fishermen Get Organized, Name Officers," *Grand Rapids Press*, 1 April 1967; Ray Voss, "Sport Fishing Club Formed in State," *Muskegon Chronicle*, 1 April 1967; "Overflow Crowd of Sportsmen," *Grand Haven Tribune*, 21 March 1969; "Spawner of the Steelheaders' to Speak, Fish Here," *Grand Haven Tribune*, 20 May 1982; Bob Campbell, "Tainted Catch," *Detroit Free Press*, 24 August 1986; Bogue maintained that sport fishing originally gained power in the Great Lakes region in the nineteenth century. See Bogue, 297–98.

26. "Letters: DNR Policies," 3 February 1970, GPHS scrapbook; Paul L. Dorweiler, *Great Lakes Trout and Salmon Fishing* (Coon Rapids, Minn.: Paul Lawrence and Associates, 1982).

27. On opposition to salmon stocking in lake tributaries, see "Reconsider, Please," [n.d.] 1970, GPHS scrapbook; "Letters to the Press: Save Our Whitefish," 2 March 1970, GPHS scrapbook; "Letters to the Press," 5 March 1970, GPHS scrapbook; "Stop the Salmon Plantings in Traverse Bay," *The Sport Fisherman's Friend* (November 1997). On support for salmon stocking, see William J. Stephenson, *Coho: Miracle Fish of the Midwest* (Kalamazoo, Mich.: Coho Unlimited, 1968); "Sees World Fame for Area Coho Fishing," *Charlevoix Courier*, 3 January 1968; "Tension Builds Along Coho Coast," *North Woods Call*, 25 July 1973.

28. On Steelheaders' opposition to tribal fishing, see Thora Layman, "Sports Fishermen Uniting Against Indian Gill Netters," *Benzie County Record Patriot*, 9 September 1978; Thora Layman "Fishing Indian Right,

Whiteman's Privilege: LeBlanc," *Benzie County Record Patriot* 13 September 1978; Gordon Charles, "TC Boat-In Lansing Rally to Show Great Lakes Threats," *Traverse City Record Eagle*, 15 September 1979.

29. Ron McCandlis, *The Fish Line* 1, no. 1 (6 May 1967).

30. On sport opposition to commercial fishing, see Clifford Ross Gearhart, *Pity the Poor Fish*, 148; Norm Spring, [Letter from Michigan Steelheaders President], *The Fish Line* 1, no. 1 (6 May 1967); "Modern Gill Nets More Lethal," *The North Woods Call*, 29 April 1970; "Anglers Demand End to Gill Nets at NRC Showdown," *North Woods Call*, 15 August 1973; "Time Sports Fishermen Got into Gill Net Row," *Petoskey News Review*, 27 August 1973; Richard C. Bishop, *Sport and Commercial Fishing Conflicts: A Theoretical Analysis* (Madison: University of Wisconsin Press, 1980); Michigan DNR, Fish Division, *The Dynamics of Competition Between Sport and Commercial Fishing: Effects on Rehabilitation of Lake Trout in Lake Michigan*, by Richard D. Clark Jr. and Bin Huang, Fisheries Report No. 1909 (Lansing: Michigan DNR, 17 March 1983).

On snagging, see Norm Spring, [Letter from Michigan Steelheaders President], *The Fish Line* 1, no. 1 (6 May 1967); Jerry Chiappetta, "Great Lakes Salmon," *Field and Stream* 72 (March 1968): 94; "Letters to the Press: This is a Crime?" 30 January 1970, GPHS scrapbook; Ben East, "Battle Over Salmon Snagging," *Outdoor Life* 155 (January 1975): 50–51.

31. Fred Vanden Brand, "Indian Fishermen Net Another Big Catch Here," *Grand Haven Tribune*, 7 July 1971 [from clipping file at the Tri-Cities Museum, hereafter TCM]; Rick Haglund, "Sportsmen Declare War on Netters," *Traverse City Record Eagle*, 20 April 1979; Rick Haglund, "New Threats Anger U.P. Indians," *Traverse City Record Eagle*, 21 April 1979; "No Room Here for Racist Tactics," *Traverse City Record Eagle*, 21 April 1979; "Organization Formed to Stop Gill Netting in Area" *Charlevoix Courier*, 25 April 1979; Doreen Fitzgerald, "SGN—Both Good and Bad," *Antrim County News*, 26 April 1979; Doreen Fitzgerald, "Anti Gill Net Group Formed," *Antrim County News*, 26 April 1979; Doreen Fitzgerald, "SGN—Prosecutors Meet with DNR," *Antrim County News*, 3 May 1979; "Gill Netting Foes Deny Condoning Any Violence," *Petoskey News Review*, 8 May 1979; "Our Gill Net Position, " *Traverse City Record Eagle*, 9 May 1979; Paula Holmes, "Charters Protest One Trout Limit," *Petoskey News Review*, September 1980; "Rally Against Gill Net Fishing Is Slated," *Muskegon Chronicle*, 25 April 1982; John Broder, "Vigilantes Greet Gill Net Fishers," *Detroit News*, 24 June 1982; Letter from Joseph Lumsden, Arthur Duhamel, and Wade Teeple to Michigan Governor William Milliken, 22 September 1982 [original in the possession of Chippewa, Ottawa Tribal fisheries Management Authority, Sault Ste. Marie, Mich.]; "Threat to Fishing," *Michigan Out of Doors* (April 1984): 1; "State Asks U.S. Court to Halt Indian Fishing," *Lansing State Journal*, 29 April 1988; Nancy Kida, "Gill-Netting Limit Sought in Grand Traverse," *Detroit News*, 29 April 1988; "Fishing Controversy Myths," 23 March 1988, Typewritten Report, Mackley Public Library Vertical File, Muskegon, Mich.; Ric Zehner, "Instead of Fishing Rights, It's Discrimination by Feds," *Traverse City Record Eagle*, 7 September 1997; Benzie Fishery Coalition, "Menace of Gill Nets May Return to Lake Michigan," *Benzie County Record Patriot*, 19 November 1997; "Be Aware and Join Up," *Traverse City Record Eagle*, 15 December 1997; Brian Springstead, "Finally ... Our Day in Court," *Grand Traverse Area Fishing Assn. Newsletter* 1, no. 1 (1998); Diane Conners, "State Wants Ruling on Salmon Fishing," *Traverse City Record Eagle*, 2 February 1998; R. Lance Boldrey, "Sport Fishers Not Alone in Protecting Resource," *Kalamazoo Gazette*, 26 September 2000; Larry Sawicki, "As I See It ...," *The Sport Fisherman's Friend* (November 1997); Richard M. Zehner, "Congress Must Act on Gill Netting Issues," *The Sport Fisherman's Friend* (November 1997); Doherty, *Disputed Waters*, 81–85

32. George Stanley, "Fishermen Seek More Alewives in Lake Michigan," *Milwaukee Sentinel*, 18 December 1990.

33. On criticism of the tribal fishing rights and the 1985 Consent Agreement, see Kuchenberg, 102–3, 202–7; "Discontent Is Being Shared Among Traverse Bay Sports Fishermen," *The Sport Fisherman's Friend* (November 1997); Larry Sawicki, "As I See It ...," *The Sport Fisherman's Friend* (November 1997); Howard Tanner, *Indian Fishing Rights and State of Michigan Responsibilities* (Lansing: Michigan Department of Natural Resources, September 1979); [Letter to the Editor], "Disagrees on Indian Gill Nets," *Petoskey New Review*,

[n.d]; Tom Nugent, "Angry Sportsmen See Indian Abuse of Fishing Rights," *Detroit Free Press*, 28 June 1971; Grand Traverse Area Sportsfishing Association, "The Treaty of 1836 and the Fishing Case" [n.l.] 17 February 1976, CRSS; Jim Doherty, "Anglers Protest Gill Nets in the Bay Here," *Petoskey News Review*, 23 May 1977; Ellen Grzech, "Indian Nets Rile Rod Fishermen," *Detroit Free Press*, 19 June 1977; Dave Guzniczak, "Fence Across Roadway Stops Indian Gill Netters," *Petoskey News Review*, 27 July 1978; Thora Layman, "Petition to Ban Indian Gill Netters," *Benzie County Record Patriot*, 30 August 1978; "MUCC Presses for Petitions to Curb Indian Trout Kill," *North Woods Call*, 20 September 1978; "Candidate Brown Sees Indian Gill Nets a Threat to Fish," *Petoskey News Review*, October 1978; Doreen Fitzgerald, "Indian Gill Netting Resumes," *Traverse City Record Eagle*, 12 April 1979, CRSS; Rick Haglund, "Indians May Fish When May 15 Ban Expires," *Traverse City Record Eagle*, 19 April 1979; Rick Haglund, "Sportsmen Declare War on Netters," *Traverse City Record Eagle*, 20 April 1979; Rick Haglund, "New Threats Anger U.P. Indians," *Traverse City Record Eagle*, 21 April 1979; "District Judge Comments on Editorial Opposing Violence," *Petoskey News Review*, 27 April 1979; Jeff Blake, "Dismayed Gill Net Foes Warn Will See Depletion of Fish," *Petoskey News Review*, 8 May 1979; Jim Doherty, "Judge Fox's Decision Is Law of the Land," *Petoskey News Review*, 9 May 1979; "MUCC Terms Fox Decision 'Outrageous,' 'Prejudiced,'" *Traverse City Record Eagle*, 9 May 1979; Marcella S. Kreiter, "Fox Warns Against Fishing Violence," *Petoskey News Review*, 9 May 1979; Eric Sharp, "Indians Win Court Fight on Fishing Rights," *Detroit Free Press*, 9 May 1979; "Carte Blanche for Indians?" *Traverse City Record Eagle*, 9 May 1979; "Milliken: Appeal Fish Ruling," *Traverse City Record Eagle*, 10 May 1979; Nancy Zeno, "Bay Sport Fishing Endangered," *Antrim County News*, 2 August 1979; "MUCC to Sue Feds, State if PBC Not Enforced on the Gill Netters," *Petoskey News Review*, 8 August 1979; Rick Haglund, "Fish Stock Dwindling, Sport Fishermen Say," *Traverse City Record Eagle*, 17 August 1979; Tom Opre; "Sport Fisherman Demands Sporting Chance to Compete," *Petoskey News Review*, 11 September 1979; "Equal Rights, Not Super Ones," *Traverse City Record Eagle*, 15 September 1979; Gordon Charles, "TC Boat-In Lansing Rally to Show Great Lakes Threats," *Traverse City Record Eagle*, 15 September 1979; "Anglers to Appeal Fox Ruling," *Petoskey News Review*, 18 September 1979; Marsha Robinson, "No Sign of Inland Fishing," *Petoskey News Review*, 18 September 1979; Eric Sharp, "Anglers Urge State to Buy Indians Out," *Detroit Free Press*, 21 September 1979; Rick Haglund, "U.S. Court Order Halts Gill Netting," *Traverse City Record Eagle*, 22 September 1979; "Plan Suggests Millions to Buy Indian Fishing Rights," *Detroit Free Press*, 23 September 1979; "Steelheaders to Battle Feds on Proposed Gill Net Rules," *Petoskey News Review*, 7 November 1979; "Statement of Thomas L. Washington on Behalf of the MUCC" [Presented before the House Subcommittee on Fisheries and Wildlife Conservation, 6 June 1980, Traverse City, Mich.], Michigan DNR File, Michigan State Archives, box 8, Lansing, Mich.; "Rally Against Gill Net Fishing Is Slated," *Muskegon Chronicle*, 25 April 1982; John Block, "Fishermen Losing Patience in Wake of Judge's Ruling on Gill Netting," *Kalamazoo Gazette*, 12 July 1992; Ken Merckel, "Who's Protecting the Fish Resource," *Great Lakes Steelheader*, February 1994; Andy Pelt, "Gill-Net Menace Threatens Return," *Great Lakes Steelheader*, February 1994; "Press Release from the Grand Traverse Area Sport Fishing Association on Native American Fishing Regulations," 24 April 1995; John Block, "More Gill-Net Fishing Controversy Surfaces," *Kalamazoo Gazette*, 8 February 1997; "Judge Oks Indian Commercial Fishing in Grand Traverse Bay," *Weekly News: Fishery News of the Great Lakes Basin*, 8 September 1997; John Block, "Truce on Indian Fishing in Jeopardy," *Kalamazoo Gazette*, 4 October 1997; Benzie Fishery Coalition, "Menace of Gill Nets May Return to Lake Michigan," *Benzie County Record Patriot*, 19 November 1997; "A Boating Hazard Is Being Created in Grand Traverse Bay and Lake Michigan," *The Sport Fisherman's Friend* (November 1997); "Be Aware and Join Up," *Traverse City Record Eagle*, 15 December 1997; Brian Springstead, "Finally . . . Our Day in Court," *Grand Traverse Area Fishing Assn. Newsletter* 1, no. 1 (1998); Kevin Clark, "Letter From the Editor, Making Heads or Tails Out of It All," *Grand Traverse Fishing Association Newsletter* 1, no. 1 (1998): 2; Steve Kellman and Diane Conners, "Grand Traverse Band Loses Bid to Expand Fishing," *Traverse Bay Record Eagle*, 5 February 1998; Diane Conners, "Attorney: Tribe May Boycott Fish Talks," *Traverse City Record Eagle*,

6 February 1998; Don Ingle, "Banquet Centered on Tribal Fishing," *Traverse City Record Eagle*, 18 April 1999; Diane Conners, "Cool Outlines Indian Fishing Issues," *Traverse City Record Eagle*, 28 April 1998; Cari Noga, "Rumblings in Air Over Tribal Fishing Rights," *Traverse City Record Eagle*, 22 June 1999; R. Lance Boldrey, "Sport Fishers Not Alone in Protecting Resource," *Kalamazoo Gazette*, 26 September 2000; Lawrence J. Thornhill, "An Invasion of Gill Nets Could be Awaiting the Great Lakes," *The Sport Fisherman's Friend* (November 1997); Larry Sawicki, "Some Blame Should Fall on Our Governor's Office," *The Sport Fisherman's Friend* (November 1997); Doherty, *Disputed Waters*, 72–85, 105–23.

On changing attitude of local press on sportsman/tribal conflict, see Doherty, *Disputed Waters*, 75–85.

34. Eric Sharp, "Chinook Bounce Back on Lake Michigan," *Detroit Free Press*, 8 August 1992.

35. Cal Johnson, "Wisconsin: Camp Sport Tour Series," *Forest and Stream* 96, no. 5 (1926): 270–72, 305.

36. Howard Meyerson, "BKD Widespread in Salmon," *Grand Rapids Press*, [n.d.] 1990, CRSS.

37. On steelhead fishing, see John O. Carter, "Fall Steelheads Are Back," *Outdoor Life* 140, (October 1967): 58–59, 148–52; Dick Swan, "Science Is Killing Us," *Great Lakes Sporting News*, June 1999, CRSS.

38. On Gordon Zuverink and the Michigan Steelheaders, see Gordon Zuverink, "Zuverink Addressess the NRC," *Great Lakes Steelheader*, March 1981; "Zuverink Farewell," *Great Lakes Steelheader*, 30 December 1982.

39. On Grand Traverse Area Sport Fishing Association, see "Press Release from the Grand Traverse Area Sport Fishing Association on Native American Fishing Regulations," 24 April 1995.

40. Rick Haglund, "Indians Make Big Whitefish Catches," *Traverse City Record-Eagle*, 19 July 1979.

41. See Fred Vanden Brand, "Indian Fishermen Net Another Big Catch Here," *Grand Haven Tribune*, 7 July 1971; Bob Clock and Fran Martin, "Enforce Park Law, Norwood Asks State Police," *Petoskey News Review*, 22 August 1978; Mike Van Buren, "Gill Netters Invade County," *Antrim County News*, 21 September 1978; Nancy Zeno, "Gill Netters Converge on Antrim County Shores," *Antrim County News*, 26 September 1979.

42. Ben East, "Bass from Carp," *Forest and Stream* 99, no. 11 (1929): 800–1, 860.

— 4 —

Government Mediation
of Fishing Claims

Regulation, Research, and the Public Trust

THE FOLLOWING TESTIMONIES, gathered from men and women who are past and present fisheries scientists, managers, and educators with state and federally funded agencies, reveal the importance of historical perspective in the development and implementation of current fisheries policy. These oral histories show that various specialists in public-sector fisheries management are sensitive to the ways in which past policy decisions affect the options they might exercise. Charged with overseeing the resource to achieve the greatest public benefit, their testimonies reveal that their application of this mandate—the public trust doctrine—is inseparable from the historical patterns, shifting and divergent perceptions, and conflicts that have engulfed each of their respective agencies. In an attempt to further their ability to make informed fisheries management policy decisions, some acquired a detailed knowledge of the history of their agencies. They supplemented this information with careful insight into the personalities and agendas of their predecessors, and balanced it with an understanding of the political contexts that influenced the work of their predecessors. In short, each of these oral history informants displayed acute awareness of the institutional cultures that preceded them, along with that which they cultivated during their tenure with state and federal agencies. The insights of these professionally trained fisheries managers show them to be among the most historically oriented of all natural resource custodians who represent the public interest.

The multitude of governmental bodies and commissions that are historically involved in Great Lakes fisheries management often make it difficult to interpret how political considerations combine with economic and social factors to influence specific decisions regarding Lake Michigan. Lake Michigan is wholly within the geographical boundaries of the United States, while the other Great Lakes are not, thus putting its fisheries issues in a unique position relative to the concerns of the U.S. federal government, the territorial jurisdiction of four U.S. states, the Canadian national government, and the provincial government of Ontario. Federal interest in Great Lakes fisheries was evident in the earliest activities of the U.S. Fish Commission and its successor agencies, the U.S. Bureau of Fisheries of the Department of Commerce and the U.S. Fish and Wildlife Service (USFWS) under the Department of the Interior. All these agencies conducted studies on commercial fish species and problems faced by commercial fishermen. Even when the Great Lakes research of these agencies did not focus expressly on Lake Michigan, their results were still germane to constituencies that used the basin's fish and resources.[1] From the late-nineteenth century to the twenty-first century, the U.S. Army Corps of Engineers and the Coast Guard regularly undertook improvements to harbors, lighthouses, and other maritime facilities which benefited the exercise of the commercial fishery. By the middle of the twentieth century, the activities of these federal agencies would be of paramount importance to the safe implementation of Lake Michigan's modern sport fishery.[2]

Responsible for the bottomlands within their borders, the state legislatures in the Great Lakes region created fisheries boards or commissions during the late-nineteenth century.[3] Dividing their time between inland lakes, rivers and streams, and the Great Lakes waters within their boundaries, state fish commissions licensed commercial fishermen, kept catch statistics, and operated fish propagation facilities. During the early 1920s these state fish commissions gave way to larger and more sophisticated natural resources agencies. For example, in 1921, Michigan replaced the Fish Commission with the Department of Conservation and gave it the power to enforce laws enacted to halt the decline of lake trout, whitefish, and other commercial species. The Michigan Department of Conservation implemented these

Dr. John Van Oosten (1891–1966) was foremost among Great Lakes fisheries scientists. Van Oosten, who received his Ph.D in zoology from the University of Michigan in 1926, spent his entire career studying Great Lakes fisheries. An employee of the U.S. Bureau of Fisheries, later the Bureau of Commercial Fisheries of the U.S. Fish and Wildlife Service, Van Oosten worked out of a laboratory located on the University of Michigan's Ann Arbor campus in the Natural History Museum. Courtesy of the Great Lakes Science Center, U.S. Geological Survey.

measures by instituting licenses for commercial fishermen, creating size limits,[4] establishing closed seasons,[5] and regulating gear—principally nets.[6]

In addition to their regulatory activities, the Michigan Department of Conservation and the Wisconsin Department of Conservation (created in 1927) undertook research on Great Lakes commercial fisheries.[7] By the 1880s, faculty members at the University of Michigan occasionally undertook scientific research projects on Great Lakes fisheries on behalf of the Michigan Fish Commission. This collaborative effort was formalized in 1929 when the university constructed a facility on campus named the Institute for Fisheries Research. The institute's first professional position was funded by the Michigan Department of Conservation and was held by Dr. Jan Metzelaar.[8] Perhaps the best known of the Great Lakes fisheries scientists who worked out of the institute's laboratory and offices was Dr. John Van

A trap-net device was set up on land by Van Oosten as part of his research on how entrapment devices affected fishery stocks. His opposition to trap nets, in part, resulted in the banning of deep nets in Lakes Michigan and Superior in the 1930s. Courtesy of the Great Lakes Science Center, U.S. Geological Survey.

Oosten. Awarded a Ph.D. from the University of Michigan in 1926, Van Oosten was one of the first modern fisheries managers to benefit from collaborative research activities taking place between the University of Michigan, the Michigan Department of Conservation, the Michigan Department of Health, and the U.S. Bureau of Fisheries. The training Van Oosten received in this collaborative context set the stage for his appointment as director of the U.S. Bureau of Fisheries Great Lakes Fishery Investigations in 1927—a research initiative that would later be placed under the U.S. Fish and Wildlife Service (USFWS).[9]

From the late 1920s through 1950, no federal or state fisheries researcher was as widely associated with the Great Lakes as Van Oosten. While much of Van Oosten's research activity can be attributed to his education, training, and employment, it also stemmed from the energy he expended with every fisheries constituency in the Great Lakes basin. He was equally at home in the fishing sheds of Great Lakes commercial fishers and at their professional gatherings as he was at conferences

The *Fulmar* was used by the U.S. Bureau of Fisheries to study the selectivity of chub gill nets in Lake Michigan in the early 1930s. Courtesy of Robert and Fern Ver Duin.

held by the American Fisheries Society (AFS). He placed Great Lakes fisheries issues at the center of national and international consideration through his participation in drafting the American Fisheries Society's North American Fish Policy in 1938 and by serving as president of AFS from 1941 to 1946. The fisheries scientists and managers interviewed for this project acknowledge that Van Oosten's lack of training in broader ecological approaches to fisheries management left him ill-equipped to deal with the catastrophic effects of sea lamprey predation. But they do not underplay the role he charted for government involvement in Great Lakes fisheries. During the course of collecting these oral histories, it was not uncommon for both commercial fishers and fisheries scientists to recall Van Oosten's activities on Lake Michigan, particularly his use of the U.S. Bureau of Fisheries research vessel *Fulmar* in his studies on the effects of gill nets and trap nets.

From the last quarter of the nineteenth century until World War II, the fisheries programs in the states surrounding Lake Michigan focused their efforts on stocking, population studies, and pollution research. But they gave little attention to the more holistic environmental context that caused the decline of most fishery stocks. Responding to the late-nineteenth-century political influence of commercial fishing interests, both Michigan and Wisconsin appropriated funds for hatcheries that raised whitefish and, later, lake trout. The first railroad car the Michigan Fish Commission customized to transport hatchery personnel and cans of fish fry was named the "Attikumaig," the Ojibway word for whitefish, or the "deer in the water."[10] The states bordering Lake Michigan stocked millions of whitefish and lake trout fry during the late-nineteenth and early-twentieth centuries before they cut back on the former in favor of game fish favored by anglers on inland waters.[11] Since the 1940s, the USFWS has provided funding for hatcheries in Michigan and the Great Lakes region to assist the states in stocking lake trout.[12]

The dwindling stock of virtually all important Great Lakes fish prompted efforts to bring Canadian, U.S., and state fisheries officials together to create uniform or compatible fisheries laws and policies. As historian Margaret Beattie Bogue has recently shown, numerous agreements and treaties were proposed and negotiated and commissions and conferences were organized. The International Board of Inquiry for the Great Lakes Fisheries, established in 1940, recommended joint control of Great Lakes fisheries under the terms of a treaty, but action was delayed until 1946. In the absence of an agency or body charged with the task of coordinating U.S., Canadian, and state agreements regarding the fisheries, these initiatives accomplished little until after World War II.[13]

The management of Great Lakes fisheries suffered not only as a result of the lack of uniform laws and regulations between the U.S. and Canada, but also because of the absence of coordination between federal and state officials. The division of responsibility between federal and state officials in Michigan waters was reportedly based on an informal agreement between John Van Oosten of the USFWS and Fred Westerman, a former hatchery worker who served as head of the Fish Division of the Michigan Department of Conservation from 1925 to 1959. Van Oosten focused federal resources on research problems relating to Michigan's Great Lakes commercial fisheries. Westerman directed the bulk of the appropriations made to the Department of Conservation to the management of the inland lakes, rivers, and streams popular with anglers.[14]

Patrol Boat No. 1 and crew, December 1929. *Patrol Boat No. 1* was used by the Michigan Department of Conservation to patrol commercial fishermen working in the state waters from 1929 to 1959. Upon the retirement of Captain Charles Allers, *Patrol Boat No. 1* was replaced by a series of smaller patrol vessels. Courtesy of the Allers-Nicolen Families.

Regardless of whether Van Oosten and Westerman actually had such an agreement, as the testimony below will show, it was widely believed that they did. Perhaps as a result of this agreement, fisheries officials have tended to downplay the initiatives undertaken by the Michigan Department of Conservation to consolidate control over Great Lakes fisheries beginning in the 1920s. The Michigan Department of Conservation's efforts to establish authority over its Great Lakes fisheries took a major step forward when it began to construct its own "conservation navy" and placed law enforcement officials on board vessels. Commercial fishermen understood the level of the Michigan Department of Conservation's commitment to managing the commercial stocks in its Great Lakes boundary waters when, in 1928, it hired Great Lakes mariner Charles Allers of Beaver Island to design and serve as captain of *Patrol Boat No. 1*. Allers, who retired in 1959, served as the one and only captain of *Patrol Boat No. 1*.[15]

Captain Charles Allers of the Michigan Department of Conservation's *Patrol Boat No. 1* measures the mesh size of a gill net. Allers, who was known to commercial fishermen throughout the Great Lakes region, was raised on Beaver Island in Lake Michigan. He would eventually recruit several of *Patrol Boat No. 1*'s crew from Beaver Island. Courtesy of the Allers-Nicolen Families.

In 1949, in response to the increasing numbers of the fishermen who were switching to trap nets, the Michigan Department of Conservation placed two, forty-two-foot steel patrol boats into service to monitor both gill-net and trap-net fishing.[16] During the 1930s and 1940s, commercial fishing operations were also surveyed from the air.[17] Lake Michigan fishermen licensed to fish in Wisconsin waters were also subject to surveillance. In 1941 the Wisconsin Department of Conservation obtained the fish tug *Barney Devine* and refitted her to monitor commercial fishermen.[18]

In the years prior to World War II, Commercial fishers frequently challenged the management practices of the U.S. Bureau of Fisheries, the U.S. Fish and Wildlife Service, state fish commissions and state conservation departments. Commercial fishermen attracted the attention of U.S. congressmen, state legislators, governors, and other elected and appointed officials by organizing the Wisconsin Commercial Fishermen's Association, the Michigan Fish Producers Association, and numerous other groups. By contrast, federal initiatives and state fisheries laws and regulations

The *Barney Devine* was a fish tug used by the Wisconsin Department of Conservation during the 1930s and 1940s to patrol state-licensed commercial fishermen. Named for the state's Chief Conservation warden from 1934 to 1940, the *Barney Devine* is now used by the Wisconsin DNR as an educational and research vessel. Courtesy of the Wisconsin Conservation Law Enforcement Museum.

that affected fishing on the big lakes were seldom of concern to sport fishermen and their groups who prior to the late 1960s focused their attention on inland waters.

After World War II, the debate over Lake Michigan's fisheries became more acute as four constituencies or interest groups (in current policy terms, stakeholders) made highly vocal and strident claims to the fisheries resources of this ecologically sensitive freshwater basin.[19] Prior to this time, the debate was more singular: the attempt to conserve the valuable lake trout, whitefish, and lake herring stocks that endowed the Great Lakes region with the largest freshwater commercial fishery in the world. But in the postwar era—one in which modernism's broadly shared assumptions gradually gave way to postmodern society's splintered sentiment— decidedly more fragmented feelings emerged over the utilization and allocation of Lake Michigan's fish. State governments—principally Michigan and Wisconsin— continued their pre–Great Depression and World War II efforts to reclaim the managerial authority many believed had been informally relinquished to the federal

Shortly after it began stocking the Great Lakes with salmon, the State of Michigan launched its new fisheries research vessel, *Steelhead*, in 1968. Based at the Great Lakes Fishery Research Station in Charlevoix, the *Steelhead* is still in use. The name of the ship was indicative of the state's new fisheries policies and its emphasis on researching and promoting sport fishing species. Courtesy of the Michigan DNR, Great Lakes Fishery Research Station.

government, and to use it to aggressively advance sport fisheries.[20] Sport-fishing constituencies, buttressed by American society's increasing affluence and interest in outdoor recreation and emboldened by state government support, saw new opportunities on Lake Michigan. They readily lent their influential cultural, economic, and political standing to the creation of sport fisheries deemed by state natural resource officials as more commercially bountiful and ecologically sustainable. Native Americans, reacting to the momentum of the American civil rights movement, began to reclaim treaty fishing rights in an act of cultural, economic, and political revitalization. Commercial fishers, crippled by years of ineffectual policy, overfishing, sea lamprey predation, and the growing power of sport-fishing interests, sought to adapt to the myriad problems that beset their occupation.

Since the mid-twentieth century, tensions among these groups vacillated greatly; the appearance of reconciliation or agreement was sometimes nothing more than an expedient guise for uneasy toleration. This era of fisheries management on Lake Michigan is more readily recognized as one punctuated by a series of flash points of regional, national, and international consequence that started in the late 1940s and continues to the present.

The first event that helped to solidify the power of the Michigan Department of Conservation over its Great Lakes fisheries occurred in the immediate postwar years. After allowing record harvests of lake trout for the war effort, the Michigan Department of Conservation now faced the possibility of the virtual elimination of these stocks due to sea lamprey predation. Other commercial species, such as whitefish and walleye, were also dangerously reduced in number by the sea lamprey. When describing the sea lamprey crisis the Michigan Department of Conservation observed, "perhaps the only redeeming aspect is that it focused public attention on the importance of Great Lakes fisheries."[21]

Although efforts to more effectively foster national, binational, and interstate oversight of Great Lakes fisheries can be traced to the closing years of the nineteenth century, these initiatives had not matured into any type of viable comanagement plan by the mid-twentieth century. But in the early 1950s, the sea lamprey crisis revived interest in these issues and prompted state, provincial, and national authorities from the United States and Canada to assemble a wide range of fisheries representatives to discuss international comanagement of the Great Lakes. These talks, which included elected officials, government-employed fisheries managers, and delegates from nongovernmental fisheries interest groups, ultimately led to the creation of the Great Lakes Fishery Commission.[22] Founded in 1955 through the ratification of the Convention on Great Lakes Fisheries, the Great Lakes Fishery Commission did not, in the end, become an international comanagement body for Great Lakes fisheries to which Michigan, Wisconsin, and the other Great Lakes states ceded or delegated power. Instead, as former Executive Secretary Carlos Fetterolf recounts, it adopted a far more narrowly defined mission—to stem sea lamprey propagation and restore lake trout stocks.[23]

Despite the efforts of scientists employed by the Great Lakes Fishery Commission, the USFWS, and state departments of conservation, by the late 1950s and early 1960s, the nonindigenous sea lamprey's biological invasion was so systemic that it precipitated widespread ecological disequilibrium—enough to gradually allow

The political and economic importance of sea lamprey control was underscored by the presence of Wisconsin Governor Gaylord Nelson at an educational program in Oconto, Wisconsin. The U.S. Fish and Wildlife Service organized an educational campaign to inform the public about sea lamprey control methods in the Great Lakes. Courtesy of Ludington Biological Station, U.S. Fish and Wildlife Service.

alewife, another nonindigenous species, to dominate the biomass of Lake Michigan. The sea lamprey problem subsided in the early 1960s through the application of lampricide (TFM—3-trifluoromethyl-4-nitrophenol) and other devices such as weirs and electric barriers developed by the Great Lakes Fishery Commission or the USFWS. The ecological devastation brought by the sea lamprey did not, however, disappear overnight.

Faced with growing stocks of alewife and other so-called rough fish in Lake Michigan, state fisheries officials began examining various ways of reducing them through the creation of a trawl fishery.[24] Although the trawling initiative required substantial technological adaptation, some fisheries managers saw it as a viable means to simultaneously reduce Lake Michigan's overabundant alewife stocks and provide commercial fishers with a high-volume fishery directed toward the animal feed market. The State of Wisconsin embraced this management strategy, but it was a short-lived option in the State of Michigan. Michigan chose to pursue far more revisionist policies that would broaden the economic matrix of Lake Michigan fisheries. To this end, in a plan that ultimately eclipsed the region, Michigan began redefining the very premise of Lake Michigan fisheries management: dramatically channel the passions of the sport-fishing community into unprecedented use-patterns of the lake and its fish.

Both states, longtime havens of American sporting life, were swept by intense postwar interest in outdoor recreation as a means of economic development; in the 1960s, it became a regional movement whose influence was so far-reaching that, in the words of environmental historian Thomas Huffman, it "provided the initial impetus for the evolution of modern environmental politics."[25] Ably positioned for such a role, Michigan and Wisconsin were already benefiting from the 1950 Dingell-Johnson Federal Aid in Fish Restoration Act—a tax on a host of recreational fishing supplies that provided states with funds to improve their sport fisheries.

Working from these precedents, particularly the financial alignments of the Dingell-Johnson Act, Michigan and Wisconsin politicians (most notably, Wisconsin governor Gaylord Nelson, the founder of Earth Day) anticipated the emergence of a postindustrial economy in which their states' natural resources

The State of Michigan has promoted fishing as a mean of increasing tourism for over half a century. This late 1940s fishing guide shows how little emphasis was placed on fishing Great Lakes waters compared to inland lakes and streams. Courtesy of Michael J. Chiarappa.

would be increasingly consumed by outdoor recreation's broadly integrated markets.[26] While these developments drove some of the political motivations behind environmental quality, they also necessitated bureaucratic changes that could respond to these new priorities. Not surprising, in order to accommodate these trends, Michigan and Wisconsin spent considerable time in the 1960s reshaping the institutional structures that implemented their natural resource management and policy. This difficult process was emblematic of a reconfiguration seeking to satisfactorily allocate natural resources with three principal concerns in mind: (1) make the conservation and availability of natural resources more readily suited to outdoor recreation's diverse marketplace demands; (2) insure the state's ability to pursue its prerogatives in its territorial waters; and (3) be cognizant of the need to comply with a growing list of federal requirements to promote environmental protection. It was a scenario that put Lake Michigan at the center of America's nascent environmental movement and, closer to home, put its fisheries at the center of an acrimonious regional debate.

Political rhetoric and cultural changes elicited new expectations for the use of Lake Michigan's fisheries resources; as the mid-1960s approached, however, the region lacked a fisheries management plan to match this sentiment. But this quickly changed. In 1964 Ralph MacMullan, the director of the Michigan Department of Conservation, hired Howard Tanner as chief of the Fisheries Division.[27] With the commercial fishing industry weakened and the public clamoring for more sportfishing opportunities, MacMullan encouraged Tanner to move boldly. The Michigan Department of Conservation began exploring the introduction of nonindigenous species such as Pacific salmon and striped bass that would hopefully support a vibrant sport fishery. Since 1921, however, the Department of Conservation had held to the belief that its indigenous commercial and sport species could be self-sustaining only by prohibiting nonindigenous introductions. This era was about to come to an end. In an ironic twist of fate, with Lake Michigan's ecology so heavily altered by biological invasions, the State of Michigan's fisheries managers were to begin its economic resuscitation through the planned introduction of nonindigenous species.[28]

Tanner worked for Colorado State University's fisheries program prior to his arrival at the Michigan Department of Conservation and his management philosophy stridently advocated sport fishing's economic and cultural benefits. A Michigan native who, as a boy, worked as a fishing guide in the bucolic surroundings of Michigan's Antrim County, he was personally familiar with Lake Michigan's under-use as a sport-fishing venue. Earlier attempts had been made to promote "deep-sea fishing" on Lake Michigan, but the initiative languished. The principal quarry of such recreational fishing effort was lake trout, a fish not generally admired for its sporting qualities and which swam at less accessible depths when most anglers pursued it in warm-weather months.

Trolling for lake trout grew in popularity in the late 1940s and the early 1950s, but enthusiasm dissipated as stocks plummeted from sea lamprey predation. These circumstances, along with few incentives to develop regionally effective tackle, impeded a serious open-water sport fishery for this or other Lake Michigan species. Compounding the situation, Lake Michigan's sport-fishing community did not have as much experience with, or accessibility to, the types of "deep-sea" boats and marina facilities used on America's east and west coasts.

Tanner had time to think about this problem while in Colorado. During his time in the West, he familiarized himself with the biology and cultivation of Pacific salmon through fish management contacts in Pacific Northwest states.[29] Just before the arrival of the Michigan State University graduate, Michigan's Department of Conservation was conducting its own investigation into the feasibility of planting Pacific salmon in Lake Michigan. It is not surprising that Tanner returned to Michigan with an idea, pursued at MacMullan's enthusiastic urging, that redefined Lake Michigan fisheries: create a Pacific salmon sport fishery in Lake Michigan by planting these non-native species in the lake's numerous tributaries. Tanner envisioned numerous benefits from the introduction of this species. At long last, Lake Michigan would not only have fish with popular sporting qualities, but they could be pursued in the spring and summer in open-water, "deep-sea fashion," and in the tributaries during fall spawning runs. Furthermore, using alewife as their forage base, Pacific salmon would control the latter's biotic dominance, as well as lessen the environmental nuisance and economic impact caused by their massive die-off along Lake Michigan's shores.[30]

Coho salmon were planted in Lake Michigan streams in the spring of 1966 and by the fall of 1967, the region's anglers were in a frenzy over this new sport fishery. With the planting of chinook salmon in 1967, interest only grew. Leading sports

Governor George Romney emptied a gold-plated bucket of kokanee salmon into Wilkins Creek, a tributary of Torch Lake in Antrium County in March 1965. Despite the great fanfare, it was coho salmon, not the kokanee, that brought Dr. Howard Tanner (standing, far left), Chief of the Fisheries Division of the Michigan Department of Conservation, widespread recognition from fisheries scientists and sportsmen. Courtesy of Howard Tanner and the Michigan DNR.

magazines and television shows assured skeptical anglers that some of the country's hottest salmon fishing was a short ride from Chicago and Milwaukee. By 1970, the initial economic benefit of Lake Michigan's new sport fishery numerically verified the immeasurable cultural excitement that was being generated throughout the region.[31]

The State of Michigan's fisheries scientists reveled in what they considered to be nothing less than a six-year management revolution. During this time, they largely obtained direct authority to dictate commercial and sport-fishing regulations and, of greater relevance, obtained the power to unabashedly privy sport-fishing interests over commercial fishing. Michigan's Department of Conservation gave precedence to sport fishing at the outset of this six-year transformation when it called for a new "fishing frontier" on the Great Lakes. As they gained greater control over Lake Michigan from federal officials who they believed were biased toward commercial fishing, the department's fisheries managers saw the success of the salmon sport fishery as legitimizing their vision. They linked their sport-fishing crusade to the State of Michigan's obligation to responsibly manage 41 percent of the Great Lakes surface area (38,575 square miles), and public enthusiasm added only greater sanction to the Fish Division's newly acquired power. To foster their program's growth, the Michigan Department of Conservation, which in 1968 became the Department of Natural Resources, encouraged fishing tackle and boating industries to prepare prescriptive literature on how to use their products in Lake Michigan's new sport fishery.[32] Like an evangelist traveling from town to town, Dr. Tanner logged thousands of miles as he went around the Great Lakes speaking to chamber of commerce and other business and tourism groups about raising salmon, and attracting salmon fishermen.[33] Tanner, along with his successor, Wayne Tody, did not limit the program's media exposure to government publications, but worked with national outdoor recreation and sport-fishing magazines to advance their cause. They in turn received national recognition for their work in creating the Great Lakes salmon fishery.

Seeking to maintain local political support, state conservation officials worked closely with the well-established Michigan United Conservation Clubs. They even went so far as to encourage the formation of an advocacy group—Michigan Steelheaders—to expressly promote Lake Michigan sport fishing's anadromous species. Michigan's successful experiment prompted Wisconsin's Department of Natural Resources to announce in 1968 that it, too, planned to give priority to sport fishing in its Lake Michigan waters. As Wisconsin proceeded with its first planting of coho salmon in its Lake Michigan tributaries, the stage seemed set for unparalleled consent among these neighboring states. What happened instead is that the similarities of the two states' policies only accentuated their differences in handling their commercial fishing constituencies. Rather than setting a stage for unanimity, the stage was being set to make Lake Michigan's fisheries management the most politicized of the Great Lakes region.

By the time the Michigan Department of Conservation began stocking coho salmon in Lake Michigan streams and tributaries in 1966–67, the U.S. Fish and Wildlife Service had already been working for more than two decades to eradicate the sea lamprey and restore the lake trout as the top predator species. The decision by the Conservation Department to introduce another exotic species into one of the world's largest bodies of fresh water not only changed its relationship with federal fisheries officials, it also placed the agency on a collision course with two other groups. The first group that challenged the agency's decision to turn Lake Michigan into a sport-fishing paradise was commercial fishermen. Reduced in number, saddled by debt or rising costs, and blamed for the decline of Great Lakes fisheries, the appeals made by commercial fishermen for the preservation of their livelihood were all but brushed aside by a state eager to see the potential economic returns offered by a successful sport fishery.

Ironically, the most formidable challenge to Michigan's plan to turn the lake over to sports fishermen proved to be from those who, at the time, were among the least politically empowered of all state residents—Native Americans belonging to the Bay Mills Indian Community, the Grand Traverse Band of Ottawa and Chippewa, and other tribes. As Howard Tanner, the father of Michigan's coho stocking program, conceded in his interview, the state's hard-line position on commercial fishing virtually forced the Indians to abandon fishing altogether or pursue their treaty fishing rights in federal court. Throughout the Upper Midwest, it is widely known that the introduction of salmon into the Great Lakes put the states of Michigan and Wisconsin in conflict with commercial fishermen and, in the case of the State of Michigan, at odds with Native Americans that claimed treaty fishing rights. By the 1980s and 1990s, however, salmon stocking also brought these states into dispute with the very interests they helped to empower—sport-fishing advocates. State and federal fisheries officials have taken positions or adopted policies on highly charged issues such as tribal fishing grounds and methods, proposed reductions in salmon stocking, regulations on commercial fishing gear, and contaminants that are opposed by sport-fishing interests.[34]

All of the fisheries managers and scientists who were interviewed for this project would vigorously agree that they are government personnel charged with upholding the public trust doctrine's goal of managing fisheries resources with the widest possible benefit in mind. When fisheries officials describe their experience in implementing various management plans for Lake Michigan's fisheries over the past half century, however, their exercise of this authority is far more political and far less inclusive than their mediating role would suggest.[35] When Michigan and Wisconsin made sport fishing a management priority in the 1960s, there were no absolute calls to eliminate commercial fishing and the appearance remained that it would receive due consideration in policy formulation. Rather than implement an outright ban, the State of Michigan made commercial fishing options so conditional that the occupation's ranks diminished significantly. Oral history from the state's former fisheries officials shows how highly reticent they were to accept input from or share power with commercial fishing interests. Conversely, the same narratives reveal the extraordinary level of cooperation and power they extended to sportfishing advocacy groups, nationally prominent tackle companies, and the tourist industry. While Wisconsin commercial fishers were not always happy with policy outcomes, they were invited to participate in regulatory affairs and, in relative terms, received a more equitable hearing from fisheries managers. Wisconsin officials remark on their efforts to simply mitigate the fear that was engendered by the far less compromising position of their Michigan colleagues.

The theme of power sharing runs far deeper in these narratives. The square mile amount of open-water space within both Michigan and Wisconsin's borders surpasses that of many ocean coast states. Exhibiting states' rights mentality, fisheries officials from each state were determined to take control of their waters. Addressing issues that have hitherto received no overt attention in written documentation, the informants describe the influence of federal fisheries officials over these waters—power that had been informally relinquished by the states in the late-nineteenth century. The federal government, because of the efforts of the U.S. Fish Commission, the U.S. Bureau of Fisheries, or the U.S. Fish and Wildlife Service, had a long tradition of being oriented toward commercial fishing interests. As each state became more inclined to use Lake Michigan for recreational purposes, its fisheries officials saw this as an untenable power-sharing relationship. Former Michigan Fisheries chief Howard Tanner simply recalls, "We were going to take control of Lake Michigan."

Over the years, regional boosterism has tended to suppress some of the less vocal division within state government over the aggressive promotion of Lake Michigan sport fishing. Local and regional business interests and most elected officials touted the economic benefits of sport fishing. State and federal fisheries managers were ill-placed to question the policy or its implementation as the manufacturing sector of Michigan and the Great Lakes region diminished and these economies suffered as a result of the Rustbelt reputation. Today, some former fisheries managers claim that they personally regretted, even at the time of implementation, the uncompromising policies that deprived commercial fishers of their income and occupational tradition. Although some of this sentiment might be fueled by hindsight, it sheds important light on the subtle fractures that are often hidden within government fisheries bureaucracies. Since the 1960s, Lake Michigan states have celebrated their ecosystem approach to managing the basin's fisheries, yet those who saw this as a new lease for the restoration of native species were concerned about the use of one nonindigenous species—Pacific salmon—being used to control the effects of another—the alewife. When chinook salmon began extinguishing the alewife that sustained the sport fishery, these orally circulated concerns began entering official records and research.

Showing the human face of the public trust doctrine, oral history exposes the tenet's inability to fully embrace inclusivity in the policy-making process. Over the course of their careers, Lake Michigan's fisheries managers have verbally acknowledged that their work is a historically oriented scientific discipline, but they have been reluctant to fully consider the managerial value of commercial (Euroamerican) and Native American fishing's folk history. While presumably open to the observations of fishers, their oral histories rigidly define scientific practice and show why fishers' traditional ecological knowledge has not received greater recognition in the planning process. Ultimately, the remarks of Michigan's former fisheries managers revealed the state's reluctance to expand the spirit of the public trust doctrine when it refused to negotiate with Native Americans who reasserted the treaty fishing rights on Lake Michigan. Recounting these events, former Michigan fisheries chief and Department of Natural Resources director, Howard Tanner, would not waver from his notion of the public trust prerogative and blamed the situation on the unforeseen consequences of imposing income qualifications on participation in the

Salmon are removed from the Little Manistee River weir for propagation and research purposes by an unidentified Michigan DNR employee. In recent years, both Michigan and Wisconsin have reduced the number of salmon eggs planted in response to a reduction of the forage base. Courtesy of Ludington Biological Station, U.S. Fish and Wildlife Service.

commercial fishery. Hardly neutral, Tanner's oral history embodies the often unacknowledged bias of government management. [36]

Interestingly, while observers often concede that the claims of Lake Michigan's commercial, sport, and tribal fishers are entrenched in the social and cultural dimensions of their activity, they are slower to recognize that such dynamics influence the legacy of government-based fisheries personnel. It is well-documented that state and federal government supported their role in mediating claims to Lake Michigan's fisheries by professionalizing their fish and wildlife management agencies.[37] However, the culture that fostered one's decision to become a government-based fisheries manager or scientist is not extensively noted. If fisheries history is going to contribute to more inclusive management schemes, it needs to delineate—just as it has done with commercial fishers, tribal fishers, and sport fishers—social/cultural factors that guide one's entry and tenure in government-sponsored fisheries projects.

The oral histories that follow reveal these factors in a variety of ways. Hardly immune from history's reach, the government fisheries managers and scientists who were interviewed for this project re-establish their connections with an occupational tradition that dates to 1874 when George S. Jerome (1819–85) was appointed Michigan's first superintendent of fisheries; his scientific knowledge of fisheries was secondary to his political, economic, and social ties. Jerome, who held the post until 1884, came to Niles, Michigan, from his native state of New York after earning a degree in law. He worked as a Berrien County attorney and judge before moving to Iowa where he served as chairman of the Republican Party and an assessor for federal revenue. In 1873, shortly after his return to Berrien County, Michigan governor John J. Bagley appointed Jerome to the newly established Board of Fish Commission, a position which he held for a month before resigning to become superintendent of fisheries.[38]

By the time the Board of Fish Commission selected Oren M. Chase (1840–83) the third superintendent of fisheries in 1882, it was convinced of the need for an individual who combined administrative skills with experience in fish propagation and eventually, advanced degrees in fisheries science. Chase became involved in fish propagation as a result of his employment by the New York Central Railroad, transporter of thousands of milk cans of fish fry for state fish hatcheries. Seth Green, a leading expert on fish propagation, encouraged George Jerome to hire Chase. The man who would be Jerome's second successor joined the staff of the Fish Commission as superintendent of the Detroit River Hatchery. Chase had been fisheries superintendent for only a short time when the ship he was aboard sunk in a November 1883 storm on Grand Traverse Bay.[39] He had been working on a whitefish hatchery project in Petoskey, Michigan.

Chase's emphasis upon fish propagation mirrored the entire orientation of the Michigan Fish Commission. The emphasis on fish propagation continued until 1921 when the Fish Commission became the Fisheries Division of the Department of Conservation—the beginning of a sustained process to professionalize the state's management of its natural resources.[40] During most of its years, the Fisheries Division of the Department of Conservation was under the direction of Fred A. Westerman— a time period spanning from 1925–59. With his father having served as an employee at the Paris Fish Hatchery, Westerman could not have been more representative of those who were gaining entrance to the profession through the modern occupational culture and networks of fisheries management.

During the 1960s, increasing specialization led to the appointment of fisheries chiefs at the Departments of Conservation in Michigan and Wisconsin who held terminal degrees in fields related to fisheries science, beginning with James T. McFadden, who served on an interim basis in 1964. McFadden's departure from the Department of Conservation for an academic appointment established a precedent followed by his successor, Howard Tanner, who received a Ph.D. in zoology in 1952 from Michigan State University and left the Department of Conservation in 1966 to join the faculty at his alma mater. Tanner was followed by another Michigan State University-trained fisheries scientist, Dr. Wayne Tody. Both Tanner and Tody, along with Wisconsin Fisheries bureau chief Ron Poff, presided over transitions within their agencies where a new, professionally trained class of fisheries scientists was supplanting the dated research methods of those who preceded them.[41] Thus, the process of developing and implementing fisheries policy on Lake Michigan was increasingly dominated by men who had studied biology, limnology, zoology, and related disciplines at the University of Michigan or land grant universities such as Michigan State University and the University of Wisconsin. This new cadre distinguished itself by moving away from narrow, singularly directed species studies to more integrated, ecosystem-based approaches of fisheries management.[42] As suggested in the testimony of Tanner, Tody, and Poff, the occupational culture and social dynamics of Lake Michigan policy makers shifted dramatically during the mid-twentieth century to a system that valued the most modern academic training that university degrees could provide.

These oral histories show that many fisheries policy makers and advocates who worked at both the state and national level during the 1950s and 1960s shared an early interest in fishing on the Great Lakes. This introduction to Great Lakes fishing typically came through the family as part of a recreation or leisure activity. The landscape of lakeshore communities, their occupational structure, and other social and economic institutions and organizations also served to educate young people about fishing on the Great Lakes. Children who grew up in or visited lakeshore communities for extended periods could observe how sport and commercial fishers utilized Lake Michigan's maritime infrastructure of harbors, channel markers and buoys, docks and piers, lighthouses and Coast Guard stations. They might have known or recognized public officials including Coast Guardsmen, lightkeepers, and game wardens who both served and regulated sport and commercial fishers. Workers whose livelihood was tied to Lake Michigan such as commercial fishermen and fish market clerks, would be familiar sights to the youth of lakeshore communities.

1. In the Midst of Fish: Government Conservation and Management Becomes a Way of Life

Stan Smith, Ph.D., a fisheries expert who retired from the U.S. Fish and Wildlife Service, recalled the pioneering research work of John Van Oosten, Ph.D., at the laboratory at the University of Michigan in Ann Arbor under the federally funded Great Lakes Fishery Investigation. Prior to 1950, many of the leading scientists involved in Great Lakes fisheries research and management were University of Michigan graduates such as Van Oosten. Bright prospects were simultaneously recruited for both the University of Michigan fisheries science (limnology) program and employment at the Great Lakes Fisheries Laboratory maintained by the U.S. Fish and Wildlife Service.

While I was a graduate student at the University of Michigan, I came to work for John Van Oosten, the chief of the Great Lakes Fishery Investigation. The Great Lakes Fishery Investigation was formed under the U.S. Bureau of Fisheries about 1928. Van Oosten also had faculty status so he could work with the students; I believe he was called a research associate. In 1940 they combined the Bureau of Fisheries with the Biological Survey and formed the U.S. Fish and Wildlife Service. The Great Lakes Fishery Investigations were under the Fish and Wildlife Service of the Department of the Interior in Washington. My research was actually directed by Dr. Ralph Hile, whose length of association with the Great Lakes Fishery Investigations were second only to Van Oosten's.[43] When I came to Ann Arbor to work with the Great Lakes Fishery Investigations under John Van Oosten, there were only three research biologists—John Van Oosten, Ralph Hile, and myself.

It turned out that I only worked for Dr. Van Oosten for one day because the very day I reported for work, in September 1949, he was called to Washington. It was

Stanford Smith received a Bachelor of Science in Fish and Wildlife Management from Oregon State University in 1943. In 1954 he completed a Ph.D in Zoology at the University of Michigan. Dr. Smith was employed as a fishery research biologist by the U.S. Fish and Wildlife Service from 1944 to 1972. He also worked as a consultant to the National Marine Fishery Service and the Great Lakes Fishery Commission. Dr. Smith served as a Research Associate and Adjunct Professor at the University of Michigan's School of Natural Resources from 1967 to 1984. Interview, 25 August 1999. Photograph by Michael J. Chiarappa.

announced that the U.S. Fish and Wildlife Service had just received an appropriation of some $200,000 for fishery research and lamprey research and control on the Great Lakes. Through negotiations, they decided that Van Oosten would become a senior scientist. As he was nearing the end of his career, Van Oosten would have the freedom to work the data and information that he had collected since 1920. Actually, he started to work on the Great Lakes earlier as a student at the University of Michigan. The U.S. Fish and Wildlife Service would look for a younger, vigorous fellow to tackle and expand the activities in the Great Lakes. That person turned out to be Dr. James Moffett, who I had worked for in California. Dr. Moffett became chief of the Great Lakes Fishery Investigation in January of 1950 and I worked for him there.[44] In the interim, Ralph Hile had been the acting chief of the Great Lakes Fishery Investigation.

Before I started, it was decided, probably by Ralph Hile, that I would work on the lake herring of Green Bay. The research would be my doctoral thesis material. At that time, the lake herring supported a very productive fishery in Green Bay. Actually, the initiation of the Great Lakes Fishery Investigation came about as a result of the collapse of the lake herring fishery in Lake Erie, which was a very, very productive fishery. They wanted to study lake herring population during its peak production, not after it collapsed, to see what it was like. That was my assignment, both as part of the research of the laboratory, and as a doctoral dissertation project. In earlier years, Dr. Van Oosten had tried to get interest in forming a Great Lakes Commission to focus on the fisheries of the Great Lakes, but no such action was taken until the sea lamprey came along.

When James Moffett became chief of the Great Lakes Fishery Investigation after the change occurred in 1949, John Van Oosten was not involved directly in any of the work on the Great Lakes. He had full freedom to work with the masses of data that had been accumulated up until that time in the library. When I was a student, and employed part-time, my office was in the Museum's Annex, which was between the building that housed the Great Lakes Fishery Investigations and John Van Oosten, who was in the University of Michigan Museum, I was the go-between for the Investigation and John Van Oosten. I needed his expertise, his knowledge of how things were put together, for my research. And so I was his contact with the work on the Great Lakes.

James Moffet was a good administrator; he took care of the administrative aspects of the Great Lakes Fishery Investigations. Moffett focused very strongly on sea lamprey because that was the major emphasis in the early days. Sea lamprey control was his main area of involvement, although as the director, the chief of operations, he was interested in all of the work.

Ralph Hile's main responsibility was in the fishery research. He was oriented toward the commercial fishing and Howard Tanner was oriented toward the recreational fishing. I was in between. I explained my position in a paper that I wrote about the surveys in Lake Michigan, "Species Succession and Fishery Exploitation in the Great Lakes." I looked at the whole picture. This was the first time somebody came along and said well, let's not put all the blame on one side or the other side, and attempted to explain the way the whole system worked. I was not particularly oriented toward the commercial fishermen or the sport fishermen. I was trying to answer the question, what was going on.

Stan Smith recalled the informal division of responsibility that existed between John Van Oosten and Fred Westerman. Under this unwritten agreement, the State of Michigan allowed federal agencies such as the U.S. Fish and Wildlife Agency to conduct research and make recommendations for the Great Lakes fisheries.

I nitially, way back in the 1920s and 1930s, there was agreement between Dr. John Van Oosten and Fred Westerman. Westerman was in charge of the fishery work in the state of Michigan. They agreed that John Van Oosten and the federal government would be responsible for the Great Lakes fishery work, and the State of Michigan would look after its inland fisheries. When Fred Westerman retired, the administration of fishery work in Lake Michigan changed. For the first time in history the State of Michigan became active in their responsibility for the Great Lakes and began looking at what was going on in them. There was also a change in emphasis. It was a rather dramatic change from an emphasis on commercial fishing to an emphasis on sport fishing. For instance, at the University of Michigan in addition to the laboratory for the Great Lakes Fishery Investigations, where I worked, Dr. Lagler organized a sport-fishing forum where people would come and hear about sport fishing in Michigan. I was given the responsibility to give talks on sport fishing in the Great Lakes in the early 1950s. The forum was arranged such that I would give my talk repeatedly and people would move from area to area to hear different subjects. I did not get many people come to listen to me and learn about sport fishing in the Great Lakes. There just was not much interest at all in sport fishing in the Great Lakes. They wanted to learn about walleye fishing, and other inland fishing, but for the Great Lakes they had little interest. There was very little interest until the salmon came along. Then the fishermen began getting equipped to go out in the open lake and fish. But before the salmon, the lake trout were out there, but they disappeared, as the sea lamprey became abundant.

Former DNR head and MSU professor Dr. Howard Tanner was aware of the informal agreement that reportedly existed between John Van Oosten and Fred Westerman.

T he Institute for Fisheries Research was adjacent to, but not formally a part of the University of Michigan. It was an office and a laboratory of the U.S. Bureau of Commercial Fisheries. One of the very important early pioneers was John Van Oosten. John Van Oosten was still living and working there when I was a student. He may have been retired when I began my vaguest participation in fisheries work in about 1947–1948. He had to be a pretty old man by then. The Fish Division in Michigan was

Howard Tanner, a veteran of World War II, received his undergraduate and graduate degrees in fisheries science from Michigan State University. After working in Colorado's fisheries, Tanner joined the staff of the Michigan Department of Conservation as chief of the Fisheries Division. During the brief time Tanner was fisheries chief, the Pacific salmon were successfully introduced into Lake Michigan. In 1966, Tanner left the Michigan Department of Conservation to teach at Michigan State University. In 1975, Tanner became the director of the Michigan DNR. Tanner continued teaching at MSU until his retirement in 1993. Interview 24 August 1999. Photograph by Michael J. Chiarappa.

dominated completely by hatchery programs. People with a hatchery background became administrators without any science background. This tradition, which lasted until about six months before I became chief of fisheries, goes clear back to the time span of fisheries chief Fred Westerman. According to a secondhand story or legend, Fred Westerman and John Van Oosten allegedly sat down over a cup of coffee and they agreed that John would take the Great Lakes and Fred would take the inland waters. The federal presence without statutory authority provided the information and, information being power, set the regulations for commercial fishing throughout the Great Lakes including Michigan.

Michigan as a state did not have programs on the Great Lakes until 1964. There was no fishing license required. There was not much to fish for. There were good populations of fish—smelt and lake trout—before the sea lamprey and commercial fishing wiped them out, but it was minimal. People also did not have the capability of utilizing those waters. The boats were not big enough. There were not enough people with motors and so on. There was a federal presence, but there was no federal authority. It was just sort of a fait accompli. It was just the way they did it, and maybe John and Fred did sit down and say this is yours and this is mine.

In addition to this alleged division between Van Oosten and Fred Westerman, there was another division between the two of the most prominent figures in early freshwater fish management and fisheries—Van Oosten and Dr. Langlois, a very powerful figure at Ohio State. Van Oosten and Langlois had a long-standing professional dispute over the impact of commercial fishing. John Van Oosten, who time has showed to be wrong, insisted that fishing harvest had minimal impact on fish stocks. Langlois said commercial fishing is the mortality factor in managing fish stocks. Their ongoing exchange or dispute can be followed in the fisheries management literature.

Wayne Tody recalled that John Van Oosten favored an increase in federal oversight of the Great Lakes.

John Van Oosten was a good fed. He foretold of the collapse of the Great Lakes fisheries before sea lampreys. He would just get on the pulpit, and his buddies in Ann Arbor in the Commercial Fisheries Bureau would disagree with him. They maintained that there is no such thing as exploitation. The stocks will always recover. The

Wayne Tody retired from the Michigan DNR in 1980 as deputy director. From 1966 to 1976, during the heyday of the Lake Michigan salmon fishery, he was chief of the Fisheries Division of the Michigan Department of Conservation and its successor agency, the Department of Natural Resources. Tody received a Ph.D in Fisheries Science from Michigan State University. During Tody's tenure, the State of Michigan's fisheries research vessel, *Steelhead*, went into service. Interview 9 June 1999.

blue pike in Lake Erie had a catch of 18 million pounds, and two years later they became extinct. Nobody can explain why. Anyway, Van Oosten spent his life studying exploitation, but he had a bad side to him. Instead of negotiating, he had the opinion that effective management will never be established on the Great Lakes as long as the control of the fisheries is divided among the nine enforcement agencies, the eight states and Ontario. He wanted the feds to take over. And there were 150 meetings where the feds tried to take over. The commercial fishermen fought them the hardest. They were afraid the feds would nail them with one set of laws.

Howard Tanner spoke of the put-and-take orientation of fisheries management prior to the time he became head of the Fisheries Division. Michigan's Fisheries Division chief Fred Westerman was typical of the administrators with a hatchery background.

The antecedents of all modern day fisheries management were the hatcheries. If you had a scarcity of fish, the solution was to plant more fish. And then you began to learn that if you planted tiny fish, they did not survive so you had to have bigger hatcheries to grow the fish to a bigger size and so you stocked fish that you thought would survive. You moved fish around. If there were not any large-mouthed bass in the Upper Peninsula, so they put large-mouthed bass in the Upper Peninsula. The brook trout was not widely distributed in Michigan. It was probably only native to the Lake Superior drainage basin. Maybe there was some in northern Lake Michigan, possibly some in the Jordan River in the Lower Peninsula. So when the grayling went down, the brook trout came in. And so the hatchery system was originally built to raise brook trout, and then rainbow and brown trout.

They found that the only way they could have an impact on the fishing public was to stock what we called a catchable sized trout, which was the legal size of seven inches. If you stocked seven-inch to nine-inch trout, they would live long enough to be caught by fishermen provided you stocked them at the target, on Friday before a busy weekend such as Memorial Day or Labor Day. The trucks would arrive and everybody went out and followed the truck and caught the fish after they were put in. The hatcheries were beautiful. Everybody liked to go see all the fish. It was a nice display;

it really was not fisheries management. The put-and-take approach provided a brief, artificial recreation. After the initial introduction, the stocked trout did not have much impact on the wild trout populations. The scientists knew that, but the hatchery system was nonscientific. That was where the budget went. If a politician wanted fish stocked in his county or his district, he would go to the Fish Division where fish were given out as political payoffs and pork barrels. It was all tied in together. That was the way the Fish Division worked.

The incongruity of the situation was that at the Fisheries Research Institute in Ann Arbor and other fisheries aspects of the university, the federal government was one of the finest sources of information in United States, maybe in North America. They were saying this is not really management. Here are the limiting factors. There are the life history studies. Here is what is destructive, and here is what you have to protect. Here is where the mortality occurs, and these are the mortality factors. All the things we now know as a background for intelligent management were coming right out of Ann Arbor. It was a good a source, and Michigan was not taking it.

Stan Lievense discussed the fisheries research projects he was involved with early in his career, including the time he attended the University of Michigan and was employed at the Institute for Fisheries Research.

I received a bachelor's degree in fisheries biology. My first assignment with the Department of Conservation was district fisheries biologist up in the Cadillac area. At that time, I had five counties to cover. The sea lamprey were showing up more and more and more. About 1948 I was given the assignment to check all the streams of western Michigan that are connected to Lake Michigan for the sea lamprey spawning runs. This study was to see how advanced they were and they were advanced. Every stream was loaded with sea lamprey. So that was really the early stage. The larvae spend three years in a stream and then drop down and then become a parasite that needs blood. So, we were after a method that would treat the streams. You can kill a three-year class at a time.

I worked there from 1947 to 1949. Then I went up to Escanaba where you have the Big and Little Bay de Noc, very fertile bays in the Great Lakes. I ran into a rather

Stan Lievense is a member of the National Fishing Hall of Fame. Shortly after earning a Bachelor of Science degree from the University of Michigan, the Holland, Michigan, native began work for the Michigan Department of Conservation as a fisheries biologist. In 1967 he began working for the Michigan Tourist Bureau where he promoted Great Lakes sport fishing. Interview, 27 August 1999. Photograph by Michael J. Chiarappa.

interesting situation there. They had fabulous walleye fishing in Little Bay de Noc and Big Bay de Noc. When I got there they were catching walleyes in the six- to eight-pound bracket in great numbers. It was not uncommon to go out and get your limit of five. Well, how would you like to be a biologist starting when the fishery is already good? This scared me. So I analyzed the situation. The first thing I did was enlist the aid of a commercial fisherman who was sucker netting. He was getting a lot of walleyes in his nets which he had to release, so I talked him into letting me take 100 of them for scale sampling. The results were tragic. All of these fish except one were from one year's hatch. When walleyes grow in Great Lakes water at a fast rate, they do not live long, six years about maximum. So go six years back and that is when you had your big survival of the young walleye. Why did this happen? That year they had massive smelt mortality in Lake Michigan, so this tells you that the smelt is a very serious predator of the Great Lakes walleye.

I was transferred down from Escanaba to Baldwin, Michigan. I was the district fishery biologist. I was in charge of the management of the waters there. I concentrated quite a bit on the steelhead runs at that time. There was some research being done on the food habits of the Great Lakes steelhead. And they found, believe it or not, that their bread-and-butter food was plankton. They are plankton feeders. Although they eat fish, plankton is what really gives them their growth and so on.

In 1950, I started in Traverse City. I was getting acquainted with these Great Lakes now. I was in Traverse City from 1950 to 1965, so I had fifteen years of it. In Traverse City, I did not work as much with commercial fishermen. They were managed pretty much out of Lansing and we did not really have much influence there. So I was working more from the sport-fishing angle like planting steelhead that would go out into the big lake and so on.

―――――――――

Wayne Tody, a retired fisheries chief from the Michigan DNR, recalled how technology was employed to make the harvesting of Great Lakes fish more successful. Commercial fishers became too efficient and depleted fishery stocks.

The fisheries started back in the early 1800s in a very primitive way with the fur companies. The Indians caught fish as employees of the American Fur Company and the Canadian Hudson's Bay Trading Company when it was partly Canadian at Lake Superior. By 1820 commercial fishing had started in the Detroit area. After 1850 steam tugs started to replace the schooners and rowboats. The commercial fishery just took off and it was tremendously productive for years. Fishermen caught a billion pounds of whitefish in those good years. The biologists have what they called a period of normalcy where the lakes were heavily exploited, heavily fished, but also recovered their productive order about as well as they could. So they were probably producing somewhat less than their maximum production of commercial fish but as good as they could with their standing crop. Then overfishing began. The commercial fisherman will tell you this is a state opinion belonging to the fish guys of the State of Michigan, but it really is not. I can give you several references by college professors in Toronto and other scholars where we all say the same thing. People do not want to admit it. Old-time commercial fishermen refuse to think you can overfish fish. The lamprey then whacked what was left of the lake trout, whitefish, steelhead, and anything big enough to get a meal of blood out of. The commercial fishermen went on fishing with more and more nylon gill nets because they were cheap. At the peak of the fishery, as some of the wildest ones set 100,000 feet of net a day for six days, then went back and run the first back, trying to get a few whitefish. They had gone; that is what we call the collapse. To make it all worse, the alewife came in.

———————

In her recent book, historian Margaret Beattie Bogue showed that throughout most of the nineteenth and early-twentieth centuries, the United States and Canada were seldom in agreement over issues involving Great Lakes fisheries. The devastation of the lake trout and whitefish stocks due to the sea lamprey was an environmental crisis of sufficient scale to incite the United States and Canada into action. Created by the terms of a treaty between the two countries, the Great Lakes Fishery Commission came into being in 1955. Since its inception the Commission has focused on two issues—sea lamprey control and lake trout restoration. Other causes of the decline of Great Lakes fisheries, including overfishing and pollution, have not been addressed by the commission perhaps because they are too politically divisive. Most important, unlike regulations on fishing and the discharge of water and other wastes into the Great Lakes, the eradication of sea lamprey and the restoration of a self-sustaining lake trout fishery were issues supported by numerous Great Lakes constituencies that could help verify the effectiveness of these programs.

The Commission successfully applied research in marine science and technology to help control sea lamprey populations in the Great Lakes. The method and approach used in sea lamprey control is slowly changing, but not fast enough for some of its critics. The lake trout restoration program has proved to be a major challenge for the commission outside of Lake Superior.

Dr. Stanford Smith, a retired biologist from the U.S. Fish and Wildlife Service, recalled the origins of the sea lamprey which, like the alewife, invaded the Great Lakes watershed from the Atlantic Ocean. He discussed how the sea lamprey crisis and the effort to restock lake trout unified both the United States and Canada as well as the Great Lakes states.

The lamprey and the alewife came up the Hudson River, the Mohawk River, through the Erie Canal, and they inhabited the Finger Lakes, Oneida Lake, Cayuga Lake, and Seneca Lake and established a viable population there. Then they moved downstream into Lake Ontario. Vernon Applegate did the research at the Hammond Bay Laboratory of the U.S. Fish and Wildlife Service that determined the temperatures that were needed for the sea lamprey to reproduce. In order for lamprey eggs to incubate and hatch successfully, the water has to warm up in the spring above sixty degrees.[45] Before the Great Lakes states were deforested, if the sea lamprey by chance came up and spawned there, the eggs would not hatch because the water did not get warm enough.

The Atlantic salmon required cold water streams to reproduce and the streams were no longer cold, so the Atlantic salmon disappeared, not because of the fishery but because of deforestation. So their range moved northward where they had cold water they could reproduce in. The lake trout thrived in Lake Ontario along with the whitefish in Lake Ontario and were exploited by the fishery. And then the sea lamprey came in and depleted them. There is not a lot of early documentation of the fishery because there was not much of a fishery. But the fishery was over-exploited. In Lake Ontario before the sea lamprey, the Canadian and U.S. fishermen moved to other lakes. So the fishermen themselves migrated. When the sea lamprey depleted the lake trout and whitefish on Lake Huron, the fishermen from Lake Huron moved to Lake Michigan and Lake Superior.

The goal of the work at Hammond Bay was to get rid of the lamprey. They were in a closed system. In open systems, such as the ocean, you do not see the harm that the sea lampreys do because there is an abundance of fish for them to feed on. The sea lamprey in a closed system could eat themselves out of house and home and they would disappear. It is just like the schooling fish in the Great Lakes. I do not think they would survive in a closed system. They would be eaten completely by lake trout or salmon. If you want to resolve the problems in the Great Lakes, do nothing. Do absolutely nothing. Just stand there and watch it. The sea lamprey will disappear. The smelt will disappear. The alewife will disappear. They will all be gone. But as the fish stocks are manipulated to favor the desired species, undesirable species will remain.

The lake trout had disappeared in Lake Huron. Reproduction of lake trout in Lake Michigan had virtually ended, and they were being greatly depleted in Lake Superior by sea lamprey predation. There was international interest in doing something about this animal that had depleted our resources. The sea lamprey depleted the lake trout first because it was the largest and most vulnerable fish for the sea lamprey to feed on. When the lake trout declined, it focused on the whitefish, another very valuable commercial species. When it reduced the whitefish, it started then on suckers and burbot and other large fish. Eventually they were all decimated. The loss of these valuable fisheries brought the states together, and the two governments of the United States and Canada to formulate a treaty and form an international Great Lakes Fishery Commission. The main responsibility, almost the total responsibility initially of the Commission, was sea lamprey control. The people most responsible in the U.S. for getting agreement among the states and the two governments were Dr. James Moffett and a fellow from the State Department named Harrington. They worked very diligently. Their main focus was the formation of the Great Lakes Fishery Commission. During that period, I was pulled into broader activities on the Great Lakes because of this increased initiative. I had to work doubly hard both as a student and a researcher in developing programs for the Great Lakes.

Dennis Lavis, a fisheries biologist who supervises the U.S. Fish and Wildlife Service's Ludington Research Station, explained the relationship between the U.S. Fish and Wildlife Service and the Great Lakes Fishery Commission.

The U.S. Fish and Wildlife Service occupies a unique role in sea lamprey control on the Great Lakes. We actually act as agents of the Great Lakes Fishery Commission, an international fishery commission between the United States and Canada. It was formed back in the mid-1950s specifically to combat the sea lamprey problem in the Great Lakes and to promote fishery research in the Great Lakes. After its formation in the mid-1950s the Great Lakes Fishery Commission contracted with the two federal national resource agencies of both countries, U.S. Fish and Wildlife Service and the Department of Fisheries, Oceans Canada, to conduct a program of sea lamprey control in the Great Lakes. The arrangement continues to this day. The U.S. Fish and Wildlife Service works under a reimbursement agreement with the Great Lakes Fishery Commission whose dollars for the program come from the U.S. State Department in the United States and a comparable agency in Canada. Our funds do not come from the U.S. Department of Interior where the Fish and Wildlife Service lies. So essentially, the commission gives cash to the service to perform this function out of the Ludington office and our Marquette office now. We work very closely with all the other natural resource agencies around the Great Lakes basin, both federal, state, provincial, tribal.

Dennis Lavis has been employed by the U.S. Fish and Wildlife Service for over twenty years and is a specialist in sea lamprey control. He holds a Bachelor of Science and a Master of Science degrees in fishery biology and management from Michigan State University. Interview, 10 June 1999. Photograph by Michael J. Chiarappa.

For example, the USFWS works with Michigan DNR, Wisconsin DNR, and all the states that border the Great Lakes, the Ontario Ministry of Natural Resources, the Chippewa/Ottawa Treaty Fishery Management Authority, and Great Lakes Indian Fish and Wildlife Commission. There are a myriad of other agencies as well as agencies within the U.S. Geological Survey, Natural Biological Resources Division, that do a lot of the research for us in the large fishery research centers in Ann Arbor and La Crosse, Wisconsin. So it is a large cooperative effort with the service and the Department of Fisheries, Oceans Canada doing the work

The Great Lakes Fishery Commission operates on a real large committee structure and all of these agencies are members of the committees. Each lake has a lake committee and lake technical committees that make recommendations on how to manage the Great Lakes fisheries. All the committees operate under a large umbrella document called the Strategic Management of Great Lakes Fisheries or SMGLF for short. It was recently revised, and all the parties to this document, all of the natural resource agencies that surround the Great Lakes as far as fisheries go, signed it again. So we are a big happy family working to manage the Great Lakes.

The commission set lofty goals back in the beginning of the 1990s, when they published their vision for the decade. Their vision for the 1990s included reduction in lamprey populations by some level from what they were in the early 1990s. We achieved that goal. We got there. They are in the process of revising their vision now for the next decade, and one of the recommendations that we made to the Commission for them to consider was to consider making eradication a goal at least in the lake basin. For example, we could conceivably get to the point where we would not have to treat any streams in Lake Superior. It is possible by using sterilized males and that sort of thing. We will not be able to eradicate them from all the lakes, but we can continue to strive toward further reductions, moving away from chemical use as much as possible to a more biological base control. That is a target to shoot for.

Part of the commission's vision, back in the 1990s, was to move away from lampricide use. They wanted to move away from a chemical means because essentially any pest control program that is totally dependent on one method is extremely vulnerable to failure at some point in time. One of the other ripples, if you will, is the fact that up until the last few years, TFM was supplied by only one German company. We are the world's only user. They were the world's only maker and supplier, so of course, we were subject to their cost. If they for some reason or another, they decided they are not going to produce it, we are out of business. We now have two suppliers, a domestic and a foreign supplier, so that helps. But just relying on one method still is tenuous. A good integrated pest program uses a variety of methods to control the pest. As a result, the Commission charged its agents back in the late 1970s and early 1980s to look at integrated pest management as a way to control sea lampreys. That is where we have headed over the last couple of decades and we will continue to evolve in that direction.

There is a lot of research being done in other areas. There is some very promising research on attractants and repellents based on the natural odors that lampreys give off. We might be able to attract lampreys to a trap, repel them from good streams, and attract them into bad streams. Sex pheromone research is another area that's very exciting because you might be able to couple that with that on sterilized males. Perhaps we can make the sterilized males exude more sex pheromone than the normal males and attract more females and thereby waste more eggs. So there are a lot of things that are being looked at, some really off-the-wall stuff that is being looked at, but you never know what is going to pay dividends down the road. So the Commission has a very active research program.

Carlos Fetterolf received a Bachelor of Science degree from the University of Connecticut and a Master of Science degree at Michigan State University. He was executive secretary for the Great Lakes Fishery Commission from 1975 until his retirement in 1992. He presently serves on the National Sea Grant Review Panel for the U.S. Department of Commerce. Interview, 10 August 1999. Photograph by Michael J. Chiarappa.

Retired as executive secretary of the Great Lakes Fishery Commission, Carlos Fetterolf recalled the influence of the late Claude Ver Duin of Grand Haven, who was appointed to the Great Lakes Fishery Commission by President Dwight D. Eisenhower in 1956.

Claude Ver Duin was extremely influential in getting the commission started. He was Mr. Great Lakes Fishery Commission. Ver Duin was very disturbed to see the gradual transition from commercial fishing over to recreational fishing. But there was not anything he could do about it. The commercial fishermen were formerly a genuine political power block. I do not know how they ever got that powerful, but commercial fishing all over the country was very important politically. In some areas they still are but in most areas the recreational fishery has supplanted that power.

Jack Bails applied for the job that I got with the Great Lakes Fishery Commission. Claude Ver Duin would not have Jack Bails because he was associated with the Michigan DNR and the recreational fishery. Well, I was in water quality and had worked on many committees that dealt with water quality and fisheries, but nothing that had to do with fisheries. Claude Ver Duin said to me, "You know Wayne Tody, chief of fisheries?" I said, "Yeah." He asked, "You work with him much?" I said, "Just very, very slightly. I do not have anything to do with the work he does except if he asks me water quality questions."

———————

Carlos Fetterolf explained the circumstances under which he joined the staff of the Great Lakes Fishery Commission in 1975 and his efforts to understand how it functioned on an international, national, regional, and local level.[46]

During the early 1970s, I had been on leave to the National Academy of Sciences but was still with the Water Resources Commission when it became part of the DNR. Lots of people knew my reputation through water quality; it was the current cause celebre. I was becoming very active with the International Joint Commission in Windsor and headed up a couple committees for them. One committee was developing the scientific basis for water quality criteria in the Great Lakes. I also chaired the water quality objectives committee which recommended water quality objectives for dissolved oxygen, for DDT, for pH, for any number of parameters. I was working on weekends down in Windsor when Stan Smith called my hotel. He was with the U.S. Bureau of Commercial Fisheries when the bureau was the major federal influence on fisheries in the Great Lakes. Stan was a leading fishery scientist and was very much associated with the Great Lakes Fishery Commission on their Science Advisory Board. He asked, "Why aren't you interested in this job with the Great Lakes Fishery Commission?" And I said, "I had not really thought much about it at all." But I drove from Windsor to his home and he told me about the commission. The next morning I called the chairman of the Great Lakes Fishery Commission and in two weeks I was interviewed and hired. So after doing my senior seminar on the sea lamprey in 1950, in 1975 I got back with the sea lamprey.

On July 1, 1975, when I went down there and took on the job, the greatest concern I had was that I did not have a current grasp of the fisheries science literature. I had been in water quality for nineteen years. I found out later that that really was not any great handicap. I needed to be familiar with fisheries science, but I needed to be very familiar with the issues and the politics of fisheries between the two countries, Canada and the United States, and the policies among the states and provinces.

When I first started with the Great Lakes Fishery Commission, Stan Smith had talked to me about its work, but I was pretty vague about what its duties and responsibilities were. They were not a well-known group in 1975. The Commission was not the high profile group it was years ago when they had started the war against the sea lamprey and there was a lot of publicity with the discovery of TFM. Stan Smith had said, "Carlos, the executive secretary of the Great Lakes Fishery Commission IS the Great Lakes Fishery Commission." And unfortunately, I believed him. When the commission first met and the chairman asked for a vote, I caught myself voting. Well, I certainly learned that I did not have a vote very, very quickly. There were dirty looks all around the table at this newcomer, but I only did that once. I told him I did not like their letterhead; I thought it was rather meaningless. I presented them with a new letterhead I had designed and, believe it or not, they liked that. I presented several items to them with my recommendations for their decision, and my batting average was about thirty percent. I thought to myself, what is wrong with me? Why don't I understand what these people want? At the end of one meeting, the four American and four Canadian commissioners all went back to their home bases to ponder a decision. I called the chairman of the U.S. section and the chairman of the Canadian section who were supposed to come up with consensus decisions of their respective sections and report them to me. They reported we cannot get these other commissioners to agree on anything. So then I understood that they would rarely all agree, and my batting average went up a lot after that. I did not try to recommend a single approach. I simply presented them with the options and consequences; it got to be a whole lot better that way.

Howard Tanner, formerly of the Michigan DNR and Michigan State University, maintained that the Great Lakes Fishery Commission was biased in favor of commercial fishing. It sought to turn back the hands of time to the days when the lakes were the domain of commercial fishermen, the sea lamprey was not a menace, and lake trout were the top predators.

The U.S. Great Lakes Fishery Commission was formed in 1955 in response to what was perceived as a crisis, the collapse of the various fisheries in the lakes. Sea lamprey and overfishing were some other factors blamed. Smelt was an important factor, in my opinion. The establishment of this joint commission between Canada and the United States would mean uniform management of the Great Lakes. Each state would have to voluntarily give the Great Lakes Fishery Commission its management authority over their portion of the Great Lakes. Seven states and the province of Ontario agreed. One state said no. That state was Ohio. Ohio had a significant sport fishery for walleye and perch in Lake Erie and a commercial fishery, and the state refused to turn its management authority over to anybody. The Great Lakes Fishery Commission decided it would manage Ohio's share of Lake Erie and so they went ahead with the formation of the commission without its management authority.

The principal mission of the Great Lakes Fishery Commission was to control sea lamprey. Secondarily their mission was to rehabilitate lake trout populations. Those are the only two missions they ever really had. Now in order to fulfill their mission, they have conducted research. Back in the early days, there was a technology portion to their laboratory where they helped to develop markets for fish products as part of an effort to help sustain a very floundering commercial fishery. The fishermen could not make a living. There was nothing left to fish for. By the early 1960s, alewife made up the vast bulk of the weight of fisheries in Lake Michigan.

The Great Lakes Fishery Commission was located in Ann Arbor. The U.S. Bureau of Commercial Fisheries was still there at the Institute for Fisheries Research. The Great Lakes Fishery Commission was pretty much totally oriented toward commercial fishing. The problem was the sea lamprey and the need to rehabilitate the principal predacious fish, the lake trout. That is very understandable; it was the way things had been and the way they were going to continue. That is why Claude Ver Duin was Michigan's representative on the Great Lakes Fishery Commission.

Myrl Keller, a retired research biologist for the Michigan DNR, discussed the coordinating role of the Great Lakes Fishery Commission.

Since the 1960s, through the Great Lakes Fishery Commission, we have met at least annually with the other state agencies and discussed management issues cooperatively. It has really worked out quite well. We have a good working relationship. For instance, on Lake Michigan, we are real close to Indiana, Illinois, and Wisconsin. We talk

Myrl Keller is from a Saginaw Bay commercial fishing family. He worked as a commercial fisherman for brief periods before he graduated from Michigan State University with a degree in fisheries science. He was previously employed with the U.S. Fish and Wildlife Service on sea lamprey control. Keller helped set up the Michigan DNR's first Great Lakes fishery station in Charlevoix, Michigan, and retired as the station's manager in 1996. In 2002 Myrl Keller was inducted into the Fresh Water Fishing Hall of Fame. Interview, 27 May 1999. Photograph courtesy of the Great Lakes Center for Maritime Studies.

to those people on a regular basis and meet with them quite regularly, even over and above the big annual meeting that we normally have once a year, usually in March.

The Great Lakes Fishery Commission works primarily with sea lamprey, but they also provide the forum for all the states, universities, other federal agencies, the tribes, and Ontario, to get together and discuss Great Lakes issues and set up cooperative research and management. And a lot of that is done through the Great Lakes Fishery Commission. The commission worked with all the agencies quite equally. They were housed for a number of years with the U.S. Fish and Wildlife Service in Ann Arbor, but their charge was to cooperatively work with all the fisheries agencies on the Great Lakes.

***

Wayne Tody, a retired DNR official from Michigan, regarded the Great Lakes Fishery Commission as a rare example of international intrastate cooperation.

Everybody always says that the states cannot cooperate, but that is not true. The Great Lakes Fishery Commission was established by the United States and Canada to control sea lamprey and to coordinate research. It is the first positive thing we had along that line. We had interstate compacts, but they were full of two-bit politicians mainly arguing how much water can be diverted from Lake Michigan and how much power can come over Niagara Falls. I went to some of their meetings, but they were nonproductive from our point of view. The Great Lakes Fishery Commission did a tremendous thing in getting the U.S. Fish and Wildlife Service and the Canadian Ministry of Fisheries organized in each of their own waters to control the lampreys with TFM lampricide and set up a funding formula. That went along great for years until the last few years, when our government has begun to renege on the appropriations, as usual. They did such a beautiful job, and delegated themselves this responsibility. The federal government has done a lot of good things, but then they screw around. They only put up $2 million, and the Commission deals in trillions. Governor John Engler, whom everybody hates environmentally, bailed out the Commission, and put up million dollars of state money, which he does not have. It was just a gift because the treaty calls for federal funding in both countries. Ontario does not put up any money either, and they own all the Canadian water of the Great Lakes. They did come through with enough money to keep the program going because there is a big build-up of sea lampreys in the Sault locks, the rapids in the river.

Carlos Fetterolf, who served as executive secretary of the Great Lakes Fishery Commission from 1975 to 1992, recalled how the commission's work assisted the State of Michigan's efforts to create a sport fishery.

After the Great Lakes Fishery Commission, through its agents the U.S. Fish and Wildlife Service and Fisheries and Oceans Canada, brought the sea lamprey under sufficient control so that fisheries could be rehabilitated, stocking of lake trout by both countries started. In the absence of predatory fish, a huge population of alewives developed. During alewife die-offs in the spring and summer their carcasses made fish chowder along the shores. Michigan believed it could rear and stock the fast-growing Pacific salmon much more efficiently than the U.S. federal government and Ontario could raise the slow-growing lake trout. Michigan also predicted if salmon stocking was successful, that a very valuable sport fishery would develop. Michigan was convinced that the sport fishery would be much more valuable socially and economically than a commercial fishery. The salmon program quickly proved to be a recreational and economic success. The word spread and soon all the Great Lakes had salmon and lake trout sport fisheries plus strong whitefish populations for commercial fisheries in the upper lakes.

At the height of the fishery, 1980, the Great Lakes Fishery Commission contracted for an economic assessment of the total Great Lakes fishery. The estimate was $2–4 billion dollars annually, with perhaps ten percent of the value being commercial. Now back in the old days before there was a strong recreational fishery, what was the recreational fishery for Lake Michigan before World War II? Oh, there were a few boats that took out some guys after lake trout with long wire lines, you know. And there was a strong fishery for yellow perch off the breakwaters. There might have been some head boats that went out, charter boats that took twenty-five to fifty fishermen. That is what you call a head boat. But what happened after World War II was that people started having money for recreation. And suddenly people began to orient toward the lakes and we had alewives for the salmon and lake trout to feed on and people went out there to catch the big fish.[47]

Wayne Tody, former chief of the Fisheries Division and assistant deputy director of the Michigan DNR, served on several committees for the Great Lakes Fishery Commission. He recalled Canadian efforts to establish splake in the Great Lakes.

I enjoyed my years on the Great Lakes Fishery Commission. They had a committee for each of the Great Lakes. Michigan was the biggest state. We had a committee member on Lake Superior, one on Lake Michigan, one on Lake Huron, one on Lake Erie. And I always volunteered for another committee besides the one on Lake Michigan. When I was on the Lake Huron committee we got in some debates with Ontario. They were good debates. They were biological debates. They did not want to introduce lake trout because the native population was extinct. They wanted a breed of splake, combination of lake trout and brook trout. It is a pretty fish, and would go to the depths that lake trout went to. The Canadians figured if they did this for five generations, the fifth could be selected to where it would have the good qualities of the brook trout, and be able to do what the lake trout does in several hundred feet of water. It did not work. But my predecessors had agreed never to plant lake trout unless the Canadians furnished us with breeding stock for the splake when they had them. Well after a few years, it became obvious that the splake were not going to work, but the Canadians would not admit it. But we have got people over on Lake Huron that are awful hungry. Remember that two-year delay? So I had to say the gentleman's agreement is hereby broken, dissolved, and buried. And we are going to plant lake trout. That is when they finally agreed. They were going try to continue with the splake, but admitted that it did not look promising.

We had a lot of disputes over size limits, bag limits, kind of gear used, and all that. But I never saw when we could not sit down at those committees and negotiate. When we went home and tried to get proposals through our commissions and legislatures where somebody else is politicking it, a lot of things died, just like they die today in committee. But that is not the end of the work.

Now retired, Wisconsin DNR biologist and fisheries expert Jim Moore discussed the role of the Great Lakes Fishery Commission in fostering cooperation among the states.

U nder the Great Lakes Fishery Commission, each of the Great Lakes has a lake committee made up of one member each from each of the management agencies on the lake. There are also various working committees called technical committees, made up of at least two biologists from each of the management agencies and some representatives from the commission. So we have at least three or four meetings of those groups every year. A lot of the programs jointly agreed upon are monitored by those groups, and we have annual meetings where we get together and report our findings and things that are going on. I am a member of the Lake Michigan Committee and Mike Toneys is a member of the technical committee for Wisconsin.

I do not know how soon after 1956, when they had the first Great Lakes Fishery Commission meeting, that each of the lake committees started meeting annually. By the time I started working in 1968, that was a pretty regularly scheduled thing. At the lake committee meetings, there was a lot of revisiting of regional goals and discussion of how to adjust to new problems. It has been quite a cooperative effort between all the states. And as much as there is cooperation, there can always be more improved

Jim Moore was a Regional Fisheries Expert for the Wisconsin DNR Division of Fisheries. Moore retired in 1999 after more than thirty years of service. Interview, with his colleague Michael Toneys, 1 and 2 June 1999. Photograph by Michael J. Chiarappa.

ways of doing it. But it is very hard when you have to deal through our own state legislatures and implement your own rules and regulations to make everything fit into a system that should be probably managed uniformly across all jurisdictions.

Carlos Fetterolf wanted the Great Lakes Fishery Commission to become more active in fostering cooperation among international, federal, and state Great Lakes fisheries policy makers. The lack of comprehensive planning for the entire Great Lakes region presented difficulties in establishing uniform fisheries policy.

The Great Lakes Fishery Commission is funded through External Affairs Canada and the State Department on the United States side. There are some six international fishery commissions funded from one budget envelope within the State Department. The State Department says these are the dollars, spread them among these six commissions. The Great Lakes Fishery Commission has the most active field program and it gets about half of that State Department budget for all these six commissions. We have always felt we needed more money to do the research that was going to give us alternative methods of control. We wanted more options for control of the sea lamprey and we fought hard for the dollars. I always felt that one of the handicaps we faced was that we had TFM. We had a chemical successful in killing a large portion of larval sea lamprey in their natal streams. We were successful in developing a world-class fishery. So why should the countries increase the GLFC budget? The Commission was doing its job without more funds. But we did not have the final solutions.

I was disappointed that the Commission, in its wisdom, did not seem to focus on the protection of the fisheries. They left that up to the state and provincial agencies to accomplish with regulations on catch, season, and gear. The Commission was very concerned that lake trout were not reproducing and was convinced the reason for the insufficient numbers was that too few fish were reaching spawning ages and sizes.

The Commission was very concerned about the tribal fisheries, but not from a standpoint that they wanted to get in and become active in the negotiations. They did not feel that was their role. Their role was to control lampreys, and bring the management agencies together, including the tribal people. But they did not care how the tribal people and the federal people and the state people were involved in this. That was not their job.

Sea lamprey control is just one of the responsibilities of the Great Lakes Fishery Commission. I think the greater responsibility comes in working with the various management agencies around the lakes and trying to facilitate their thinking on establishment of their goals so they were thinking alike and working toward the same end points. That is the biggest role that the Commission plays. And in order to facilitate that, along about in the late 1960s, there was talk of starting a strategic plan for management of Great Lakes fisheries. Actually the Great Lakes Basin Commission (which was in existence then and has since been phased out) made that suggestion. The Basin Commission said we will be glad to do this for the Great Lakes Fishery Commission. I went to the Commission and asked, "Are you going to hand over this great opportunity to the Great Lakes Basin Commission when it should be our responsibility to do this?" New York and Ontario biologists committed to leadership and the Commission agreed to take it on.

Ken Loftus, a commissioner representing the Ontario Ministry of Natural Resources, knew that in order to come up with a strategic plan for management of the Great Lakes fisheries we would need the endorsement of each agency involved. The Commission could not work only with its lake committees and agency biologists and planners. We had to have the approval of top administrators. So the Commission created the Committee of the Whole, made up of directors of the state, provincial, and federal agencies with Great Lakes fishery responsibilities. Given veto power, the directors gave the go ahead for several meetings working with their personnel at their own agency's expense.

After a year and a half of negotiations, the team came up with several principles for management and several strategic procedures to follow in developing the fishery. All of the agencies agreed with the proposal. Some seven or eight years later, the tribal groups signed on as well so that there were definitely uniform goals that were being— that we were all striving to achieve in the various lakes.

Finally we began to get the research money but it was awfully difficult. I spent much time in Washington and in Ottawa. Often there was really no hope for getting more money at that time, but eventually your message gets through if you keep pushing.

———

Since the late 1940s and early 1950s, there have been state, provincial, and federal efforts for sea lamprey control. The first of these were physical and electrical barriers and traps. The search for a selective lampricide started with the Fish and Wildlife Service and continued support from the Great Lakes Fishery Commission. After TFM came into use, other methods followed: Bayluscide, low head barriers, attractants and repellants, and sterilization. Funding for sea lamprey control is provided to the U.S. Fish and Wildlife Service and Fisheries and Oceans Canada. These agents form the Great Lakes Fishery Commission.

Carlos Fetterolf recalled what he knew about the days when scientists were working to find an effective lampricide.

Vernon Applegate and his coworkers worked on sea lamprey up at the Hammond Bay research laboratory. It was started under the Fish and Wildlife Service and funding has continued from both Canada and the U.S. under the Great Lakes Fishery Commission. The discovery of TFM was almost a handicap for the Great Lakes Fishery Commission. The public and funding agencies thought we had this silver bullet sort of a thing. I, for one, never thought TFM was a silver bullet. It kept the sea lamprey under

Sea lamprey control devices such as electrical weirs were used in both Michigan and Wisconsin by the U.S. Fish and Wildlife Service to help aid the recovery of Lake Michigan's devastated stocks of lake trout, whitefish, and other species. Prior to the creation of the bi-national Great Lakes Fishery Commission, these weirs were constructed with federal and state on the Kewaunee River in Wisconsin in 1952 and the Whitefish River in Michigan in 1955. Courtesy of the Ludington Biological Station, U.S. Fish and Wildlife Service.

a reasonable control but could not completely solve the problem, besides it involves putting a toxicant into water supplies, and I advised the commission we are going to get in trouble with this. Even though our research shows that this is not consequential to nontarget organisms and there is no evidence that it has any effect on people who are drinking this water. There is going to be a backlash in that people are going to say we want the best quality water we can possibly have and we are not getting it if you are going to be putting TFM in it. There was even a person at the University of Wisconsin who actually figured out how many parts per trillion there were of TFM in Lake Superior water. I urged that we go forward, and discover and work with alternative methods of lamprey control. The commissioners were angry with me. Their attitude was that we have a method that is working and we do not need to spend money to go out and look for other methods. Their attitude changed over the years with the greening movement where people wanted the best possible environment they could have, and they wanted it chemical-free.

When I first went with the Commission in 1975, they were phasing out the use of electricity in weirs, barriers, and traps.[48] They were used as monitoring devices to judge how many lamprey there were in a given lake. The Commission's agents had about ten monitoring stations along Lake Superior. Every spring when the lampreys were migrating upstream, they would count the numbers in a trap. The staff members were glad when the electrical weirs and barriers were phased out because they were so afraid they were going to electrocute somebody. They did kill deer and there were some close calls. I felt it was a mistake to phase out the electric lamprey control method. After we dropped it, other fishery research people continued to work with electricity and developed new techniques. Electricity was eventually restored to our program with a barrier at Custer, on the Pere Marquette River. The Smith-Root barrier has lines of electrically charged wire placed across the river on an inclined ramp. When a sea lamprey starts to go up, it gets a continuing and increasing dose of electricity. The hope was that the steelhead would be more tolerant of the electrical charge and be able to get up over the weir.

The electric barrier at Custer was put into operation the same night that Michigan played for the national championship in basketball. It interfered with the television reception in the Ludington area. It was a very unpopular start. Besides that, the barrier created a short in the electrical system. Nearby cows received a shock through their teat cups when they were milked, and the next night, they would not come back into the barn.

A side channel with pumped attraction flows was later installed. The channel passes steelhead, but traps lampreys. Some low head barriers have now been modified with water level sensors connected to computers in headquarters. The height of the barrier can be adjusted remotely by inflating a rubber tube to compensate for changes in flow.

We found that Bisagine, a potent carcinogen, was very effective in sterilizing sea lamprey males when it was absorbed through the skin. For effectiveness, you had to keep the lamprey in this solution for certain periods of time so that they absorbed the Bisagine, became sterile, but still retained their libido. It was decided that the immersion system was too dangerous and an injection system was developed. At first we did hand injections to see how it was going to work. Then we built a sterilization facility up in Hammond Bay. Our goal was to capture sexually active males, sterilize them, and release them into a stream to outnumber the potent males. A large percentage of the eggs of a breeding female will thus not be fertilized. If you do this through enough generations, you are going to flood out a population. I am not sure how well it is working.

One of the more recent lamprey control techniques involves the use of pellitized Bayluscide. Around the early 1960s I worked with John Howell, a scientist at Hammond Bay. We did an experiment on Houghton Lake where we set up plots and I spread Bayluscide to control the snails, which were the host of the organism causing swimmer's itch. John Howell came down with little mesh-covered bread tins containing live brook lamprey. They are nonparasitic species but, of course, they are a lamprey. If Bayluscide affected brook lamprey, it would also affect adult lamprey or larval lamprey. It was a very successful experiment. Bayluscide has been reformulated and it is being applied from helicopters in selected locations in the St. Mary's River. The St. Mary's River seems to be the most important single source of lamprey in both Lake Huron and Lake Michigan. Where the St. Mary's River comes out of Lake Superior there are thousands of lamprey larvae. We drop coated granular Bayluscide in selected areas. When it gets to the bottom it releases its toxicant. We think that it is going to be very, very effective treatment because this area is the major source of lamprey to Lake Huron and to Lake Michigan. If we can control it this treatment is going to be a great success.

Dennis Lavis of the U.S. Fish and Wildlife Service's Ludington Research Station discussed how sea lamprey reached the Great Lakes. Lavis saw the discovery of the chemical compound tritryfloromethylfornitrophenal, known as TFM, as a major turning point in saving the Great Lakes fisheries.

I was not around when the lamprey problem first began; I am not that old. Sea lampreys are native to the Atlantic Ocean. For thousands of years, they ascended coastal streams to spawn. The larvae lived in the coastal streams along the Atlantic Seaboard. Then they go to the ocean and enter the parasitic phase. For thousands of years, they could come as far inland as Lake Ontario, but they could not go any further because of

TFM (3-trifluoromethyl-4-nitrophenol) was a chemical compound (lampricide) developed in the 1950s by fisheries scientists funded by the Great Lakes Fishery Commission to control sea lamprey propagation. Still in use today, TFM eliminates this parasite while it is in its larval stage and is one of several measures U.S. Fish and Wildlife Service officials use to keep sea lamprey infestation in the Great Lakes to a minimum. Courtesy of Ludington Biological Station, U.S. Fish and Wildlife Service.

Niagara Falls. Then in the early 1800s, the Welland and Erie Canals were built to provide ships a way around Niagara Falls and ply the upper Great Lakes for the booming lumber and mining industries. And once those canals were built, it allowed ships to come into the upper Great Lakes. The lampreys just swam right along in with the ships. It took a while for lampreys to become established in the Great Lakes. I believe the first sighting was about 1930 in Lake Erie. But by the close of that decade, by 1940 or so, they essentially spread throughout the Great Lakes and were fairly common. By the mid-1950s, they had completely destroyed the lake trout fishery and were working on many other species in the Great Lakes. Essentially the lake trout were extirpated from Lakes Huron and Michigan. Some remnant stocks remained in Lake Superior when the control program first was started and the first stream treatment occurred about 1958 once TFM, the lampricide that we use today, was discovered. From that point on, the lampreys quickly became under control and so we have been doing this kind of work since the late 1950s.

Sea lampreys have a fairly complex life cycle. They spend four or five years developing as immature larvae in the stream. They are harmless in that stage. They do not have any eyes. They do not have the sucker feeding mouth that they have in the parasitic phase. The lamprey burrow in the stream bottom and filter things coming downstream. After they spend four-five years there, they reach a certain size. Then they undergo transformation where they get eyes, and the filter feeding mechanism changes to the parasitic mechanism with all the teeth. The animal leaves the stream, and goes to the Great Lakes to feed on lake trout and salmon for a year or twenty months, depending on whether it comes out in the spring or fall of the year. After that twelve- to twenty-month period, it returns to a stream, spawns, and dies. So a lamprey generation is about seven years total from egg to death. It is during that larval phase of four to five years when they are vulnerable to our control methods. A stream that is infested with lamprey becomes infested every year. For example, Marquette River right here is one that becomes infested every year. A new class of lampreys becomes established each year, but you do not have to go in there and treat it every year because they are sedentary for four to five years. So you can let four to five year classes build up, then you go in and treat the stream and destroy four to five year classes all at once. So streams, on the average, require treatment every three to five years depending on the growth rate, infestation, and things like that.

When our crews are in the field, they are doing a myriad of things. At the Ludington Station, there are basically two units, an assessment unit and a lampricide control unit. Assessment units basically are search and destroy people. They are out with electrofishing gear, conducting surveys on Great Lakes tributaries to determine the extent of infestation of larval sea lampreys and how large the populations are. Our lampricide control unit, on the other hand, is out there actually treating tributaries to the Great Lakes with TFM to destroy larval populations. When they are out in the field, they determine stream discharges and water chemistries, and conduct bioassays. There are a lot of things that they do.

The lampricide control unit is somewhere between ninety-seven and ninety-eight percent effective. In a stream like the Marquette, you will have upwards of a million larvae in the stream. And so even when you leave one or two percent of a big number, that is still enough to continue the life cycle, transform, go out in the lakes, feed on fish, return, spawn, and die. And the average adult female lamprey lays about 80,000 eggs and only a small percentage of those survive. But once they hatch and get into the larval phase, the actual mortality rates are not all that high. They are significant, but they are pretty much home free for the most part because they are unavailable to other fish in the stream as food. The most vulnerable period of life is when they transform, and from the time that they transform to their first feeding in the lake. They have fairly high survivability. There are enough that survive treatments to continue the whole process.

———

Ralph Hay of the Michigan DNR's Division of Fisheries explained how the Great Lakes Fishery Commission works through the U.S. Fish and Wildlife Service to aid the state's fishery program.[49]

The Great Lakes Fishery Commission adopted a policy to control sea lamprey through the use of TFM chemical treatment as the primary method of control. It is still a major method of sea lamprey control. In the late 1950s lampricides were developed which would kill the young sea lamprey larvae while they were still in the stream bed. All the Great Lake states and the province of Ontario have pooled their resources together and have selected the U.S. Fish and Wildlife Service to control the

Ralph Hay's involvement with the DNR began in 1968 when he was a student at Michigan State University. Since that time, he has worked for the Michigan DNR Division of Fisheries in various capacities, principally in areas involving fish propagation. Interview 26 May 1999. Photograph courtesy of the Great Lakes Center for Maritime Studies.

sea lamprey. So on the one hand we wanted to control the sea lamprey population. The best way to do that was through chemical treatment on those streams that were identified as producing large numbers of lamprey. On the other side, we needed to rehabilitate the lake trout population and so that was done through large stocking programs of lake trout and the lake trout that we got were from different sources. Some were from Lake Superior, and others were from some large inland lakes in Michigan and Wisconsin that had native populations. So on the one hand we were controlling the parasite and on the other hand, we were trying to reestablish the species lake trout through a massive stocking program.

Today there is a continual program of sea lamprey control with chemicals, but we are looking at other means of controlling sea lamprey such as sterilization of males through radiation and physical barriers that prevent the adults from migrating upstream to spawn, and electrical barriers. We have kind of shied away from the electrical barriers now because of some health concerns and safety issues. More emphasis is being placed on physical barriers and sterilization because of the cost and source of TFM. We have one sole producer of it in Europe and it is very expensive. A reduction in the use of TFM is also sought by people who are concerned from the environmental point of view about the use of chemicals.

Lamprey control is strictly a function of the U.S. Fish and Wildlife Service. That is where the expertise lies and that is where their funding is. Their staff has identified all of the streams that are major producers of sea lamprey larvae. Michigan DNR staff is not involved in the actual work on lamprey control. We do talk to the U.S. Fish and Wildlife staff and we do some fine tune coordinating as to when we want treatments done in select streams. We do not want them to treat a stream when we have large fish runs in particular streams.

Dennis Lavis of the U.S. Fish and Wildlife Service's Ludington Research Station discussed the various forms of sea lamprey control used by the agency. At the outset of the sea lamprey control program, there was a great deal of trial and error.

TFM, or trifluoromethyl-nitrophenal, is a compound. Back in the 1950s, scientists looked at about 6,000 different compounds and discovered that TFM was extremely toxic to larval sea lampreys as they reside in stream beds, but its toxicity on higher vertebrate fish was not nearly as great. Lampreys die when exposed to TFM in very low concentrations. A lamprey might need a part per million TFM to die; a brown trout or a rainbow trout might need twenty-five parts per million before they would start to show effects. So there is a wide working range that provides the selectivity so that we can continue to remove larval lampreys.

I do not believe TFM has any other purpose. Where it came from, I am unclear. It was just a compound they discovered. It has not been used for anything else since then. I know we are the world's only user of it. The TFM is metered in over about a twelve-hour period, and then it starts to move downstream in a block or a bank. The trick, if you will, is to expose larval lampreys to a minimum lethal concentration for about nine hours. As soon as you start putting it in the stream, it begins to break down. It breaks down under sunlight and is constantly diluted by small springs. We account for major tributaries that commune into the mainstream of a system, and add chemical as this block of TFM moves downstream. You are constantly adding more just to maintain the concentrations you need. It rapidly breaks down. Once that twelve-hour block passes by, it is not detectable. If you were able to freeze it in time, it would break down and go away within twenty-four hours roughly to nondetectable forms.

That is why we have been able to do this for fifty years, and not fill the Great Lakes full of TFM.

We try to supplement lampricide control by trapping the returning adult spawning phase lamprey after they have done their damage out there in the lake. We destroy the female lampreys. We cart the male lampreys over to our sterilization facility on Lake Huron near Roger City. There we sterilize the male lampreys and then turn them loose. All of them right now are going into the St. Mary's River to actually reduce the reproductive capacity of that system. We also install low head barriers in some select streams that keep lampreys from reaching spawning grounds or minimizing the amount of habitat that larval lampreys can inhabit as a means to supplement this lampricide control. But once they transform, leave the stream, there is really nothing you can do with them until they come back to spawn and die and, of course, by that time they have done the damage. So it is either get them in the larval phase or reduce the number that are producing during those subsequent matings several years later.

The St. Mary's River has always been one of our major thorns. It is a large river system that connects Lake Superior to Lake Huron. The St. Mary's River drains Lake Superior essentially, and has a vast area of larval habitat. The river system is too big to treat conventionally with TFM. It would take our whole budget to buy just the lampricide, and it would not be effective anyway. We have learned a lot over the last few years. We are starting to attack the problem. But we need help from our partners to do it. We put the word out, and get assistance from other federal and state agencies. That is one of the ways that we have worked together out there on the ground.

The technology has come a long way in the last decade. The advent of global positioning systems, GIS computer technology, and our own deep-water sampling gear has improved our ability to locate larval lampreys. Our traditional means to sample for larval lampreys is backpack electrofishing gear. It works great in shallow, wadeable waters. But as soon as you get in waters that you cannot wade anymore, it is ineffective. We developed new deep-water sampling techniques that use electrofishing and a suction pump so we can energize a bell on the bottom twenty feet down. The lampreys come squiggling out of the bottom, and they get sucked up and brought up to the surface where they can be enumerated and things like that.

That technology, coupled with GPS and GIS, have allowed us to completely map the St. Mary's River in terms of larval infestation and densities. We know exactly where they are. The lampreys are patchy in their distribution because they favor some types of habitat and not other types of habitat. We have been able to tell where all these clumps are and we have another lampricide that is a granular formation. It kind of looks like fertilizer. The lampricide is coated in a sand grain and then it is encapsulated with a time-release coating like you have on a contact. You can broadcast the lampricide out over the surface of the water and target the high-density areas with this granular formation. It spreads out over the water and sinks to the bottom. The coating dissolves, and the lampricide comes off the sand grain, sets up a toxic layer a couple, three inches off the bottom, and destroys the lampreys right there on the bottom.

We had a helicopter that applies the stuff. We started that work last year. We are going to continue it this year. We are going to treat about 2,000 acres aerially. We are going to be able to reduce the contribution of sea lamprey from the St. Mary's River to Lake Huron a projected eighty-five percent. We have also increased our capability to trap returning adults in the rivers, so we are taking as many adults out of the river as possible. We are returning all of our sterilized males to the St. Mary's River. So we are putting about somewhere between 17,000 and 24,000 sterilized males into the system every year to kind of overwhelm that system and to keep the recruitment down. So once we knock the larval population down, and continue down this road of sterilized males and increased trapping, we are confident that it is going to significantly reduce contribution to the St. Mary's River. We may never have to go back in there and use granular lampricide again.

In the case of the sterilized male program, there is a point of diminishing returns. The fewer lampreys that are out there, the fewer you have to sterilize. We are now doing research on bringing Atlantic-run male lampreys into the Great Lakes and using them in the sterile male program. And there are lots of things to overcome. We have to make sure that they are disease- free. You do not want to bring something into the Great Lakes that is going to wreak havoc even though that is where the lamprey originally came from. The Atlantic males are about twice as big as Great Lakes lampreys. Are these big male lampreys going to overpower the poor little female Great Lakes lampreys? Maybe they will not be as competitive or maybe they will be too competitive. There is work being done to determine whether that difference in size is a function of the environment, or is there some genetic thing there? If an Atlantic-run male lamprey was not sterilized 100 percent and they produced lamprey, would it make for a larger Great

Lakes lamprey? There are a lot of things that need to be done and once again, it hinges on some dollars.

At the very onset of the program they were grasping at anything they could to control the lamprey populations. And, of course, the first thing they did was try the tried-and- true traditional means of trapping aquatic animals in streams with mechanical weirs and barriers, traps if you will. They did not work. They flooded and washed out. Then they turned to electricity, and put electrical weirs in with direct current fields and alternating current fields. They worked real well as long as the water levels stayed stable and did not come up. As soon as the water levels came up, they would wash out the barriers and the lampreys would swim around them. There was no evidence that either of those two methods were having a dent on returning lampreys or lamprey populations in the Great Lakes. So you could classify those as failures, if you will, but it is more like a learning experience. They did not work, essentially. When TFM was discovered, that worked. TFM has had its ups and downs initially. They knew it killed lampreys. They had an idea of how much TFM was needed to kill lampreys, but they did not have a real good idea on how to do this. Your fishery textbooks on river systems say you cannot treat flowing waters. The old guys in the program, the initiators, were determined to prove that wrong.

There were some significant fish kills in the early days of the program, when they would put TFM in, but they could not control it. And we pay for those failures today, because people have long memories. The people who live on rivers have extremely long memories and they can remember back in the early 1960s, when they came to treat this stream the first time. They killed lampreys, but they also killed thousands of suckers or something else. And so you live that down to this day. But all of that has evolved into a science that is extremely precise and accurate today. We go through the whole field season, and you could probably count on all hands and have some fingers left the number of nontarget organisms you can observe. These types of failures, if you will, are all part of learning things, part of the evolution of this program. In fact, we are returning to electrical devices as barriers today because again, the advent of technology has allowed electronic components to evolve to a point where we can now build a gradient field electric barrier, and a pulse direct current barrier that lampreys cannot get through. Unfortunately, fish cannot get through them either. But we also are applying technology to make fish ways around these. So we are coming back to an electrical device to block lampreys, but now we also know how to trap lampreys. Back in the early days of electrical, they really did not know how to trap lampreys either. All that in combination will make a very efficient device.

The Great Lakes Fishery Commission has focused on the restoration of self-sustaining populations of lake trout as one of two major issues of concern since it was created by the United States and Canada in 1955. Despite nearly a half century of efforts, the lake trout population still is not self-sustaining except in Lake Superior. Critics of the lake trout program have charged that the Great Lakes Fishery Commission refuses to admit there is no returning to the days when the lake trout was the top predator fish in Lake Michigan. Stan Smith, formerly of the U.S. Fish and Wildlife Service, recalled how the research vessel *Cisco* was used in 1953 to gather data in Lake Superior for the restocking of lake trout.

M uch of my early research work evolved into close association with the research vessel *Cisco*, when the U.S. Fish and Wildlife Service got this big lump of money, and they needed a research vessel. It was one of the biggest commitments of the first increase in the budget for fiscal year 1950. The money was received in September of 1949, and the vessel was built. The first year the *Cisco* was built, the funding for its operation was greatly reduced. It would not have been operated at all if it were not for a geologist named Dr. Jack Huff from the University of Illinois. Jack Huff had a grant to study the sediments in Lake Michigan. His grant financed a two-week cruise in Lake Michigan. A fellow named Bill Glidden who was responsible for collecting data on Lake Erie, and I served as biologist on the *Cisco*. The next year, the funds still were not increased for the vessel as the major emphasis was on trying to find a way to control the sea lamprey. The vessel could not operate at full time, so it was used primarily in Green Bay to primarily collect information on the lake herring of Green Bay, which I used for my thesis. We made exploratory runs into Lake Michigan and Lake Huron to test equipment and for data collection.

The *Cisco* was built by a naval architect who built Great Lakes fish tugs, but he never built a research vessel. He did not know about trawling or an oceanographic boat. We got this vessel and nobody knew what to do with the equipment. We tried to figure out how to work it, and that effort really did not turn out very well. We had all this oceano-graphic equipment that had been ordered out of a catalog, but nobody knew how to work it. The U.S. Fish and Wildlife Service sent me to the Gulf of Mexico to go on a cruise on the research vessel Alaska, which was under the Galveston laboratory of the Fish and Wildlife Service. I learned how to operate oceanographic instruments and collect and record oceanographic data. We got that down pat and came back. We knew how to operate the gill-net lifter because it was characteristic of the Great Lakes. We wanted to do some trawling. They rigged up some trawling drums and gear on the boat and we tried to trawl, but nobody knew how to trawl. We could not figure it out and it did not seem to work right. So they sent me to Gloucester, Massachusetts, to spend some time on the in-shore commercial trawling boats which were similar size to the *Cisco*. I learned about the trawls—the gear that you need, the rigging, and the actual procedure you go through to do trawling. I came back and started working on Green Bay in 1952 and we worked on the methodology for doing the oceanographic work and the fishing work on the *Cisco*. It was a very interesting period. It was not built right to begin with so we had to rebuild a lot of the rigging on the boat so that it could handle trawls.

The *Siscowet* was originally a fishing boat called the *Iva May*. It was originally assigned to the U.S. Fish and Wildlife Service's Marquette station for biological research on fish, but when the sea lamprey program received more emphasis, they turned the operation at Marquette into a sea lamprey program.[50] Subsequently, in the late 1950s, we opened up a field station in Ashland, Wisconsin. It became the headquarters for biological research on Lake Superior. They had the *Iva May*, but it was completely inadequate for that type of work. We could not get money to build a new boat. There was a freeze on building, but we could remodel boats. So we took the *Iva May* and we cut it off at the water line at the Peterson Shipbuilding Company in Green Bay. We built a vessel on top of the hull of the *Iva May* that was designed by a naval architect at the University of Michigan, a student named Finn Nicholson, and renamed it *Siscowet* and used it for research at Ashland.

The *Cisco* was used for the first year of fishery research on Lake Superior. This was open-lake research. Before the Ashland station was formed, the *Cisco* went to Lake Superior. We spent a whole year in Lake Superior in 1953 studying the lake trout. We had very little information about juvenile lake trout. This information was needed because we were building hatcheries to restore the lake trout once the sea lamprey was under control. Paul Eschmeyer directed the research on the early life of the lake trout in Lake Superior in 1953. Paul Eschmeyer was another University of Michigan graduate who they brought back when they got the budgetary increase in 1950. He was in charge of finding as much as possible about the lake trout, both in Lake Superior and what was left of the lake trout in Lake Michigan. In Lake Michigan he contracted with a number of commercial fishermen to gather small lake trout. There were no large lake trout left. The only lake trout left were the ones too small for the sea lamprey to feed on.[51]

All of the large lake trout were gone because the sea lamprey needs a large fish to feed on. It attaches itself to the fish and sucks the blood from the fish as it rides with the fish. The fish have to be big enough to carry the sea lamprey. If it is a small fish, the sea lamprey and the fish would fall to the bottom. There were still juvenile lake trout left, but none old enough to reproduce, so there were no very small lake trout, no lake trout fry in Lake Michigan. Under the direction of Paul Eschmeyer, we gathered information in Lake Michigan by riding the commercial chub boats that caught lake trout incidental to their chub catch. We had to ride the boats because some commercial fishermen seemed to feel guilty about catching the lake trout and they did not want people to know that they caught a lake trout. We rode the boats, and were right there watching the lake trout come up out of the water. We took scales and measurements from the lake trout and recorded information like the depth and where it was caught and so on and so forth. We would occasionally catch a commercial fisherman trying to shake a lake trout off in the water before we saw it.

Carlos Fetterolf, formerly of the Great Lakes Fishery Commission, recalled the difficulties federal fisheries officials have encountered in their attempts to restore a naturally sustaining lake trout population.

The Great Lakes Fishery Commission was confident that its efforts in sea lamprey control were adequate to protect the fish and the fisheries, so that there were sustainable fisheries coming along. Once they were able to say yes, we have adequate control, they were concerned the fish populations were not adequately protected. What the Commission wanted was to get self-sustaining populations of lake trout and whitefish back. Those were the species that were very important in pre-lamprey times. Lake trout and whitefish were the species they wanted to put the effort into. The whitefish came back to historically high levels in Lake Michigan. The lake trout reproduction is still hampered. One popular belief is that contaminants are the reason, but no one has really been able to prove that it was contaminants. The lake trout population is self-reproducing in Lake Superior and there is some reproduction in Lake Huron. Unfortunately, at this time there is no lake trout reproduction in Lake Michigan.

During the time of the alewife die-offs, the Great Lakes Fishery Commission was working with the U.S. Fish and Wildlife Service to restock lake trout. The U.S. Fish and Wildlife Service established the Jordan River hatchery for lake trout. No one knew how to raise lake trout. This was a new species and it was a tremendous problem. At first, the lenses of their eyes popped out because the trout were exposed to too much light. No one knew this before. Then they started building covers over the raceways to give the fish some shade. Gradually we found out that it took a hell of a long time to raise lake trout and it was an expensive proposition. You put them in the lake and they grow very slowly. It takes seven years or so for males to reach a reproductive stage. It might take seven, eight, nine, ten years for a female lake trout to reach her reproductive stage. Instead, you could raise salmon by the zillions, put them in the lakes, and get a great return to the rod.

Along towards the end of the 1970s Wisconsin figured—and I have not got these numbers exactly right—if you stocked a pound of brook trout fingerlings you would get back a pound and a half to the rod. If you stocked a pound of steelhead, you got back five pounds. If you stocked a pound of brown trout, you got back ten pounds. If you stocked coho salmon, you got back twenty-five pounds and if you stocked a pound of chinook salmon, you got back 200 pounds. Now what do you stock? Then there was a real and very logical argument that you cannot stock chinook salmon only. You cannot just stock lake trout. You cannot just stock one species of fish. You have got to have a community of fish that you are working with because if disease attacks one species, it will drop out. Suppose that was your main species? What takes its place? We have had diseases in Lake Michigan that have severely impacted the recreational fishery. If that recreational fishery was entirely dependent on chinook salmon and there was a disease of chinook salmon, then that is really going to hurt so there must always be a fallback position. You could fall back to lake trout. You could fall back to coho or silver salmon.

554

———————

Dennis Lavis, a fisheries biologist who supervises the U.S. Fish and Wildlife Service's Ludington Research Station, speculated on possible reasons that the lake trout program has been far more successful in Lake Superior than the other Great Lakes.

The sea lamprey control program allowed Lake Superior to basically revert back to a wild lake trout population. Wild lake trout now account for upwards of the high ninety percent of all lake trout in Lake Superior. So a few years ago, the Great Lakes Fishery Commission and the Fish and Wildlife Service and all the agencies involved with management of Lake Superior declared Lake Superior rehabilitated. The impact of lampreys is basically minimal in Lake Superior. In the other Great Lakes, they are still stocking lots of fish. It is estimated that lampreys probably still take as many trout and salmon as fishermen do every year in most of the other lakes. There are other things going on in Lakes Huron, Michigan, and Ontario and the far eastern end of Lake Erie that preclude self-sustaining stocks of lake trout. There is a lot of controversy as to why they are not reproducing like they are in Lake Superior. Even though the stocking has been going on for thirty to forty years and there are large numbers of lake trout, they are not reproducing. Opinions range everywhere from changes in habitat in the lakes to contaminant levels in the fish and lots of different things.

I guess I subscribe to all of those camps. Lake Superior is still pretty much the way it was when lampreys decimated lake trout. There have not been a lot of ecological changes in Lake Superior, not only from a physical standpoint in terms of the lake and the quality of water, but also in terms of the fish community and the other parts of the aquatic community. Exotic fish and the other things they have stocked are but a small percentage of what is in Lake Superior. The non-native stocks are not reproducing well. The lower lakes are kind of a big fishpond. There are a lot of non-native fishes in the lower lakes. The whole ecological status of the lakes is not anything like it was when the lake trout were the only predator in the lake, before the lampreys. Now we are trying to introduce the native predator back with lots of other predators. Who knows what all those linkages are? Ecology is a lot more complex than rocket science. You bring two compounds together, create an explosion, and the rocket goes up. When you have all these linkages out here, you do not know what is causing what not to work.

Retired in 1972 from the U.S. Fish and Wildlife Service, Dr. Stanford Smith recalled how the agency hired two University of Michigan graduates who had formerly been employed by the State of Michigan for key roles in sea lamprey control and lake trout restoration.

Dr. Vernon Applegate worked for the State of Michigan until about 1949. He and Dr. Paul Eschmeyer worked for the State of Michigan at the Institute for Fishery Research while they were students getting Ph.D. degrees at the University of Michigan. Paul Eschmeyer went to Missouri to work after he got his degree in 1949. I cannot recall where Vernon Applegate went. But they were both brought back to Michigan. Vernon Applegate was put in charge of the sea lamprey research in Hammond Bay under the direction of the Great Lakes Fishery Investigation's. Eschmeyer operated from the Ann Arbor laboratory. He was interested in lake trout wherever they were, and at that time, there were only two places in Lake Superior and Lake Michigan. They were completely gone on the U.S. side of Lake Huron. There were still some lake trout in Georgian Bay, on the north side of Lake Huron. They were the subject of work by Dr. Fred Fry of the University of Toronto. They had a field station at South Bay on Manitou Island. They did laboratory work at the university on lake trout pressurization to determine what happens to lake trout at different depths and the depths they prefer. They put them in a vertical pressurized tank trying to learn as much as possible about the biology of the lake trout. Nobody knew anything about lake trout, and the information was needed to use in the rehabilitation process.

Where do we put the young lake trout of various sizes, where do they physically occur in the lake? We found out where three-inch lake trout were in the lake. We knew that they occurred in certain areas on the lake, so boats were built that would carry them out and release them at those depths on those areas. But it turned out that lake trout were homing like salmon are. The lake trout will spawn on a reef, lay its eggs on a reef, and the eggs will hatch and the young will move steadily out to deeper water. Then when the lake trout mature, they will come back to that very same reef where they hatched to spawn. But if we took juvenile salmon from a hatchery and planted them out in the lake in the region where we found fish of their size, they would not know

Ron Poff spent a total of 41 years working in different positions in fisheries management for the Wisconsin DNR. He retired in 1998 as chief of Fisheries. Interview 9 June 1999. Photograph by Matthew Anderson.

where the spawn reefs were. All they knew was to go back to the place where they were planted. So they did not show up on the spawning grounds. Experiments were conducted where eggs were placed on the lake trout reef in cages and mats, so the eggs would hatch where they would normally if the lake trout had laid them there. Once the fry develop, they would move into deep water. Then they would come back to that reef to spawn as the adults. And that is a long-term operation because it takes quite a few years for a lake trout to become mature.

Retired Wisconsin DNR official Ron Poff spoke of sport fishers' opposition to the creation of trout refuges in Wisconsin's Lake Superior waters.

The lake trout are still pretty much stocked populations in Lake Michigan. In Lake Superior, at Gull Island and Devil Island shoals, we have native lake trout. They never lost the native stocks up on Lake Superior like they did on Lake Michigan. There is natural reproduction on Lake Superior in Wisconsin waters. A lot of people did not understand the nature of these fish populations. When we first created trout refuges on Lake Superior, we held public hearings. Our rationale for creating the refuges was that we were losing the large lake trout spawning stock, and we were concerned about it, so we wanted to create a spawning refuge. And a charter boat operator out of Cornucopia got up and said this was one of the reefs he was fishing and we were going to put him out of business. He said, "Last year alone, I harvested 500 large lake trout off of that reef." And I just chuckled and I said, "Well, why the hell do you think we are making this refuge? You are a good reason. Those stocks are not that abundant." The guy just did not understand. Sure, we are putting him out of business, but he would be out of business anyway if he continued that kind of harvest, and that was exactly what we were trying to protect from.

———————

Reflecting on his more than thirty years with the Wisconsin DNR, Jim Moore observed that of all the commercial and sport fisheries issues he has addressed, the most challenging issue or project was lake trout restoration.

When the *Barney Devine* was acquired by the Wisconsin DNR, they believed it would be only a matter of time before the lake trout would be naturally reproducing. As the population increased we would use the boat for setting our own research nets and looking for spawning areas. Despite all we did, the lake trout did not reproduce. We have gotten a lot of data over the years to try and answer questions why they have not reproduced. It was anticipated that with the stocking of lake trout and other trout and salmon species, the program would get bigger and bigger and it did.

It has been frustrating trying to figure out why the lake trout do not reproduce naturally. It has been over thirty years. In some respects we are still struggling trying to pinpoint the exact reasons why lake trout have not reproduced. That has probably been the biggest ongoing struggle and challenge. All lake trout are raised by Fish and Wildlife Service in federal hatcheries and stocked with state coordination. There is pretty much unanimous agreement on the management goals of stocking lake trout between all the states on Lake Michigan. There is in effect a partnership arrangement concerning lake trout management. It is to the point where a lot of people are questioning why we continue stocking so many, especially when there are questions about forage availability and it is expensive. Why not cut back the numbers, and just go to a put-and-take fishery? These are all legitimate questions that as a working group, the states have to address. Next year there is going to be a State of the Lake report prepared by all the management agencies for Lake Michigan. I am sure some of those questions will be raised by the public, so we will have to be prepared to give some progress reports and recommendations on what to do in the future regarding lake trout as well as all the other species.

The emphasis on lake trout goes back to the convention between the United States and Canada to establish the Great Lakes Fishery Commission, which was established primarily to gain control over the sea lamprey. Early on, it was decided that the number one goal should be to try and reestablish lake trout in Lake Michigan because there was such a historical native lake trout commercial fishery over the years with production reaching 5–6 million pounds annually at times. So from the get-go, the federal government and Canada were going to underwrite and fund sea lamprey control and raise lake trout for restocking into Lake Michigan and all the Great Lakes. So that was outlined in the language that set up the Great Lakes Fishery Commission and still continues to be some of the things that drive a lot of the programs on the Great Lakes.

More and more evidence and information suggests that lake trout and other trout and salmon species raised in the hatchery system are affected by the interactions between thiaminase and thiamine. And it has been pretty well documented that alewives and other species have a high level of thiaminase. I think chubs and smelt also fairly compare to other species with high levels of thiaminase. I suspect as long as we have got forage levels that are very high in thiaminase, the thiamine levels in lake trout and some of our other salmon species are not going to allow large-scale natural reproduction in Lake Michigan. When we see problems developing in some of the fish that we are rearing in hatcheries, it is just amazing that by treating them with thiamine, they snap out of it almost immediately. So this is my own personal opinion that to me we probably should have recognized this thirty years ago when mink farmers were feeding their mink large quantities of alewives and it was recognized at that time that thiaminase was causing severe reproductive problems in mink. So we had a lot of early clues we probably should have followed and looked at it a lot closer than we did. Again, that is my own personal opinion based not on a lot of conclusive factual data to date, but we will see.

John McKinney is a Michigan Sea Grant agent in the Traverse City area. He has worked as a commercial fisherman both in the United States and Ireland. Interview, 28 May 1999. Photograph by Michael J. Chiarappa.

Michigan Sea Grant agent John McKinney discussed the politics of the lake trout restoration program.

There is always politics certainly, probably of necessity. There is a range of opinion of what is the best way to manage the fishery, if you assume it is going to be a managed fishery. It comes from the guys down here clear up through the government, where the EPA is trying to mandate these lakewide management plans which include the fishery component. It has been politically manipulated, but originally, the plan talked about returning Lake Michigan to its natural state from a fishery standpoint. Define natural state. When? Where? It is an impossible thing; we are not talking about something that is doable here. We cannot really do this, but there are many efforts to do that. Lake trout is part of the classic example. For twenty-five to thirty years the federal government has been pumping a lot of money into the hatcheries to plant lake trout out there to restore a fish that is maybe never going to be restored. However, in Lake Superior, they just declared that it is now self-reproducing. They have said that

Lake Superior now can reproduce itself in lake trout. So it has been done. They claim this is a success, although that was the place they were going to succeed if anybody ever succeeded getting lake trout back. Lake Michigan is not that far along. Lake Superior has fewer problems. It was more likely that they would be able to succeed up there, although that is not their ideal arrangement. These are the better lakes for it, but there is so much else going on, much more competition, more human impact, they are preventing the fruition.

The lake trout are seen as a federal resource in the sense that it is a multistate and international issue. I do not know if I can describe why politically that has been done, but lake trout was a U.S. Fish and Wildlife Service issue long before I was around. The Fish and Wildlife Service controls the lamprey research and control process. The lamprey was the main, one of the main causes for the decline of lake trout, so there is a parallel there. They are both Fish and Wildlife Service issues that are part of a federal mandate.

Mike Toneys of the Wisconsin DNR, discussed political perceptions of the lake trout program in Wisconsin.

The lake trout restoration program pervades almost everything else we do on Lake Michigan. It is one of the major restoration efforts we have going. It is something that people have been involved in for thirty years, and the frustration level is incredibly high among people like Jim Moore and I who are, and have been, real close to the project. It is a contentious issue with the sport-fishing public because they see us pouring a lot of money into what seems like a dead-end project in species. They would just as soon see that money spent on things like chinook, fun fish to catch. The program has been a bane for commercial fishermen because of the incidental kill problem. It is our responsibility to try and reduce the amount of mortality on lake trout, so we can keep enough out there to mature and hopefully successfully reproduce. So it essentially pervades everything we do out here. It has been the reason for a lot of the sport and commercial regulations we have put into effect over the years. It has raised issues with other agencies around Lake Michigan with regard to our continuing to allow gill nets in the commercial fishery because of the incidental kill problem in those nets, especially with lake trout.

Mike Toneys is a fisheries biologist and Lake Michigan Sub-team Leader for the Division of Fisheries of the Wisconsin DNR. He graduated from the University of Wisconsin with a Bachelor of Science degree and completed a Master of Science degree in fisheries science at the University of Wisconsin at Stevens Point. Interview, with his colleague Jim Moore, 1 and 2 June 1999. Photograph by Michael J. Chiarappa.

Of all the projects we have worked on, I think lake trout has probably given Jim Moore and I more gray hairs over the years than anything else for a number of reasons. We still believe it is a worthwhile project, but it is frustrating as to why things have not happened. It is possible Lake Michigan has changed too much. Lake trout seem to thrive in a simple environment, a simple community, and we do not have that out there anymore and probably never will because of all the exotic species that we know about, and some that we do not even know about. I am not sure that lake trout are ever going to be back to a sustainable status throughout the lake. We might find pockets here and there, such as the southern midlake refuge and the northern refuge, where we have pinned a lot of our hopes. Historically, they were productive areas, and we are thinking that if anything is going to happen, that is where it is going to happen. Maybe that is the only place we can hope for it to happen. And if anything is going to happen in the southern refuge, we are probably on the brink of it now. We have a fantastically large, diverse population of mature fish out there that should be doing something right now. For whatever reason it is just not happening.

For some individuals, lake trout restoration is almost a religious experience. They have been at it a long time and firmly believe that what we as managers and biologists should do everything we can to return Lake Michigan to an earlier state. And that earlier state had lake trout as the top predator out there. Most of those same people believe that if we were to have a more stable system out there, it is probably the predator best adapted to Lake Michigan and, therefore, that is where we ought to be putting our efforts, not into things like Pacific salmon, for instance. There are some of us who believe that as well, but also believe there is room for other species out there. We have got naturalized species like the Pacific salmon that are reproducing very well in streams over in Michigan, and are probably responsible for a fair amount of the fishable biomass of Lake Michigan. Jim Moore and I are more pragmatic. We think there is room for things other than lake trout. Considering the changes that have occurred both biologically and culturally, what are you going to return Lake Michigan back to? I am not sure how much energy we should put into trying to return the lake to some earlier state. I am not sure it is possible anymore.

In some ways, maybe it is a romanticized vision that some hold more dear than others. Fish and Wildlife Service have lake trout as a trust species, and they are firmly committed to trying whatever it takes. The federal government has a unique responsibility to protect and encourage lake trout as a trust species because it is an endangered or threatened native species like the sturgeon. I do not know where the end point is located, when they would finally give up whatever it takes to reestablish lake trout in Lake Michigan. State agencies around the lake are a little bit more pragmatic, and are working with the federal agencies as well as the Native American tribes to try and restore lake trout to some sustainable status out there. You are not going to have lake trout on a lakewide basis like we used to have because things have changed so much. I do not know if Jim Moore and I are at one extreme and the federal agencies and maybe some of the university people are at the other extreme. Everybody else in the middle has different agendas perhaps, but most are committed to seeing this lake trout experiment through.

Retired fishery biologist Stan Smith of the U.S. Fish and Wildlife Service recalled the concern about how the stocking of salmon would affect the lake trout restoration program.

On the other side of Lake Michigan and Lake Huron from Michigan, the goal of sea lamprey control was to bring back the lake trout. The Canadians still had that goal for the east side of Lake Huron, and there was quite a bit of negotiation between them and the State of Michigan about planting salmon in Lake Huron. Salmon in Lake Huron was contrary to their goal of having the lake trout the predominant fish species in the lake. It was quite a political football at that time.

The lake trout would have been a good sport fish, but lake trout do not catch like salmon. The lake trout fed on chubs primarily and sculpins, which live on the bottom of the lake and are widely scattered. The lake trout grew very slowly because they had to go from here to there to find a fish to eat. The alewife and the smelt were the first species in the Great Lakes that were schooling fish. A species like the Pacific salmon that is accustomed to feeding on schooling fish, lock into a school of fish, and then they just go chomp, chomp, chomp, chomp, chomp. They grew very rapidly, and were easier to catch by sport fishermen. The lake trout are widely scattered and the salmon are more concentrated. You can take a boat out and find the Pacific salmon a lot easier than you could find the lake trout. And that is probably why there was not much lake trout fishing in the lake. They were more difficult to catch. But as far as the schooling fish and the lake trout are concerned, the lake trout growth increased sharply in the presence of schooling fish. When we got lake trout back into the lake after the sea lamprey control, they benefited from the schooling fish, the smelt and the alewife.

Hatchery-stocked lake trout were used to try to rehabilitate the species in the Great Lakes. There probably were not any schooling fish in the Great Lakes initially. Back during the glacial periods when the Great Lakes were opened and then shut off from the ocean, there were not any schooling fish in Lake Ontario below the Niagara Falls and the St. Lawrence River. In a closed system, apparently you do not have schooling fish because a predator like a lake trout or the Atlantic salmon in Lake Ontario would eat all of the schooling fish, and they would disappear. Schooling fish are too vulnerable to being eaten. So if we want to get rid of the alewife and the smelt in the Great Lakes all we have to do is introduce lots of large predators or let nature take its course. And that is what happened in the planting and the stocking of lake trout and stocking of salmon; they planted enough that they depleted the smelt and the alewife.

The decision made by the Michigan Department of Conservation in 1966 to stock its Great Lakes waters with salmon was, in the view of most "Fish for All" project participants, the major demarcation point in the history of fisheries policy. Salmon were stocked in the Great Lakes waters of Michigan at a time when the state was losing manufacturing jobs and seeking ways to foster economic growth through tourism.[52] The devastation of lake trout and whitefish populations by the sea lamprey during the 1940s and 1950s and the alewife population explosion of the late 1960s suggested that the harvest of commercial stocks of Great Lakes fisheries had come to an end. The Michigan Department of Conservation seized upon the environmental crisis and turned it into an opportunity to reorient the Great Lakes toward greater recreational and leisure use. Senior staff member and fisheries scientist Dr. Howard Tanner was given the power to decide to stock the Great Lakes with salmon. Tanner and his successor, Dr. Wayne Tody, foresaw a day when thousands of Chicago and Milwaukee area sportsmen would regard the Great Lakes, and Lake Michigan in particular, as a sports-fishing haven right in their own backyard.[53]

The Michigan Department of Conservation altered the ecosystem of the one of the world's largest resources of freshwater without holding public meetings and hearings, conducting exhaustive scientific studies, and writing environmental impact statements. As Howard Tanner acknowledges below, the views of fisheries officials representing the American Indian tribes who claimed treaty fishing rights, the United States, Canada, and the other Great Lakes states were not seriously considered. More important, the Department of Conservation used its political power to overcome opposition such as that from Fenton Carbine of the U.S. Fish and Wildlife Service.[54] The exclusionary process employed by the Michigan Department of Conservation would, as Tanner observed, ultimately create numerous problems with both commercial and treaty fishing interests. The state's hard-nosed policy practically forced American Indians who claimed treaty fishing rights to take legal action and become more politically active.

Stanford Smith recalled that prior to Michigan's decision to plant Pacific salmon in the Great Lakes in the 1960s, earlier efforts had been made to establish the species in the lakes.

Back in the old Bureau of Commercial Fisheries days, they introduced fish all over the United States just sort of willy-nilly. They brought the German carp into the United States only to have it become a nuisance fish. This recent introduction of salmon was not the first introduction of salmon on the Great Lakes. They tried to establish the salmon in the Great Lakes in the late 1800s and early 1900s, and they would not take. The early introductions of the salmon in Lake Michigan did not reproduce very well. The only salmon that took off on its own in the Great Lakes was the pink salmon in Lake Superior. They brought pink salmon eggs to a hatchery in Thunder Bay to be hatched and then taken up and planted in Hudson Bay or someplace up north. And after the planting was over, the hatchery manager pulled the plug and let the remaining salmon go into Lake Superior, and forgot about them. A few years later, there were pink salmon spawning in Lake Superior tributaries and they took off and reproduced and are there today.

Howard Tanner recalled how the DNR planted kokanee salmon in several inland lakes in 1965, before introducing coho salmon into Lake Michigan the following year. Chinook salmon were introduced in 1967.

When I came back to Michigan from Colorado in September 1964, I came in with a Michigan background but I also had western fishery experience. I belonged to the Pacific Coast Fisheries Biologists Association and had contacts with the Pacific fisheries salmon biologists. Dr. Ralph A. MacMullan, rest his soul, greeted me by saying, "I want you to take charge of this fisheries group you got. I want you to bring them together. I want you to do something very visible and if you can make it spectacular, please do so." That was about as much instruction as I got from Ralph MacMullan. It was a wonderful, wonderful introduction to my job.

The first thing I did was import kokanee salmon to put in certain inland lakes. Kokanee are a land-locked, sock-eye fish that I thought would do very well in a number of inland lakes. So I called up some of the Colorado people I had personal involvement with over the years. They agreed to give us kokanee eggs if we sent a crew to Colorado to help take them. We sent a crew to Colorado on an airplane. They took a million kokanee eggs and brought them back to Michigan.

We got the kokanee eggs in the fall of 1964, and we stocked them in the spring of

1965 in Wilkins Creek, a tributary of Torch Lake, in my home county of Antrim County. Gov. George Romney was there with a golden bucket stocking the fish. We planted the kokanee salmon in Torch Lake and Higgins Lake. Almost nothing came of the effort. We managed them for a little while, took eggs and put them in other lakes and so forth, but whatever impact they had was very insignificant. They are now gone as far as I know; it would be very unlikely if there are any kokanee in Michigan.

About the time we got the kokanee started, I learned that there was a surplus of coho eggs on the West Coast. This was unheard of because for many years the Columbia Basin states agreed not to ship any salmon eggs out of the basin for any reason because there were not enough fish for the hatcheries to get enough eggs to renew the next batch. We started working on coho while I was chief of fisheries research in the state of Colorado. We stocked Granby Reservoir and we had a biologist looking at them. They grew, and people caught them, but the coho were not huge because they did not have a big food supply. The notion that coho salmon could not survive in a totally fresh-water environment was largely a mental barrier. We knew better. Montana had raised coho ten to twenty years before. California had raised coho through a life cycle at their hatcheries. Salmon have to come to freshwater to spawn, but there is no obligatory reason for them to go to saltwater except in search of food. One type of salmon or another had been stocked in the Great Lakes at least thirty-five times that we could document prior to our attempts in 1964 and 1965. The efforts were principally by Ohio and New York in the lakes of Erie and Ontario. There may well have been others. The Bureau of Commercial Fisheries and the U.S. Fish Commission made eggs and fish available upon request. They were stocked as fry and in essence, there were no results. The reason they were all total failures was that there was not enough understanding of life history at that time to make it work.

Everybody wanted to know where I got the idea to stock coho. I did not get the idea. I do not claim to be the originator of the idea. That idea obviously had been around a long time. What I do take credit for was I take the responsibility for doing it. Whenever somebody wants to criticize it, they criticize me. When everybody wants to compliment, they can just as well compliment me, because I took the responsibility. I was allowed to make the decision to stock the coho salmon. Ralph MacMullan could have made the decision, but he allowed me to make it. The Commission could have made the decision, but they allowed me to make it. I took the idea and I sold it.

First of all, I knew how to get the surplus coho eggs on the West Coast. I called ahead of time. I wrote to Oregon and Washington and asked them to send us a million eggs. Both agreed to give us a million coho eggs provided we followed a whole set of directions of how to manage them. We were delighted to take their advice. They told us to stock them in large groups, do not scatter them all over, stock them at a certain size, stock them at a certain time, stock them in this kind of a stream, and feed them on Oregon moist pellet, and so on. We got the eggs beginning in late December of 1964, and January of 1965. Washington was unable to deliver. Some politicians got a hold of what was going on, and they said you cannot do that. Oregon came through with the first million eggs.

Wayne Tody was Michigan's fisheries chief for ten years beginning in 1966. He recalled the early skepticism toward the salmon-stocking program.[55]

At that point in time no one, including some biologists, thought salmon would survive here and thrive. A few of us had faith these saltwater fish would thrive in the Great Lakes. The salmon were part of a plan to rehabilitate the Great Lakes prepared around 1966. The plan did not all work out, but we even set dollars on it, which was kind of brave.

People thought the salmon could not regulate in freshwater, they could not acclimate in freshwater, but they can. They have the same kidney that brown trout and all the other anadromous selmonites have so they can, and we had the proof. Some thought the eggs would not be fertile. Actually, salmon succeeded so damn well, we broke the world's record with a thirty-three-pound coho. It did not count as a world record because it was not sport-caught. Weir-caught fish and commercially caught fish are not eligible for the record, but they offered us the trophy for the world's largest coho from the west coast, because it was a lot bigger than anything ever got in the ocean. Of course like all introductions, the coho had this tremendous peak and then died down.

In the spring of 1967, the coho salmon had been planted the year before. The chinook were planted that spring, but were not of predator size yet. Alewife formed windrows that deep along the Chicago waterfront. They smelled so bad people evacuated residential areas for two or three blocks back from the lake. And our state parks were all unusable clear up to probably Manistee, and even beyond that. People were highly concerned then. There was great pressure on us to get the salmon fish going. There was great pressure on the commercial end to catch the alewife for meal. They had no other value other than chicken and agriculture feed. We stuck to our guns. In the fall there was a coho run that was revolutionary here in terms of sport fishing. Everybody went out with a rowboat and anything else they could to catch an eighteen-pound salmon. They just went wild. I could tell you a lot of stories about guys bringing up fishing rods that they just designed at Shakespeare Company in the back seats of their cars. Then we settled down and we rebuilt all the state hatcheries. We put in egg-taking facilities for the steelhead and the salmon, so we could take millions of eggs and spread them to the other seven Great Lake states and Ontario.

Howard Tanner recalled how his decision to stock coho salmon in Lake Michigan placed the Michigan DNR in conflict with federal officials, such as those from the U.S. Bureau of Commercial Fisheries and later, the U.S. Fish and Wildlife Service.

Supported by Ralph MacMullan and the Fish Commission, the Fish Division decided Michigan needed to manage its share of the Great Lakes. Instead of managing the three percent of the state's waters, which are inland waters, we were going to manage the total area of Michigan waters. We had never managed the vast waters out there that belong to the State of Michigan. We did not have any program and we did not have any research. We immediately came into conflict with the U.S. Bureau of Commercial Fisheries, which was based in Ann Arbor. They had always managed Michigan's Great Lakes waters. They did not manage the lakes intensively, but were oriented towards commercial fishing.

We concluded that the Michigan fishing public had the leisure time and the transportation to travel to have a quality fishing experience. We decided that we were not going to manage the resource for the commercial fishery. We were going to manage for sport fisheries. Now we were really in conflict with the U.S. Bureau of Commercial Fisheries who saw the lakes as their turf. The commercial fishermen were up in arms too.

The resource must be managed for the greatest good for the greatest number for the longest period of time. If you are allowing commercial fishing to harvest fish, say hypothetically at a dollar a pound, and the sport fishermen by their amalgamation of money spent in their effort to catch fish will spend $20 a pound, then the dollar a pound does not make any sense at all. Now in those areas where you cannot demonstrate a demand for sport fishing, commercial fishing is fine. If there is a lack of interest in a certain species or particular area, commercial fishing is fine. But where there is a demand or a higher value, then that is what you should manage for. That is the philosophy, which makes lots of sense to me. Except for the tribal fishing, the commercial fishing that is left can be meshed quite well with the sport fishing. But you cannot have, for example, nonselective gear such as gill nets. Commercial fishermen have to be told what species they can harvest, and they must harvest them with minimal impact on sport fishing. That is the key value concept where you have several uses, but one value is supreme.

When the DNR announced it was going to manage the Great Lakes for sport fishing, we also announced changes for commercial fishing. The first thing we did was introduce limited entry. It used to be that anybody who wanted a commercial license could buy one for twenty-five dollars. We were not going to have an unlimited capitalization of this resource. Commercial fishermen whose income averaged more than $5,000 for the last three years could retain their licenses. Otherwise, their licenses were canceled. That is where the blood, sweat, and tears came from on both sides.

Fenton Carbine, the director of the Bureau of Commercial Fisheries in Ann Arbor, resisted our salmon program. He wrote a famous letter to the governor when the appropriation for $500,000 I secured on a promise to the state legislature that there would be a salmon fishery, had passed the House and the Senate. We had the coho eggs in the hatchery. He wrote the governor and said, this is ludicrous; it is a terrible thing. You must veto this. Romney was governor at the time. His procedure was that when letters came in, somebody on his staff would send them to the relevant department. So they sent the Carbine letter over to Ralph MacMullan's office—what we called the head shed—at the DNR. They sent it down to the Fish Division, so the letter came to me. I had to respond to this federal official who is now meddling in state affairs by asking the governor to veto our appropriation for raising coho. The letter got leaked out. Perhaps about 10,000 copies went all over the state as evidence of what the federal government was trying to do. I responded for the governor. Soon after that, the Bureau of Commercial Fisheries was removed from Ann Arbor and it became a part of the U.S. Fish and

Wildlife Service. Fenton Carbine was sent to Peru, where he worked the rest of his career on anchovies.

—————————

Retired Michigan DNR fisheries chief Wayne Tody recalled that the agency's plans to develop a Great Lakes sport fishery were resisted by the federal agencies such as the Bureau of Commercial Fisheries.

The federal government responded to the alewife by going into the meal plant fishery, a commercial deal with trawls. This is where we begin to get into fights. The Michigan DNR advocated converting the tremendous forage base to high-value fish like lake trout, salmon, coho, chinook, steelhead, or brown trout, because of Lake Michigan's cold, oligotrophic water. The State of Michigan got into a battle then with the Bureau of Commercial Fisheries. Michigan claims ownership of the fish and the bottom. The fish and game belong to the state, and are held in trust for the people in the state. The State of Michigan has ceded wildlife management rights only in a few instances such as national parks like Sleeping Bear Dunes. The federal government was going to enforce the commercial fishery's right to take all the alewife they wanted for the meal plants. They had a big meal plant in Wisconsin, which we did not control. The federal government wanted to build some in Michigan, but we balked.

My director, the head of the Bureau of Commercial Fisheries, and I got together and we finally had it out. The federal representative got a solicitor general's opinion that they had some rights to do what they wanted in U.S. waters. Lake Michigan was not U.S. waters; much of it was Michigan waters. They made the mistake of writing a letter to our governor, George Romney, who said you cannot do that. This happened back in the days of state's rights. The net result of it all was that the Bureau of Commercial Fisheries was kicked out of Michigan, out of the Great Lakes, except for the research and lab things. We became part of the Gloucester region in the east. This all came to a head in 1967, when the great alewife die-off occurred.

We had people from the saltwater come in and volunteer to eliminate the alewife with an underwater suction pump factory ship. They said they could wipe them out in a year. We had to fight them off. We did not fight them off. We told them no deal, but keep your mouth shut. This was after the big die-off of alewife. If they had gone public with the proposal, it would have gone through politically. There was panic. But they were good guys and they did not. The proposal remained in the bottom drawer where it belonged. I do not think they could have done it anyway, but they thought they could because they eliminated the menhaden in the Atlantic Ocean.

Howard Tanner recalled the preparations to begin salmon stocking that took place in 1964 when he was fisheries chief of the Michigan Department of Conservation.

We had the coho eggs in the hatchery in 1965. I was going around the state stumping the sale of the salmon program. Bill Mullendorr was doing a magnificent job of publicizing it. The fish were kept at the Platte River Hatchery for a year and a half, so the first official stocking of coho was on the 2nd of April, 1966. At that time, the Platte River facility was a small rearing station. Now it has grown into a very large hatchery.

The coho were also raised at the Oden hatchery. When we were trying to get the $500,000 appropriation for the salmon program through the legislature, Sen. Joe Mack from the Upper Peninsula, an infamous character, was chairman of the Senate Appropriations Committee. He said you can get your $500,000 through my committee provided you stock some fish in Lake Superior in my district. So 150,000 fish were stocked in the big Huron River, a tributary to Lake Superior, and the other 650,000, which were the survivors of the original one million eggs, were stocked in Platte River and Bear Creek.

There was some minimal stocking a day or two before that but the ceremony, the golden bucket and so forth, was the 2nd of April at the Platte River. Earlier, there was some stocking in late March of 1966 at Bear Creek, a tributary of the Manistee River. Bear Creek runs into the Manistee downstream from the first barrier dam, so it was important. That was the first stocking. We said these fish are going to grow, they are going to get big and come back. It was all pie in the sky, but you have to remember at that time, anybody in Michigan who caught a ten-pound fish was in the newspaper. You would be on Morton Neff's *Michigan Outdoors* show, which at that time, was a big deal. It did not matter whether it was a bass or a pike or what it was. There were not very many big fish being caught.

We stocked the coho salmon in the spring of 1966. The alewife die-offs each year were humongous. There were dead alewives for 300 miles up and down the beach. They came right at the peak of the beach-oriented tourist season in West Michigan. I was engaged in this conflict with the Bureau of Commercial Fisheries. Their solution was to get seven huge beach sweepers to sweep up the alewives. We said it is a far better idea to turn those alewives into coho salmon. On the West Coast, alewife feed on anchovies, a fish that is similar to alewives. The coho are going to eat alewives and we are going to have a fine sport fishery.

I left the fish division in June or July of 1966. Michigan State, my alma mater, asked me to come back as a full professor with tenure and take an administrative position over all of natural resources. The university offered me almost twice as much money as I was making in the Fish Division. Most important, the job would change the fact that I was never home. I was all over the state during the turmoil of the late 1960s when I had three sons going into their teenaged years. I could see the signs; I could not do both things. And Wayne Tody was there. Wayne Tody was very capable, and could take over in my stance, and do very well. And he did. I sold the program, I initiated the program, I take responsibility for it, but he continued the fight with the commercial fishing interests, and got a magnificent new hatchery system built to support the program. I was at Michigan State, and I had no more responsibility for the program. But I was well known and I had a foot in both camps, so everybody helped us sell it. We had been managing three percent of the water. Now we had a hundred percent of the water to manage. It was a huge expansion of responsibility.

————————

Howard Tanner indicated that the foremost purpose behind the salmon program was to create a Great Lakes sport fishery, not eliminate the alewife problem. The introduction of salmon into Lake Michigan took place at nearly the same time that the population of another non-native species, the alewife, crashed.

I t really upsets me to have people say that we put the coho in the Great Lakes to control the alewife. We were sport fishing oriented. We were going to build a great sport fishery and alewife was the food supply. If you are going to build something, you have got to have something to make it work. The alewife was the food energy to make it work. I would never say the salmon program was there to control alewives. It was there to take advantage of the alewives.

We stocked the first coho in 1966. The alewife die-off was terrible that year. We were still in all these conflicts. We had not really won anything. There are precocious salmon who run a year early. They are mostly males, and are called jack salmon. We got a jack run in the fall of 1966; they were coming in from four to seven pounds. We wrote to our contacts in Oregon and Washington which later did supply eggs. We told them we were seeing a few jacks that were running four to seven pounds. They said that cannot be. We said we will pay your way to come back and look. So we paid their way, they came back, and looked. They told us to get ready because we were going to have a big jack run. We got probably 10,000 jacks that fall. They were terribly surprised and so were we. There was a lot of excitement. They were caught in the rivers and Platte Bay in the fall of 1966.

In 1967, 650,000 fish were stocked in Lake Michigan. The summer of 1967 was the worst alewife die-off that anybody had ever seen. That fall, the adult coho came in. This was the bonanza. This was the coho explosion. This is what generated all the excitement. We were in the right place at the right time. There was a terrible alewife problem in 1967 and then a huge successful fishery in the fall. Everybody was catching coho. I have got a million stories about the craziness of the coho bonanza. In 1968, there were no dead alewives. Everybody said, the salmon ate them all. And we said it could not possibly be true. We made that argument probably for maybe a minute, maybe two minutes. But then we said, okay we did it. What had happened was the population of an introduced species oftentimes goes up to a peak until it hits some ceiling, usually a food ceiling, and it crashes. That is what really happened in Lake Michigan. The alewife population crashed in 1967. The salmon could not possibly have had a significant impact that first year. There was not enough fish out there to have a significant impact. There were billions of pounds of alewife. The salmon ate the alewives until they were big fish, but they did not make a dent in the population. The alewife died from lack of food and that is why there were so many on the beach in 1967 and there were none in 1968.

When the fish were caught in the fall of 1967 and then in the spring of 1968, there were no dead alewives, everybody thought that the salmon had eaten the alewives. The state legislature could not give us enough money. They thought this was wonderful.

One newspaper called the salmon program one of the ten most significant effects or events of 1967 or 1968. That is the first time I ever knew that an outdoor fish or wildlife event ever competed successfully with strikes and earthquakes.

———————————

Stanford Smith recalled how the alewife crisis prompted the agency to work with Wisconsin and Michigan commercial fishermen in establishing experimental trawling operations.

After the *Cisco* spent 1953 in Lake Superior, it was brought to Lake Michigan to study the chub population, which supported the main commercial activity in Lake Michigan. Small chubs known as "bloaters" and yellow perch had not yet disappeared because they were too small for the sea lamprey to eat. And small chubs were rapidly becoming much, much more abundant. They were so small, they were of very little food value. In 1954 and 1955 I conducted a study to get an idea of what was going on with the chubs in Lake Michigan with respect to the sea lamprey, the fishery, and the environment. The resulting study was published under the title "Species Succession and Fishery Exploitation in the Great Lakes." I used all of the data that we gathered in 1954 and 1955 and data gathered by the *Fulmar*, which was operated under John Van Oosten in the 1930s in Lake Michigan. I was able to describe the interactions of the various species and the sea lamprey, which resulted in the bloater becoming extremely abundant, and then subsequently, the alewives became extremely abundant and the bloater declined very sharply. This was an interaction between the fishery and the sea lamprey and competition amongst the various species.

The alewife ate the bloater out of house and home. The alewives became extremely abundant in the late 1960s. In 1967 we had a massive die-off. Then that became my main focus of research. The alewife crisis brought research money. I went back and researched the history of the alewife in the Great Lakes. When it first became established in Lake Ontario, it underwent a similar type of massive explosion and die-off when it reached peak abundance. It ate itself out of house and home and became a very stressed species. The same thing happened in Lake Michigan, and to a lesser degree in Lake Huron. In Lake Huron the die-offs were not as well documented and may not have been as noteworthy because they were not in highly populated areas such as southern

Lake Michigan and in the Chicago area where there is a massive human population. The stench of rotting alewives raised considerable concern by the residents of that area. They wanted to know what is happening out there. Why do we have these tons of dead fish on our shore?

The *Kayho* was built to explore commercial fish potential and was asked to evaluate the great abundance of bloaters in Lake Michigan. What do we do with all of these fish that the commercial fishermen do not have a market for? After the Bureau of Commercial Fisheries was formed, they brought an exploratory fishing program into the Great Lakes. Fenton Carbine moved from Washington to Ann Arbor to become the regional director of the Bureau of Commercial Fisheries for inland waters. The *Kayho*, which was an experimental commercial fishing research boat, was used to find ways to catch large quantities of bloaters and use them for cat and dog food, fishmeal and oil, and other products. When the bloater declined, they moved their focus to the alewife which had become extremely abundant. They wanted to see how to catch large quantities of alewife with trawls. The people from the *Kayho* taught commercial fishermen how to make the transition to trawling for chub and alewife during the 1960s. But the State of Michigan, Howard Tanner, and Wayne Tody came in with other ideas. They said we have all these alewives out here. They are the natural food of the salmon, and so let us bring some salmon in to eat the alewives and the salmon will be a nice desirable species for recreational fishing. So that is how the salmon introductions got started. The catch per unit of effort of lake trout in the Great Lakes was much lower than for salmon, and was not enough to stimulate the emotions of a sport fisherman. Sport fishermen also love salmon because they jump out of the water and fight. They are easier to find and catch than lake trout.

––––––––––

Ralph Hay, of the Michigan DNR's Division of Fisheries, recalled the relationship between the depletion of commercial fishing stocks, the explosion of the alewife population, and the agency's attempt to create a sport fishery.

I came on board at the Michigan DNR when we had the alewife problem. Back in the early 1960s the non-native alewife population just exploded because there were no predators, mainly the lake trout. The stock of lake trout was depleted due to overfishing from the commercial fishermen and the invasion of the sea lamprey. So we were faced with some tremendous die-outs of the alewife along the shorelines of Lake Michigan and Huron in the 1960s. It was bad. There were times when I was in high school and college the die-offs were so extensive, people could not utilize the beaches. Windrowed alewives blocked people's access to vast sandy beaches.

The DNR embarked on a program to try and control or at least utilize the abundant forage base. We considered introducing a couple of different species of fish into the lake systems to control the alewife population. We looked at striped bass, a fish common to the waters of the Atlantic Ocean and East Coast because it is a ferocious, voracious eater known to utilize a lot of its prey species. We looked at several species of salmon, namely the coho and the chinook, and had long debates and studies and opinions on which species to go to. I think the decision to go with the coho and the chinook was based on the fact that the lakes currently are being managed for selmondid species, cold-water species. We wanted to continue to manage it with those species in mind, so that is probably why the DNR ultimately chose to introduce the coho and chinook salmon.

When we first made the introduction back in the mid-1960s we had both the coho and the chinook salmon from the West Coast. And we had unbelievable survival and growth on those species. We had rates of growth and survival the West Coast had never experienced in recent time because we had tremendous forage base. There were no predators out there. These fish had an unlimited food source so their survival and growth was phenomenal.

During the late 1960s and early 1970s the problems we faced were a result of too many salmon in our streams. I mean they were literally overrun with coho and chinook salmon. And Michigan anglers had never, ever seen that many large fish before in the state. Prior to that, our biggest game fish was northern pike and muskee. And now there are thousands and tens of thousands of fish anywhere from eight to thirty pounds jamming up every little stream they could find. When you have that kind of numbers of fish, it brings out the worst behavior in people. We ended up having a lot of problems with trespassing, littering, spearing, and clubbing. People just absolutely went berserk when they saw all these huge fish. And the fact that they were going to die within a few months even compounded the problem because their feeling was well, they are going to die anyway. So we were blessed with the opportunity to turn those alewives into something useful, a good sport fishery with coho and chinook. But on the other hand we created some problems on our inland waters with too many of these fish and people problems.

———————

Stan Lievense discussed how, during the mid-1960s, his work for the Michigan Department of Conservation became increasingly oriented toward not only sport-fishing research, but promotional activity as well. As a staff member he worked to further sport-fishing interests through the creation of the Michigan Steelheaders.

I had a lot of interaction with sport fishermen. I recognized that all the fishermen were my bosses, and so I really worked very closely with all the sportsmen's clubs and cooperated with them all I could. A good classic example is the Benzie Sportsmen's Club over by Beulah. They complained that the brown trout in the Platte River were down and they wanted us to plant more. I said, "I disagree with you. I think we got a very healthy brown trout situation." So I said, "I will tell you what we will do. We will have a demonstration day. I will come with the electric shocker and we will test the stream right by the highway where it has heavy fishing." Every bit of cover that we ran into we turned two, three nice brown trout, so their eyes were opened. So then they wanted another area planted. I went there and found the water was too warm. However, there were some springs—strong spring streams that would enter and in testing with the electric shocker again, you get all kinds of warm-water fish and then all of a sudden you get a trout. So that is how I worked with the sportsmen.

As part of my involvement with sportsmen's associations and clubs, I did a lot of talking to bring out the news and developments. My involvement with Michigan Steelheaders was when I was part of the Fish Division staff. After being in the field, I went to staff. I was brought in there because of the salmon fishery. Dr. Tanner was the one credited with the introduction of the salmon. He knew that I was a very avid brown trout fisherman. He knew that I managed a lot of the inland lakes for trout, so I was a specialist in trout lake management. Anyway, Dr. Tanner wanted me.

Dr. Tanner was at the DNR for a short time when he got a promotion and went to Michigan State University. Wayne Tody became fisheries chief. Wayne Tody saw the need for the sportsmen to get into this new salmon program, so he gave me the assignment to see if I could establish a Great Lakes sport-fishing association. I worked with Norm Spring, the first president of Michigan Steelheaders. I found him to be very knowledgeable; he was a key fisherman.

When I went to staff, I was put to work mostly on sport-fishing promotion. I was the salmon and bass promoter, more or less, for the State of Michigan. I spoke. I had to get out the first fishing brochure on salmon fishing. I did not know salmon fishing, but I had to find out, so I leaned heavily on the West Coast. I went on a trip to Seattle at my expense, gained this information, and made a good brochure—I had lots of examples. For instance, on the West Coast dodger squids are popular among king salmon and coho fishermen. A dodger is a big attractor which offers awful clumsy fishing, but it is very, very effective. Those are things that I learned from the outside and put in the salmon brochure.

I also did a lot of speaking, television work, and radio work to promote salmon. It grew out of the state; Wisconsin called me first, then Illinois, Minnesota, Ohio, Pennsylvania, and New York. I got around. I had one of our artists make me a black-and-white tin drawing of a large chinook salmon and what we could expect. When I talked, I would say, "Well, here's what's coming." It really made a lot of excitement and it has not held up. Now that was a fifty-pounder and they have not hit a fifty-pounder yet. They had one at forty-nine pounds, a big fish.

While I was promoting sport fishing, commercial fishermen were concerned—nothing outright, but they were afraid. They were afraid that sport fishing might get too strong, which it has. Their livelihood has been threatened greatly.

Myrl Keller, retired manager of the Michigan DNR's research station, recalled the reorientation of fisheries policy from sport to commercial during the late 1960s.[56]

I was the first biologist hired to work specifically on the Great Lakes with Howard Tanner, who was the chief of fisheries at that time. Wayne Tody was the assistant chief of fisheries. During that period, Walt Crowe and I actually wrote the policy that said we would spend the bulk of our efforts in managing recreational fisheries and commercial fisheries would take the surplus fish. This was totally opposite of the practice of that time where the fishery was dominated by the commercial fisheries. So there was a policy change about 1967.

When I started in the early 1960s we could go from Charlevoix all the way to St. Joseph, and rarely see a sport-fishing boat on the Great Lakes. The sea lamprey were really abundant. Around 1967 one of my first assignments was to measure the wounding rates on lake trout. Lake trout were first planted in 1965 to get an index of lamprey abundance. They were very abundant and so was the alewife. In 1967, we had a massive die-off of alewife. We had to literally wash down the beaches and unplug the fish from water intakes. At that time it was figured the state lost approximately $55 million in tourist revenue as a result of the big die-off.

The salmon program was started to develop a recreational fishery utilizing the undesirable alewife as forage. Socially we set up something that the public of the Great Lake states could enjoy, that was also of economic benefit to the state. It worked actually far beyond our dreams. It was primarily Wayne Tody who came up with the idea of using a predator on alewife. The federal government proposed an exploratory program where alewife would be harvested and rendered into meal at plants all up and down the lakes. We were totally opposed to this. We thought that it would benefit the public of Michigan much further to use the alewife to support a more desirable fish like trout or salmon. So that is the path we took. The exploratory harvest of alewife type fishery kind of went by the wayside over a period of years.

Our plan initially was to develop a recreational fishery on the Great Lakes because our inland waters, at least in Michigan, were fairly saturated with sport fishermen. We looked at the fisheries resource, at least in Michigan, as being a publicly owned resource. We asked how can we best serve the majority of the people and we decided we could do that through a recreational fishery. Some of the other user groups were not happy with the decision at that time. We were supported by the legislature and the governor, so we went forth with the program.

We only knew of one location in Alaska where salmon reproduced in the freshwater environment. But we felt that they would do fine in the Great Lakes system. Wayne Tody did most of the research and looking into it. Right off the bat, he predicted what the salmon would do when we introduced them into the system. They are voracious feeders. The salmon feed on herring-like fish such as alewife, and so it all fit; it would be ideal. We also based our decision on the fact that chinook and coho are a relative to the rainbow trout or steelhead, which are in the salmon family. They were very successful since the late 1800s in the Great Lakes system.

It is comical today when we look back, to consider the federal fisheries officials, in particular the director of the group at that time Fenton Carbine, tried every method to stop us from introducing salmon. He personally wrote a couple letters to the governor totally against the salmon introduction. Carbine did not realize that the governor sent most of the letters relative to fisheries matters over to the fisheries division, so we had to answer the letters. But the U.S. Bureau of Commercial Fisheries dominated the Great Lakes scene prior to the time Michigan started the salmon programs. They were not part of the program so they were apparently rebelling.

It turned out to be just an absolute phenomenal fishery. The lake trout planted first in 1965, the coho planted in 1966, and the first chinook planted in 1967, plus brown trout and steelhead just made a spectacular fishery, both near shore and offshore. The offshore fishery developed in the 1980s when the steelhead fishery developed in the center part of the lake. Alewife provided an excellent forage base. Alewife numbers were reduced. The stocked fish also fed on chub. We had a pretty good balance overall until the late 1980s when there were too many predators out there for the forage base to sustain. There were too many fish being planted, so since that period all the states have reduced their planting numbers to try to establish a better predator-prey relationship out there.

The success period was a great surprise. We felt that it would make a great contribution, but nothing like that early fishery that was so spectacular. Even today it is great. I have talked to salmon fishermen in Seattle, for instance, who are happy if they catch two or three salmon in a season. In Michigan, people can catch two or three in one trip and think nothing of it. A few years ago, the fishery was so great it was not anything to catch fifteen or twenty in one day. So the program has just been phenomenal. Probably no place in the North American continent and possibly the world, has developed such a spectacular sport fishery as what these salmonoids have provided. When I speak of salmonoids I am speaking of salmon and the trout fisheries.

Wayne Tody was head of the Fish Division of the Michigan DNR from 1966 to 1976. As fisheries chief, he chose to concentrate the agency's resources on Lake Michigan and defer attention to Lake Huron.

Lamprey control was well established in Lake Superior in 1966. Lake trout were planted to reestablish the population, although they never went entirely extinct. We had a sufficient degree of control in Lake Michigan so that by the time our steelhead, salmon, brown trout, and lake trout got up to prey size, the lamprey would be under control. It worked beautifully. We had to hold off a couple years in Lake Huron. Lake Huron had to wait for lamprey control. Naturally, all those nice folks wanted to keep up with Lake Michigan, and they could not for a couple of years, so they got kind of hard on us. But they got in the swing of things and really have the best fishery of the two at the moment, because there are not so many people working on it. Right when we got everything going great, we ran into all kind of problems with DDT and pesticides contaminating the fish, and had to quit the commercial sale of a lot of them. The state had this big surplus of salmon at our weirs too. We tried to work out deals with the commercial fishermen to process them, but they could not do it. They just were not equipped for it, so we had packing plants do it by contract. I think it is still done that way today.

Ralph Hay of the Michigan DNR's Division of Fisheries noted the significance of Michigan's decision to create a sport fishery in the Great Lakes and not to support the economic and environmental recovery of commercial fishing.

For many years the emphasis on the Great Lakes fishery was commercial. The alewife and the sea lamprey practically killed the commercial fishery. With the commercial fishery on a downward spiral there was an opportunity for us to not only control the alewives, but in doing so, create a very viable sport fishery. When you look at it from an economic point of view, more people are going to benefit from a highly viable sport fishery than you would sustain with a commercial fishery. So Michigan and the Great Lakes, in particular Michigan, made a very bold move back in the 1960s to go from a commercial fishery to a sport fishery. And the alewives and the salmon really at that point in time helped make that transition. We still have a commercial fishery in the Great Lakes, not only tribal fishers, but nontribal commercial fishers as well. The emphasis of the commercial fishery is on those species that are not of high sport value, like chubs and whitefish. In certain areas, commercial fishers are allowed to take lake trout and perch, although the perch commercial fishery has already been curtained in Michigan and to a lesser degree, in some of the other states. The early 1960s saw a vast change in philosophy from commercial to sport.

Myrl Keller, a retired DNR fisheries biologist, discussed the research work done by the state on Great Lakes fisheries.

The staff at the Great Lakes fishery research station in Charlevoix did not make policy. We advised from the research we generated. We made recommendations based on the information we collected. Policy was set at the Lansing level. They generally took our advice. Of course, they obtained information from other sources as well before they made recommendations or set policy, so we worked quite well together.

The Great Lakes fishery research station is a research facility. The staff reports directly to Ann Arbor, the Institute of Fisheries Research. It is kind of unique with regard to how it functions and how it is administered. Its jurisdiction extends through five districts and three regional areas. We have always worked cooperatively with the district field people and regional field people and it has worked out quite well.

The Great Lakes fisheries research station's main piece of research equipment initially was the sixty-foot research vessel, the *Steelhead*.[57] It was built in Escanaba in 1967. More or less, the ship was our platform for using trawling gear for surveying young fish and gill-netting gear for adult fish. And it is still the basis of much of their work at the research station. Since that time, however, we have set up a number of studies of salmon and trout with microtags. We also monitor the sport fishery through interviewing and observing catches of sport fish. All the information is funneled into the Charlevoix station for all the Great Lakes. All the charter boat harvest figures also go to the Charlevoix station for all the Great Lakes. So there has been a number of other programs added to evaluate the fishery stocks. Initially it involved the use of research-type vessels and then coordinating information gathering with the other states and the

U.S. Fish and Wildlife Service. We also evaluated the stocks with onboard monitoring of commercial fishing vessels. We gave special permits to evaluate certain species of fish in areas where commercial fisheries did not operate.

———————

Jim Moore of the Wisconsin DNR recalled how, in the late 1960s, the Great Lakes fisheries, and specifically Lake Michigan fisheries, began to receive more attention from researchers.

When I was hired as a biologist in 1968, there was some concern for whitefish because our commercial production had been down for many years. One of my main projects was to look at whitefish and gather some of the biological data and hopefully, implement rules and regulations that would protect whitefish over the long haul. I also worked with lake trout. I was actually funded under a federal lake trout project for a good percentage of my time, so those were two of my key areas when I first started working as a biologist.

After I became a fisheries biologist, I had routine contact with the commercial fishers. I would do a lot of the same types of things that we do today. We would ride their boats and monitor their catch, looking for incidental fish and verifying some of the things that we would observe. They would have to report monthly catch reports and we were responsible for logging those in. We would do a lot of cross checking on them. We had a pretty active tagging program both for whitefish and lake trout for the first few years. We would track the fish and try to get tags returned from the fishermen. So it was primarily keeping abreast of what was going on, and also looking at some of the issues, whether it was contaminant issues, incidental kill issues, or whatever, and just building a database to have information when you dealt with all that stuff.

When I was hired, there was an understanding that the DNR would establish a Lake Michigan fishery station somewhere on the lake. I figured if I found the property in a place I thought it looked to me like I would like to live, that would be a bonus. So fortunately, I found some property in Sturgeon Bay and we developed our first station across the bay where the new convention center is being built. I moved up to Sturgeon Bay in the fall of 1969, and slowly started putting together the various pieces of our Lake Michigan program.

About 1968–1969, we went through a mini-reorganization, and lot of the things that Lee Kemen initially did with the trout and salmon program out of Green Bay were transferred to me up here in Sturgeon Bay. So after a few years working initially mostly with commercial fishermen with whitefish, we became more involved up here with all aspects of the trout and salmon program. So we have dealt both with the sport and commercial fishery issues. We acquired an old commercial fishing tug around 1970 or a little earlier. Our law enforcement people used the *Barney Devine* for many years. We hired a boat captain and a mate, and started out pretty slowly with just myself working on the lake proper. The boat was built in Manitowac by Burger Boat Company. I think it was owned by a gillnetter on the Michigan side. It was originally owned by our Law Enforcement Division, and used primarily for law enforcement work on Lake Michigan.

Back in the 1950s, one of the biggest issues and controversies raging on Lake Michigan was the size of gill nets to use for fishing for chubs. There were various conflicts, sometimes referred to as the "chub wars." Wardens were sneaking around trying to catch commercial fishermen using undersize mesh. And we had elaborate ways of the wardens going to fishermen's net sheds and measuring the mesh size on their gill nets. That was probably the single biggest issue in fisheries involvement in law enforcement. Once that finally subsided, Law Enforcement really did not have much use for the boat. When we started with the modern day trout and salmon program in 1968, the boat had been sitting for some time tied up at a dock. They used it once or twice a year just to keep it operable. We made a pitch that they transfer it to the Fisheries Division, which they did. And so that is how we acquired the *Barney*, and over time it has worked out to be quite a valuable fisheries research vessel for us. It is only set up for gill netting, but it does that very well and we have got lot of good use and good information over the last thirty years with it.

I was the first biologist that the Wisconsin DNR hired to work exclusively on Lake Michigan. Prior to that time, Larry Wiegert had Lake Michigan responsibilities, including the minor stocking that they had done with rainbow trout and a few brown trout. His main responsibility was tracking commercial catches. At that time, the commercial fishermen would mail their monthly fish reports to Green Bay. He would log them in, bundle them up, and send them over to the Ann Arbor Great Lakes fish lab. He was the only person who had any involvement with fishing for all of Lake Michigan from

Marinette all the way down to Racine-Kenosha. Obviously, he was not able to spend a lot of time on it. He also had an inland area he was responsible for. So the commercial fishery up until that time was relatively unregulated. Some of the laws had been on the books for many years. Some of them were more set by whims than science or anything that had anything to do with biological concerns. And at the time, obviously the sport fishery had not developed to the point where there were big conflicts with the commercial fishery yet. It took a number of years for the sport fishery to start really getting to the point where there were large numbers of sport fishermen demanding this or demanding that. So it gave us an opportunity to start gathering information and looking at some of the biological aspects of the regulations that we had at the time. Our program grew over time. We hired more people. Lee Kemen and I were the only two people working on Lake Michigan at that time. Now we have probably twenty or twenty-five people including our central office, who work on Lake Michigan most of their time.

Jim Moore indicated that the agency had cordial relations with sport-fishing interests compared to commercial fishing, especially during the peak years of the salmon fishery.

There have been a few issues where sport fishermen have not seen eye to eye on things that we wanted to do, but by and large it is a whole different situation than commercial fishing. We are not impacting their livelihood. The sport fishermen are out there primarily for recreation. It is hard for them to argue based on what they could do in the early 1960s versus what they could do as far as trout and salmon fishing now. By and large, it has been just nothing but success until we had some problems in the late 1980s with the chinook salmon fishery. Any time we go to change a rule or regulation, whether it is adjusting the bag limits for yellow perch or whatever, they come and scream and holler. They call you names and all kinds of stuff, but that is just part of doing business, I guess. It has never been quite as contentious working with the sport fishery as the commercial fishery. I think it is mostly due to the fact that the DNR is not a threat to their livelihoods. I guess if I was a commercial fisherman, I would probably be looking at it a lot differently, too.

There were a few guys from Door County who started charter boat fishing back as early as 1968 or 1969 in the first days that we started seeing salmon. It took many years after stocking to where they could go out there and catch species other than lake trout. I do not know if our charter catch reports show the trend in licenses, but back in the mid-1980s, there were upwards of 500 charter licensees on Lake Michigan. Now it is down. It is probably running at a couple hundred right now. It has dropped off because they cannot go out there and catch twenty or thirty chinook salmon, and half the catch weighs twenty pounds or better. That is not all bad. Our sport fishermen were very spoiled. A lot of people go out there fishing for the first time and catch a twenty-five-pound fish, and think you can go fishing any place and catch fish like that. It is unbelievable how spoiled a lot of people were with the success of Lake Michigan fishing. Their expectations were much higher than what they ought to be for anything. At that time, salmon fishing was ten to twenty times better than anything you could hope to experience on the West Coast. It probably still is considerably better. The golden years of the salmon fishery were from 1980 to 1987. There were six or eight years around that time where it was not uncommon to go out there and catch hundreds of pounds of fish in a short trip.

Myrl Keller recalled that DNR fisheries chief Howard Tanner's decision to stock salmon in Lake Michigan brought about a shift in the balance of power that existed between Michigan and federal fisheries officials.

Most of the management people in the State of Michigan's old Department of Conservation relied heavily on the recommendations of the Bureau of Commercial Fisheries—before it was the U.S. Fish and Wildlife Service—regarding how the various fish populations should be managed. They had tremendously strong input on what was done for many, many, many years on the Great Lakes. The Bureau of Commercial Fisheries was pro-commercial fishing and anti-hatchery. They pretty much dominated the scene.

Michigan's salmon program brought a whole different look to the Great Lakes fisheries resources. Up until that time (as biologists) we were literally writing the obituaries on each of the species as they went by the wayside. We wanted to stop that and apply new management skills and better manage the resource for the public. We decided we could best serve the public if we rewrote the whole program and took a different management philosophy.

Michigan DNR fisheries research biologist Jory Jonas noted the effects of the state's decision to favor sport over commercial fishing interests.

The tendency in the past may have been to side with the anglers because they seemed like they were the underdogs out there. The argument weighed the angler who takes one or two fish versus a commercial fisher who may take hundreds or thousands. But there are also some innate, cultural things to be considered regarding commercial fishing. You have to consider generations of people fishing and living a hard lifestyle to make a dollar. Commercial fishing has a long and ancient history. From a cultural perspective it is fascinating to have people working out there, who know the system and work with it. It is possible for the two groups to exist in the same system. The main key to their coexistence is good monitoring and scientific data and proper controls on both groups to require them to act in a way in which protects the fishery.

Jory Jonas indicated that when she first left graduate school, she was considered radical because she opposed the introduction of non-native species such as salmon into the Great Lakes. Over time, however, she altered her view. Jonas was among those who saw the introduction of salmon as primarily an alewife-control measure.

Lake Michigan is a mess but it did not start with chinook salmon stocking. It started with the St. Lawrence Seaway. I did a lot of research on the history of fisheries management by looking at some old management documents and some of the letters that went back and forth among the biologists at that time. I was trying to get a sense of where they were coming from. They felt a definite need to act. They had three feet of alewives on beaches. The alewife die-off was not like anything you see now when you have an alewife die-off. It was huge. It was something that the public was not going to stand for. The alewife came in through the St. Lawrence Seaway when we opened up the lock system. So you had that problem to deal with and that is where the chinook

Jory Jonas is a fisheries research biologist at the Michigan DNR's Great Lakes Fishery Research Station in Charlevoix. Jonas holds Master of Science degree in fishery science from the University of Illinois at Champaign–Urbana and has previously been employed by the Wisconsin DNR and Wisconsin Sea Grant Institute A specialist in lake trout and steelhead. Interview 27 May 1999. Photograph by Michael J. Chiarappa.

salmon came from. It was an alewife-control measure. They were not trying to create a fishery or bring new things in. They had to put something in the lake to eat the alewife, and they succeeded. The chinook is very focused on the alewife.

Everybody was just so happy with this tremendous sport fishery. There were parades. Everybody said the fisheries managers are great; they brought chinook salmon in. Then some disease and genetic issues came up. Like computers, a lot of these genetic concepts were not understood until the 1980s and 1990s. Decisions were made in the 1960s and 1970s, when the knowledge just was not there. It is easy to jump on the bandwagon and point fingers and say now what should have been considered then. It is too late. We have this system to deal with it. The chinook became a problem when they reached these tremendous numbers and sizes. Then the population crashed in the mid-1980s for reasons that are still not clear to us. What we do know about chinook salmon is that when there are high densities, the population crashes. Now whether it is because of reduction in the forage base or disease or whatever, they have what is called a density dependent effect.

Howard Tanner recalled that the communities near the places where the salmon runs occurred in the fall of 1968 were unprepared for the beginning of the coho craze.

Everybody was catching big fish. Before this time, there had not been any big fish. The coho craze was centered on Manistee. There was total lack of facilities. You waited two hours to launch a boat. There were not very many places to launch boats. The first lure that worked was the flatfish, the silver flatfish. The tackle stores ran out of silver flatfish. Then they ran out of silver paint that they were painting other flatfish with. Then they rented flatfish. They ran out of beer. There was a real crisis. There was a mass of people on the coho coast.

Ralph Hay (Division of Fisheries of the Michigan DNR) recalled that the state was not well prepared for the salmon fishing bonanza of the late 1960s and early 1970s.

I was here when the salmon boom was on, so to speak. And I was here when these rivers were overrun with salmon. In some instances, you could literally walk across the rivers on the backs of salmon. It was almost chaos. I can remember salmon fishing out on the Great Lakes when you could go out and catch your limit in no time at all. In fact, a lot of people went out two or three times and fished their limit. It was just unbelievable fishing. It was a new program and people were just getting into it. And if you were one of the first, it was a bonanza. Like any new fishery, things boom and then they bust. The populations declined, then they rebounded a little bit, and they declined again. Today, we have a more stable salmon fishery.

When people talk about the good old days of salmon fishing, they mean the late 1960s and early 1970s. It is nothing like it used to be. I realized that that kind of fishery cannot be maintained over the long haul. The fishing bonanza created many problems such as snagging. Snagging is where you take basically just a big treble hook and just drag it through the water until you put the hook into the back of the fish. You capture them—capture them—you put the hook into the body wherever you can. To some, snagging is unsportsmanlike because the fish is not biting the lure. You are just putting the lure into him someplace, whether it is in the back or the tail or the belly or whatever. It is sort of like spearing in a way; the fish is not coming to you. You are going to the fish.

The DNR allowed snagging because we had a lot of public pressure put on us to harvest those fish in a quick and efficient manner. And then when the population levels declined and we did not have those numbers of fish, there was no need to use that gear type to take all the fish. They just were not available. And so we eventually eliminated snagging. So I went through the era where we did not have snagging, we had snagging, and then we had to eliminate snagging.

Ron Poff, formerly of the Wisconsin DNR, maintained that the economic influence of sport fishing has given rise to its political influence.

The sport fishery has done its share in attracting visitors. Towns like Algoma and Kewaunee were dead towns for a long time until the sport fishery started to pick up. Then all of a sudden we got all these charter boats. Funny things would happen at times, especially the salmon fishery. I was on my way up to Manitowoc one day for a commercial fishing board meeting, and it seemed like every other car on the road was a pickup truck with a piggyback camper on it from Iowa. I pulled into one parking lot and ninety-five out of one hundred cars were trucks from Iowa. It was in the fall, and they were all headed to Manitowoc to fish salmon. These guys would come up there with a coffin-sized cooler on the back of their truck. They would go out snagging salmon, which was legal at that time, and can them right there. Then they would head home with a trunk full of canned salmon. It was an attractive fishery and that meant money to the communities. But it also created another edge to the sword. Now there was an economic value of significance—fresh dollars coming in from out of state. It was not just a transfer from some other activity to fishing.

One result of the creation of the sport fishery on Lake Michigan was a growing relationship between the Michigan DNR and Michigan State University. Howard Tanner, who served both as director of the Michigan DNR and director of natural resources at Michigan State University, contributed to the growing ties between the two.

I was not a unique individual, but I was one of the relatively few faculty members who had hands-on experience. I got that experience in Colorado, and I got that experience in Michigan. I found the students very appreciative of somebody who could say they had been there or done that. It was helpful to me, it was helpful to the students, and it was helpful to the faculty.

I did whatever I could to improve the lines of communication between fisheries and wildlife downtown at the Michigan DNR and fisheries and wildlife at Michigan State University. The overall capability of the University of Michigan in fisheries and wildlife has declined very substantially, while Michigan State has grown. They are working in cooperation with the department downtown. Bill Taylor, John Robertson, and others have created a partnership in ecological research and management. The DNR funds faculty positions in fisheries and wildlife. Much of the credit for this cooperative work should go to Bill Taylor.

Michigan State also has a lamprey professor funded by the Great Lakes Fishery Commission. He works on the physiology of sea lamprey looking for controlling mechanisms. There are three fisheries positions funded by the DNR Fisheries budget. There are three wildlife positions funded by the Wildlife Division of DNR. There is now an inner exchange of information and factual data and the application of it. I liken it in a slight way to the cooperative extension service of every land grant college. They have faculty doing research on campus and they also have a delivery system to each county largely, but not exclusively, in agriculture, but also in forestry and community problems and activities. What I see growing between the Michigan DNR and Michigan State University in fisheries and wildlife is a pipeline from the source of information out to delivery points where it makes application.

---

2. TAKING CHARGE OF LAKE MICHIGAN'S FISHERIES:
FROM GENTLEMEN'S AGREEMENTS TO BELLWETHERS
OF STATE IDENTITY AND ECONOMIC BENEFIT

Dr. Stanford Smith of the U.S. Fish and Wildlife Service discussed how the agency gradually moved to an ecosystems approach to fisheries management on the Great

Lakes after Dr. John Van Oosten stepped down as chief of the Great Lakes Fishery Investigation. He also reflected on the changing nature of education and research in fisheries science.

D r. John Van Oosten was a very precise person, a very methodical person. This is probably why they thought that it would be good to have a fresh, dynamic person with a broadened new emphasis. John Van Oosten would not have fit that picture. He was very precise and methodical. His preciseness and methodical nature was very important in the work that had been done up until that point. Similarly, they brought in a whole new generation of younger officers to fight World War II because it was fought in an entirely different way than World War I.

What Van Oosten did in his work as a student at the University of Michigan was to determine fish age and growth from fish scales. The federal government financed his work as a student at the University of Michigan. That is why federal fishery research on the Great Lakes dates back to 1920. He worked with a fellow named Walter Koelz, who got his Ph.D. at the University of Michigan. Walter Koelz worked on the chubs, the deep-water ciscoes mainly. At that time, they needed to be identified. They did not know how many species there were, so chubs were his focus. John Van Oosten was mainly interested in the lake herring in Lake Erie and Saginaw Bay. And that was the way work was done up until this revitalization of the Great Lakes. In those days there was little thought about looking at all of the species or of the whole system at once. Van Oosten was very intrigued when I talked to him about the new work. He thought that was great, but through his background, he just was not keyed in to that type of thought process.

Dr. Ralph Hile was more oriented toward an ecological approach. Hile had more of a broader mindset in looking at problems than Van Oosten. So he was very well set up for this type of change in the type of operation that occurred, the change that occurred in 1949–1950.

The systems approach brought me to the University of Michigan. There were other things happening there and I did not know how to delve into and understand. I did not have enough basic ecology and biology. They did not teach that type of thing at Oregon State, where they taught primarily how to manage fish and wildlife. At the University of Michigan, they taught the biology and ecology underneath that. They had excellent staff members such as Dr. Paul Welch who was a limnologist at University of Michigan. Jim Moffett got a doctorate in limnology at the University of Michigan under Paul Welch. Fortunately I was there the last year before Dr. Welch retired and was able to sop up as much of his knowledge and understanding of limnological processes as possible. Dr. Karl Lagler was in charge of the fish work. Dr. John Bardock was not there very long. They had excellent people in aquatic botany and invertebrate and vertebrate biology and so I got all of the things that I needed to be able to look at the broad picture.

Stan Smith recalled that political pressure from commercial fishing interests brought about a bureaucratic reshuffling in 1970.[58] Until 1972 when the National Marine Fisheries Service hired him, Great Lakes commercial fishermen did not have any federal fishery advisor available to them.

I retired from the U.S. Fish and Wildlife Service, Bureau of Sport Fisheries and Wildlife in 1972, shortly after it took over the laboratory in Ann Arbor in 1970. In 1970 there was a restructuring within the Department of the Interior. The commercial fishing interests felt they were not getting a fair shake from the Bureau of Commercial Fisheries under the U.S. Fish and Wildlife Service. They yearned to have it back like the old days when the Bureau of Fisheries was under the Department of Commerce. In 1970 commercial fishing activities that involved the federal government were moved back to the Department of Commerce under the National Marine Fisheries Service. The commercial fishery responsibility of the Great Lakes went to the National Marine Fisheries Service. The laboratory in Ann Arbor, the Great Lakes Fishery Laboratory as it was called then, had no responsibility for answering the questions or attending the meetings for the commercial fishermen in the Great Lakes and responding to their needs. So when I left the laboratory on the last day of June in 1972, the regional director of the National Marine Fisheries Service, who had responsibility in the Great Lakes, contacted me. He was located in Gloucester, Massachusetts. He asked me to help him. Since 1970, the Great Lakes commercial fishermen had been asking for somebody from the National Marine Fisheries Service to talk to about their interests. They were promised there would be someone to talk to. He asked me to talk to these fishermen and explain things to them, tell them what was going on, and what it means. I was hired as a consultant to the National Marine Fisheries Service to fulfill their responsibility to the commercial fishery in the Great Lakes. And I served in that position until 1978, until there was so little commercial fishing in the Great Lakes, the people at the National Marine Fisheries Service decided that they did not need this type of help.

The day before I retired, I was appointed adjunct professor in the School of Natural Resources at the University of Michigan. I moved to an office in the School of Natural Resources at the University of Michigan. From that location I did my National Marine Fisheries Service work plus my I gave lectures and taught classes at the University of Michigan. And as the work with the National Marine Fisheries Service grew, I could not handle it all. We hired a fellow named John Carr who was a biologist at the Fish and Wildlife Service in Ann Arbor. He became in charge of looking after the federal responsibility for the commercial fishing interests in the Great Lakes rather than me. So this took the pressure off of me, and I became more of a consultant and my work with the University of Michigan mainly dealt with their Sea Grant program, which I continued until 1984.

Wayne Tody, who retired from the Michigan DNR as deputy director in 1980, indicated that prior to the introduction of the salmon, the DNR faced a legislative mindset that linked the Great Lakes with commercial fishing and inland lakes and streams with sport fishing.

Michigan had another row to hoe in the Great Lakes. It did not have a sport fishery as such on the Great Lakes; there was not even a license. Sport fishing was inland waters and commercial fishing was the Great Lakes; that was the political understanding. It got bitter at times. Around 1900, the state legislature told the fish chief that it would not appropriate one more red cent for planting fish in the Great Lakes. The budget was cut in half, and all activities were confined to the inland waters. The commercial fishermen would never agree to any rules and regulations. They lobbied themselves out of it every time. Two or three years later, they restored their budget, but the legislature never encouraged them to ever look at the Great Lakes again, which is a tragedy. In 1968 we finally got a license through. We got a lot of things through after the salmon run. The sport fishing in the inland waters peaked about 1954, and then went into a fairly sizable drop. It kept right on dropping until salmon were planted.

―――――――

Jory Jonas discussed the role of politics in the management of Lake Michigan fisheries resources.

The DNR does a good job of explaining when science is not playing a role in fisheries management decision. If politics comes down and overrides the science, they still give me the ability to express my opinion. The best I can do is to say what I think the biology is telling me, or what we need to do to get the information we need to make a decision. And sometimes politics can override that decision. Right now, I feel really comfortable with fisheries management as our division carries it out. Politics are not running things a whole lot here.

―――――――

Myrl Keller, who served as a fisheries biologist from the Michigan DNR's Great Lakes fisheries research station from 1967–96, discussed the impact of politics on fisheries management.[59]

You are trained as a biologist. You deal in facts from research. You get information on a population of fish and you know the proper management, but sometimes it just is not suitable politically, so it does not fly, or it just does not come into being. It is frustrating. It is our job to get more involved in the political process, to educate our politicians, our legislature, and then possibly, some of those things that we would like to implement would be easier to do.

I have not had any problem working with any of the fisheries user groups. They have all been easy to work with. The sport fishermen have been just wonderful to work with. The charter boat folks have been great. Once the commercial fishers understand what you are trying do they are not difficult to work with. Some of the tribal issues have been frustrating but as time progresses, the tribes are going to have to accept the responsibility for what they are doing. I think they are going to be much more cautious and are going to better conservation practices to manage the stocks of fish they

Myrl Keller (left), of the Michigan DNR Great Lakes Fishery Research Station in Charlevoix, examines salmon caught by unidentified representatives from the Shakespeare Company who are testing equipment. Government fisheries officials worked closely not only with sport fishing tackle companies, but also with sport fishing organizations, to promote sport fishing on the Great Lakes. Courtesy of the Michigan Department of Natural Resources, Great Lakes Fishery Research Station.

are harvesting out there. I think they will be responsible people down the line. If they are not, they will not have a fishery to fish. History will repeat itself. They will overfish and nobody will benefit.

Stanford Smith noted how politics and funding influenced the research agenda at the Ann Arbor laboratory.

I n fish management and research the tendency is to focus on crisis problems like the alewife or the bloater. Here are all these bloaters or small chubs and what do we do with them? Or all of these smelt, what do we do with them? The collapse of the lake herring in Lake Erie and pollution were crisis problems. Stillman Wright had a boat on Lake Erie and he did some surveys on the pollution problem. Fisheries management is still and will always be a political process. Money comes from crises.

The focus of my research was species interaction, the interaction of the fish and the environment. The fishery ecology of the Great Lakes was my main interest, regardless of commercial, sport, whoever was involved. I became involved in the pollution problem in Lake Erie. The talk I gave on Lake Erie pollution had probably the most significant impact of any that I gave.[60] It really was not significant from the biological standpoint, but from the political standpoint, it was extremely significant. I worked with a fellow named Al Beeton, who focused on limnlogical aspects of the Great Lakes. We had the research vessel *Cisco* in Lake Erie for two years to intensively study the ecology of Lake Erie. We discovered that as a result of the oxygen depletion in Lake Erie, the blue pike had disappeared and the species composition was changing rapidly. The commercial fishery and the sport fishery were having trouble for lack of fish to catch. Al Beeton and I were given the responsibility to go around and talk to people, and try to stir up an interest that something should be done about this just like the crisis that occurred earlier with the lamprey problem. People were shrugging their shoulders and nodding their heads; they agreed with what we had to say that this is a serious problem and something should be done about it, but nothing happened.

In October 1961, Fenton Carbine, the regional director, was invited to talk to the Lake Erie Resources and Recreation Council at Vermilion, Ohio. He did not like to talk to groups and that was something that I did regularly, so he asked me if I would talk to these people about the problems in Lake Erie, and explain how serious they are, and the need for something to be done. I said yes, as I dutifully would to a superior. Carbine told me you have got to say something different than what you have been saying before because it really has not been getting their attention; it has not been hitting home. So I took my usual talk and I consulted with Ralph Hile to come up with something different to say. So I added a paragraph, the last paragraph to my usual talk, which said, "The status of Lake Erie as a useful freshwater resource has become uncertain. As impressive as the conspicuous changes have been, there may still be more dire consequences from slow yet undetected accumulation of common detergents, toxic chemicals that continually enter the lake. Lake Erie can be described accurately as a dying lake and because of the subtle cumulative effects of the sewage and industrial waste, it may be dead even before we are aware of it."

The meeting was attended by two reporters from the Cleveland paper. They took that one paragraph and said Lake Erie is dying and we have got to do something about it. Within six months, we had the Federal Water Quality Administration calling and had an explosion of activity on the Great Lakes dedicated to water quality as a result of that one paragraph. The U.S. Congress came to the Great Lakes and held hearings after that. What is going on? What are we going to do? Finally, we hit a nerve by saying something is dying. It was not my responsibility, I just happened to be the guy who was there. The reason I came up with the thought of calling it a dying lake is because the last thing I heard about the work on Lake Erie before getting the assignment to give this talk was that commercial fishermen were lifting their trap nets, and they were covered with slime. There were little or no fish in the nets or what few fish they had were dead.

The Canadians had a field station in Wheatley, Ontario. They had just conducted a trawling transect where they went from north to south across the lake and trawled to see what fish they caught. The closer they got to the U.S. shore, the fewer fish they got. When they got to the U.S. shore, they caught none. So these reports triggered the thought to call it a dying lake because in essence from a fishery standpoint, on the south shore, it was dead. In the Northern Hemisphere, water circulates counterclockwise—you flush a toilet or drain a sink, the water will go clockwise. Well, the contaminants from the Detroit River and the eastern part, industrial part, of Lake Erie, hug the south shore as the water goes counterclockwise in that direction. That is why the south shore, the U.S. shore was affected and the Canadian shore was not. That is why there were no fish in the south shore. So indeed, something needed to be done, and within a year, we had everybody here. We had federal and state laboratories in New York, Cleveland, and Chicago all dedicated to clean up all the Great Lakes. And the fishery got emphasis from that too. The whole thing got emphasis.

Suttons Bay–based Tom Kelly is a fisheries biologist and educator. He discussed the influence of politics on fisheries policy.

Tom Kelly is a marine biologist who founded the Inland Seas Education Association in Suttons Bay, Michigan, in 1989. In addition to being the organization's executive director, he is also captain of its marine education vessel, the *Inland Seas*. He has a Bachelor of Science degree in Natural Resources Management and a Master of Science degree in Marine Science from the University of Michigan. He was previously employed by the Michigan Sea Grant program and as a commercial fisherman. Interview, 28 May 1999. Photograph by Michael J. Chiarappa.

I did some work in commercial fisheries when I was at the university, mainly ocean stuff, marine fishery management. And when I got up here, I ran into a number of people who were in the commercial fishery here. They were interesting people, so that is how I got to know them a little bit. In those years, there was quite a lot of animosity between the commercial fishermen and the state DNR. The sport-fishing groups were aligned with the state DNR and generally tried to shrink or eliminate the commercial fishermen, particularly the gillnetters. They had some genuine concerns in trying to protect the sport fishery from over-harvesting and accidental harvest, by-catch, from the commercial fishermen. But as happens oftentimes, the techniques used were so heavy-handed. Most of the commercial fishermen thought they were getting a raw deal, and so there was a lot of animosity and hard feelings. There were two camps, those that were allied with the state and the sport fishing, and people in the other. I remember going to public hearings where these issues were being discussed, and it was a very heated atmosphere.

Just stepping into that arena and presenting information such as scientific data, not necessarily for or against either side, was a political act and made friends and enemies for you whether you wanted to or not. When I first moved to Traverse City there was an organization called the Boardman River Advisory Council. It was a citizen's group that was working with the state to get the Natural Rivers Act to include the Boardman River and they were working on management and that sort of thing. And they asked me to join because I was one of the few people around here at that time who had any technical knowledge of the fisheries and that sort of thing. There was also a DNR biologist in the town at that time. They asked me to serve as a technical advisor to that committee which I thought was a rather innocuous thing at the time. But somehow word got back to the DNR in Lansing, and the next thing I knew my boss was calling me from Ann Arbor. He said his boss had been contacted by the head of the DNR, who was wondering what Tom Kelly was doing in Traverse City and get him the hell out of there. It was kind of an unpleasant experience to have somebody trying to take your first job for what was basically a misunderstanding. But the times were so heated, anybody that was not on their side was against them. But a lot of the DNR people in the field, the technical people that worked in the field, were probably more closely allied with the sport fishing. Most of the people I worked with on a one-to-one basis in the field were pretty levelheaded, and could see both sides. They were interested obviously in protecting the fishery, but I think the higher up you went in the organization, the closer you got to Lansing, the more politicized it became.

I never had any problem getting along with the DNR fisheries people in the field. I had a pretty good working relationship with Myrl Keller up in Charlevoix. He told me one time that he was told by the people in Lansing not to be too cooperative with me or give me any information or anything like that. And he said that even though that was what he was told, all of the files and records at the Charlevoix lab were public information available to the public and that included me, too. He was not going to do that although he had to follow what he was told. On a one-to-one basis, we had a pretty good working relationship over many, many years even though we did not always see the issues the same way. On a professional level, I was able to work with him and a lot of other people in the DNR too.

Jim Moore, former fisheries official for the Wisconsin DNR, discussed the public view of the DNR.

The DNR has some supporters, but as in many states, it is the state agency people love to hate. There are so many things that we are involved with that impact their lives, whether it is going to a park, raising the fees for their hunting or fishing licenses, issuing permits for them to build something or something they need for business. In their eyes, there is hardly anything we are not meddling with. Criticizing the DNR is a good way for politicians to get votes. They promise they are going to do this or that to the DNR, or make sure they do not do something to you. It has been kind of tough over the years to sit back and watch politicians get elected by badmouthing the DNR, and then turn around and find out the reality of things after they are elected and start looking into things. They often end up eating their words, backpedaling, or doing things exactly opposite of what they ran on when they were seeking office. That has been going on for the thirty-plus years that I have been working. I do not think you will ever get away from it. Whether it is regulating the sport or commercial fishery, if you base it on good biological facts and information and lay your cards on the table, more often than not, they have supported the rules as they go through the legislative process for approval. Every now and then, it might get to the point where decisions are made based on politics. Those cases they usually come back to haunt them, and we end up in the not-too-distant future having to go through a lot of grief trying to reverse those types of decisions. We are always going have to deal with that kind of stuff.

Ralph Hay of the Michigan DNR Fisheries Division recalled how agency policy makers consulted with the staff and sought public input on issues pertaining to fisheries management and policy.

We would have staff meetings and we would sit down and we would talk about the problems that we might have such as how are we going to control the abundance of salmon in certain rivers. Out of these meetings would come some strategies to deal with these problems. We also developed policy regarding where we would plant fish, how many we would plant, whether we would open rivers, gear restrictions, seasonal restrictions, and that sort of thing.

Before the DNR can revise its own cold-water regulations on trout in inland waters, for example, we will have numerous public meetings. We have had focus group sessions where people would be called in and asked questions about what they thought about cold-water fishing. And we have had external committee meetings where we have had select private people working with department people to come up with proposals. We will hear from the regulations committee, made up of strictly internal people who can hash out the problem. And then we go to the public—the anglers—to find out what they think about these proposals. Then we take what we gather at public information meetings, and run it back through the committees again, and hopefully go before the Natural Resources Commission with a proposal.

We also get feedback at the local level because we are constantly meeting the public on a day-to-day basis. For example, information about stream surveys is distributed at sportsmen's clubs meetings, and wildlife association meetings. Their members bring questions to the DNR staff members. We offer suggestions and they will offer their opinion. Our creel census clerks have been interviewing anglers on the Great Lakes for about fifteen years. They offer a very front-line initial contact with our clientele group. People offer opinions to them and their comments are passed on up through the chain of command.

Jim Moore indicated that throughout his career, the state attempted to work with both sport and commercial fishing organizations in the policy-making process.

During the late 1950s the sea lampreys were having an effect on whitefish and lake trout. Alewives were running rampant. Whether or not they were having any impact on whitefish reproduction survival, I am not sure we will ever know. I think the huge biomass of alewives was a real detriment to everything in the lake at that period of time. Regulations were minimal and enforcement was minimal. There was one warden assigned to all of Lake Michigan. How could one guy oversee the whole lake and do anything meaningful? At the time, we had probably very close to 300 commercial licenses. Today we are under 100 and a lot of those are families like the Weborg family or the Hickeys, who have multiple licenses. So if you actually cranked it down to how many family, commercial operations you have got going, it would probably be in the fifties somewhere. There are a lot of things that have changed from that standpoint, too.

When I started working in the late 1960s, there was still an active board called the Commercial Fishing Advisory Board. It was made up of five or six fishermen and one sport-fishing representative. And during the 1970s when a lot of this contention occurred, I was at a meeting in Manitowoc or Two Rivers with our fisheries chief, Jim Addis. I was trying to explain some new rule or regulation and was getting beat up pretty bad by some of the commercial guys there. Addis got so mad, he went back to Madison and abolished the Commercial Fishing Advisory Board. He said "That's it. We are not putting our people through any more of this." But at the same time, as we were starting to look towards quotas, he also proposed a Lake Michigan Commercial Fishing Board which was very active in coming up with recommendations and responsibilities for determining how quotas were going to be allocated.

The Commercial Fishing Board is still in existence, but a lot of the quota allocation responsibilities have now been transferred back to the department. The board is more or less just an advisory to the department on those types of things. Over the thirty years I worked for the department, both of those groups have functioned in an advisory capacity or been involved directly with some of the commercial rules and regulations. In Wisconsin, we also have what is known as the Wisconsin Conservation Congress, whose delegates include sport-fishing and hunter groups. They have got about twenty different committees active in that group, including turkey, deer, bear, and Great Lakes sport fishing. It is almost a study in itself to follow the way that organization has worked over time. And then we have big sport-fishing organizations such as the Great Lakes Sport Fishing Federation and the Council of Great Lakes. It is hard to keep all the names straight. There are real active groups that we work with on the sport side, too. There are also local groups. Door County has its own commercial fishing association. The trawlers have their little association. We also have the southern Green Bay perch fishermen. There are a lot of little smaller groups within the commercial fishing industry as well and port or big city groups of sport fishers who belong to the federation clubs. We spend a lot of time working with all those groups and individuals over time. Those people are usually pretty well informed on the issues. Sometimes people are not as informed as they should be, even to argue their own concerns.

Public apathy over what goes on is probably worse now than back when the programs were thriving. We will hold a public information meeting and advertise the heck out of it, and it is about normal if a half a dozen to a dozen people show up. Oftentimes, there are more DNR people there to help answer questions than members of the public. I do not know how you can do a better job of trying to educate people to the issues you are dealing with.

———————

Mike Toneys of the Wisconsin DNR noted that nearly all fishing groups are becoming more politically aware and seek input in the policy-review or policy-making process.

B oth the sport and commercial fishermen have become political, very politically savvy I would say, especially in the last ten years. Often the few people who show up at public meetings are always the same people, the very vocal, and the most controversial. Some have axes to grind or are politically connected. In the twenty years that I have been here, people have become more politically connected. They are more apt to go to politicians, legislators, and even our administrators in Madison and work with them directly, rather than work with field people as closely as they used to. It is kind of a power game. Why waste time with people like Jim Moore and I to settle conflicts and issues when they can go right to the top? It certainly has not made life any easier for us, because we are reacting to legislators or some of our administrators who are getting nasty-grams from the public about this or that issue. It has made things harder than they should be. When I first started, people were more apt to come to the local fishery managers, the biologists, and talk over issues. If they could not get satisfaction, they chose another route. Now they choose the other route more often than not first.

Our relationship with the commercial fishermen has gotten more rational and gentlemanly in the years that I have been here. We spend a lot of time with them; sometimes we spend more time than we probably should. We have got fewer fishermen to deal with. Most of the ones that are left in the fishery are professional, serious, full-time fishermen. We may not agree on issues, but we spend a lot of time with them sitting down. Jim Moore is involved in a rather large effort involving commercial, sport, the general public, and law enforcement to rewrite some of our commercial rules right now. That process is going along quite well. The last major controversy we had and are still facing is the cutback in chinook stocking. It has been a lakewide issue since the late 1980s when the chinook population crashed. Dealing with the sport-fishing public has been contentious at times. But if we do some decent biology and are working as one voice among all the agencies around the lake, we can usually hold sway in a proposal. It worked out that way with the chinook.

Some of the most contentious players and issues often arise in the southern metropolitan Milwaukee-Racine-Kenosha area. Some of the more vocal spokespeople for the sport-fishing concerns come from that Milwaukee area. Perhaps there is something in the water or the air, or just living in close proximity with each other, but they are some of the more angry people we have to deal with. And some of those who are vocal with us are well connected politically and will call a representative at the drop of a hat. If they do not think they are getting a fair shake from the department people, they will go to their legislators very quickly, probably faster than a sport or commercial group in northern Wisconsin, although commercial interests in general have become savvier politically. They have looked to their legislators to bail them out on a number of issues or soften the blow of some of the regulations. Fortunately, I have not had to deal with that group down there as much as some of the local DNR folks have that are stationed right down there. You hear some war stories that make you appreciate the peace and quiet of Door County.

Usually there is either a phone call or a letter that we receive at the local level from that representative that needs to be answered. Often you have to spend more time on an issue than perhaps you would have otherwise. Most of the legislators I have dealt with are pretty understanding. They are just working on behalf of their constituents. We have some in our legislature that like DNR more than others and vice versa, so it makes for an interesting workday at times.

We have to go through a long process just to get a rule into effect. We propose a rule. It goes to what is called a Natural Resources Board, a citizens policy board for DNR. They either accept or reject the proposed rule change. Their recommendation then goes to legislative review. People who disagree with the proposed rule can go to their legislator, seek a legislative hearing, and it can be thrown out at that point for commercial rules. For sport-fishing rules, we have got the Conservation Congress that acts as a hearing body. Sport rules can go to legislative review. There are checks and balances; we are accountable. For the last three or four years, the governor has selected the DNR secretary. The Natural Resources Board used to pick our secretary, so it has become more politically oriented than it used to be. Perhaps change was made on behalf of the critics who said we were not accountable enough. Maybe that was their answer—to have the secretary picked by the governor and made a cabinet position.

The bumper sticker "What God Giveth, the DNR Taketh Away" is a reminder of the way things used to be, in contrast with how much more rational and fun they are now. I started in 1980 at the end of the wars that went on in the 1970s. The first commercial boat I monitored in Door County had the sticker above the door. When I stepped on Don Voight's boat back in the 1980s, that sticker was posted above his door. It says "What the Lord giveth, the DNR taketh away." The Voights are a very religious family. Their boats are named *Faith* and *Hope*.

The bumper sticker has been a constant reminder of the kind of a history I have been involved in up here with the commercial fishery, and it is near and dear to my heart. It is something I can look at and get a dose of reality.

Wisconsin DNR fisheries official Ron Poff, who retired after forty-one years of service, noted that fisheries managers play a difficult balancing act weighing what is best for the resource against other political, economic, and social realities.

I t is always tough when you work with commercial fishermen and any of these industries—sport, the charter trawlers, tournament anglers, private fish hatcheries, and net fishermen. They are harvesters, and they make a living off of it. It is not just a hobby with them. They are not out there strictly for the fun of it. You are a regulator, and you have a lot to do with the well-being of the fish population they are harvesting or making their money off of. So you get kind of a thick skin after a while. The only way you survive in the job is to say, "I know where you are coming from, but in the long run, it is the well-being of the fish stock that is going to contribute to your well-being." You develop an interesting attitude working with the people. It has been fun. I really enjoy working with people. Most recently, I was working with private fish hatchery operators and tournament anglers, but it has all been essentially the same kind of a thing. You have to be a hell of a negotiator sometimes. You are what one management style calls blue. The reds make snap decisions; the greens need more data to make a decision; and the blues strive for a decision. So they are accommodating. You have to accommodate and you realize to win everybody has to lose a little bit. That is the way it works.

I have fond memories of a lot of the commercial fishermen I worked with. Jeff Weborg up in Gills Rock was kind of a rambunctious kid at the time. Elaine Johnson ran a grocery store up there; she is probably still around. She called me one day to pick my brain about something about walleye fishing in Green Bay and some commercial fish act money we had gotten. She was a feisty one. I will never forget they organized a busload of people to come down to a hearing in Manitowoc, Wisconsin. This great big bus shows up with banners on the sides. They had gotten word that one of the networks was going to film a talk I was giving. I must have talked for a couple hours, and the network probably got a couple minutes condensed out of it, but it was quite an experience. So they made their showing. It was fun. But you keep coming back. You just do not go away, so it is kind of frustrating for them. You are there. It is your job. You are going to keep coming back.

We developed some pretty interesting ways of operating. We ended up creating commercial fishing boards, one for each lake, that were comprised of fishermen representing each of the major commercial fishing groups on the lake. There might of even been sport-fishing interests involved also, but the commercial fishermen said we should worry about the biology of the fish and the well-being of the fish, and they will worry about the well-being of the fishermen. In essence, that translated to you tell us what the total allowable catch should be, we will accept the responsibility for apportioning that amongst the total allowable number of fishermen. And they had a heck of a struggle on their hands with that task. We debated and debated on some of these. One of the first fisheries that came to their attention on Lake Michigan was the chub fishery. Around 1974, we had to close the chub fishery. We allowed some harvest, but only under assessment contracts. A group of biologists from Lake Michigan including the Fish and Wildlife Service folks at Ann Arbor, created a chub technical committee. We looked in depth at the stock and decided when we would be able to reopen the chub fishery. In 1977 or so, we reopened the fishery.

In order to close the chub fishery, we had to convince people that the fishermen were literally fishing up the stocks. Chubs are a species that exist in somewhat independent stocks across the whole lake, up and down the coast, and the fishermen are mobile. So even though the stocks are becoming depressed, it is not reflected in the catch rates. They will fish up one stock to the point where it becomes no longer profitable. Then they will move to another stock. They were literally harvesting their capital out there, and we convinced them of it. We were able to close the fishery, provided we could give out some pretty decent assessment contracts. It worked.

The fishery that has always amazed me is whitefish. In my mind, whitefish are the bread and butter of the Lake Michigan fishery. Door County would not be Door County without whitefish. Despite all of the other things that were going on, we were able to continue whitefish fishery at a million pounds or more a year, at an annual mortality rate of up around fifty to sixty percent of the stock. That is at the knife's edge. When you are managing whitefish at that level, they could crash or go the other way, but instead, it has been consistent. In fact, since limited entry came in, it has been a much better fishery. The average before limited entry was more like 400,000 pounds a year for the Wisconsin fishery.

We had some pretty big operators like the Smith brothers in Port Washington, who were represented on the Commercial Fishing Board. They basically said that with the harvest of up around three million pounds of chubs, they could sustain the market with a good returning price to the fishermen. If it went above that, then the price to the fishermen would go down. You have got to balance this thing and work in favor of establishing some sort of a quota to keep the price supported. You must also keep the harvest low enough so you got a continuing operation there. There have been other fisheries that have had problems such as the yellow perch and lake herring up on Lake Superior. There are the alewife fishery, the smelt fishery, and the continual battle with the trawlers.

In the early 1970s Wisconsin DNR Fisheries official Ron Poff was caricatured in a well-known billboard constructed by Northeast Wisconsin's commercial fishing community. The billboard was in Algoma, Wisconsin, and Poff commented on how it was emblematic of a host of problems that afflicted late twentieth-century fisheries management on Lake Michigan.

The billboard poster is a story in itself. We had been paying the fishermen for icing and boxing illegally caught lake trout. The lake trout fishery had been closed, I think, in 1955 or so because of the sea lamprey, but the commercial fishermen were still catching them in whitefish nets. And rather than have them go to waste, we allowed them to ice them and box them, and then the wardens would handle their dispensation. We started out giving them around eight cents a pound, which is peanuts. Then it went to fifteen cents, and then up to forty cents a pound. We reasoned that at forty cents a pound, they were being amply compensated and then they would go ahead and sell the fish as well, and give us the difference between the fisherman's returning price and forty cents a pound. Well the way it worked out, we ended up getting about a dollar a pound, but the fishermen also ended up getting about a dollar a pound, because in most cases he is also the processor. He has one price that's the dockside price. He has another price that is the market price. And we sort of looked the other way on that and said fine, that's good. We are getting a dollar a pound for those fish. That is okay by us.

And then along came the Department of Agriculture and State Division of Health who said the fish are contaminated with DDT, and we could not allow the fishermen to market them. We had to write a letter for Secretary L. P. Voight's signature saying we've got to discontinue this process. We spelled out the reasons why we had to discontinue it but, of course, the backlash was at the department. And so came the billboard behind Steel Winery in Algoma, showing my boss, John Brasch and I, putting a wood screw through a commercial fisherman. It was all about the DNR denying the fishermen this right. There was not a word about the State Division of Health or Department of Agriculture or anybody else. It was the DNR.

Jim Moore noted that while the policy-making process was highly politicized, the enforcement of fisheries laws and regulations rarely created political problems.

Over my career, there were relatively few instances when the governor's office, the secretary, or the regional director told a supervisor that a certain individual should be reassigned. I am not aware of anybody who has ever been fired or accused of wrongdoing or heavy-handed tactics related to enforcement of regulations. If I get a speeding ticket and I was going only a few miles an hour faster than what I was supposed to, I might view that as heavy-handed, too, as opposed to getting a warning. So sometimes it is the perception of those who might be violating the law or stretching the law. I guess you would almost have to deal with those on individual cases and try to make your own decision on whether it was heavy-handed or not. You would have to look at both sides of the argument.

Jory Jonas, a research biologist at the Great Lakes fisheries research station operated by the Michigan DNR, discussed the cooperation among the states bordering Lake Michigan and between the states and the federal government.

Each of the agencies that manage Great Lakes fisheries has different constituent groups and different abilities to communicate with them. Each state has a different government and way to make an action occur. We are getting better at working together to manage the Great Lakes. We have a Lake Michigan committee that is comprised of fisheries policy makers and managers from all of the different agencies that work on the lake, including Wisconsin, Michigan, Indiana, Illinois, and each of the tribal representatives. The Lake Michigan committee is supposed to address issues that are of concern to everyone on the lake. Underneath the Lake Michigan committee is the lake technical committee. It is comprised of people like myself, scientists who do research on the lake and provide scientific, technical, or expert advice to the members of the Lake Michigan committee to help them get the answers they need to make effective management decisions.

We have had success in working together to reduce chinook salmon stocking on Lake Michigan. It took five to eight years of planning and getting everybody oriented in the right direction before we could actually begin stocking reduction. There were many governmental and political considerations that had to be addressed particularly with the anglers' groups. Fisheries management is tough; it gets frustrating sometimes. Communication is so important. We need to get the information flowing in the right way at the right time. We developed a series of five presentations to get information out to the public on the whole Lake Michigan/chinook salmon/alewife phenomena. We present the top ten reasons why the DNR felt we should reduce chinook salmon densities in Lake Michigan. This information is available on our site on the World Wide Web.

Sea Grant agent John McKinney spoke of his role to provide the public with the results of recent research and information relating to Michigan's Great Lakes waters and their fisheries. His goal is to avoid advocating a particular view or position.

All Sea Grant extension people are links; we are networkers. At one end, we are linked to the university and on the other end we are out here with the public. We are part of that two-way stream of information. Working with the public, we hear things and funnel them back. Research is done or other things happen. That is one angle—one approach to it. But what hopefully I have done is served as an unbiased source of information. I have many roles. I conduct, host, or convene fishery workshops and meetings to provide a forum for exchange of ideas. They address specific issues like the safety guidelines for fish handling mandated by the federal government. I try to bring resources to whoever needs them so that they can make better decisions. That is really what it is. Most of us at Sea Grant do this kind of thing. It is a continuous challenge not to become biased, not to become an advocate or identified with one side or the other. You have to continually try to be available to everybody and in some ways, that is an ideal position, because you do not have to take sides. You can be neutral. You can be out there by yourself sometimes. You are nobody's friend or you are everybody's friend. That is the role I think I have to play. There are times when you stray one way or the other, but over the longer term, I would hope it balances out.

Jim Moore, who worked in the Wisconsin DNR's fishery program for nearly thirty years, recalled when trawling first began in Wisconsin waters in the late 1960s. He noted that in recent years, trawling had become increasingly controversial.

When I started working in 1966, trawlers had already operated for a little while on Green Bay—trawling for alewives. I do not know if it was Art Swaer or the LeClairs out of Two Rivers, who got the idea of using gulf-style trawlers on Green Bay and Lake Michigan to catch large quantities of alewives. I think they approached some of my predecessors and broached the idea of using that type of gear on Lake Michigan.

And because of the severe problems during the mid-1960s with dead alewives on the beach and at the time, most of the biomass of fish in Lake Michigan was alewives, those fellows were actually encouraged to look into the gear. It was operated for many, many years under a special permit type arrangement. There were a lot of concerns within the commercial industry, and part of the reason I rode fish tugs sometimes three days a week during the summer of 1966, was to see what impact they were having on yellow perch in Green Bay.

The Wisconsin DNR began allowing the harvest of alewives by trawling in the days when alewives were very abundant and washing up on the beaches and chasing tourists out of the county. Now there are more than enough trout and salmon out there to maintain and keep the alewives in check. We are even concerned there are too many salmon out there, so we have reduced stocking this year. Pete LeClair has been involved in trawl fishing for over thirty years on Lake Michigan; trawling continues to be one of our biggest controversies. We just went to the Natural Resources Board with a reduced smelt quota because the smelt population has not been doing real well over the last few years even though Pete LeClair's catches were up this last winter. There is nothing biologically to suggest that there are more smelt in the lake than there have been over the last few years. We probably spend as much time working on that issue, one way or another, than any aspect of the commercial fishery that we manage over the last fifteen years. There are three or four other trawler operators besides Pete LeClair. There is an operator out of Cedar River, Michigan, named Bob Ruleau, who trawls in Wisconsin as a nonresident. Trawling has probably been one of the biggest areas of contention, continuously back and forth between the politicians, sport groups, or Pete LeClair and his continual requests of one sort or another.

Ron Poff recalled how Wisconsin regarded trawling as one solution to the alewife problem.

Trawling on the Great Lakes was quite a thing. It came in a couple years before I started working on the Great Lakes, when they had the big alewife die-offs in 1967 or so. We had sent some folks down to Mississippi to look at the side trawlers on the Gulf, and they came back with the idea that maybe this is a way of harvesting some of these masses of fish in Lake Michigan. The federal government jumped in after the big die-offs and funded a skimming operation to benefit all of the states on Lake Michigan. For example, the water intake for industrial use in Chicago was threatened with all these dying alewives. So the federal government came in, and funded contracts with trawlers to operate skimming nets on the lake. They used big monster nets. They put a trawl on each end, and dragged these fairly shallow skim nets to concentrate the alewives. The theory was you could put out a floating fish pump into this mass of fish, pump them into a truck, and haul them to a landfill. There was a little problem in getting landfills to accept millions and millions of pounds of alewives, so it did not last very long. It was also a difficult operation with the winds that we encountered on the lake and getting people to fish these nets. The theory was fine, but it did not quite work. The fish pump idea was petering out at the time that I started on the Great Lakes. In fact, Wisconsin's two fish pumps never did get used on the Great Lakes; they sat in a warehouse. The pumps might still be there, unless they finally got rid of them.

Trawling became a pretty effective method of harvesting alewives, smelt, and sheepshead on Lake Winnebago. There was a time when it was not unusual for Swaer fisheries out of Pensaukee to have trucks running with 30,000 pounds of alewives out of places like Two Rivers. I will never forget a truck with 30,000 pounds of alewives headed to Pensaukee lost its tailgate in Green Bay. They spread alewives down this one street for quite some distance. And of course, the fisherman, one of the LeClairs, was nonplused. He just did not understand how this could have happened. He ended up paying for a cleanup. It was quite a thing.[61]

I have been out on LeClair's trawlers, and he does take a lot of juvenile fish other than what he is targeting. When they are trawling, it is damn near impossible to avoid it. You cannot tell what some of the stuff is. It is just little translucent fingerlings. By the time they come in a smelt trawl, they are mush. We kept working with him to try and get a different time of the day to trawl or a different season to trawl to try and avoid nontarget fish. He makes a good share of his money on the smelt fishery.

There is a certain amount of animosity between the types of fisheries. The chub gillnetters are not too happy with trawlers that might trawl for chubs. Actually, at one time, the trawlers were encouraged to trawl for chubs. Chubs were all over the place just before the alewife fishery. There are also the gillnetters and the poundnetters on whitefish fisheries. I have always encouraged the state, probably wrongfully so, not to try and ban the large mesh gill net. We have a size limit of seventeen inches for whitefish. A gillnetter uses four-and-a-half-inch mesh gill nets. Probably less than two percent of what he catches is below seventeen inches. The average size of the whitefish taken in the gill nets is more like nineteen inches. Michigan got rid of the gill nets, or at least they were going to. I do not know where it stands now with the treaty fisheries.

Trapnetters are a little hard on a fish compared to pound nets. It is because they pull the whole net, the harvest, so the fish get beat up quite a bit. There is not a high mortality, but it is significant. The big bugaboo for gill nets is the incidental catch. If we could get the whitefish fishermen to avoid or to not have a high incidental catch of lake trout it would be great. It is hard to do, though, when there are lake trout all over the place.

One of the most controversial policy issues involved the regulation of gill-net fishing. During the 1970s, the State of Michigan sought to drastically reduce and ultimately eliminate the use of gill nets in its Great Lakes waters. Commercial fishermen, many of whom had fished with gill nets their entire lives, opposed this action. Some lacked the capital necessary to buy a trap-net boat and gear. Others remained unconvinced that gill nets were really the killer nets critics alleged. They maintained that most fishermen used gill nets properly and were able to target species with minimal incidental catch. Today, the tribes license most of the Lake Michigan fishermen who gill net in Michigan waters.

Howard Tanner believed that it was necessary for Michigan to ban the gill net in order to protect the budding sport fishery.

In 1964 the conflict with the commercial industry was very, very difficult and it was not fun. There are a lot of good people who are commercial fishermen. There are some scoundrels, but there are scoundrels everywhere. The commercial fishermen had been there for generations when we came along and said we are going to take it away from you. One of the things I left undone that my successor, Wayne Tody, finished was the banning of the gill nets. We said, "You cannot fish with gill nets. You can fish with trap nets, with impounding gear where you can keep those fish that we decide that you are entitled to, like whitefish. The fish you are not entitled to which we are declaring to be game fish, can be safely released with minimal mortality with impounding gear." Some commercial fishermen would accept that, and a lot of them would not. It took seven years of court action to finally close down the gill-net fishery. Gill nets were still in use in 1972–1974 because the fishermen had appealed our decision. It went clear to the Michigan Supreme Court, which ruled that the DNR did have the authority to ban the gill net.

Michigan DNR fisheries division chief for ten years, Dr. Wayne Tody was convinced of the need to ban gill nets in order to protect the salmon fishery.

My biologists who were assigned to the Great Lakes station told me I had a real problem. They told me the salmon are going to be sitting ducks for the large mesh gill nets. The large mesh gill nets, uncontrolled as they were then, will hurt the stocks when the fish are small and when they are big. We have got to manage both simultaneously. We then recommended a law banning large mesh gill nets because they would catch salmon, lake trout, or steelhead and so on in waters shallower than forty fathoms. Few fish are alive in a gill net. A few of them are, but they will not live if you let them go. Not very many will live for several reasons. Dieresis is one. Build up of lactic acid is another. Destruction of their mucous coat making them susceptible to fungus is another. If you let that kind of fish go, you are going to get delayed mortality. They swim away and look healthy, but they are not.

The gill-net ban hit the commercial fishermen awful hard because that was mainly what they were fishing. The sport-fishing lobby was very strong and financed us, so obviously we were biased. We were also trying to rehabilitate the Great Lakes and convert alewife to valuable fish and so on. So we proceeded through all the court battles and political battles and helped organize the sport-fish lobby to get rid of the gill nets, the large mesh gill nets. We left the commercial fishermen small mesh for chubs in the deeper waters. The trapnetters were maintained.

At the same time in fisheries, a move was going on around the world to limit entry to where people could make a decent living fishing. The old notion of the commons where everybody could go out and get what he can get the quickest and let the devil take the hind, was mostly gone. Now there were going to be quotas and catch numbers for the people. The commercial fishermen just could not understand this. It was totally foreign to them. I think it is every place in the world where they have done the old tragedy of the commons so long and so much. You are not going to get this story from them, but that is what this is all about.[62]

As executive secretary of the Great Lakes Fishery Commission from 1975 to 1992, Carlos Fetterolf was in a unique position to observe changes in Michigan's approach to fisheries management and policy.

The gill netting ban controversy was one that Michigan wanted to push very hard and Michigan did push it. The DNR was able to get the laws changed so that there was not any gill netting in Lake Michigan in Michigan waters. Then this gradually spread around all the other states. To my way of thinking, a fish is just as dead if it is dead in a gill net, trap net, or an angler's ice box. But the gill nets were nonselective and they did kill a lot of fish that were not targeted species. It is a form of management that is very popular with states and very unpopular with commercial fishermen. If I had one thing to pick out as the saddest event that took place while I was with the Great Lakes Fishery Commission from 1975 to 1992, it was watching the demise of the commercial fishery in a lot of areas. I have always felt that commercial fishing can be viable along with recreational fishing but the regulation has to be very tight on it.

The Michigan DNR's increased emphasis on sport fisheries in its Great Lakes waters and the declined population of lake trout and other native species ultimately led to the near-elimination of gill nets by state-licensed commercial fishers. Jory Jonas, a research biologist at the Michigan DNR's Charlevoix research laboratory, discussed how her views on gill nets changed over time.

There is a lot of debate around gill net versus trap net. When you are fishing a gill net, most of what you catch dies. You can release some stuff alive, but most of the bi-catch is not going to make it. The gill nets are not very selective. You can set the gill nets in a way to make them more selective, but it is pretty difficult not to trap other nontarget species as well. Whatever is swimming by is going to end up trapped in the gill net.

When the trap nets are pulled, the fish are alive. You can sort them by size and species and release them. I started out thinking gill nets were bad. My opinion has been turned around by my own boat crew, consisting of two commercial fishermen with long histories on the Great Lakes. They get lots of hours to batter me with concepts on the boat. They have convinced me that gill nets may have a place in commercial fishing. When there is ice out there, there is no way you are going to be able to deal with a trap net. Gill nets are relatively easy to handle, even under the ice. The other benefit of a gill net is that it is inexpensive relative to a trap net, although the latter will likely cost less to maintain and repair. There may be seasons and opportunities where there are concentrations of the fish species targeted by commercial fishers where gill-net use could be an option. There may be a way to work the gill nets into some type of a fishing regime where their use would not seriously harm fish stocks.

Wisconsin fisheries biologist Mike Toneys reflected on the state's decision to retain the use of gills nets in commercial fishing in its Great Lakes waters.

It has been our position to work towards a viable commercial fishery on Lake Michigan's Wisconsin waters. One of the things we have tried to do was to make regulations as flexible as possible for the commercial fishermen so they had a variety of gear to use out there. One type of gear does not fit all situations for harvesting. And yet we have tried to control the amount of gill net used and where it was used, to minimize incidental kill. Fishermen from other states around Wisconsin have put pressure on sport fishermen here to put pressure on the DNR to get rid of the killer gill net. It has caused us a lot of headaches over the years, and we have had to spend a lot of time trying to defend our position on the use of gill nets in the commercial fishery.

It is probably fifty-fifty right now, although in the last ten years or so, it has gone more towards trap nets. There are some years when some of the fishermen feel compelled to go back to fishing gill nets, because the trap nets are not getting the fish they need. They are not getting deep enough with them. We have gone probably more so to an entrapment-gear fishery than a gill-net fishery, but the fishermen like to have the option of using both. We have allowed them to continue using both, although it has created a lot of management headaches and user conflicts. We have tried to walk a fine line and leave those options out there, and yet try to placate sport fishermen and keep the lake trout program going. It is much more difficult to administer than Michigan policy; they just outlawed the gear, period.

———————

Former DNR fisheries chief Wayne Tody of Michigan is critical of tribal fisheries management because it permits gill nets. Tody opposes gill nets because they harm fisheries resources.

I do not like the way the fishery is organized. With fair negotiation and realistic nego- tiation the issue could be resolved. I feel bad about the guys we took the licenses away from. They cannot get them back because of the Indians. We banned gill nets by law and I do not think anybody is going to revoke that law. We do not think gill nets should be used. I do not think you will get anybody to disagree with that. I hope not. The Indians are using them in ways that we outlawed so that we could manage the fish, not to keep them from ever getting caught, but get them up to a healthy and mature size, mostly for in the sport catch, but in the commercial catch too. In spite of what anybody may tell you, the quality of gill-net-caught fish is often poorer than that caught in trap nets. Any fish gets soft you let it hang there in a net for two or three days and if there is a storm, those guys are adrift in those nets in thirty-foot waves. Do not let them kid you. If there is fish in the nets it will spoil. I am not going to defend gill nets—large mesh nets in less than forty fathoms of water. We banned them once and they are going to stay banned, I hope.

The Indians fish under the federal protection. They have spread their fishery quite broad and wide. I know they are fishing in Grand Traverse Bay and they are always arguing how many salmon they want to catch. The sport-fishing interests are griping. They had a pretty good fishery for sport fishery on East Bay, but it seems to be gone. Myrl Keller told me that the Indians are fishing all the way from Drummond Island down well into Green Bay. They have got major fishery I think going up to Keweenaw Bay and, of course, at Sault Ste. Marie and Whitefish Bay. The Indian fishery is getting pretty widespread and bringing us right back to gill nets where we were in 1967. I do not think it was a great thing.

———————

Ron Poff expressed frustration with sport fishers' hostility toward commercial fishers. He argued that the value of the commercial fishing industry is too often calculated only in monetary terms.

A t the time when we were harvesting a million pounds of whitefish, several million pounds of chubs, and probably 27 million pounds of alewives a year out of Lake Michigan, we also had probably the best sport fishery for trout and salmon that we have ever had. And yet sportsmen were saying that the commercial fishermen were raping the resource and we had to get rid of them. It used to really grate me. At the time, Michigan went through a dozen different bouts of ban the gill nets, and finally ended up going to trap nets for whitefish. It just did not make a whole lot of sense, but we got caught up in it too. We created a fantastic fishery in Green Bay, for example, with stocking levels that were not modest but were substantial, but not outrageous. And yet our own managers kept asking for more fish to stock. Well, we have never had the kinds of catch rates that we had in the mid-1970s, until about 1976 which was one of the peak years despite the fact that we had been stocking more and more fish for the sport fishery.[63]

There has been more and more pressure against commercial fishing largely because of the high incidental catch of sport fish in commercial nets. It seems like it is either black or white with people. It is either pro or con. There is no room in this fishery for resolution when they are constantly battling each other.

Conflict continues today. There have been little inroads now and then, when the fishermen try and get together, but the conflict is still there. Maybe if the sport fishery mellows a little bit, it might be better. We will never have the monster commercial fisheries of 100 years ago, that is for sure. We will never have those kinds of commercial fisheries. It just is not in the cards. Remember fish is a luxury item when you consider the prices for perch and whitefish and lake trout. Hamburger is a lot cheaper.

There is room for a commercial fishery. There is always going be room for it, I think. One of the major benefits is not just the fact that they are harvesting fish and selling them so there are new dollars coming into a community. It is not as though somebody is switching from bowling to sport fishing, so there is just a transfer of funds. This is new money harvested from the public trough. It is a public resource that they are harvesting. But it does bring new dollars coming into a community. So there is that value, but there is also a value just in the sociology of it. What would Door County be if there was no commercial fishery? No fish tugs, no fish boils, no whitefish boils? Bayfield is the same way. Those communities would lose something fairly significant if they did not have a commercial fishery. Commercial fishing is one of the things that attracts people to those areas. Tourism is the biggest buck, and commercial fishing is an essential element.

Jim Moore recalled the situation faced by commercial fishermen in the 1950s and 1960s, before the Wisconsin DNR faced conflict with Lake Michigan sport fishermen.

The commercial fishermen were coming out of a rather depressed time. In 1957 or 1958, their whitefish catch for all of Lake Michigan in Wisconsin waters was only about 9,000 pounds. The sea lamprey had probably pretty well not only decimated lake trout, but it knocked whitefish production down to the point where a lot of those guys had dropped out of the ·fishery just because it was not economically feasible. The big herring fishery had pretty much collapsed. They were still catching some perch, but it was not anywhere near enough to keep everybody going. The chub fishery was still fairly good, and a number of guys were involved with it. There were not incidental lake trout problems at the time, or other salmonids interfering with that they were doing.

I think some of the smarter ones could see it coming as fish were being stocked. It was one of those things that as more and more fish are stocked in the lake, and more and more sport-fishing pressure started building and more obvious problems not only of incidental fish, but also, illegal fishing activities. Guys were setting nets and catching lake trout and selling them illegally. Everything kind of started out slowly, and just built and built and built. We have been working on problems of one sort or another ever since. I am not sure how best to characterize the Wisconsin commercial fishermen's attitudes other than very much from the beginnings of the trout and salmon program, it was pretty clear that one way or another, there was going to be a commercial fishery existing with the sport fishery. It was decided there would be a viable commercial fishery, and that has pretty much guided us ever since.

There has always been one issue or another that has caused conflict between the sport and commercial fishermen, whether it was incidental catches, or the question of harvesting forage fish or whatever. So a lot of our work over the years has been trying to gather data to answer questions when these conflicts have arisen and manage the various species, whether it is sport or commercial, in between all the other problems that keep arising over time.

Jim Moore recalled that early in his career, many commercial fishers were suspicious or hostile toward the DNR and its management efforts on Lake Michigan.

The bumper sticker "What Lord Giveth the DNR Taketh Away" sums up the attitude of many of the commercial fishermen. When I started working, the commercial fishermen thought they could catch out of the lake whatever the Lord had provided. Just because they were the ones who were out there with the gill-net boats and the gill nets, they felt they could keep harvesting as long as they wanted. They believed that is the way it should be. A lot of these fishing families are very religious and well-intentioned. They look at things from the standpoint that the Lord provideth all this. We will go out and take advantage of it. And when times get slack, we will go grow our strawberries, or do whatever until the fish come back. They have no concept at all of the fact that some management might provide things over a long sustained period without all these peaks and valleys. And over time, through our management system with quotas and everything else, I think we have finally shown a lot of the guys that are left in the fishery that good biological management is possible. We have convinced them that you do not have to take the years of nothing versus waiting for fish to recover on their own, and that maybe there are good reasons for some of the rules and regulations that we have instituted over the years.

Mike Toneys of the Wisconsin DNR found commercial fishermen reluctant to accept the growing role of the state in managing Lake Michigan, but noted the improvement of relations between the DNR and the state's commercial fishers since the mid-1980s.

The commercial fishermen were slow to realize they are not the only ones out there using the lake in fishing. They do and can have an impact out there with their nets, and it is not always a good impact. As the years went on, the 1970s, 1980s, and 1990s, it became more obvious that more and more people were out there sport fishing. Conflicts were arising and they were going to have to deal with them and work with us. We try to keep them in business, and keep the other side happy so they can both be out there. There is plenty of room. Each needs to understand how the other works. If they abided by the rules, they would probably be able to coexist. And I think it has worked out a heck of a lot better than they thought it would. People have adjusted.

There are some commercial fishermen who are still fighting those old wars. There are some that every time you meet them, some heated discussion takes place. There are some that will take that right to the grave. And there are probably some people in the department that harbor ill feeling from way back when. Commercial fishing is a damn hard way to make a living. Commercial fishermen are very individualistic people. They are proud of what they do. They work hard. They do not like people telling them how to make a living. They do not like a lot of rules and regulations. They are a lot like farmers; they have a very insecure way to make a living, and it is their perception that we just make things that much more difficult at times. I understand they can be bitter and frustrated with us at times. That is understandable and why I think it is helpful to sit down and talk with them and get their input when we are thinking about regulation changes and before problems arise. They often come up with some pretty good ideas that help make the process work a heck of a lot better in the long run. Communication has been a big part of the improvements. Better law enforcement has certainly been a big part of it, too. It is a lot easier to talk with these people rather than have shouting matches or end up in court with them, having lawyers arguing both sides. When you get to that point, you know you have lost; everybody has lost. You try and do something more proactive well ahead of that situation.

Wayne Tody maintained that Michigan wanted to establish limited-entry fishing as in the case of Alaska and Wisconsin. He maintained that the tribal fishing issue prevented the realization of these plans.

During the late 1960s, the fish were still in terrible shape, even after we banned gill nets. Zones were created for the Great Lakes.[64] We were going to divide the lake. Surprisingly enough, this was happening but in an awful haphazard way. Commercial fishing zones were the best fishing grounds. The Naubinway grounds are great for whitefish. Saginaw Bay is best for perch and so on. Sport fishing had already been established in Grand Traverse Bay and Isle Royale National Park. And the rest of the areas were to be rehabilitation zones. And when the fish were recovered, sport-fishing areas would fill in along the coast line with the demand. Commercial and sport fishing are not compatible. They have never been compatible. A gill net cannot compete with a trawling line with one hook on it. It is that simple. Commercial fishermen can fish until the stock is nearly gone and still catch a few fish to sell, but you are not going to attract sport fishermen to those kind of waters.

I tried hour after hour with a few commercial fishermen, young guys, to sell them on the concept of franchise fishing. Fishermen like Walt Stoddard, a perch fisherman, a trapnetter, understand the concept, but their roots go back to the bitterness of commercial fishing, fighting regulations, and they do not want to get branded as selling out to the state.[65]

We got the law through giving us the authority to limit the number of commercial fishing licenses to be issued and determine the qualifications for such licenses. We did it very painfully. We said that anyone who had fished fifty days, lifted nets for fifty days in each of the past three years, could retain the license. We would either convert him to trap nets or we would buy up his gear and he is out of business.

We also knocked down the number of so-called sport commercial fishing licenses. We had a couple thousand fifteen-dollar licenses out that let the licensee set a gill net under the guise of commercial fishing. Sportsmen with a gill-net license called a commercial fish license were whacked right up. We eliminated the license. There is no economics involved in that. This cut the number of commercial fishermen down to like 100 or 200 from previous thousands. They have been dropping out because they are starving to death over the years; they go broke. They could not even buy gas for their boats and stuff. The law permits us to fix and determine the amount of fish taken in a space at a particular time, which had never really been done since 1800. We never had effective laws on how many fish could be taken. We have sport-fishing limits, but not on the commercial fish. The law allowed us to designate the areas where commercial fishermen could conduct operations. They could fish any place except what was zoned sport, on top of each other if need be. We could also specify methods and gear and provide a catch fee for the value of the fish taken.

We collected about $30,000 from the sale of commercial fish licenses and about $10 or 15 million from sport fishermen. We spent $400,000 on patrol boats to police the fishery. The sport fishermen quickly caught onto the fact that they were financing the people who were getting their fish. This was their attitude. Limited entry went through in Alaska, and it has the best commercial fishery in the world. I have been up there three or four times as a guest of the state or the federal fisheries managers. With limited entry, some Alaska fishing licenses are worth half a million bucks. They can be transferred or inherited, but are negotiable. That is the concept we had in mind. We were calling it a franchise fishery. Let us say here is a commercial fishing area. We would license fish people to fish here even for some game fish like brown trout where it would not hurt anything and there is a surplus, and whitefish and chubs, which are primarily for the commercial fishery. It would have been a beautiful setup. This is why I am bitter. We were moving in the direction of limited-entry fishing when Indian treaties came in.

Ron Poff recalled the details of the passage of legislation that brought limited-entry fishing to Wisconsin's Great Lakes waters.

When the Wisconsin DNR instituted limited entry on Lake Michigan, we worked through Larry Van Sistine, a legislator from Green Bay. He was the one who finally agreed to consider introducing some legislation. The agency cannot draft the legislation; it has got be drafted by somebody other than us if it is going to get anywhere. The first limited-entry legislation proposed for Lake Michigan was called Senate Bill 409 or SB 409. I actually appeared in opposition at a public hearing on it in Racine. I said it had a lot of good points, but it went too far in some respects. Then the bill came back as an Assembly Bill in a revised version. Both houses supported it with some fairly modest amendments and it was all a matter of just working across the street with a few of the legislators. My boss at the time was Jim Addis and that was his forte. He realized his strong point was in the political arena, so he spent his time working over there. I spent my time working with the fishermen. It worked out real well. Clyde Porter, the legislator up in the Door County-Green Bay area, introduced twenty-six proposed amendments to this piece of legislation, and they all failed. And once the word got out that he was doing this, every one failed a little bit worse than the one before it, till by the end, there were not any votes in favor except probably his own. His comment was Agents Poff and Addis are in the back room rubbing their thumbs. We got out of the legislature about five o'clock that night after a long day.

When the legislature is meeting on what we thought was a major piece of legislation, you have to be there. The pages keep running back into the anteroom. They will say somebody out there wants to know about this or that, you write a brief note, and you will send it in by a page. Well, those guys were running crazy on that one. We had a tough day that day but, of course, getting the statute through is only part of it. And after, came a whole series of meetings with the commercial fishermen on the administrative rules. The statute established limited entry and created a fee structure for license and relicensing fees. It said the state shall establish relicensing criteria, so we had to develop administrative rules. NR25 is the part of the administrative code that contains commercial fishing regulations and rules determining our operating procedures, how the fishery is going to be licensed, how we are going to regulate it, and the kinds of gear that can be used. The statute allows us to regulate such things as the kinds and amounts of gear. It also gave us the right to limited entry and the quantity of fish that could be harvested and those sorts of things.

In order for the agency to develop a set of administrative rules, I held seven meetings, night meetings, with commercial fishermen. I think I had well over 150 commercial fishermen attending these meetings in fish houses. They were tough. We started at 7:00 pm and a lot of times, we did not get done till midnight. Then we broke out the smoked chubs or the smoked bullheads. I was at an Oconto fish house meeting with about forty guys. I had a rough draft of this chapter of the administrative rules. My job was to go through that rough draft and get their reaction to any changes from previous commercial fishing regulations. I would come back from every one of those meetings with a big pile of paper that was just my own notes. When it was all over, out comes a couple of boxes of smoked chubs or smoked bullheads and we would sit around, have a beer, and drink till one o'clock. Two days later, I am in Racine at another meeting in another fish house.

We made a lot of points with the industry in doing things that way. We had a lot of supporters. They recognized the value of limited entry and playing an active role in developing the rules to go with it. But it is hard. You can read things into what they are saying, so you have got to be careful what you say. The key is not to create a whole lot of enemies in the fishery. It just makes your work that much harder. You can have enemies, but they can be friendly enemies. They can be ones who are not afraid to debate you in public. It is the ones that go back door on you, through the legislature or something like that. They are the ones that are hard to work with. Elaine Johnson, Jeff Weborg, and those folks were right up front.

Ron Poff discussed the origins of the state's decision to adopt limited entry and quotas for Great Lakes fisheries.

I n the late 1950s and early 1960s I worked mostly inland. I knew the Great Lakes fishery had been somewhat depleted for years and years. The Great Lakes fisheries were going to hell. They were overfished. There were hundreds and hundreds of miles of gill nets being set in the Great Lakes. In 1874, the federal government established fish commissioners and the states created a department and a state fish commission and we started getting fish from the federal government to plant. During the first year of its operation, the Wisconsin Fish Commission spent under $400 to plant fish. Actually, the federal commissioner got $500 to buy the fish for the state, so it was not a big operation. The federal government provided millions and millions of fry mostly, fry and even eye eggs at times. It was an effort aimed strictly at replenishing what was considered a food supply, partly, perhaps, because there were a lot of immigrants coming into the country and they needed food. The government perceived this need for food, and the stocks were already overfished at that time. Overfishing went on and on, throughout series of ups and downs and regulations, until finally in 1967, Lake Superior became limited entry. Lake Michigan became limited entry in the mid-1970s.

Prior to the introduction of limited entry in Wisconsin, a gentleman from Michigan, Asa Wright, and I attended a limited-entry symposium in Denver, an international affair. We had had some experience with the Lake Superior limited-entry program, so we had an inland pilot project. Prof. Rich Bishop on the Madison campus published a paper and presented it at the limited-entry symposium in Denver. It got us thinking about what was necessary to keep this kind of fishery going. You cannot limit entry in terms of limiting the number of anglers. You have to have some sort of quota control at the same time, so it is not a monster horse race out there, and the few people who are in the fishery are not overcapitalizing to get the lion's share. Some major debates went on about limited-entry fisheries. They still are, I guess.

The philosophy that came out of the limited-entry symposium was that if you are going to have limited entry, you have to have quota control, and you probably will eventually need some system so that the quotas have value. They can be transferred to maintain a viable fishery. Those were all philosophies that were kind of talked about at that time. At the federal level, coastal management councils were created, with representatives from all the oceanic fisheries. They were, of course, involved in limiting entry, especially in the Alaska fisheries. In Gloucester, up on the New England coast, they were talking about limited entry. People in the fisheries profession probably were not that aware of the impact of limited entry on the social aspect of population. The Gloucester fishermen, the Portuguese fishermen in that part of the country, looked at limited entry as a hell of a threat and, of course, so did our fishermen in Door County. These commercial fishermen are a close-knit group; they are very tight with each other. It is a way of life. And when you talk about limiting numbers of people, it is a threat to their way of life. I had an interesting job in that I had to kind of weigh all these sort of things and act as sort of the go-between in some cases between the fishermen and the bureaucracy even though I was part of the bureaucracy. I would say, now wait a minute. We have got to be aware of what this is going to do to the local community. We have got to think about that and try and resolve some issues other than just the biological issues.

When I started, there were sixty-eight licenses on Lake Superior and about 260 on Lake Michigan. I had been hired for the Great Lakes position to implement limited entry. The legislature passed a resolution around 1967 that said the state should limit entry to the fishery. The first thing we did was freeze the number of licenses. Then we had to work on a process, in order to be constitutional, that would allow a way for new fishermen to get into the fishery. Some sort of criteria or test that had never been run before had to be established for them to meet. It had to give them a chance to compete for a position in this fishery. The rules were that the fisherman had to show an investment of a certain size or amount of gear in order to get a license, or they had worked as a member of a crew for a number of years as though they were apprenticing into this fishery. It worked out pretty well. We lost the fishermen who were pretty much the part-time fishermen. We lost some just through attrition; these were the people that were getting older and could not fish anymore. And we created a fishing board to review the licensing process, and if somebody had a definite hardship, the board could address that and allow them to keep their license. They would consider a medical disability or something of a temporary nature in their decisions. It was an interesting fishery to work with, mostly because it was small.

By the time I had moved on to another job, we were down to twenty-one, non-Indian licenses on Lake Superior with quota control in the lake trout fishery and a pretty good set of relicensing criteria. Then, of course, we got into limited entry on Lake Michigan and that was another matter. That was quite a battle. I do not exactly know how many licenses Wisconsin has right now on Lake Michigan. The number had been dropping rather dramatically. With the decline in the stocks out there, we have seen a lot of fishermen drop out of the fishery, and that is probably good. It allows the ones who are left a little more of a chance to properly capitalize their operations and still maintain a decent price in the marketplace.

Looking back on his forty-one years with the Wisconsin DNR in the fisheries bureau, Ron Poff was convinced that the state had been too harsh in its treatment of commercial fishermen when limited entry was introduced in order to appease sport and charter boat fishing interests.

My first boss in the bureau was named Ed Schneberger. He was the first fisheries biologist we hired in this state in 1934; he had a Ph.D. in limnology. He was the bureau director, and he used to get into some awful battles with the Lake Michigan fishery. One day they were down in Milwaukee and they almost came to fisticuffs with

Butch LaFond and a couple other guys down there. He had a story about driving north to a meeting up at Manitowoc, when a group of fishermen followed him. He was afraid that they were going to stop him and beat him up. It got pretty close. In Green Bay at one of the hearings held on NR 25, a commercial fisherman came into the courthouse. He was a little bit plastered. Nobody knew he had a gun until he told everybody, and then of course, two of the wardens got on him right away, and shepherded him out.

In Racine, a fisherman came up to me after the hearing. He was a guy who fished all by himself. He had a chub tug, and he would disappear for two weeks at a time all by himself out on the lake. He thought our limited-entry program was going to put him out of business. He literally cried on my shoulder. It makes you feel bad when somebody does that, but he was still in the fishery ten years later as far as I know. How do you assuage the guy? How do you say do not worry about this, even though you are worried. It is fine to worry about it a little bit, but let us plan ahead and see how you might be able to make something out of this. You are a good chub fisherman. You will get a quota.

I was almost glad to go to the inland fishery when I did after twelve years of working on the Great Lakes because the sport fishery was becoming more and more dominant and more and more irrational. It was not that kind of sport fisherman like my next door neighbor who goes over to Lake Michigan to fish. It was the charter boat operator and the people who had a lot of money, and for whom it was literally an economic concern. They could take their clients out and fish and make money off of them. It used to grate the hell out of me to see those folks with this kind of holier-than-thou attitude when I knew they were commercializing on that resource. And yet they held sway. Politically that was the thing. There were thousands of sport fishermen and a couple hundred commercial fishermen. I felt sorry for the commercial fishermen because in some respects, the cards were stacked against them. But at least with our limited entry and quota control, we prevented them from overcapitalizing on the fishery. In other words, they did not get into quite as many horserace-type fisheries. I did not see anybody building monster fleets out there, and we were able to keep a significant number of boats coming into a significant number of harbors. I think the fishery still exists, and is still something that people who go to Door County and up along the lakeshore can look for.

———————

Mike Toneys of the Wisconsin DNR explained the establishment of the quota system in Wisconsin.

The quota system in Wisconsin started back in the early 1980s with chubs. Later quotas were established for perch and all the rest of the species including whitefish in 1989. Basically, biologists in Wisconsin come up with an annual allowable harvest of each of these target species on a lakewide/baywide basis. In turn, each of those quotas is individually allocated to licensed commercial fishermen. Each fisherman's quota is based originally on his past history of harvest of these particular species fisheries. We looked at each individual fisherman's catch during a target group of years, averaged it, and then came up with a percentage of the total harvest that that licensee was responsible for. Once we allocated the quota, what portion each person got was based on that percentage of past history in the fishery.

For example, Neil Teskie, whose quota is seventeen percent, is one of the bigger fishermen, especially in the whitefish fishery. The total allowable harvest annually for whitefish, for instance, is divided into three fishing regions or zones. One of them is southern Green Bay. There is a zone that encompasses the bay and lake sides of Door County, and then all of the rest of Wisconsin waters south of approximately Door County. Most, if not all, of his whitefish quota comes out of that portion of the quota allocated to the Door County area. A substantial portion of the total whitefish quota is allocated just in the waters of Door County, probably about eighty percent of it. And right now that quota is right around 1.7 million pounds annually. Teskie has to take his seventeen percent in his specific zones. If he has quotas in other zones he is allowed to take them, but I think most of Neil Teskie's quota comes out of the zone right around Door County.

Some fishermen have multiple zones. We allow the fishermen to either temporarily or permanently transfer part or all of his quotas among other fishermen. It is part of our initiative to keep this a viable fishery, so if some people want to sell out, they can transfer that and get paid for it, before they get out of the business. If some people want to get bigger, then they can buy up if there is quota to be had. So I have no idea what Neil Teskie started out with, but I think he probably has purchased excess quota over the years as other fishermen have gotten out of the business.

———————

Jim Moore, who retired from the Wisconsin DNR in 2000, acknowledged that it was possible for fishermen to cheat under the quota system. He recalled a major initiative among state wildlife and law enforcement officials to stop illegal perch fishing.

S ome of the gross violations of fisheries laws came out of the big sting operation called CanAm. The wardens actually set up a dummy fish buying company that focused primarily on the yellow perch fishery, especially on the southern end of Lake Michigan down to the Milwaukee area. They documented literally thousands of pounds of unreported yellow perch. A number of commercial fishermen spent quite a bit of time in jail. Some lost their licenses. A similar effort took place over in the Marinette-Menominee area with similar results.

There are various ways a fisherman could cheat on the quota. They are required to fill out quota books when they are out on lake fishing. They have to be filled out prior to reaching shore. But if they thought there was no warden around, they might fill out an estimated catch. And that is an area that law enforcement is not comfortable with. The task force is looking at how to get fishermen to more accurately report their catch on a daily basis. Those who are interested in the long-term health of the fishery need to realize that without good numbers on daily catch and harvest and everything else, it is going to be difficult for us to generate realistic quotas.

Look what went on in the perch fishery; it is a good example. On southern Lake Michigan, the commercial fishery has now closed the yellow perch. I am not saying that it was due to over-exploitation by the commercial fishing industry, but I dare say it played a role in a more sudden collapse of the yellow perch fishery on southern Lake Michigan, at least in Wisconsin waters. So some of them cheated, some of them made big bucks, but some of them are now out of business with no chance of getting back in the fishery because of it. A lot of others are paying the price for some of the stuff that took place.

We are looking at how much money commercial fishing must generate to pay its own way as far as the cost of the enforcement of management programs. There are

agreements going back to a 1974 task force that included commercial fishing representatives, recognizing that they should be paying more of their own costs for us to
allow them to do business, but there have not been increases in commercial license
fees. The fees do not come anywhere close to covering the actual costs.

Mike Toneys noted the difficulties in enforcing the Wisconsin DNR's quota system.

There has been concern among our law enforcement people that there has been X
amount of cheating on quotas, misreporting, and false reporting. Wardens feel in
general that it is very difficult to enforce the quotas. They are looking for some rule
changes now to tighten that up a bit. Jim Moore is involved with a committee that is
working on that problem. The committee is made up of sport fishermen, commercial
fishermen, and DNR representatives. The quota system is tough to enforce. It takes a lot
of time and money. There are some that abide by it, probably to the letter. There are
some that cheat once in a while, perhaps inadvertently. There are some that knowingly
cheat. Some have been caught. Some have not. It is something that we have to be constantly vigilant of as far as enforcement. We try and prevent loopholes from entering
into these regulations whenever we can, but it is a fairly intensive management scheme
that requires enforcement. We could put all the rules on the books we want, but if it is
unenforceable, if we do not have the wardens to enforce it, then it is probably not
worth the paper it is written on. To some extent, we have to depend on the honesty of
the fishermen and that runs the gamut. Some are very honest; some are not. Hopefully
we have weeded out a lot of those that are not or are in the process of doing it, but it
is tough. We have chosen the quota system as a management scheme and we are paying somewhat of a price for it in the cost of enforcement, regulations, and vigilance.

There is a fairly stringent reporting system. Every two weeks, the fishermen are
required to report what they catch so there is a paper trail that law enforcement can
do a pretty good job following. There are sting operations run by the wardens. The wardens are pretty savvy people; they know the good players, the bad players, and the
problem areas. They do their best to try and get at some of the people who are cheating the system and sometimes they get a small fine. Sometimes we send them to jail.
But it is a never-ending process.

A number of the bad actors have either died, been kicked out of the fishery, have quit, or have reformed. Some of the animosity is still there but I do not think it reared its ugly head like it used to. There are a couple of hotheads who will die feeling vengeful towards the department for causing them untold problems. I started at a good time, and things have gotten progressively better in the twenty years I have been associated with the commercial fishery and the sport fishery. Things have changed and for the most part, we work with a pretty good set of clients. There are more rational than irrational people, and people understand the limits of the lake better than they used to. And if we have taught them nothing else, it is that things do change out there. Nothing remains the same. And it is not an unlimited bounty out there.

Jim Moore recalled when the DNR attempted to step up enforcement of the quotas on chub. The crackdown and the resistance were known as the chub wars. He argued that the Wisconsin DNR and its quota system had helped the state's commercial fishery become both more productive and profitable.

During the chub wars, Don Euers was the Lake Michigan warden. The wardens liked to use the *Barney Devine*. If they could get positioned right, they could sneak up behind them and get up close enough where they could jump across onto a fishing boat. They would throw their net measuring device on their chub nets and if they were too small, they "gotcha," and gave out a ticket. Pete LeClair's dad (Joseph LeClair) and Pete LeClair were on the boat, if I remember correctly. They saw the *Barney* coming, but they pretended like they did not and went about their business. As soon as Don Euers jumped over on their boat, they cut their nets off, closed the doors, and took off. Their boat was faster than the *Barney Devine*. This was during a period of the year when it was very cold out. Don was stuck on the roof of Pete's dad's boat, getting colder and colder and more desperate. He decided that if he took his heavy jacket off and stuffed it down the exhaust pipe, he will snuff the engine out. So he took his jacket off and stuffed it down the pipe. His jacket burned up and it did not stop the boat. Well, now he is up there really freezing his buns off and I guess they had him pretty much crying uncle before they finally decided, "Oh, gee, there must be somebody on the roof of our boat."

There were lots of incidents. Two Rivers was one of the big hot spots. There would oftentimes be incidents where the wardens would go there, and somebody ends up standing close to the edge of the dock and before long, somebody would be in the river. There were lots of little incidents over the years and stories like that. But with regard to the boat ride, I have heard Pete LeClair's version, and I have heard Don Euers' version, and they pretty much coincide so I think it was an actual event.

I would like to talk to those people that still harbor ill feelings towards the DNR. Let them go back to the late 1960s and the early 1970s when they obviously thought we were trying to put them out of business. In 1957 or 1958, Wisconsin commercial fishermen only caught about 9,000 pounds of whitefish in Wisconsin waters of Lake Michigan. Our recent quota was 1.7 million pounds. Ask anybody who is rational at all to explain to me how he can harbor ill feelings towards our department for trying to put them out of business. In a lot of respects, we have made some of these guys very wealthy individuals. Granted, they may not have liked some of the rules and regulations that we adopted or put into effect for whatever reason at the time. They might have thought something was going to threaten their livelihood, but I will not listen to any argument they put forth telling me that we were not doing the right thing and protecting not only their interests, but those of all the citizens of the state of Wisconsin. A lot of their animosity is driven by emotions at the time and other things like personal greed and human nature. A lot of these people will probably never forgive and forget some of the hot issues that happened in the past.

Jory Jonas, a research biologist at the Michigan DNR's Great Lakes fisheries research station in Charlevoix, compared her fisheries work in Wisconsin and Michigan.

People in Michigan are not as adversarial with the DNR as they are in the Green Bay/ Door County shoreline in Wisconsin. I have not noticed any major differences in the way the agencies behave, but I think there are some cultural things going on there as well. When I was in Wisconsin, I did feel that there was a lot of animosity. Maybe it has been remedied in recent years and enough time has passed on both sides. But at the time, the DNR was viewed as the regulators and the people that take away. There was resistance to moving from a basically unregulated system to one that is regulated. In Michigan, we have a pretty good working relationship with the public. I have not been a meeting yet where I felt a lot of animosity. In fact, I have almost always felt support. I know that is in part because my predecessors had some level of respect and credibility with the public.

Another major difference between Wisconsin and Michigan relates to the public perception of the DNR. In Wisconsin the angling groups are not organized as they are in Michigan. In Michigan the large Steelheader organizations meet together and provide a place where DNR officials can go and communicate with them annually or evenly monthly. We do not have to depend on a press release to translate our ideas to the public, which goes a long way in building a strong relationship. In Wisconsin, the fisheries managers are more dependent on the press to communicate with fishermen, and the anglers themselves are not organized into these nice groups that you can get to talk to.

Retired Wisconsin DNR fisheries official Jim Moore indicated that Michigan and Wisconsin differ in both the management of commercial fishery and the way fishing is approached.

In the State of Wisconsin it is part of our natural resources board policy and statutory code that we will have a sport and a commercial fishery on the Great Lakes. We will not favor one over the other, and both are viable to whatever rules we think we need to keep them both viable. So it is not only policy, it is the law that we operate under. Michigan went a completely different direction. When salmon were first introduced over in Michigan, the state made a decision that in order for the sport fishery to really thrive, they were going to have to probably really clamp down on the commercial fishery and do away with gill nets. So early on, that was one of their big pushes. They finally succeeded in banning gill nets in Michigan, and put a lot of pressure on us here in Wisconsin to follow suit because the sport fishing got better, and our sport fishermen became more politically active. They just assumed that a good sport fishery could not survive in the face of a commercial fishery that used gill nets in any quantity. Michigan started out with a program called zone management where they zoned the lake and eventually eliminated gill nets. I am not sure where the whole tribal issue came into play, what time period, but that kind of complicated some of the things that they hoped to achieve.

In Wisconsin we chose to go a little slower. We were doing some modified zone management. In the early days when I was working with the commercial fishery, we restricted gear from certain areas by permits. All the commercial fishermen were required to have permits for large mesh gill nets or trap nets which authorized how many boxes of nets they could set and in some cases, the location. But we never looked at it from the standpoint that it was going to be necessary to eliminate most of the commercial fishery in order to have a sport fishery thrive in Wisconsin.

Back in the early 1970s there was a big blue ribbon task force appointed by the governor to look at what Wisconsin had to do to maintain a viable commercial fishery. It came up with a natural resources board policy that would guide us in the management of the fishery resources for both sport and commercial use. There were many meetings in the late 1960s and through the 1970s, where we had a lot of hotly debated issues involved with how Michigan or Wisconsin were actively managing the fishery. The debates have been interesting over the years.

Looking at Michigan's situation now, where they have got some areas almost wide open to tribal fisheries, I wonder what they gained from putting the clamps on their nontribal fishermen. The bottom line is that you can still have pretty good success through introductions of trout and salmon and still have commercial fisheries, even ones still using gill nets heavily. You must identify areas where you could work on problems, and get the commercial fishermen to understand there might be times of the year or depths that we can guarantee their continued fishing on the lake, and still have an active sport fishery. So I think over time, we probably did it the right way and it has worked out well in Wisconsin. There are still problems. A lot of the sport fishermen would not cross the street to save the commercial fishery if there were a choice, but I think we have been able to maintain not only a good sport fishery, but a pretty viable commercial fishery.

When I started work in 1968 as a biologist, I was the first fisheries biologists assigned to Lake Michigan on a full-time basis. Up until that time, there had not been much done in the way of rules and regulations aimed at the commercial fishery that were based on going out and gathering biological data. Sure, they knew when fish spawned and when to close the season, but there were a lot of things they just did because it sounded good or looked good. And as we stocked more fish and the problems with incidental catch became greater, we started making rules and regulations that our commercial fishermen felt were going to nickel and dime them, and put them out of business. They saw what was going on across the lake in Michigan, and assumed that Wisconsin was going to put the stranglehold on till the point where they were going to be out of business, too. Combine that with the fact that during the 1970s there was a very, very active illegal trade in lake trout. Even though the lake trout were not reproducing, they were certainly surviving very well. These fish quickly grew to size.

The illegal trade was big time. There are even some of our current fishermen who probably made lots of money bootlegging lake trout. There were years where the wardens would be chasing down trucks or following up on tips or leads of lake trout stashed in a cooler or freezer. There was an incident in Jacksonport, where the wardens went in to check some freezers and they made some arrests. One of the people at the restaurant where the arrests took place threw a knife at one of the wardens. I do not know how close it came to him, but it was close enough that he was lucky somebody did not draw a pistol and shoot him. Fortunately, we have not had any deaths, but just guys getting frozen on the top of fish tugs, pushed in the water, and a couple scuffling matches on the docks. That is about all it has amounted to. But in that instance, someone came pretty close to getting seriously hurt.

Eventually, the U.S. Fish and Wildlife Service wardens stepped in to enforce a federal law called the Lacey Act, which prohibited the shipping of illegal fish across state lines. We were able to help put a lot of the illegal lake trout activity out of business.

It took some real enforcement efforts on the part of our state wardens and the U.S. Fish and Wildlife Service federal wardens to finally get our commercial fishermen to the point where they would not jeopardize their licenses and access to a rapidly improving whitefish fishery to bootleg lake trout. The illegal lake trout activity also declined as a direct result of contaminants. People were going to go to jail for a long time for shipping illegal fish across state lines, especially contaminated fish. I think that finally scared a lot of guys out of that whole scenario.

There were a lot of growing pains. There were a lot of rules and regulations that the commercial fishermen did not like. Nobody had ever come in and started enforcing how long they could leave their gill nets out, how much gear they could set, or where they could set gear. There were lots of tickets being written for one thing or another, whether it was bootlegging fish or doing things that violated the permits we issued for gear and that type of thing. During the 1970s and probably into the early 1980s, there was just one battle after another, whether it was chasing fish trucks down the road and ripping open cases of fish to look for lake trout, or hot battles in court over particular issues.

We had a couple attorneys here in town who were the primary representatives for the commercial fishermen whenever there were court cases. There were lots of heated meetings discussing and debating the merits of rules and regulations and why we were doing things the way we were doing it. The tension subsided when the enforcement people finally got the attention of the commercial fishermen, and convinced them that if they continued to bootleg lake trout, they were probably going to be out of business. At the time, our whitefish kept increasing in value. I think a lot of these guys just decided it was not worth their time and effort to jeopardize their livelihood to continue doing something that caused a lot of animosity in the sport fishery when it was splashed in the newspapers probably two or three times a week. The controversy has died down over the last fifteen years or so. One of the reasons things are a lot less stressful today is that we work our way through some of these problems.

Retired Michigan DNR fisheries biologist Myrl Keller regarded Michigan as the leading Great Lakes state in fisheries management.

M ichigan was the first to ban the gill nets. We were the first to introduce the salmon. We were the first to set up a very intensive research program on the Great Lakes and we have always worked cooperatively with the other states. We were first to set up quite a large hatchery system throughout our state. The other states followed. Probably Michigan was first because we had a larger stake in the Great Lakes than most other agencies.

Fisheries biologist Mike Toneys of the Wisconsin DNR maintained that his Michigan counterparts often objected to Wisconsin's policy to allow commercial fishers to continue to use gill nets and develop a sport fishery at the same time.

Over the years, we certainly have taken criticism from biologists in Michigan about our stand on commercial fishing, and the way we manage our commercial fishery. In some cases, we have not only tolerated, but also in some cases promoted a commercial fishery over here. Michigan essentially decided that the way to go was to nurture a sport fishery at the expense of many of their commercial fishermen. It is not a policy that we followed over here. We certainly have had our disagreements about gear. The Michigan commercial fishery outside of Native Americans is essentially an entrapment-gear fishery, which cuts down on the incidental catch. We still allow a variety of gear, including the infamous gill net. They have sometimes been baffled, maybe even astounded, how we can maintain good to great sport fishing right on top of a commercial fishery. One of the prime examples is in northern Door County up in the Washington Island-Gills Rock area where we have the heaviest amount of large mesh gill-net fishing going on and yet have prime chinook fishing. And some of the commercial fishermen are working as sport fishing guides part-time. Sport fishermen are using docking facilities owned by commercial fishermen, and people get along fairly well. They understand each has a place out there and they respect each other. They get along very well and sometimes, that has been baffling to Michigan. We take a lot of pride in that.

We have bent over backwards to try and work with both groups whenever possible, and get them together. Both commercial and sport fishers were involved in a task force that recently reviewed the major policy decisions that we have made over the years involving fisheries. For instance, we come up with management plans for Lake Michigan fisheries about every five or six years. As we are formulating these plans, we get together sport and commercial fishermen to get their input and reaction. Over the years, we have tried to do a better job of communicating with these people. Some of them do not get along now, and have never gotten along. There are still bitter feelings up there. But more often than not, they get along much better than you would expect, considering the histories of both and the contentious issues back in the 1960s and 1970s, when the commercial fishery was recovering and the sport fishery was starting to grow. There were some growing pains there, but I think both sides have adapted fairly well. People that disagree can still sit down and discuss things and in many cases, come to some decent resolutions of issues.

Howard Tanner from the Michigan DNR acknowledged that state policy prompted tribal members to seek legal redress in federal court. The former Michigan State University faculty member and former Michigan DNR head drew distinctions between the tribal fishers who have joined together under the Chippewa Ottawa Treaty Fishery Management Authority.

D uring 1965 we had coho eggs in the hatcheries, and were getting money and the authority to require a license to fish on Lake Michigan. We were closing down the commercial fishery. We made a hard-and-fast rule if you have not reported $5,000 average, you do not have a fishing license. When we did that, we eliminated all the tribal fishermen. With hindsight, that was an obvious mistake. That is when they took us to court. That is when they won. And that is why they have been able to sustain a fishery beyond state authority today. That decision was the genesis. Big Abe LeBlanc out of the Bay Mills Tribe took us to court. It was the way to go towards limited entry. But if we had had the benefit of hindsight, we would have avoided a tribal problem and made an exception.

The way I perceived it originally was that commercial fishing should be strictly a secondary activity. It could function as long as it did not impinge upon our opportunity to build sport fishing to its maximum. When the tribes came in and insisted on being able to fish with gill nets in the manner and place of their own choosing, it was completely opposed to what I sought to do. It is opposed to what I would term my resource philosophy because it does not constitute the greatest good for the greatest number. It is an illogical allocation of a public resource. I have a hard time encompassing the idea of separate rights for the tribes. The courts have obviously ruled that they have those rights and I will abide by the law. The courts say that is the case, and I accept that. That does not mean I like that, and I do not think it is good overall resource management. But given the fact that we have to accommodate that, the 1985 agreement does reasonably well in that it allocates space and fishes to the tribes in areas that are of least interest to the sport fishing. I do not mean to suggest that there were not sport-fishing interests in these areas, but if you have to have it somewhere, that is a pretty good place for it. There are conflicts on the two fronts. Overall, the judge and the parties involved did a pretty good job of accommodating two groups and equal rights to the resource. It is tolerable. I would like to see it continued substantially in the way that it has been in the past. I think the resource could be managed so that it was more valuable to more people, but given the legal constraints that have been placed on it, so be it.

Since 1985, a lot of things have changed in the relationships between the tribes and the state. At that time, the only area of contest between the tribes and the state was the fishery resources. Now casinos are the item. There are a number of agreements on other matters between the tribes and the state regarding taxation and a variety of things. I think we are now more interdependent upon one another. I am not personally involved in any way, but I believe that there is room for a solution that minimizes the friction. The last thing that anybody wants is illegal violence of any kind. That must be avoided; it is no solution to anything.

The three principal tribes do not represent a single unit. They have different interests. They have different ways. The Sault St. Marie Tribe has done a fine job of managing their monies, much of which has come from their casino. Their monies have gone into the tribe, not to the individuals. The tribe owns a lot of land and buildings in Sault Ste. Marie. They have built a community hospital and community service buildings. They have demonstrated citizenship in their own community, and are to be highly commended.

There is more animosity with the Grand Traverse Band. Sometimes it comes down to individuals on both sides. Some of the friction is deliberately created. There are attorneys who are not particularly helpful. Grand Traverse is now making demands for inland management of fisheries and inland management of game. It seems to me that the tribes would be well-served to think carefully about how they are viewed by the rest of the Michigan population. I do not think it is to their overall benefit to do certain things that are particularly obtrusive to the rest of us such as demanding inland hunting and fishing prerogatives, and that everybody else get a license from them in order to participate. There are relatively few tribal members that will benefit. They ought to think about animosity. They are poorly served by their leadership if they go that way. They have a right to let the courts decide on the issue and I hope the courts limit that right. They are members of the community. Some tribes do a good job and others, particularly the Grand Traverse group, are not doing a very good job. Their legal leadership is taking them in the wrong direction.

———————————

Tom Kelly, captain of the *Inland Seas,* a research sailing vessel, commented on his acquaintance with Skip Duhamel, son of American Indian activist Art Duhamel.

I n any situation there are always going to be some people that are sort of out in the front. Some people just gravitate toward a situation that needs to have something done. And so Skip sort of takes that role and his father did that before him. I knew Art a little bit, but I do not know how the other fishermen who are just out there trying to earn a living, how they feel about him. I guess you would have to ask them.

I think Art was genuinely concerned about the future of the Native peoples here. This was way before the casino and it was a very depressed area, very poor. And I remember him talking to me one time about some young person in the tribe he was encouraging to go to college and go into fisheries biology or some natural resources management kind of thing so it would benefit their tribe. I knew at the time that the Indians did not have to pay tuition; they basically had free education, college education. And I asked him how many people from the tribe were going to college, and he said there was almost none. Even though the opportunity theoretically was there, culturally, it was not happening. So I think a lot of things have changed since then. That was twenty-five years ago or so. I mostly saw him in either a social situation or a business situation. I never saw him in a confrontational situation. What he did I think was fairly well thought out. When he broke the law there was a purpose to it. He expected to be arrested and there was a reason for doing it. So it was civil disobedience for a purpose. In my meetings with him, I never got the impression of him as being a wild man who was flaunting the law or anything. He knew what he was doing and had a purpose in doing it.

———————————

Wayne Tody recalled that after observing West Coast Indians obtain treaty fishery rights, he anticipated Michigan would no longer be able to deny the tribes the right to fish in Michigan waters in the manner of their own choosing.

I knew what was going to happen because one of my closest colleagues was the chief of fisheries in the state of Washington.[66] And the feds attacked Washington for fifty percent of the fisheries to be turned over to the Indians. That was a tremendous hardship to the non-Indian commercial fishermen and the sportsmen both. The federal judge that conducted these hearings on treaties decided everything in favor of the Indians. In Michigan, we were a sitting duck. You have probably gathered by now that we were not too courteous at times when the federal government interfered with what we thought were our state rights and prerogatives. One Indian went out, caught four lake trout, and allowed himself to be arrested by a state conservation officer. Some of us knew where we were headed because it was an obvious, voluntary thing. The district and circuit courts found him guilty. Federal court found him innocent. The state appealed and protested vigorously to Soapy Williams [G. Mennen Williams], the former governor who got appointed to the Michigan Supreme Court. On the Supreme Court, he wrote an opinion that treaty rights are the law of the land, and are irreproachable. They cannot be questioned or played with. And the Indians, as far as he was concerned, had treaty rights to the fish, rights; they actually had never ceded them. They controlled them.

The feds and the Indians organized and spent a year or two getting all their stuff together and taking depositions from all of us. They went before another federal judge, Noel Fox, and he interpreted the case right along the same line as Soapy Williams, which there is some truth to. The Indians really did not know what they were signing; the language in the treaties is meaningless. But because they are sovereign people, they have rights. Nevertheless, we ended up with two management agencies in the field, the DNR Fisheries Division and Indians. The Fisheries Division is backed up by the State of Michigan and the legislature, and the Indians are backed up by the Department of Interior, the Bureau of Indian Affairs, the federal register, and by the federal judges. Obviously, there is quite a bias there towards the Indians and not to the State of Michigan, and that is why I am bitter. I am still for negotiation. I am still for the United States to control it, and if we are going to recognize the Indians' treaty rights, then that should be put on a level field. It seems to me that the nine or ten million people in Michigan ought to have actually some little bit of precedent on these fish.

We know that the state, the federal master, and the Indians are renegotiating the 1985 Consent Agreement. I might go so far as to write a white paper of things to consider and why. I would like to get one or two other of my old cronies to help write it. We have raised some interesting points about jurisdictional things that I never hear, unless you are just going to sweep them aside with discrimination. I do not know what is the matter with my successors, why have they failed to remind the feds of their limitations? Now you cannot lick the federal judges. They have got the power. The Great Lakes will never be rehabilitated by timid men. If you are going to do it, you have to get in there and fight. And we did and we made a hell of a lot of progress. The fishery is a lot better than it was. And so why not? Why not give them some suggestions? I do not think that is interfering with anybody who is taking responsibility and the credit for things today.

———————

Myrl Keller noted how the Michigan DNR promoted the growth of sport fishing and at the same time, tightened its restrictions on commercial fishers. Further changes in regulation and policy came about when the tribes were awarded the right to self-regulated fisheries.

The DNR enacted certain management regulations for the commercial fishery. We limited their entry. We banned gill nets, which are a malicious, destructive mode of fishing. We encouraged the use of the trap net, which can selectively take the targeted species and allow for the escape alive of the unwanted or protected species. The tribal folks used gill nets and would not listen to alternative fishing techniques simply because the gill net is quite easily fished. It does not take a lot of experience to know how to fish a gill net whereas the successful use of the trap net requires a little bit of experience and a great financial investment. Those were frustrating times because we saw when the tribes were targeting for whitefish, for instance, they were killing large numbers of lake trout that everybody, specifically the federal government through the Great Lakes Fishery Commission, wanted to see successfully reproduce. In Grand Traverse Bay, the tribes practically annihilated the lake trout that were planted in just a few years. There were a lot of confrontations, arrests, and court cases. The judges decided that the tribal folks had the right to do this, so that is where it is today.

The process was frustrating as a biologist, very frustrating. We knew what worked for the system and what was healthy for the system. Here was a group of people, resource users that really we did not have any control over. And in order to manage the resource you had to have some control over it and we simply did not. I testified in a lot of court cases, including the one in Grand Rapids with Judge Fox. He made the final decision and that said that the tribal fisheries could fish where there were fish to be found in the ceded waters of the treaty.

For quite a number of years, almost a hundred percent of my time was taken up with those issues. We gathered information on the harvest from Grand Traverse Bay that was submitted to the federal court in Grand Rapids and many others. We monitored a lot of tribal fisheries initially. Many meetings were held with tribal people, federal people, and representatives from the Great Lakes Fishery Commission and the other states bordering on Lake Michigan. It took up a lot of my time.

I did not have any personal experience with the violence that took place on the lake, but I had heard about different things that had taken place. A lot of the folks in the Grand Traverse area were quite upset with what was going on, but really there was not much they could do about it.

The 1985 Consent Order had a big effect on the program that we had set up initially for the Great Lakes. The Consent Order allowed almost exclusive tribal regulation of a big area of Lake Michigan, a large area of Lake Superior, and also a large area of Lake Huron. We have not been able to develop viable recreational fisheries in those areas. What makes a good sport fishery is a surplus of fish, an abundance of fish. And because the resource is being exploited by the tribal fishery, the fish simply are not there for the recreational fishery. So we have not ignored those areas by any means. We are still concerned about the fish populations in those areas. But it simply is not possible to develop them for a viable recreational fishery.

If the tribes want to go back to square one and fish from Grand Haven north on Lake Michigan, for instance, they can do it if they want to. They have proven that already through the court system. But it is going to be detrimental to the recreational fishery. I am sure that the decision will not be popular with many citizens of Michigan. Public opinion keeps the tribes from pushing into areas that are well-developed now for the recreational fishery.

Stan Lievense, now retired from the Michigan DNR, maintained that the highest rate of economic and social return on the state's investment in fish was in sport fishing. As a result, he favors limits on treaty fishing rights.

The American Indians are now netting the nice game fish. Our side of the picture is that sport fishing is the greatest participant sport of all in the United States. And yet, the day is coming, in my estimation, where there is not room for a net being set and coming in with thousands of pounds of these nice fish, when one trout will be recognized as providing many, many hours of recreation potential.

Sport fishing really is much more valuable in terms of the recreation it provides and from a monetary standpoint. I hate to put the money value in there but it is a necessity. In assessing the issue you have got to recognize the American Native has treaty rights. We cannot do too much with them, but I think they should get together. We do not like Indian fishing for the simple reason of what they are doing to our sport. They are afraid of us, which is bad. I do not want to dislike them. I think something should be worked out where Grand Traverse Bay should not be net-fished in large numbers. Maybe open it all up to sport fishing, and perhaps allow the Indians to license it, have control of the fishery, and we pay a fee. I mean, that is a theoretical thing, but something like that should be worked out.

Tom Kelly, a marine biologist and educator, expressed concern about negotiations for the renewal of the 1985 U.S. District Court Consent Agreement.

Here in Grand Traverse Bay, a lot of it comes down to management and tradition. There are sort of equity things that get you into another whole ballpark. I would imagine that most of the tribal fishery will probably be trap nets, but there will still be some near-shore gill nets into the future. I do not know how it is going to shake out. Of course, next year they are supposed to renegotiate the consent order. You would not want to have the Fish for All project stir up the pot, and bring up animosities from the past that may be best left to lie. The most important thing is to get the Consent Order renewed in a way that is acceptable to all the parties. None of the parties are going to agree to everything because they are just too far apart. But at least there has to be a meeting of the minds and an agreement that we are going to live by this, whatever it is. Things were really nasty here for maybe the three or four years leading up to the Consent Order. There were vigilante groups running around at night confronting the Indian fishermen. There were lots of threats of violence and property damage. There was fallout in the schools. The Indian kids were being harassed at school and it was a very ugly time. It is not something anybody wants to return to. I certainly would not want to see it again. So I am hoping that the Consent Decree will get renewed in some form. Again, nobody is going to be happy with all of it, but I hope that it will be something that everybody can live with because it is certainly something that we do not need to go backwards on that.

There has to be accountability. Everybody wants a good ecological system, a stable ecological system, and one that is going to produce fish for everybody. So there are some things everybody can agree on. And then when you get down to who is going to get what, where, when, and how, those are things that get contentious, but I think they can be worked out. There has to be a feeling on all sides that the fishery is being monitored and policed and that whatever laws are, they are being obeyed.

One of the more contentious issues recently has been whether the Indians should be allowed a piece of the salmon pie, which are mostly all planted fish. There are a couple places where they can fish for salmon legally. I think that is probably going to continue, but it is pretty localized. It is not everywhere. I think as long as the sport fishermen do not see the Indians out wholesale slaughtering their fish they will be able to live together. And mostly the Indians are targeting whitefish around here anyway.

One time an Indian gill-net tug had stopped at the end of the cold dock down at the end of Suttons Bay. Somebody came down there and threatened them. I do not know whether they were armed or not. That was typical of what might happen. There was not very much latitude for trying to understand what each other was up to, why they were doing it, and what they were like as people. It was them against us kind of thing. And there were mostly instances that I read about in the paper. In Suttons Bay for whatever reason, the village people—the people in the government—tended to try to not meet the issue head-on. It worked out better for them in the long run whereas in Leland and Northport, they tried to keep the Indian fishermen out and there were lawsuits filed. The two towns ended up losing the case and spending a lot of money and time and energy. But for whatever reason, that type of head-on thing did not happen in Suttons Bay. I am not sure why or why not. Of course, in any given community there are going to be people who are vehemently opposed and other people that do not care much one way or the other. It is not all black and white. Except for that one incident that I witnessed, it was mostly the undertone you could sense in the community. It was the topic of conversation in the grocery store, the barbershop, and wherever you were. People were talking about it, and mostly it was not pleasant stuff. Because a particular ethnic group was involved, there is another element to it there that you do not know how deep that goes. So that is why I say one of the most important things to do is get this Consent Order renewed so that we do not go back into that sort of racially charged issue.

We work professionally with the biologists up at the tribe. We meet at least once a year. We have a big meeting of all the people that are doing environmental research on Grand Traverse Bay. For about a year or so, I was hired as a consultant to do some research for the tribe. I wrote a series of papers for them on fishery management options and a history of the fishery in this area. At that time, they were still negotiating the Consent Decree, and were looking for information that they could use. They were also looking ahead to managing their fishery and how best to do it—what techniques to use. I do not know whether any of that information was actually used or not. I just turned in my reports and got my check and went home. They pretty much decided what to do with it. I had some contact with some of the fishermen who worked out of Suttons Bay before they built the harbor up at Peshawbestown, the new harbor. There were a number of fishermen who worked out of Suttons Bay, so I would see them almost daily. I got a chance to talk with them about what they were catching and what was going on and stuff. In the last few years, I have had very little contact with them just because our paths do not cross. Most of the Indians are just regular folks trying to make a living. They are as concerned with the ecology of the lake as anybody else because that is their livelihood. So you get down to the allocation issue. There is only so much fish. Who is going to get what, how much—these are the things that the Consent Decree has to deal with.

John McKinney began his career as a Michigan Sea Grant agent in 1979, when the controversy over state efforts to end or curtail commercial fishing combined with tribal efforts to secure fishing rights.

There were some very angry people because certain fishery groups felt threatened by the actions of the state and federal government. There was potential violence. I do not know that actual violence ever occurred, but there was certainly damage to gear. There were people doing things to each other and there was a lot of potential for serious problems. There were attempts to defuse it. There were attempts to rationalize it out and to "educate" people to the fact that certain things were happening, and certain interpretations were being placed on old treaties. There were some things being looked at in the court system, and they were going to impact local people. This was not very clearly understood back then and maybe not now so much, but certainly back then. Most people had not even heard of these treaty issues, and they were looked at as something that was invasive of the rights of the people of Michigan. Where did it come from? And it was an attempt to point out that this was being done legally and it was being done under the system that we all adhere to and whether that was going to be acceptable or not was up in the air at the time. There were lots of people who did not agree with that. Probably the same people still do not agree with it, but they have learned to accept it and at least to realize that it was going to be mandated by the system and they cannot do much about it.

At the same time or I guess prior to that even, the controversy was over the commercial fishing versus the recreational fishing. The state was in the process of buying out licenses and trying to eliminate or cut back on the commercial fishing. The rationale for this was not always clear, but they felt that the recreational fishery was more important and in ascendancy, was taking over. That situation was happening before the tribal issue entered into it. Then you also get into a three-way tussle, which in some ways, is still going on. In a lot of areas, the commercial fishermen, the licensed state commercial fishermen, are a thing of the past almost. Certainly in this area, that is almost true. There is not much commercial fishing left. So in the evolution, it has come through several phases.

Retired Wisconsin DNR fisheries official Ron Poff observed there is not a strong tribal fishing presence in Wisconsin's Great Lakes waters today. He recalled the conflict that existed over tribal fishing earlier in his career, during the 1960s.

O ur wardens had arrested a couple of Indians on an inland lake for spearing suck-ers, of all things, out of season and that kind of started it all off. We had some problems on Lake Superior with commercial fishing when we had to deal with both the limited number of non-Indian fishermen and Indian fishermen, the Bad River and Red Cliff bands, to get an agreement about the harvest up there. We already had limited entry on Lake Superior at that time, and were down to twenty-one licensed commer-cial fishermen, a couple of whom were Indian fishermen. Then everything kind of blew up. It seems that the court cases have been pretty good to us in Wisconsin, especially with the inland walleye fishing, the spearing. We have a formula-based fishery there that is probably as conservative as you can imagine. And on the Great Lakes, it is a shared fishery on Lake Superior. I do not think we have any Indian commercial fisher-men on Lake Michigan in Wisconsin at this time.

Jory Jonas was one of the fisheries biologists the State of Michigan relied upon for information in negotiating the renewal of the 1985 Consent Agreement.

O ne misconception that exists in the public is that the DNR has the ability to stop the tribes from commercial fishing. That is not possible. The tribes have won that right and they will have it. Now we are in the position of working with them to find the best way to allow for tribal fishing and other uses as well. The tribes share the DNR's concern with public opinion. I doubt they want to enter into fights with people any more than the DNR wants to enter into a fight involving other parties. It is an issue of allocation now. We will base our decisions on the facts and science and biology, and what we know about population dynamics.

On Lake Michigan, there are really good working relationships between the biol-ogists who work for the tribes and those who work for the state. We are starting some cooperative assessment work. Thus far, we have discussed the methodologies we will use to do our assessments in fisheries. We want to be sure we are all on the same page now that there are more of us out there now doing this work. Instead of one agency trying to assess the entire northern Lake Michigan, we now have six that are each responsible for their portion. The tribal agencies tend to monitor the shoreline areas. The DNR has a large research vessel, so we have been focusing our efforts offshore. The cooperative assessment effort has turned out some neat information, and we are looking forward to keeping that kind of thing going through time. We have databases that all synchronize now. As part of the negotiations for the renewal of the 1985 U.S. District Court Consent Order, models were developed to predict the impact of fishing in Lake Michigan. The gathering of information for the preparation of models forced us to come together and share information. We have agreed to come together and share information. It has not been an adversarial process, at least from the biological standpoint. We sit in a room. We all get along and it has been positive so far.

Jim Moore, retired Wisconsin DNR fisheries expert, expressed concern about the renegotiation of the 1985 Consent Agreement.

Obviously the fish that we stock swim over into Michigan waters. A lot of them could end up in tribal fishing areas, so there is concern over what types of rules and regulations they would be looking at, and their impact on our sport fishery and our commercial fishery. If they have unlimited harvest on whitefish and allow liberal catches for trout and salmon, it is going to have a bearing on the rest of the lake. So only time will tell what kind of discussions they have, which direction they go in. Wisconsin is not directly in the negotiations, just the tribes, the federal government, and the State of Michigan. There ought to be representation from the other states and, as far as I know, there has not ever been much.

NOTES

1. On federal involvement in Great Lakes fisheries during World War I, see Margaret Beattie Bogue, *Fishing the Great Lakes, An Environmental History* (Madison: University of Wisconsin Press, 2000), 275–78. During the Great Depression, see "Unfair Trade Practices for the Great Lakes Fisheries," *The Fishing Gazette* 50, no. 12 (1933): 29; "To Build New Dock for Fishermen in Marinette," *Atlantic Fisherman* 20, no. 4 (1939): 18; Kenneth L. Peterson, "Hatching Some Fishing Fun," *Michigan Natural Resources* 55, no. 4 (1986): 7–8. On

World War II, see "Food for Wartime," *Michigan Conservation* 12, no. 4 (1943). "Great Lakes Fish Production Threatened by Ceilings," *Atlantic Fisherman* 26, no. 7 (1945): 28. On federally financed studies of Lake Michigan fisheries, see "Great Lakes Fishermen to Benefit by Low Cost Government Loans," *Atlantic Fisherman* 20, no. 8 (1939): 12; "Fishermen Ask for Net Loans," *Atlantic Fisherman* 20, no. 12 (1940): 19; "Fishermen to Get Loans for Lost Nets," *Atlantic Fisherman* 22, no. 1 (1941): 9; "New Fish and Wildlife Station Opened," *Atlantic Fisherman* 31, no. 8 (1950): 20; "Fisheries Statistics Office Established," *National Fisherman* 36, no. 2 (1955): 35; "New Fishery Statistical Office in Wisconsin," *National Fisherman* 36, no. 5 (1955): 16; U.S. Congress, House of Representatives, *Executive Hearings Before the Committee on the Merchant Marine and Fisheries,* 79th Cong. 1st sess., 19 and 21 February 1945; "Commercial Fish Material: Fish Hatcheries for Commercial Species, 1918–1955," State Archives of Michigan, Michigan Historical Center, Lansing, Michigan, 75–34, Box 13, File 3; Bogue, *Fishing the Great Lakes,* 35–47, 182–86, 195–203, 254–61, 294–96, 298–320, 324–30; Tom Kuchenberg, *Reflections in a Tarnished Mirror: The Use and Abuse of the Great Lakes* (Sturgeon Bay, Wisc.: Golden Glow Publishing, 1978), 202–3; U.S. Fish Commission, "Laws, Correspondence, and Judicial Proceeding, Regarding Fish Culture Work in Michigan," in *Report of the Fisheries Commission for 1904* (Washington, D.C.: U. S. Government Printing Office, 1905); "Census Report on Lake and River Fisheries," *The Fishing Gazette* 28, no. 25 (1911): 769–70; U.S. Department of Commerce, Bureau of Fisheries, *Fishing Industry of the Great Lakes,* by Walter Koelz, Bureau of Fisheries Document no. 1001 (Washington, D.C.: U. S. Government Printing Office, 1926); John Van Oosten, "Scientific Investigations of [Great Lakes Fishery by] the Bureau of Fisheries," from *Second Great Lakes Fisheries Conference* (Lansing: Michigan Department of Conservation, 1928); John Van Oosten, "Some Fisheries Problems on the Great Lakes," *Transactions of the American Fisheries Society* (reprinted from vol. 59, 1929); John Van Oosten, "Investigation of Method of Measuring Twine in Great Lakes District," *Michigan Fisherman* 14, no. 4 (1930): 1, 6; "Strong Current Hinders Fishing," *The Fisherman* 2, no. 1 (1932): 12, 14; John Van Oosten, "Review of Great Lakes Work Conducted by the U.S. Bureau of Fisheries," *The Fisherman* 2, no.1 (1932): 3–4, 8; John Van Oosten, "Preliminary Report on Investigation of Chub Net Meshes in Lake Michigan," *The Fisherman* 2, no. 4 (1933): 3–4, 8; John Van Oosten, "Questionnaires Prove Valuable to Fisheries," *The Fisherman* 4, nos. 6–7 (1935): 1–2; John Van Oosten, "Dr. Van Oosten Reveals Startling Data," *Gold Medal Netting News* 9 (May 1936): 1–2; John Van Oosten, "The Great Lakes Fisheries: Their Proper Management for Sustained Yields," *Transactions of the American Fish Society* 66 ([n.d], 1936): 131–38; John Van Oosten, "Net Selectivity on the Great Lakes," *Gold Medal Netting News* 10 (July 1936): 2–3; John Van Oosten, "Doom of the Great Lakes Fisheries," *American Forests* 43, no. 3 ([n.d.] 1937): 103–5, 144–45; John Van Oosten, "Michigan's Commercial Fisheries of the Great Lakes," *Michigan History Magazine* 22, no. 1 (1938): 3–39; John Van Oosten, "The Extent of the Depletion of the Great Lakes Fisheries," in *Proceedings of the Great Lakes Fisheries Council* (1938): 10–17; John Van Oosten, "From Cisco to Perch to Pike: The Fish by Fish Account of Depletion of Great Lakes Fisheries," *State Government* 11, no. 3 (1938): 55–57; Oliver H. Smith and John Van Oosten, "Tagging Experiments with Lake Trout, Whitefish, and Other Species Fish from Lake Michigan," *Transactions of the American Fisheries Society* 69 (1939): 63–84; John Van Oosten, William C. Adams, William L. Finley, and Fred Westerman, "Migratory Fish, A Problem of Interstate Cooperation?" *Transactions of the North American Wildlife Conference* 4 (1939): 25–43; John Van Oosten, "Can the Great Lakes Fisheries Be Saved?" *American Wildlife* 28, no. 3 (1939): 129–35; John Van Oosten, "A Common Concern . . . Great Lakes Fisheries for Angler and Fishers," *Michigan Game Trails* 1, no. 15 (1939): 1–2; "US Coast Guard Studies Plan for Marking Gill Nets," *Atlantic Fisherman* 22, no. 1 (1941): 9; "Recommendations Presented," *Atlantic Fisherman* 23, no. 6 (1942): 18; John Van Oosten, "Lake Trout," *U.S. Fish and Wildlife Service Fisheries Leaflet,* no. 15 (1944); "Great Lakes Research Institute to Investigate Waters," *Atlantic Fisherman* 26, no. 6 (1945): 28; "Fish and Wildlife Service Tag Yellow Perch," *Atlantic Fisherman* 29, no. 7 (1948): 18; "Urges Greater Govt. Interest in Fisheries," *Atlantic Fisherman* 29, no. 8 (1948): 28; John Van Oosten, "The Present Status of the United States Commercial Fisheries of the Great

Lakes," *Transactions of the North American Wildlife Conference* 14 (1949): 319–30; "Wants Tagged Perch Reports," *Atlantic Fisherman* 32, no. 6 (1951): 18; Ralph Hile, "25 Years of Federal Fishery Research on the Great Lakes," Special Scientific Report no. 85 (Washington, D.C.: U.S. Fish and Wildlife Service, 1952); "Persons Urged to Report Drift Bottles," *National Fisherman* 36, no. 9 (1955): 20; Ralph Hile, *U.S. Federal Fishery Research on the Great Lakes Through 1956,* Special Scientific Report no. 226 (Washington, D.C.: U.S. Fish and Wildlife Service, October 1957); "Studying Fish in Isle Royale Area," *National Fisherman* 39, no. 10 (1958): 33; U.S. Department of the Interior, Fish and Wildlife Service, *U.S. Federal Research on Fisheries and Limnology in the Great Lakes through 1964: An Annotated Bibliography,* by Ralph Hile, Special Scientific Report-Fisheries no. 528 (Washington, D.C.: Government Printing Office, March 1966); Alfred Beeton, "Ahead of the Game," *Michigan Natural Resources* 55, no. 3 (1986): 90–91.

On public trust doctrine, see D. B. Reynolds, "Who Owns the Fish and Game?" *Michigan Conservation* 5, no. 1 (1935): 1, 8. On cooperation between the Michigan Department of Conservation and the U.S. Bureau of Commercial Fisheries, see Walter R. Crowe, "Profile of an Industry," *Michigan Conservation* 36, no. 2 (1968): 18–22. On fishery policy in international perspective, see James R. Coull, *World Fisheries Resources* (London and New York: Routledge Press, 1993).

2. On federal aid to Great Lakes ports, see "Pentwater Harbor Re-Conditioned," *The Fisherman* 1, no. 1 (1931): 1; John E. Hubel, "Great Lakes Has New Commercial Fishing Zones Established," *Atlantic Fisherman* 20, no. 2 (1939): 14; "Rivers and Harbors Program," *Atlantic Fisherman* 27, no. 7 (1946): 26; "Funds Approved for Rivers, Harbors Project," *Atlantic Fisherman* 29, no. 5 (1948): 18; "Grand Marais Harbor Dredged," *Atlantic Fisherman* 29, no. 10 (1948): 23; "Claim Dredging Procedure Detrimental," *Atlantic Fisherman* 30, no.1 (1949): 28; "Grand Marais Gets Stronger Light," *Atlantic Fisherman* 31, no. 7 (1950): 27; "Harbor Projects Delayed," *Atlantic Fisherman* 31, no. 9 (1950): 21; "New Channel Light Being Constructed," *Atlantic Fisherman* 31, no. 10 (1950): 21; "Radar Buoys to be Tested," *Atlantic Fisherman* 31, no. 10 (1950): 21; "Beaver Island Harbor to be Improved," *National Fisherman* 36, no. 11 (1955): 27.

On the economics of conservation, see R. D. Burroughs, "Conservation is Big Business," *Michigan Conservation* 20, no. 2 (1951): 6–8. On the early efforts to link fishing and tourism, see "Passenger Department of the Grand Rapids and Indiana Railroad," *A Guide to the Haunts of the Little Fishes* (Chicago: Culver, Page, Hoyne and Co., 1875); Marston J. DeBoer, "Michigan's Sport Fishing at the Crossroads," *Michigan Conservation* 6, no. 7 (1937): 3–4; Mel Ellis, "The Door to Fishing Paradise," *Field and Stream* 71 (May 1966): 52–55, 88.

3. Nicholas V. Olds, "Who Owns the Great Lakes," *Michigan Conservation* 20, no. 6 (1951): 11–14; Jack D. Bails, "Who Owns the Great Lakes?" *Michigan Natural Resources* 44, no. 3 (1975): 5–9.

4. "Legal Limit for Perch Remains," *Atlantic Fisherman* 23, no. 11 (1942): 15; "Size Limit for Perch Reduced," *Atlantic Fisherman* 29, no. 10 (1948): 23. On unsuccessful efforts to save the grayling see "Plantings May Perpetuate Grayling Fauna in Michigan," *Michigan Conservation* 6, no. 7 (1937): 5–6.

5. On theories of fisheries management, see Robert T. Lackey, "Fisheries Management: Integrating Societal Preference, Decision Analysis, and Ecological Risk Assessment," *Environmental Science and Policy* 1 (1998): 329–35. On Michigan commercial fishing regulations, see "Commercial Fish Material: Areas Closed to Commercial Fishing, 1929–1950," State Archives of Michigan, Michigan Historical Center, Lansing, Mich., 75–34, Box 12, File 27; "Commercial Fish Material: Commercial Fish Licenses, 1920–1965," State Archives of Michigan, Michigan Historical Center, Lansing, Mich., 75–34, Box 12, File 25; "Commercial Fish Material: Spawn Taking Records—Lake Trout and Whitefish, 1927–1930," State Archives of Michigan, Michigan Historical Center, Lansing, Mich., 75–34, Box 14, File 1; "Commercial Fish Material: Fish Hatcheries for Commercial Species, 1918–1955," State Archives of Michigan, Michigan Historical Center, Lansing, Mich., 75–34, Box 13, File 3; "Commercial Fish Material: Commercial Fishing Questionnaire, 1928–1940," State Archives of Michigan, Michigan Historical Center, Lansing, Mich., 75–34, Box 13, File 2; "Commercial Fish Material: Fishing Laws and Regulations, 1926–1960," State

Archives of Michigan, Michigan Historical Center, Lansing, Mich., 75-34, Box 12, File 29; "Commercial Fish Material: History of Commercial Fishing," State Archives of Michigan, Michigan Historical Center, Lansing, Mich., 75-34, Box 15, File 4; Bogue, *Fishing the Great Lakes*,181; Kuchenberg, *Reflections in a Tarnished Mirror*, 134-38; Shari L. Dann, *The Life of the Lakes: A Guide to Great Lakes Fishery* (East Lansing: Michigan State University, Department of Fisheries and Wildlife, 1994); "Michigan Fisheries," *The Fishing Gazette* 38, no. 11 (1921): 59-60; U.S. Department of Commerce, Bureau of Fisheries, *Fishing Industry of the Great Lakes*, by Walter Koelz, Bureau of Fisheries Document no. 1001 (Washington, D.C.: Government Printing Office, 1926); John Van Oosten, "Lake States Change Fishery Regulations," *The Fisherman* 4, no. 10 (1935): 1-2; "Important Changes Effected in Commercial Fishing Laws," *Michigan Conservation* 5, no. 2 (1935): 6; "New Fishing Laws," *The Fishing Gazette* 52, no. 12 (1935): 31; John Van Oosten, "Net Selectivity on the Great Lakes," *Gold Medal Netting News* 10 (July 1936): 2-3; Russell J. Martin, "Great Lakes Industry Is Full of Drama and Adventure; Each Season Has its Tragedies," *Michigan Conservation* 6, no. 3 (1936): 3; "The States Should Agree," *Michigan Conservation* 6, no. 12 (1937): 2; Harold Titus, "Fisheries in Distress," *Michigan Conservation* 8, no. 5 (1939): 3, 9; John Van Oosten, William C. Adams, William L. Finley, and Fred Westerman, "Migratory Fish, A Problem of Interstate Cooperation?" *Transactions of the North American Wildlife Conference* 4, (1939): 25-43; Russell J. Martin, "Yellow Pickerel Run," *Michigan Conservation* 8, no. 9 (1939): 6-7; "Michigan Bans Fishing Permits," *Atlantic Fisherman* 20, no. 12 (1940): 19; "Michigan Fishermen Restricted to Fifty Mile Radius," *Atlantic Fisherman* 21, no. 6 (1940): 13; "Derelict Stirs Memories of Brave Men," *Michigan Conservation* 9, no. 10 (1940): 1; "Pickerel Season Opens," *Atlantic Fisherman* 26, no. 3 (1945): 34; "Illegal Fish Nets Surrendered," *Atlantic Fisherman* 26, no. 11 (1945): 38; "Whitefish More Plentiful," *Atlantic Fisherman* 28, no. 1 (1947): 20; "Great Lakes Fishing Laws Are Revised," *Atlantic Fisherman* 28, no. 7 (1947): 26; "Great Lakes Whitefish Hauls Show Gain," *Atlantic Fisherman* 28, no. 8 (1947): 30; "Great Lakes Whitefish Catch Shows Big Gain," *Atlantic Fisherman* 29, no. 1 (1948): 22; "Search and Seizure Law Discussed," *Atlantic Fisherman* 29, no. 2 (1948): 25; "Search and Seizure Bill Passed," *Atlantic Fisherman* 29, no. 5 (1948): 18; "Great Lakes Whitefish Catch Shows Marked Increase," *Atlantic Fisherman* 29, no. 8 (1948): 28; "Recovers Cost of Lost Nets," *Atlantic Fisherman* 30, no. 4 (1949): 20; "Changes in Michigan Laws," *Atlantic Fisherman* 30, no. 6 (1949): 21; "Perch Fishing Allowed in St. James Harbor," *Atlantic Fisherman* 30, no. 12 (1950): 22; Spencer M. Bower, "Great Lakes Fisheries," *Michigan Conservation* 19, no. 5 (1950): 7-10; "More Conservation Officers for Bays de Noc," *Atlantic Fisherman* 32, no. 1 (1951): 22; "Bill Would Allow Keeping of Nets," *Atlantic Fisherman* 32, no. 4 (1951): 30; "Great Lakes Bill Would Curb Commercial Walleye Fishing," *Atlantic Fisherman* 32, no. 5 (1951): 26; "Bills Before Legislature," *Atlantic Fisherman* 32, no. 6 (1951): 18; "Michigan Makes Several Changes in Fishing Regulations," *Atlantic Fisherman* 32, no. 10 (1951): 23; Ralph Hile, "Fishing Regulations," *The Fisherman* 20, no. 3 (1952): 5, 12, 14; "Adson Casey, "Commercial Fisherman," *Michigan Conservation* 24, no. 4 (1955): 15-18; "Fish Sorting Device for Hatcheries," *National Fisherman* 36, no. 10 (1955): 31-32; Justin Leonard, "Our Stake in the Great Lakes," *Michigan Conservation* 26, no. 5 (1957): 9-13; "New and Current," *Michigan Conservation* 31, no. 3 (1962): 2; Wayne Tody, "The World's Finest Fishery?" *Michigan Conservation* 36, no. 3 (1967): 2-7; Walter R. Crowe, "Profile of an Industry," *Michigan Conservation* 36, no. 2 (1968): 18-22; "Michigan Officials Are Granted Broad Powers Under New Fishing Regulations," *The Fisherman* 23, no. 2 (1968): 1; "DNR Tightens Rules Governing Commercial Fishing," *Charlevoix Courier*, 25 November 1970; Martin Glass, "Commercial Fisherman Loses License for not Fishing Enough," *National Enquirer*, [n.d.], 1973; "The Latest DNR Decisions," *Northland Press*, 26 July 1973; "Last Days of the Wolverine," *Michigan Natural Resources* 43, no. 1 (1974): 20-21; Jil Gahsman, "The Old Fish Car and its Legacy," *Michigan Natural Resources* 49, no. 2 (1980): 34-37; Jack D. Bails, "Waters of Change," *Michigan Natural Resources* 55, no. 3 (1986): 45-55. Jack D. Bails and Mercer H. Pat Riarche, eds., *Status of Selected Fish Stocks in Michigan's Great Lakes Waters and Recommendations for Commercial Harvest*, Technical Reports 78-10, 11, 32 and 33 (Lansing: Michigan DNR, Fisheries Division, January 1974); Thomas M. Kelly, *Purse Seining on the Great Lakes: Catches*

Effort, and Problems (Ann Arbor: Michigan Sea Grant Publications Office, September 1979); Michigan Sea Grant, *The Michigan Purse Seining Demonstration Project* (Ann Arbor: Michigan Sea Grant Publications Office, [n.d.]); Thomas M. Kelly, *Purse Seining on the Great Lakes: Vessels, Gear, and Operation* (Ann Arbor: Michigan Sea Grant Publications Office, January 1979); "Michigan Task Force Studies Needs of Rural Areas and Small Communities," *The Fisherman* 34, no. 3 (1982): 3, 8, 17; Ronald W. Rybicki and Philip J. Schneeberger, *Recent History and Management of the State-Licensed Commercial Fishery for Lake Whitefish in the Michigan Waters of Lake Michigan,* Fisheries Research Report no. 1960 (Lansing: Michigan DNR, 5 April 1990).

On the deep trap-net controversy in Michigan, see "Commercial Fish Material: Fish Hatcheries for Commercial Species, 1918–1955," State Archives of Michigan, Michigan Historical Center, Lansing, Mich., 75–34, Box 13, File 3; Frank W. Jacobs, "Deep Traps Nets," *The Fisherman* 1, no. 3 (1932): 1; John Van Oosten, "Department of Commerce, Bureau of Fisheries, University Museums Building," *Michigan Tradesman,* 19 December 1934; Arthur J. Blume, "Deep Trap Net Banned," *Atlantic Fisherman* 15, no. 3 (1934): 12; "Michigan Passes Bill Prohibiting Trap Net Fishing on Two Great Lakes," *Atlantic Fisherman* 16, no. 5 (1935): 20; Charles R. Hoskins, "Depletion of Fish in the Great Lakes," *Atlantic Fisherman* 20, no. 6 (1939): 7; John Van Oosten, Ralph Hile and Frank W. Jobes, "The Whitefish Fishery of Lake Huron and Michigan with Special Reference to the Deep Trap Net fishery," *U.S. Fish and Wildlife Service, Fishery Bulletin* 50 (1946): 297–394; Michigan Department of Conservation, *1921–1946: Twenty-Five Years of Conservation in Michigan* (Lansing: Michigan Department of Conservation, Office of Information and Education, 1960), 17.

On gill nets (nontribal) in Michigan, see Bogue, *Fishing the Great Lakes,* 39–40, 93–102; Clifford Ross Gearhart, *Pity the Poor Fish, Then Man* (Au Train, Mich.: Avery Color Studios, 1987), 193–94; Kuchenberg, *Reflections in a Tarnished Mirror,* 90–92, 146; Lawrence J. Thornhill, "Large Mesh Nets Banned in Michigan 1968!" *The Sport Fisherman's Friend* (November 1997); Michigan United Conservation Clubs, "Ban Gill Nets Now" [n.d.], Michigan United Conservation Clubs files, Lansing, Michigan; Wayne Tody, Letter to Norm Spring, 14 June 1967 (original in possession by Norm Spring); "Gill Net Hearing September 27," *Charlevoix Courier,* 30 August 1967; Glen Sheppard, "Let's Get Answers From Conservation Dept. at Hearing," *Charlevoix Courier,* 27 September 1967; "Hearing Tonight," *Charlevoix Courier,* 27 September 1967; "Says Justice Denied," *Charlevoix Courier,* 27 September 1967; Tom Opre, "Those Gill Nets Must be Banned," *Detroit Free Press,* [n.d.] 1973, CRSS; "Myrl Keller Won't Write Obituaries," *North Woods Call,* 13 June 1973; Al Wolff, "Gill Net Ban Debated by DNR This Week at Cadillac Meet," *Petoskey News Review,* 13 July 1973; "Controls Needed to Preserve all Fishing—DNR," *Northland Press,* 26 July 1973; "A Century of Disgrace—Use of Gill Nets," *North Woods Call,* 8 August 1973; "Gill Nets Must Go, or Fish Will—DNR's Keller Argues," *Petoskey News Review,* 9 August 1973; John Swartley, "Battle Lines Drawn Here for Gill Net Debate," *Petoskey News Review,* 9 August 1973; "Anglers Demand End to Gill Nets at NRC Showdown," *North Woods Call,* 15 August 1973; "Fish Boycott to Stay Over Ban on Gill Nets," *Petoskey News Review,* 23 August 1973; "Time Sports Fishermen Got into Gill Net Row," *Petoskey News Review,* 27 August 1973; "Sees Propaganda War in Gill Net Boycott," *Petoskey News Review,* 28 August 1973; John Swartley, " First it Was Beef, Now Fish Short on Menus," *Petoskey News Review,* 28 August 1973; "Phony Blackmail Charged by DNR in Fish Boycott," *North Woods Call,* 29 August 1973; "Gill Nets Continue Lethal Assault," *North Woods Call,* 12 September 1973; John Swartley, "Gill Nets—It's Up to the Legislature," *Petoskey News Review,* 18 October 1973; "All Present Gill Net Fishermen to Have Opportunity to Convert to Impounding Gear," *The Fisherman* 26, no. 1 (1974); Michigan Department of Natural Resources, *Michigan Fisheries Centennial Report, 1873–1973* (Lansing: Michigan DNR, Fisheries Division, April 1974), 46–48.

On commercial fishing regulations in Wisconsin, see "Commercial Fish Material: Fishing Laws and Regulations, 1926–1960," State Archives of Michigan, Michigan Historical Center, Lansing, Mich., 75–34, Box 12, File 29; Walter Scott and Thomas Reitz, *The Wisconsin Warden, 100 Years of Conservation Law and Enforcement History* (Madison: Wisconsin Department of Natural Resources, July 1979); Bogue, *Fishing the Great Lakes,* 181; Kuchenberg, *Reflections in a Tarnished Mirror,* 76–79, 104–108, 202; *Biennial Report of the*

Commissions of Fisheries and the State Fish and Game Warden of Wisconsin, 1897–1898 (Madison: Democrat Printing, State Printer, 1899); "Lake and River Fisheries," *The Fishing Gazette* 36, no. 6 (1919): 212; James Nevin, "Commercial Fisheries of Wisconsin," *The Fishing Gazette* 38, no. 2 (1921): 45, 47; "Regulations For Wisconsin Became Effective February 4," *The Fishing Gazette* 55, no. 2 (1938): 9; John E. Hubel, "Lake Fishing and Wisconsin Conservation," *Atlantic Fisherman* 19, no. 8 (1938): 7; "Great Lakes Fish Net Ruling Still a Matter of Debate," *Atlantic Fisherman* 20, no. 11 (1939): 16; "Wisconsin Governor Takes Hand in Mesh Ruling," *Atlantic Fisherman* 20, no. 12 (1940): 19; "Wisconsin: Conservation Commission Upheld by Supreme Court," *Atlantic Fisherman* 21, no. 6 (1940): 13; "Spawn Fishing in Wisconsin," *Atlantic Fisherman* 21, no. 10 (1940): 13; "Bill to Prevent Pollution," *Atlantic Fisherman* 22, no. 2 (1941): 17; "Great Lakes Conservation Agitation Not New," *Atlantic Fisherman* 22, no. 5 (1941): 10; "Wisconsin Issues Fishing Law Modification," *Atlantic Fisherman* 22, no. 6 (1941): 15; "Argue in Favor of Present Mesh Size," *Atlantic Fisherman* 23, no. 3 (1942): 19; "To Collect Spawn," *Atlantic Fisherman* 27, no. 10 (1946): 22; "Control of Lake Michigan Unchanged," *Atlantic Fisherman* 28, no. 7 (1947): 26; "Fishermen Favor Hatchery Program," *Atlantic Fisherman* 28, no. 10 (1947): 33; "Urges Propagation Program for Whitefish," *Atlantic Fisherman* 29, no. 4 (1948): 23; "Wisconsin Whitefish Season Extended," *Atlantic Fisherman* 29, no. 10 (1948): 23; "Asked to Report Taking of Tagged Perch," *Atlantic Fisherman* 30, no. 4 (1949): 20; "Great Lakes Fishing Laws Liberalized," *Atlantic Fisherman* 30, no. 10 (1949): 26; "Smaller Nets to be Tried," *Atlantic Fisherman* 31, no. 11 (1950): 27; "Wisconsin Size Limits and Closed Seasons," *Atlantic Fisherman* 31, no. 12 (1951): 22; "Shorter Season for Yellow Perch," *Atlantic Fisherman* 32, no. 9 (1951): 49; Ralph Hile, "Fishing Regulations," *The Fisherman* 20, no. 3 (1952): 5, 12, 14; "Report on Commission Actions," *National Fisherman* 35, no. 9 (1954): 18; "Studying Pollution and Fish Tastes," *National Fisherman* 39, no. 1 (1959): 28; Wisconsin DNR, Division of Forestry, *Wildlife and Recreation, Wisconsin's Lake Michigan Commercial fisheries: 1940–1973*, by Ronald J. Poff, Fish Management Section Report No. 75 (Madison, December 1974); Wisconsin DNR, *Lake Michigan Fisheries Management Plan* (Madison: Bureau of Fish Management, DNR, 1986); University of Wisconsin, Sea Grant Institute, *The Fisheries of the Great Lakes* (Madison: University of Wisconsin, 1988).

By 1938 Wolf Lake State Fish Hatchery, Michigan's largest, no longer raised commercial species. See Jay G. Marks, "Michigan Hatchery Largest of Its Kind," *Michigan Conservation* 7, no. 10 (1938): 7. On limited entry fishing, see Ray Voss, "State Adopts Strict Commercial Fishing Rules," *Grand Rapids Press*, 8 November 1969; Ronald W. Rybicki and Philip J. Schneeberger, *Recent History and Management of the State-Licensed Commercial Fishery for Lake Whitefish in the Michigan Waters of Lake Michigan*, Fisheries Research Report no. 1960 (Lansing: Michigan Department of Natural Resources, 5 April 1990). On zone management, see Kuchenberg, *Reflections in a Tarnished Mirror*, 89, 106; Wayne Tody, "Zones for the Big Lakes," *Michigan Natural Resources* 39, no. 2 (1970): 3–9; Michigan Department of Natural Resources, "Zone Management for the Great Lakes," (Lansing, Mich: DNR, 1970).

On Indiana fishing regulations, see Kuchenberg, *Reflections in a Tarnished Mirror*, 118–20, 146; *Biennial Report of the Commissioner of Fisheries and Game for Indiana, 1907–1908* (Indianapolis: Wm. B. Burford, Contractor for State Printing and Binding, 1908); "The Status of Fish in Indiana, 1776–1976," in *Fish and Wildlife in Indiana, 1776–1976*, Proceedings of the Joint Meeting American Fisheries Society and The Wildlife Society (Bradford Woods, Ind., February 1976); H.E. McReynolds, "Fisheries in Indiana, 1900–1940," in *Fish and Wildlife in Indiana, 1776–1976*, Proceedings of the Joint Meeting American Fisheries Society and The Wildlife Society (Bradford Woods, Ind., February 1976); Frank R. Lockard, "History of Fisheries Activities in Indiana, 1950–1976," in *Fish and Wildlife in Indiana, 1776–1976*, Proceedings of the Joint Meeting American Fisheries Society and The Wildlife Society (Bradford Woods, Ind., February 1976); Indiana Department of Natural Resources: Division of Fish and Wildlife, *Fisheries Management: The Indiana Coastal Zone Management Program*, Technical Report no. 308 (Indianapolis: State Planning Services Agency, May 1979); Tom Flatt and Gary Hudson, *Who's Managing the Fish* (Indianapolis:

Indiana DNR, 1987); Dan C. Brazo, *Indiana Great Lakes Fishery Assessment* , 1987 (Michigan City: Indiana DNR, 17 March 1988), submitted to the Great Lakes Fishery Commission; and Dan C. Brazo, *Fisheries Research Report and Management Report from the Indiana Waters of Lake Michigan, 1990* (Michigan City: Indiana DNR, 1991), submitted to the Lake Michigan Committee of the Great Lakes Fishery Commission. On Illinois fishing regulations, see Kuchenberg, *Reflections in a Tarnished Mirror*, 93–94.

6. On regulation of drop nets in Wisconsin, see "Fish Protection on the Great Lakes," *The Fishing Gazette* 52, no. 6 (1935): 9; "Bill on Fyke Nets Passed," *Atlantic Fisherman* 16, no. 7 (1935): 22–23; "Wisconsin Passes New Laws Regarding Fish Nets," *Atlantic Fisherman* 16, no. 8 (1935): 22, 24; "New Rule on Fyke Net Licenses," *Atlantic Fisherman* 19, no. 3 (1938): 12. On the regulation of gill nets in Wisconsin, see "Lake and River Fisheries," *The Fishing Gazette* 36, no. 7 (1919): 252–53; "Wisconsin Fishermen Fight New Law," *The Fishing Gazette* 46, no. 4 (1929): 37; "Wisconsin Shelves Plan to Increase Mesh," *The Fishing Gazette* 46, no. 6 (1929): 39; "Wisconsin Fishers Ask for Smaller Mesh," *The Fishing Gazette* 46, no. 10 (1929): 63; "No Further Concessions to Lake Michigan Fishermen," *Atlantic Fisherman* 21, no. 1 (1940): 9; "Fishing Conditions at Two Rivers Not Changed," *Atlantic Fisherman* 21, no. 3 (1940): 13; "Judge Reis Upholds Commission's Net Ruling," *Atlantic Fisherman* 21, no. 4 (1940): 11; "Wisconsin Fishermen Still Dispute Regulations," *Atlantic Fisherman* 21, no. 7 (1940): 18; Walter Scott and Thomas Reitz, *The Wisconsin Warden, 100 Years of Conservation Law and Enforcement History* (Madison: Wisconsin DNR, July 1979), 74a-c.

   On other nets, see "Dispute Over Net Fishing," *Atlantic Fisherman* 17, no. 4 (1936): 26; "New Net Sizes Ordered by Conservation Board," *Atlantic Fisherman* 22, no. 5 (1941): 10; "Wisconsin Retains Mesh Size," *Atlantic Fisherman* 23, no. 6 (1942): 18; "Wisconsin Commission Changes Size Requirements," *The Fishing Gazette* 60, no. 3 (1943): 73; Ernest Swift, Madison, Wisconsin, to David LeClair, Two Rivers, Wisconsin, 4 November 1947, Wisconsin Fish Producers Association, Gold Meijer Library, University of Wisconsin-Milwaukee; "Pound Net Law Revised," *Atlantic Fisherman* 29, no. 2 (1948): 25; "Use of Seines Protested," *Atlantic Fisherman* 30, no. 6 (1949): 21; Michigan Department of Natural Resources, *Michigan Fisheries Centennial Report, 1873–1973* (Lansing: Michigan DNR, Fisheries Division, April 1974), 47.

7. On Michigan DNR fisheries research, see Michigan Department of Conservation, Institute for Fisheries Research, *The Improvement of Lakes for Fishing: A Method of Fish Management,* by Carl L. Hubbs and R.W. Eschmeyer, Bulletin of the Institute for Fisheries Research no. 2 (Ann Arbor: University of Michigan Press, May 1938); "Researchers Use Underwater Diving Gear," *National Fisherman* 36, no. 3 (1955): 23; "Divers Study Walleyes," *National Fisherman* 36, no. 8 (1955): 26; Justin W. Leonard, "The Forward Look in Conservation Research," *Michigan Conservation* 25, no. 1 (1956): 9–11; Ralph Hile, *U.S. Federal Fishery Research on the Great Lakes Through 1956,* Special Scientific Report no. 226 (Washington, D.C.: U.S. Fish and Wildlife Service, October 1957); Michigan Department of Natural Resources, Fisheries Division, *Institute for Fisheries Research 1930–1980, Fifty Years of Fisheries Investigations,* by W.C. Latta, Fisheries Research Report No. 1882 (Lansing: Michigan DNR, 10 July 1980); Diane Conners, "State's Declining Lake Trout Population Can't be Blamed on Tribal Fishing Alone," *Traverse City Record Eagle,* 2 February 1998.

   On Wisconsin fisheries research, see G.E. Sprecher, *Wisconsin Fisheries Program: Common Questions and their Answers on Fish Propagation* (Madison: Wisconsin Conservation Department, 1941); "Report on Whitefish Studies," *National Fisherman* 39, no. 12 (1959): 26; Russell Daly, *The Lake Trout: Its Life History, Ecology and Management* (Madison: Wisconsin Conservation Department, 1965);"Survey to Determine Lake Fish Condition," *Charlevoix Courier,* 12 November 1969, CRSS. On the Institute of Fisheries Research, see "New Director Is Named for Fisheries Institute," *Michigan Conservation* 5, no. 4 (1935): 8; R.W. Eschmeyer, "Fish Need Oxygen," *Michigan Conservation* 5, no. 10 (1936): 3, 11; O.H. Clark and Albert S. Hazzard, "Census—Fisheries Style," *Michigan Conservation* 9, no. 8 (1940): 3, 11; "Cousin of the Whitefish," *Michigan Conservation* 13, no. 4 (1944): 4.

8. "Science Has Steered Changes," *Michigan Conservation* 15, no. 5 (1946): 4; Michigan Department of Conservation, *1921–1946: Twenty-Five Years of Conservation in Michigan* (Lansing: Michigan Department of Conserva-

tion, Office of Information and Education, 1960), 18; Jim Meritt, "Planting Fish and Playing God," *Field and Stream* 102 (June 1997): 127–29.

9. Van Oosten's works include: John Van Oosten, "Department of Commerce, Bureau of Fisheries, University Museums Building," *Michigan Tradesman*, 19 December 1934; John Van Oosten, "The Great Smelt Mystery," *Michigan Conservation* 13, no. 6 (1944): 8; John Van Oosten, Ralph Hile, and Frank Jones, *The Whitefish Fishery of Lakes Huron and Michigan with Special Reference to the Deep-Trap-Net Fishery,* U.S. Fish and Wildlife Service Fishery Bulletin 40 (Washington, D.C.: U.S. Government Printing Office, 1946). On Van Oosten, see "Commercial Fish Material: Commercial Fishing Questionnaire, 1928–1940," State Archives of Michigan, Michigan Historical Center, Lansing, Mich., 75–34, Box 13, File 2; Bogue, *Fishing the Great Lakes*, 299, 301; "Arrival of Deep Trap Rigs Stirs Grand Haven Fishermen," *The Fishing Gazette* 51, no. 9 (1934): 37; Jack Van Coevering, "Drastic Changes in Chub Net Fishing Necessary, Says Dr. Van Oosten," *The Fishing Gazette* 52, no. 2 (1935): 4–5; A.J. Blume, "Great Lakes News," *Atlantic Fisherman* 18, no. 1 (1937): 13; "Commercial Fish Menaced," *Michigan Conservation* 6, no. 9 (1937): 11; Harold Titus, "Fisheries in Distress," *Michigan Conservation* 8, no. 5 (1939): 3, 9; "Great Lakes: Negotiations for Board of Inquiry Completed," *Atlantic Fisherman* 21, no. 4 (1940): 11; "Great Lakes 'Trouble-Shooter,'" *The Fishing Gazette* 62, no. 5 (1945): 76; "Great Lakes Official Urges Uniform Regulations," *Atlantic Fisherman* 26, no. 11 (1945): 38; Helen Lee Foster, "Twenty Five Year Record is Reviewed," *Michigan Conservation* 15, no. 5 (1946): 3–4; "Big Nylon Net Catches Cause Concern," *Atlantic Fisherman* 30, no. 8 (1949): 23; "Changes in Service's Great Lakes Staff," *Atlantic Fisherman* 30, no. 10 (1949): 26; Ralph Hile, "25 Years of Federal Fishery Research on the Great Lakes," Special Scientific Report no. 85 (Washington, D.C.: U.S. Fish and Wildlife Service, 1952); Ralph Hile, *U.S. Federal Fishery Research on the Great Lakes Through 1956,* Special Scientific Report no. 226 (Washington, D.C.: U.S. Fish and Wildlife Service, October 1957).

10. Michigan Department of Conservation, *1921–1946: Twenty-Five Years of Conservation in Michigan* (Lansing: Michigan Department of Conservation, Office of Information and Education, 1960), 16.

11. Ibid., 11.

12. On lake trout, see Bogue, *Fishing the Great Lakes*, 153–56; Gearhart, *Pity the Poor Fish, Then Man*, 99; Kuchenberg, *Reflections in a Tarnished Mirror*, 56–58; United States Fish Commission, "Laws, Correspondence, and Judicial Proceeding, Regarding Fish Culture Work in Michigan," in *Report of the Fisheries Commission for 1904* (Washington, D.C.: GPO, 1905); Richard E. Smith, "Are Lake Trout Decreasing," *The Fishing Gazette* 53, no. 11 (1936): 12; "Largest Catches of Trout Ever Reported," *Atlantic Fisherman* 21, no. 1 (1940): 9; "Closed Season Lengthened," *Atlantic Fisherman* 22, no. 10 (1941): 10; "Lake Michigan Trout," *Atlantic Fisherman* 22, no. 10 (1941): 10; "Catches over 1,100 Pounds of Trout," *Atlantic Fisherman* 22, no. 12 (1942): 15; John Van Oosten, "Lake Trout," *U.S. Fish and Wildlife Service Fisheries Leaflet,* no. 15 (1944); "Big Lake Trout Hatch," *Atlantic Fisherman* 26, no. 1 (1945): 30; "Great Lakes Trout Relieving Food Shortages in Andes," *Atlantic Fisherman* 26, no. 10 (1945): 34; "Making Good Trout Catches," *Atlantic Fisherman* 28, no. 6 (1947): 21; "Check Value of Lake Trout Planting," *Atlantic Fisherman* 28, no. 8 (1947): 19; "Making Good Lake Trout," *Atlantic Fisherman* 28, no. 11 (1947): 20; "Great Lakes Trout Large in Late Spawning Run," *Atlantic Fisherman* 28, no. 12 (1948): 51; "Trout Staging Comeback in Green Bay," *Atlantic Fisherman* 29, no. 1 (1948): 22; "Munising Fishermen Bobbing For Trout," *Atlantic Fisherman* 29, no. 1 (1948): 22; "Lake Superior Trout: Traits of this Versatile Fish and Methods of Catching," *Atlantic Fisherman* 29, no. 3 (1948): 17, 33; "Great Lakes Fishermen Make Sizable Trout Catches," *Atlantic Fisherman* 29, no. 5 (1948): 18; "Superior Fishermen Taking Unusually Large Trout," *Atlantic Fisherman* 29, no. 6 (1948): 25; "Good Trout Takes in Lake Superior," *Atlantic Fisherman* 29, no. 8 (1948): 28; "Superior Trout Catches Good," *Atlantic Fisherman* 29, no. 12 (1949): 36; "Trout Yield Good in Marquette Area," *Atlantic Fisherman* 30, no. 3 (1949): 25; "Sizable Trout Hauls from Lake Superior," *Atlantic Fisherman* 30, no. 12 (1950): 22; "Lake Superior Trout Catches Improving," *Atlantic Fisherman* 31, no. 5 (1950): 28; "Great Lakes Trout Catches Show Improvement," *Atlantic Fisherman* 31, no. 8 (1950): 20; "Trout Second in Michigan's June

Catch," *Atlantic Fisherman* 31, no. 8 (1950): 20; "Make Good Trout Hauls," *Atlantic Fisherman* 31, no. 10 (1950): 21; John Van Oosten, "Progress Report on the Study of Great Lakes Trout," *The Fisherman* 18, no. 5 (1950): 5, 8–10; no. 6 (1950): 5, 8 5, 8; "Want Fish Hatchery Constructed," *Atlantic Fisherman* 32, no. 2 (1951): 17; "Lake Superior Trout Yields Better," *Atlantic Fisherman* 32, no. 4 (1951): 30; "Trollers Making Good Trout Catches," *Atlantic Fisherman* 32, no. 8 (1951): 25; "Results of Lake Trout Study," *National Fisherman* 35, no. 5 (1954): 32; "Asked to Report Marked Trout," *National Fisherman* 36, no. 8 (1955): 26; John Van Oosten and Paul H. Eschmeyer, "Biology of Young Lake Trout (Salvelinus namaycush) in Lake Michigan," *U.S. Fish and Wildlife Service, Research Report no. 42* (1956); "Trout Free of Lamprey for Three Years," *National Fisherman* 39, no. 10 (1958): 33; W.F. Carbine, "One Answer for a Fishery," *Michigan Conservation* 29, no. 4 (1960): 25–27; Woodie Jarvis, "New Trout for the Great Lakes," *Field and Stream* 66 (March 1962): 86; "Lake Trout Comeback," *Michigan Conservation* 32, no. 6 (1963): 24–29; Russell Daly, *The Lake Trout: Its Life History, Ecology and Management* (Madison: Wisconsin Conservation Department, 1965); "Too Many, Too Early," *Michigan Conservation* 36, no. 4 (1967); Richard L. Lehman, "Swimming Room Only," *Michigan Conservation* 37, no. 1 (1968): 24–27; Walter R. Crowe, "Profile of an Industry," *Michigan Conservation* 36, no. 2 (1968): 18–22; Bob Clark, "Ban Commercial Taking of Lake Michigan Lake Trout," *Petoskey News Review*, 25 April 1969; "Lake Trout Confuse, but Please DNR," *North Woods Call*, 29 October 1969; Tom Opre, "Comeback of Lake Trout Rated No. 1 in State," *Detroit Free Press*, 16 August 1970; John A. Scott, "Great! Lakers are Back," *Michigan Natural Resources* 40, no. 3 (1971): 24–27; Dave Otto, "Up the Down Lakers," *Outdoor Life* 148 (July 1971): 56, 76, 78, 80; Michigan Department of Natural Resources, *Michigan Fisheries Centennial Report, 1873–1973* (Lansing: Michigan DNR, Fisheries Division, April 1974), 17–38, 39–41, 107–25; Gerald Myhre, Michael Rindfleish *and Randal Rossing, History of Conservation Laws in Wisconsin* (Madison: Wisconsin DNR, July 1979), 71–72; "Tanner Predicts End for Lakers," *North Woods Call*, 22 September 1979; Robert H. Longstaff, "Large Areas of the Great Lakes Maybe Closed to Trout Fishing," *Grand Rapids Press*, 28 June 1980; "Cut Lake Trout Limit to One in this Area Sunday," *Petoskey News Review*, 8 August 1980; Rick Haglund, "State Resources Commission Eases Rules for Trout Fishing," *Traverse City Record Eagle*, 12 January 1981; "U.S. Fish and Wildlife Service Reiterates Policy for Trout for the Great Lakes," *The Fisherman* 34, no. 3 (1982): 9, 10, 22; Michigan Department of Natural Resources: Fish Division, *The Dynamics of Competition Between Sport and Commercial Fishing: Effects on Rehabilitation of Lake Trout in Lake Michigan*, by Richard D. Clark, Jr. and Bin Huang, Fisheries Report no. 1909 (Lansing: Michigan DNR, 17 March 1983); William H. Eager, *Lake Trout Rehabilitation Management Plan for the Michigan Waters of Lake Superior, Huron, and Michigan: 1985–2000* (April 1984), Michigan DNR File, Michigan State Archives, Box 8, Lansing, Mich.; Diane Conners, "State's Declining Lake Trout Population Can't be Blamed on Tribal Fishing Alone," *Traverse City Record Eagle*, 2 February 1998.

On lake trout propagation, see Steve Zucker, "Commercial Fish Material: Fish Hatcheries for Commercial Species, 1918–1955," State Archives of Michigan, Michigan Historical Center, Lansing, Mich., 75–34, Box 13, File 3; "Lake Trout Cross Lake Michigan Both Ways," *The Fishing Gazette* 51, no. 6 (1934): 23; "Million Trout Released in Lake Michigan," *Atlantic Fisherman* 21, no. 10 (1940): 13; "Propagation of Whitefish and Trout," *Atlantic Fisherman* 22, no. 3 (1941): 18; "Bill for Charlevoix Hatchery," *Atlantic Fisherman* 26, no. 3 (1945): 34; "Small Amount of Spawn Taken From Lake Trout," *Atlantic Fisherman* 26, no. 11 (1945): 38; "Charlevoix Hatchery Operation," *Atlantic Fisherman* 27, no. 8 (1946): 31; "Lake Trout Planting Experiment in Lake Michigan," *Michigan Conservation* 16, no. 5 (1947): 6; "Great Lakes Hatcheries May Be Re-established," *Atlantic Fisherman* 28, no. 6 (1947): 21; "Trout Fingerling Planted in Lake Huron," *Atlantic Fisherman* 28, no. 9 (1947): 14; "Lake Trout Fry Plantings," *Atlantic Fisherman* 29, no. 5 (1948): 18; "Lake Trout Planted," *Atlantic Fisherman* 30, no. 1 (1949): 28; "Great Lakes Seek Federal Hatchery Program," *Atlantic Fisherman* 30, no. 2 (1949): 25; "Congressman Potter Seeks Fish Hatcheries," *Atlantic Fisherman* 30, no. 4 (1949): 20; "House Approves Hatchery," *Atlantic Fisherman* 30, no. 6 (1949): 21; "Superior Trout Propagation Favored," *Atlantic Fisherman* 30, no. 7 (1949): 23; "Hatchery Approved by Senate," *Atlantic*

Fisherman 30, no. 8 (1949): 23; "Profits From Fin-Clipped Trout," *Atlantic Fisherman* 30, no. 9 (1949): 28; "Fishermen Request Hatchery," *Atlantic Fisherman* 30, no. 11 (1949): 30; "Great Lakes Trout Problem to be Object of Study," *Atlantic Fisherman* 30, no. 12 (1950): 22; "Trout Eggs Received at Hatchery," *Atlantic Fisherman* 30, no. 12 (1950): 22; "Great Lakes Testing Value of Lake Trout Planting," *Atlantic Fisherman* 31, no. 2 (1950): 22; "Fishermen United in Drive for Hatchery," *Atlantic Fisherman* 31, no. 3 (1950): 23; "More Fin-Clipped Trout Recovered," *Atlantic Fisherman* 31, no. 3 (1950): 23; "Great Lakes to Have Trout Hatchery," *Atlantic Fisherman* 31, no. 4 (1950): 24; "Hatchery Project Halted," *Atlantic Fisherman* 31, no. 10 (1950): 21; "Trout Spawn Plan Turned Down," *Atlantic Fisherman* 31, no. 10 (1950): 21; "Hatchery to Plant Lake Trout," *Atlantic Fisherman* 32, no. 4 (1951): 30; "Lake Superior Gets Trout Fry," *Atlantic Fisherman* 32, no. 6 (1951): 18; "To Resume Construction on Hatchery," *Atlantic Fisherman* 32, no. 6 (1951): 18; "Great Lakes Patrol Boat Plants Trout in Lake Superior," *Atlantic Fisherman* 32, no. 8 (1951): 25; "Trout Planted in Lake Superior," *Atlantic Fisherman* 32, no. 9 (1951): 49; "Plant Trout in Lake Superior," *National Fisherman* 35, no. 6 (1954): 18; "Raising Lake Trout Stock," *National Fisherman* 35, no. 11 (1954): 22; "Great Lakes Fishermen Favor Trout Hatchery Expansion," *National Fisherman* 36, no. 9 (1955): 20; "Lake Trout Spawn to be Collected," *National Fisherman* 36, no. 10 (1955): 31; "Plants 75,000 Lake Trout in Leland," [n.d.], CRSS; "100,000 Lakers for Charlevoix" [n.d.], CRSS; "E.D. Mason to Stay Here," *Charlevoix Courier*, 16 August 1967; "Charlevoix Lake Trout to Supply Hatchery Eggs," *Charlevoix Courier*, 25 October 1972; Al Wolff, "Lake Trout Egg Taking on at Charlevoix," *Petoskey News Review*, 27 October 1972; Michigan Department of Natural Resources, *Michigan Fisheries Centennial Report, 1873–1973* (Lansing: Michigan DNR, Fisheries Division, April 1974), 31–32, 125; Tom Dammann, "Are Michigan's Planted Lake Trout Reproducing on Their Own or Not?" *Charlevoix Courier*, 15 May 1974; Gordon Charles, "Astroturf Helps to Develop Lake Trout," *Traverse City Record Eagle*, 23 November 1997.

On criticism of lake trout propagation, see Walter R. Crowe, "The Lake Trout Are Back," *Michigan Conservation* 34, no. 4 (1965): 2–7.

13. On American-Canadian fisheries relations, see U.S. Congress, House of Representatives, *Executive Hearings Before the Committee on the Merchant Marine and Fisheries*, 79th Cong., 1st sess., 19 and 21 February 1945, 3; "Commercial Fish Material: History of Commercial Fishing," State Archives of Michigan, Michigan Historical Center, Lansing, Mich., 75–34, Box 15, File 4; Kuchenberg, *Reflections in a Tarnished Mirror*, 43–45, 148–51, 212; "Best Plan to Foster Supply of Whitefish in Great Lakes," *The Fishing Gazette* 28, no. 29 (1911): 897–98; "Lake and River Fisheries," *The Fishing Gazette* 32, no. 17 (1915): 524; "Notes from the Second Great Lakes Fishing Conference" (Lansing, Michigan, 8 February 1928), File 7, Box 5, Michigan State Archives, Lansing Michigan; Piscator, "Saving the Great Lakes Fisheries," *The Fishing Gazette* 46, no. 1 (1929): 45; "Great Lakes: Fishermen Seek Tariff Protection," *Atlantic Fisherman* 19, no. 4 (1938): 12; "Great Lakes: Fishermen Oppose Treaty with Canada," *Atlantic Fisherman* 19, no. 11 (1938): 11; Harold Titus, "Fisheries in Distress," *Michigan Conservation* 8, no. 5 (1939): 3, 9; John R. Schacht, "Great Lakes Fishermen Opposed to Treaty with Canada," *Atlantic Fisherman* 20, no. 1 (1939): 9; "Oppose Treaty Between U.S. and Canada to Regulate Great Lakes Fisheries," *Atlantic Fisherman* 20, no. 2 (1939): 11; "Schacht at Washington," *Atlantic Fisherman* 22, no. 1 (1941): 9; "Great Lakes-Canadian Treaty Being Considered," *Atlantic Fisherman* 26, no. 4 (1945): 38; "Joint Meeting Recommends Treaty," *Atlantic Fisherman* 26, no. 9 (1945): 27; John R. Schacht, "Proposed Great Lakes Fishing Treaty," *Atlantic Fisherman* 26, no. 12 (1946): 19, 43; "Great Lakes-Canadian Treaty Signed," *Atlantic Fisherman* 27, no. 3 (1946): 34; "Great Lakes Treaty to be Delayed," *Atlantic Fisherman*, 27, no. 4 (1946): 33; "To Continue Pound Net Rule Waiver," *Atlantic Fisherman* 27, no. 3 (1946): 34; "Great Lakes Fisheries Treaty Is Before Senate," *Michigan Conservation* 15, no. 5 (1946): 14; "International Treaty Is Discussed," *Atlantic Fisherman* 27, no. 7 (1946): 26; "The International Treaty," *Atlantic Fisherman* 27, no. 10 (1946): 53; "The Great Lakes Treaty," *Atlantic Fisherman* 27, no. 12 (1947): 53; "Great Lakes Fishermen Ask Rejection of Treaty," *Atlantic Fisherman* 28, no.5 (1947): 18; "Canadians Confiscate American Nets," *Atlantic Fisherman* 28, no. 10 (1947): 33; "Illegal Operations by Canadian Boats," *Atlantic Fisherman*

28, no. 10 (1947): 33; "Wisconsin Conservation Commission Supports Treaty," *Atlantic Fisherman* 29, no. 4 (1948): 23; "Open Drive Against Canadian Poachers," *Atlantic Fisherman* 30, no. 7 (1949): 23; "Canadians to Engage in Restocking Program," *Atlantic Fisherman* 31, no 11 (1950): 27; "Seek Ratification of International Treaty," *Atlantic Fisherman* 32, no. 5 (1951): 26; "Competition From Canada," *Atlantic Fisherman* 32, no. 10 (1951): 22; "Lake Huron Waters Being Studied," *National Fisherman* 35, no. 9 (1954): 18; "Restocking Program Being Studied," *National Fisherman* 36, no. 10 (1955): 31; "Bill Lets U.S. Fisheries Use Canadian Boats for Alewife," *Grand Rapids Press*, 31 January 1968; "Canadians Take Coho By the Ton," *Grand Rapids Press*, 2 May 1969; Margaret Beattie Bouge, "To Save Fish: Canada, the United States, the Great Lakes and the Joint Commission of 1892," *Journal of American History* 79, no. 4 (1993): 1429–54; Kurkpatrick Dorsey, *The Dawn of Conservation Diplomacy; U.S.–Canadian Wildlife Protection Treaties in the Progressive Era* (Seattle: University of Washington Press, 1998): 19–104; "Great Lakes: International Board to Hold Public Hearings," *Atlantic Fisherman* 21, no. 5 (1940): 19; "Fisheries Hearing to Be Held," *Atlantic Fisherman* 21, no. 9 (1940): 17; "Great Lakes: International Board of Inquiry Holds Hearings," *Atlantic Fisherman* 21, no. 10 (1940): 13; "Great Lakes: Investigation Continues in Progress," *Atlantic Fisherman* 21, no. 11 (1940): 13; "Wisconsin Holds International Board Hearing at Bayfield," *Atlantic Fisherman* 22, no. 7 (1941): 18; John Van Oosten, "The Great Lakes Fisheries: A Review of the International Board of Inquiry for the Great Lakes Fisheries," *State Government* 15, no. 11 (1942): 212, 219–20; Hubert R. Gallagher, A.G. Huntsman, D.J. Taylor and John Van Oosten, *Report of the International Board of Inquiry for the Great Lakes Fisheries*, Report and Supplement (Ann Arbor: International Board of Inquiry for the Great Lakes Fisheries, 1943): 1–24; Hubert R. Gallagher and John Van Oosten, *Supplemental Report of the United States Members of the International Board of Inquiry for the Great Lakes Fisheries*, Report and Supplement (Ann Arbor: International Board of Inquiry for the Great Lakes Fisheries, 1943), 25–213; "International Treaty to Regulate Great Lakes Fisheries Is Recommended," *Michigan Conservation* 13, no. 4 (1944): 5.

On interstate cooperation, see Kuchenberg, *Reflections in a Tarnished Mirror*, 43–45; A. J. Blume, "Great Lakes States May Enter into Compact to Regulate Lake Fisheries," *Atlantic Fisherman* 19, no. 1 (1938): 13; A.J. Blume, "Great Lakes Problems Being Studied," *Atlantic Fisherman* 19, no. 2 (1938): 14; "Fisheries Conference Held," *Atlantic Fisherman* 19, no. 2 (1938): 14; John Van Oosten, William C. Adams, William L. Finley, and Fred Westerman, "Migratory Fish, A Problem of Interstate Cooperation?" *Transactions of the North American Wildlife Conference* 4 (1939): 25–43; "Are the Great Lakes Fisheries Doomed?" *Atlantic Fisherman* 20, no. 4 (1939): 7; "Unification of Great Lakes Fishing Laws Needed," *Atlantic Fisherman* 26, no. 8 (1945): 7; Michigan Department of Conservation, *Notes from the Tri-State Fisheries Conference*, Roscommon, Michigan, 14–15 February 1946 (Lansing: Michigan Department of Conservation, 1946); "Tri-State Conference Scheduled," *Atlantic Fisherman* 32, no. 9 (1951): 48; "Fisheries Legislation," *National Fisherman* 35, no. 11 (1954): 22; "Lake Michigan Compact Approved," *Michigan Conservation* 37, no. 4 (1968): 8–9; Walter Scott and Thomas Reitz, *The Wisconsin Warden, 100 Years of Conservation Law and Enforcement History* (Madison: Wisconsin DNR, July 1979), 7.

On state boundaries, see "Michigan Wins Valuable Fishing Grounds As Boundary Dispute Is Settled," *Atlantic Fisherman* 16, no. 11 (1935): 14; "Michigan Department Seizes Fish Nets," *Atlantic Fisherman* 26, no. 7 (1945): 28; "Great Lake State Boundaries Set," *Atlantic Fisherman* 27, no. 10 (1946): 22; "Boundary Lines for Fishing," *Atlantic Fisherman* 28, no. 4 (1947): 28; "Michigan Ratifies Water Boundaries," *Atlantic Fisherman* 28, no. 7 (1947): 26; "Marinette Tugs Fishing in Michigan Waters," *Atlantic Fisherman* 28, no. 10 (1947): 33; "Asks Congressional Consent to Boundary Pact," *Atlantic Fisherman* 29, no. 4 (1948): 23.

14. On Westerman, see "Commercial Fish Material: Commercial Fish Licenses, 1920–1965," State Archives of Michigan, Michigan Historical Center, Lansing, Mich., 75–34, Box 12, File 25; "Commercial Fish Material: Spawn Taking Records—Lake Trout and Whitefish, 1927–1930," State Archives of Michigan, Michigan Historical Center, Lansing, Mich., 75–34 Box 14, File 1; "Commercial Fish Material: Fish Hatcheries for Commercial Species, 1918–1955," State Archives of Michigan, Michigan Historical Center,

Lansing, Mich., 75–34, Box 13, File 3; "Commercial Fish Material: Pound Nets, 1928–1950," State Archives of Michigan, Michigan Historical Center, Lansing, Mich., 75–34, Box 14, File 6; F.A. Westerman, "The Deep Water Trap Net and Its Relation to Great Lakes Fisheries," *The Fishing Gazette* 50, no. 5 (1933): 4–5; F.A. Westerman, "Water," *Michigan Conservation* 24, no. 2 (1955): 3–5; "Last Days of the Wolverine," *Michigan Natural Resources* 43, no. 1 (1974): 20- 21; Michigan Department of Natural Resources, *Michigan Fisheries Centennial Report, 1873–1973* (Lansing: Michigan DNR, Fisheries Division, April 1974), 162, 164.

15. John Gray, "A Man, A Boat, An Era," *Michigan Conservation* 29, no. 4 (1959): 22–26.

16. Robert E. Ellsworth was the captain of the first boat used to monitor the fisheries in Lake Michigan Waters from 1916 to 1917. See "Robert E. Ellsworth," *Michigan Conservation* 10, no. 2 (1940): 10. See also "Michigan Department Gets New Patrol Boat," *Atlantic Fisherman* 29, no. 7 (1948): 18; "New Patrol Boats," *Atlantic Fisherman* 29, no. 12 (1949): 36; "New Patrol Boat for Lake Superior," *Atlantic Fisherman* 31, no. 12 (1951): 22; "Airplane Patrol Effective," *Michigan Conservation* 6, no. 5 (1936): 11; "Half Million Trout Placed in Waters of Superior," *The Mining Journal* (Marquette, Michigan), 20 July 1951 [from the Gerald LaFreniere Clipping file, hereafter, GLCF, Beaver Island, Michigan]; Al Barnes, "Era Ends with Retirement of Famed Skipper," *Traverse City Record Eagle*, 14 May 1959; John Gray, "A Man, A Boat, An Era," *Michigan Conservation* 29, no. 4 (1959): 222–26; Charlie Moore, "Historic Craft Heads for Oblivion," *Grand Rapids Press*, 30 June 1974; "Patrol Boat No. 1," *Michigan Natural Resources* 66, no. 4 (1996): 14; "Cruises Great Lakes Beat: Patrol Boat Taps Violators for State Navy," [n.l.] (16 November 1951) [From the Beaver Island Historical Society, hereafter, BIHS].

17. "Aerial Patrol Effective for Great Lakes," *Atlantic Fisherman* 17, no. 11 (1936): 11; "Busy Season," *Michigan Conservation* 9, no. 8 (1940); "Great Lakes Air Patrol," *Atlantic Fisherman* 21, no. 12 (1941): 17; "Using Planes for Law Enforcement," *Atlantic Fisherman* 27, no. 12 (1947): 26; Duward Robson, "Airplane's Uses in Conservation Work," *Michigan Conservation* 17, no. 5 (1948): 8–9; "Two forty-two Gasoline Powered Steel Boats," *Michigan Conservation* 17, no. 12 (1948): 13.

18. "Wisconsin Buys Fishing Tug for Conservation Work," *Atlantic Fisherman* 22, no. 2 (1941): 17

19. On postwar emphasis on recreation and leisure see Ralph A. MacMullan, "Manifest for Natural Resources," *Michigan Natural Resources* 38, no. 1 (1969): 2–7.

20. On DNR empowerment of sport-fishing interests, see Clifford Ross Gearhart, *Pity the Poor Fish, Then Man* (Au Train, Mich.: Avery Color Studios, 1987), 204–5. On the promotion of sport fisheries, see "Upper Michigan Places Hope in Tourists," *Michigan Tradesman*, 19 December 1934; Mel Ellis, "Big Three of the Great Lakes Country," *Field and Stream* 61 (December 1956): 52–69; "Best Fishing Spots in All Fifty States," *Field and Stream* 75 (February 1971): 109.

21. Spencer Bower, "Do You Know?" *Michigan Conservation* 21, no. 3 (1952): 32.

22. "Fishery Commission Elects Chairmen," *National Fisherman* 39, no. 12 (1959): 26. On the Great Lakes Fishery Commission, see Kuchenberg, *Reflections in a Tarnished Mirror*, 147, 206; U.S. Congress, House, *Preservation of the Fisheries in Waters Contiguous to the United States and Canada*, doc. no. 315, 54th Cong., 2d sess., 1897; "A Joint Strategic Plan for Management of Great Lakes Fisheries" (Ann Arbor: Great Lakes Fishery Commission, December 1980); Edward H. Brown, Jr., Ronald W. Rybicki, Ronald J. Poff, "Population Dynamics and Interagency Management of the Bloater (Coregonus Hoyi) in Lake Michigan, 1967–1982," Technical Report no. 44 (Ann Arbor: Great Lakes Fishery Commission, March 1985); Randy L. Eshenroder, Mark E. Holey, Thomas K. Gorenflo, Richard D. Clark, Jr., "Fish-Community Objectives for Lake Michigan," Special Publication 95–3 (Ann Arbor: Great Lakes Fishery Commission, November 1995).

23. On sea lamprey, see "Commercial Fish Material: History of Commercial Fishing," State Archives of Michigan, Michigan Historical Center, Lansing, Michigan, 75–34, Box 15, File 4; Bogue, *Fishing the Great Lakes*, 163–64; Kuchenberg, *Reflections in a Tarnished Mirror*, 51–55, 60–67, 197–98; Jan Zita Grover, *Northern Waters* (St. Paul: Graywolf Press, 1999), 79–87; Carl L. Hubbs and T.E.B. Pope, "The Spread of Sea

Lamprey through the Great Lakes," *Michigan Conservation* 6, no. 12 (1937): 5–6; "Sea Lamprey Threatens Fisheries," *Atlantic Fisherman* 19, no. 1 (1938): 13; "Large Sea Lamprey Caught," *Atlantic Fisherman* 20, no. 11 (1939): 16; "Fishes Enemy," *Michigan Conservation* 13, no. 6 (1944): 3, 11; "Great Lakes Trapping Sea Lampreys," *Atlantic Fisherman* 26, no. 5 (1945): 28; "Great Lakes Making Study of Lamprey Control," *Atlantic Fisherman* 26, no. 8 (1945): 34; "To Trap Lampreys," *Atlantic Fisherman* 27, no. 1 (1946): 29; "Seek Removal of Lamprey Eels," *Atlantic Fisherman* 27, no. 5 (1946): 31; "Great Lakes Lamprey," *Atlantic Fisherman* 27, no. 5 (1946): 57; "Great Lakes Lamprey to be Investigated," *Atlantic Fisherman* 27, no. 6 (1946): 27; "Great Lakes Lamprey Bill Is Passed," *Atlantic Fisherman* 27, no. 7 (1946): 26; "Great Lakes States Unite Against Sea Lamprey," *Atlantic Fisherman* 27, no. 11 (1946): 25; "Sea Lamprey Control Campaign Studied," *Atlantic Fisherman* 28, no. 3 (1947): 18; "The Menace of Sea Lamprey," *Michigan Conservation* 16, no. 4 (1947): 6; "Sea Lamprey Run Smaller," *Atlantic Fisherman* 28, no. 6 (1947): 21; "Sea Lampreys," *Atlantic Fisherman* 29, no. 1 (1948): 22; "New Type Sea Lamprey Trap Being Built," *Atlantic Fisherman* 29, no. 2 (1948): 25; "Sea Lamprey Runs to be Studied Again," *Atlantic Fisherman* 29, no. 3 (1948): 20; "Status of Sea Lamprey Problem," *Michigan Conservation* 17, no. 5 (1948): 12; "Biologist Assigned to Thompson Hatchery," *Atlantic Fisherman* 29, no. 5 (1948): 18; "Fishermen on Lamprey Committee," *Atlantic Fisherman* 30, no. 11 (1949): 30; "Asks Funds for Lamprey Study," *Atlantic Fisherman* 32, no. 2 (1951): 17; "Mackinac Straits Fishermen Blame Sea Lamprey," *Atlantic Fisherman* 32, no. 9 (1951): 49; "Sea Lamprey Invades Rifle River System," *Atlantic Fisherman* 32, no. 10 (1951): 23; "Market for Lampreys," *National Fisherman* 35, no. 5 (1954): 32; "Chestnut Lampreys Found on Trout," *National Fisherman* 35, no. 8 (1954): 24; "Lamprey Eel May Prove Beneficial to Science," *National Fisherman* 36, no. 3 (1955): 23; Horace Loftin, "Nature Ramblings," *Science News Letter* 70 (6 October 1956): 224; Jim Doherty, "Lookin' em' Over" *Petoskey News Review*, 16 June 1970, CRSS; John A. Scott, "Great! Lakers are Back," *Michigan Natural Resources* 40, no. 3 (1971): 24–27; Michigan Department of Natural Resources, *Michigan Fisheries Centennial Report, 1873–1973* (Lansing: Michigan DNR, Fisheries Division, April 1974), 97–106; Richard C. Bishop, *Sport and Commercial Fishing Conflicts: A Theoretical Analysis* (Madison: University of Wisconsin Press, 1980).

The U.S. Fish and Wildlife Service (USFWS) worked as servicing agency in American waters for the Great Lakes Fishery Commission. See Ted Bentz, "Progress Made Against Sea Lamprey Menace," *Atlantic Fisherman* 29, no. 6 (1948): 17, 45; "Joint Authority Needed to Control Lamprey," *Atlantic Fisherman* 30, no. 4 (1949): 5; "Elvers May Solve Lamprey Problem," *Atlantic Fisherman* 30, no. 4 (1949): 20; "Weak Point in Sea Lamprey," *Atlantic Fisherman* 30, no. 9 (1949): 28; "Lamprey Eel Appropriation," *Atlantic Fisherman* 30, no. 10 (1949): 26; John Van Oosten, "Progress Report on the Sea Lamprey Study," *The Fisherman* 17, no. 3 (1949): 6, 9–10; John Van Oosten, "The Sea Lamprey—A Threat to Great Lakes Fisheries," *State Government* 22, no. 12 (1949): 283–84, 289; Cleland van Dresser, "The Battle for the Great Lakes," *Popular Mechanics* 93 (1950): 159–61; "Lamprey Traps Planned," *Atlantic Fisherman* 31, no. 2 (1950): 22; "Electronic Device for Destroying Lampreys," *Atlantic Fisherman* 31, no. 6 (1950): 21; James Moffett, "Sea Lamprey Control," *Michigan Conservation* 19, no. 4 (1950): 18–20; "Bid Accepted for Lamprey Boat," *Atlantic Fisherman* 31, no. 7 (1950): 27; "Repair Lamprey Trap," *Atlantic Fisherman* 32, no. 4 (1951): 30; Ralph Hile, "25 Years of Federal Fishery Research on the Great Lakes," Special Scientific Report no. 85 (Washington, D.C.: U.S. Fish and Wildlife Service, 1952); "Cisco to Study Lampreys," *National Fisherman* 35, no. 5 (1954): 32; "Lamprey Take Increases," *National Fisherman* 35, no. 6 (1954): 18; "Treaty Will Aid Lamprey Control," *National Fisherman* 36, no. 3 (1955): 23; "Joint United States-Canada Attack on Lamprey," *National Fisherman* 36, no. 5 (1955): 16; "Sea Lamprey Take Increases," *National Fisherman* 36, no. 6 (1955): 40; "Isle Royale Streams Surveyed for Lampreys," *National Fisherman* 36, no. 7 (1955): 24; Ted Bentz, "Lake Superior Gets Priority in Lamprey Campaign," *National Fisherman* 36, no. 9 (1955): 15; *The Sea Lamprey, Its Effect on Great Lakes Fisheries and the Status of Efforts to Control It* (Ann Arbor: Great Lakes Fishery Commission, 1956); Ralph Hile, *U.S. Federal Fishery Research on the Great Lakes Through 1956,* Special Scientific Report no. 226 (Washington, D.C.: U.S. Fish and Wildlife Service, October 1957); Woodie Jarvis, "New Trout for the Great Lakes," *Field and Stream*

66 (March 1962): 86; Walter R. Crowe, "The Lake Trout Are Back," *Michigan Conservation* 34, no. 4 (1965): 2–7; United States Department of the Interior, Fish and Wildlife Service, *U.S. Federal Research on Fisheries and Limnology in the Great Lakes through 1964: An Annotated Bibliography*, by Ralph Hile, Special Scientific Report-Fisheries no. 528 (Washington, D.C.: Government Printing Office, March 1966), 1–3; "Lamprey Program in Trouble," *Michigan Conservation* 37, no. 3 (1968): 27–28; "Lakes Commission Has Plan For Sea Lamprey Removal," *National Fisherman* 39, no. 6 (1958): 13; "Lake Trout Comeback," *Michigan Conservation* 32, no. 6 (1963): 24–29; Paul C. Neth, "Operation Coho—Plus!" *Conservationist* 26 (April 1972): 14–17; "Sea Lamprey Populations Reduced 90% in 25 Years of Commission Activities," *The Fisherman* 34, no. 3 (1982): 13, 15; Great Lakes Fishery Commission, *TFM vs. The Sea Lamprey: A Generation Later*, Special Publication no. 85.6 (Ann Arbor: Great Lakes Fishery Commission, 1985).

24. W. F. Carbine, "One Answer for a Fishery," *Michigan Conservation* 29, no. 4 (1960): 25–27; Edward E. Schultz, "Three New Fish," *Michigan Conservation* 32, no. 2 (1963): 33–35.

25. Thomas R. Huffman, *Protectors of the Land and Water: Environmentalism in Wisconsin, 1961-1968* (Chapel Hill: University of North Carolina Press, 1994), 9. On the creation of the Wisconsin DNR, see Huffman, 136–67. For a study showing how Michigan's environmental politics paralleled Wisconsin's, see Dave Dempsey, *Ruin and Recovery: Michigan's Rise as a Conservation Leader* (Ann Arbor: University of Michigan Press, 2001).

26. Glenn C. Greg, "Men, Land and Leisure," *Michigan Conservation* 36, no. 1 (1967): 2–7.

27. Ralph A. MacMullan, "We Will Move Ahead," *Michigan Conservation* 33, no. 3 (1964): 29; Ralph A. MacMullan, "Manifest for Natural Resources," *Michigan Natural Resources* 38, no. 1 (1969): 2–7; Jerry Chiappetta, "The Coho Craze in Michigan," *Field and Stream* 72 (January 1968): 42–43, 103–5, 113; Luther J. Carter, "Lake Michigan: Salmon Help to Redress the Balance," *Science* 161 (August 1968): 553, 555; "The Meandering Line," *Michigan Natural Resources* 40, no. 6 (1972): 1–2; "School Named as Living Tribute to MacMullan," *Michigan Natural Resources* 40, no. 6 (1972): 31; Michigan Department of Natural Resources, *Michigan Fisheries Centennial Report, 1873–1973*, (Lansing: Michigan Department of Natural Resources, Fisheries Division, April 1974), 2; [Nancy Kida], "The Gill Net and State Policy," 17 March 1984, Typewritten Report, Mackley Public Library, Muskegon, Michigan; [Nancy Kida], "Fishing Controversy Myths," 23 March 1988, Typewritten Report, Mackley Public Library Vertical File, Muskegon, Michigan.

28. State fisheries officials had introduced smelt in Great Lakes tributary lakes earlier in 1906. See Michigan Department of Conservation, *1921–1946: Twenty-Five Years of Conservation in Michigan* (Lansing: Michigan Department of Conservation, Office of Information and Education, 1960), 14.

29. On Howard Tanner, see Kuchenberg, *Reflections in a Tarnished Mirror*, 78, 146, 205; Robert Doherty, *Disputed Waters: Native Americans and the Great Lakes Fishery* (Lexington: University of Kentucky Press, 1990), 109–17; Howard Tanner, *Indian Fishing Rights and State of Michigan Responsibilities* (Lansing: Michigan DNR, September 1979); Gearhart, *Pity the Poor Fish*, 149, 200; "People and Their Stories," *Michigan Conservation* 34, no. 2 (1965): 1; Howard Tanner, "Great Lakes Sport Fishing Frontier," *Michigan Conservation* 34, no. 6 (1965): 2–3; Jerry Chiappetta, "Big Steelhead Are Back," *Field and Stream* 70 (April 1966): 47–49, 177–81; Jerry Chiappetta, "Salmon Succeed in Great Lakes," *Field and Stream* 71 (December 1966): 10–15; "Fish Expert Says Can Raise Our Own Salmon," *Charlevoix Courier*, 27 September 1967; "County Must Move Now to Get in Salmon Business," *Charlevoix Courier*, 4 October 1967; "Chambers Plan Salmon Meeting," *Charlevoix Courier*, 4 October 1967; "We Need Tanner to Answer Puzzle on Salmon," *Petoskey News Review*, 14 December 1967; Wally Loder, "Chamber Chat," *Charlevoix Courier*, 20 December 1967; "Dr. Tanner Urges Area Prepare for Coming of Coho, Steelhead," *Charlevoix Courier*, 20 December 1967; "Dr. Howard Tanner 'Father of Coho' Predicts Tremendous Economic Gains," *East Jordan News Herald*, 21 December 1967; "Are We Going to be Ready," *Charlevoix Courier*, 3 January 1968; Jerry Chiappetta, "Great Lakes Salmon," *Field and Stream* 72 (March 1968): 62–63, 92–94; Dick Kirkpatrick, "The Coming Salmon Boom," *National Wildlife* 6 (August 1968): 42–45; Bob Clark, "MUCC Told Coho May Become an

'Ecological Disaster' in Lake," *Petoskey News Review*, 21 June 1969; "Coho Originator Denies 'Ecological Disaster' Quote," *Grand Rapids Press*, 28 June 1969; Bill Mullendore, "World's Greatest Fishing Hole," *Michigan Natural Resources* 39, no. 6 (1970): 21; Michigan Department of Natural Resources, *Michigan Fisheries Centennial Report, 1873–1973* (Lansing: Michigan DNR, Fisheries Division, April 1974), 86–87; "New Director Takes Helm of DNR," *Michigan Natural Resources* 44, no. 2 (1975): 6–7; "Rule Treaties Don't Cover Planted Fish," *Petoskey News Review*, 10 May 1979; "Milliken: Appeal Fish Ruling," *Traverse City Record Eagle*, 10 May 1979; Rick Haglund, "Indian Fishing 'Destructive' Tanner Says," *Traverse City Record Eagle*, 10 August 1979; "DNR Chief Warns Nets May Wipe Out North Lake Trout," *Petoskey News Review*, 13 August 1979; Tom Opre, "No Hope for Stocks if Netting Continues," *Detroit Free Press*, 2 September 1979; "Tanner Predicts End for Lakers," *North Woods Call*, 22 September 1979; "Statement of Howard Tanner to U.S. Department of Interior Concerning Amended Rules for off-Reservation Treaty Fishing on the Great Lakes," 13 May 1980, Lansing Michigan, Michigan DNR File, Michigan State Archives, Box 8, Lansing, Michigan; Robert H. Longstaff, "Large Areas of the Great Lakes Maybe Closed to Trout Fishing," *Grand Rapids Press*, 28 June 1980; Rick Haglund, "Charter Boat Business Hurt by DNR Plan," *Traverse City Record Eagle*, 2 July 1980; N.B. Sawyer, "Watt Outlines Indian Gill Net Zoning Proposal," *Grand Rapids Press*, 8 May 1982; [Kida], "The Gill Net and State Policy"; [Kida], "Indians, Fishing and the Economy," 17 March 1984, Typewritten Report, Mackley Public Library, Muskegon, Michigan; [Kida], "Fishing Controversy Myths,"; "Salmon Are Not a Native of the Great Lakes," *The Sport Fishermen's Friend* (November 1997).

30. On alewife, see Bogue, *Fishing the Great Lakes*, 162–63; Kuchenberg, *Reflections in a Tarnished Mirror*, 71–72, 197–98; "Alewife Taken from Lake Michigan," *Atlantic Fisherman* 32, no. 5 (1951): 26; "Alewife Causes Concern," *National Fisherman* 39, no. 10 (1958): 32–33; "Bill Lets U.S. Fisheries Use Canadian Boats for Alewife," *Grand Rapids Press*, 31 January 1968; "Understanding Alewife," *Michigan Conservation* 37, no. 4 (1968); "Alewife Decrease Feared by Many," *Milwaukee Sentinel*, 23 May 1984.

In 1963 the Michigan Department of Conservation looked forward to the day when alewife would provide forage for recovering Lake Trout stocks. See Edward E. Schultz, "Three New Fish," *Michigan Conservation* 32, no. 2 (1963): 33–35; Michigan Department of Natural Resources, *Michigan Fisheries Centennial Report, 1873–1973* (Lansing: Michigan DNR, Fisheries Division, April 1974), 123–25. On economic impact of alewives, see Russell McKee, "Fishstory," *Michigan Conservation* 36, no. 6 (1967): 2–8; "Alewives, Pollution Harsh Words for Great Lakes Resorts," *Petoskey New Review*, 9 June 1970.

31. On economic impact of salmon, see: Kuchenberg, *Reflections in a Tarnished Mirror*, 80–81, 84–86; McKee, "Fishstory," 2–8; "Dr. Tanner Urges Area Prepare for Coming of Coho, Steelhead," *Charlevoix Courier*, 20 December 1967, CRSS; "Dr. Howard Tanner 'Father of Coho' Predicts Tremendous Economic Gains," *East Jordan News Herald*, 21 December 1967; Jerry Chiappetta, "The Coho Craze in Michigan," *Field and Stream* 72 (January 1968): 42–43, 103–5, 113; "Are We Going to be Ready," *Charlevoix Courier*, 3 January 1968; "Coho Impact Series Opens Here with Fishery Chief," *Petoskey News Review*, 13 January 1968; "Coho Impact," *Petoskey News Review*, 24 January 1968 [photograph]; "Fish Chief Speaks Thursday at First 'Coho' Meet Here," *Petoskey News Review*, 24 January 1968; "Hodge Sees Great Area Salmon Potential," *Petoskey News Review*, 24 January 1968; "Coho Session Set Tomorrow," *Charlevoix Courier*, 24 January 1968; "The Outdoors," *Time* 92 (27 September 1968): 63; Wayne H. Tody, "100,000," *Michigan Conservation* 37, no. 5 (1968): 27; "The Fish That has Them Hooked," *Business Week* (5 October 1968): 160–61; Al Stark, "Honor Coho," *Field and Stream* 74 (May 1969): 58, 118; Jim Morris, "Diving for Baits," *Michigan Natural Resources* 38 no. 3 (1969): 13; "Festival Atmosphere of Coho Fishing [Photo]," *Michigan Natural Resources* 38, no. 6 (1969): 33; "Salmon Fishery at Peak in Huron, Michigan," *North Woods Call*, 12 September 1973; Pete Sandman, "Indian Rights Decision Will Affect Multi-Million Dollar Business," *Great Lakes Steelheader*, (July 1979): 1.

32. On boats and gear for salmon fishing in the Great Lakes, see Hank Babbitt, "Boom and a Blunder on Lake Michigan," *Sports Illustrated* 27 (6 October 1967): 67–68; Jerry Chiappetta, "The Coho Craze in Michigan,"

Field and Stream 72 (January 1968): 42–43, 103–5, 113; Howard A. Tanner, "Text of Address" (speech given at the annual industry breakfast jointly sponsored by American Fishing Tackle Manufacturers Association and National Association of Sporting Goods Wholesalers, Chicago, 5 August, 1968), [mimeographed copy] original in possession of Dr. Howard A. Tanner, Haslett, Michigan; Wayne H. Tody, "100,000," *Michigan Conservation* 37, no. 5 (1968): 27; "The Fish That has Them Hooked," *Business Week* (5 October 1968): 160–61; Jerry Chiappetta, "Coho—Fish of Surplus," *Field and Stream* 73 (December 1968): 42–45, 82–84; "New DNR Fishing Rig Locates Huron Salmon," *Grand Rapids Press*, 24 July 1969; Tom Dammann, "Handicapped Turn Out a Trout Lure," *Grand Rapids Press*, 8 November 1969; Henry F. Zeman, "Surf Fishing, Michigan's Newest Sport," *Field and Stream* 74 (February 1970): 150–61; A.J. McClane, "Salmon Potpourri," *Field and Stream* 75 (December 1970): 88–90; Stanley J. Lievense, "Spoonful of Fun," *Michigan Natural Resources* 40, no. 1 (1971): 25; "Tips for Tackling Chinook," *Michigan Natural Resources* 40, no. 3 (1971): 29; Russell McKee, "Are Fiberglass Boats Safe?" *Michigan Natural Resources* 40, no. 4 (1971): 19–23; Jim Roe, "Coho Catcher," *Popular Science* 205 (October 1974): 80–81, 166; Ken Schultz, "Far-Out Fishing," *Field and Stream* 101 (May 1996): 106–7.

33. On the late-1960s introduction of salmon in the Great Lakes, see Kuchenberg, *Reflections in a Tarnished Mirror*, 77–83, 198; Doherty, *Disputed Waters*, 51–66; Dempsey, *Ruin and Recovery*, 119–23; Mel Ellis, "Big Three of the Great Lakes Country," *Field and Stream* 61 (December 1956): 52–69; Howard A. Tanner, "Coho Salmon," [mimeograph copy] original in the possession of Howard A. Tanner, Haslett, Michigan; "People and Their Stories," *Michigan Conservation* 34, no. 2 (1965): 1; Howard Tanner, "Three Fine Fish," *Michigan Conservation* 34, no. 2 (1965): 16–21; Howard A. Tanner, "Recreational Fishing in the Great Lakes (speech presented at the Recreational Fisheries Conference, Haven Hill Lodge, 2 August 1965), [mimeograph copy] original in the possession of Howard A. Tanner, Haslett, Michigan; Howard Tanner, "Great Lakes Sport Fishing Frontier," *Michigan Conservation* 34, no. 6 (1965): 2–3; Michigan Department of Conservation: Fish Division, *Coho Salmon for the Great Lakes*, by Wayne H. Tody and Howard A. Tanner, Fish Management Report No. 1 (Lansing: Michigan Department of Conservation, February 1966); Jerry Chiappetta, "Salmon Succeed in Great Lakes," *Field and Stream* 71 (December 1966): 10–15; Michigan Department of Conservation, *Status Report on Great Lakes Fisheries*, by David P. Borgeson and Wayne H. Tody, Fish Management Report no. 2 (Lansing: Michigan Department of Conservation, March 1967); A.J. McClane, "Where East Meets West," *Field and Stream* 71 (April 1967): 78–80, 89–92; Wayne Tody, "The World's Finest Fishery?" *Michigan Conservation* 36, no. 3 (1967): 2–7; "All Outdoors: Michigan Second in Sales," *Michigan Conservation* 36, no. 4 (1967): 27; "Coho Runs Underway," *Michigan Conservation* 36, no. 5 (1967): 23; "Coho in the Round," *Michigan Conservation* 36, no. 5 (1967); Hank Babbitt, "Boom and a Blunder on Lake Michigan," *Sports Illustrated* 27 (6 October 1967): 67–68; "753,000 Coho Hatching at Charlevoix," *Petoskey News Review*, 29 November 1967; William J. Stephenson, *Coho: Miracle Fish of the Midwest* (Kalamazoo, Mich.: Coho Unlimited, 1968); "Sees World Fame for Area Coho Fishing," *Charlevoix Courier*, 3 January 1968; "Coho Session Set Tomorrow," *Charlevoix Courier*, 24 January 1968; "80,000 More Coho Die at Wolf Lake," *Petoskey News Review*, January 1968; "Seek Reason for Salmon Die-off at Charlevoix," *Charlevoix Courier*, 31 January 1968; Jerry Chiappetta, "Great Lakes Salmon," *Field and Stream* 72 (March 1968): 62–63, 92–94; Nick Drahos, "The Silver (Coho) Salmon," *Conservationist* 22 (April-May 1968): 2–3; "Salmon Plantings Completed for '68," *Michigan Conservation* 37, no. 3 (1968): 27; Wynn Davis, "More on Coho," *Outdoor Life* 142 (July 1968): 62–66, 91; Dick Kirkpatrick, "The Coming Salmon Boom," *National Wildlife* 6 (August 1968): 42–45; Howard A. Tanner, "Text of Address" (speech given at the annual industry breakfast jointly sponsored by American Fishing Tackle Manufacturers Association and National Association of Sporting Goods Wholesalers, Chicago, Illinois, 5 August, 1968), [mimeographed copy] original in possession of Howard A. Tanner, Haslett, Michigan; "Coho Running Strong in Western Michigan," *Ludington Daily News*, 9 August 1968; Luther J. Carter, "Lake Michigan: Salmon Help to Redress the Balance," *Science* 161 (August 1968): 553, 555; "Canadians Take Coho By the Ton," *Grand Rapids Press*,

2 May 1969; Vlad Evanoff, "The Coho Catches On," *Motor Boating* 124 (October 1969): 63, 107; "Surplus Salmon Handout Sunday in Manistee," *Grand Rapids Press*, 4 October 1969; Michigan Department of Natural Resources: Fish Division, *Coho Salmon Status Report, 1967–1968*, by David P. Borgeson, Fish Management Report no. 3 (Lansing: Michigan DNR, February 1970); Dave Borgeson, "Log of the Chinook," *Michigan Natural Resources* 39, no. 5 (1970): 3–5; "Best Fishing Spots in All Fifty States," *Field and Stream* 75 (February 1971): 71–75, 99–115, 162–93; Paul C. Neth, "Operation Coho—Plus!" *Conservationist* 26 (April 1972): 14–17; Michigan Department of Natural Resources, *Michigan Fisheries Centennial Report, 1873–1973* (Lansing: Michigan DNR, Fisheries Division, April 1974), 121–25; "Tension Builds Along Coho Coast," *North Woods Call*, 25 July 1973; John O. Carter, "Chinook: Mystery Heavyweight of the Great Lakes," *Outdoor Life* 157 (May 1976): 78–79, 146, 148–51; "Salmon Are Not a Native of the Great Lakes," *The Sport Fishermen's Friend* (November 1997): 1.

On the management of the Great Lakes salmon fishery, see Hank Babbitt and Dave Kitz, *Catching Coho: The Complete Guide to Freshwater Cohos Salmon Fishing* (Ann Arbor: Sports World Publishing, 1968); John A. Scott, "Salmon 1969," *Michigan Natural Resources* 38, no. 5 (1969): 28–29; Victor R. Patrick, "Salmon Water Patrol," *Michigan Natural Resources* 39, no. 5 (1970): 16–19; Richard J. Enger, "Grand Traverse Bay: Melting Pot for Game Fish," *Field and Stream* 78 (April 1974): 182–88; "The Lady Who Holds the World Record," *Michigan Natural Resources* 40, no. 1 (1971): 31; "Coho Salmon," *Outdoor Life* 159 (1977): 66–67; Ken Schultz, "The Great Great Lakes," *Field and Stream* 87 (February 1983): 79–84; Russ Fimbinger, "Salmon Bonanza," *Michigan Natural Resources* 54, no. 4 (1985): 39–43; Ken Schultz, "Great Lakes Fall Salmon," *Field and Stream* 90 (September 1985): 42–44; Ken Schultz, "Salmon in the Spring," *Field and Stream* 90 (April 1986): 64–65, 126.

34. On pollution and contaminants, see Gearhart, *Pity the Poor Fish, Then Man*, 163–65, 183–87; "Letter to the Editor from Paul F. Kempton," *Michigan Tradesman*, (19 December 1934): 9; Luther J. Carter, "Lake Michigan: Salmon Help to Redress the Balance," *Science* 161 (August 1968): 553; "Ask U.S. Wait on Fish DDT Residue Level," *Petoskey News Review*, 23 April 1969; "Lake Michigan Fishing May be Dealt Setback," *Charlevoix Courier*, 23 April 1969; "DNR Says FDA's DDT Level Will Change Commercial Fish Methods," *Petoskey News Review*, 24 April 1969; "CMU Launches Study of Torch Lake Trout," *North Woods Call*, 30 April 1969; "Don't Go Near the Water?" *Newsweek* 73 (5 May 1969): 75; Richard Morscheck, "Minding Our PCB's" *Michigan Natural Resources* 45, no. 2 (1976): 4–7; Walter Scott and Thomas Reitz, *The Wisconsin Warden, 100 Years of Conservation Law and Enforcement History* (Madison: Wisconsin Department of Natural Resources, July 1979), 27, 29, 41, 61–62, 89, 91; Ken Schultz, "The Great Great Lakes," *Field and Stream* 87 (February 1983): 79–84; Jack D. Bails, "Waters of Change," *Michigan Natural Resources* 55, no. 3 (1986): 52–53; Jim Kingham, "Pure and Secure," *Michigan Natural Resources* 55, no. 3 (1986): 78–81; Alfred Beeton, "Ahead of the Game," *Michigan Natural Resources* 55, no. 3 (1986): 89–93; Kuchenberg, *Reflections in a Tarnished Mirror*, 167–94, 200–2; Bob Campbell, "Tainted Catch," *Detroit Free Press*, 24 August 1986; Howard Tanner, "Restocking of Great Lakes Fishes and Reduction of Environmental Contaminants, 1960–1980," in *Toxic Contamination in Large Lakes, Volume II: Impact of Toxic Contaminants on Fisheries Management*, ed. Norbert W. Schmidtke (Chelsea, Mich.: Lewis Publishers, 1988): 209–27; John E. Grant, "Michigan's Process for Regulating Toxic Substances in Surface Water Permits," in *Toxic Contamination in Large Lakes*, ed. Schmidtke, 2:317–29; Frank M. D'Itri, "Contaminants in Selected Fishes from the Upper Great Lakes," *Toxic Contamination in Large Lakes*, ed. Schmidtke, 51–84; Carlos M. Fetterolf, Jr., "Uniting Habitat Quality and Fishery Programs in the Great Lakes," in *Toxic Contamination in Large Lakes*, ed. Schmidtke, vol. 2, 85–100; Niles Kevern and H. Francis Henderson, "Impact of Toxic Contaminants on Fisheries Management," *Toxic Contamination in Large Lakes*, ed. Schmidtke, vol. 2, 1–4.

On tribal accounts of the destruction of fisheries habitat, see Bogue, *Fishing the Great Lakes*, 109. Great Lakes fisheries habitat was altered by nineteenth-century agriculture development and runoff. See Bogue, 9–15, 23–27, 113–48, 279–86, 331–37.

35. On management of sport fisheries in Michigan, see "Commercial Fish Material: History of Commercial Fishing," State Archives of Michigan, Michigan Historical Center, Lansing, Michigan, 75–34, Box 15, File 4; Bogue, *Fishing the Great Lakes*, 184–87; Michigan Outdoor Publishing Co., *Fishing in Michigan: A Michigan Outdoor Guide* (Kalamazoo: MOPCO., 1965); Gearhart, *Pity the Poor Fish, Then Man*, 203–7; Hank Babbitt and Dave Kitz, *Catching Coho: The Complete Guide to Freshwater Cohos Salmon Fishing* (Ann Arbor: Sports World Publishing, 1968); Paul L. Dorweiler, *Great Lakes Trout and Salmon Fishing* (Coon Rapids, Minn.: Paul Lawrence and Assoc., 1982); Michigan Department of Conservation, Institute for Fisheries Research, *The Improvement of Lakes for Fishing: A Method of Fish Management*, by Carl L. Hubbs and R.W. Eschmeyer, Bulletin of the Institute for Fisheries Research no. 2 (Ann Arbor: University of Michigan Press, May 1938); Steve Zucker, "Planting Time," *Petoskey News-Review*, [n.d.]; David S. Shetter, "Catch Restore Can Help All of Us," *Michigan Conservation* 17, no. 4 (1948): 6–7; "The General Creel Census of Fish, 1947," *Michigan Conservation* 17, no. 12 (1948): 8–9; Kenneth E. Christensen, "Liberalized Fishing Regulations," *Michigan Conservation* 19, no. 4 (1950): 8–9; Wayne H. Tody, "Operation Rifle River," *Michigan Conservation* 20, no. 1 (1951): 15; Stanley Lievense, "A Fisherman's Challenge," *Michigan Conservation* 21, no. 3 (1952): 9–10; "Fish for More Fishermen," *Michigan Conservation* 24, no. 3 (1955): 15, 18; Russell McKee, "25 Busy Years in Conservation," *Michigan Conservation* 26, no. 1 (1957): 2; J.W. Leonard, "Sport Fishing in 1990," *Michigan Conservation* 28, no. 6 (1959): 40–43; James T. McFadden, "Blueprint for Better Fishing," *Michigan Conservation* 33, no. 4 (1964): 3–7; "19 Points of the Law," *Michigan Conservation* 34, no. 1 (1965): 9; Jerry Chiappetta, "Big Steelhead Are Back," *Field and Stream* 70 (April 1966): 47–49, 177–81; Michigan Tourist Council, "Coho, Chinook, and Steelhead in Michigan" ([n.1.], 1967); Wayne Tody, "The World's Finest Fishery?" *Michigan Conservation* 36, no. 3 (1967): 2–7; Michigan Department of Conservation, Fish Division, *Status Report on Great Lakes Fisheries, 1967*, by David P. Borgeson and Wayne Tody, Fish Report no. 2 (Lansing: Michigan Department of Conservation, March 1967); Michigan Department of Conservation, Fish Division, *Coho Salmon Status Report, 1967–68*, by David P. Borgeson, Fish Management Report no. 3 (Lansing: Michigan Department of Conservation, February 1970); Michigan Department of Conservation, Fish Division, *Status of Michigan's Fisheries Management, 1971*, by David P. Borgeson, Fish Management Report no. 4 (Lansing: Michigan Department of Conservation, February 1972); Wayne Tody, Letter to Norm Spring, 14 June 1967; Richard L. Lehman, "Swimming Room Only," *Michigan Conservation* 37, no. 1 (1968): 24–27; John A. Scott, "Great! Lakers are Back," *Michigan Natural Resources* 40, no. 3 (1971): 24–27; "Controls Needed to Preserve all Fishing—DNR," *Northland Press*, 26 July 1973 [CRSS]; Norris McDowell, "The Perch Are Back," *Michigan Natural Resources* 45, no. 3 (1975): 22–25; Jil Gahsman, "The Old Fish Car and its Legacy," *Michigan Natural Resources* 49, no. 2 (1980): 34–37; Robert H. Longstaff, "Large Areas of the Great Lakes Maybe Closed to Trout Fishing," *Grand Rapids Press*, 28 June 1980; Rick Haglund, "Charter Boat Business Hurt by DNR Plan," *Traverse City Record Eagle*, 2 July 1980; Michigan Department of Natural Resources, Fisheries Division, *Institute for Fisheries Research 1930–1980, Fifty Years of Fisheries Investigations*, by W.C. Latta, Fisheries Research Report no. 1882 (Lansing: Michigan Department of Natural Resources, 10 July 1980); Rick Haglund, "State Resources Commission Eases Rules for Trout Fishing," *Traverse City Record Eagle*, 12 January 1981; "Know Your Great Lakes Salmon and Trout," (Lansing: Michigan DNR, Fisheries Division, 1983); Ken Schultz, "The Great Great Lakes," *Field and Stream* 87 (February 1983): 79–84; Michigan Department of Natural Resources: Fish Division, *The Dynamics of Competition Between Sport and Commercial Fishing: Effects on Rehabilitation of Lake Trout in Lake Michigan*, by Richard D. Clark Jr. and Bin Huang, Fisheries Report no. 1909 (Lansing: Michigan DNR, 17 March 1983); Russell McKee, "Winning Ways for Deep Water Anglers," *Michigan Natural Resources* 53, no. 3 (1984): 47–51; Russ Fimbinger, "Salmon Bonanza," *Michigan Natural Resources* 54, no. 4 (1985): 39–43; William G. Milliken, "A Great Lakes Vision," *Michigan Natural Resources* 55, no. 3 (1986): 95–97; Kenneth L. Peterson, "Hatching Some Fishing Fun," *Michigan Natural Resources* 55, no. 4 (1986): 4–11; University of Wisconsin, Sea Grant Institute, *The Fisheries of the Great Lakes* (Madison: University of Wisconsin, 1988); Jean White, "Lake

Michigan Fishing: No Shore Thing," *Saturday Evening Post* 261 (September 1989): 86–87; Gerald P. Rakoczy and Richard D. Rogers, "Charter Boat Catch and Effort from the Michigan Waters of the Great Lakes, 1989," presented at *Regional Charter Boat Workshops* (winter 1990); Chuck Stafford, "Consumers Power Biologists, 2 Others Face Net Charges" *Ludington Daily News*, 10 August 1992; Bob Knigsley, "DNR Seeking Valuable Information," *Muskegon Chronicle*, 15 August 1992; Larry Sawicki, "Some Blame Should Fall on Our Governor's Office," *The Sport Fisherman's Friend* (November 1997); Diane Conners, "State's Declining Lake Trout Population Can't be Blamed on Tribal Fishing Alone," *Traverse City Record Eagle*, 2 February 1998.

On sport fisheries management in Wisconsin, see Wisconsin State Conservation Commission, *Where to Fish in Wisconsin*, (Madison: Wisconsin Conservation Commission, 1925); Dave Otto, "Up the Down Lakers," *Outdoor Life* 148 (July 1971): 56, 76, 78, 80; Bob McNally, "Hottest Lake in the U.S.," *Outdoor Life* 167 (1981): 34–35, 110–112; Wisconsin Department of Natural Resources, *Lake Michigan Fisheries Management Plan* (Madison: Bureau of Fish Management, DNR, 1986).

On sport fisheries management in Indiana, see "Cohos on a Shoestring," *Outdoor Life* 144 (July 1969): 34–35; James D. Absher and John R. Collins, "Southern Lake Michigan Sportfishery: Angler Profile and Specialization Index for Illinois and Indiana" ([n.l].: Illinois-Indiana Sea Grant Program, [n.d.]).

On ecosystem management, see Shari L. Dann, *The Life of the Lakes: A Guide to Great Lakes Fishery* (East Lansing: Department of Fisheries and Wildlife, Michigan State University, 1994); Nicholas V. Olds, "Michigan Leads the Way," *Michigan Conservation* 21, no. 1 (1952): 6–8; F. A. Westerman, "Water," *Michigan Conservation* 24, no. 2 (1955): 3–5; "A Look to the Watershed," *Michigan Conservation* 24, no. 3 (1955): 15, 18; C. R. Humphrys, "Are there Wrongs in Water Rights," *Michigan Conservation* 26, no. 3 (1957): 22–27; Justin Leonard, "Our Stake in the Great Lakes," *Michigan Conservation* 26, no. 5 (1957): 9–13; G.A. Walker, "Dollars and Cents," *Michigan Conservation* 34, no. 1 (1965): 4–5; Gerald E. Eddy, "Clean Water on the Way," *Michigan Conservation* 35, no. 3 (1966): 3–7; Ralph A. MacMullan, "Manifest for Natural Resources," *Michigan Natural Resources* 38, no. 1 (1969): 2–7; Ralph A. MacMullan, "The Michigan Plan," *Michigan Natural Resources* 39, no. 6 (1970): 3- 8; "Lakes Fishery Threatened," *Michigan Natural Resources* 40, no. 3 (1971): 29; Ralph W. Prudy, "The Trouble with Nuclear Power," *Michigan Natural Resources* 40, no. 1 (1972): 2–7; Russell McKee, "Chlorine," *Michigan Natural Resources* 40, no. 3 (1972): 29–33; Howard A. Tanner, "Putting Waste in Its Place," *Michigan Natural Resources* 40, no. 6 (1972): 3–7; "Last Days of the Wolverine," *Michigan Natural Resources* 43, no. 1 (1974): 20- 21; Stanley J. Lievense, "Michigan's Forgotten Fishing," *Michigan Natural Resources* 43, no. 5 (1974): 10–13; Ned E. Folgle, "Michigan's Oldest Fish," *Michigan Natural Resources* 44, no. 2 (1975): 32–33; Richard Morscheck, "Minding Our PCB's" *Michigan Natural Resources* 45, no. 2 (1976): 4–7; Jack D. Bails, "Waters of Change," *Michigan Natural Resources* 55, no. 3 (1986): 45–55; Jim Kingham, "Pure and Secure," *Michigan Natural Resources* 55, no. 3 (1986): 78–81; Billy Goodman, "Keeping Anglers Happy Has a Price," *Bioscience* 41 (May 1991): 294–99; Wisconsin Department of Natural Resources, *Lake Michigan Integrated Fisheries Management Plan: 1995–2000* (Madison: Wisconsin DNR, 1995); John Robertson, "Role and Responsibility of Management," in *Fishing For Solutions: Sustainability of Commercial Fishing in the Great Lakes, Conference Proceedings* (Great Lakes United, December 1995), 75–78; Margaret Dochoda, "Role and Responsibility of Non-Regulatory Agencies in Great Lakes Fish Management," in *Fishing For Solutions*, 79–84; Dave Dempsey, "Role and Responsibility of the Stakeholders in Great Lakes Fishery Management," in *Fishing For Solutions*, 85–88; "Fisheries Legacy," in *Fishing For Solutions*, 91–93; Ronald J. Poff, *From Milk Can to Ecosystem Management: A Historical Perspective on Wisconsin's Fisheries Management Program, 1830s–1990s* (Madison: Wisconsin DNR, 1996); Jim Meritt, "Planting Fish and Playing God," *Field and Stream* 102 (1997): 127–29.

On zone management, see Kuchenberg, *Reflections in a Tarnished Mirror*, 89, 106; Wayne Tody, "Zones for the Big Lakes," *Michigan Natural Resources* 39, no. 2 (1970): 3–9; Michigan Department of Natural Resources, "Zone Management for the Great Lakes" (Lansing: Michigan DNR, 1970); Michigan Tourist

Council, "Fishing in Michigan" [n. 1.: n.d.]. On water quality, see Kuchenberg, 139–44, 154–66, 196–202. On Stanford Smith and water quality, see Luther J. Carter, "Lake Michigan: Salmon Help to Redress the Balance," *Science* 161 (August 1968): 551–55.

36. On Michigan opposition to tribal fishing rights, see Kuchenberg, *Reflections in a Tarnished Mirror*, 100–1, 121–33; Charles E. Cleland, *Rites of Conquest: The History and Culture of Michigan's Native Americans* (Ann Arbor: University of Michigan Press), 279–87; Doherty, *Disputed Waters*, 1–6, 67–139; Larry Sawicki, "As I See It . . . ," *The Sport Fisherman's Friend* (November 1997); "Discontent Is Being Shared Among Traverse Bay Sports Fishermen," *The Sport Fishermen's Friend* (November 1997); Diane Conners, "Federal Judge Will Rule on Tribal Fishing," *Traverse City Record Eagle*, [n.d]; "Will Indians Ruin Fishery," *Charlevoix Courier*, 11 August 1971; "Indian Commercial Fisherman Issued Compassion Licenses in Michigan," *The Fisherman* 24, no. 2 (1972): 10; Jack D. Bails, "Who Owns the Great Lakes?" *Michigan Natural Resources* 44, no. 3 (1975): 8–9; "Reverse Discrimination Ruled Out by Judge in Case Involving Indian Fishing," *The Fisherman* 28, no. 2 (1976): 10; "Strong Resolution on Indian Fishing Adopted by Michigan's Natural Resources Commission," *The Fisherman* 29, no. 6 (1977): 2; Tom Opre, "A Veiled Attack on Treaty Rights?" *Detroit Free Press*, [n.d.] 1979, (CRSS); Gordon Charles, "Indians Fish 800 Miles of Nets," *Traverse City Record Eagle*, 7 April 1979; Doreen Fitzgerald, "Indian Gill Netting Resumes," *Traverse City Record Eagle*, 12 April 1979; Rick Haglund, "Indians May Fish When May 15 Ban Expires," *Traverse City Record Eagle*, 19 April 1979; Rick Haglund, "New Threats Anger U.P. Indians," *Traverse City Record Eagle*, 21 April 1979; "New Study May Ease Indian Fishing Dispute," *Traverse City Record Eagle*, 28 April 1979; Kendall P. Stanley, "Prosecutors Warn Gill Netters, Vigilantes," *Petoskey News Review*, 30 April 1979; Marcella S. Kreiter, "Fox Warns Against Fishing Violence," *Petoskey News Review*, 9 May 1979; Jim Doherty, "Judge Fox's Decision Is Law of the Land," *Petoskey News Review*, 9 May 1979; Eric Sharp, "Indians Win Court Fight on Fishing Rights," *Detroit Free Press*, 9 May 1979; "Rule Treaties Don't Cover Planted Fish," *Petoskey News Review*, 10 May 1979; "Milliken: Appeal Fish Ruling" *Traverse City Record Eagle*, 10 May 1979; Rick Haglund, "Some Chippewas to Resume Fishing," *Traverse City Record Eagle*, 10 May 1979; "Depletion of Traverse Bay Fishery Predicted by Fall," *North Woods Call*, 25 July 1979; Tom Opre, "Gill Netting: Will the Indians Catch Cost Lake Michigan Too Much?" *Detroit Free Press*, 5 August 1979; Rick Haglund, "Indian Fishing 'Destructive' Tanner Says," *Traverse City Record Eagle*, 10 August 1979; "DNR Chief Warns Nets May Wipe Out North Lake Trout," *Petoskey News Review*, 13 August 1979; Tom Opre, "No Hope for Stocks if Netting Continues," *Detroit Free Press*, 2 September 1979; Rick Haglund, "Milliken Asks Halt to Fishing, New Rules for Indian Netters," *Traverse City Record Eagle*, 15 September 1979; "Tanner Predicts End for Lakers," *North Woods Call*, 22 September 1979; Rick Haglund, "U.S. Court Order Halts Gill Netting," *Traverse City Record Eagle*, 22 September 1979; "State Appeals Judge's Gill Net Ruling," *Detroit Free Press*, 23 September 1979; "State Is Trying to Save Fishery," *Detroit Free Press*, 26 September 1979; Tom Opre, "Kelley Asks New Ban After Gill Net Tangle Deepens," *Detroit Free Press*, 30 September 1979; "Steelheaders to Battle Feds on Proposed Gill Net Rules," *Petoskey News Review*, 7 November 1979; Rick Haglund, "Court Decides Gill Net Ban is Limited to 1 Indian Band," *Traverse City Record Eagle*, 5 December 1979; "Statement of Howard Tanner to U.S. Department of Interior Concerning Amended Rules for off-Reservation Treaty Fishing on the Great Lakes," 13 May 1980 (Lansing: Michigan DNR File, Michigan State Archives, Box 8, Lansing, Michigan); "Statement of Thomas L. Washington on Behalf of the MUCC" [presented before the House Subcommittee on Fisheries and Wildlife Conservation, 6 June 1980, Traverse City, Michigan], Michigan DNR File, Michigan State Archives, Box 8, Lansing, Michigan; Robert H. Longstaff, "Large Areas of the Great Lakes Maybe Closed to Trout Fishing," *Grand Rapids Press*, 28 June 1980; Rick Haglund, "Charter Boat Business Hurt by DNR Plan," *Traverse City Record Eagle*, 2 July 1980; Rick Haglund, "State Resources Commission Eases Rules for Trout Fishing," *Traverse City Record Eagle*, 12 January 1981; John Broder, "Vigilantes Greet Gill Net Fishers," *Detroit News*, 24 June 1982; Letter from Joseph Lumsden, Arthur Duhamel, and Wade Teeple to Michigan Governor William Milliken, 22 September 1982 [original in the

possession of COTFMA, Sault Ste. Marie, Michigan]; [Kida], "The Gill Net and State Policy"; [Kida], "Treaties: Yesterday Lives On"; [Kida], "Indians, Fishing and the Economy"; [Kida], "Fishing Controversy Myths"; [Kida], "State Asks U.S. Court to Halt Indian Fishing," *Lansing State Journal,* 29 April 1988; "Threat to Fishing," *Michigan Out of Doors* (April 1984): 1; [Kida], "Gill-Netting Limit Sought in Grand Traverse," *Detroit News,* 29 April 1988; Bill O'Brien, "Court Rules in Favor of Mooring Right," *Traverse City Record Eagle,* [n.d] 1995; John Block, "More Gill-Net Fishing Controversy Surfaces," *Kalamazoo Gazette,* 8 February 1997; Diane Conners, "Court Won't Hear Gill-Net Dispute Until December," *Traverse City Record Eagle,* 28 August 1997; "Nets Pulled for Weekend," *Traverse City Record Eagle,* 31 August 1997; "Nets Pulled for Weekend," *Traverse City Record Eagle,* 31 August 1997; Eric Sharp, "DNR, Indians Should Compromise to Avoid Fishing Battle," *Traverse City Record Eagle,* 4 September 1997; "Judge OKs Indian Commercial Fishing in Grand Traverse Bay," *Weekly News:" Fishery News of the Great Lakes Basin,* 8 September 1997; Steve Kellman, "Tribe Ends Talks for New Fishing Agreement," *Traverse City Record Eagle,* 10 September 1997; Diane Conners, "Fishing for Some Answers," *Traverse City Record Eagle,* 1 February 1998; Diane Conners, "State Wants Ruling on Salmon Fishing," *Traverse City Record Eagle,* 2 February 1998; Diane Conners, "State's Declining Lake Trout Population Can't be Blamed on Tribal Fishing Alone," *Traverse City Record Eagle,* 2 February 1998; Steve Kellman and Diane Conners, "Grand Traverse Band Loses Bid to Expand Fishing," *Traverse Bay Record Eagle,* 5 February 1998; Diane Conners, "Cool Outlines Indian Fishing Issues," *Traverse City Record Eagle,* 28 April 1998; Bill O'Brien, "Walleye Stocking Dispute Ignites," *Traverse City Record Eagle,* 3 July 1998; "Cost, Benefit Don't Balance in Tribal Mooring Right Case," *Traverse City Record Eagle,* 18 July 1998; Connie Stafford, "Gill Nets in the Water for Assessment," *Alpena News,* 24 October 1998; Bill O'Brien, "Fishing Case at End of Line," *Traverse City Record Eagle,* 8 December 1998; "Mooring Rights Lawsuit Wasted Time and Money," *Traverse City Record Eagle,* 14 December 1998; Michigan Legislative Service Bureau, *Michigan Indian Rights Controversy,* by Paul G. Connors, Legislative Research Division Report, vol. 19, no. 3 (Lansing: Michigan Legislative Service Bureau, July 1999); "More Gill Nets Reportedly Recovered in Petoskey," *Petoskey News Review,* 14 October 1975; David Averill and Bill McCulloch, "Feds Open Dunes Area to Indian Fishing," *Traverse City Record Eagle,* 17 August 1979; N.B. Sawyer, "Watt Outlines Indian Gill Net Zoning Proposal," *Grand Rapids Press,* 8 May 1982; "Nets Pulled for Weekend," *Traverse City Record Eagle,* 31 August 1997; John Block, "Truce on Indian Gill Fishing in Jeopardy," *Kalamazoo Gazette,* 4 October 1997; Connie Stafford, "Gill Nets in the Water for Assessment," *Alpena News,* 24 October 1998.

37. James Nevin, "Educating Young Men for Fish Culture Work," *The Fishing Gazette* 37, no. 8 (1920): 54; "Evolution of a Conservation Officer," *Michigan Conservation* 9, no. 10 (1940): 4; "Fisheries Science Course Broadened," *Atlantic Fisherman* 31, no. 12 (1951): 22. On fishery careers, see "Stanley R. Shust," *Michigan Conservation* 17, no. 8 (1948): 12; "Justin W. Leonard Appointed," *Michigan Conservation* 20, no. 5 (1951): 3. On fish and game wardens, see Lewis C. Reimann, *The Game Warden and Poachers* (Ann Arbor: University of Michigan Press, 1959); Clarence M. Taube, *Michigan Fisheries Centennial Report, 1873–1973* (Lansing: Michigan DNR, Fisheries Division, April 1974), 153–75 and Jim Chizek, *Protectors of the Outdoors: True Stories from the Frontline of Conservation Enforcement* (Lodi, Wisc.: Flambeau River Publishing-Leopard Press, 1999).

38. Clarence M. Taube, "Biographical Profiles: Persons Notably Engaged in Michigan's Fisheries," *Michigan Fisheries Centennial Report, 1873–1973* (Lansing: Michigan DNR, 1974), 153–54.

39. Taube, "Biographical Profiles," 156; Harry Westers and Thomas M. Stauffer, "A History of Fish Culture in Michigan," in *Michigan Fisheries Centennial Report, 1873–1973* (Lansing: Michigan DNR, 1974), 109–10.

40. Taube, "Biographical Profiles," 156–75.

41. On Ron Poff, *see:* Kuchenberg, *Reflections in a Tarnished Mirror,* 109–14. *See also:* Poff, *From Milk Can to Ecosystem Management.*

42. Frank N. Egerton, "Missed Opportunities: U.S. Fishery Biologists and Productivity of Fish in Green Bay, Saginaw Bay, and Western Lake Erie," *Environmental Review* 13, no. 2 (1989): 33–63.

43. On Ralph Hile, see Ralph Oscar Hile, *The Collected Papers of Ralph Hile, 1928–1973* (Washington, D.C.: Department of the Interior, U.S. Fish and Wildlife Service, 1977); "Biologists Oppose Walleye Bill," *Atlantic Fisherman* 32, no. 3 (1951): 21; Ralph Hile, "Fishing Regulations," *The Fisherman* 20, no. 3 (1952): 5, 12, 14; "Great Lakes Lamprey Trapping Program Shows Results," *National Fisherman* 35, no. 8 (1954): 24.

44. On James Moffett, see Kuchenberg, *Reflections in a Tarnished Mirror*, 202; "Great Lakes Campaign Against Lampreys Being Organized," *Atlantic Fisherman* 30, no. 11 (1949): 30; "Lamprey Control Program Intensified," *Atlantic Fisherman* 31, no. 3 (1950): 19, 35; "Sea Lamprey Blockade," *Atlantic Fisherman* 31, no. 4 (1950): 24; "Great Lakes to Have a New Fishery Research Station," *Atlantic Fisherman* 31, no. 6 (1950): 21; James Moffett, "Sea Lamprey Control," *Michigan Conservation* 19, no. 4 (1950): 18–20; Ted Bentz, "Commercialization May Solve Lamprey Problem," *Atlantic Fisherman* 32, no. 11 (1951): 17; "Sea Lamprey Boat Laid Up," *Atlantic Fisherman* 32, no. 12 (1952): 36; "In Memoriam," in Ralph Oscar Hile, *The Collected Papers of Ralph Hile, 1928–1973* (Washington, D.C.: Department of the Interior, U.S. Fish and Wildlife Service, 1977).

45. On Vernon Applegate, see Vernon Applegate, "The Menace of Sea Lamprey," *Michigan Conservation* 16, no. 4 (1947): 6; "More Streams Infested by Sea Lampreys," *Atlantic Fisherman* 28, no. 8 (1947): 30; "Great Lakes Trying to Eradicate Lamprey," *Atlantic Fisherman* 28, no. 9 (1947): 14; "Great Lakes Lamprey May be of Value in Medical Research," *Atlantic Fisherman* 32, no. 7 (1951): 24; "Find New Lamprey Weapon," *National Fisherman* 36, no. 10 (1955): 31; "Find New Chemicals that Kill Lampreys," *National Fisherman* 39, no. 3 (1958): 29; "New Chemical Effective Against Sea Lamprey," *National Fisherman* 39, no. 5 (1958): 32.

46. Carlos M. Fetterolf, Jr., "Why a Great Lakes Fishery Commission and Why Sea Lamprey International Symposium," *Canadian Journal of Fisheries and Aquatic Science* 37 (1980): 1588–93; Bob Campbell, "Tainted Catch," *Detroit Free Press*, 24 August 1986.

47. "Lake Trout Comeback," *Michigan Conservation* 32, no. 6 (1963): 24–29

48. "Swedish Pattern Used for Sea Lamprey Weir," *Michigan Conservation* 17, no. 3 (1948): 15; "Lamprey Weir Being Built," *Atlantic Fisherman* 29, no. 9 (1948): 23; "Catch Lampreys in Weirs and Traps," *Atlantic Fisherman* 31, no. 9 (1950): 21; "Lamprey Weirs Being Closed For Season," *National Fisherman* 36, no. 7 (August 1955): 24. On barrier dams, see "New Type Barrier Dam for Lampreys," *Atlantic Fisherman* 31, no. 8 (1950): 20. On electronic fish barriers, see "Sea Lamprey Test Planned," *Atlantic Fisherman* 31, no. 10 (1950): 21; "Electric Shocking Fails to Kill Lampreys," *Atlantic Fisherman* 32, no. 4 (1951): 30; "Sea Lampreys Stopped by Electrical Barrier," *Atlantic Fisherman* 32, no. 5 (1951): 26.

49. On Ralph Hay, see "DNR Plan Would Close Boardman Fish Weir," *The Sport Fisherman's Friend* (November 1997).

50. "Great Lakes Gill Net Tug Is Converted to Research Vessel," *National Fisherman* 39, no. 7 (1958): 11.

51. On Paul Eschmeyer, see "Producers Association Discusses Lamprey," *National Fisherman* 36, no. 1 (1955): 18.

52. Keith Wilson, "80 Snug Harbors," *Michigan Natural Resources* 38, no. 2 (1969): 25–28.

53. On Wayne Tody, see Kuchenberg, *Reflections in a Tarnished Mirror*, 97–101; Jerry Chiappetta, "Big Steelhead Are Back," *Field and Stream* 70 (April 1966): 47–49, 177–81; Jerry Chiappetta, "Salmon Succeed in Great Lakes," *Field and Stream* 71 (December 1966): 10–15; Wayne Tody, Letter to Norm Spring, 14 June 1967; Jerry Chiappetta, "The Coho Craze in Michigan," *Field and Stream* 72 (January 1968): 42–43, 103–5, 113; "Coho Impact Series Opens Here with Fishery Chief," *Petoskey News Review*, 13 January 1968; "Coho Great, But Wait'll You Meet Chinook, Tody Promises," *Petoskey News Review*, 24 January 1968; "Fish Chief Speaks Thursday at First 'Coho' Meet Here," *Petoskey News Review*, 24 January 1968; "Hodge Sees Great Area Salmon Potential," *Petoskey News Review*, 24 January 1968; Jerry Chiappetta, "Great Lakes Salmon," *Field and Stream* 72 (March 1968): 62–63, 92–94; Luther J. Carter, "Lake Michigan: Salmon Help to Redress the Balance," *Science* 161 (August 1968): 553; Dick Kirkpatrick, "The Coming Salmon Boom," *National Wildlife* 6 (August 1968): 42–45; Jerry Chiappetta, "Coho—Fish of Surplus," *Field and Stream* 73 (December 1968):

42–45, 82–84; "The Meander Line," *Michigan Natural Resources* 39, no. 4 (1970): 1; Bill Mullendore, "World's Greatest Fishing Hole," *Michigan Natural Resources* 39, no. 6 (1970): 21; "The Lady Who Holds the World Record," *Michigan Natural Resources* 40, no. 1 (1971): 31; "Time Sports Fishermen Got into Gill Net Row," *Petoskey News Review*, 27 August 1973; John Swartley, "Gill Nets—It's Up to the Legislature," *Petoskey News Review*, 18 October 1973; Michigan Department of Natural Resources, *Michigan Fisheries Centennial Report, 1873–1973* (Lansing: Michigan DNR, Fisheries Division, April 1974), 11, 43, 45–60; [Kida], "The Gill Net and State Policy"; [Kida], "Treaties: Yesterday Lives On"; [Kida], "Fishing Controversy Myths"; "Salmon Are Not a Native of the Great Lakes," *The Sport Fishermen's Friend* (November 1997).

54. Carbine worked for the Michigan Department of Conservation before joining the U.S. Bureau of Commercial Fisheries in 1948. See W.F. Carbine, "One Answer for a Fishery," *Michigan Conservation* 29, no. 4 (1960): 25–27.

55. "Letter to the Editor: Fish Compromise?" [unidentified newspaper clipping], 6 March 1970, Garden Peninsula Historical Society Scrapbook, [hereafter GPHSS].

56. John Swartley, "Charlevoix Fisheries Station to Expand with Lease from City," *Petoskey News Review*, 10 August 1973.

57. The *Steelhead* was commanded by C. E. Belfy. Belfy's father, Edwin E. Belfry served on board *Patrol Boat #1*, captained by fellow Beaver Islander Captain Charles Allers. See "Commercial Fish Material: Commercial Fish Licenses, 1920–1965," State Archives of Michigan, Michigan Historical Center, Lansing, Michigan, 75–34, Box 12, File 25; "Commercial Fish Material: Spawn Taking Records—Lake Trout and Whitefish, 1927–1930," State Archives of Michigan, Michigan Historical Center, Lansing, Michigan, 75–34, Box 14, File 1; U.S. Congress, House of Representatives. *Executive Hearings Before the Committee on the Merchant Marine and Fisheries*, 79th Cong., 1st sess., 19 and 21 February 1945, 30–31; Francis E. Martin, "The Last Days of the Fishing Business," *Journal of Beaver Island History* 4 (1998): 191–211; "Back on the Job," *Michigan Conservation* 14, no. 6 (1945): 7–8; "Erwin Belfy Honored," *Charlevoix Courier*, 18 April 1957; Fran Martin, "C. E. Belfy, New *Steelhead* Skipper, No Lakes Stranger!" *Petoskey News Review*, 24 July 1970; Kahlenberg Brothers Company, "A Low Repair Cost Operating Record," Bulletin no. 58 (Two Rivers, Wisc.: Kahlenberg Brothers, n.d.). For a picture of *Patrol Boat #1*, see Kahlenberg Brothers Company, *Kahlenberg Marine Diesel Model C Series* (Two Rivers, Wisc.: Kahlenberg Brothers, [n.d.]).

On the *Steelhead*, see "Vinette Builds Boat for State Fish Study," *Escanaba Daily Press*, 28 December 1966; "Boat Ordered for Fish Study," *Ironwood Daily Globe*, 29 December 1966; "60-Foot Steel Boat to Probe Fish's Secrets," *Escanaba Daily Press*, 29 December 1966; "U.P. Firm Given Order for Fisheries Research," *Marquette Mining Journal*, 31 December 1966; "State's New Fishery Research Craft to be Launched at Escanaba Dec. 21," *Escanaba Daily Press*, 7 December 1967; "Launch Floating Laboratory," *Charlevoix Courier*, 24 December 1967 [Photograph]; "Fish Finding Aboard 'Steelhead," *Petoskey News Review*, 25 June 1969; "Inland Seas Fact Finder," *Michigan Natural Resources* 38, no. 4 (1969): 21–24; "Here Comes the Fish-Finder's Showboat," *Grand Rapids Press*, 17 September 1972; Michigan Department of Conservation, Great Lakes Fisheries Station, Charlevoix, Michigan [Dedication Program for Fisheries Survey vessel *Steelhead*], original in possession of Norm Spring; "Fisheries," *Michigan Natural Resources* 66, no. 4 (1996): 43.

On Wisconsin patrol boat the *Barney Devine*, see Walter Scott and Thomas Reitz, *The Wisconsin Warden, 100 Years of Conservation Law and Enforcement History* (Madison: Wisconsin DNR, July 1979), 79.

58. Stanford H. Smith, *Species Succession and Fishery Exploitation in the Great Lakes, Contribution no. 368* (Ann Arbor: Ann Arbor Biological Laboratory, U.S. Bureau of Commercial Fisheries, 1968).

59. On political support for the DNR, see Suzy Averill, "Sport Fishing Is Number One," *The Weekender*, 14 May 1970; "Press Release from the Grand Traverse Area Sport Fishing Association on Native American Fishing Regulations," 24 April 1995.

60. Standford H. Smith, "The Changing Ecology of Lake Erie" (mimeograph copy of talk given to the Lake

Erie Resources and Recreation Council, Vermillion, Ohio, 20 October 1961); Kuchenberg, *Reflections in a Tarnished Mirror*, 214.

61. The state of Wisconsin encouraged consumption of rough fish, including carp and sheepshead. *See* Vern Hacker, *A Fine Kettle of Fish* (Madison: Wisconsin DNR, 1982); "Wisconsin Product Tripled Since 1934," *The Fishing Gazette* 55, no. 6 (1938): 38

62. "DNR in Session at Blaney," 7 June 1969, GPHS scrapbook; "Consumer Suffers Under 'Zone Plan,'" 22 October 1969, GPHS scrapbook; "Commercial Fishery Gets Little Relief," 13 April 1970, GPHS scrapbook; "Whose Fish? Michigan Shows Way," 23 March 1975, GPHS scrapbook.

63. Linda Weimar, "Wisconsin Fishery Administration and Biologist Support Gill Nets in Open Hearing," *The Fisherman* 28, no. 4 (1976): 5, 10.

64. Ray Voss, "New Great Lakes Fishing Regulations Ready for State OK," *Grand Rapids Press*, 4 October 1969.

65. "Future Management of Michigan's Commercial Fisheries Under Study," *The Fisherman* 25, no. 1 (1973): 1, 10

66. On Michigan's efforts to settle treaty fishing rights, see "Gill Netters and Foes Huddle With Milliken," *Petoskey News Review*, 15 September 1978; "High Court Agrees to Take State of Washington Indian Treaty Fish Case," *Petoskey News Review*, 17 October 1978; Russell W. Brown, Mark Ebner, and Tom Gorenflo, *Great Lakes Commercial Fisheries: Historical Overview and Prognosis for the Future* (Woods Hole, Mass.: National Oceanic and Atmospheric Administration, 1995?); Bob Gwizdz, "A Negotiated Settlement on Indian Fishing?" *Kalamazoo Gazette*, 21 February 1998; Bill O'Brien, "Plan for Fishing Treaty Unveiled," *Traverse City Record Eagle*, 27 June 1998; Bill O'Brien, "State, Tribes Ordered Back to the Bargaining Table," *Traverse City Record Eagle*, 9 September 1998; Cari Noga, "Rumblings in Air Over Tribal Fishing Rights," *Traverse City Record Eagle*, 22 June 1999; R. Lance Boldrey, "Sport Fishers Not Alone in Protecting Resource," *Kalamazoo Gazette*, 26 September 2000.

Fishing Claims Converge

Everybody's Lake, Everybody's Fish—A Shared
Environmental History and Its Contemporary Concerns

I N THE COURSE OF COLLECTING oral history for the *Fish for All* project, testimonies were obtained whose content linked—in some cases united—the observations of all the stakeholder groups. While the oral histories of the project's four stakeholder groups frequently identify the differences that separate them, their recollections show that they are all shaped by Lake Michigan and thus share the experience of its environmental history and the contemporary concerns it creates. But environmental policy, whether it focuses on fisheries-related issues or other natural resources, often becomes so polarized that participants cease to recognize mutually compatible viewpoints. The preceding sections show that the history of Lake Michigan's fisheries deliberations have not been immune from these contentious dynamics—a postured tone that characterizes most of modern America's natural resource legacies. As much as Lake Michigan's ecosystem frames the experience of each group, there are historical and cultural misunderstandings that impair more balanced, consensus-driven decisions.

This concluding section contains oral testimony that challenges the methods and assumptions that have guided natural resource policy deliberation on Lake Michigan. Addressing a distinctly local situation, the unifying themes of these narratives offer insight on how to productively channel the commitment of each group rather than have it waylaid into the divisiveness that surrounds so many common-property resources. These historical and cultural perspectives hardly diminish the differences of each group; indeed, the division and consensus that one can discern from any fisheries situation is as entrenched in the enterprise as the tradition and innovation that continually fuels it. But these concluding oral testimonies—presented in an integrated format of environmental concern—do reveal points of convergence that stand to mitigate obstructions in the policy-making process. The following testimonies show that each group, historically, has struggled with issues such as nonindigenous species, pollution, the broader wildlife ecology of the basin, outdated management strategies, problems with stocking programs, and resource-use ethics; in short, these groups find common ground in some of Lake Michigan's most fundamental environmental problems.[1] One cannot expect these shared perspectives to settle the differences among Lake Michigan's fisheries stakeholders, but their careful consideration can inform a more studied and less reactionary context among these groups and the public at large.[2] For each group given a voice in *Fish for All*, history and tradition empower their devotion to Lake Michigan and its fisheries resources. The oral histories of these groups—applied in policy-making, museum exhibition, public programming and, of course, the workings of everyday life—clarify their divisions and agreements and set the stage for a new era of fisheries management on Lake Michigan.

John McKinney, who has served as Michigan Sea Grant Agent since 1979, indicated that ongoing controversies about the public health risk posed by the consumption of Great Lakes fish have political, economic, and cultural overtones.

The issue involving most of my time and maybe the most continuous issue in my career has been the health issue relating to the eating of the fish. People are being educated to the fact that there are contaminants in most things. The fish seem to be highlighted in this unending battle to tell the public what they should and should not do relative to eating fish. Again, as much as that is an educational issue, it is certainly the most persistent question that people ask. And I have lots of literature in my files on the history of health advisories and it blows hot and cold in a cyclical way, depending on who wants to make an issue of it. The fish are there and the contaminants are in them. Biologically, you can test them and there are certain trends that can be identified.

I have often been asked to speak about these trends. Are they safer this year than last year? Well, maybe. It depends on which fish, where you catch them, and who measured it. I am not the one who tests the fish. I am not the guy in the laboratory who says these are the numbers. But we certainly are given numbers, and depending on who is interested in it, or whose political agenda it is most important to at the time, you can get different sets of information. It is tough to know. I can give my opinion based on what I know, but it intrigues me, because I am never sure how right I am or how wrong I might be. I trust my sources. I think my sources, in this case they are typically university-based, are probably as good as anybody's. It is the best source of information and that's what I base it on. But there's an endless flow of information, documentation, and calls for testing. Let us test them one more time and know for sure. And it never ends. The fact that it has not ended has had a lot to do with the success and failure of many fishing people. There are some years when the headlines are condemning the fish of Lake Michigan and that can be national headlines. People go out of business because of that. They have a percentage bad year and a lot of that contributes to this mix of who is doing the fishing now. Commercial fishermen and charter boat fishermen, for example, are pretty vulnerable to that. Sport fishing is somewhat immune to that because people do not listen to it anyway because they do not think they eat enough of it to make a difference.

There is no right or wrong. There is a range of knowledge, a range of reactions, and a range of things that anybody can do. Educationally, you just do so much with it. I have gotten calls from state legislators collecting opinions. They get the official version from the Department of Health, and then they want a range of things and maybe that is our process. You collect the range of opinions, and then you have to make a judgment or in the case of these legislators, they may have to vote on something. It may be whether to build more hatcheries, whether to plant fish here or there, whether to reinstate the DNR budget, whether to fire the fisheries chief. There are issues that they may have to deal with, but it may revolve around some opinions they collect from people like me and that makes it—I think it is important that I try to be as informed as I can. I feed into the process; I am just one of many.

Door County, Wisconsin–based fish broker and former fish processor Elaine Johnson saw politics complicate efforts to curb pollution in the Great Lakes.

The money spent to plant walleye came out of the Commercial Fisheries Act. All the money that was spent came from the commercial fisheries, through the Commercial Fisheries Act for the enhancement of the commercial fishery. Now, they have never got a piece of that action because of the pollution that was done by the paper mills. I do not know why the Fox River has not been cleaned up. You could take a walleye that the sports people caught, you could hang him up by the tail and shut your lights off and there would be such a glow in the room you could read your Bible. That's pretty contaminated.

They put out warnings, do not eat this fish, but nobody listens to warnings. The sportsmen say, "I look all right. My fingernails are growing. Nothing's crooked. I got one head. Let's eat it." The commercial people—and so it should be—are regulated by the FDA. They were down here. They inspected these whitefish. To begin with, they would take these fish and they would put them in homogenizers and they would grind them up and they would get an emulsion and test the emulsion. They took the fins, the scales, everything, and the emulsion—although the law said you test the edible portion of a fish. You do not test the whole fish, but to get the count high enough so that commercial people could not fish them, they tried every which way they knew.

Tom Kelly, a marine biologist who directs the Inland Seas Education Association based in Suttons Bay, Michigan, noted the complex ecological history of Lake Michigan's fisheries. A former staff member of the Michigan Sea Grant Program, he has worked with every fisheries stakeholder group on Lake Michigan.

The whole lake is much different now than it was twenty years ago, or twenty years before that, or twenty years before that, and it is never going to be the same. It is never going to go back to being the way it was. I think that the problem with the lake trout is the genetic stocks that were there prior to the crash in the 1950s are gone. That genetic makeup is gone, and for whatever reason, the fish that had been planted have just not been able to do very well. I do not think anybody's sure what the reason is—

toxic chemicals, changes in environment, or different players in the ecosystem. But it is never going to go back to the way it was, especially now that we have zebra mussels, spiny water flea, gobies, the roughy and other species that were not here before.[3]

Commercial fisherman and fish buyer Bill Carlson of Leland, Michigan, expressed concern about Lake Michigan's ability to sustain the fisheries. He notes that Lake Michigan's biomass has been so transformed by human factors that it is difficult to characterize it as a "naturally" managed ecosystem.

I think the big surprise is yet to come. The environment we are living in has changed rapidly in the last few decades. The water quality has changed dramatically. The species that inhabit it are exotic. They are not even natural. We do not know what effect the zebra mussels are going to have.[4] I would assume they are going to have a very dramatic effect on a lot of the fish population because they take out the microorganisms that fish need when they first hatch. The water quality looks a lot better, but that could be a bad thing. We do not know. But there is very little natural ecosystem left. It has changed so much that we do not know what is going to happen next. They might as well manage these fish with aquaculture theory or an aquaculture concept because the salmon are not natural. The alewife are not natural. The zebra mussels are not natural. The lake trout are natural, though the planted ones we have here evidently cannot reproduce in the environment. We have a few species that are natural and we can see some stress on them, especially the chub populations. They seem to be stressed and that could have a lot to do with the water quality. But we do not know. I do not know. Maybe somebody knows, but they are not being heard because it is not a good time to hear that sort of thing or it is not fitting in with negotiations (renegotiation of the Consent Order of 1985) that we have to have at this point.

Lake Michigan is like a fish farm without the controls that you need to be able to have a fish farm. If you were raising fish in an aquaculture situation, you would have controls over almost all the factors. Once in a while, something would happen like a whirling disease that could hurt your stock, but you have basic control over a lot of it. Here in the lake, you do not have any. There is political control, but you do not have environmental quality control. There are a couple of new exotic species of fish that have just been showing up here in the last year or so. There is the roughy and a couple others that we have been seeing. And there is no control over how those develop or expand or where they live or what they eat. Just like there's no control over the zebra mussel and whatever else might be in there that we do not even know about yet, but that we are going to see in the next few years. I do not worry about it anymore. I just do what I am allowed to do and make the best of it.

Ralph Hay of the Michigan DNR's Division of Fisheries indicated that management of the Michigan's Great Lakes ecosystem is complicated by loss of habitat for fish breeding.

The water quality in the Great Lakes has improved in many cases, as a result of environmental laws passed in the 1970s. Water quality continues to improve in general. Our big issue now is habitat loss or degradation. You can have clean water that is safe to drink, but if you do not have habitat for aquatic organisms, there are not going to be any. For instance, for trout species to successfully breed, you need not only cold water, clean water, but also gravel for them to spawn in. You need to have the right type of gravel to attract the insects the fish eat. You need to have woody debris and need places for little and big fish to hide.

Urban development gobbles up lots of land. It impacts the environment and affects fish habitat. People think it is a good idea to get all the wood out of a stream and put a lot of sand in the streams so you can walk. But those are things that are not good for aquatic organisms. We need to educate people in what is good for the animal and what is good for the resource is good for us. The number of anglers stays steady despite the reduction in habitat conditions. They are all vying for the few remaining streams and lakes that still have good fisheries. We have to deal with an allocation issue.

There are still some areas that we plant for a put, grow, and take fishery. The DNR puts them in, lets them grow up, and people take them out. There are a few places where it is just strictly a put-and-take. You put them in and take them out. However, we seem to be trained to move in the direction where we want to improve the habitat. We can improve the natural reproduction. We want to ultimately get as many naturally produced fish in the environment that we can for a couple of reasons. First, naturally spawned fish seem to be hardier through the natural selection process. They tend to have better survival rates. Second, it is a lot cheaper in the long run. It is very expensive to raise fish in a hatchery environment. It takes a lot of money and if we can turn the habitat around so that it can produce those fish naturally, then we can cut back on the number of fish that we have to stock. If we can encourage the propagation of natural fish through natural selection, better survival rates, and better habitat conditions, then we can reduce the amount that we have to stock.

Research biologist Jory Jonas, who is employed in Charlevoix at the Michigan DNR's Great Lakes Fisheries Research Station, discussed the ongoing challenges in managing Michigan's Great Lakes fisheries.

There is no evidence in the 1990s to show that we are out of the woods in terms of pollution in Lake Michigan or Lake Ontario. Often, the demise of the lake trout and other native species is blamed on the invasion of sea lamprey and commercial fishing. I would also put toxins right up there, because research shows that certain mixes of PCBs can damage the reproductive potential in fish and other aquatic species.[5] We are just beginning to gain an understanding of those types of influences. There is not a straight-line answer to what caused the demise of lake trout and other native fish populations. We would have the answer for you if it were commercial fishing or a specific contaminant. Right now, I think we have some interactive effect going on that is not real clear. We need to look at multiple avenues and how those things work together to create this type of situation. It is troubling that whitefish, which were heavily fished, seemed to survive, while lake trout nearly did not. There are some strange things that do not fall in place.

Whitefish populations have rebounded. Burbot densities are at all-time highs because they do not have any competitors in their deep-water environments. The lack of lake trout at their density has opened up a niche for the burbot. On Lake Ontario, the goby populations are taking off and small-mouth bass are becoming so abundant in that system, it's incredible. Zebra mussels, exotic zooplankton, and new fish such as the goby, the rough, and the three-spine stickle back, are all the wild cards. I do not know how they are all going to interact and cause changes. I think it is more of a changing system where some things are winning and some things are losing because you have all these little aspects tweaking them that were not always there. I do not know that it is possible for us to ever go back to what it was. But we need to find out why some of these things are failing, like lake herring and lake trout. To me, the fact that we do not have an answer for that is troubling and I think it is critical that we understand what is going on out there ecologically.

Ralph Hay of the Michigan DNR's Division of Fisheries observed that the state and the sport-fishing organizations have taken on the role of exposing youth to fishing—a task once undertaken by the family. He points out the challenges of providing young anglers with an education about Lake Michigan's fisheries ecology.

The Michigan DNR is concerned about the future of fishing in Michigan. License sales and other studies show that kids are not becoming involved in fishing even though every kid wants to fish. If you go to a school and talk about fishing to young kids in second, third, or fourth grade, they all want to go. They all want to go camping, but they do not have anybody to take them. A kid is not going fishing on his own unless he has been out there before with an adult. There are a lot of single parents, especially the women, who do not have the time or the knowledge to take their kids hunting and fishing. You need somebody to mentor these kids. You need to take them out and show them. Another reason why kids do not fish is because there are so many things for them to do. Many other sports are available to them. They have electronic media, videos, and computer games. When I was a kid, there were not as many choices.

Under Director K. L. Kool, the Michigan DNR has made a concerted effort to reach out to youth and help get them fishing. We have fishing clinics. The free fishing weekend is another opportunity for anybody to fish; you do not need a license. Various sportsmen's clubs in communities offer clinics and will provide the gear. They show kids how to catch trout in a pond, and how to make lures and tie flies. That kind of exposure not only helps the kids, but the parents as well. We want the youth to not only support our fisheries programs, but we need them to support environmental issues both now and in the future. If they hunt, fish, camp, and hike in the woods, they will have a much better appreciation of the environment when related policy issues come up.

My dad took me hunting and fishing and I take my daughter out fishing. My daughter is fifteen and she still loves to fish. She goes fishing every night that she does not have a softball game or choir practice or concert practice. I took her fishing when she was little, and she learned how to do it. Now she likes to do it. With many youth, they love fishing when they are real young. When they get to be teenagers, I hate to say it, but the hormones change. They become interested in other things and lose interest in fishing. But if they have that exposure to hunting and fishing before that hormonal change takes place, they will go back to it. I did a lot of hunting and fishing when I was real young, then I got on to other things. Later, I got back into it. In a very short period of time, my daughter will probably lose a little interest in fishing. But if she gets married and has kids, she will be in a position to take her kids out and show them how to hunt and fish.

A life-long enthusiast of sport fishing, Roy Holmquist discussed the importance of teaching children how to fish.

All our kids are pretty well hooked into fishing. We started them when they were young. They were fishing by the time they were two and a half. And it has worked out great. My youngest son, he has got a twenty-one-foot boat back in Illinois. I got kids in New York, Arkansas, and Florida, and they are all fishermen. My daughter from New York, my granddaughter and my great-granddaughter just visited. My great-granddaughter said, "Papa, how come you do not come to New York and take me fishing?" I am just not enthused about going to New York—with all that traffic and what have you. I am sort of spoiled since we came to Wisconsin. We lived in the city, but we made sure that we took our kids out and got them fishing. To start the kids out right, get them to a pond where they have blue gills, a lot of blue gills, so they are interested, because kids will lose interest in a hurry. But once they start getting into it, they get hooked on it and I will tell you, it is a great sport to be hooked into. Like I say, we have been awful fortunate. I have a lot of friends that come up and then being involved with the club, you are always doing something.

South Haven–based charter boat operator Don Nichols observed the changed in the market for excursion sport fishing.

My fishermen here are basically retired or forty on up. We are not getting the teenagers. We are not getting the twenty-year-olds; they are just not there. The state is aware of this and is on a big campaign to try to promote fishing. They have a free fishing weekend. They have a great deal for children now. You can get a patch and all this. But we have been doing it for the last—heavily for the last five years. Schools are looking for a class picnic or field trip or something of this order. And by going on shorter trips, working harder, and providing more experiences, it is working. It is working pretty well. It is catching on. We have got a lot more schools yet to run here in the next couple weeks. It is probably the hardest trips we do as far as the crew and everything goes, but it is very, very rewarding. Even for my young crew, it is rewarding to them. We run a lot of class groups now because we give our reduced price. The schools love it because the kids are here for the experience. If they catch a fish, that is a bonus. But it is the experience of going fishing and learning how it is done.

Myrl Keller, a retired Michigan DNR fisheries biologist, discussed the ongoing challenges presented by the Great Lakes sport fisheries.

The growth of the salmon has declined because there is no longer a superabundance of alewife like there was in the late 1960s and early 1970s. This is probably one of the first indicators to tell you that too many salmon are being stocked for the forage base to sustain. We have to also learn that these species are opportunistic. They will feed on alewife because they were the easiest to get and they occupied the same pelagic or the midwater strata and are easy to feed on. When their numbers came low, the salmon shifted to feeding on chubs, a native species and a member of the whitefish family, which prefers the deep water and the lake bottom. The salmon started feeding on chubs, so they are a very unique species.

The greatest threat to Great Lakes fisheries today is man and what he will do for his greed and personal wealth and good. If good conservation practices are not employed, the Great Lakes and their resources will suffer. And I am fearful right now with the present leadership that we have in Michigan that maybe conservation practices are not being attended to quite as well as they should. I know that in the early part of my career, we were pretty sincerely convinced that what was best for the resource is best for the resource users.

Man has probably made the greatest changes to the lakes and I think he will continue to in the future. He can do very well for the resource. Everybody ought to be very sincere about protecting this resource because it is so unique. The resource can be used forever if it is wisely used. But sometimes people just do not treat it as kindly as they should. History has taught us so much—there has been so much damage, but it can be corrected. So the stewards, the people that watch this body of water, it is very important that they sincerely do the right things.

Former Michigan State University faculty member and Michigan DNR director Howard Tanner regarded the lack of uniform regulations as harmful to the Great Lakes region.

If they would make me czar of Lake Michigan, I could do it right and there would be uniform regulations throughout the Great Lakes. They should be managed with a substantially uniform set of regulations based on population demand and the movement of fish around the lake, particularly the forage fish such as alewives, which are crowded in the southern third of the lake all winter. In the areas where there is minimal recreational interest, commercial fishing should be allowed to dominate. North of Petoskey, with limited exceptions on the southern shore of the Upper Peninsula and portions of Wisconsin, Lake Michigan waters could be zoned commercially. I would still restrict them to impounding gear. I would not permit them to take lake trout and salmon. These options are possible. Every time somebody talks about having uniform regulations on Lake Michigan, it turns out that they want to put a federal presence in that role and I am adamantly opposed to that. The federal government is not in the business of managing fisheries. They are not a management agency with the exception of places like national parks and national monuments. They do not have management authority on the Great Lakes and generally throughout the inland areas. On the oceans, it is quite a different situation. The federal government is not a management agency and I do not want them to be a management agency. That does not mean I am happy with a divided management philosophy of four states. So, with tongue in cheek, I would say, let's vote shares based on acreage of ownership on Lake Michigan. Michigan will get sixty-one votes and Wisconsin will get about seventeen, Indiana will get two, and Illinois will get what's left, and we will settle things my way. In other words, the right way. But that's not going to happen.

Sport fisher Gordon Zuverink expressed concern about the future of the salmon fishery in the Great Lakes. He believes that organizations such as Michigan Steelheaders can play a vital role in maintaining support for the sport fishery.

We want fish, but we know that you can have too many fish out there. Then you are not going to get healthy fish. That is what happened in 1987, one of the better fishing years we had since the introduction of salmon. In 1988 and 1989, it collapsed. Fishing—bay and lake fishing—was shot. Fishermen got out of it; they started selling their boats and went playing golf instead. They were not going to waste their time going out there to catch a fish or two, particularly if it was not a chinook and maybe only a lake trout. After all, the number one thing they wanted was salmon, big salmon. So we had to realize that there is a balance. We were the first ones to admit that we want a healthy fishery. When the fishery collapsed, the reasoning was that the fish were not healthy and bacterial kidney disease took over. Bacterial kidney disease came from the northwest; it is like a common cold to the fish. If a fish is healthy, he will not get sick from it and die.

The thing that we are concerned with is having a healthy fishery and maintaining a world-class fishery. It is good for the economy when the fishing is good. We get people from all over the country. I have had people from England fish with me, come over here charter fishing. In fact, for years, I had a group from Iowa City, Iowa, and others from Des Moines and Davenport. One notable person was Hayden Frye, the football coach at the University of Iowa, who recently retired. He and a group of his friends came fishing with me for three or four years in a row. I have some pictures of Hayden Frye with some of his friends on my boat holding up fish. It is a boom to the economy here. It is a multimillion dollar industry for the Great Lakes and the Great Lakes Basin.

Holland is one of the Steelheader's best chapters because we seem to have developed a following of younger personnel joining our chapter. Many of the chapters are run by older members. I refer to them as burned-out members, not active enough anymore. The young kids are more enthusiastic than many older people who become more negative, less positive, and less enthused. You have got to have good young members coming in and every year more of our members are younger, kids in their twenties and early thirties, and not the old gray-haired guys. I challenged them at the state board. I said, years ago, "Guys, look around the table. It is all gray hair around here." I said, "It is all old people, lots of them retired." I said, "We have got to get young blood in here. If we expect this organization to keep going and be a factor, we have to have young blood." Since that time, we have gotten some very enthusiastic young board members. They are taking a leadership role and doing a good job and it is a healthy organization with young ideas. I did not want to hurt anybody's feelings, and we still need some of the old guys around when these young guys come up with an idea to say, "Hey, guys, we have been there and done that. Do not do it. We made that mistake before. Do not do it again." So that's where seniority—generational members help. Do not make the same mistake twice.

Brian Price is a former commercial fisherman who now directs a nonprofit land trust. With an education in geology, he observes that as an ecosystem, the Great Lakes has been characterized by instability.

There are a number of really fascinating research projects taking place. There are many open-ended questions, especially given the huge disruptions brought on by zebra mussels and other exotic species. Many people have this vision in their mind that there was once this primeval lake ecology and system that was in perfect balance with everything in its perfect little niche. The Great Lakes is a very young system; it was less than 10,000 years since the glacier left. This amount of time is nothing compared to the time that it takes for species to migrate back in, reestablish their territories and their spawning populations and get things worked out. In a young system like the Great Lakes, there were probably always some larger fluctuations than we ever realized in terms of populations of fish. It was a young, somewhat unstable system in the first place. It was rapidly evolving and becoming a little more stable, when settlers cut down all the forests, dammed all the spawning streams, and introduced non-native species for sport fish like smelt, brown trout, and carp. It was just one question mark after another after that.

Nobody can ever predict what is going to happen on the Great Lakes. Every time somebody thinks they have got a handle on what is going to happen next ecologically out there, something entirely different comes up. The last time that the state thought they had a good handle on this they started dumping too many salmon into the lake. As a result, a couple of things happened. Bacterial kidney disease started and some of the salmon hatcheries were closed. The alewife population crashed. They had built this enormous sport fishing industry on an assumption that there would always be abundant stocks of alewives. Well, that is not out there anymore, so the fish got smaller and they started to feed on other fish. It was thought they would not feed on chubs, well they do feed on chubs. It was thought that they would not feed on young whitefish, well they do feed on young whitefish. It is a seesaw that is never quite in balance.

Neil Teskie expressed the view that commercial fishermen need to comply with too many regulations, particularly if they sell fish for human consumption. He suggests that Lake Michigan's fisheries stakeholders show mutual empathy for each other's endeavors.

R egulation would be the biggest threat—not only commercial fishing regulation but agriculture regulation and building regulation. We need regulation, but it seems like I have more permits and licenses than I ever dreamed I would have in my in my life to operate a business. To a small businessman it's sometimes overpowering. You do need regulation, but you could be over-regulated. I mean, you cannot have a regulation that allows fishing all year long and with no size limits. The task force or the DNR should ask themselves, "Would I want to do this myself?" That is the bottom line for me. It is easy for somebody to sit back and say have all your fish dressed and weighed before you leave the boat. Well, you saw how many fish they had today. Was there any way you could dress those before you left the boat? No way. Sometimes they do not really know what fishing requires. That is why I like to explain to people or show people what I do. I would say that these issues are the biggest threats to commercial fishing. I do not see environmental threats right now. I do not see fish populations being threatened. I think we are always going to have some environmental problems with chemicals and PCBs. I think that things have cleaned up quite a bit compared to what it used to be. I do not see a sea lamprey disaster like in the 1950s. The legislature and the DNR could go off the deep end and say we do not want any more commercial fishermen. That would be the other threat. I do not see that happening in the immediate future. I understand that we have to have regulation. I understand it is to protect the public. But it starts adding up. For years we cleaned fish in that shed down there and nobody ever got sick. Now, I have my little shed down at the dock and it is FDA-approved. I have had the FDA down there and I have got it approved for doing caviar or whatever. In a way, I am glad it is that way. I like to reflect that everything is in line at this place. I have always been one to have my nets in good repair, my boats in good repair—everything.

Kevin Naze, a sport-fishing writer and fishing guide from Door County, Wisconsin, discussed health concerns relating to the consumption of Great Lakes fish.

Back in 1986 the State Division of Health wanted to start a study testing what they called lifetime and major fish eaters. You had to have eaten an average of a pound of fish a week over the course of a year. We had to keep notebooks and so forth. I volunteered for the study because, as a writer, I did not believe in it. I volunteered in 1986 and again in 1991 in a follow-up test. Five years later, they followed up on both tests. I went through about thirty pages of paperwork. The bottom line was I had no significant accumulation of PCBs in my blood—no more than the average person walking the street or working in a factory. And I am a heavy fish eater, a lifelong fish eater. Before I knew about these advisories, I used to fish for rainbows in the streams and so forth. I would consume a big, seven- to eight-pound rainbow trout by myself in two days. I love fish. I fillet it and grill it. I fry it, deep fry it, and bake it. I just love eating fish.

I believe that the PCBs can accumulate in your tissue, but I also believe that many of these studies have never proven a thing. Some contradict each other. At first they were grinding up the guts, the skin, everything, and then they were taking these PCB readings off of that. The results will vary according to whether a person knows how to properly clean the fish. One study said there are lower birth weights for babies born of mothers who ate Great Lakes fish and lower IQs for their kids. I am going to do a study one of these years on how many of our valedictorians and salutatorians in Door and Kewaunee Counties ate fish all their lives growing up and whether their mothers ate fish while they were pregnant. I think that would be very interesting because fish eating is huge around here. There is a fourth-generation fishing family in Algoma. They have smart, healthy twins.

You see these pictures of cross-billed gulls and cormorants. They have got to look awful hard for those because I have been fishing my whole life, and I have never seen one. The gulls and cormorants are reproducing like mad. There are more cormorants and gulls than ever before. So they are not having problems with their eggs. I swear sometimes these studies are about getting grants and grant money. They are scaring people. Back in the late 1980s the National Wildlife Federation came out with this fish cancer scare. It made national headlines. I think it was 1987 or 1988. If you ate Great Lakes fish, you had a 1 in 100,000 chance of getting cancer. Those reports scared the pants off of people. The findings were reported by Dan Rather on television, and on every major talk show and newspaper. It was sensationalism. The American Cancer Society says 1 out of 3 of us is going to get cancer in our lifetime. All right, 1 out of 3. So what is 1 out of 100,000 risk? That was the point I tried to make. We worked really hard for a couple years to get people to come back to the lake. It scared them for a while. You could not eat those fish.

My wife is pregnant right now and I know that they recommend not giving any Great Lakes fish to anybody who is pregnant or in their childbearing years, but I am being real picky. I am being selective. I am taking the lowest fat, leanest fish. I am not going to give her any lake trout or any big fatty fish. So far, she has eaten brown trout, perch, smelt. Dangerous as it might sound, I want to show that our baby is not going to have a low birth weight, heaven forbid. I want to show that it has got a high IQ. This could be some story years down the road, but I just really think that this is all over-sensationalized. Sometimes I think they are using the Great Lakes fishery as a sacrificial lamb to try to get the industries to clean up more. They are scaring people with the fish. I know there are problems. I would not eat a fish out of the Fox River or Green Bay. There are heavily contaminated fish and ducks there. The cross-bill thing really gets on my nerves. I do bus tour talks for the "Lake Circle Tours," as they are called. I hop on the bus either from Green Bay to Sturgeon Bay or Sturgeon Bay to Algoma. Every year, there are more and more. I think I am up to fifteen this year. The people on the Lake Circle Tours are from all over the country. In the last ten years, I have educated a lot of them. I bring up the issue of eating fish every time. I ask people if they have heard you cannot eat fish from here. They have heard you cannot. They are mostly retired people. I tell them when you go back home, tell people here is the story. Boy, they are glad to hear that. I think the word needs to be spread a little more that properly cleaned and cooked, there are more advantages to eating fish than disadvantages. They are high in Omega-3 fish oils and in protein. Fish is low in fat. They are just good for you. They are brain food.

We would try to tell people about eating fish at sports shows. Different charter captains would cut out my articles, lay them out in a book and say, "Here, read what this guy has to say." It was also spread through word of mouth. The state has gotten so much pressure from us, they also helped us out a little. They came out with these fish advisories that are put out twice a year, around April and October, in all the states around the Great Lakes. They will tell you to not eat more than one meal of this per day, week, month, or year. They will break it down on a fish from ten inches to twenty inches or whatever. They have it broken down by size and species. There's some fish on a "do not eat list," but most of them you can eat safely and most of them the average charter boat customer who is coming once a year could never eat enough to worry about it. But again, the headlines scare them. But slowly they are figuring it out. You could say do not eat a hot dog or any smoked meats because of all the nitrates. There are so many things we cannot eat nowadays because they are supposed to be bad for us. God forbid, if I get cancer and somebody says it is from the fish, maybe it was from a burnt hot dog that I ate. Burned meat is a carcinogen. If 1 in 3 of us are going to get it anyway, I am going to live my life eating what I want to eat and not really worry about it. I will cut off the skin on a bigger fish and the fat off of all the fish, but I do eat the skin on the small fish that are only a year old.

Fisheries biologist Mike Toneys of the Wisconsin DNR expressed concern about the impact of exotic species on the Lake Michigan ecosystem.

We know the exotic species have had an impact. We know they continue to have an impact. We know if we did not have a control program on sea lamprey, in a few short years, we would be back to what we had in the 1950s, which was just about zilch other than alewives. Some exotics we can control; some we cannot. They are all having an impact out there, some more insidiously than others. The exotic species problem may be one of the major reasons lake trout cannot get a foothold again. So from my perspective, we have a disturbed system out there because of exotic species. They are probably the major problem of the future as far as any kind of management scheme goes. It is a moving target. It is dynamic. Nothing is forever and some of the changes that happen are unexplainable. We are still not sure what happened to chinook back in the late 1980s. Some of the best fishing in Wisconsin took place in 1986–1987. In 1987–1988, mature adult chinook started rolling up on beaches dead. Within a couple of years, the majority of the chinook population was dead, probably as a result of bacterial kidney disease brought on by some one or more stresses out there such as a lack of enough forage to keep them going. We may never know exactly what happened, but we think we have got a pretty good idea. It was totally unanticipated and happened so dramatically, so quickly, it scared the hell out of a lot of us.

Here was an example of one exotic, salmon, that we introduced, dependent for survival on another exotic, alewives, that we did not introduce. It becomes a real balancing act to manage things out there when you have got natives competing with exotics and in some cases the natives winning out, and in some cases the exotics winning out. It is a real crapshoot out there. It is a way for somebody to get gray fast. And the expectations of the public do not help because they do not understand that Mother Nature has the final say out there. They think that if we shove more fish in or if we do this or that, everything will be fine. It is not that simple. And sometimes they get impatient when we try and explain the complexities and the uncertainties. We do not know everything. We barely know what is going on out there half the time. We spend a lot of money and time out there and we barely understand a fraction of it.

We have had to deal with the consequences of zebra mussels. It is really no control method. We have watched them spread. They are alive and well and probably having some impact on water clarity in especially protected bays such as Sturgeon Bay. They probably have had an impact on food chains in parts of the bay and the lake. Maybe they are part of the problem we are seeing with perch and chubs. So they are here, and we are essentially trying to work around them. We answer numerous questions from the public about them. In the last few years they have become so abundant that during storm events they are washing up in windrows on people's beaches and creating problems people have never had to deal with before. Rather than sand, they are walking on a foot, two-feet thick of zebra mussel shells and they are not real thrilled about it. They are looking for some relief, and unfortunately there is none. The zebra mussels have found Green Bay and the near shore area of Lake Michigan to their liking and we are dealing with them.

Dennis Lavis, a marine biologist who supervises the U.S. Fish and Wildlife Service's Ludington Research Station, reflected upon some of the contemporary issues facing managers of Great Lakes fisheries.

We have got a whole suite of exotic species that have come in over the last several years from other parts of the world via ballast water primarily. They have put a lot of pressure on the systems and things are changing out there. Unfortunately, the animals have not been around long enough to see and be able to predict the impact of many of those changes. We are just now seeing things happening in the lake and trying to understand what is causing them to change. Just when you think you are headed down the right direction and you think you might be getting a handle on why things are changing, something else crops up and you have to scratch your head and say well, what is going on here? Yellow perch are an example. Yellow perch in Lake Michigan have been just going straight downhill for the last half dozen years. And, of course, the people who manage the perch populations have speculated everything from too many alewives, which compete with yellow perch, to zebra mussels cleaning up the water and lowering productivity. Then last year we had one of the largest classes of yellow perch produced on record from a very small standing stock of perch. Now you go back and look at your data some more, and try to get a little better understanding of what's going on. The alewife population is going down, and so maybe that's part of it. Only time will tell where it goes from there.

In terms of priorities for the Great Lakes fishery management agencies, the sea lamprey program has been and probably always will be, the number one priority on their agendas because they cannot have any kind of fishery out there without lamprey control. That is the way it is today. If we stop lamprey control today, within a matter of a few years, lampreys would quickly take over once again and the fishery that we enjoy today would be gone. It is like keeping your thumb on a coiled spring. You take pressure off and that spring just goes up and that is just what lamprey populations have the potential to do. And so everybody recognizes this. So lamprey control is well funded. The only time there was pressure from governments to cut back funding for this program, the management agencies and the fishing public rallied to the defense of the Commission [Great Lakes Fishery Commission] and picked up the phone and wrote letters. The lawmakers have always backed off and said, "Okay, we will fund you."

Commercial fisherman Steven Peterson (Fairport, Michigan) expressed concern that the fisheries were threatened both by cormorants and zebra mussels.

The cormorants are getting thicker every year. There are a lot more cormorants in the last five years. The fish have little scars on them because they dive down pretty deep. We were showing the two old guys that went with us today. Their bills are hooked and they will snag the fish. They cannot get the bigger fish but they definitely get the smaller ones. They can dive down pretty deep. They eat their weight per day of fish, whatever small fish they can get. The zebra mussels are just starting. The last couple of years they have been working their way up north. They do not like the colder water as much, but they have been coming this way. They are getting thicker the last two years up this way. The zebras clear up the water, but you do not know whether it is good or bad. There are a lot of them towards Escanaba, and wherever it is shallow water. Some of the fish are starting to learn to eat them even though they are hard shelled. We have been finding the whitefish are starting to eat them, which they have never done before.

Leon Voight, a commercial fisherman based out of Gills Rock, Wisconsin, discussed his concerns about the effect of non-native species on whitefish and other indigenous stocks.

L ampreys are coming back again. We know that. We have seen many marks on the fish. We have seen this in the last few years with the whitefish. When we harvested fish from lower Green Bay they were all full of lamprey marks. We are starting to see a few more lampreys in the nets. They quit treating some of the rivers on the other side of the bay here quite a few years ago. They are going to have to start looking at them again because we are starting to see small ones. The zebra mussels rip our nets; we really take a trashing from them.

The cormorants are getting to be an awful nuisance. They go down and stab the whitefish and rip their bellies open. There are times when you will get a whitefish, the stomach is healed but the guts are hanging out of them and they are still living. But cormorants, they are getting to be a nuisance because all it knows is to kill. Even though it has got a full stomach it kills and kills and kills. When you have a group of them come into an area such as Sand Bay you get thousands of them chasing baby whitefish around. They are not only eating them, but they are killing them. The cormorants really multiply. We have a lot of smaller islands where nobody lives. The birds nest in the trees and have killed the entire habitat on these islands.

Richard Stevenson, a charter boat operator who fishes out of Sturgeon Bay, Wisconsin, maintained that cormorants were a threat to the fisheries.

A cormorant is a bird used for fishing. Probably ten years ago, we first started seeing them coming around. I used to see a pair here, and a pair there, every once in a while. No one knew what they were. We would ask the customers, but most had never seen them before. Now there are just flocks all over the place. They are a fish-eating bird and they are very good at it. They can dive twenty feet down to catch fish. And they put a big dent in the trout population. When the game wardens stock the trout, they just come in and it is lunchtime for them. They will take out twenty percent of the trout in no time. It is a big problem. You cannot shoot them. They are going to be a big problem because they are populating pretty quick. I think they are probably just as much of a problem as zebra mussels. I think they are a bigger problem than lamprey eels. The thing is, a lot of people do not even look at cormorants.

The DNR is still trying to figure out what they are going to do about the zebra mussels. They are all over. They are everywhere. I do not know how far down they go. I know we have caught them from the bottom out in Lake Michigan over the rock pile in 100 foot of water. You cannot kill them all. Now you put something in the water, you kill everything. I think you kind of have to let them cycle themselves out and it is something people are going to have to live with.

The impact of cormorants and zebra mussels on fisheries stocks has convinced Don Bell, a fisherman and fish buyer, that they are a significant problem.

The lakes have really changed in the last four or five years because of those damn cormorants. For awhile, the sportsmen were thinking the Indians were fishing out all the perch. Well, they could not fish out all the perch because they were not fishing perch that hard, especially over around Cedarville and Hessel. That used to be a real good perch ground for the sportsmen. Then, after a couple of years of raising hell and bitching at the Indians, they finally realized it is the cormorants. For instance, the fishermen out of St. Ignace have trap-net rigs. They take off early in the morning because they like to be to their first net when the day breaks because around ten o'clock in the morning the winds start picking up. So, if they get to their net at seven o'clock or six thirty when that day starts to break, they have two or three hours. They can get a lot of work done if that wind does pick up at ten o'clock like it generally does. So they are trying to make a living that way but it is a hard way to do it. As they are leaving, they get over by those islands and their boat is chugging along making a lot of noise. They say that in the morning, the sky will turn black with all the cormorants that live on those islands.

In the Orient, they put rings around the cormorant's neck and use them for fishing. Well, these birds do not have rings on their necks. These bays around here, they are only forty to fifty feet deep, so your perch, bass, sunfish, blue gills, menomoniees—all your small fish—those cormorants are just going right after them. When the DNR dumps all these little baby salmon and baby trout, those birds just sit back and say here comes supper. Those damn fish, they do not have a chance.

Roy Holmquist of Ellison Bay has been fishing the waters off Door County, Wisconsin, for sport fish for nearly thirty years. He suspects that cormorants and zebra mussels could be contributing to the decline of sport stocks such as perch.

Our perch fishing used to be fabulous. We used to fish off of Nicolet Bay. You could go out there in the evening and catch your twenty-five perch like no problem. All you had to do was find bait fish and then you had perch under them. It was great. There is nothing better eating than a perch, except maybe a walleye.

There was great fishing at every one of these piers around here. Way back, when we first started, no matter where you went, if you went to Egg Harbor you got perch, if you came to Sister Bay you caught perch, if you went to Ellison Bay you caught perch. There were perch all over. But our perch fishing has really gone downhill. They said there has not been a lot of good recruitment and we do not know what is causing that—if it is the other species that came in here that is getting to them—if it is the zebra mussels or cormorants eating the little ones. So that is still up in the air. They are still trying to figure that one out.

Cormorants are a touchy subject with the fishermen. They are supposed to be an endangered species, which is a joke because you come out to North Bay in the spring and there are flocks of 2,000, 3,000 of them, flock after flock. I have seen them where they get in a line and they just keep moving these fish and just keep eating them. They drive them like cowboys with the cattle. When we stock fish up here, Mike Toneys calls me to get some fishermen to keep scaring the birds away while they stock. They give you these little noise rockets to shoot. At Sister Bay, they usually stock the browns in the fall and little browns will hang in the harbors for about a week whereas the kings—when you stock the kings—they are gone in about two hours. But the crazy little browns hang there. And then as soon as the cormorants realize that, they are in there in droves. I think that is what is cleaning up some of our browns. Somebody told me that cormorants can eat nine pounds of fish a day—that is a lot of little browns. And they can swim underwater, I guess, at twenty-seven miles an hour. The little fish probably do not have a chance.

Our DNR wants to get rid of the cormorants. It is the feds now, it is the federal government, and I wrote letters to the senators through the club—let us eliminate some of the cormorants, open up the season on them. The DNR is all for it. The DNR has the legal right to get rid of them if they come near the hatcheries. They do multiple damage to our stocks when they first put the little fish in, especially with the browns. Kings are not so bad, but who knows what happens when they get them out in the lake? In fact, Europe Lake near here—the little inland lake—was loaded with perch. We used to go there and catch perch all the time. It was sort of a pain, you know. You would try to fish for northern pike or bass or walleyes and you would be catching perch. Two or three years ago I went over and fished it and I never caught a perch. I asked Lyle Teskie, "What happened to the perch in Europe Lake?" He said about three years ago, a flock of cormorants moved in and wiped out all the perch. Those perch were there forever. It was just loaded with perch. You could not put a worm down because you would have a perch. Now you cannot even catch a little perch. It is a crime. I used to take my one granddaughter over there all the time in the winter for ice fishing. I would put on a wax worm and let her fish for perch and she had a picnic. She would come home and tell grandma, "I caught a bunch of fish but papa did not catch any."

It is just amazing how the zebra mussels have multiplied. I have gotten hung up on them a couple times fishing for bass—fishing on the bottom and pulling up zebra mussels. There would be a little clump of them and the big one might be an inch and then there's all little tiny ones hanging on there. And I do not know if that really has anything to do with the water—the water clarity is just unbelievable. When we were fishing in this last brown trout tournament, I could see bottom in thirty-five foot of water. I could not believe it. It is just amazing. When you come to the different harbors and you look along the bottom, you see these zebra mussels all over. I do not know if they are taking all the plankton out of the water that the little fish are feeding on. That may have something to do with why we are not getting recruitment with the perch. But DNR is working on it, so let us hope. But how are you going to eliminate the zebra mussels? I do not think they have a natural predator.

Lyle Teskie, a charter boat operator, discussed his belief that exotic species were primarily to blame for the lack of forage food for fish and shorebirds. He laments the effects of nonindigenous species on the cultures of commercial fishing and sport fishing.

The DNR is focused in on pollution and that is good because PCBs and chemicals affect us. They affect the fish, too, so that's important. But as far as the ecology of the lake, the foreign species coming through the St. Lawrence Seaway has probably hurt Lake Michigan, all the lakes, more than pollution. I am not saying throw the pollution laws out, but that's the way it is. I guess you cannot be in every place looking at everything all the time but there are a lot of zebra mussels.

It is horrible to live on a beautiful place like the lake and see the seagulls sitting on the beach. Seagulls should be flying. That is what tells you that there are fish. It is sad to see them sit there on the beach like there is nothing to fly for. Do you know what that says? There are no fish there. The northerns are starving. There is no food. There are no little fish anymore for the northerns to feed off of. Everything is getting so scarce. They are going up to the surface and a fish does not really like going to the surface. When you see things like that, it tells you that there is something wrong. You can see it in the fish you catch. The heads are bigger and the bodies are smaller and leaner. You can see the fish are starving. It is sad. The sad part about it is I am in the fishing business. People come on my boat. Most people do not know. Most people want to have a good time, so you do not tell them. But when somebody asks you, you got a choice. Either lie or tell the truth. And the truth is right there. It is not because I have studied it. It is just that you see it. All the crabs in the harbor have died the last couple of years. My brother is in the commercial fishing business and he is still getting good lifts of whitefish, but they are getting lean too. The oil content is falling way down. The whitefish is the most abundant of the fish in Lake Michigan and I hope it survives. It may not. It used to be a cycle of fishing of good year-bad year-good year. Now, the cycle will probably go over generations. The zebra mussel—because it is dominant—will run it right back in the hole so the cycle will never really ever get back to the way it used to be.

Ten or twelve years ago, just before the perch disappeared, I used to go perch fishing with a small rowboat. It was just fun. That is fishing to me. The charter fishing that I do, I do not consider that as much fun because only a few can do it. It is expensive to do it, so not everyone can do it. Not every family can take their kids out charter fishing. The wealthy can do it. That is why I am disappointed to see the perch and the bass disappear, not for any other reason than you could fish them off the dock. Kids could fish them off docks. You did not have to pay sixty-five dollars to go on my boat to get one.

Washington Island commercial fisherman Ken Koyen expressed concern that the zebra mussels and the cormorants may, in part, account for the fact that fishing stocks were down.

When I started in 1971, the industry was basically providing the same amount of fish we are getting now. The last three or four years have been real lean, and I think it's all due to the zebra mussel moving in. And I do not know what is going to happen. It is not looking good. I know the DNR did some testing west of the island this morning. I called them because I was hoping they found some whitefish out there. A friend of mine came back from there and he says it is not good. I have not had a chance to talk to him on the phone to find out just how bad it was, but he said a lot of dirt and no fish.

Years ago, when the lake trout was first being planted, commercial fishermen were supposed to get a fishery out of it. To date all we have gotten is a little incidental catch. That is it. I remember a meeting with the DNR when they wanted to plant German brown trout, which is not native to these waters. One of the fishermen that knew what he was talking about got up and said, "Do not put anything in the lake that is not there already." If you look at it—the overall picture—your alewife were not here, zebra mussels were not here. Anything, your white perch, gizzard shad, all trash that came in, has caused nothing but havoc. They keep trying to get one species to fish out the other. I do not know what they are going to fish the zebra mussels out with but they better find something or the whole fishery is going to be in trouble. I am not talking about us as much as the sport fishery. There is a lot more money out there in the sport fishery than there is in four fish tugs, although we do feed a lot more people than the sport fishery does. And as far as marketing, our biggest problem is imports from Canada—Lake Superior whitefish. Canada subsidizes their fishermen. What we get is what we get. Over the border, the fish are sold in one location, but the fisherman gets a constant price.

The cormorants are like the geese in the cities. It is the same thing. They have got to do something and pretty damn quick too—the cormorants are after your minnows. The only fish that are safe here in the harbor are the ones hiding under the boats. Everything is steel. Your fish cannot get into the cribbing [older dock foundations] anymore. Years ago you used to be able to walk over and drop a line next to the wood crib and catch all the rock bass you would want. Now you cannot find one. First, you cannot find the crib, and secondly, you cannot find the rock bass.

I have seen 10,000 cormorants trying to chase deer out. I have seen them up north here on a dead, calm morning when they would go down in a long line. There might be a line of them two miles long and they just keep tumbling. It is like they are driving, headed towards the shallow water. Whatever they were after, they were chasing it into the shallow water.

Outdoor writer and fishing guide Kevin Naze discussed cormorants and other threats to fishery stocks.

The double-crested cormorant is a fish-eating bird. There are a lot of studies on what they eat in the Great Lakes, but most of them come from Lake Ontario. We are pushing pretty hard for a study in the Sturgeon Bay, Algoma, and Green Bay areas to show their impact. We want to know if they really are preying on a lot of yellow perch, small-mouthed bass, small trout and salmon—like fishermen think—or are they just taking more minnows and alewife and so forth. It is to the point where some of the angry sport fishermen are ready to test the law and kill them. They are a protected bird like a herring gull. If the DNR cut them open themselves when they saw them diving they would find ten trout in their stomach. There are some pretty big sport groups out there like the Great Lakes Sport Fishing Council and some of these groups might help you fight something like that because the Fish and Wildlife Service seems to be dragging their feet on it. The sport-fishing community is really upset because we spend millions of dollars stocking trout and salmon. Every fisherman who fishes the Great Lakes has to buy a stamp. And that $7.25 goes toward restocking fish, and hatcheries, and so forth, and when they see birds eating these fish up, they are not too happy. So that is a hot issue right now.

Alewives seem to be coming back, but then the last couple years they seemed to be going down again. Back in the late 1980s and early 1990s, the salmon crashed in Lake Michigan. One of the theories was bacterial kidney disease caused by a stress of not having enough nutrition. Michigan did not believe it. They were the only state that failed to cut back their salmon while the other three states did. Now Michigan has decided to cut back. This year is the first year of a big cutback. I think they are cutting back like forty-five percent or better in salmon numbers and the rest of the states are to a lesser degree. Michigan has great natural reproduction over there. I believe they are now estimating that one out of three chinook is naturally reproduced over there. So they think there may be more trout and salmon in the lake than ever before, so they are worried that the predation on the alewife is so intense that the alewives are going to go down again. And if they crash again, the whole fishery might crash because the fish do not seem to want to switch over to the bloater chubs.

The chubs are out there in increasing number. I think the forage has flip-flopped in twenty years. The bloaters used to be maybe twenty percent of the population, the alewife was eighty, and now I think it is vice versa. Fishermen also are concerned about the rainbow smelt declining rapidly, although commercials in Two Rivers this year had a superb year for trawling for smelt. Maybe the zebra mussels and all these other exotics that are clearing up the water so much are possibly influencing the fact that smelt do not come so close to shore anymore. Maybe there never will be a great inshore run like there used to be. That's a tradition has been lost in the 1990s—people throwing their nets off the piers and pulling in these huge buckets of smelt.

Lyle Teskie, who worked as a commercial fisherman before starting a charter boat operation, regards cormorants as destructive to both the fisheries and the larger environment.

The cormorant was on the endangered species list and environmentalists wanted it off the list. So the issue went to the legislature and it was pushed through. They wanted the bird in the water but they never thought about what would the bird do to the other things. But somebody should know that. It is common sense. This bird is what you call a fish-eating machine by design. If you are on the lake, you see what they do. I watch them outside the dock here. They are just as efficient as can be. But why would anyone do that to a lake? They claim they can eat five pounds of fish a day. I do not want a species to be endangered. But to enhance one species that really is not any good to the lake anymore—to put something like that into Lake Michigan or Green Bay and have it destroy what's still there naturally, I think that is more of a tragedy than anything else. The cormorant has wrecked Pilot Island. They have taken over Spider Island and Gravel Island, which were nesting grounds for the seagulls. They kicked them right off those two islands. What I do not understand is why they get grants to study the cormorant.

These tanker trucks used to put fingerlings under the ice when there was not a cormorant around. But then they started planting these fingerlings when the cormorant was here. They would dump in 10,000 or 20,000 fingerlings that had been raised in a hatchery where they feed off of these pellet machines so these little fish are all looking on top of the water for their food after months of being in the hatchery. Now you put them in Lake Michigan, and they are on the surface looking for their food. And here is the cormorant. So I really came to the conclusion that the DNR actually was planting the fish to feed the cormorant with the taxpayers' money. That is one of the things that drew me to telling the truth. If the DNR would blatantly do that, they do not feel that anybody can do anything about it or touch them. Now you could tell them and they would kind of laugh at you. Shoot at my boat, give me a thrill, but do not put fish in the lake and then put a bird there to eat it. It might slap you in the face. It is kind of humiliating.

Ben Peterson, who held both a tribal fishing license and a commercial fishing license from the State of Michigan until 2000, is concerned with how disease and exotic species will affect the whitefish.

The DNR knows about BKD and how the salmon transferred it to the whitefish. Our bays could be a problem. We could have big problems here eventually. The kidney disease is still a problem. I think the newer breed of salmon that they hatch now does not have the kidney disease, but a lot of the ones that went into the lake did. It is something they picked up from the hatchery. There is a lot of competition with the lake trout now, zebra mussels, and kidney disease. We fish for whitefish—a fish that eats plankton. Zebra mussels eat plankton. The whitefish are trying to adapt. All the fish are trying to adapt by eating something else, so we are finding the fish in different areas than we have found them in the last couple of years. The numbers are down some in the bay, I would say. Who knows if it is on account of the kidney disease, on account of the zebra mussels, the fish went deeper. The sport fishermen are finding the DNR planted a lot of walleyes, but when the zebra mussels come in, clear the water completely up, it is a lot more difficult to catch them. They move out in the deeper water.

Neil Teskie (Gills Rock, Wisconsin) expressed apprehension with whitefish stocks. He was especially concerned about the effects of the zebra mussel. His recollections focus on how exotic species disrupt the traditional ecological knowledge of commercial fishers.

Well, for the last couple of years, the whitefish fishing has not been real good. I have always been a believer that we need rain. If you do not have rain, you do not have runoff. If you do not have runoff, you do not have blooms in the water and you do not have little bugs growing in there. Well, there are two things that fish do. They spawn and they eat. That is what drives the fish population. Water temperature as well. But if the water temperature is close and there is a lot of food there or if the water temperature is close and there are females there, and it is spawning time, they are going there. The water temperature is not going to totally keep them away. So we know that is what drives these things. Now this year, we have had rain and right away I can see that the fish are coming in and they are full of food because of the rain. Of course, the water temperature is real cool. They like the cooler water but they also like the food. Last year was not that good because I have always been a believer that the rainwater going into the lake has an effect on the fishing, especially in the spring of the year. That brings them into the beach. I do not think it is the temperature as much as the fact that water running off puts nutrients in the water and that allows the bugs to hatch out.

The zebra mussel concerns me but it is a concern that I do not really have a good handle on yet. We have had some fluctuations in the fishery. Last year (1998), the whitefish would not come into shallow water. Now was that because of the sunlight penetration or was it because it was dry weather because of no rain? Now this year we still have the zebra mussels and it looks like the whitefish are going to come into the shallow areas more than once. Last year they came in once and I had the nets up in North Bay area; I have a couple of nets that are way up in thirty-five feet of water up in there. In previous years, June used to be a good time of year up in there. Last year,

I could not catch whitefish up in there at all. I would lift up the net and look on in there and it would be pathetic. This year looks all right, but it is not all written down yet. I have to wait for June to go along. But the other day there was 1,300 pounds in one trap net.

So zebra mussels concern me because maybe they are changing the patterns of the fish. They concern me because they are taking all the nutrients out—creating less zooplankton and phytoplankton. But without little shrimps and snails there is not enough food for the whitefish and that is what the DNR is concerned about—the whitefish growth rates are slowing—they are like a year to two years behind in their growth rates. They are afraid that there's not enough food out there for the whitefish. Now is that because of zebra mussels or is that because they placed us on a quota system? There have been so many fish out there and we used to be able to go get them. But we were hardly fishing any netting. Did they eat up their food supply and then move out into the lake? Was that the reason or was it because of zebra mussels? I mean, things are coming at the same time so we do not know what to blame. There are a lot of fish in the bay but there are lots of sub-legals and lots of skinny ones. The bigger fish are in the lake. Now is that because there is not any food there? I do not know. It has changed and it could be because they ate up their food supply.

———

Based in Gills Rock, Wisconsin, fisherman Rick Johnson is fearful that the zebra mussels will destroy the whitefish fishery.

My biggest concern right now is the zebra mussels—the effect they are having on the spawning beds. I mean, the major spawning bed around here is in North Bay and Moonlight Bay. The number of zebra mussels in the nets are up. Three years ago, you never saw a zebra mussel. Zebra mussels are getting in all that honeycomb rock where the whitefish spawn. The rocks are getting filled up with zebra mussels. What happens when the whitefish come to lay their eggs? To me, that is the biggest concern in the fishery right now. All they are worrying about is the nuclear plants and plants that take in water to cool their systems down. But as far as I know, there is nothing being done about zebra mussels. I do not even know if there is any research being done, to tell you the truth. In the spring, when we had a bad storm and they washed up on the Lake Michigan shores—two or three feet thick on the shore—just windrows of them. Obviously, they have the effect of helping clean the water. I mean, you can see down seven or eight feet now. You can see the bottom where you could not see it five years ago. But what is it doing to the rest of the lake—are they eating the same food as the whitefish and what are they doing to the spawning beds?

Ron Poff, formerly of the Wisconsin DNR, speculated on the impact of exotic species.

The cormorants are back in spades. There are cormorants all over the place. For a while they were threatened and, in our infinite wisdom, the DNR created a breeding grounds in Green Bay by putting in some telephone poles with nesting platforms on them in the southern part of the bay. At the same time, the pesticide DDT was creating a soft shell problem with the bysivorous birds that were being diminished. All of a sudden, we get cormorants all over the place. They were catching them in pound nets, trap nets, and even gill nets that are shallow enough for them to get into. It is one of those things—Mother Nature kind of swings the pendulum on us every now and then. Zebra mussels are going to be a tough one. Right now the east shore of Green Bay along Dikesville and in areas with the low water, apparently they are having a heck of a time with zebra mussels. There is as much as 200 feet of three-feet high of zebra mussels in some spots. There are some good things to it. It is a filter feeder so they are filtering contaminants, but the bad thing is what do you do when you got a bunch of dead zebra mussels? How do you get rid of them? They are all contaminated. You cannot very well put them into a landfill someplace.

Bithotripes are another problem. This is a little spiny water flea that is ingested by juvenile perch and their spiny tail does some damage on a juvenile fish. And so I suspect that when the minute perch get into a situation where they are big enough to start scavenging on spiny water fleas, they will get into trouble. I am sure there are other things to it too. Other exotics include the white perch and the European rough. Thank heavens we have not seen tench lately. Tench or tinkatinka is a commercially reared fish in Europe that looks like a big guppy and is tolerable of low oxygen levels. I have always been afraid of something like that coming in, especially in an area where we may have a contaminant problem and just being able to survive like no other species. And who knows what the next exotic will be? Could be another mussel out there, could be some more zooplankton or more fish. We have to be alert all the time. Our managers are constantly on the watch for more exotics showing up. And there are the battles that are being fought on bilge water. That will become interesting because there are economic issues there.

I am not as concerned as some about the yellow perch fishery, which was probably never that large a fishery on the Wisconsin side of the lake proper, not including Green Bay. I do not know what the chub fishery will do. The whitefish fishery is key to maintaining the kind of fishery I envision operating in places like Baileys Harbor and the little ports up along the Door Peninsula. We must maintain the whitefish fishery. It is an excellent fish. It should draw top dollar, and it will certainly attract tourists to the area. Hopefully, there will be some limited lake trout harvest associated with it, too, for years to come, because there certainly are plenty of lake trout out there. I doubt if we will ever see commercialization of coho or chinook. They have had too many problems. The salmon are an exotic, and they had too many problems of their own. They created a heck of a fishery, but like most exotics, the salmon are likely to only be able to sustain themselves at relatively low levels at some time in the future.

The big concerns are things like zebra mussels and bithotripes. The water is as clear as it has ever been out there with all these zebra mussels around filtering and operating on the low end of the food chain. You have got to have phytoplankton and zooplankton, or you are not going to have anything. I do not know what is going to happen there. The history with exotics is they explode on the scene and then they sort of level off at some much lower rate. I do not think there will ever be significant voids in the fish population. Some species will fill any voids. There has always been talk about the possibility the alewives would crash, and there would be no forage for the coho and chinook. Well, that did not prove itself out. When the alewives crashed the last time, there was a modest explosion of chubs. If the chubs go down, the smelt and the yellow perch may come back. Who knows what will happen there? I doubt you are going to see any big voids in the food pyramid out there. The species composition will shift.

Mark Weborg, a commercial fisherman based out of Gills Rock, Wisconsin, expressed concern that the forage base for valuable commercial fishing stocks such as whitefish was diminishing as a result of the zebra mussel.

Cormorants are causing havoc on the fishery. It is a known fact they eat six to eight fish a day. They are basically a nuisance bird. They have no value whatsoever and they are here by the thousands. They have taken beautiful islands that were nice green islands and turned them into nothing, because their excrement kills everything. Zebra mussels are going to be the major problem in the near future. We have seen that they are clearing the water up to the point where the whitefish feed on fresh water shrimp and algae in the water and they have changed the whole algae base—where that is. The top thirty-five feet of water was the first thermal climate and that was where you would see algae. Now it grows from the top all the way down to 130 feet of water. Also, zebra mussels are eliminating the freshwater shrimp. We are hardly seeing any. We have seen alewife in the whitefish—that is not a good sign. For them to be eating that, that means they are very, very hungry and increases the amount of contaminants in their bodies.

John McKinney, who has been a Michigan Sea Grant agent since 1979, considered it impossible to accurately predict the changes exotic and other nonindigenous species might bring to the Great Lakes fisheries. He credits the insights of commercial and sport fishers who observe fish habitat everyday.

Nobody knows better than the guys who are out there on the water if the non-indigenous species are causing change. They know better than I what is actually happening; they can see it every day. And that change is likely to be more disruptive to the system than anything else. It is kind of the next step although we have had nonindigenous species out there for a long time. Some of the main things they catch are nonindigenous; it is just how you define nonindigenous. The zebra mussel, potentially the goby, the rough, some others, and of course the lamprey, have been an issue out there for a long time. Cumulatively speaking, nonindigenous species are probably having more impact now than they ever have. The spiny water flea is less visible, but may be making just as traumatic changes in the food chain as the zebra mussel. I could agree with those that they should be nervous about this; it is going to change. Now change does not always mean all bad. The change might in the long run be good, or there might develop some other kind of fishery they can capitalize on. But in the interim, they may begin to see some problems with the fishery. No one knows for sure.

Jim Moore, who recently retired after serving the Wisconsin DNR since 1968, emphasized the rapidly changing nature of Lake Michigan fisheries.

People assume that zebra mussels are going to have a major impact on the fisheries. To date, we have not seen anything that we could directly attribute to zebra mussels as having any great effect on the fisheries. Zebra mussels have been in Lake Erie for many more years than they have been established here, and their fishery is still thriving. It does not seem to be impacted directly by zebra mussels. Perhaps over long periods of time, you might be able to attribute something to zebra mussels such as water clarity, which might, over time, have some negative or beneficial impacts. It is hard to say which it might be. Right now, it would be hard to even guess what some of those impacts might be, if any. Those are some of the things you just deal with; you are not going to do anything about it. People should not be fearful that it is going to have detrimental effects to the point where there are not going to be various sports species around to catch, because that certainly has not been the case.

The lake is changing constantly. It always amazes me how fast things can change. Back in the early 1980s, we were catching probably a million or two fish through the ice in Green Bay. Four or five years later, you could throw a stone or shoot a gun across the bay and not hit an ice-fishing shack. So you are always going to see these changes, whether it is with a sports species or a commercial fish species like whitefish, that has been on a roll now for the last ten or fifteen years and just does not show any signs—right now—of having any problem areas. But then there are other commercial species like chubs, where we saw such lows in the early 1970s we had to close the fishery. Then there were great big highs, and all of sudden it looks like we are heading for some problems again. A lot of the indicators of problems in the early 1970s are happening again now. In a few more years we will know whether it runs the same cycle or not. You are always going to have these cycles, and you can never predict where they are going to pop up. If you are a sports fisherman, take advantage of the opportunities, and wait out the years when the species that you like to fish are at a low point. Hopefully, you are going to get another crack at them. And the same holds true for the commercial fishery. There are a lot of things we can do management-wise, but the bottom line is still Mother Nature—she is a lot stronger and has more impact on what is going to happen out there than the sport fishermen, commercial fishermen, and the DNR.

Mike Toneys of the Wisconsin DNR suggested that the public does not understand the complexity of managing the fisheries resources of the dynamic Lake Michigan ecosystem.

Contaminants are always out there as an issue. And even though we review and publish guidelines annually, it still does pop up every once in a while as a contentious issue, especially with sport trollers and those whose business might be impacted. It is our responsibility, along with all the agencies around the lake, to deal with that and we will have to continue to deal with that. So that is out there as a continuing issue and sometimes it flares up, but people have pretty much been made aware of it, know it is there, know the guidelines, and are able to live with that.

The lake is biologically changing. I do not know what the—there does not seem to be an end point. It seems to be dynamic; it is kind of hard to predict what is going to happen. I think the sport fishery is still alive and well. We have weaned them off of a single species and tried to tout the benefits of a variety of fish, not only trout and salmon but also small-mouthed bass, perch, pike, and a variety of others, rather than just concentrating on king salmon. The commercial fishery, at least in Wisconsin, is aging. There is not a lot of new blood coming in, so I would guess that it is going to continue to contract. When I started there were about 230 licensees. Now we are below 100, and every year we probably lose another one or two. I would think there is going to continue to be a commercial fishery at some level, but it will probably be smaller in the future than it is now. Hopefully, a little less controversial. Even now, it is a lot less controversial than it used to be.

Elaine Johnson, a Wisconsin-based fish producer, maintained that pollution problems should receive greater attention from DNR fisheries managers.

The fish out there are my resource and they are yours. Because of money, the paper companies have polluted our Fox River and Lower Green Bay. You cannot fish walleye down there because they are so polluted with PCBs. They have contaminated all these fish. This big industry can get by without cleaning up that water before they release it back into the Fox River. Now that is a dirty damn shame that they do this. I am an environmentalist, I think. When I am chewing a candy bar, the wrapper goes in my pocket. Even the gum wrappers go in my pocket. We recycle. We try to do our thing.

I do not think anyone realizes how fragile the lake and its resources are. Everybody has to realize, it is their resource. It does not belong to the fishermen. It does not belong to DNR. It is everybody's resource and it is fragile. Let us protect it. Look how they polluted the harbors up in Michigan. Look at the paper mills. Look at the chemical companies. Look at the sewers. Open up the gates. Dump her in Lake Michigan.

The zebra mussels, as I understand it, came from the Caspian Sea. They got into Lake Erie and southern Green Bay. The fishermen tell me now that when they were out lifting in seventy feet of water you can see to the bottom. It is crystal clear.

Then you have the underutilized species; there is no pressure on them at all. We never used to have that many "lawyers," or burbot in the lake. But there is no pressure on them, no harvest of them. Years ago, the DNR was going to see if there would be a market for them, but what they say and what they do are two different things. Suckers and these underutilized fish seem to be flourishing because there is no pressure on them, no market for them.

The lake can only take care of so much. With the zebra mussels, they are taking the nutrients out of the freshwater column. There is nothing in the water now for some of the fish to eat. So who is to blame for that? Who is to blame for the pollution of the fish? Are the mussels? Is it the growth of the underutilized species? It is not the fishermen out there making their living on the waters. What's the DNR doing about it? They do not know what to do. They put all these exotic species in the lake. Took the Lord thousands of years to do it right, but the DNR comes along, snaps their finger, and makes a judgment. Oh, God this is the thing to do. We will show you how to run this thing.

It is not just the DNR. Just as soon as man gets into anything, he has got to screw it up. That is his first step. Let us screw it up. But that's politicians. The sports people have got backing because they have got money. There is no question about that. There are no commercial fishermen in Indiana, Minnesota, Illinois, and nothing in Michigan except the Indians and a handful of others. There are about twenty-seven of us up here, just a few scattered down the way. That is nothing. We had the biggest fishery in the Great Lakes up here in Wisconsin, but it is not a fishery anymore.

Wisconsin fisherman Don Stiller began fishing in the 1940s. Now retired, he reflected on how commercial fishermen and Lake Michigan fisheries both in the past and today pay the costs of industrial pollution by paper companies and other manufacturers.

There was one time—I would say in the early 1960s—that the pollution was so bad out there that the nets would come up out of the water and it was like cow dung. You had to wring the water out or you would not have been able to get the nets on the boat. It was like paper pulp. In fact, that is what it might of been and it would dry on the nets and we would put them on the reel and then we would try to rub it out and at that time we did not have all nylon netting. If you had all nylon netting, you could just put the nets in the tub and cover them up for a week. When you put them back in the water you would put a clothespin on your nose and spin them back in again because it smelled just like clear sewage. I do not know if the paper mills are still leaving a little PCBs in the bay or not. But you read this in the paper every day. They are talking about digging out the whole Fox River for a section of twenty-one miles and transporting it. But they are going back and forth with the landfill business. It is going to be an astronomical project. They say the east shores are mostly polluted because the pollution leans to the east shore. Then they came out and said that they were finding tumors in the walleyes from the PCBs. Green Bay white perch are not marketable. I think they still import some in from Lake Erie, so I guess they are all right. There was a fairly decent market for them. They are not a bad tasting fish. People say, "Well, they do not taste like a yellow perch." Well, nothing tastes like a yellow perch. But you can see what this pollution probably does.

My books show that we had a nice lake herring fishery—which is one of the seven types of ciscos. In about 1955, they started blaming the smelt on the herring disappearing. About 1955, the herring catches started going down and the perch catches started coming up. By 1965, the herring were practically gone and the perch had taken over. But we concentrated more on herring than we did on perch at the time. That was one of the nicest tasting fish I can remember. I preferred those over yellow perch. I can remember, we would come in on a Friday night and my mother would say get some herring. I would clean up four or five herring and she would put them in a crock and stick them in the oven and you would be eating high off the fish at suppertime about an hour later. But then they got—they called it gassy. They had kind of a sulfur-like taste to them and maybe fifty percent of them did not taste good. If you put them in the pan, you could smell them. Sometimes you could smell them when you cleaned them and we always said it was like sulfur. Some fish smell that way today. If you fish down in the south end of Green Bay, the whitefish will pick that up very quickly. If they pass the outside light and get down into the south end and you catch them on the way back, they are going to be strong tasting. It does not take them long to pick it up. So there are a lot of aspects to what is going on.

I do not know what the future of the fishery is. It does not look too good to me—I think that their aim is to get the amount of fishermen down. They have got to have designated ports to come into so they can keep a line on them. Of course, in the wintertime, they are out there and nobody is watching too much and they are fishing and they will come into some resort and land their catch and not put it in the book or something. I will not say it does not happen, because I know it does. There was a big scam up in Marinette a couple of years ago, where a lot of fishermen got cited. So, I am glad I fished when I did. It was hard work, but you got out in nature. You had to fight the elements. You would grumble at them sometimes, but then you got those days when it is just beautiful. You got the days when the walleyes rolled in and you could see the dollar signs in their eyes and then you got the days when the pollution came up. So it all settles out.

Commercial fisherman Mark Weborg (Gills Rock, Wisconsin) expressed concern about how zebra mussels and declining water levels would affect Lake Michigan fisheries.

T he biggest challenge right now is the zebra mussel and what they are going to do to the whole structure of the lake—whether it is commercial, sport, whatever it might be, it is changing everything. It is forcing the whitefish out in much deeper water. We have been fishing whitefish out in 200–250 feet of water, which is unheard of. Normally, you never catch any outside of 180 feet. The zebra mussels are changing all their feeding patterns, and I have no clue what they are going to do to the fishery. I have no solution.

Another big factor in the fishing industry has been the water level. For years, it went on a seven to ten year cycle from top to bottom. Well, we have not had any low water now since 1966. Many people feel it is low now, but it is really not much under average. Every time the water level went low, our fishing almost went extinct. We do not know if that is going to happen this time. It is got about two feet to go to go real low. When it goes low, it changes the spawning patterns of the fish. Normally, they are spawning in two or three feet of water. Now, they only have six inches of water or less and then the waves come in and it smashes them to pieces. That is our theory. We know when it is low water, we have very poor fishing. So that is another question mark out there, what the water level is going to do. Some people feel they have control over it, but they do not. They think they do.

Daniel "Pete" LeClair expressed concern that the younger generation is not interested in learning how to acquire the traditional ecological knowledge and experience necessary to run a trawler or another fishing rig and crew. He sees this development as adversely affecting management schemes that will benefit all who use Lake Michigan's fisheries resources.

I t takes a long, long time to get these captains experienced on the operation of the net, the equipment, where to fish, and so forth. Once you lose these guys, there is no way you are coming back. There are no young people coming into the industry because there is no future in it. There are lots of young kids that would like to fish, but under the present management system they are not going to stay and they are all going into the factories. I think this is the last generation of commercial fishing on Lake Michigan. When my kids are gone there is not anyone coming up after them. We are the last family of Le Clairs that fish out of Two Rivers where there used to be eighteen boats out of Two Rivers—now we are down to two and that is part-time.

Our family fishery is on its last leg. We are more or less going to get out of commercial fishing and just run our fish market with smoked salmon, lake trout, eel, and perch from Canada. Canada is really the backbone of the whole Great Lakes fishery. They produce a lot of fish and they have a good management and research program. These lakes can produce good fish. In Wisconsin, Michigan, and Illinois all the fish is going towards sport fishing. There is no management or research for the commercial fishery. How can you manage it if you do not know what is in the lake?

We would like to be a good research team with the DNR—take the DNR people out there and monitor our catches, study the classes, study the gross factors, study the sex ratios and really know what's going on out on that lake. If you have more forage fish, you have to plant more predator fish. If the forage fish is down you plant less predator fish. If you do this, you can maintain a perch fishery, maintain a sports fishery and a commercial fishery that produces food for human consumption. This is what this is about. This lake has to produce food for your human consumption. You cannot have a great lake like this and use it for a playpen. This is totally uncalled for. That is not the way it started, but that is the way it is going now.

Yvonne Walker Keshick of the Little Traverse Bay Bands of Odawa discussed the need for education about fishing and the environment and a broader, ecosystem approach to fisheries management.

The tribe has been thinking about going into either buying ten sixteen-foot boats or one big tug. They brought it up a few years ago. I voted against the tug because with a tug only three people benefit, the captain and the crew. You buy ten boats and teach thirty young people how to fish, then they benefit and the tribe benefits and they pass on part of the fishing culture. That is part of the curriculum I am writing up. It also includes first aid, swimming, fishing regulations, boarding rules, and so forth. We are also going to include what to look for if they find contaminated fish. The curriculum will be used if the tribe goes for it. I do not see how the tug benefits anyone. We were also talking about raising our own perch. We're pushing for aquaculture in educational programs. We are in early stages of curriculum development, gathering materials. We are trying to put it in some kind of order and develop programs.

I think that if more people learn how to fish, then they would be more inclined to help raise fish and put them back. Just like I believe that people who cut timber should plant trees, not just scrubby pine like all these things out there that will grow any place, but native trees. Put in birch and maple and all the others that used to be there, put in native trees. That is what we told the tribe to do when they started building houses. Do not go in there, chop down everything, make it all flat, put your houses in, and then stick grass and strange, non-native trees in there. Put our own in there. Keep our own trees. And for every tree they cut, they should plant two. You would clean up the world a whole lot quicker.

As long as the water is clean and usable everybody wants it and tries to claim it. When it gets contaminated and dirty and nobody wants to use it, then they try to shove it back to the government for cleanup. The government does not want to clean it up. The DNR will say the job belongs to some other department. John Keshick was talking back in the late 1970s, how the bilge on the ships should be dumped or filtered before they were allowed into the Great Lakes. He was saying it back in the 1970s before the zebra mussels. Back when we were fishing, too, they were blaming us for all the fish being gone. Back then, the cormorant became a protected bird and they multiplied and ate a lot of the fish.

The salmon do not hesitate to eat perch. The perch might hatch out, but they might not make it to maturity because there's so many salmon. We would watch the DNR plant salmon and trout in the bay in the daytime. John says plant them at night. The seagulls are not there to eat half a million before they get away. Why don't they plant fish at night? They cannot blame the tribes for loss of fish. I think they are planting them at the wrong time of the day for the fish's protection. There are a lot of things that contribute to the problem of no fish. There are fish there.

The DNR makes a big thing of it when they plant fish. It got into the local paper because that's a positive thing. Then they print a story about some of these nets that are washing up on shore, but with no names. We know nonlicensed fishermen who fish with nets. And we know that it is probably their nets that washed ashore with a couple hundred pounds of rotten fish in it. And it is a sportsman who openly fights against gill netting. We know who he is, and yet he sets nets himself.

NOTES

1. For more on the legacy and politics of pollution and water quality, see Robert Doherty, *Disputed Waters: Native Americans and the Great Lakes Fishery* (Lexington: University of Kentucky Press, 1990), 36–50; Tom Kuchenberg, *Reflections in a Tarnished Mirror: The Use and Abuse of the Great Lakes* (Sturgeon Bay, Wisc.: Golden Glow Publishing, 1978), 172–215; Dave Dempsey, *Ruin and Recovery: Michigan's Rise as a Conservation Leader* (Ann Arbor: University of Michigan Press, 2001), 184–93, 245–82; William Ashworth, *The Late, Great Lakes: An Environmental History* (Detroit: Wayne State University Press, 1987), 154–72. On exotic species to the Great Lakes, see John Flesher, "Great Lakes Invaders," *Kalamazoo Gazette,* 23 July 2000; Kuchenberg, *Reflections in a Tarnished Mirror,* 52–73; Joseph H. Leach, Edward L. Mills, and Margaret R. Dochoda, "Non-Indigenous Species in the Great Lakes: Ecosystem Impacts, Binational Policies, and Management," in *Great Lakes Fisheries Policy and Management,* ed. William W. Taylor and C. Paola Ferreri (East Lansing: Michigan State University Press, 1999), 185–207; Jon Schmid, "Area Beaches Dodge First Wave of Dead Alewives," *Chicago Sun-Times,* 1 March 1999.

   On destruction of fish stocks, see Walter Scott and Thomas Reitz, *The Wisconsin Warden, 100 Years of Conservation Law and Enforcement History* (Madison: Wisconsin DNR, July 1979), 29–30. On recent issues surrounding perch, see Tom Vanden Brook, "Researchers Find No Sign of Yellow Perch Reproducing," *Milwaukee Journal Sentinel,* 4 September 1999.

2. On new interpretations of fisheries management for Lake Michigan, see "Grant to Help Hatcheries," *Kalamazoo Gazette,* 2 October 1999; Randy Eshenroder, "Sustaining Ecosystem Structure and the Fishery: The Challenge," *Fishing For Solutions: Sustainability of Commercial Fishing in the Great Lakes, Conference Proceedings* (Great Lakes United, December 1995), 5–18; Randy L. Eshenroder and Mary K. Burnham-Curtis, "Species Succession and Sustainability of the Great Lakes Fish Community," in *Great Lakes Fisheries Policy and Management,* ed. Taylor and Ferreri, 145–84; Jack D. Bails, "The Great Lakes Fishery Trust," *Michigan Natural Resources* 69, no. 2 (1999): 21–25. On recent activities of the Great Lakes Fishery Commission, see Great Lakes Fishery Commission, "Strategic Vision of the Great Lakes Fishery Commission for the Decade of the 1990s" (Ann Arbor: Great Lakes Fishery Commission, February 1992); Great Lakes Fishery Commission, "A Joint Strategic Plan for Management of Great Lakes Fisheries" (Ann Arbor: Great Lakes Fishery Commission, June 1997).

   For more on how the perspectives of Lake Michigan's four principal fisheries stakeholder groups can be related to contemporary ecosystems management of the Great Lakes, see Lynton K. Caldwell, ed., *Perspectives on Ecosystem Management for the Great Lakes; A Reader* (Albany: State University of New York Press, 1988); Theodora E. Colborn, Alex Davidson, Sharon N. Green, et al., *Great Lakes, Great Legacy?* (Washington, D.C.: The Conservation Foundation, 1990).

3. On gobies, see John Myers, "Goby Find Confirms Fears," *Duluth News-Tribune,* 5 August 1995; Gene Schabath, "Goby Threatens State's Game Fish," *The Detroit News,* 23 March 1998; Doug Schmidt, "Killing Lake Invaders," *Windsor (Ontario) Star,* 24 October 1998.

4. On the zebra mussel, see Jim West, "Mussel Menace," *Michigan Natural Resources* 59, no. 4 (1990): 4–12; Conners, "Biologists Sound New Alarm on Zebra Mussels," *Traverse City Record Eagle*, 15 December 1997; *Zebra Mussels: A 1991 Great Lakes Overview* (New York: Sea Grant Institute, May 1991).

5. On PCBs, see Dempsey, *Ruin and Recovery*, 273–82; Lauri Harvey, "PCBs Most Stubborn Contaminant," *Hammond Times*, 13 June 1999.

Index

of Names, Places, and Vessels